Karl Radek on China

Historical Materialism Book Series

The Historical Materialism Book Series is a major publishing initiative of the radical left. The capitalist crisis of the twenty-first century has been met by a resurgence of interest in critical Marxist theory. At the same time, the publishing institutions committed to Marxism have contracted markedly since the high point of the 1970s. The Historical Materialism Book Series is dedicated to addressing this situation by making available important works of Marxist theory. The aim of the series is to publish important theoretical contributions as the basis for vigorous intellectual debate and exchange on the left.

The peer-reviewed series publishes original monographs, translated texts, and reprints of classics across the bounds of academic disciplinary agendas and across the divisions of the left. The series is particularly concerned to encourage the internationalization of Marxist debate and aims to translate significant studies from beyond the English-speaking world.

For a full list of titles in the Historical Materialism Book Series
available in paperback from Haymarket Books, visit:
https://www.haymarketbooks.org/series_collections/1-historical-materialism

Karl Radek on China

*Documents from the Former
Secret Soviet Archives*

Edited by
Alexander V. Pantsov

Translated by
Richard Abraham
Steven I. Levine

Haymarket Books
Chicago, IL

First published in 2020 by Brill Academic Publishers, The Netherlands
© 2020 Koninklijke Brill NV, Leiden, The Netherlands

Published in paperback in 2021 by
Haymarket Books
P.O. Box 180165
Chicago, IL 60618
773-583-7884
www.haymarketbooks.org

ISBN: 978-1-64259-599-4

Distributed to the trade in the US through Consortium Book Sales and Distribution (www.cbsd.com) and internationally through Ingram Publisher Services International (www.ingramcontent.com).

This book was published with the generous support of Lannan Foundation and Wallace Action Fund.

Special discounts are available for bulk purchases by organizations and institutions. Please call 773-583-7884 or email info@haymarketbooks.org for more information.

Cover art and design by David Mabb. Cover art is a detail of *Rhythm 69 no.20, (William Morris Block Printed Pattern Book, with Hans Richter Storyboard, developed from Hans Richter's 'Rhythmus 25' and Kazimir Malevich's film script 'Artistic and Scientific Film – Painting and Architectural Concerns – Approaching the New Plastic Architectural System')*, paint and wallpaper on canvas (2007).

Printed in the United States.

10 9 8 7 6 5 4 3 2 1

Library of Congress Cataloging-in-Publication data is available.

In memory of my teacher,
Mikhail Filippovich Yuriev

Karl Radek
RUSSIAN STATE ARCHIVES OF SOCIAL AND POLITICAL HISTORY, F.490. OP.2.PHOTO 282

Contents

Preface XI
Abbreviations XII

Karl Radek – Sinologist   1
    by Alexander V. Pantsov

1 On the Fundamentals of Communist Policy in China
  22 June 1926   16

2 History of the Revolutionary Movement in China: The 1926–7 Lecture Course
  Fall 1926 – Early 1927   22

3 Controversial Questions of Chinese History: Lecture to the Society of Marxist Historians
  26 November 1926, Stenographic Report   208

4 On the International Situation of China
  11 March 1927, Stenographic Report   226

5 Driving Forces of the Chinese Revolution: Lecture to the Communist Academy
  13 March 1927, Stenographic Report   248

6 Concluding Word to the Lecture 'Driving Forces of the Chinese Revolution'
  27 March 1927, Stenographic Report   283

7 The 'Betrayal' of the National Movement by the Chinese Upper Bourgeoisie
  Early May 1927   306

8 Speech at the Institute of World Economy and World Politics of the Communist Academy during the Discussion of the Lecture by L.N. Geller on the Chinese Workers' Movement
  17 May 1927, Stenographic Report   370

9 A New Stage in the Chinese Revolution: From Chiang Kai-shek to Wang Jingwei
2 July 1927, G.E. Evdokimov, G.E. Zinoviev, K.B. Radek, G.I. Safarov, L.D. Trotsky 385

Appendix 1: Letter from L.D. Trotsky to K.B. Radek
26 June 1926 419
Appendix 2: Letter from L.D. Trotsky to K.B. Radek
14 May 1927 420
Appendix 3: Facts and Documents Which Should Be Available for Verification by Every Member of the AUCP(b) and the Whole Comintern: Chronological Information
21 May 1927, G.E. Zinoviev and L.D. Trotsky 423

Biographical Dictionary 434
Works Cited 471
Bibliography of the Published Works of K.B. Radek on China and Literature about K.B. Radek 482
Index 490

Preface

This work has been carried out as part of the implementation of an academic project with the overall title 'The Russian Left Opposition and the Chinese Revolution: Documents and Materials from the Former Secret Soviet Archives'. The project received financial assistance from the Chiang Ching-kuo Foundation for International Scholarly Exchange (Taipei, Taiwan), from DePaul University (Chicago, USA), and also from Capital University (Columbus, Ohio) to all of which I would like to express my profound gratitude.

I also wish to express my warmest acknowledgment to Dr. Alexander L. Chechevishnikov, at the Scientific Research Institute of Social Systems of Moscow State University, for his selfless assistance in the discovery of documents, and also to the former Director of the Institute of Modern History of Academia Sinica (Taiwan), Professor Ch'en Yung-fa, who collaborated with me in determining the direction of my investigations. In addition, I am also indebted to the translators of the book, Dr. Steven I. Levine who translated Chapter 2 and Richard Abraham who translated the rest of the book. My heartiest thanks too go to Dr. Richard Ashbrook, Dr. Denvy Bowman, Dr. Mechthild Leutner, Dr. Mikhail Serafimovich Meyer, Dr. Pierre Broué, Father Thomas Croke, Dr. Jean-François Fayet, Dr. Irina Nikolaievna Sotnikova, Dr. Yu Miin-ling, to my mother Nina Stepanovna Pantsova, my daughter Dr. Daria Aleksandrovna Arincheva, my stepdaughter Ekaterina Alekseevna Gribova, Dr. Iurii Mikhailovich Ovchinnikov, Danny Hayward, Hilde Kugel, and also to Dr. Sébastien Budgen.

I value very highly the cordial attitude to my work shown by colleagues in the Russian State Archive of Social and Political History (RGASPI) and the Archive of the Russian Academy of Sciences (ARAN), in particular by Dr. Kirill Mikhailovich Anderson, Dr. Valerii Nikolaevich Shepelev, Svetlana Markovna Rozental, Larisa Aleksandrovna Rogovaia, Liudmila Mikhailovna Kosheleva, Larisa Nikolaevna Malashenko, Liudmila Konstantinovna Karlova and Iuri Tikhonovich Tutochkin.

Finally, I would like to express unlimited gratitude and the warmest recognition to my wife, Ekaterina Borisovna Bogoslovskaia, my closest friend and assistant, whose contribution to the preparation of this work for the press was especially valuable.

A.V.P.
Columbus, Ohio
1 January 2020

Abbreviations

ACCTU	All-China Confederation of Trade Unions
AN	Akademiia Nauk (Academy of Sciences)
ARAN	Arkhiv Rossiiskoi Akademii Nauk (Archive of the Russian Academy of Sciences)
ARCEC	All-Russian Central Executive Committee
AUCEC	All-Union Central Executive Committee
AUCP(b)	All-Union Communist Party (Bolsheviks), 1925–52
AUCUTU	All-Union Council of the Union of Trade Unions
AUkCEC	All-Ukrainian Central Executive Committee
Bund	Allgemeiner Jüdischer Arbeiterbund (General Jewish Labour Bund)
CC	Central Committee
CCC	Central Control Commission
CCP	Chinese Communist Party (Zhongguo Gongchandang)
CEC	Central Executive Committee
C-in-C	Commander-in-Chief
CLD	Council of Labour and Defence [Sovet Truda i Oborony]
Comintern	Communist International
CP(b)Uk	Communist Party (Bolsheviks) of Ukraine
CPC	Council of People's Commissars
CPPCC	Chinese People's Political Consultative Conference
CPSU	Communist Party of the Soviet Union, 1952–91
CP USA	Communist Party of the United States of America
CYI	Communist Youth International
CYL	Communist Youth League
CYLC	Communist Youth League of China
Donugol	Donetskii ugol (Donetsk Coal State Trust)
ECCI	Executive Committee of the Communist International
ECCYI	Executive Committee of the Communist Youth International
GMD	[Chinese] Nationalist Party ([Zhongguo] Guomindang)
Gosbank	Gosudarstvennyi Bank (State Bank)
Gosizdat	State Publishing House
Gosplan	State Planning Agency
GPU	Gosudarstvennoe Politicheskoe Upravlenie (State Political Administration)
IWE&WP	Institute of World Economy and World Politics
Kadet	K.D. (Constitutional-Democrat, member of Party of People's Freedom)

Khimkombinatstroi	Chemical Trust Construction
Komsomol	Communist Youth League
KPD	Kommunistische Partei Deutschlands (Communist Party of Germany)
KUTK	Kommunisticheskii Universitet Trudiashchikhsia Kitaia (Communist University of the Toilers of China)
KUTV	Kommunisticheskii Universitet Trudiashchikhsia Vostoka (Communist University of the Toilers of the East)
Kuzbasstroi	Kuzbas Metallurgical Trust Construction
Left-SRs	Party of Left-Socialist Revolutionaries – Internationalists
Medgiz	Medical State Publishing House
MPR	Mongolian People's Republic
MRC	Military Revolutionary Committee
NKPS	Narodnyi Kommissariat Putei Soobshchenii (People's Commissariat for Transport)
NPC	National People's Congress [of the People's Republic of China]
NRA	National Revolutionary Army
OGPU	Ob"edinennoe Gosudarstvennoe Politicheskoe Upravlenie (Joint State Political Administration)
Orgburo	Organisational Bureau
Partizdat	Party Publishing House
Politburo	Political Bureau
PRC	People's Republic of China
Profintern	Internatsional Profsoiuzov (Trade Union International)
RCP(b)	Russian Communist Party (Bolsheviks), 1918–25
RCYL	Russian Communist Youth League
Revcom	Revolutionary Committee
RGASPI	Rossiiskii Gosudarstvennyi Arkhiv Sotsial'no-politicheskoi Istorii (Russian State Archive of Social and Political History)
RMC	Revolutionary Military Council
RMCR	Revolutionary Military Council of the Republic
RSDLP(b)	Russian Social Democratic Labour Party (Bolsheviks) (Rossiiskaia Sotsial-Demokraticheskaia Rabochaia Partiia [Bolsheviks]), 1903–18
RSFSR	Rossiiskaia Sovetskaia Federativnaia Sotsialisticheskaia Respublika (Russian Soviet Federal Socialist Republic)
SDKPiL	Socjaldemokracja Królestwa Polskiego i Litwy (Social Democracy of the Kingdom of Poland and Lithuania)
Sibmashstroi	Siberian Machine Tool Trust Construction
Sovinformburo	Soviet Information Bureau

SPD	Sozialdemokratische Partei Deutschlands (Social Democratic Party of Germany)
SRINCP	Scientific Research Institute on National and Colonial Problems
SRS	Socialist Revolutionaries
SSNE	Supreme Soviet of the National Economy [Vysshyi Sovet Narodnogo Khoziaistva]
TASS	Telegraph Agency of the Soviet Union
Tsentrosoiuz	Tsentral'nyi Soiuz Potrebitel'skikh Obshchestv (Central Union of Consumer Societies)
TUC	Trades Union Congress [of Great Britain]
USA	The United States of America
USSR	Union of Soviet Socialist Republics
UTK	Universitet Trudiashchikhsia Kitaia (University of the Toilers of China)
Uralmash	Urals Machine Tool Trust
WPRA	Workers' and Peasants' Red Army

Karl Radek – Sinologist

by Alexander V. Pantsov

Karl Bernhardovich Radek was a distinguished activist of the Russian and international workers' movement, a senior official of the Bolshevik Party and the Comintern, an active participant in the left Trotskyist Opposition, and one of the main accused in the ill-famed show trials of the late 1930s. He was a man of many parts. Generously gifted by nature, he spoke fluently and wrote in six languages, and possessed remarkable oratorical talents, allowing him to retain the attention of his listeners for hours at a time and to address a variety of audiences. He was widely educated and erudite, and he also impressed with a surprising sense of humour.

Radek belonged to that galaxy of revolutionary intellectuals for whom social revolution was an object of creativity. A historian by education, a journalist and politician by vocation, above all he saw in the revolutionary movement an engaging subject, requiring the play of his outstanding mind.

Radek participated actively in practical administrative work: he was the head of a department of the People's Commissariat of Foreign Affairs of the Soviet government, head of the department of foreign relations of the All-Russian Central Executive Committee (ARCEC), secretary of the Executive Committee of the Communist International (ECCI), and head of the bureau of international information of the Central Committee of the All-Union Communist Party (Bolsheviks) (AUCP[b]). He took part in the organisation of the First Congress of the Communist Party of Germany (30 December 1918–1 January 1919), in the leadership of the October (1923) revolution of the German proletariat, and also frequently carried out a variety of commissions of the Bolshevik Central Committee (CC) in various countries. But despite all this he was not an enthusiast for organisational work. Above all, he was a theoretician of revolution, belonging to the left wing of European socio-political thought, known under the name Marxism, or more accurately to its most radical, extremist current – Bolshevism.

On some readings at least, for adherents of this tendency a voluntarist attitude to the laws of social development was characteristic, together with an underestimation of the principles of scientific-historical evolution of human society, an absolutisation of the role of the masses and of class struggle in history, a total denial of the rights of property as well as a marginalisation of the question of individual rights, a certain casual attitude to violence that sometimes became a tendency to make a virtue out of a necessity, and also a rather blithe approach in general with regard to humanitarian values including ethics and morality, religion and civil society as generally understood. For many Bolsheviks, a simplified, superficial conception of the socio-economic, political and ideological structures of capitalist and pre-capitalist societies, which failed to take into account the full heterogeneity of social systems, was also typical. In their views of world development they were radical internationalists, striving to establish the only thesis acceptable to them of the inevitability of world socialist revolution.

All these characteristic traits of the Bolshevik worldview were reflected in full measure in the works by Radek on China, 1926–27, published in this collection. These works are the clearest possible example of a schematic, Communist and narrow-minded class approach to the most complex questions of socio-economic and political development of oriental civilisations, their history and ideology. The works are extremely politicised, but reasonably logically structured and goal-directed. They are passionate, emotional, polemical and occasionally naïve, but at the same time characteristically reasoned. The whole epoch of Russian Bolshevik Sinology of the 1920s is reflected in them more than anywhere else. At the same time, they bear all the hallmarks of the sharp intra-party discussion in the AUCP(b) and the Comintern, conducted by a minority of party members (the so-called Left Opposition) with the Stalinist bureaucratic majority, about the problems of the revolutionary movement in China among other things. That is precisely why they are interesting today, as a model of a particular, left-radical Bolshevik tendency in Russian Sinology, and as a source on the history of political struggle in the USSR.

These works provoke particular interest by virtue of the fact that they were written by a man who was considered one of the most outstanding specialists in the sphere of Soviet Sinology in those years – notwithstanding all his differences with the leadership of the AUCP(b) and the Comintern over these same Chinese problems. After all, it was Radek himself who in 1925–27 headed the Chinese university in Moscow, the so-called Sun Yat-sen University of the Toilers of China (UTK), a special institute of higher education, founded for the theoretical preparation of both Nationalist (Guomindang) and Communist cadres of the Chinese revolution. He was known to a wide reading public as a Sinologist at that time, and he was accepted in Soviet academic circles as an expert on China, mainly on Chinese history and politics. And all this despite the fact that he came to the subject of China completely accidentally, having no special preparation in Sinology. He did not even know the Chinese language. By his whole experience of life and revolution, and even his formal education right up to 1924, he had hardly any contact with China. For most of his life, Radek moved in circles remote from Chinese studies.

Karl Bernhardovich Radek (original name Sobelsohn)[1] was born on 31 October 1885 into a family of 'prosperous, progressive'[2] Germanised Jews in Galicia, which then belonged to Austria-Hungary. Until the age of five, he lived with his parents and his elder sister in the city of Lemberg, better known under the Slavonic name L'vov (Lwów or L'viv). After the death of his father, he moved in 1890 with his mother and sister to the city of Tarnów (Western Galicia). In 1902, he passed the gymnasium final examination as an external student, and in 1905 he graduated from the history department of Kraków university (in those days, Kraków also belonged to Austria-Hungary). Already during his years of study at the gymnasium, as well as in the university, Karl (or 'Lyolik' as he was then called by his friends and relatives) was carried away by Marxism, becoming one of the most active members of the European Social Democratic movement. In 1902, he entered the Polish Socialist Party, and became a member of the Russian Social Democratic Labour Party (RSDLP). In 1904, he joined the special territorial organisation of the RSDLP embracing Marxist groups active in Russian Lithuania and Poland, the so-called Social Democracy of the Kingdom of Poland and Lithuania (SDKPiL). In 1905–7, while in Warsaw, he took an active part in the 1905 Revolution, but emigrated upon its defeat. In 1908, he entered the German Social Democratic Party, where, alongside Rosa Luxemburg and Karl Liebknecht, he became one of the most outstanding representatives of the left-wing.

In 1903–17, Radek collaborated with the Polish, Swiss, German and Russian Social Democratic press. He was 'the sparkling pamphleteer'.[3] In the period of the First World War, he spoke from radically antimilitarist positions, took part in the international conferences of Social Democratic internationalists in Zimmerwald (1915), Kienthal (1916) and Stockholm (1917), and joined the Zimmerwald Association of left Social Democrats. After the February Revolution of 1917 in Russia, he became a member of the foreign representation of the RSDLP in Stockholm.[4]

---

1 Karl Bernhardovich Sobelsohn had many pseudonyms: Paul Bremer, K. Bremer, Berliner, Andrei, B. Karlson, Ramsey Carlson, Alfred J. Chili, Max, Obozrevatel (Observer), Parabellum, Porebski, Ramsay, Konstantin Romer, Arnold Strutan, Artur Shtrutkhan, Sergei Volkov, Viator; see Broué 1997, p. 1069; Artemev 2000, p. 4. However, he remained well known under the surname 'Radek', which he chose for himself while still a youth under the impression of the 1897 novel *Syzyfowe prace* by the Polish writer Stefan Żeromski. One of the characters in the novel, the Polish revolutionary Andrzej Radek, became his favourite literary hero; see Lerner 1970, pp. 5–6; Fayet 2004, pp. 31–4.
2 Leviné-Meyer 1977, p. 200.
3 Ibid., p. 206.
4 For more detail, see Radek 1989, pp. 138–67.

Radek arrived in Russia shortly after the Bolshevik October Revolution of 1917 and was accepted for work in the People's Commissariat of Foreign Affairs in the capacity of head of the Central European department. Ever since his period in emigration, he had enjoyed good relations with Leon Trotsky, the People's Commissar then in office. At the same time, Radek also headed the department of foreign relations of the All-Russian Central Executive Committee. In December 1917, he was included in the Soviet delegation for peace negotiations with Germany and her allies at Brest-Litovsk. However, he spoke out sharply against the conclusion of peace, in effect sharing the views of Nikolai I. Bukharin, who then headed the inner-party group of so-called 'Left Communists'. In November 1918, shortly after the beginning of the German revolution, he was sent illegally into Germany as a member of the Soviet delegation to the congress of German Soviets. The German police offered a high price for the capture of such a famous Bolshevik, who 'dominated the German scene'[5] and in February 1919, after the First Congress of the German Communist Party, he was arrested, but was soon released and deported to Russia in December.

In March 1920, Radek was transferred to work in the newly-formed Communist International and right up to the beginning of 1924 he was a member of the Presidium and secretary of its Executive Committee (ECCI). In 1919–24, he was a member of the CC of the Russian Communist Party. In 1920, he was a member of the so-called Polish Revolutionary Committee and took part in the invasion of Poland by the Red Army, which ended in defeat. At the end of 1920 – early in 1923, he frequently travelled to Western Europe, to Germany, Holland and Norway, participating in the organisation in those countries of a united front of left-wing forces.[6]

In October 1923, he was again sent to Germany, that time to prepare a new large-scale Communist uprising in that country: in the Comintern, they considered the German revolution of 1923 as essentially the most serious attempt since October 1917 to ignite the fire of world revolution. However, the Bolshevik putsch in Hamburg, in whose preparation Radek played a leading role, ended in total defeat. Radek returned to Moscow, where he was subjected to criticism for the 'mistakes' committed in Germany. In effect, he was removed from Comintern affairs.[7]

It was at this point, in 1924, and motivated by personal interest, that he first began to concern himself seriously with China. After the defeat of the Ham-

---

5 Leviné-Meyer 1977, p. 203.
6 Radek 1989 [1927], pp. 167–8; Khazanov 1993, pp. 270–1.
7 See Lerner 1970, p. 129.

burg uprising of 1923, he had plenty of free time as he was no longer permitted to take part in European affairs. Meanwhile, a national-liberation movement rapidly began to develop in China in 1924, directed against economic and political exploitation by foreign imperialism. This undoubtedly fired his interest in this distant oriental country. Until then, he dealt with China only intermittently as secretary of the ECCI, although he succeeded in leaving a substantial trace in the history of both the Chinese Communist Party (CCP) and the Chinese Nationalist Party (Guomindang, GMD). At the end of July 1922, it was Radek himself who had compiled the text of the most important instruction from the ECCI to Hendricus Sneevliet (Maring), as guidelines for his work in his capacity as Comintern representative in South China.[8] In this instruction the idea was expressed for the first time, as a substantive directive of the supreme organ of the world Communist movement, that the CCP should enter the Guomindang with the aim of forming a united anti-imperialist front in China.

From July 1924, Radek's articles on Chinese problems began to be published in *Pravda*, and then in *Izvestiia, Kommunisticheskii Internatsional*, and other party publications.[9] In the autumn of 1924, his first public speech on China took place in the Bolshoi Theatre; this also received widespread attention.[10] None of this provoked any critical comment on the part of the leadership of the AUCP(b) and the Comintern, since at that time and right up to the summer of 1926 Radek fully supported the ECCI line on China. And although from the autumn of 1923 he took part in the left Trotskyist Opposition, and together with the other oppositionists conducted a heated polemic with the Stalinists on questions concerning the bureaucratisation of the Party, economic development in the USSR, and the victory of socialism in one country, in relation to everything concerning China he stood essentially with the Comintern point of view.[11] In his articles he actively defended the necessity of the participation of the CCP in the anti-imperialist front, underlining the progressive character of the Guomindang as the party uniting all the revolutionary forces of China. It was no accident therefore that in the spring of 1925 Radek again received real work, this time connected with China. He was appointed to a commission alongside the Rector of the Communist University of the Toilers of the East

---

8   See Radek 1991 [1922], pp. 328–9; Pantsov and Benton 1994, pp. 61–3.
9   For a list of Radek's publications for 1924–26, see the bibliography included in this collection.
10 Radek 1924a, pp. 23–61. This same lecture, read on 22 September 1924, was published in the collection *Ruki proch' ot Kitaia!* See Radek 1924b. In 1925, it appeared as a separate publication with the Simferopol publisher Krymgosizdat. See Radek 1925a.
11 For more, see Pantsov 2001, pp. 166–7.

(KUTV), Grigorii I. Broido, and the deputy head of the Eastern Department of the ECCI, Grigorii N. Voitinsky, responsible for the organisation in Soviet Russia of the Sun Yat-sen University of the Toilers of China.[12] In November 1925, he became head of this university.

Radek's first doubts concerning the correctness of the China policy of the ECCI emerged at the beginning of 1926, apparently after contacts with students, the first group of whom arrived from China in November 1925. He raised the question of the utility of the continued presence of the CCP in the Guomindang in 'conversations with the comrades guiding ... [Comintern] policy in China' – apparently with Grigorii E. Zinoviev and Voitinsky. But they did not attach serious significance to his doubts, and Radek accepted their arguments.[13]

But the further development of the situation in China forced Radek to reconsider the problems of a united front. On 20 March 1926, in the city of Guangzhou (Canton), the soon-to-be Commander-in-Chief (C-in-C) of the National Revolutionary Army (NRA) of the Guomindang, Chiang Kai-shek, used military force against Chinese and Soviet Communists (that is, Soviet military and political advisers in China) and their attempts to consolidate their influence in the Guomindang.

Chiang Kai-shek's 'coup', although bloodless, led to the establishment of a barely veiled military dictatorship of 'right' Guomindang and centrists on the territory under the control of the National government of the GMD. Its consequence was a marked weakening of the positions in the Guomindang not only of the Communists, but also of the 'left' Guomindang, grouped around the Chairman of the National government, Wang Jingwei. It was of the most serious significance for the CCP that shortly after the 'coup', in May 1926, Chiang Kai-shek's group made a series of demands to the CCP aimed at a considerable limitation of its political and organisational independence within the Guomindang. In this connection Radek prepared a fairly sharp polemic on 22 June 1926, 'On the Fundamentals of Communist policy in China', in which he expressed himself emphatically in favour of the exit of the CCP from the Guomindang (see document 1). He acquainted his comrades in the Opposition with this material.

Radek's position attracted the attention of Trotsky, and on 26 June 1926, the latter wrote Radek a letter in which he expressed his solidarity with Radek's positions (see document 10).

---

12   See the letters of G.N. Voitinsky to L.M. Karakhan of 4 June 1924 and 22 April 1925; RGASPI, collection of unsorted documents. The last of these letters was published in 1994; see Titarenko 1994–96, Volume 1, pp. 549–53.

13   See the first document in this collection, 'On the Fundamentals of Communist Policy in China'.

In late August and early September 1926, Radek presented his new views, admittedly with great caution, in letters to the Stalinist leadership of the AUCP(b).[14] He received his 'answer' in October 1926 from the head of the Eastern department of the ECCI, Fedor F. Raskol'nikov. In an address to the 15th Conference of the AUCP(b), Raskol'nikov unexpectedly subjected Radek to caustic criticism.[15] Such an unusual reaction to Radek's letters was obviously planned by the Politburo of the CC of the AUCP(b), which was not prepared to tolerate any doubts concerning the correctness of Comintern policy (that is, essentially their own policy).

The departure of the Communists from the Guomindang was unacceptable to Stalin, even after 20 March, in view of the fact that the Politburo under his direction aimed for a radical alteration in the class and political character of the Guomindang itself by means of a seizure of power within this party by the left Guomindang and the Communists. This was precisely how it perceived the tactic of a united front. In accordance with Stalin's directives, transmitted by the Politburo of the CC of the AUCP(b) through the Comintern to China, members of the CCP were obliged to use their presence in the GMD so as to convert this organisation into as 'left' an organisation as possible, and specifically into a 'people's (worker-peasant) party'. They were supposed to achieve this by means of the ousting and subsequent expulsion from the GMD of 'representatives of the bourgeoisie'. Following this, they were to subject their 'petty bourgeois' allies to their influence, so as ultimately to establish the 'hegemony of the proletariat' in China not directly through the Communist Party, but through the Guomindang.

This conception was, in its very essence, purely bureaucratic and based almost entirely on abstract considerations about the balance of power in the Guomindang. It could not be successful in a China embraced by the flames of a national revolution. In contrast to the degraded AUCP(b), the Guomindang was a revolutionary party in 1925–27, and its anti-Communist military faction enjoyed popularity not only within the officer corps, but also among significant layers of Chinese society. Simply ousting members of this group from their own political organisation was impossible. However, Stalin refused to recognise this. Being extremely skilful himself in everything concerning intrigue by the apparatus, he must have been absolutely convinced of the inevitable success of his policy. At this very time, he was occupying himself by ousting his principal antagonists from the leadership of the Bolshevik Party.

---

14 See 'Letter of K.B. Radek to the Secretariat of the CC of the AUCP(b) of 31 August 1926'; Titarenko 1994–96, Volume 2, p. 353; 'Letter of K.B. Radek to the Politburo of the CC of the AUCP(b) of 28 September 1926'; Titarenko 1994–96, Volume 2, pp. 469–70.
15 See AUCP(b) 1927b, p. 87.

The Chinese Communists were objectively hostages to Stalin's line. The dependence of the CCP on Soviet financial assistance predetermined the inevitable acceptance of Stalin's course by the leaders of the Chinese Communist Party. At the same time, it was impossible to carry out the directives for the communisation of the Guomindang without risking the severing of the united front. Leaving the GMD meant burying all hopes for the conversion of this party into a 'worker-peasant' party.

Stalin found himself effectively trapped in a situation of his own making. Within this situation, he should have contented himself with the anti-imperialism of the GMD, effectively making concessions to Chiang Kai-shek, so as to preserve the CCP within the Guomindang.[16]

Finding himself under fire, Radek also fell into confusion. For a while he stopped making any further attempts to extort from the Politburo the acceptance of a decision for the withdrawal of the CCP from the Guomindang; he seems to have retreated into academic educational work. In the final months of 1926, Radek was actively involved in a reworking of a teaching course on the history of the Chinese revolutionary movement for the Sun Yat-sen University of the Toilers of China. He continued this work in 1927. It is true that he only succeeded in preparing 17 lectures embracing only the pre-history of this movement. They were organised in three cycles: the first of which was dedicated to a comparison of the basic regularities of the development of China and of the West in ancient and medieval times, with particular regard to land property rights, commercial capital, a bureaucratic state, and peasant uprisings (lectures one through five); the second to the specific features of the economic and political evolution of China in the nineteenth-century under the influence of foreign capitalism (lectures six through fourteen); and the third (lectures fifteen through seventeen) to the characteristics of social class relations in China at the end of the nineteenth- and the beginning of the twentieth-centuries. These lectures were published in a small tirage (from 250–300 copies) in the UTK Press at the very end of 1926 and the beginning of 1927. In themselves, they undoubtedly deserve attention (see document 2).

Although some lectures were extremely well researched and presented (especially lectures six through ten dedicated to the Sino-Japanese, Sino-Russian, and Sino-German relations as well as the imperialist encroachment on China in the nineteenth century), the general outline of the course was fairly original. According to Radek, who relied not only on his own research but also on that of his colleague at the university, Mikhail P. Zhakov, who had specialised in the

---

16 For more on this, see Pantsov 2001, pp. 125–46, pp. 178–224, pp. 296–8.

philosophical legacy of Mencius,[17] feudal relations in China had dominated it only until the third century BCE. After that, in his view, a struggle for dominance by commercial capital had begun, ending with the latter's victory in the thirteenth and the fourteenth centuries. This was followed by a weakening of commercial capital, connected with the disintegration of the Mongol empire and the corresponding loss of an enormous foreign market for Chinese goods. (This was the reason, in Radek's opinion, for China's subsequent lagging behind the West.) A new strengthening of indigenous commercial capital had begun, in Radek's view, in the 1840s under the influence of foreign capital. Basing himself on his hypothesis, Radek concluded by formulating the thesis that, although modern capitalism had taken over only the coastal regions of China, the age of feudalism in China had largely become a thing of the past. Radek characterised the exploiting class in the Chinese countryside of his day (the large landowners and owners of medium-sized land holdings), not as feudal (or semi-feudal) but as capitalist.

Radek's hypothesis was not purely abstract and scholarly in nature. Radek was trying to demonstrate that the theory of social development worked out by Marx and Engels based on their study of European civilization was entirely applicable to Chinese history as well. This conclusion made it easy for him to overlay upon backward China the pattern of social relations characteristic of the more advanced countries. Furthermore, this enabled him to apply rather freely to China certain tactical prescriptions from the arsenal of the Bolsheviks. Such tactical prescriptions included those which, from his point of view, were aimed at helping the CCP to gain hegemony within the national-revolutionary movement, and then further to consolidate this hegemony. Among these tactics were strengthening the alliance of the proletariat, the peasantry, and the urban petty bourgeoisie; placing the revolution on the 'worker-peasant foundation'; and isolating the national bourgeoisie, so that subsequently a revolutionary democratic dictatorship of the proletariat and peasantry could be established and the bourgeois revolution be switched over onto the socialist track.

In addition to these lectures, Radek's speech 'Controversial Questions of Chinese History', with which he addressed the Society of Marxist Historians of the Communist Academy, is also included in the present anthology (see document 3). The original conception of Chinese history expounded in this individual lecture fully corresponds to the scheme presented by Radek in the series of lectures developed for his course on the history of the Chinese revolutionary movement. His speech aroused a lively but overall friendly discus-

---

17 See Zhakov 1927.

sion. (Researchers such as Boris I. Gorev, Michael P. Zhakov, Michael N. Pokrovskii, Michael A. Rubach, and Grigorii S. Fridliand took part in the discussion.)

At the beginning of 1927, Radek corrected his position in respect of the united front in China, giving it a certain flexibility. He no longer demanded the departure of the CCP from the Guomindang; he formally agreed with the possibility of achieving the hegemony of the CCP through the Guomindang. However, as distinct from Stalin, Radek renounced any tactical concessions to Chiang Kai-shek, insisting on the immediate adoption of determined measures directed towards the realisation of this hegemony. He argued for the immediate establishment of the 'worker-peasant foundation' under the revolution, and for the isolation of the national bourgeoisie (the 'right-wing' Guomindang) with the subsequent establishment of a revolutionary-democratic dictatorship of the proletariat and peasantry, and the switching of the bourgeois revolution onto socialist rails. In substance, the realisation of such a policy would undoubtedly have led to a severing of the united front and the departure of the CCP from the Guomindang. One can hardly believe that Radek failed to understand this. He was simply manoeuvring.

Amongst the Left Opposition, Zinoviev and his partisans, the so-called Leningrad group, shared Radek's views. (Right up to the end of 1926, Zinoviev had been chairman of the Leningrad Soviet.) However, Trotsky and many of those who thought like him considered Radek's manoeuvres to be 'concessions' to Stalin, and considered the immediate departure of the CCP from the Guomindang to be vitally important.[18]

Radek presented his new views in the clearest possible form in March 1927 in the literary-political journal *Novyi Mir*,[19] the newspaper *Izvestiia*,[20] and a series of lectures on the international situation of China, the Chinese revolution, and the life and activities of Sun Yat-sen, the deceased leader of the Guomindang. These were delivered in various institutions, including the N.K. Krupskaia Communist Pedagogical Academy,[21] the club of the Sun Yat-sen University of the Toilers of China,[22] and the Communist Academy. (12 March 1927 was the second anniversary of the death of Sun Yat-sen). The stenographic texts of two of these lectures are published in this collection (see documents 4 and 5).

---

18   For more, see Pantsov 2001, pp. 161–224, pp. 298–9.
19   See Radek 1927a, pp. 146–59.
20   See Radek 1927b.
21   RGASPI, F.532, Op.4, D. 311, L.32.
22   *Pravda*, 15 March 1927.

Radek's speeches were widely noticed, especially his lecture to the Communist Academy, delivered on 13 March (document 5). Together with Raskol'nikov's lecture, made on the same day, and the speech of the General Secretary of the Profintern Solomon A. Lozovskii on the 17 March, this lecture provoked a prolonged and lively discussion. In the course of two days (20 and 27 March) no fewer than 17 people spoke, including spokesmen for the official line Moisei G. Rafes, Alexander S. Martynov, Boris Z. Shumiatskii, Zhou Dawen and others,[23] as well as the oppositionists Sergei A. Dalin, M. Alsky, Semen V. Gingorn, Mikhail P. Zhakov, Abram G. Prigozhin and Abram Ia. Guralskii. On 27 March, Radek summed up the results of the discussion (see document 6).

Of course, the Stalinists could not accept Radek's demands, all the more so because in his speeches he had informed society about the events of 20 March 1926 without the sanction of the Politburo (until then only a narrow circle of highly placed functionaries knew about Chiang Kai-shek's coup). On the 16 March, an editorial appeared in *Pravda* (judging by its style, its author was Bukharin, who was then an ally of Stalin), in which 'several "experts" on the Chinese question' were condemned in the sharpest form, as they had allegedly fallen for 'the imperialist theory of the degradation of the Chinese revolution'.

In Moscow, many people began to talk about differences in the AUCP(b) over the China question. A fairly clear indication of the way in which events subsequently developed is given in the 'Chronological Information' compiled by Zinoviev and Trotsky for the 8th Plenum of the ECCI, summoned in May 1927 in Moscow (document 12). The Left Opposition rose to Radek's defence at the end of March 1927, developing a real attack on the positions of the Stalinist majority over questions of the Chinese revolution. Trotsky was especially active; he made a compromise with Radek and Zinoviev over the question of the presence of the CCP in the Guomindang in the interests of an anti-Stalinist bloc. Stalin, Bukharin and other leaders of the Politburo and Comintern were drawn into an extremely sharp discussion. They also began to use their administrative power against oppositionists. On 6 April 1927, they dismissed Radek from his post of Rector of the Sun Yat-sen University of the Toilers of China. In the meantime, on 12 April 1927, Chiang Kai-shek carried out a new anti-Communist coup in Shanghai, this time a bloody one. The Stalinist policy of concessions was totally discredited. However, Stalin himself did not recognise this, con-

---

23 Carr mistakenly asserts that Voroshilov was present among the opponents of Radek in the Communist Academy. In actual fact, Voroshilov's secretary for foreign political affairs, S.S. Ioffe took part; see Carr and Davies 1969–1978, Volume 1, p. 132.

tinuing as before to insist on the presence of the CCP in the Guomindang, but this time within the left Guomindang, led by Chiang Kai-shek's opponent Wang Jingwei.

Shocked by the coup, Radek prepared a major report at the beginning of May, which he intended to publish in the form of a pamphlet (obviously, it could not be published at that time). In the report, he systematically analysed the basic factors which, in his opinion, led to Chiang Kai-shek's coup (document 7). Both Trotsky and Zinoviev devoted great attention to this document. Trotsky formulated a series of critical notes to the author (document 11), while Zinoviev fully agreed with Radek. Zinoviev even borrowed several ideas from Radek in his essay 'Lessons of the Chinese revolution', on which he was working at that time, lifting heavily (without any acknowledgment to the author) from Radek's chapter 'The Comintern warned, the Chin[ese] Com[munist] P[arty] knew the danger', which Trotsky had criticised more than any other chapter.[24]

On the 17 May, Radek again subjected the China policy of the Comintern to public criticism, speaking in the Institute of World Economy and World Politics during debates on the lecture by the Stalinist Lev N. Geller on the workers' movement in China (document 8). However, neither Radek nor the other oppositionists were in a position to change the situation. The 'left' faction of the Guomindang, which had continued to co-operate with the Communists after Chiang Kai-shek's coup, collapsed. Alarming news was coming from China. In these circumstances and under pressure from Trotsky, Radek made a decision to raise once more the question of the immediate withdrawal of the CCP from the Guomindang in public. This time Zinoviev and the other participants in the Opposition supported him. The leaders of the Opposition decided to send a collective letter to the Politburo, the Presidium of the Central Control Commission, and the Executive Committee of the Comintern. The only thing that embarrassed them was the need to explain why they had not openly demanded the departure of the CCP from the GMD earlier. Naturally, they did not wish to expose the existence of their own internal disagreements before their opponents. The discussions within the faction took up several days. All agreed that they should declare something as follows: although the opposition had not openly proclaimed the slogan of a break with the bourgeois elite in China, in essence those conditions which they had put to the Guomindang (namely, full independence of the CCP), 'in practice and on paper' excluded the possibility of the Chinese Communist Party remaining any further in the GMD. However,

---

24   See RGASPI, F.324, Op.1, D.350, Ll. 14–18, 43, 48–51a. See loc. cit. for manuscript of Zinoviev's own essay, Ll. 1–68.

Zinoviev and Trotsky evaluated this policy differently. The former considered that the Opposition had 'turned out to be right all along',[25] while the latter proposed admitting mistakes.[26] Radek agreed with Trotsky.[27] In the end, Zinoviev's explanations were employed. Zinoviev therefore emerged as the basic author of an essay on this question, which was completed on 2 June 1927 (document 9). The essay was sent to *Pravda*, but was obviously not published.

In December 1927, the 15th Party Congress expelled Radek and other active participants in the Opposition from the Party.[28] In January 1928, Radek was exiled to Tobolsk, before being transferred to Tomsk a few months later, where he remained until May 1929. He was returned from exile and reinstated as a Party member only when he capitulated to Stalin, after making a declaration that he was leaving the Opposition. In 1930, he again began to speak on the Chinese question; however, now he spoke from orthodox Stalinist positions. Radek openly ingratiated himself with Stalin, who publicly humiliated him: it is no accident that Radek's most embarrassing essay – with its shameless criticism of oppositional views – was published in the journal of the Scientific Research Institute on China, whose leadership included his former colleagues of the Sun Yat-sen University of the Toilers of China, which he had once headed.[29] From 1932 to 1936, Radek headed the bureau of international information of the CC of the AUCP(b), but he no longer intervened in discussions over the problems of the Chinese revolution, only infrequently publishing informational essays on the situation in China.[30] He was already a broken man, and according to an eyewitness, '[i]t was already natural for him that no one should dare have an opinion of their own or to say something which Stalin would not like to hear'.[31]

In September 1936, Radek was arrested and again expelled from the Party: a vengeful Stalin had still not forgiven him for his participation in the Opposition. Together with other former Trotskyists, Iurii L. Piatakov, Leonid P. Serebriakov, Iakov A. Livshits, Nikolai I. Muralov, Iakov N. Drobnis, Mikhail S. Boguslavskii, as well as Grigorii Ia. Sokol'nikov (who had never been a Trotskyist) and sev-

---

25 See Zinoviev's 'Notes on the question of the withdrawal of the CCP from the Guomindang', RGASPI, F.324, Op.1, D.351, Ll. 5–8; see also Zinoviev's notes on the margins of Trotsky's declaration to the Presidium of the CCC. RGASPI, F.324, Op.1, D.354, Ll. 1–12.
26 See Felshtinskii 1988, Volume 3, pp. 130–1.
27 See Radek's notes on the margins of Trotsky's declaration to the Presidium of the CCC, RGASPI, F.362, Op.2, D.95, Ll. 165–76.
28 See AUCP(b) 1928, pp. 1317–19.
29 Radek 1930, pp. 10–20.
30 See the bibliography included in this collection.
31 Leviné-Meyer 1977, p. 208.

eral others, Radek was accused of participation in the so-called 'Parallel Anti-Soviet Trotskyist Centre'. (This 'centre' was given this name because, according to 'the investigation', it had existed in parallel to the so-called 'Anti-Soviet United Trotskyist-Zinovievist Centre', headed by Zinoviev and Kamenev. Sixteen persons involved in the case of the 'united centre' had been sentenced to the highest measure of punishment on 24 August 1936 and immediately shot.)

Between 23 and 30 January 1937, Radek, along with the other accused (there were seventeen persons in all), stood before the Military Collegium of the Supreme Court of the USSR including V.V. Ulrikh, I.O. Matulevich and N.M. Rychkov, with the participation of the Procurator of the USSR, A.Ia. Vyshinskii. Despite the ludicrous nature of the accusations, all of them confessed under the pressure of the investigation to 'conspiratorial crimes' and were found guilty of sabotage and diversion, spying (for the benefit of the German and Japanese secret services) and terrorist activity. Thirteen of them were sentenced to shooting, three of them, including Radek, to ten years' deprivation of liberty. One of the accused received eight years' imprisonment.

However, Radek was not destined to survive Stalin's prisons. On 19 May 1939, he was stabbed to death by fellow prisoners in the Verkhneuralsk isolation prison as a result of a fight that had broken out. It only remains to speculate as to who directed the hand of the assassin.

On 13 June 1988, on the basis of a thorough and comprehensive investigation of the materials of the case, and materials of a subsequent review of it, the plenum of the Supreme Court of the USSR resolved to cancel the sentence of the Military Collegium of the Supreme Court of the USSR in relation to Karl Radek. His case was halted in view of an absence of a *casus delicti*, and Karl Bernhardovich Radek himself was posthumously rehabilitated.[32] It took 51 years for this decision of the Supreme Court of the USSR to be handed down.

∴

Twelve archival documents are included in this collection: Radek was the author of eight, and co-author of one. Trotsky's letters to Radek and the 'Chronological Information' by Zinoviev and Trotsky, are arranged as appendices. These documents significantly complement the basic material. None of them has ever been published in English.

---

32   See Yakovlev 1991, pp. 210–35.

Ten of the documents are preserved in the former Central Party Archive of the Institute of Marxism-Leninism of the CC of the CPSU in Moscow, which is the biggest depository of documents on the history of the world Communist movement. In October 1991, the Archive was reorganised and renamed the Russian Centre for the Preservation and Study of Documents of Contemporary History, and in June 1999, after amalgamation with the former archive of the All-Union Leninist Communist Youth League, received the title Russian State Archive of Social and Political History. Altogether, around two-million manuscript documents, 12,105 photographic materials and 195 documentary films, distributed in 669 thematic collections, are located in the archive.

Two documents – Radek's lecture to the Society of Marxist Historians 'Controversial Questions of Chinese History', and his 'Speech at the Institute of World Economy and World Politics of the Communist Academy during the Discussion of the Lecture by L.N. Geller on the Chinese Workers' Movement' – were discovered in the Archive of the Russian Academy of Sciences (ARAN).

The documents are preserved in the following archival collections:

1. The Russian State Archive of Social and Political History (RGASPI):
   F 17, Op 71. Documents of the Internal Opposition in the AUCP(b) (1921–1937)
   F 326. Karl Bernhardovich Radek.
   F 495, Op. 166. 8th Plenum of the Executive Committee of the Communist International.
   Collection of unsorted documents.
2. Archive of the Russian Academy of Sciences (ARAN):
   F 350. The Communist Academy.
   F 377. The Society of Marxist Historians.

The collection is organised chronologically and embraces the period from June 1926 until July 1927. Contemporary orthography and punctuation are used in the documents. Chinese names and titles are given in contemporary transliteration, excluding those which could not be established. Stylistic inaccuracies and other eccentricities of the text are basically preserved – a few small abbreviations have been made in those cases when they are absolutely necessary for transmitting the author's meaning. These abbreviations are shown by dots placed in angle brackets. Supplementary fragments are put into square brackets.

CHAPTER 1

On the Fundamentals of Communist Policy in China

22 June 1926

1. The sources of the Chinese revolution consist in the mismatch between the developing productive forces of China (a commodity economy in the countryside and its social differentiation, the development of capitalism in the cities) and the political fragmentation of China and its dependence on foreign imperialism, as well as a mismatch between the political awakening of the masses and the absolutism of the provincial little tsars supported by international imperialism.[1] The revolutionary forces growing on the basis of this contradiction are the working class, the many million-strong mass of artisans and generally the urban poor, and the peasantry. The upper bourgeoisie in the shape of the comprador one is linked to world imperialism and plays a counter-revolutionary role. The independent commodity bourgeoisie and the industrial and banking bourgeoisie have an interest in the struggle with foreign capital, so long as it controls the customs and is in competition with it.[2] But it fears the unfolding class struggle of the proletariat. While exploiting the vacillations of the bourgeoisie, the Chinese proletariat after all should remember that the victory of the Chinese national revolution depends on its [proletariat's] link with the mass of artisans, peasants, and the urban poor. The intelligentsia and student body are simply representatives of these classes. The struggle of the artisans is directed against capitalist competition, which is ruining them, but it is directed in the first place against the strongest capitalist competition, which is foreign. The mass of the artisans will still continue to play a revolutionary role for a considerable period to come. The revolutionary role of the peasantry is deeper, owing to the relative overpopulation of the countryside, which cannot find accommodation for its surplus in the city, whose development is held up by foreign capital. The massive social dislocation penetrating the countryside makes it a powder keg. The sufferings of the countryside, pro-

---

1 On the first page of the copy of the document, on the top left hand corner there is a note in Trotsky's handwriting: 'Return to Radek'.
2 Radek is mistaken. In China of the time there was no a sharp division of the bourgeoisie into a national one and a comprador one. All business of the Chinese bourgeois who held nationalist views was also closely connected with foreigners. See in detail Bergère 2009.

voked by the wars of the appanage satraps compels the countryside to be a partisan for the reunification of China to a greater extent than was the case in Western Europe.

2. Whether the Chinese revolution concludes with the worker-peasant democratic dictatorship which would unite China for the struggle with imperialism, but which would also inaugurate a period of capitalist development, or whether it leads directly to the socialist revolution evading the bourgeois-democratic phase, depends to a considerable degree on the course of events in Europe. If the proletariat is victorious in a series of industrial countries in the immediate future, then it is not excluded that the Chinese revolution, like the Russian one, will reduce to a minimum the period of time taken by the transformation of the bourgeois-democratic into the proletarian revolution. Irrespective of either prognosis, the link between the working class and the urban and rural petty bourgeois strata is an obligatory precondition of victory. In the first case, the democratic-revolutionary phase will end temporarily with the crossing over of the petty bourgeoisie to the side of the upper bourgeoisie, by the liquidation of the democratic-revolutionary dictatorship and the foundation of a bourgeois government. In the new situation, the proletariat will then have to seek a coalition with plebeian elements, at whose expense the bourgeoisie will try to organise its regime. In present circumstances the elements for the resolution of the revolutionary tasks of China along Russian lines are not yet apparent. The Communist Party should attempt to determine these questions, by means of an 1848,[3] so as to bring about an acceleration of the transformation of the national-bourgeois revolution into a socialist revolution, to the extent that the sharpening of international and Chinese circumstances will in future permit. The immediate objective of this will be a democratic-revolutionary dictatorship of workers, peasants and artisans.

3. The necessity of a link between the working class and the petty bourgeois strata does not in any way pre-determine the form of this link. Even in the Russian revolution these forms changed in shape very much. We took power with the well-known neutrality of the Left-SRs, and subsequently found ourselves in a coalition government with them which ended with their uprising against us.[4]

---

3   This refers to the bourgeois-democratic revolutions of 1848 in a series of European countries: France, Austro-Hungary, Germany, and Italy. Only the French Revolution was successful: in February 1848 the Second Republic was proclaimed in France.
4   The Party of Socialist-Revolutionaries (SRs) was formed in Russia in 1901–1902. It defended the interests of the poor and middling peasantry. Its leader was Victor M. Chernov. In 1917 the left wing withdrew from it and began to collaborate with the Bolsheviks. Radek is inaccurate: the Bolsheviks took power in October 1917 not with a certain neutrality, but with the

And now we maintain a link with the peasantry directly, relating to the poor and middling masses without the intermediary of a peasant party.

4. In the Chinese revolution the question of the form of the connection between the working class and petty bourgeois elements already has a history of its own. When the Chinese Communist Party was founded as the party of the progressive Chinese intelligentsia, the petty bourgeoisie had its own vanguard in the shape of the Guomindang. Neither this organisation nor the Communist Party yet had serious contacts with the popular masses. The advantage of the Communists in relation to the Guomindang consisted not just in a fully developed ideology received from the European proletariat but in the fact that the USSR stood behind the Communists. Sun Yat-sen began moving towards an alliance with the Communists from considerations of international policy in the first place. Having lost faith in liberalism and American assistance, he set course for a link between the Chinese revolution and the world revolution and moved towards a coalition with the Chinese Communists. The young Chinese Communist Party, being more disciplined than the Guomindang, which represented the ideological current of supporters of Sun Yat-sen but not an organised party, was able to conquer a series of commanding roles for themselves in this bloc. Relations between the Communist Party and the Guomindang worked out so that the CCP entered the Guomindang, influenced its policies, and took part in its leading institutions, all the time preserving its organisational independence. To understand this peculiar situation, one must take into account that unlike in Western Europe, there is no excretion of workers' democracy out of petty bourgeois democracy in China, but to a considerable extent there is a conquest of the administration of a petty bourgeois party by the Communist Party.

5. This situation, which gave the Communists significant advantages, was only possible for so long time until the Communist Party and the Guomindang began to attract the masses. Now it threatens to change from an element for the development of the revolution into an element weakening it. It threatens the link of the working class with the petty bourgeois elements or the independence of the workers' movement. Having grown up into a mass party, the Guomindang found control by the Communists irksome. It feels the abnormality of the situation, which consists in the fact that the Communists are

---

direct support of the Left SRs, headed by Boris D. Kamkov, Mark A. Natanson, and Maria A. Spiridonova. A month after the revolution seven Left-SRs entered the Council of People's Commissars. Their collaboration with the Bolsheviks continued right up to 6 July 1918, when they tried to organise a putsch as a sign of protest against the signature by Bolshevik Russia of a separate Brest-Litovsk peace treaty with Germany and her allies.

members of Guomindang organisations and take part in their leadership. The Guomindang is not a member of Communist organisations and has no control over it [must be them]. In this area endless wrangles occur, which threatens a rift. The Communists on their part, having a formally contractual influence over the Guomindang, do not make any effort to win over the confidence of the Guomindang masses, and try to decide questions by means of giving orders or behind the scenes intrigues. On the basis of this situation frictions appear which threaten the existence of the Canton government and provide a basis for the right wing of the Guomindang, which aims for a break-up of the bloc with the working class. From that situation there are two possible outcomes. Either a renunciation by the Communists of their own independent policy, a complete subordination to the Guomindang – the left Guomindang member Su-Chen[5] in a letter to me[6] demands that the Communists accept the three pillars of Sun Yat-sen[7] as their platform – or it is necessary to move from the present form to a bloc with the Guomindang as an alliance of independent parties.

6. This transition is demanded by the entire political situation. The present form of contact with the Guomindang necessarily involves the fostering of illusions among the popular masses concerning the Guomindang. A condition of a bloc of a workers' party with a petty bourgeois party, a condition which we cannot renounce, consists in the freedom to criticise the ally. The social composition of the Guomindang is variegated, containing within itself the likelihood that some of the members of the Guomindang will go over to the positions of the upper bourgeoisie, but even the leftist members of the Guomindang will strive [to go over to the position of the upper bourgeoisie], even when it is a matter of civil war in the name of the interests of petty bourgeois strata, for example the peasants. The most left-wing members of the Guomindang demonstrate a failure to understand the inevitability of a civil war for the liberation of the peasants from exploitation by the leaseholders[8] and the gentry.[9] Only the pressure from the Communists, and pressure not behind closed doors but before the face of the masses, will push the Guomindang to the left. In the present situation we are not only whitewashing the essential character of the

---

5   This probably refers to the well-known member of the left wing of the Guomindang, Xu Qian, though it cannot be excluded that a certain student of the UTC sent the letter to Radek.
6   Document not found.
7   This refers to Sun Yat-sen's Three Principles of the People: Nationalism, Democracy and People's Livelihood (Radek called it Socialism), which comprised the essence of his political platform.
8   Thus in the text. It should read: 'landowners'.
9   Gentry – thus at that time in Soviet literature devoted to China they termed *shenshi*, the Chinese feudal intelligentsia.

Guomindang, but we are pushing it towards a politics of pretence. Under our influence the Guomindang are taking on Communist phraseology and are even competing with us among the masses of the workers. Already the question has arisen as to whether or not to allow the Guomindang to enter the trade unions. In addition, instead of pushing the Guomindang to organise the peasant masses and the artisans on the basis of their real interests, we are wasting our time with getting the Guomindang to adopt revolutionary declarations, which are not inspired by any revolutionary policy, not even of a covert nature. Changing all this is possible only with an open discussion of the question of a bloc between us and the Guomindang, as of a bloc of a workers' party with petty bourgeois [elements].

7. Before an enlarged plenum of the Executive Committee[10] I raised these views in conversations with the comrades guiding our policy in China.[11] To my great surprise, these comrades then rejected them. They spoke up in defence of these views at the very moment when the right-wing Guomindang were demanding a breach with the Communists. In defending my views in the Politburo, I then spoke out against the implementation of their views at a moment of a right-wing attack, considering that one should not overload the horses when the river threatens to sweep the cart away.[12] But the attack of the rightists was repelled, and now the moment has arrived, when we must table the question of altering the form of the relations between the Guomindang and the CCP. In putting forward this question, we must propose as the central idea the necessity of a link between the working class and the revolutionary petty bourgeoisie of the cities and countryside. For this link the creation of an independent, mass petty bourgeois party is vital. The form of the bloc with it must take into account the desire for independence that has been unleashed within it. The Guomindang and the Communist Party must have independent local and central organisations. The connection between them must be realised through coalition committees in the centre and in the localities. It is understood that it is impossible to foresee all the transitional forms from the present situation to such a bloc. These forms must be worked out in practice while allowing continuously for two objectives: the foundation of an independent mass Communist Party and its ties with the party representing the petty bourgeoisie.

---

10 This refers to the Sixth ECCI Enlarged Plenum, which took place in Moscow on 17 February to 15 March 1926.
11 Apparently Zinoviev and Voitinskii.
12 This refers to Radek's speech at the Politburo session of 29 April 1926 against proposals by Voitinskii and Zinoviev for a withdrawal of the CCP from the Guomindang. For more detail see Pantsov 2000, p. 114.

8. The working out of a concrete programme of the Communist Party with reference to the peasantry and the artisans will play a major role in the effective strengthening of this bloc. The elaboration of this programme and the agitation for it among the masses will force the Guomindang to address these questions and move from an intelligentsia policy to one of mass democracy.

Karl Radek
22.VI–26
RGASPI, F.514, Op.1. D. 181. Ll. 66–70
Typescript, original.
RGASPI, F.326, Op.2. D. 24. Ll. 102–6.
Typescript, copy

Publication: Titarenko, M.L. et al. (eds) 1996, *VKP(b), Komintern i natsional'no-revoliutsionnoe dvizhenie v Kitae. Dokumenty*, (Volume 2), Moscow: AO 'Buklet', pp. 262–5.

CHAPTER 2

History of the Revolutionary Movement in China: The 1926–7 Lecture Course
Fall 1926 – Early 1927

Lecture One

The Chinese Revolution contributed to Sunyatsenism three fundamental principles: democracy, nationalism, and socialism. These three principles are the programme of the national movement in China, a programme that is binding upon both Guomindang members and the Communists inasmuch as the Communists have entered the Guomindang party.

But if we approach these three principles and uncover their contents, we will see at once that these are merely general slogans and that the task of revolutionaries is not only to assimilate these three slogans, but also to understand their concrete meaning.

What does 'democracy' mean? Formally, it means the solution of all problems of state by the people themselves. In reality, up to now democracy has always been achieved as the rule of the bourgeoisie.

But Sun Yat-sen put forward the slogan of socialism.

What is the relationship between socialism and democracy? What is the relationship between socialism, as the organisation of the economic forces of the country in the interest of the labouring masses, and the contents of democracy if the latter represents the rule of the bourgeoisie?

Moreover, democracy signifies a unified state, a union of the whole people.

China is broken up into territorial fragments which are fighting against each other. There are districts occupied by Zhang Zuolin; there are districts occupied by Wu Peifu, by the Canton government, and so forth. China has been torn apart into pieces. What has brought about the splintering of China? How can China achieve unification?

These are a series of vital questions. How may they be resolved? How may Sun Yat-sen's slogans be put into practice, where shall we look for the answer?

Numerous Chinese writers concerned with Sun Yat-sen's three slogans have tried to accomplish the task by following an exclusively logical path. But I have already shown that the slogan of democracy contradicts the slogan of socialism and the slogan of unity contradicts the contemporary reality of China. The path to unity is unknown. It is clear that a Chinese revolutionary cannot search for a solution in word games, in the logical counterposition of one to another. He must seek the path through analysis, in studying the development of Chinese reality. That is the path we are taking now. When we finish our course, Sun Yat-sen's three slogans will appear before us not as abstract, contradictory concepts which thought tries to squeeze into a single framework, but as conclusions replete with lively content, the result of analysing the motive forces at work in contemporary China. We will see that Sun Yat-sen, who did not take his stand on the ground of contemporary Marxism, but only approached it, was not an accidental plaything of fate, but of powerful forces of historical development which he studied and thought about seriously, that he was led onto the path of the Chinese revolution, that he was truly great, a leader who pioneered the nationalist development of China. Only the study of Chinese reality will give us the opportunity to understand the true path of its development as it opened up before Sun Yat-sen, and which we must elaborate on the basis of more contemporary methods than those which Sun Yat-sen had at his disposal.

1   *The Condition of China at the Beginning of the Introduction of European Capitalism*

The subject of the course upon which we embark today is contemporary China which has given birth to the Chinese revolution, the national revolutionary movement. The introductory lectures in this course must be devoted to the condition in which China found itself when European capitalism intruded into the country, the moment when its influence began to change the social conditions of China and shattered old forms, created and summoned into life this mighty revolutionary movement of which you constitute a small part.

China encountered the capitalist world as an *agricultural* country; therefore, the first question we must consider when we wish to study the influence of capitalism on Chinese development is the question of Chinese agriculture. This general question must be subdivided into a series of questions. The first question: *Did private property in land exist in China*? The second question: *How was this private property distributed*? Were there large landholdings? Did renting of land exist? Were there hired agricultural labourers? The third question: Was Chinese agriculture a *natural economy* or had it entered into the *whirlpool of commercial circulation*? What degree had the commodification of the Chinese economy reached at the time when China encountered Europe, for the influence of European capitalism would proceed precisely along these two lines: commodification and the differentiation of the Chinese agricultural economy.

A   Did Private Property in Land Exist?

Bourgeois scholars and bourgeois pundits who study the history of China have managed to create an extraordinary muddle regarding the first question: Did private property in land exist in China? So great is the fog generated by the literature on this basic question – who were the owners of land in China when China came into conflict with the capitalist world? – that even in the literature that the Russian revolution created to illuminate Chinese questions, we find the assertion that even at present land in China is nationalised. Three serious works with which we must familiarise ourselves exist on this question. The first is a work by the Russian Sinologist [Ivan Ilyich] Zakharov, appearing in 1854 [1853] under the title 'Pozemel'naia sobstvennost' v Kitae' ['Landed Property in China'], and constituting the basic work on the history of the development of agrarian relations in China.[1] Then there is the work of the English Sinologist [George] Jamieson, chairman of the China Branch of the Royal Asiatic Society, which appeared in 1889 [1888] under the title 'Tenure of Land in China and the Condition of the Rural Population'.[2] Finally, the work of the German Sinologist Franke which appeared in 1903 [1908] and studied legal relations in agriculture.[3] (I do not know the Chinese literature and, therefore, cannot say whether it contains more valuable works, but according to those who know Chinese, there are no such works.) These three works must serve as the foundation for study of the problem. These works complement each other. The first is purely historical; the second describes the economy of agriculture in the 1880s, and the work of Franke, as I have already noted, is juridical in character.

What results do these three sources lead us to?

Zakharov says that under the last – the Qing – dynasty land was divided between state and private property owners and the allocation of land remained as before. *Private agricultural property remained inviolable*, excluding the loss of private persons occurring during times of political upheavals. The right of ownership in any quantity, the sale, purchase, and the mortgaging of land – all on the previous bases – was provided at will to everyone. The government assumed the responsibility of defending this property against unjust appropriation, and bent every effort to ensure that cultivable land was not left idle, the quantity of which increased many-fold during the period of disarray and troubles which put an end to the Ming dynasty, and, by so doing, to stop vagrancy.[4]

---

1 See Zakharov 1853.
2 *The Journal of the China Branch of the Royal Asiatic Society.* V, XXIII, 1888. *Radek's note.* It refers to Jamieson 1888.
3 See Franke 1908.
4 Zakharov, 'Pozemel'naia sobstvennost' v Kitae ('Landed property in China'), *Trudy* [*chlenov*]

Thus, Zakharov demonstrates that there existed in China the right to own unlimited amounts of land, the right to sell, buy, and mortgage it. In a word, with certain exceptions which shall be discussed later, private property in land existed.

Jamieson's work consists of two parts: of his own generalisations and of a series of answers to questionnaires. They are valuable in providing concrete answers to what agricultural property is like in certain provinces – in Manchuria, Zhili, Shandong, Guangdong, etc. – rather than constituting unsubstantiated assertions. Relying upon these concrete descriptions of the situation in these provinces, Jamieson gives the following answer to the core question:

> Whether the absolute ownership of the land may more properly be described as vesting in the people or in the Crown is a question of an academic rather than of a practical nature. The answer to that would depend, as in similar cases in Oriental countries, on the degree of interference which the Government reserves to itself in dealing with the land, and the greater or less latitude it allows its subjects in the disposition of their holdings. To some extent also it would depend on the amount of which the Government exacts as land tax relatively to the gross produce; if large enough to be called a fair rent or a full rent there would be little or nothing left for the cultivator to call his own, and the land would properly be said to belong to the Government, the cultivator being a mere tenant.
>
> In China the authorities generally hold that theoretically the land belongs to the Crown, on the general principle embodied in the maxim that all under the sun belongs to the Emperor, and all the people are his servants. On the one hand, the Crown or Government is the nominal owner of all waste lands, and is the final reversioner of all arable lands which for any reason become tenantless, as from failure of heirs, or from being abandoned on account of famine, civil war and so on. *Original grants of such land may be had from the local representatives of the Government by the first comer on his undertaking to bring it under cultivation and pay the usual taxes. Titles so obtained are good against all the world. On the other hand, land once in private hands may be dealt with at pleasure. It can be freely sold, mortgaged or leased without interference on the part of the Government, and the same terms are used to express the sale and purchase of land as those expressing the sale and purchase of ordinary personal chattels.* The land tax is in general moderately light, amounting on an average

---

Rossiiskoi dukhovnoi missii v Pekine (Works of the members of the Russian ecclesiastical mission in Beijing). *Radek's note.*

to 1/20 or 1/30 of the gross produce. It is not on the better soils anything like a full rent, and owners who do not farm their own lands can always let them at a rent which leaves something considerable over after paying the Government demands.

It may therefore be said that private owner of land has as absolute a property in China as he would have in any other country (under the power of any other government).[5]

Therefore, Jamieson gives an answer similar to that which we have already seen from Zakharov: private property in land exists.

What sort of exceptions are there to this private ownership of land? First, if the land is not cultivated, it may be confiscated by the government. Second, fallow land belongs to the government. Third, alluvial land created by rivers is considered the property of the state. Professor Franke demonstrates that the latter two exceptions also exist in Germany on the basis of prevailing civil law.

The third book I mentioned, the book by Professor Franke, explains from where the notion that land is the property of the Emperor derived. He points out that this is the result of Confucian legends about land which formerly were communally owned. In the *Shijing*[6] we find the words, that everything 'Under the wide heaven, All is the King's land. Within the sea-boundaries of the land, All are the King's servants'.[7] This is a religious formulation which reflects the transition from communalism to feudalism, to a social order in which the Emperor, the seignior, was the juridical owner of the land. But Professor Franke demonstrates that this was not actually the situation from the very earliest historical times, and he repeats exactly what Jamieson said, that

> the character of private property in land in China is just as complete as in any other state in the world. *One may speak of the superior or universal right of property of the state or the Emperor only to the same extent as in other countries of Europe and America, and there is no basis for saying that the situation in China is exceptional.*[8]

---

5 G. Jamieson, 'Tenure of land in China and the Conditions of the Rural Population', *Journal of the China Branch of the Royal [Asiatic] Society*, Vol. XXIII, 1888, pp. 61–2. *Radek's note and emphasis.* In Jamieson's text the last phrase is slightly different: 'It may therefore be said that private owner of land has as absolute a property in it as he can have under any government' (Jamieson 1888, p. 62).
6 *Shijing – The Book of Songs*, the ancient Chinese classic of poetry.
7 Legge 1960, Volume 4, p. 360.
8 Dr. O. Franke, 'Zemel'nye pravootnosheniia v Kitae' ('Land laws in China'), Vladivostok, 1908, 25. *Radek's note and emphasis.*

This demonstrates that at the time China came into contact with the capitalist world, China was not an exception to other countries with respect to private property in land.⁹

In any case, in response to the first central question – did private property in land in China exist at the beginning of the nineteenth century? – we can answer, yes, it existed. China encountered the capitalist world as a country with private property in land. All the profound questions posed in the European literature about the nature of landed property in China are the result of ignorance, the result of reports by European tourists and superficial writers about China who heard that the Emperor is considered a god, that he is very strong and is a landowner. Then, without any attempt at verification or criticism, they conveyed this information to their readers. Sometimes our comrades, too, instead of reading the basic works, read and continue to read this commentary and are therefore unable to dissipate the fog created around these most important questions.

I would again like to draw attention to the fact that Zakharov and Franke and Jamieson themselves knew Chinese; they all made use of Chinese sources. Moreover, Jamieson, who was chairman of the British Society of Sinology, depended, as I have said, on questionnaires which presented a concrete picture of the situation in various regions of China.

B   Did Large Landholdings Exist?

The second question to which an answer must be given is the question of the distribution of landholding.

Usually, China is depicted as a country of exclusively small proprietors, as a country in which there are no large landowners.

The question of whether or not there were large landowners in China is one of *enormous theoretical importance*, because if we want to understand *what the Chinese state represented, what class did the mandarinate headed by the Emperor represent*, then it is obviously very important for us to know whether in China there was only a class of small peasants or there were also large landowners.

This is one of the central questions of Chinese historiography. Without an answer to this question one cannot even attempt a Marxist interpretation of Chinese history or understand the great struggle which unfolded in China in the nineteenth century.

---

9   It is revealing, by the way, that Franke, whose work is valuable only in that he studied the juridical aspects of the question, in order to enhance its value, stops quoting Jamieson at the moment when he begins his factual content, thereby distorting the latter's point of view. *Radek's note and emphasis.*

The conventional answer, which is presented in numerous writings, and even in supposedly Marxist works, is that there was no large landed property in China, but the work of Jamieson, who supplies more or less precise factual material on this question for many provinces, confirms the existence of large landholding. By way of 'eyewitness indicators', let us look at some of the replies to the questionnaire distributed by the British Society of Sinology.

Here, for example, is the reply provided by John Ross, an English missionary in Manchuria. He reports that the average size of a peasant holding is 5–10 English acres, while holdings of 10–30 acres are quite common. In Jilin province there are wealthy peasants with twice as much land who live better than peasants anywhere else in China. Moreover, he testifies that there are very many landholders in Manchuria who have 100 acres, and not a few with 200 acres. Although it is rare, there are even those with more than 500 acres. Someone with 100 acres is considered a wealthy person. Such is the situation in Manchuria.[10]

We have additional evidence from Shandong. There, to be sure, the missionary Medhurst says there are no particularly large landholdings, but in the very same district where Medhurst lived he identified 8–10 persons who owned 500–600 *mu*[11] and one or two who owned as much as 1,000 *mu* while he estimated that 10 *mu* is the average size of a peasant holding in this district of Shandong province. In his opinion, 10 percent of the agricultural land is rented out to peasants by landlords. A peasant pays a portion (up to half) of his summer harvest as rent.[12]

The English missionary Bagnall, who was in Shanxi, reports that there, too, there were large landlords who rent out land and employ hired labour. He says there are huge estates in the southern part of Shanxi. Landlords own more than 1,000 *mu*. He writes, 'About three years since, while traveling in the north of the province outside the barrier, I found there were land-owners who held much larger quantities and worked it by employing labourers by the job'.[13]

The report of the English consul Oxenham in Jiangsu about the situation in that province is very interesting. Interesting because it sheds light on the Taiping revolution.[14] One of the questions in dispute about the Taiping revolution

---

10   Jamieson 1988, pp. 79–80.
11   *Mu* is equel to 0.16 acre.
12   Jamieson 1988, p. 86.
13   Ibid., p. 90.
14   This refers to the Taiping Rebellion (1851–64), i.e., the war of the poor classes in South and East China.

is whether it was a peasant struggle aimed against officials, did it only concern the reduction of taxes or was it also directed against landlords. Oxenham writes the following:

> Since the Taiping Rebellion no large proprietors remain, only peasant holders ... In the north of Jiangsu more large proprietors exist, and a considerable proportion of the land is rented. Formers, when lessees, do not cultivate more than 50 to 100 *mu* each as a rule.[15]

This means that earlier there were large landlords, but that during the Taiping Rebellion they were destroyed and only peasants remained. But in northern Jiangsu, which the Taiping Rebellion did not reach, there are a significant number of large landlords and Oxenham gives completely exceptional numbers which, unfortunately, I am unable to confirm. It is of interest to those of us who will be engaged in scholarly work on these issues, using Chinese sources, to confirm this. He says,

> As was stated above, the number of large proprietors to the south of the River (Yangzi. – K.R.) is very small, and the same may be said of the country within 30 miles of the north bank of the Yangzi. Farther north, however, large landed proprietors are more common, and peasant owners are rare. One family, named Chen, is said to possess 400,000 *mu* (66,000 acres), and its properties extend into the provinces of Hubei and Anhui. Another person, named Yang, owns 300,000 *mu*, whilst owners of 40,000 to 70,000 *mu* are numerous. These large properties are situated in the more northerly portions of the province of Jiangsu, but at Xinghua and Taizhou there are also large proprietors owning from 1,000 to 10,000 *mu*.[16] The Taipings, who almost extirpated or drove out the inhabitants living near Jinjiang, and who burnt, with the Yamens [offices] they destroyed, the land registries, did little damage in the northern prefectures of Jiangsu, and the old families retained their land. To the south of the Yangzi the land, after 1865, was occupied by the first comer, to whom a title was given after some years' occupation, and the payment of land tax was allowed. Of course, under such circumstances, none but poor cultivators who could make a living out of the produce of their farms would take up land, and then only in small quantities.[17]

---

15   Ibid., pp. 98–9.
16   In Jamieson's text: 'from 10,000 to 1,000 *mu*'.
17   Ibid., p. 100.

In this report, Oxenham gives us an entire spectrum from small and medium landlords to very large ones who hold in their hands large chunks of provinces.

Thus, even without turning to Chinese sources, one can find a considerable amount of information about the existence in China of large landholding in the mid- and late nineteenth centuries.

The missionary Boden, who worked in Hubei province, reports that in this province a holding of 300 *mu* was a large property and even a proprietor with 200 *mu* could be considered a landlord. And there were such landlords in Hubei province. The same thing was reported from Zhejiang.[18] And so forth.

I will not exhaust you with additional citations. You will find a summary of the reports used by Jamieson in the table composed on the basis of these reports.[19]

Since we are not dealing with precise statistics covering massive phenomena, but only with eyewitness reports, it is self-evident that, on the basis of this material, we cannot tell with assurance what is the true extent of landlord holdings nor what was its role and proportion, but the fact that has been denied – the existence of huge landholdings as a phenomenon encountered in all provinces – after Jamieson's work this fact is no longer subject to any doubt whatsoever.

Before turning to the question of the condition of the peasantry, of the degree of commodification of the peasant economy, we must first consider certain circumstances.

Where did landlord holdings in China come from?

There were several sources. One was the grant of land by the imperial court to the upper bureaucratic and military aristocracy. However, the high officials who were granted lands comprised only one component of the large landlords. A second group was recruited from officials who squeezed considerable wealth from the mass of peasants by means of collecting taxes, a portion of which they retained for themselves as their personal income (we will have more to say about the system of taxation), and then, if they did not invest these funds in commercial enterprises, bought land. The third source of landlord holdings was the purchase of land by merchants. The landlord class was composed of these three parts.

Landlords themselves did not cultivate their land. Absentee landlordism, a phenomenon characteristic of a number of other capitalist countries with declining agriculture, was extremely common in China. Landlords either did

---

18   Ibid., pp. 103, 105.
19   The table is missing.

not till the land at all, or only tilled an insignificant portion of their holdings. A majority of them lived in towns, in their own residences, and the land was let out to peasants to work. According to Jamieson, the usual rent paid by peasants was half of the basic harvest.[20]

Apart from landlord and peasant holdings, in China up to the nineteenth century there were also so-called banner lands and military settlement lands. Zakharov asserts that under the Ming dynasty one-seventh, and, in the eighteenth century, about one-twentieth of all arable land was military and not subject to alienation and, consequently, withdrawn from circulation among the peasantry. With the passage of time, however, for various reasons the military lands gradually passed over to the peasantry, and in keeping with the growth of a commodity economy, the Manchu regiments were less and less able to retain these lands in their own hands. They began to mortgage and sell them, and Zakharov demonstrates that beginning in the eighteenth century, the government, which wanted to maintain the material basis for its own armed forces, was forced to spend significant sums on purchasing land that had been sold or rented out by the commanders of Manchu troops. By the mid-nineteenth century the government's struggle against the dispersal of military lands into the general peasantry and landlord holdings had become completely futile. Toward the end of the century banner and military agricultural holdings had all but disappeared.

This concludes our survey of the state of landholding in China around the time China came into contact with European capitalism. We may shift to the next lecture, to the question of the commodification of the peasant economy and then, continuing, draw a more or less complete picture of social conditions in China in the period that interests us the most – the beginning and middle of the nineteenth century.

Lecture Two

The previous lecture was a response to the overall question about Chinese agriculture and, consequently, generally speaking, what was China's economic development in the early and mid-nineteenth century.

Sometimes unreliable answers were given by some Marxist writers as well. Thus, for example, in 1889, Kautsky, a man from whom we once learned a lot, asserted in his work *China and Europe* that China's stability and stagnation

---

20   Ibid., p. 108.

was largely due to the fact that China encountered the capitalist world, having preserved, if not quite primitive communism, then, at any rate, autonomous peasant communes, an economy limited within the confines of an 'extended family' which satisfied all its needs. No matter what happened on the surface of Chinese life, there inside, in the depths nothing ever changed, there the masses of people lived in a natural economy, producing everything they required and needing neither money nor anything produced by other households.[21]

We have already seen, however, that private property actually existed in China, and that the rural population was divided into landlords, peasants – small proprietors and renters – and that both landlords and proprietors made use of hired labour to a significant degree. This would be quite enough to conclude that Kautsky's assertions are wrong. But we have lots of additional evidence regarding the fantastical nature of his assertion that in nineteenth century China the natural economy and the 'extended family' were the basic unit of Chinese society during this period.

Not only in the nineteenth century, but throughout the Christian era, a money economy developed in China. China made use of money – and not only metallic, but paper money as well – from the beginning of the European chronology. And if one should suppose – also contrary to fact – that in the Yuan dynasty (1260–1368), in the era of Mongol rule, when China experienced a rebirth of feudalism and when Marco Polo saw castles in which feudal lords lived, that in this time the money economy embraced only the apex of feudal society, and hardly extended down to the village level, and that trade was primarily external, then it is abundantly clear that in the nineteenth century China could not do without domestic trade which, in any case, embraced a certain part of the needs of the broad masses of people.[22] Within the developed feudal order, trade served primarily to satisfy the needs of the grandees, mostly in luxury goods, and the commercial centres themselves usually doubled as administrative centres where the grandees lived in the castles allotted to them. Similar trade existed in China in the thirteenth century when merchants imported various valuables, including wine from Persia and Italy, Indian, Persian, and Arab fabrics and damask.

But in the nineteenth century, commerce in China was quite unlike medieval commerce.

---

21   Radek is mistaken. In 1889 Karl Kautsky did not publish a work titled *China and Europe*. Radek must have had in mind Kautsky's article titled 'The Chinese railroads and the European proletariat', published in 1886; see Kautsky 1886 and Blumenberg 1960.

22   According to recent discoveries, Marco Polo never travelled to China; see Wood 1995. Radek is incorrect. The Yuan dynasty was established in 1271.

If, as we have noted in the first lecture, disputes arose in the European literature about the existence of landlords in China fifty to one hundred years ago, then it is self-evident that a landlord economy was not dominant, that landlords were not the main organisers of the economy as they were during the era of feudalism, and it was not their need for luxury goods which defined the parameters of commerce.

It is true that we have no general works on the state of Chinese domestic commerce in the nineteenth century, but we can easily draw a picture of it using data collected from various sources. I cite one of these sources, '*Tagebucher aus China*' ('Letter from China'), which is the diary of [Baron Ferdinand von] Richthofen, a German geographer who travelled throughout China in the [18]60s and [18]70s and, as the fruit of his travels, compiled an enormous work on the geography of China.[23]

If we examine this work for a description of commercial cities, a list of goods which moved along China's internal roads, what do we see? What is being transported along these trade routes, on the Grand Canal, on the main highways? We find the following goods: iron from Shandong province and Shanxi, cotton from central and southern China, tobacco, grain and salt. These were the main items of domestic trade at the time of Richthofen's observations.

The literature on China is full of talk about opium, but Richthofen informs us that peasants did not smoke opium; it was too expensive for peasants, and the masses of peasants despised opium-smokers. Most of those who smoked were in the cities. Goods traded were necessities of the peasant masses and the urban population of craftsmen, merchants, and so forth.

Peasants produced not only to satisfy their own needs, but also to make money, part of which they paid in taxes and used to purchase necessities for their households such as iron, salt, and cotton. This is how we must understand Richtofen's description.

That the peasant economy was drawn into commercial exchange and that the trade served the peasant market is eloquently confirmed by the questionnaires to which we turned for clarifying the question of large-scale landholding. A feature of the answers Jamieson provides is that their authors, for the most part English missionaries, give exceptionally precise and detailed, almost exhaustive, data *about the prices of the most important products of the peasant economy* – rice, millet, wheat, which, of course, they would have been unable to do if these products were not regularly available at markets. In almost all

---

23   Five volumes 'On Social Relations in China' and two volumes of 'Letters'. *Radek's note*. It refers to Richthofen 1877–1912 and Richthofen 1907.

provinces, to a greater or lesser degree, we find *monetary rents*, and the unavoidable payment as well of at least part of taxes in money. We know of a large number of districts in Shandong province, Guangdong, Hubei, Gansu, etc. where, from time immemorial, exclusively *market cultures* have flourished in cotton, tobacco, silk, poppies, sugar cane, etc. People from various provinces tell us of the higher or lower price of peasant land depending upon the ease of *transportation*. We are informed of the cost of cotton clothing bought by peasants, of agricultural implements, fertiliser, and so forth. One may conclude without any doubt that the scale of commodification was very significant from the fact that the government purchased a large quantity of grain for its granaries. In the invaluable work by the Russian monk Iakinf, *Kitai, ego zhiteli, nravy, obychai, prosveshchenie*, published in 1840, we find a special, very interesting chapter on food stores ('measures of national provisioning in China') and we have the following picture in this chapter: The government collects the land tax partly in money and partly in grain. The grain collected in this manner is stored in state granaries in the event of famine. Moreover, the peasants collect a certain amount of grain themselves and store it in village storehouses toward the same end. Regarding the government granaries, Iakinf writes:

> Officials in charge of the granaries, noting changes in [the price of] grain, can sell it at a lower price, and, in the autumn, replenish their stock by purchasing new grain. In this way, the older grain is replaced with new grain.
>
> Up to three-tenths of the grain, stored in provincial state granaries, can be sold, while seven-tenths remains in reserve. However, depending on the soil, in some places one-half or even seven-tenths may be sold, but in years when the harvest is good, no more than one-tenth or two-tenths is sold. In good harvest years, grain from the granaries is usually sold at a twenty percent discount, but in poor harvest years at ten percent off the referenced market price. After the autumn harvest, the granaries are replenished with new grain purchased for a stipulated sum.[24]

---

24 Iakinf, 'Kitai' ('China'), pp. 287–8. The author even makes it possible for us to calculate the amount of grain bought and sold annually by officials, since he inserts into his work a table of the amount of grain in state warehouses by province. He gives the total amount of rice, millet, and wheat in state warehouses all over China as 41,049,991 sacks of 160 *jin* [one *jin* is approximately equal to one lb.] each, that is, approximately 200 lbs. Thus, in years of good harvest, officials sold from 20 to 40 million *poods* [one pood is 36.11 lbs] and during partial harvest failures, the total evidently reached as much as 100 million *poods* or more. *Radek's note*. It refers to Iakinf (Bichurin) 1840.

This means that peasants consigned a part of their grain, and a rather significant part at that, to the market.

Further. We know what role the salt monopoly played in state finances. And here is what the monk Iakinf, naming the sources from which he accumulated his capital, has to say:

> Merchants are usually the wealthiest of private persons in China, among them in particular are several of the possessors of salt mining privileges ... The next wealthiest among private persons are members of the *Cohong* [Gonghang. i.e. state owned trading company]. The property of Panikqua,[25] the number one merchant of this society is estimated at 4 million *taels* or 6 million *piasters*.[26]

But what does this indicate? It shows that one of the most important sources of capital accumulation (more important than foreign trade which the *Cohong* conducted) and of state revenues, derived from the power of the countryside, that is, the main consumer of salt, of course, was the peasants. Naturally, it would be wrong to think that Chinese peasants produced everything for the market. Like peasants in all undeveloped capitalist countries, Chinese peasants consumed most of what they produced. But Chinese farmers were connected to the market, and as Richthofen shows, it was very common in many places that their links to the market were significantly greater than in backward regions of Europe. Richthofen says, for example, that nineteenth century Balkan peasants were less connected to culture and the market than Chinese peasants. Many misunderstandings regarding the condition of Chinese farmers and the social conditions of the Chinese peasantry derive from the fact that travellers did not notice the difference between the *state of the economy* and *political forms* in which the countryside lived and which, to a significant degree, only reflected the past organisation of the village economy. For example, Richthofen says that there is no other country in which villagers lived as democratically as in China. In his book *L'empire chinoise*, published in 1854, and considered at the time one of the basic works about China, Huc provides the following picture of this village democracy. Villages followed their own

---

25 Thus in the text.
26 Iakinf, 'Kitai' ('China'), 338–9. The excerpt presented here is one of the 'responses' of Mr. Krusenstern to questions given him by Mr. Virst. Iakinf supplements this response with a report about other capitalists, in particular Beijing lay bankers, without, however, disputing the words cited by Krusenstern. *Radek's note.* It was first published in Iakinf (Bichurin) 1827.

customs in settling disputes; it was not the state bureaucracy, but their own village elders, the most respected fathers of peasant families who were also responsible persons vis-a-vis the state administration, utilising this democratic apparatus to bring relief to themselves and to collect taxes and conduct state policy. The state viewed the village as a unit responsible for the conduct of its own affairs.[27]

In the economy, therefore, each family was an individual unit, but each village functioned as a single entity vis-a-vis the state.

As in Russia, where a communal economy has not existed for a long time and every peasant conducts his own economic affairs independently, the commune continued to exist as an apparatus which partially substituted for the state administration and facilitated its work, so in China, too, political power in the countryside was exercised through delegates from among the peasants who were heads of households, and this is one of the reasons why many researchers concluded that communal landholding still existed in nineteenth-century China. In reality, as we now know, there was no such thing.

---

27 'Each village stood before the state, to which it was obligated to pay taxes, as a single and consolidated whole. At the head of this whole unit was an elder (*sian-yo*) [*xiangzhang*] chosen through universal suffrage. Perhaps nowhere else in the world did communities have such complete and consummate organisation as in China. Its officials were freely chosen by laymen, while state officials (the mandarinate) did not propose candidates or influence the course of elections. Every member of the community possessed the right to choose and to be elected, but in reality the choice usually fell upon persons who enjoyed universal respect by virtue of their venerable age, character, and prosperity. We will encounter many such Chinese elders, and it cannot be denied that on the whole they are fully worthy of having been chosen by their fellow villagers. Their term of office varies by locality. They oversee the police and, in cases which exceed their competence, they serve as intermediaries between their electorate and the mandarinate'. Huc. *L'empire chinois*, 1854, [Vol.] 1, pp. 97–8. *Radek's note*. Radek's translation from French into Russian is not entirely accurate; he is also mistaken in paging. It refers to Huc 1854, Vol. 1, pp. 96–7. The correct English translation of this piece by Huc is as follows: 'The villages are collectively responsible to the Exchequer for the discharge of all fiscal impositions, and they have at their head a mayor called *Sian-yo*, who is chosen by universal suffrage. The communal organisation is perhaps nowhere else as perfect as in China; and these mayors are chosen by the people, without the Mandarins presenting any candidates or seeking in any way to influence the votes. Every man is both elector and eligible for this office; but it is usual to choose one of advanced age, who both by his character and fortune occupies a high position in the village. We have known many of the Chinese mayors, and we can affirm that in general they are worthy of the suffrages with which they have been honoured by their fellow-citizens. The time for which they are elected varies in the different localities; they are charged with the police duties, and serve also as mediators between the Mandarins and the people, in matters beyond their own competence' (Huc 1855, p. 88).

If one asks (as Kautsky posed the question), why did China's economy change so slowly, one must seek the answer not in the countryside in its sham backwardness and primitiveness, but in the cities, in the state of Chinese handicrafts and manufacturing.

In lectures I gave last year, I already talked about how Marco Polo described Chinese handicrafts in the thirteenth century. He spoke of them in such a way, and provided a picture that left no doubt whatsoever that Chinese handicrafts in the thirteenth century were at a higher level than even the best European handicrafts at that time in Venice, Milan, and other centres in Italy which, at the time, was the most advanced capitalist country.

If one looks at Chinese handicrafts of the late eighteenth century, it was not only the Chinese Emperor who could then say to the British ambassador Macartney that there is nothing we need to buy from you, nothing we want, for what we produce is no worse than what you produce. Such was also the view of a large number of travellers who compared the state of Chinese handicraft industry at the end of the eighteenth century with the European crafts of the same period prior to the beginning of the Industrial Revolution.

The similarity here was not simply external or technical. Just as in Europe, handicrafts in China in the eighteenth century not only attained perfection, but also outlived itself. The destruction of medieval relations in the handicraft industry in China went even further, perhaps, than in Europe. At any rate, Iakinf asserts that guilds and medieval corporations no longer existed in China in his time there, and that only memories and fragments remained. Even the very term for medieval corporation or guild (also meaning boundary, line, series, condition) had lost its meaning.

'In China the word Hang [guild] exists only as a name'. Handicraftsmen still often occupy separate streets according to each craft and organise traditional handicraft holidays, but there are no written regulations or rules.[28] Chinese handicrafts not only incorporated the highest level of the division of labour, enormous specialisation, but on the foundation of this specialisation already had become transformed into manufacturing. The works of many authors whom I have already cited, such as Huc and Richthofen, contain descriptions of Chinese manufactures – porcelain, textiles, silk – descriptions which demonstrate that the technical mastery of Chinese craftsmen was in no way inferior to European. Richthofen even says that the Chinese took the techniques of their craft to such a level that each craftsman functioned like an automatically operating machine. The division of labour in Chinese manufacturing

---

28   pp. 343–5. *Radek's note*. This in the text. It is not clear what Radek refers to.

was much more advanced than in Europe. A well-known example is the production of porcelain. Each Chinese porcelain factory had its own specialty and, moreover, was divided into departments for the special manufacture of a particular kind of crockery. For example, the large imperial porcelain factory, which had opened as early as the fourteenth century, had twenty-two departments. Within each of these departments the strictest and most detailed division of labour prevailed. 'Each worker', Huc says,

> had his own specialty, his own special talent. One paints flowers, another birds, one applies red dye, another blue. I have calculated that by the time a porcelain vase assumes the final form in which it will go on sale, it has passed through the hands of fifty workers.[29]

Naturally, a worker who has performed only one of these fifty operations throughout his life has brought it to the highest level of perfection and efficiency.

In addition to handicrafts and manufacturing there also existed 'domestic industry' – working at home to fill the orders of a buyer. The peasant cum part-time craftsman was at the beck and call of the buyer who brought him orders and purchased the products of his work. The Russian monk Iakinf, whom I have already cited, a man who displayed great interest in economic questions and especially questions relating to banks, percentages and so forth, where he adduces Krusenstern's reply to the question of whether factories existed in China or whether wares were produced by families, and what was the relationship between masters, assistants, and apprentices, confidently corrects his predecessor:

> Both silk and cotton fabrics are also produced by family workshops, but more according to orders from factory owners and from manufactured materials. Village inhabitants, preparing raw materials, have neither the time nor means to process them any further.[30]

These peasants prepare the raw materials, buyers purchase these raw materials and give them to other peasants to process.

---

29 Radek is mistaken. This is a quotation from Renard 1863, p. 533.
30 Iakinf, 'Kitai' ('China'), Chapter IX. 'An explanation of Mr. Krusensterns's answers', p. 350. This entire chapter of Iakinf's book consists of commentaries on the brief and sometimes unreliable reports of the traveller Krusenstern, which the latter obtained second-hand in Canton from Englishmen. *Radek's note.*

Iakinf also speaks of the existence in his time of numerous large and small 'workshops' of various kinds, more likely manufactories. For example, porcelain manufactories near Canton, state silk mills in Nanjing, Suzhou and Hangzhou. I would also like to draw the attention of the comrades to a new work by ([William F.] Collins, *Mineral Enterprise in China*, [Revised ed.], Tientsin: [Tientsin Press], 1922)[31] which, on the basis of Chinese sources, provides an outline of the coal and metallurgical industries of China prior to China's encounter with European capitalism. Collins shows how in this 'heavy industry' – rather than cotton or silk – we see the kind of development that Europe surpassed only after the employment of steam-powered machines ...

The only remaining question is why China did not advance from handicraft manufactures to modern industry, in other words, why the Chinese did not invent steam-powered machines. But this question is for persons who like to split hairs. We must take as a given that modern machinery was invented in England. Why not ask why Germans didn't invent steam-powered machines even though it is said that it was a German who even invented the ape? Why did the French not invent the machine? The obvious fact is that owing to well-known historical conditions, which I shall touch on below, the invention of modern machines occurred in England. It is ridiculous to ask why did the Chinese not invent these machines since all other peoples apart from the English are in the same position.

Are there reasons why it was in England that the shift from handicraft manufacture to modern industry occurred?

If we examine the history of technology, we will see that, in essence, attempts to effect a transition to modern machinery took place in three countries. First of all – at the end of the Middle Ages – in Italy. We know how the brain of a genius such as Leonardo Da Vinci laboured over technical questions. And probably not in vain; he did not labour fortuitously. His was part of a general search for a breakthrough beyond the bounds of handicraft manufacturing. The second country was Holland, and the third country, where these efforts led to a solution of the problems, was England.

Why did the efforts to escape the limits of the technological achievements of handicraft manufacturing take place in these three countries and not in others?

These were maritime countries, living by foreign trade and colonial plunder. In these countries there was a growing need for a breakthrough to mass production. England turned out to be best situated for this because, as we know, Italy's role ended from the moment when the Arabs and then – decisively –

---

31 See Collins 1922a.

the Turks cut off the peoples of the Mediterranean Sea from the East. Holland had too small a territory and too few of its own resources for the technical tasks of mass production to acquire the intensity and acuteness necessary to engage in sustained experiments. England possessed a much larger territory and inexhaustible mineral wealth. Moreover, during the heyday of handicraft manufacturing, it was experiencing competition from East India … China, an enormous country rich in natural resources, was heading in the same direction as these other countries as early as the thirteenth century when the Mongols held all of Asia in their hands, when Chinese money circulated from the Pacific Ocean to the Persian Gulf and the Caspian Sea, when the existence of commercial turnover throughout Asia stimulated the rapid growth of Chinese merchant capital and encouraged the development of manufacturing. But the collapse of Mongol rule, struggles among the rising Muslim states, the conquest of India, and the decline of Persia led to the break-up of Asia and the fragmentation of an enormous common market. Chinese merchant capital was denied the opportunity of trading on the continent of Asia, and there was nowhere it could go by sea. At the time the Pacific Ocean provided so little scope for the development of trade that the Chinese dredged and maintained the Grand Canal parallel to the sea, because it was cheaper and more convenient than to subject ships to monsoons and risk battles with the pirates who controlled the coast. Chinese merchant capital was confined to China itself, cut off from all foreign markets, and after the fall of the Yuan dynasty one of the main domestic markets for infant capitalism also disappeared since the triumph of the peasantry and the destruction of feudalism meant the disappearance of the courts of the feudal nobility. Chinese manufacturing, highly developed in the mid-fourteenth century, remained at almost the same level from then on, unable to move forward.

It is amusing when people like the bourgeois scholar Weber say, and following him, our own comrade Varga repeats, that the reason why the Chinese economy stalled was because the natural sciences failed to develop in China.[32] This is utterly absurd. It is not because the natural sciences develop that capitalism develops but the natural sciences develop where capitalism develops and there is a corresponding need for them. Another absurdity is that the reason for the absence of such development, that is, of a transition to capitalism, is the lack of strong state power which could compel peasants to submit to authority and work in factories. Once again, capitalism is not created on the foundation of state power, but state power on the foundation of capitalism. Moreover, Chinese state power was sufficiently strong at the time the Manchu dynasty

---

32   See below.

was established to drown all of North China in blood and suppress a peasant rebellion that had been going on for fourteen years. It coped with a series of peasant uprisings and continued to exploit the peasants mercilessly. All these theories run counter to the fact of a considerable intensification of the division of labour in the countryside. It had nothing to do with the absence of a strong authority or insufficient advancement of the natural sciences, but everything to do with the constraint on Chinese merchant capital. We must seek the primary explanation of why Chinese capitalism failed to make the transition from handicraft production to factory production in the fact that it was unable to engage in colonial expansion.

Owing to these factors, in mid-nineteenth century China we do not even see the crystallisation of a special class of industrial bourgeoisie. Crafts remain in the hands of small-scale proprietors, and manufacturing in the hands of merchants. The merchant class was the incarnation of the Chinese bourgeoisie, impeding its development.

It would be incorrect to say that there were only petty merchants in China. If we sum up what we know about transport enterprises in China, of the shipping of rice, cotton, iron, salt, and grain over enormous distances, shipping not only with the assistance of the state apparatus which compelled peasants to perform unpaid work for the state, but also by means of private merchant capital, then the existence of a large stratum which accumulated significant amounts of capital in its hands will become evident.

To the question of where and how significant were trade fairs and trading places, Krusenstern, after first enumerating the ports for foreign trade, replied, 'All large cities serve as *places for warehousing goods for domestic commerce and for the manufactures of their own province, and especially those located on large rivers and canals*' and that 'in the interstices between the wharves trade is taking place almost everywhere.' Iakinf considered 'this reply very satisfactory' and added that temporary markets in China include 'the ranks of selling points and bazaars' in unimportant points, and in place of large-scale trade fairs 'there are quite a few storerooms which, judging by the extent of their trade, could be considered trade fairs, if their wares were central, and not just going in one direction'.[33]

All of this clearly demonstrates that apart from local, small-scale commerce, there was also large-scale trade on a national scale.

Merchant guilds have been disbanded almost completely since individual capital has exceeded the bounds of the guilds. To be sure, 'dealers in canvas and

---

33   Iakinf, pp. 345–6. *Radek's note and emphasis.*

owners of tea plantations annually gather in a place designated by their leaders where, in a general meeting, they set prices according to which their goods will be sold in various places', but, on the other hand, for example, merchants who are members of the *Cohong*, senior members of the guilds, who are supposed to represent only thirteen kinds of goods in Canton, in reality are monopolistic brokers 'who are shearing the wool from all their merchant brethren.'[34]

Thus, there can be no doubt of the existence of large-scale merchants and highly-developed merchant capital.

This is likewise confirmed when we read works dedicated to the development of credit. In addition to the books of English authors, we now have the work of the Chinese Ku Sui-lu on the development of types of bank transactions in domestic Chinese trade.[35] Ku Sui-lu's book, which is devoted to the development of credit institutions, their turnover, etc., fully confirms in its essentials what Iakinf reported on the condition of banks. Iakinf writes that, 'in Beijing alone there are as many as 200 private lending banks and the poorest among them has not less than a million rubles (in paper currency) in circulation'. What these banks are engaged in is very interesting. First of all, merchants themselves never carried with them significant amounts of money from one city to another. They deposited money in the bank of a large commercial city and received a check on the bank of a province to which they were going. Upon selling their goods, they took payment not in cash, but in a promissory note on another bank. These promissory notes were honoured not only by the bank from which it originated, but also by banks networked with that particular bank. In this fashion, we have a system which is conceivable only in the context of a high volume of trade and in which merchant capital plays an important role.

No less indicative of the level of development of Chinese merchant capitalism is the existence of private postal stations, excellent book-keeping which merchants conduct, price-lists which they post in their shops and so forth, all of which our Russian missionary, so well-informed on commercial matters, relates painstakingly.

The merchant bourgeoisie in China was not a ruling class just as it was not in any other absolute monarchy. Both in eighteenth-century France, and in Germany under Frederick the Great, merchant capital did not directly dictate government policy, although it had already begun to become the dominant force in the national economy. Even on the basis of the scant information we

---

34 Iakinf, pp. 345–6. *Radek's note.*
35 It refers to Ku Sui-lu 1926.

possess, there can be no doubt whatsoever that merchant capital in China controlled enormously valuable goods, that it influenced the entire national economy, and that it was one of the dominant forces in the country. We cannot arrive at an accurate picture of the dimensions of monetary merchant capital since, understandably, we lack any statistical data, but we already know, for example, that according to Krusenshtern, Panniqua, the head of the *Cohong*, the privileged group of Canton merchants which the government had granted a monopoly of foreign trade in Canton, possessed four million taels, a sum which, Krusenstern added, probably was understated since Chinese merchants were unwilling to discuss their finances lest they be subjected to higher taxes. It is not for nothing that such an expert on world trade as Cobden, the leader of the English Liberal Party, in his speech on the occasion of the opium conflict, bows before Panniqua's firm, calling it 'one of the most important firms in world trade'.

Of course, the group of merchants who constituted the *Cohong* did not fall from the sky. It was just one of a number of powerful merchant alliances in China. Krusenstern even places the wealth of its members below that of the salt monopolists. Where did these merchant firms come from? Where did their capital come from? The same Iakinf gives a highly embossed response to this question.

> There are many extremely rich men in China, and the number of well-to-do capitalists is very great. They come from among the officials, but even more from among merchants. Their wealth consists of land, buildings, and moveable property such as silver and goods.

Later he speaks of loan-granting banks, and then continues,

> In China almost all the land belongs to landowners. As a matter of preference, everyone, regardless of their status, tries to maintain part of their capital in land, for such capital provides a reliable income and, moreover, is not liable to any unforeseen dangers apart from political upheavals. But no one refers to those who possess land as landlords.[36]

What do we see in this? On the one hand, a commercial revolution is taking place in the country which is mobilising cash capital, a part of which, especially in years of drought or other disasters, goes into interest-bearing loans,

---

36   Iakinf, 'Kitai' ('China'), p. 398. *Radek's note.*

is invested in domestic special-order production, or in manufacturing, thereby accelerating the process of monetary accumulation in merchant hands. The accumulation proceeds more quickly than market growth and the merchants invest a part of their money in land. The officials, who enrich themselves at the expense of the masses of people, do the very same, investing money, on the one hand, in land, which secures them an honoured position in society, and, on the other hand, directing a part of the income into trade and thereby enriching themselves.

Such is the general position of the Chinese economy which one may deduce on the basis of the several more sober and business-like reports at my disposal rather than the information usually provided by tourists and superficial observers. I am convinced that any comrade who avails himself of similar high-quality material will reach the same conclusions. All of the mystique concerning the economic realities of China which emanates from the superficial literature, dissipates as soon as one turns to studying the testimony of thoughtful and serious observers.

We may be assured in advance that both the essentials of state power and the class character of the mandarinate will become wholly clear to us if we are able to free our understanding of the Chinese state from fantastic overlays.

When, in the following lectures, we will provide an analysis of the Chinese tax system, the system of power, and of administration, we will see that all the tales alleging that the Chinese bureaucracy supposedly constitutes a supra-class type of power are unreliable. We will probably see in this connection a whole series of distinctive phenomena, because in the economic development of China as well there were distinctive delays and divergences, but in its essential structure both the society and state power in China were just like the structure of society and state power in all other countries with a commercial economy in which merchant, rather than industrial, capital played the leading role.

Lecture Three

In the two preceding lectures, I tried to present a very general picture of the social structure of China at the time of the incursion of European capitalism. We saw that there were no significant differences between the social conditions of China in the middle of the past century and the social conditions of West European countries in the epoch prior to the development within them of modern industry. We saw an agricultural country consisting of small proprietors experiencing a process of differentiation which under the influence of a money economy, created poor and well-to-do peasants, landlords, traders, merchants, capitalists, an urban poor of workers labouring in manufacturing and handicraft industry or in their own workshops. Now we take up *the question of the nature of state power* which found expression in the alternation of Chinese dynasties, and its final development prior to the 1911 revolution[37] in the mandarinate of the Qing dynasty.

If, with regard to social conditions in China we heard an enormous quantity of variegated fabrications, understandable in view of the fact that the Europeans did not know Chinese, or of those who did, only in rare instances did they live outside a few port cities, in regions more distant from the seacoast, then with regard to the nature of state power all of the European literature is fantastical without exception. In brief, we may say that if Confucianism in China itself is now in the process of disintegration, then *a Confucian take on the nature of the Chinese state reigns unchallenged in the European literature*. In China perhaps there are no such orthodox Confucians as we encounter in European, so-called scholarly literature dedicated to China.

I will touch only upon the historical-theoretical literature.

To comrades who know German, I would like to recommend as the best bourgeois work which attempts to present the sociology of China, to ponder the nature of China, and its similarities and differences with Europe, the work of the German sociologist Max Weber, dedicated largely to Confucius, but embracing all of the main questions of Chinese history.[38]

Even in this best work, the author wholly endorses the Confucian legend that Chinese state power was a *supra-class* power, the power of scholar-bureaucrats who were not defending any particular class interest. With the materials he had at hand, Professor Weber tries to prove this in detail.

This view is so widely dispersed that not only the bourgeois scholar Weber, but also our comrade, Varga, a leading specialist on the world economy, in his book on the Chinese revolution could write the following:

> It seems to us that the reason for the non-emergence of indigenous Chinese capitalism is the following: 1) There was no completely powerful state organisation, built on coercion, which could compel workers to serve capitalists. Central and local government authorities arose in China from the need to regulate water supply, protect against floods, and

---

37 It refers to the Xinhai Revolution of 1911–12 that overthrew the Manchu Qing dynasty. On 1 January, 1912 China was pronounced a republic.

38 Max Weber, 'Gesammelte Aufsätze zür Religionssoziologie', Tübingen, 1922. I.B. *Konfuzianismus und Taoismus. Radek's note and emphasis.* It refers to Weber 1922, pp. 276–536.

ensure irrigation of the land. Thus, authority arose for profoundly peaceful goals, and not as in Europe, from the struggle of monarchical power with feudal lords and the military-style organisation of the urban bourgeoisie. Since, moreover, given the enormous size of the state, especially after construction of the Great Wall, many regions of China remained devastated as a result of civil wars, state power acquired a purely pacifist character. The result was the formation of a ruling class of a very special type, unknown in the realm of European culture, namely, a class of literaten [literati].[39]

What does comrade Varga say in his article? 1) State power arises not from class struggle, but in the struggle with nature to irrigate the land. 2) State power does not lead to wars; 3) State power cannot coerce, lacks the means to coerce the popular masses. In general, in this article Varga repeats the same Weberian theory that the Chinese bureaucracy constitutes a special scholarly stratum which, not being tied to any classes, defends the general interests of the country, irrigates this country, constructs dams, canals, and so forth. I said this is a Confucian view. Anyone who knows Confucianism, who knows the contemporary Chinese literature on Confucius and, generally, those views which are widely disseminated about the essence of the power of the Chinese mandarinate, will see here a total reiteration of these views.

I want to give only one example, namely, a remarkable chapter from *Mencius*. As is known, Mencius, more broadly than Confucius, poses and discusses general problems of state.

The remarkable passage which I wish to mention is dedicated to explaining the general character of state power. This passage is from Book Three where Mencius is conversing with farmer-scholars coming from various regions to the principality of Tang who were attracted to the small principality by reports about a very good prince there.

These scholars came to this fortunate country and, in conversation with Mencius, expressed surprise as to why the prince, instead of earning his own bread by tilling the land, collected taxes and lived off the people? Mencius begins by asking his interlocutor: 'And does the honourable Xu [Xing] (the person who had expressed his dissatisfaction with the prince) sow his own grain and eat it?'

---

39   Varga, 'Ekonomicheskie problemy revoliutsii v Kitae' (Economic problems of the revolution in China), *Planovoe khoziaistvo* (Planned Economy), No. 12, 1925. *Radek's note.* It refers to Varga 1925.

'It is so', was the answer.
'The honourable Xu, of course, weaves his own cloth, and then makes his own clothing?'
'No', was the response. 'No, he dresses in a simple caftan.'
'Does the honourable Xu wear a hat?'
'Of course.'
'What sort of hat?'
'A simple one'.
'And does he make it himself?'
'No, he receives it in exchange for grain.'
'Why does he not make it himself?'
'Because it would prove injurious to his farming'.
'Does he use cauldrons and pots to prepare his grain and does he plough with iron instruments?'
'Of course'.
'Does he make them himself?'
'No, he receives them in exchange for grain'.

Thereupon, Mencius said,

> The exchange of instruments for grain does not constitute a form of oppression for the potter or the blacksmith. How, then, could the potters and blacksmiths, who receive grain in exchange for their products, be oppressors vis-a-vis the farmer? Then, why does the honourable Xu not make himself into a potter and a blacksmith and supply everything he needs from his own home? Why does he continually resort to exchanges with craftsmen? Why does the honourable Xu not fear disturbances?

Chen [Chan] Xiang replied, 'In no way can handicrafts be equated with farming'.

To which Mencius replied,

> Does that mean that only rule by the Emperor may be equated with farming? *Superior persons have their own affairs and petty persons theirs*. To demand that each person do for himself everything that is done for him by every conceivable sort of craftsman, would lead to a situation in which everyone would scurry about incessantly. Therefore, it is said that '*some labour with their minds, others with their muscles (strength); those who labour with their minds rule over the others; those who labour with their*

muscles are the ones who are ruled over. Those who are ruled over provide food for the others; and the rulers are fed by the others. This is a universal law of justice.[40]

Mencius propounds the theory that state power is the power of mind workers who must help the people maintain order, without which the work of society is impossible. Further on, when Mencius takes up the theme of what rule is, he says that the exercise of power is not a struggle between classes, but is a struggle to control water, just what comrade Varga said, only two thousand years earlier. Mencius says that Yu brought the rivers under control, regulated their flows, that owing to the labour of Chinese Kings who engaged in the irrigation of China, the country flourished.

Thus, you see that the fundamental view which bourgeois scholarship defends, and which even Marxists uncritically accept, is wholly based upon Confucian scholarship which was created at the time when feudal society, at an early stage without a distinctive bureaucracy, crystallised a bureaucratic stratum as a ruling apparatus.

When we critically examine this theory, we see that it is ridiculous. One need not even know all the fine points of Chinese history; it is enough to be in possession of well-known facts to jettison this theory. Class struggle in China did not begin with the development of capitalism; it began with the decline of the primitive commune, and Chinese literature is replete with historical documents devoted to this struggle, documents in which this struggle is clearly reflected. On their foundation, we may easily understand the truth about the nature of the state.

Let us examine how the Chinese state came into being. Here we must repeat a lot of what we went over last year, but we must do so because the Chinese mandarinate was not created after the Manchus came to power, but was inherited by the Manchu dynasty from the preceding dynasties, and its antecedents go back to the feudal epoch.

What truth is there in the connection between the rise of state power and the struggle against floods? There is probably a kernel of truth in it. When the Chinese became farmers, then their most important regular task was the battle against floods, and there can be no doubt that to a significant degree the authority of the ancient tribes was grounded in their possession of the means to regulate irrigation. At most, this might be the basis for the rise of local power in

---

40   *Mengzi*, III, 1, IV, 4–6. *Radek's note and emphasis*. For a slightly different translation see Legge 1960, (Volume 2), pp. 247–50.

China as one sees in all other countries where artificial irrigation plays a role. But in China one cannot speak of a significant facilitation or acceleration of the process of national unification owing to the seizure of the means of irrigation such as occurred in ancient Egypt. *The difference in the nature of irrigation between China and Egypt in itself rules out the establishment of an authority controlling a large territory on the basis of irrigation.*

If one takes ancient Egypt for comparison, where political power was also created through class struggle, and where the centralisation of authority did not occur immediately, there history unfolded around one river which supplied water to the entire territory of the state, a river whose regulation required a knowledge of astronomy and mastery of the highest level of technology known to ancient history. Since it was impossible to regulate this river in parts from the Blue Nile to the delta, we see in the history of Egypt that in order to guarantee a supply of water to all of Egypt the pharaoh's power had to extend throughout the Nile valley. In our time, when Kitchener tried to seize Abyssinia,[41] he essentially followed the same route that Egyptian pharaohs did long ago. A single river flows throughout the country, therefore, the fate of Egypt depends upon who controls its sources and what kind of order he has established.

China is crossed by three rivers, and agriculture is not restricted to narrow strips of land along the banks of even these three rivers. Thousands of tributaries of these rivers and an abundance of lakes around them guarantee a supply of water everywhere, and, therefore, an enormous state with centralized power could not be constructed on the basis of irrigation.

The Chinese state did not arise in a struggle for water or in a struggle against water. It suffices to point out the simple fact that if the Manchus came to China in the seventeenth century and the Mongols in the thirteenth century, it was obviously not because they had nothing to do at home and decided to grace the Chinese with their presence and help them in the struggle to control water.

The Chinese state arose *in the context of a struggle between agriculturalists and nomads.* This was one starting point. The second was *the division into classes and class conflict within the Chinese nation itself.*

I will pause here to say a few words regarding the first point. All of ancient Chinese history is full of echoes of the struggle for expansion of the main body of the Chinese people which, most likely, was located in Shanxi [Shaanxi]. Even if one discards all the conjectures holding that the Chinese came from other countries – from Northern India, Mesopotamia, or from Central Asia (the

---

41 Radek is mistaken. Field Marshal Herbert Kitchener conquered Sudan (in 1898), not Abyssinia (Ethiopia).

Tarim Basin) – still the heterogeneous character of the Chinese nation is indisputable. The national language indicates that in China we have an amalgam of various ethnological elements. The southern Chinese language is closer to Indochinese than to northern Chinese. This speaks to the point that when a part of the current Chinese people developed agriculture in Shanxi [Shaanxi], became firmly established, and began to spread out, they entered into conflict with a population that was at a lower cultural level and occupied their land. In this struggle, the elders of the tribes, just as occurred with the creation of irrigation, enhanced their own power. But the historical development of the Chinese did not occur in empty space. The nomadic Tatar-Mongolian peoples who were living in the north constantly tried to frustrate the Chinese people's transition to agriculture, and if one looks at the classical works of the Confucian era – the *Shijing*, the *Liji*,[42] etc. – you will find hundreds of references to the struggle against the Tatar-Mongolian peoples who are called the Hunnu [Xiongnu] in these sources. Last year a work appeared by a German historian who extracted all kinds of information about the struggle of Chinese agriculturalists against the nomadic Tatar-Mongolian northern peoples.[43] In these battles political power embracing larger territories was crystallised and Chinese military organisation developed. Since it was difficult for agriculturalists to engage simultaneously in both farming and warfare, *princely militias* began to be formed, special units of armed persons who waged the struggle against these Tatar-Mongolian tribes. A knighthood developed that no longer tilled the land, but lived on the labour of peasants. This is how feudal power arose.

Feudal power did not unite all of China into a single set of hands. Hundreds of feudal principalities existed because, without merchant capital, without developed commerce and the corresponding means of transportation, feudal authorities lacked the material means and conditions to control such an enormous state. We see that the subsequent history of China developed along a path *of struggle among the various feudal principalities*. Why was there such a struggle? Each feudal commander wanted to gather into his own hands as much land and as many people as possible in order to feed his army. Feudal expansion was a struggle for peasants, a dispute over which of the princes would have the most peasants. During the course of a thousand-year struggle among various feudal princes, an endless war took place over the peasants.

Thus we see – in response to those who talk about the pacifist character of Chinese power – that, like all political power, it arose in wars. Even after

---

42   *Liji – The Book of Rites*, an ancient Chinese classical text.
43   It might refer to Krause 1924, although this article was published in 1924, i.e., two year prior to Radek's lecture.

the decline of feudalism, the history of China was still one of endless wars. In these wars dynasties arose and fell, struggles among various dynastic lines occurred as in Russia, France, and England, and then there occurred the two great conquests of China by foreign peoples – the Mongols and the Manchus. All of this is quite unlike pacifism. The Mongols conquered China and reestablished feudal power, which had already disappeared, once more. The Manchus came to China as the suppressors of a popular peasant insurrection, they came to power through an alliance with the feudal aristocracy of the Ming dynasty. They fought for twenty years to subdue China and, thereafter, unable to subdue all of China, they had to establish large, autonomous principalities in the south which submitted to them only in name. This was still wholly possible. We know that in the eighteenth century even pirates existed as an autonomous force, controlling China's seacoast and that the Manchus were unable to cope with them.

You see that arguments about the pacifist origins of Chinese political power are wholly fantastical.

Let us switch now to the language of class and ask ourselves whether, as Confucian legend and comrade Varga say, this state power which developed peacefully lacked the means to coerce the popular masses? We will look at the most basic facts from the perspective of class struggle which has occurred throughout Chinese history.

Class conflict, from which state power arose – and state power is always the power of one class over another – was initially a struggle of the feudal princes and the knights to subordinate the peasantry so that the peasant clan commune was subordinated either to a feudal lord directly in control of land or a feudal lord resident at the court of a prince and who had been granted the right to receive tribute from certain peasant communes. This period is reflected in ancient Confucian literature. In his article which we are trying to have translated into Chinese, your teacher comrade Zhakov has worked on the book *Mencius* from the perspective of delineating the class composition of Chinese feudal society.[44] In this work you will find many quotations from Mencius in which the latter speaks about the exploitation of peasants indicating that at the time which he praises – the flowering of Chinese feudalism during the Zhou dynasty – feudal power waged a struggle to assimilate peasant communal land and to receive tribute from a peasantry who were trying to preserve their old clan way of life.

---

44   'Otrazhenie feodalizma v knige *Men-tszy*' ('The Reflection of feudalism in the book *Mencious*'). It refers to Zhakov 1927.

This process culminated in the so-called 'well-field system'[45] in China, which signified the subordination of the old clan communes to feudalism.[46]

Depending on how close the land was to the city, the subordination of the peasants in this second period assumed various forms. In the picture which Mencius presents, we see that in the land located closer to the city, the feudal lord received a quit-rent of payment-in-kind from all the peasant land; further from the city the knights seized part of the peasants' land, and subordinated the peasants by means of the 'well-field system', making use of unpaid peasant labour (corvee labour), and so forth.[47] We see significant discontent and ferment on the part of peasants who often stake all their cards on the feudal lords in their wars among themselves.

The third stage of class warfare begins with the decline of feudalism. This stage is the struggle around the introduction of private property in land and the striving to consolidate private property. The peasant commune was breaking down, the better-off peasants wanted to withdraw from it; the middle peasants and the poor resisted and this struggle continued for centuries. In his work on the history of land relations in China, the Russian Sinologist Zakharov extracted from the Chinese literature a series of quotations regarding the struggle that went on everywhere even after the emergence of private property in land. The peasants wanted to return to the well-field system as they found even this feudal form beneficial to them inasmuch as it preserved the commune and left the peasants with the means to support themselves after they had paid their rent and taxes. Relaying the views of Han dynasty bureaucrats, Zakharov says,

> The poor, having fields, even though not their own property, harvest everything from them and use the grain to feed their families and need not suffer hunger; the wealthy, deprived of the right to own large tracts of land, begin to till the land themselves and use the entire harvest for them-

---

45   The so-called 'well-field system' is a special form of land use, which existed in ancient China. In this system the fields belonging to the agricultural commune were divided by four boundaries into nine equal parts like the character 'well' (*jing*) [or as in Western noughts and crosses. *Trans.*]. Each of the eight outer allotments were worked by a different courtyard for their own needs. The ninth allotment in the centre was worked collectively and the harvest from it went into paying taxes.

46   It would be a great mistake to consider the well-field system a form of primitive communism. What characterised it was that the part of the land which formerly was deemed communal land now belonged to the feudal lord. *Radek's note*.

47   *Mengzi*, III, 1, III. *Radek's note*.

selves. In this way, everyone's condition is greatly equalised. The state receives a reliable revenue from each tract of land tilled by eight families.[48]

On the basis of Chinese sources, he relates that this class warfare, which continued for hundreds of years, was expressed in the form of various parties, including inside the bureaucracy itself, and in literature there are representatives of tendencies defending the peasant feudal commune. We know it was the same in Russia where, during the struggle for peasant reform, within the landlord bureaucracy there were elements who deemed it more advantageous for the ruling class to restore the commune and elements which opposed it.

This, then, is the third phase of class conflict which did not terminate with a single victory. Right up until the tenth century we frequently see attempts to restore the well-field system.

Did the struggle of state power against the peasantry end when the feudal order was completely destroyed and centralised power, no longer depending upon feudalism, but on large landowners and merchant capital, came into being?

By no means. The very same Weber, whom we spoke of above, a scholar who based his conclusions on a vast literature and tried to present a sociology of China, himself provides many simple, concrete facts which demonstrate that his entire theory is not worth a rotten egg. He speaks in the first place of the enormous state transportation system designed to carry all over China whatever the state needed. Grain, salt, silk, tea, and iron were shipped from one end of the country to the other. This required an enormous amount of unpaid peasant labour not only for the transportation itself, but for upkeep of the roads, bridges, etc., and an enormous number of lost workdays for peasant households, and so forth. We can judge the dimensions of this loss if only from the following: If one needed to ship one cartload of grain from southern to northern China, this necessitated 182 cartloads of provisions and fodder.[49] The cost of transportation was astronomical. This indicates how much labour power the state required and the general nature of exploitation of the peasantry. Peasants were obliged to serve as an unpaid working force. The state found means of imposing this upon them. After this, to say that capitalism

---

48   Zakharov, 'Pozemel'naia sobstvennost' v Kitae' ('Landed property in China'), 'Trudy chlenov russkoi dukhovnoi missii [v Pekine]' ('Works of the members of the Russian ecclesiastical mission [in Beijing]'), Vol. 2 (Beijing, 1910), p. 11. *Radek's note*.
49   M. Weber, 'Gesammelte Aufsätze', p. 327. *Radek's note*.

could not develop because the state lacked the ability to compel is, of course, nonsense.⁵⁰ E. Reclus, according to Max Weber, calculated that for the construction of the Great Wall of China, peasants had to excavate 160 million cubic meters of earth. 300,000 people were engaged in this work.⁵¹ I do not know how much labour power was involved in making the Grand Canal, but judging by its dimensions hundreds of thousands must have been involved in digging this immense construction, labouring under the lash of the state power which arose on the ruins of feudalism.

In the fifteenth century, as many as 550,000 people worked in the gold and silver mines where they extracted the metals for the minting of coins and other necessities.⁵²

How could all of this have been done without coercion? The popular masses did not submit to this at once; an endless struggle went on between them and the state authorities. What forces were employed to bring down the monarchy of Qin Shi Huangdi, the first Emperor who tried to create, not a feudal, but a centralised power based on merchant capital?

To be sure, the old feudal bureaucracy revolted against him (I return again to the factional struggle within the bureaucracy). But the main force opposing him was the toiling armies of peasants which he created to execute the large-scale works which the new state authorities had undertaken. It is very interesting to take note of who led the armies which rose up against Qin Shi Huangdi. According to Chinese sources, the head of these armies was Chen Gu,⁵³ a former craftsman, and Liu Bang, a peasant. The peasant Liu Bang founded the Han dynasty.

Whose interests did the Ming dynasty represent? It represented the peasantry which rose up against the mighty empire of the Mongols, this bloc of new feudal lords who came from abroad with merchant capital.

I have already spoken of the Manchus. You know how they came to power. It was in a struggle against the peasant uprising which continued for fourteen years, as a power which represented a bloc of the Manchu feudal knights with the remnants of the Ming feudal lords who had not yet been eliminated by the peasantry.

Now that we have seen that in China state power is *class* power, as is the case always and everywhere throughout the world, the questions before us are

---

50 The word 'nonsense' is in English in the original Russian. *Trans.*
51 Ibidem. *Radek's note.*
52 M. Weber, 'Gesammelte Aufsätze', pp. 280–1. *Radek's note.*
53 Radek is mistaken. He might have assumed Chen Sheng (alias Chen She), a captain who led the first rebellion against the Qin.

extraordinarily interesting. If you have been listening attentively to what I have been saying, then you will already have thought of the most important among them.

I said that the *Ming dynasty* came to power as a representative of the peasantry which rose up against the bloc of Mongol feudal lords and merchant capital. Then I said that the Manchus came to power as a bloc of the Manchu knights and the remnants of the *Ming feudal lords*. Initially, I say, they came as the expression of peasant interests, then I mentioned that they had feudal lords. Where did these come from? Here we arrive at the question which more than anything else has confused and obscured the class essence, the degeneration of power. We see that even after feudalism was destroyed, it recrystallised, and we see that *peasant dynasties degenerated into feudal dynasties*. We are approaching the most interesting questions of Chinese social history which we must grapple with very thoughtfully, because they possess the greatest political significance, especially for you, revolutionaries from a peasant country.

In China the peasantry has come to power many times and many times this power has degenerated into feudal power.[54] Why has this happened and *what guarantee is there that if peasant power arises in China now that it will not transmogrify into something else, for example, contemporary bourgeois power?* Why was the peasantry unable to found its own dynasty even though they fought and were victorious? Why, even when they had taken power into their own hands, did that power again become feudal? But we can finish up the question of the nature of the state in China only next time.

Lecture Four

We already know that the Chinese state was a class state, that it conducted wars, and so forth, but we have not yet answered the question of just what classes it served.

Throughout the existence of historical China, as we know on the basis of written sources, the Chinese state developed either as a *landlord* state serving the landlord class or a *peasant* state serving the peasantry. These were the two boundaries between which the development of the Chinese state took place.

I will not go through a chronological change of dynasties, but try to show these two streams of Chinese history, analyse the reasons for them, and try to

---

54 Radek is mistaken. Before the twentieth century the peasant leaders had come to power in China only twice. These were Liu Bang, the founder of the Han dynasty, in 202 BC and Zhu Yuanzhang, the founder of the Ming dynasty, in 1368.

show why the first stream – the development of the state as a form of landlord class power – was the basic one while the peasant state was only episodic, although a recurring episode in Chinese history.

China enters history as a feudal state. I have already pointed out how here in our university comrade Zhakov attempted, on the basis of the book *Mencius*, to provide a thoroughly concrete depiction of this feudal period. Therefore, I will focus only on the basic facts which characterise the state structure of feudal China to the end of the Zhou dynasty.

This state did not differ essentially from European feudal states. We see that it was a very poorly connected system of a large number of territorial principalities of individual petty states distributed throughout the entire space of China. The central authority in it arose as follows. The strongest of the feudal lords subdued through warfare a number of surrounding feudal principalities, subordinated them to himself and gathered into his own hands enough power to project his rule to more distant principalities and domains. We have here a *system of feudal vassals* such as exist in all feudal countries. The Emperor exists as the head of state, but in reality his power does not extend throughout the entire empire. Formally, the princes received power from his hands, but in reality this power was wholly in their hands. Why? For the simple reason that taxes could be extracted only in kind; given contemporary means of transportation, it was impossible to transport it over enormous distances across the territory of the state. In essence, the central authorities lived on whatever the Emperor received from the properties he controlled directly, from his own lands, and the princes paid him tribute in a certain amount of precious objects, very irregularly and rarely, and the farther they were from the center the less the amount of their tribute.

What was the bureaucracy like in such a state? There was simply no central bureaucracy. The King or Emperor did not dispatch officials to all the provinces; local officials were subordinate only to their own princes. If you read Confucius and Mencius, you will see that everywhere there were courts of the territorial commanders on the model of the Emperor's court and with the same kind of officials. How were these bureaucrats paid? They were paid in a feudal manner. The princes allot land to their officials; they distribute small holdings, and the officials support themselves on these holdings just as the princes do on their estates. For the most part the bureaucracy comes from the same feudal clans. As in feudal France or Germany, or in old feudal Russia, in feudal China positions in the bureaucracy were mostly filled by the sons of the aristocracy. Such was the state structure in the initial period of Chinese history. It literally differs not at all from the feudal order of any country. Several historians have tried to discover differences between European and Chinese feudalism by pointing to the theocratic nature of the Chinese Emperor, to the Emperor being the 'Son of Heaven', the religious head of the country, but we know that the same tendencies existed in Europe during the Middle Ages. The Kings and Emperors likewise believed they were directly subordinate to God, 'anointed by God', and likewise wanted to be the religious heads of their countries. No particular mentality or adherence to idealist philosophy was required for this. They lived at the expense of the peasant, and it was perfectly clear to them how splendid religious authority was as a means of holding the people in a state of submission. However, they did not fully succeed in concentrating religious authority in their hands since in Europe feudalism inherited the international organisation of the Catholic church from the Roman empire in mature form and the church was able to consolidate its power before monarchical power was capable of struggling against the clergy. In any case, the monarchs struggled to subordinate the clergy and the church and, to a certain degree, they shared religious authority with them over the minds of the exploited masses.

The class essence of the Chinese feudal state consisted in its being a mechanism enabling the landlords to exploit the agriculturalists, although there can be no doubt that this period was not one of the greatest exploitation of the peasantry. In general, history shows us that under conditions of an economy-in-kind, the degree of exploitation of the popular masses is never as high as it is in a money economy, even if it is only in the initial stage of merchant capital. Moreover, in the feudal epoch, to a certain degree the vestiges of communal landholding – in China the well-field system – protect the peasantry from ruin.

The transition from the feudalism of the classical era, as depicted by Mencius, to the following stage of development of the Chinese state, took place over a very long time, and the core of this development was that China began to transform from an economy-in-kind to a money economy, which led to improvements in the means of production and transportation and, therefore, prepared the soil for the emergence of a more centralised power.

The revolution carried out by Qin Shi Huangdi, which was essentially premature, far exceeded the stage of historical development. This revolution was precisely an attempt to create a *wholly centralised state relying upon a monetary economy*. It was the political expression of the process of economic centralisation that began with the development of a money economy.

What was the nature of Qin Shi Huangdi's revolution?

First of all, Qin Shi Huangdi tried to get rid of the old feudal bureaucracy. The old feudal bureaucracy was tied to the local landowners and independent of the central government. Qin Shi Huangdi tried to eliminate the individual princes. He proceeded to do this with methods very reminiscent of those employed by Ivan the Terrible in sixteenth-century Russia. He confiscated land from the princes, and evicted the representatives of the feudal aristocracy from the lands where they possessed influence over the petty landlords, and tried to destroy the bureaucracy, drawn from the strata of the nobility, which congregated around the princes. He appointed special officials from the centre to exercise control over the local bureaucracies – the so-called 'imperial censors' – which remind one of the institution of the *missiae domini* [*missi dominici*],[55] envoys of the King, which existed in Europe. He began to promote officials who were not from among feudal circles, but from among persons whose sole claim to receive official posts was their knowledge of literature. He divided officials into sixteen ranks, and during his time they were paid for their labour not only with a parcel of land for a designated period, but also received certain sums of money.

Qin Shi Huangdi proclaimed the principle that the will of the Emperor was superior to the behests of antiquity. The class of feudal lords who had been overthrown counterpoised the traditions of antiquity to the attempts to establish a centralised state. He replied that the Emperor and his decrees are superior to any traditions. Since Emperors conducted their arguments not only by means of decrees, but also with material force, there is nothing improbable about the report that Qin Shi Huangdi had 460 scholars, who defended the old view of the state, burned to death.[56] However, the books of Confucius, which set forth the entire system of the ancient feudalism, remained. Qin Shi Huangdi did not limit his efforts to bolster his ideas by burning to death Confucius' disciples, he also had the books of the Teacher burned as well.

At one time disputes took place in Chinese literature as to whether Qin Shi Huangdi's actions were good or bad from an ethical perspective, but it is ridiculous to pose the question in this way. We are dealing with the rise of absolutism, and it is perfectly clear that this absolutism was battling against ideas which interfered with his efforts to strengthen his power by all the means at his disposal.

On whom did Qin Shi Huangdi rely? From what I have already said two points may be noted. First is that Qin Shi Huangdi paid the bureaucracy a salary in cash; second is that the bureaucracy was not recruited exclusively from feudal strata. These facts alone indicate that a large change had occurred in the

---

55   *Missi dominici* – envoys of the lord (Latin).
56   Radek is mistaken. According to the official legend, Qin Shihuang did not burn them to death, but buried them alive. However, as the Soviet historian E.P. Sinitsin proved, Qin Shihuang never killed 460 Confucianists at all. The story was made up by Confucian historians of the Han dynasty; see Sinitsin 1974, pp. 147–199.

economy compared to the feudal era, namely, that a money economy had taken the place of an economy-in-kind. Peasants produced part of their products for the market rather than for themselves. A market already existed. We already see signs of the existence of a market and of peasant links with it in the works of Mencius at the end of the feudal era. And if there is a market there are also *merchants*.

In his struggle against the feudal lords, Qin Shi Huangdi relied upon representatives of the money economy – on the *service nobility and merchants*. In this connection the legend of how Qin Shi Huangdi came to power, as related by Sima Qian, is not without interest and suggestion. Sima Qian tells the story of Lü Buwei, a wealthy merchant who assisted Qin Shi Huangdi's ascension to the throne.[57] I have no doubt that comrades who know Chinese will be able to find more concrete evidence of the role of merchant capital in China at this time in the pages of ancient Chinese books. But even the scant data which, willy-nilly, is all I have to go on, suffices to delineate the general character of the process which was expressed politically in the short-lived Qin dynasty. Toward the end of the development of feudalism, new classes emerged from within the depths of feudal society itself – classes representing merchant capital – and monarchical power relied upon these classes in its struggle against the old feudal lords.

One additional important fact is linked to the name of Qin Shi Huangdi in Chinese history, without which the nature of the changes taking place in the economy would not be wholly clear, namely, the destruction of the vestiges of communal landholding. The well-field system was decisively buried under Qin Shi Huangdi. Of course, this was not the result of a singular act which the Chinese chronicles ascribe to a specific year (241 BCE), but Qin Shi Huangdi apparently completed the process which had begun long before his revolution.[58] The communes were preserved until the time that peasants were drawn into commodity exchanges and had not transitioned to private property in land. On the other hand, until there was private property in land, a swift and broad development of the market and money economy was impossible. The commune was the form in which an economy-in-kind was preserved, and its destruction was the *foundation* on which Qin Shi Huangdi's attempt to establish a centralised state became possible. The destruction of the commune was more the prerequisite than the result of the political revolution. The same thing happened in European countries during the Middle Ages: the vestiges of the

---

57   Szuma 1974, pp. 152–8.
58   Radek is mistaken. In 241 BC in China there was no Qin Shihuangdi. Radek has in mind Ying Zheng, King of Qin, who would be proclaimed Qin Shi Huangdi only in 221 BC.

commune existed everywhere, but as the money economy developed the same forces that were battling the feudal lords also destroyed communal landholding.

But along with the obvious destruction of the commune, peasants were deprived of the help of their neighbours, lost the last means of salvation from ruin and, therefore, the peasantry become extremely dissatisfied. With whom? Against the state and those social elements upon which the authority of the state rested. The state, the central authority, battled against feudalism, it took away its role of parasite over the communes and, in this way, clashed directly with the peasantry. A peasant is unable to analyse the objective processes of development, but he is clear about the intensification of exploitation which the development of the money economy engendered, and they saw the growth of inequality and the power of money in the countryside under the new conditions, they saw the taxes, the military service, and the state duties which the new state authorities imposed. Meanwhile, this same state came out against the peasantry as the destroyer of the foundations of communal life and the liquidator of the old patriarchal society. We can easily understand why a certain portion of the peasantry viewed the state and the new ruling classes with the same hostility as did the old feudal aristocracy.

Who rebelled against Qin Shi Huangdi? Here we see what is a very interesting interweaving of classes. The old feudal lords rebelled – the disenfranchised princes, the feudal bureaucracy, but the peasants also. Why? For the simple reason that this centralised state, undertaking gigantic military and commercial construction, organising an army, and pursuing a policy of high taxes – this state embodied all of the hostile forces, not only from the viewpoint of those who had been ousted from power, but also from the perspective of the peasant masses whose lives were easier under the old patriarchal order when the landlords, in order not to lose the peasants who tilled their land, were compelled to help during times when the crops failed. The landlords could not kill the goose that laid the golden eggs. But from the moment when the land became private property, when the money economy expanded, the peasants were wholly at the mercy of the elements – not the natural elements, but the social elements that were ten times more dangerous. Peasants could flee from the cruel caprice of rivers in flood if they lacked the strength to do battle against them, but when they became indebted to the merchant or the usurer, when they lost their land, they had nowhere to turn to escape the misfortunes of poverty.

Now we understand how the dominant feudal elements made common cause with the peasant masses.

This is nothing new in history. If you consider such episodes in modern history as the destruction of feudalism in France at the end of the eighteenth century, you will see that it was not only the aristocracy that battled for the ancient regime, but in the Vendée, for example, the entire mass of peasants was on the side of the ancient regime since the new order brought with it a money economy which bore heavily on the peasantry.[59]

The Qin dynasty was short-lived. Like Peter the Great in Russia, Qin Shi Huangdi was ahead of his times. A struggle to destroy his accomplishments began very soon. However, during his rule we see an attempt to create the type of governing authority for which a struggle continued thereafter for many centuries and which became firmly entrenched only under the Yuan dynasty, and then existed even later in China in the form of the rapidly transforming Ming dynasty and in the last – the Manchu – dynasty.

The line of development which commenced from the rule of Qin Shi Huangdi was repeatedly interrupted, but since our task is not that of characterising dynasties in chronological order, but following two lines of development of the Chinese state throughout Chinese history, therefore, I will allow myself to skip at once over many centuries. Later I will again return to this epoch to show in the example of the Han dynasty how a peasant government degenerated under the influence of economic development. Right now I will focus on the Yuan dynasty, which was the highest stage of development of Chinese absolutism, reminiscent of the typical absolute monarchies of late eighteenth-century Europe.

It is not by chance that the Yuan dynasty presented itself as a type of class state, a state of landlords allied with merchant capital in its pure form. The period of rule of the Yuan dynasty was a time of the greatest economic development of China. I already told you in a previous lecture that the foundation of this economic flowering was the expansion of the Mongols throughout Asia, the creation of a single Asian market. The wealth of all of Asia was concentrated then in the hands of the Mongols and through those hands the products of Chinese handicrafts and manufacturing went far beyond the borders of China. The Mongols came as conquerors and they brought with them social organisations that were wholly feudal. It is not for nothing that Marco Polo in each of his descriptions of various provinces repeats the invariably stereotypical phrase, 'there are many cities and *castles*'.[60] All across China, every twenty to forty miles, these feudal fortresses were scattered. In describing regions, for example, the one he calls 'Mangi' [Manzi] with its capital Hangzhou (then named Lin'an or Rinshi), he says,

---

59   It refers to the 1793–4 peasant uprising in the Vendée region in west-central France against the revolutionary National Convention.
60   Emphasis by Radek.

> The Great Khan hath distributed the territory of Mangi into nine parts, that is, he placed there nine great princes, and a great principality for each of them, but each of the princes was subordinate to the Great Khan. Every year each one in his principality collected both revenue and all kinds of good for the Great Khan.[61]

Thus, Polo provides a description of a feudal organisation of governance.

But in social organisation the Yuan dynasty was not a feudal state, but a bloc of landlords and merchant capital. At the time merchant capital in China was developed to such a degree that Polo, a representative of the leading country in Europe in the thirteenth century, expressed amazement at the flowering of trade, handicrafts, and the means of communication with which nothing in Europe could compare, the riches of the country and the power of the authorities. Hundreds of fabulously wealthy, densely populated cities, which in Europe at the time could evoke only astonishment and disbelief, pass before us in his description, with various kinds of craftsmen and trade and the invariable refrain: '*The city is large and wealthy; there are many merchants there; the people are commercial and artisanal; large numbers are engaged in the production of silk*' (or 'of various goods' 'weapons and harnesses' etc.).[62]

He describes in detail the superior constructions of paved roads and bridges, an excellently organised state postal system with stations at distances of 20–30 miles and hundreds of horses and riders at each station; he never tires of enumerating the types of goods, the sources of state income, the military might, the unusual quantity of large riverine and sea-going commercial vessels, etc.

Let us take, for example, his description of the commerce in the Han [Chinese] capital of Beijing which the Mongols named Khanbalyk. The first thing that impressed our Italian was the number of prostitutes.

> There were a good twenty thousand of them there. All were working for money and all of them were busy as every day a large number of merchants and foreigners were coming and going. If there were so many 'worldly women', it is easy to understand how many people there were in Khanbalu [Khanbalyk]. In no other city in the world were so many precious and expensive things conveyed. I will first tell you they were brought here from India: precious stones, gems, and every sort of expensive things. Every fine and precious thing from China and other regions was brought

---

61 Minaev 1902 [1298], chapter CLII-A.
62 Emphasis by Radek.

> here; and all of this for the sovereign's officials who live here, for their wives, for the princes, for the immense number of military men, and for those who come to the court of the Great Khan. Therefore, as I have said, conveyed here are the most precious and high-priced goods, and in an abundance unseen anywhere else in the world; many goods are bought and sold here. Know that every day more than a thousand carts loaded with silk arrive here; fabrics with gold and silk are woven here. All around this city, from near and far, are some two hundred cities from whence travellers come to make purchases; everything one needs is here; it is not surprising that in Khanbalyk one can procure everything of which I have related. Now you can understand.[63]

We should not suppose that Marco Polo was talking exclusively about trade in luxury articles and, more generally, necessities of the ruling classes. He presents a picture of the salt trade which provided a colossal income to the state, and of the organisation of state purchase and sale of grain.

> When the Great Khan knows that there is an abundance of grain and it is cheap, he orders that a large quantity be purchased and poured into large granaries; so that it will not spoil in 3–4 years, he orders that it be looked after carefully ... If there is a shortage of grain and the price rises, the Great Khan releases his grain. If a measure of grain is selling for a *besant*,[64] then he will give four measures for the same price. As much grain is released as is needed to supply everyone.[65]

But the clearest expression of the development of merchant capital during the Khan's dynasty is seen in the monetary system, more particularly in the very large role that paper money played at that time. Polo goes into detail about the preparation of state letters of credit and their free circulation throughout the empire and their exchange by the state for new credits or precious metals.

From the moment that Mongol domination of Asia ended and strong, independent monarchies emerged in the south and west of the Asian continent, and China lost its trade connections, the role of merchant capital also diminished inside the country, and its influence on state power declined. Not only did state power no longer patronise imports, on the contrary it tried to lock China up within four walls.

---

63   Minaev 1902 [1298], chapter xcv.
64   *Besant (bezant)* – a medieval Byzantine gold coin.
65   Minaev 1902 [1298] Chapter ciii.

Nevertheless, there was not, and could not be, a return to pure feudalism. All of China was now a money economy and the role of trade and handicrafts could not be extirpated. In previous lectures we have already heard how the Chinese bureaucracy invested part of its capital in land and part in trade, and if we ask what did the Ming dynasty represent in class terms after it stopped pursuing its initial peasant policy (I will discuss this later), and what did the Manchu dynasty represent, then it is obvious that these dynasties no longer represented feudal-landlord power; it was landlord power allied with merchant capital. And this type of state power was preserved in China until recently. There is nothing unusual for a European in the character of Chinese state power. What we who are accustomed to a European type of development find strange about China, what distinguishes it from European countries, is that in the thirteenth and fourteenth centuries merchant capital was not developing but withering, growing weaker. It was unable to make the leap from handicraft manufacturing and, therefore, a strong bourgeoisie capable of destroying absolutism did not develop in China. This delay in the development of the bourgeois character of state power, delay in the transition from absolutism which depended upon landlords and merchant capital to the domination of the bourgeoisie, was fully expressed in the changes taking place in the bureaucracy.

The bureaucracy ceased being an aristocratic bureaucracy. In China in the sixteenth through the eighteenth centuries, the state recruited officials not only from the ranks of the landholders, but also from the ranks of the petty bourgeoisie, merchants, craftsmen and even the peasantry. The high level of culture in China allowed this class-based state to find bureaucrats among a very wide range of the population. Tens of thousands sat for the examinations which qualified persons for bureaucratic posts. On the basis of numerous sources, Weber calculates that in China there were more than 30,000 persons who belonged to the upper levels of the bureaucracy.[66]

Given the weakness of capitalist development, that is, a weakly centralised economy, the inadequacy of means of communication, etc., how did this landlord-merchant state defend itself against a return to the time when the country was essentially a federation of disparate regions, when the bureaucrats could freely exercise rule in their own domains?

China developed an entire system suitable to the task of preventing a return to the feudal order which, at the same time, acted as a brake on a transition to the bourgeois order. The Chinese censorate was an expression of this sys-

---

66   Weber wrote 'about 30,000' (Weber 1922, p. 331).

tem. Another expression of it was the fact that by law, high-level officials could only serve in a particular territory for several years. What was the state trying to achieve by this means? It was trying to avoid re-feudalisation, because if an official remained in a given province for a long time, he would be able to accumulate substantial material means in his hands, could invest money in land and commerce – mainly in land – since moveable property was easier to lose. After ten to twenty years, he would let go of his original roots, become a huge landlord who wielded total power independent of the principality. Therefore, the central authorities would not allow him to live for long in one place where he would accumulate many ties. A Chinese official arrived in a province with a small staff and in a majority of cases did not even know the language of the province. He was dependent on petty local officials; all of the actual work was in their hands. He only supervised their work for a period of no longer than three years. In this way the state guaranteed that this important official would not be able to head the province. To make himself independent of the state.

However, in the absence of real control over the governance of the province and given the tenuousness of the ties between the provinces and the centre, the state had to yield to the bureaucracy in another dimension. Officials had long since not been assigned a specific sum which they had to transfer to the state from the taxes they collected. For quite some time officials gambled on what constituted the maximum number of misfortunes and the minimum number of persons they could report to the central government. I think that half of the errors in Chinese statistics, especially the exaggeration of disasters from huge floods, drought, and robberies, may be ascribed to a significant degree to the artifices which officials use to conceal part of the levies they collect from the people and divert to their personal use. Doubtless this circumstance also explains the unprecedented surge in the number of the population. It is indicative that when a compromise was reached in 1713 which freed officials from the fear that one fine day the government would again elevate its demand for money, suddenly, according to the statistical data, the population began to grow rapidly. The compromise which the Manchu dynasty agreed to was that the government stipulated a firm sum which the head of the provincial authority was obligated to pay the government in Beijing. He could increase taxes locally, but no additional sum would be required of him, the sum was limited and fixed once and for all. From then on an official had no interest in concealing the growth of the population. On the contrary, it was in his interest to boast about how the welfare of his province had increased under his leadership, and we see how the size of the Chinese population leaps up by millions according to the Chinese statistics.

In principle the compromise of 1713 had great significance. It indicated the limits of state centralisation that China could reach without capitalism. The state secured for itself a large-scale, specified income; the central authorities were strong enough to do what they had been unable to do during the feudal period – compel officials to hand over a specified sum in taxes – but it was not sufficiently strong to compel officials to increase the amount in accordance with the growth of the country. It ceded to officials to a certain degree governance of a province for a specified period, and allowed them to levy as much in taxes as they wished from this province, but in return they were obligated to turn over to the state a specific sum.

Thus, if we ask what, from a class perspective, did the Chinese state represent, we may say that in the main line of its development in ancient times it was a typical feudal state, the power of landlords, and in the Christian Era, in the most critical point of Chinese history, it represented absolutism, based upon a bloc of landlords and merchant capital. We know from European history as well that during the period when merchant capital was dominant, almost nowhere was the bourgeoisie able to take power into its own hands in a significant territory. Almost everywhere in this period we see the predominance of absolutism. But just as it would be absurd to repeat after German professors that Frederick the Great represented the interests of the nation or, as historians say 'the categorical imperative of state duty' rather than the class interests of the landlords and merchant capital, it would be just as absurd to repeat the assertions of European and Chinese historians that the Chinese bureaucracy represented the scholars who exercised a mediocre dominion over the country, and did not represent any class interests.

Summing up what I have said in this present lecture, you will see, of course, an enormous gap – entire centuries – about which I have said nothing. I have not told you what state authority represented in these centuries; we have said what it represented at the beginning of the Han dynasty, what it represented during the Ming dynasty, what was the content of Wang Anshi's social reforms, etc.

What was hiding in these periods which European historians usually characterise as periods of disorder and turmoil or as periods of adventurist reform? In front of me is the newest history of China written by Professor Krause.[67] He uses identical words to stigmatise the beginning of the Han dynasty, the initial steps of the Ming dynasty, and the reforms of Wang Anshi. He sees these as periods of rule by robbers and the fabrication of senseless reforms, impractical, and

---

67   See Krause 1924a or 1925.

devised for who knows whom. In reality, when we examine these periods, we see that they were times when an overwhelming majority of the Chinese peasantry tried to establish their own class ruling power, to defend the interests of the peasantry.

But I must devote a special lecture in order to examine these periods and not give short shrift to the themes which are of the greatest interest to us.

The attempts to establish peasant power are the most unique and original features of Chinese history. We also have peasant wars in Europe, but apart from the period of the Hussite wars,[68] not even in a single country have we had any such prolonged rule of peasants at the beginning of the epoch of merchant capital. Therefore, the Chinese peasant movements, which had their own raison d'être, deserve a rather long discussion. For us an examination of this historical problem is even more important since it leads us to one of the most important contemporary problems in China: In general is petty bourgeois power, as a continual power, possible in a large country?

Lecture Five

Beginning with the epoch of Qin Shi Huangdi, China did not experience the rule of landlords in the state without power being shared with other classes. But China also did not experience the rule of the bourgeoisie. Rule of the bourgeoisie signifies, first of all, its complete predominance in the economy, and then its guiding role in state policy so that even if the bourgeoisie shares power with other classes (with landlords as was the case in Europe in the nineteenth century for example, in Prussia), nevertheless the interests of the bourgeoisie predominate.

A money economy in China developed only up to the point at which merchant capital dominated, but it did not produce a modern industrial bourgeoisie. But, as I have said, what is distinctive about Chinese history is that it contained a period of peasant rule, the dominance of peasant interests, and it is to this special feature of China that I wish to devote my lecture today.

What brought about the birth of the Han dynasty?

The victory of the peasantry. The fall of Qin Shi Huangdi was the result of the struggle of a coalition of feudal sovereigns, the old feudal bureaucracy, and peasants against Qin Shi Huangdi and elements upon which he depended. But

---

68   The Hussite wars which took place in Bohemia in 1419–34 were wars between Hussites (those who followed the Christian reformer Jan Hus) and many Catholic states of Europe.

as soon as Qin Shi Huangdi was defeated, this coalition fell apart. The classes comprising it – the old landlords and the peasantry – clashed. Liu Bang led a struggle against feudal princes and achieved a string of victories. The peasantry was victorious initially in a certain territory; elsewhere, the feudalists remained, but over time the government became sufficiently powerful to subdue these feudal rivals as well.

What, however, was the result of this victory?

We see – and this marks all of Chinese history – that the administrative structure of the Han dynasty represents a compromise between the centralising tendencies of Qin Shi Huangdi and decentralisation of the feudal type. This compromise is seen in the fact that Liu Bang was compelled to appoint the top administrators from among the circle of old princes, but at the same time he maintained in his hands the right to control them. The power of the Han dynasty was stronger than that of the last Emperors of the Zhou dynasty, but it was not as centralised as that of Qin Shi Huangdi.

How can we explain this? Peasant power triumphed, but having triumphed, by its very nature it was unable to rule a great state directly through its own governing apparatus. A centralised state could exist only by relying upon the class which centralised the economy. Merchant capital was the core of the centralising economy. But the Han dynasty could not depend directly on the merchant bourgeoisie, because it had come to power in a struggle against a governing authority that had itself relied upon merchant capital. It expressed tendencies which were counter to the interests of merchant capital. This was the soil on which a bloc between the peasantry and feudal lords was created prior to the victory over Qin Shi Huangdi. Merchant capital itself was still not sufficiently strong either to break up the bloc from the very beginning or to subordinate the peasant element to itself when the latter launched a struggle against the feudal lords. But left to their own devices, the peasantry could administer villages, districts, and generally extend its influence and power as far as its connections went. In his work on economic history the German economist Büchner[69] poses the question: At what distance from the village can a city be located so that it will be worthwhile for a peasant to go there with his goods? How far can a peasant ride on his horse in one day? He can ride no more than twenty *verst* [one *versta* is 0.66 mile] a day, and to return, he must lose another day. In any case, unless he derives special benefits from it, a peasant cannot lose more than a

---

69   Radek must assume Karl Bücher, the famous German economist whose works were very popular in Russia. Before 1927, twelve works by Bücher have been translated into Russian. His most populer work was *Arbeit und Rhythmus*, which was translated in Russian and published in Russia twice – in 1899 and 1923. See Bücher 1896, 1899, and 1923.

few working days on his travels, and his connections cannot extend more than a couple of dozen miles or so. Paraphrasing Bücher, we may say that peasant power extends as far as a peasant may absent himself from his village in order to bring his goods to market. Only a governing power which enslaves the peasant, which is able to drive him further by force or by the lure of commercial profit, can extend itself beyond the nearest town. Prior to the construction of railroads, Russian peasants transported salt from the Black Sea and the Azov Sea; they rode for weeks, but they made money this way, so they did it voluntarily. The merchants who hired them, paid them in cash. The tsarist government was not only able to drive peasants all over Russia, but also, for example, to throw peasant forces to fight against Napoleon, beyond the Alps, to a country where oranges grow.[70]

But as long as a peasant government remains a peasant government it lacks the economic and administrative means to coerce the peasants, and this is expressed in the political weakness of peasant governments. But there are more profound reasons for the compromise of which we spoke. We can pursue them by dwelling on the economic policies of peasant governments.

When we ask ourselves why the Han dynasty or the Ming dynasty, which came to power as peasant governments, later followed policies of landlords and merchants, the first answer that occurs to us is a conjecture about the degeneration of the governing power itself, of its downward slide from representing the perspective of the peasantry to that of other classes. The peasant must always take into account this degeneration of a peasant governing authority. The peasantry in all countries is wholly sceptical of power which it itself wants to have. Those who work among the revolutionary peasantry know this best of all. Twenty-five years ago I myself had occasion to speak at a peasant meeting in that part of Poland which had the strongest peasant movement. After the meeting an old man – a peasant – said to me, giving me a friendly pat on the back, 'See that you don't betray us. We have been betrayed many times'.

Why are peasants so convinced that peasant power will betray them? Governing power is violence, and violence provides the opportunity for gain, the opportunity to accumulate riches, meaning, the opportunity to detach oneself from one's class.

There can be no doubt whatsoever that this process of the degeneration of peasant power really played a role in the history of the Han and Ming dynasties. Representatives of the victorious peasantry, after installing themselves

---

70   Radek assumes that in 1799 the Russian Emperor Paul I sent the Russian army to fight Napoleon in Italy.

in sumptuous palaces, began to live the good life, exacting taxes and levies from the peasantry. Waging wars, they accumulated significant wealth, acquired land, and invested money in trade. But this is not what was of decisive importance.

The Han dynasty really tried to defend the interests of the peasantry. In his work, *Landed Property in China*, Zakharov says the following,

> The Han government was not indifferent to the hardships of the people, and it implemented various measures either to enrich them or, at least, to put them in a condition to gain sufficient means of nutrition. It distributed at no cost all of the vacant lands, public and imperial gardens, encouraged officials with rewards, constantly forgave taxes, covering its expenses with the sale of offices and titles, admonished subjects to help each other in the labour of farming with loans of seeds and livestock. If there were insufficient draft animals, it advised tillers to harness themselves to the plough and use human labour power in place of animal power. It devised methods of tilling the soil – plough furrows one foot wide and deep in order to weed and water the roots of grain-bearing plants more conveniently during windy weather and intense heat so that, by these means, the protected and covered roots would yield a much greater harvest.

Trudy chlenov rossiskoi dukhovnoi missii [*v Pekine*] ('Works of the members of the Russian ecclesiastical mission [in Beijing]'), Vol. 2, Beijing, 1910, p. 10.

Thus, in the beginning the Han dynasty was concerned about the peasantry and defended the interests of the peasantry, but it encountered many failures along this path. Farther on we will see what it was that destroyed its defence of peasant interests.

The four-hundred year reign of the Han dynasty is considered a golden age in Chinese history, and in the north of China educated Chinese often call themselves the sons of Han. Peasant tendencies were so powerful during the reign of the Han dynasty that for the entire four hundred years, the bureaucracy, a significant part of which was recruited from among the peasantry, struggled over the question as to whether private property should be abolished and should they return to the well-field system. A struggle of opinions and among political parties was waged over this question, Zakharov tells us, citing authentic documents from that time. Thereafter this question arose again many times throughout the course of Chinese history and is again a central point of contention among the political parties. 'These opinions with respect to seizing land from the rich and restoring a system of communal tillage', Zakharov writes, persisted through all times and during the subsequent dynasties, and were expressed in virtually the same words in reports submitted to Chinese sovereigns. Although many of the thoughts set forth in them did not demonstrate any profound views on the subject or sound judgments, still these ideas occupied the minds of Chinese for centuries and guided the actions of governments.[71]

Why did the question of destroying private property arise? For very simple reasons. The money economy which began to develop toward the end of the Zhou dynasty led to a large-scale breakdown of the peasantry, initiating a process which we call a process of peasant differentiation. A stratum of poor peasants who had lost their land came into being. Large landowners began to buy up and seize the land. Qin Shi Huangdi sanctioned this change in landholding by abrogating the judicial vestiges of communal landholding, but the peasant dynasties, still remembering the communal traditions, and confronting the impossibility of correcting the situation through palliative measures, asked: Since the money economy and private property led and continue to lead to the breakdown of the peasantry, shouldn't we return to the commune? Others opposed such thoughts. They pointed out that the money economy had been developing for a long time and private property had existed; changes in the economy were so great that a return to ancient relations was impossible even from a technical standpoint. Moreover, various strata – poor and rich – had come into being, and if the poor were prepared to help take land from the rich, the rich in turn were prepared to do battle. Characteristically, among the Han bureaucracy were persons who said there was nothing to fear from an uprising of the rich. Moreover, we should provoke a rebellion of the rich so that we may seize their land. Zakharov tells us that at this time some members of the government, especially scholars with fiery dispositions, proposed to secretly arouse the indignation of the wealthy in order to take advantage of this circumstance and make it more convenient for the state to seize their land under the pretext of punishing them for their uprising and opposition to the government.

We see here the great tension of class struggle, because the rulers-bureaucrats would not have pulled the wool over their own eyes in vain and would not have put forward such plans had the masses not been exerting pressure on them.

The matter ended, however, with the needs of the developing money economy victorious. All the broader masses of proprietors had an interest in the

---

71   Zakharov 1853, p. 15.

preservation of private property in land as did all those tied to the market economy. In the soil of this property and commercial relations a new class of landlords grew and became firmly established, distinctly different from feudal-type landlords. With the development of local markets a class of merchants acquired more importance and influence. As time passed, the government had to reckon more and more with the new ruling classes; increasingly it had to adopt their viewpoint (and the degeneration of the government facilitated this process). Less and less did it view the fragmenting peasantry as a force which could overthrow the landlords.

Such was the evolution of the peasant government at the beginning of the Han dynasty; such was the prototype of the changes which subsequently occurred in the same form and order at the beginning of another peasant dynasty – the Ming.

But even with the triumph of the money economy over the commune, its victory, which made the abolition of private property in land and a return to the well-field system impossible, still the peasant question did not disappear. Peasants continued to live in poverty. Then, having abandoned the idea of revolution, the government considered the option of reform, of how, at least, to alleviate the poverty of the peasantry via reforms. By this time, the Han dynasty had already completely lost touch with the peasantry. It was itself a huge landowner and connected with landlords and merchants. Nevertheless, the government, in the person of the usurper Wang Mang, during the first years of the modern era [CE] posed the question of agrarian reform.[72] It posed the question not because Wang Mang was returning to the ancient traditions of the Han dynasty, it did so despite the fact that the government continued not to be a peasant government. We see a completely analogous phenomenon when Wang Anshi again proposes the same reforms in the eleventh century. The reasons were the extreme dearth of land in what was an overpopulated China. The overpopulation was felt even more keenly, because only the land in river valleys was cultivated. The population was concentrated along the banks of the Yellow River, the Yangzi River, the Pearl River and their tributaries. Given the natural conditions and the technical means of tilling the soil, farming was feasible only where irrigation could be deployed.

Given the shortage of land, the agrarian question was extremely sharp and attracted everyone's attention. There were peasant uprisings in every dynasty. The Red Eyebrow, Yellow Turban, [White] Lotus[73] and other rebellions – all

---

72   Wang Mang's reforms of 9–23 CE were aimed at the liquidation of private property in China and the land redistribution among tillers in accordance with the well-field system.

73   The peasant Red Eyebrow rebellion took place in 17–27 CE and was mainly aimed against

these peasant movements had one and the same cause, and when the peasants applied pressure, even the landlords' government had to pose the question, 'What next? Will the peasant overthrow the landlord if his situation is not alleviated?'

What were Wang Mang's reforms? He tried to limit the amount of land that a single individual could possess; it was forbidden that an individual own more than one *qing*, that is, more than 100 *mu* of land. The state would confiscate land above that limit and distribute it to those without. He issued an edict according to which anyone who considered this law unreasonable was subject to being exiled from China while those who directly violated the law on landed property and those who bought or sold land in excess of the stipulated maximum would be subject to more decisive measures – beheading. Wang Mang's reforms were in place for only three years. He himself had to retract his laws.

If we shift to the reforms of Wang Anshi, we see that although they lasted longer – about twenty years – they also failed in the end.

All the victories of peasant uprisings, all the efforts to institute reforms from above ended with the triumph of the money economy.

How did this happen? How did the money economy defeat all the judicial challenges to it? In the time of the ancient Greeks it was said that the mightiest city walls could not stand against an ass loaded with gold. A golden ass could even make its way through the walls of a fortress. And laws are weaker than fortress walls. If it was forbidden to sell land and buy more than one *qing*, then it was said that the land was not purchased; legally it was considered the property of whoever worked it, but in fact it belonged to someone else, and the nominal owner paid the real owner half of his harvest. With respect to similar land laws in the Tang dynasty, Zakharov writes,

> It is true that the buyer, notwithstanding his wealth, could not acquire more than the amount of land prescribed by law, but apart from abuses which were always possible, additional land that a rich person bought could be ascribed to the name of somebody else in his household; thus, he himself owned only a small and legal parcel of land, but as the head of the family, he possessed tens and hundreds of hectares.[74]

Thus there were always poor and ruined peasants (Ibid., p. 23), so when there was a poor harvest or war broke out and the peasant needed cash to pay

---

Wang Mang; the Yellow Turban rebellion occurred in 184–205 and was against the Han dynasty, the [White] Lotus rebellion took place in 1796–1804 against the Qing government.

74   Zakharov 1853, p. 23.

taxes or to buy livestock, seeds for planting, etc., he borrowed what he needed from the rich, and the latter, enslaving the peasant in debt he could not repay, subsequently took over the land of the debtors or used the land and labour of the peasant without transferring the land to himself. This was typical not only of China. In the USSR, for example, agrarian laws forbade the sale of land and until recently even prohibited the renting out of land; meanwhile, during periods of famine rich peasants attempted to take the land into their own hands, rented it out illegally to day labourers and bound poor peasants to work the land as sharecroppers or under other exploitative conditions.

Why did we change this law last year and legalise rentals? To defend the interests of the peasantry, because earlier inasmuch as rentals were done secretly, the renters told the poor peasants, who provided the land against their will, that they did so at their own risk and stipulated exploitative conditions. Considering that a money economy still existed in the countryside, the Soviet government had to solve the rental problem. Since the money economy exists, it could not permit such restrictions. Only to the extent that elements of a socialist economy displaced that of a money economy could the consequences that derived from a money economy wither away. The Soviet government possesses the means and appropriate conditions to supplant the money economy … The Chinese reformers were in an entirely different condition; given the strength of development of commercial relations they were able to resist only the threat of exile and the death penalty. If peasants produce a significant part of their output not for personal consumption, but for sale, if the goods are denominated in monetary terms, then this indicates that commercial relations have already taken firm hold in the economy and that attempts to limit individual accumulation in the countryside under what is solely a commercial economy are doomed to failure.

The peasant government in China became bankrupt not only because it cut itself off from the peasantry and adopted the position of other classes, but also because in the context of a money economy there were no means of protecting the interests of the peasants. The very fact that the government shifted from the peasant position to that of other classes was merely the expression of this circumstance. If the Han dynasty did not and could not possess the means to defend the interests of the peasantry, then it had to go over to defending the interests of the merchants and landlords. The free will and personal position of the ranks of the Han bureaucracy, the fact that they sat in their palaces and did not want to part from them, is of secondary importance in comparison to the basic reason for the failure of peasant government. Soviet Russia also has no guarantee against the degradation and abandonment by a certain part of the bureaucracy as long as the vestiges of a commercial economy exist in the USSR. No matter how much there may be a higher and more conscious relation of the proletarian party to this type of phenomenon, our strength consists not so much in the personal characteristics and quality of the persons who comprise the ruling apparatus of the country as it does in the economic guarantees of defending the interests of the toilers, and Lenin, at the Eleventh or Twelfth Congress, said that only naïve people can rely exclusively on the fact that our leadership is drawn from among honest revolutionaries; we possess a better guarantee for defending the interests of the proletariat and the peasantry – an economic foundation, our developing industry.[75]

The Soviet government permits rental, because it possesses the means by which it can influence the countryside – industry, transport, etc. It can retreat one step, because it has enormous levers with which to elevate the position of the peasantry. Under developed capitalism, which prepared the soil for socialism, it is possible to defend the interests of the peasantry until such time as the strengthening of socialist industry provides the opportunity to refashion peasant relations and the countryside.

In the early stage of a money economy, without industry and without a working class that is linked to the peasantry and defends its interests, this task is utopian, a utopia like that of nineteenth-century socialists such as Proudhon who thought it possible, without touching the market or the money economy, to establish workers' banks which would make workers independent of the market.

A peasant government was impossible as a permanent factor, because the peasantry could not defeat capitalism which was just beginning to develop in the form of merchant capital. Capitalism grows from a commercial economy, from a money economy in which the peasantry also exists, but capitalism signifies the enslavement of the peasantry. Capitalism means splitting the peasantry into the poor, who are pushed into the ranks of the proletariat, and the rich who climb into the ranks of the bourgeoisie. Between these two is a broad middle mass which oscillates between the poor and the rich peasants. Where industry develops, the proletarianised peasants enter industry. But industry in China existed only in the form of artisanship – and later – as handicraft manufactur-

---

75 Lenin did not take part in the Twelfth Party Congress due to illness. At the Eleventh Party Congress on 2 April 1922 he said something different from what Radek recalls: 'If indeed we had before us a naïve twelve-year old young lady who yesterday heard that there was communism in the world and put on a white dress with red ribbons and said that Communists are simply merchants, it would be funny and we could laugh good-humoredly' (Lenin 1970 [1922], p. 135).

ing. Therefore, from the first centuries C.E., millions of peasants sold their land, but could not find work in the cities. It was impossible then to solve the problem which the first peasant government in China faced. Therefore, quite apart from climbing down, the peasant dynasty – the Han dynasty – was doomed to failure. Much later, but for the very same reasons, the Ming dynasty was similarly doomed.

If time permitted me to examine this process in greater detail, then we would find in the Ming dynasty many analogous features with the Han dynasty. It came to power as a peasant dynasty and later, in the seventeenth century, it was brought down by a peasant rebellion, because long before its end it ceased being a peasant dynasty and stood for the rule of landlords and merchant capital.

I cannot analyse the history of the peasant rebellions with you in detail. Since I don't know Chinese I have insufficient materials for this. We have arranged for comrade Ivin [Aleksei Alekseevich Ivanov] to work on the history of these rebellions using Chinese sources, and then we will look more closely at their content. But in general, which is how I know it, the history of peasant uprisings in China teaches us that even though the victory of the peasantry is possible, these victories are historically barren. There has not been and cannot be the kingdom of the peasantry on earth, for a peasant kingdom is a kingdom of the market, of the money economy, and a money economy and the market signify the existence of poor and rich and the enslavement of the former by the latter. Sooner or later, any governing power which the peasantry establishes in China must exit the stage as a peasant power, be smashed by the element of the market, must perish or transform into the power of landlords and merchant capital.

In this connection the collapse of Wang Anshi's reforms is very interesting. They tell us directly what the consequences of his reforms were: rising prices, a market revolt. Merchants, who had invested money in land and from whom the land was taken, revolted. Complete chaos reigned in the market as a result of the reforms. Even now bourgeois historians write about it as an adventurous fantasy. In reality, we see not an adventure, but the tragedy of a class which was unable to establish its dominion, its rule (which it viewed as the rule of equality and justice), in the soil of a money economy, and at the same time could not escape the orbit of a money economy.

I will conclude the introductory series of my lectures which is intended to provide a starting point for examining the motive forces of the Chinese revolution.

I began my lectures by pointing out that both Chinese scholars and Europeans tell us that China is a peculiar state, which is impossible to understand, that it is a country in which everything is upside down; a peasant country in which the peasants do not own land, a country with a money economy, but one in which there is no differentiation in the countryside, no landlords, and all the land is divided into small peasant parcels, an enormous state with almost three thousand years of reliable written history, but in which classes do not exist and power is in the form of a corporation of scholars who have no ties with anyone or anything.

As we have seen, not a shred of this legend remains. We have a very poor knowledge of Chinese history. I do not want any of you to think that I claim to be a Sinologist. I do not know the language and I have not studied Chinese problems for long, but the little that I know and that other comrades know, and what we have been able to verify from the best works of bourgeois Sinologists, is sufficient to discredit the legend.

We have seen that the development of China led to the appearance of classes, that there was a class of commercial bourgeoisie, craftsmen, poor and rich peasants, landlords, and so forth. When we proceeded to study the nature of the Chinese state, to investigate what it represented in class terms, then we clearly saw the absurdity of this theory, which began with Confucius and was willingly accepted on faith in Europe by bourgeois scholars. Confucius had the right to take a class point of view: when he lived (if he generally lived in the times in which the books ascribed to him were concerned with)[76] classes were only beginning to form, and the wisest man, in the simplicity of his soul, could identify the interests of the ruling class with the interests of the whole people. But that contemporary scholars accept this theory merely demonstrates the mendacity of bourgeois class scholarship. We knew *a priori* that this was nonsense. The state always possesses a class character. It was thus in China. During the development of the money economy in China, those classes ruled whose interests were the driving force of all the changes – the merchant class and the landlord class. In the entire interval of Chinese history beginning from the time of Qin Shi Huangdi, the bureaucracy represented the interests of these classes. But since these classes destroyed the peasantry, but capitalist development was delayed, it did not provide an outlet for the peasantry; industry was insufficiently developed for superfluous peasants to go there, therefore, in China, unlike in European states, we see periods in which the peasants are victorious and establish their own governing power. In these periods, the bureaucracy is not a supra-class apparatus, but an apparatus representing the interests of the rural petty bourgeoisie, the peasantry. These

---

76   In fact Confucius himself did not write any such book.

periods in which peasant power dominated are a unique feature of Chinese history, a peculiarity which we do not encounter in Europe. However, owing to the tendencies of historical development, ruling strata crystallise from within the petty bourgeoisie, slowing and suppressing the implementation of peasant reforms.

Such are the similarities and differences in comparing Chinese history with that of Western Europe. The enchanted kingdom about which nothing can ever be fathomed turns out to be completely accessible to our analysis, and we discovered firm points of departure for our subsequent examination of the history of the driving forces of the Chinese revolution.

I propose to devote the next series of lectures to an examination of the changes which contemporary capitalism brought to China.

This series of lectures will provide us a foundation to study the changes which began to take place in Chinese classes and after these lectures we will engage in a survey of class relations in China and those movements in which these classes entered upon the stage of history, and then the contemporary Chinese revolution.

Lecture Six

Today we begin a series of lectures devoted to the social development of China, from the time that foreign capital first entered China up to the Chinese Revolution of 1911, which had already matured on the basis of those changes which European capitalism and the capitalism of America had evoked. This series must begin with the history of the development of Chinese commerce between 1860 and 1895, because trade was the initial means by which foreign capital penetrated China and began to exert influence on the country.

In the *Communist Manifesto* of 1847,[77] Marx [and Engels] wrote,

> The bourgeoisie, by the rapid improvement of all instruments of production, by the immensely facilitated means of communication, draws all, even the most barbarian, nations into civilisation. The cheap prices of commodities are the heavy artillery with which it batters down all Chinese walls, with which it forces the barbarians' intensely obstinate hatred of foreigners to capitulate. It compels all nations, on pain of extinction, to adopt the bourgeois mode of production; it compels them to

---

77 Radek makes a mistake. Marx and Engels published *The Communist Manifesto* in 1848.

introduce what it calls civilisation into their midst, i.e., to become bourgeois themselves. In one word, it creates a world after its own image.[78]

In 1847 [1848] Marx supposes that the bourgeoisie, by virtue of the cheapness of its goods, also smashes 'the Chinese wall', the isolation of China, its special peasant way of life. We know that in reality cheap goods could not have forced their way into China had the bourgeoisie not first tried to clear the path with cannons. It had to employ real artillery to be in a position to bring cheap goods into China. With the help of two wars – the first and second Opium Wars – from the 1840s to the 1860s,[79] the international bourgeoisie actually used armed force to smash 'the Chinese wall', but not, of course, the one that exists in the north, but the political-economic wall which separated China from the rest of the world. However, as we shall see further on, even this destruction was not enough to push these cheap goods into China, destroy the Chinese peasant economy, and jump start Chinese capitalism. The views of Marx which I cited were expressed under the strong influence of the era of free trade which was then beginning. Historical experience indicates that it was not free trade with its cheap goods, but imperialism with its cannons, with its loans, and its construction of railroads that facilitated the penetration of cheap goods into this country of underdeveloped capitalism.

I presented the history of the Opium Wars last year, so I will not dwell on it now. Let us only recall what political results the Opium Wars left in their wake. These results were embodied in two treaties – the Treaty of Nanking in 1842[80] and the Treaty of Tianjin in 1858.[81]

What did the Treaty of Nanking give the foreign bourgeoisie? First, it forced the Chinese government, which prior to this time had allowed goods in only through Canton, to open up five ports: Canton, Xiamen, Suzhou,[82] Ningbo, and Shanghai. Further, the Treaty of Nanking dissolved the merchant guild in Canton – the *Cohong* – which had monopolised the trade with foreigners. Until this time, foreign merchants coming to Canton could only purchase goods

---

78 Marx and Engels 1969 [1848], p. 112.
79 The first Opium war between Britain and China took place from 1839–42; the second one, between Britain and France, on the one hand, and China, on the other hand, from 1856–60.
80 The Treaty of Nanjing was signed on 29 August 1842.
81 Radek is mistaken. The Treaty of Tianjin of 1858 was not ratified by the Chinese government and the second Opium War continued until 1860, when the Conventions of Beijing were signed.
82 Radek is mistaken. It must be Fuzhou.

furnished to them by a small handful of monopolists, and had to buy them at prices dictated by this small number of merchants. Now the *Cohong* guild was disbanded, and in the five designated ports foreign capitalists could buy goods from whomever they pleased. This signified the expansion of their influence.

Prior to the Treaty of Nanking, foreigners coming to Canton could not move about freely, could not purchase land, build houses, hire servants themselves, could not have free intercourse with Chinese authorities, but had to make use of the guild – the *Cohong* – as their intermediary. The Treaty of Nanking recognised the right of extraterritoriality for foreign merchants;[83] they were not subject to Chinese courts; they were subject to the laws of their own country administered by consuls, and the consuls had the right to present their interests directly to the Chinese authorities, in the open ports they had the right to buy houses, and to arrange them as needed for trade. In the Treaty of Nanking, moreover, the government pledged to conclude a special treaty on tariffs, and a year later, a supplementary treaty of 1843 stipulated that tariffs should not be more than five percent of the cost of goods. If the goods cost 100,000 rubles, then the tariff paid on importing it would be 5,000 rubles. Likewise on exports, the tariff should not be higher than five percent with the exception of tea, on which it could be up to 10 percent.

Such were the provisions of the Treaty of Nanking. Seventeen years later the foreign capitalists achieved new concessions in the Treaty of Tianjin.

First, every European state had the right to station an ambassador in Beijing. Before this, if any given state had litigation or a quarrel with local authorities in Hong Kong, Shanghai, etc., then the local authorities could say, 'It's none of our concern; we know nothing. In Beijing sits the Great Khan, he decides, we can say nothing in reply'. Now the presence of an ambassador in Beijing enabled the capitalists to pressure the central government. Moreover, ten new ports were opened in addition to the five ports that had been opened in 1842. At that time there were no railroads in China and the condition of the roads was abysmal, and if the foreigners had access to five ports they could engage in trade only with the population adjacent to these five ports. The ten new ports opened up additional space for foreigners to trade in China.

Furthermore, foreign merchants received the right to travel about China. Now they could receive thirteen-month visas on their passports and with these in their pockets they could force their way into the interior of the country and

---

83 Radek is mistaken. The right of extraterritoriality was recognized by the Anglo-Chinese treaty of Humen on 8 October 1843.

find out what to buy and sell. In this connection, the provision of religious tolerance by the treaty was a matter of no little importance. It may seem that religion is a lofty matter which, supposedly, has no connection with trade. But when asked why he was concerned about missionaries, one British foreign minister replied, 'The missionaries are cotton'. Needless to say, this did not mean that cotton goods were made out of missionaries, but it means that missionaries, who under the guise of religious propaganda forced their way into China, were splendid economic spies and intelligence agents who opened the way for British cotton goods. Moreover, when missionaries succeeded in converting Chinese to Christianity, then in the persons of these neophytes, foreign capital already had in place local Chinese agents. The missionaries intervened in the courts and with the authorities on behalf of their converts, and this was sufficient to tie these people to them and make them agents of foreign capital.

A further concession in the Treaty of Nanking[84] was the abolition of *lijin*[85] for foreign capitalists. It was introduced during the Taiping war to cover the expenses of the Chinese government in its struggle against the Taipings. The *lijin* was a significant obstacle to trade. Instead of *lijin*, foreigners paid 2.5 percent, apart from the tariff, which freed them from extortions at the numerous toll barriers. Finally, the last important concession was legalising the importation of opium which had been imported as contraband for the past forty years. Now it was openly imported with a duty of seven percent.

In the following years, the right of foreign capital to enslave the Chinese people was significantly enlarged. At first it only affected the ports and maritime trade and did not extend to land, but the foreign capitalists strived to extend the treaties to cover overland trade, using a series of conflicts toward this end. When the British conquered Burma and dispatched a special mission to Yunnan to collect economic intelligence, a British officer was killed by Chinese.[86] The Chinese government was forced to pay for this by expanding the rights of foreigners – in particular it had to agree to trade between Burma and China.[87] When a conflict erupted over French seizure of Tonkin, the French gained the same right.[88] The basic point in this treaty was the 'Great Charter' –

---

84 Radek asuumes the treaty of Tianjin, not Nanjing.
85 *Lijin* – an internal transit toll, collected in China. Chinese merchants continued to pay *lijin* until 1 September 1927.
86 This refers to the murder of the British diplomat and traveler August Raymond Margary and his entire staff on 21 February 1875.
87 This refers to the Agreement between Great Britain and China signed on 13 September 1876 in Zhifu (an island off the Shandong north-east coast).
88 This refers to four treaties signed between France and China in 1885–7.

the point about the freedom of foreign capital in China. Let us now examine how foreign capital began to develop its trade on the basis of this freedom.

We are looking at an issue which has not only historical significance, at an institution which possesses enormous economic and political importance in Chinese history up to the present and which we must know very thoroughly so that, subsequently, we can understand the various strata of the Chinese bourgeoisie. We are addressing the question of the rise of compradors – by means of which foreign capital, having gained the freedom to enter China, began to develop trade in China.

What obstacles stood in the path of the introduction of European capital into China? The first obstacle was that China was not a country, but an entire continent broken up into a series of provinces, each with its own distinctive way of life. China was familiar with and possessed internal trade which unified it to a certain degree; iron came from the north and was distributed throughout all of China, salt and grain from one province was shipped to others, but this did not negate the fact of China's economic fragmentation, a consequence of which was the absence of a real network of roads.

Domestic Chinese trade made do with the existing roads in China, but these roads were unsuitable for the penetration of European capital. 'North China', Richthofen said, 'is a land of roads; there are both good and bad roads there, but especially many bad and even outright impossible ones, while South China is a land of waterways and footpaths'. The condition of the roads was much worse in the nineteenth century than it had been under the Yuan dynasty. 'Those among the twenty-one imperial highways which survived', E. and O. Reclus wrote in their book, *The Middle Kingdom*,

> bore witness to the advanced civilization the Chinese had attained in the Middle Ages, and this explains the enthusiastic views of Marco Polo and other travellers of that time. These highways cut through heights via trenches or even underground tunnels, and through low-lying land via embankments. In the steppes they were 20–25 meters wide. They were paved with granite slabs and trees were almost always planted along the sides like European avenues. Every five kilometres along the roads there were guard towers, inns, watering stations, places to change draft animals, and military sentries to protect travellers. Markets were also constructed at regular intervals. Monumental bridges were built across rivers.[89]

---

89   E. and O. Reclus, *Sredinnaia imperiia* ('The Middle Kingdom'), pp. 175–6. *Radek's note.* It refers to Reclus 1902.

But the vestiges of these highways were only pleasant memories. In the nineteenth century, the picture was generally entirely different.

China was fragmented into a series of very poorly connected geographical regions, and since capitalism was not immediately able to introduce railroads into China, the modern means of transportation, in regard to China it was essentially in the same position as, for example, Phoenician merchants who wound up in Europe in ancient times or Byzantine and Italian merchants who traded with northern Europe in the Middle Ages. If you study the economic history of Europe in the Middle Ages, you will see what enormous difficulties merchants had to overcome, for example, when the Italian municipal republics, which had developed considerable trade, were not yet able to construct ships which could sail directly from Genoa to England or to Flanders. The Italian merchants had to send goods via the Rhone and Rhine rivers to Flanders, and from there via sea to England. As soon as they learned to build ships that could sail to London in three or four months, then the trade which the German Hanse[90] conducted via the Rhine river dropped by half. In China there was no river which crossed the whole country in the main direction from north to south. The Yangzi linked eight provinces economically, and in the south there was a good network of waterways, but land transportation was the only way to connect the south with the north.

You know the Chinese roads better than I do. You have probably had the pleasure of riding on them; I have bumped along them only in books. But from the description of these roads it is obvious they were an obstacle to trade rather than a means of conducting it.

In another section of their book E. and O. Reclus wrote,

> Thanks to the introduction of steam power, communication between coastal China and the rest of the world has become much more convenient and lively, but the roads and canals in the interior of China remain probably worse than during Ming times, that is, three or four hundred years ago. With the exception of Shandong, Gansu, Sichuan, and several parts of Hunan, as well as localities adjacent to ports open for foreign trade, everywhere the old roads are ruined; in many places they are blocked by landslides and are dug up; bridges have collapsed. In many places instead of roads all that remains are paths winding alongside

---

90   Hanse (Hansa, The Hanseatic League) in the late thirteenth to early nineteenth century was a commercial and defensive organisation that united North German merchant guilds to dominate the Baltic sea trade routs.

where roads once were. On the rice fields which occupy a significant part of the territory of the country, the majority of roads consist of a series of slabs half a meter wide or no more than one meter wide lying higher than the level of the water which floods the fields. There is barely space on such roads for palanquin bearers; horses make their way forward single file, one after the other. There is a Chinese proverb about the paved roads: 'They are good for ten years and no good for ten thousand years' ... If these paths were paved with slabs their entire length, then one could not complain about them very much. But in any case, these are famously inconvenient roads with steep ascents and descents. In general they are laid out on a geometric axis: a straight line is the shortest distance between two points. They advance boldly forward in a straight line, not deviating to the side so much as an iota. (Incidentally, the ancient roads in France and Italy, preserved from the time of the Emperors, are the same.) In some places they have grades of twenty-seven or even thirty-six percent, and in such places they are not roads, but ladders. They pass over high ridges without paying any attention to passes and sometimes run right alongside them.[91]

Given the condition of the roads it is not surprising that in Shanxi coal costs 70 centimes per ton, but 40–50 kilometres distant it costs no less than four *taels*, that is fifteen francs in French currency, and 100 kilometres distant one had to pay seven *taels* or more than 26 francs. For every additional kilometre one paid an additional two and a half francs per ton.

The second enormous difficulty was that the monetary system in China mirrored the economic fragmentation of the state. The *chokh* or 'cash' as the British called it, was a very cumbersome monetary unit. One *liang*[92] had 1,000 *chokh* (not always, however), sometimes an official would calculate 3,000 or 2,600 *chokh* to the *liang*, when it was a matter of taxes, and one would need a carter to bring the money for the merchant. The higher monetary unit was different in different provinces. When the *haiguan tael* [Customs dollar] was introduced into ports, at the same time the government *tael* was introduced for accounting with the government. Also in circulation was the so-called Spanish dollar; the Mexican dollar also existed, moreover, each province and every city circulated its own Chinese dollars. The diversity of monetary units was an enormous obstacle to trade.

---

91   Ibid., p. 173. *Radek's note.*
92   In the middle of the nineteenth century one silver *liang* was equel to 0.67 U.S. golden cents.

The third obstacle which European capital encountered was the existence of merchant guilds. The *cohong* – the guild that monopolised foreign trade – had been disbanded, but throughout the country local merchant guilds existed. They were not only organisations for mutual aid, but also corporations which fixed prices, set the exchange rate, and in trading with foreigners represented the force of resistance of Chinese merchants. From the stories of foreign merchants one can see how they feared these guilds. The guilds could declare boycotts of foreign merchants, raise prices on goods, and so forth.

To these fundamental obstacles we may add the foreign merchants' lack of acquaintance with the Chinese language and their ignorance of local customs. All of these constituted significant obstacles to foreign merchants' penetration into the Chinese countryside to extract raw materials.

Foreign merchants found a way out by creating the institution of the comprador. The word comes from the Portuguese word 'comprare' which means 'to sell'.[93]

The comprador acted as an intermediary between foreign capitalists and the Chinese market. In China the concept of economic intermediary covers many different functions which we must distinguish from each other. One type of such intermediary was a 'gobemen' person (in 'pigeon' ['pidgin']),[94] someone who goes from one to another ['go-between']. This was a buyer who bought products from peasants when the prices for such products were low or who knew when the products of a bankrupt foreign merchant were being sold at auction in a port city, or generally bought warehoused products on sale cheaply to sell at higher prices whatever goods they might be. He sought only two contractors, one from whom to buy, the other to sell to. He worked with a small amount of capital.

A second type of comprador was a kind of stockbroker [...] (from 'fee' and 'take')[95] who bought and sold nothing himself, but was exclusively a middleman. He moved simultaneously among the circles of petty Chinese merchants and peasants, looking for goods, and among European merchants. But 'gobemen' and 'fustook'[96] were not the main instrument for the penetration of European capital. With the passage of time, European merchants became connected not with buyers and petty brokers traveling from village to village, but with the leading Chinese merchants. They became connected with merchants

---

93 Radek is mistaken. 'Comprare' is an Italian word that means 'to buy'. The same word in Portuguese is 'comprar'.
94 The word 'pidgeon' in Radek's text is written in English.
95 Words 'fee' and 'take' in Radek's text are written in English.
96 Thus in text.

who embodied the power of capital, and who already possessed influence. This kind of comprador is not merely a middleman as he is usually thought of in Europe. Essentially, one may use the term 'junior partner' to define a real comprador, a junior partner of the trading firm.[97] The comprador has his own work space (office),[98] he supervises all the Chinese personnel of the European trading house; he vouches for the accuracy of transactions in the cash box. The guarantees he provides are various, depending on the turnover of the trading house, but I have found information in the materials on compradors that there was a rather broad stratum of compradors who secured sums of up to half a million Mexican dollars.

What does a comprador do? Acting in the name of the firm, the comprador sets out to make deals. He buys raw materials in the countryside, pays for these materials, escorts them to the firm's warehouse, and attends to all the arrangements with the authorities en route. When payment of *lijin* is required, it is done on his account. The goods bought by the comprador are usually taken by the firm, but it is not obligated to do so. It might consider the deal disadvantageous, in which case the comprador must either sell the goods himself or lower the price. Furthermore, the comprador conducts all the relations with the Chinese merchants, purchasing goods from the European capitalists. For all of this, the comprador first of all was reimbursed for his expenditures by the firm, and compensated by the Chinese sellers of local products and the foreign merchants selling imported goods from half up to twice the value of the goods. Thus, he has an interest in all of the firm's transactions.

There were various types of compradors, depending upon the kind of trading operations in which the foreign firms were engaged. The large firms which have commercial dealings with the government, supplying arms to the government, uniforms (later when we take up railroad construction, we will see that the same holds true for the supply of railroad materials) have special compradors to lease with the government. These compradors are not concerned with ordinary trade; their stock-in-trade is influence on the central government and local officials. One German author – Benke, a professor at the Academy of Commerce in Berlin, who studies the question of compradors – says very openly that these compradors serve to bribe the Chinese government and Chinese officials.[99] The comprador might have to act only once or

---

97   The words 'junior partner' are in English in the original text. *Trans.*
98   Words 'junior partner' and 'office' in Radek's text are written in English.
99   It is not clear whom Radek had in mind. There was no any Benke (or Wenke) in the Academy of Commerce in Berlin.

twice a year, but he received an enormous salary from the firm as an indispensable intermediary between it and the government bureaucracy. This author states very discreetly that when compradors of this sort began to operate, and it turned out that they were very well paid, then many important officials abandoned their posts and many highly educated literati dropped their classical studies and took up this not very respected occupation, serving as an intermediary in transmitting bribes from foreign capitalists to Chinese officials.

Incidentally, if this German professor, who viewed Chinese officials and literati so condescendingly, studied not only China, but also Germany, France, and England, he would come across the same kind of comprador. In all countries, from the moment that powerful cartels and trusts appear, we see the phenomenon of many high-ranking officials who served in ministries where they had excellent connections, now working in the cartels and trusts for their new masters and using their old connections while earning three times their previous salaries. We know of even juicier instances in European practice. For example, in England, when the chief executive of the metallurgical firm 'Baldwin Limited'[100] was appointed prime minister [Stanley Baldwin], naturally he could not simultaneously trade in locomotives and head the British government. Then Baldwin placed Sir Robert Horn at the head of his firm, and Sir Robert Horn, who yesterday was a British minister, buying locomotives from Baldwin, was now selling him locomotives in the name of the firm. But when the bourgeois professor studies social phenomena, he understands with regard to China what he neither sees nor understands in his own country. In Germany and England everything is perfectly fine, but the Chinese are such a contemptible people that high-ranking officials and scholars sell out to foreign capital for cash.

To what I have said about the functions of a commercial comprador must be added the following. When a comprador clinches a deal, he accepts money in various forms: he receives ingots – large silver money worth 1,000 *liang*; various kinds of *taels*, he receives all kinds of foreign currency, and in order to verify the amount and quality of the sums he has received he has a special assistant who is called a 'shroff' (from the Arabic '*sarfar*' or banker).[101] This is essentially a responsible cashier who can attest that the money taken in from the deals is sound money and at the stipulated price. Compradors function something like the shroffs for foreign capital.

---

100   Words 'Baldwin Limited' in Radek's text are written in English.
101   'Sarfar' is usually translated as a server.

Trade requires not only dealing with the authorities, but also dealing between foreign banks and Chinese merchants. Therefore, each bank has its own banking comprador. He sits in a special office and deals only with Chinese. He is responsible for ascertaining whether the persons to whom credit is extended are credit-worthy or not. If he advises the bank to extend credit to someone who declares bankruptcy the next day, he must cover the debt with his own property.

The same is true for all insurance deals. In Europe there were special insurance societies, but in China during the period we are talking about each trading firm also underwriting its own operations. So a specialist comprador was also required, someone who knew local conditions, judicial norms, people, and so forth. The same held true for shipping. Foreign ships were leased to the comprador who paid a certain sum of money for them and was responsible for shipping. Thus, we see that foreign capital handled the Chinese market with roughly the same facility I display in this auditorium where comrade Chugunov [Zhou Dawen] serves as my comprador.[102] We see what enormous technical difficulties foreign capital had to deal with. At the same time, all this indicates to us how foreign capital finds in the Chinese merchant bourgeoisie a stratum which it binds to itself, and we will encounter this stratum in subsequent lectures when we address questions of politics and the role of those groups which began to form among the Chinese bourgeoisie.

No matter how great were the technical obstacles to the penetration of foreign capital into China and no matter how complicated were the means which foreign capitalists had to resort to, the main obstacle, of course, was not these, but the condition of the Chinese economy. We will see further on that during a period of 35 years, from 1860 to 1894, owing to all these obstacles, especially the latter one, even the cheapest goods were unable to smash the 'Chinese wall', and only very slowly was European capitalism able to take root in the Chinese economy.

If we take the figures for the period when European trade with China was just beginning to develop and look at what foreigners were trading with the Chinese, we will see at once that there was not a close link between the capitalists and the Chinese masses, the Chinese peasantry. Let's take, for example, Chinese imports in 1867. What was imported? Of the imports 21 percent was cotton textiles, 10 percent was silk fabric, 2 percent was metal goods, and 46 percent was opium. Thus, half of all imports into China consisted of opium.

---

102   Zhou Dawen was interpreting Radek during his lectures.

Generally, during the nineteenth century the trade in opium developed very successfully, but until the end of the century it was the only imported commodity which was growing by leaps and bounds. In 1821, it began with 4,600 chests, in 1830 it reached 18,700 chests, and in 1832 as much as 23,600. Subsequently, because of the efforts of the Chinese government, it declined, but after the Opium War it skyrocketed to 30,000 chests in 1850, and 83,000 in 1860. After this the import of opium declined somewhat, but in the four-year period 1877–80 it again reached an average of 86,700 chests. Only in the years following do we see a decline in the opium trade.

What did the Chinese export? For the entire period up to 1898, almost exclusively they exported tea and silk. The dimensions of this export, calculated in millions of customs *taels*, is presented in this table:

	Exports of silk	Exports of tea
1867	18.7	33.0
1870	24.0	30.0
1878	25.1	32.0
1887	31.6	30.0
1893	57.0	26.0
1894	61.0	28.5
1897	70.0	29.2

These data indicate that foreign capital, bursting its way into China, initially for a long period of time, did not produce any revolution in the peasant economy. Silk and tea had been produced in China since ancient times and had long since been foreign trade commodities. These were also the goods European capital sought to acquire. Subsequently, the trade in tea declined under the influence of Indian and Ceylonese tea which was processed more cheaply by machine, silk exports grew steadily despite competition from Japan.

The import of opium, generally speaking, in no way served as an indicator of the penetration of European capitalism or of European industry in China, but if one considers the importation of cotton and silk textiles, typical products of mass production of European industry, and if we look at the figures in this sphere in which Europe enjoyed an enormous technological advantage, then we will see that the enormous European textile industry promoted its wares slowly and with difficulty, mostly serving an urban population in the port cities and better-off peasants in localities adjacent to the ports.

The import of products of the textile industry in the second half of the nineteenth century (in millions of Customs *taels*) is as follows:

Year	Cotton textiles	Silk cloth
1867	14.6	7.3
1870	22.0	6.5
1878	16.0	4.8
1887	37.0	5.4
1893	45.1	4.5
1894	52.1	3.5
1897	78.6	4.8

If each year the European capitalists sold to each Chinese peasant just one pair of underwear, this would in itself constitute a much larger sum than what we see in this table. The table shows they were unable to break their way through into the Chinese countryside.

Let us look at metal products. China possessed only a weakly developed, primitive metallurgical production, yet the importation of foreign metal wares was insignificant.

Year	Metal wares (in millions of Customs *taels*)
1867	1.6
1870	3.9
1878	4.1
1887	5.7
1893	7.1
1894	7.5
1897	8.1

The total sum (in millions of Customs *taels*) of imports and exports and all of Chinese foreign trade in various years of the nineteenth century gives us the following picture:

Year	Imports	Exports	Overall trade
1805[103]	4.2	4.6	8.8
1827	13.8	12.8	26.6
1833	15.9	13.8	29.7
1842	17.0	17.0 (including 7.4 million in silver)	34.0
1845	14.2	25.9	40.1
1864	51.2	54.0	103.2
1866	74.5	56.1	130.6
1876	70.2	80.8	151.0
1877	73.2	67.4	140.6
1884	72.7	67.1	139.8
1886	87.4	77.2	164.6
1893	151.3	116.6	267.2
1894	162.1	128.1	290.2
1897	202.8	163.5	366.3

If one takes only the figures from the second half of the nineteenth century and compares, for example, 1866 and 1886, it turns out that over the twenty years imports only increased by thirteen million *liang*.

Just how little capitalism was able to develop the Chinese economy or, at least, to destroy Chinese relations by means of cheap goods, to differentiate the population, and compel it to sell is demonstrated by the fact that imports – even the sickly, consumptive imports – were almost always higher than exports, and in 1881 were 20 million *liang* higher, and in 1885, 25 million *liang*, in 1888, 32 million *liang*. China had to export silver to cover the deficit in the balance of trade.

Comrades, what does all this signify? Often the social-democratic gentlemen try to persuade the capitalists:

> You don't need imperialism. Why do you need cannons and ships? Imperialism is a mistake of capitalism. Sell cheap goods and you will find mar-

---

103   The sums from 1805 to 1845 are converted from Spanish dollars to Customs *taels* at the rate prevailing in 1840–60, when one Customs dollar was quoted at .66 *liang*. *Radek's note.*

kets in Africa and Asia where every Negro and Chinese is expecting that you will save their souls and sell them warm drawers.

In reality, imperialism is not an invention, an unnecessary luxury. If European capitalists want to thrust their goods upon people who are at a pre-capitalist stage of development, they must carry out an imperialist policy. And we see that the real expansion of imports and exports begins only after the Sino-Japanese War when, seeing the weakness of this giant – China – all the capitalist nations began to impose loans on China, seize concessions in China, cut up China into 'spheres of influence', and to build railroads through China. In order to push their goods, they first needed to carry out a revolution in transportation, to build railroads in China. We will devote the next lecture to the 'struggle for concessions', the period when capitalism came to realise that the artillery of cheap goods was unable to bring down the Chinese wall, and that it had to build railroads for this.

Lecture Seven

12 November 1926

The transformation of the situation in the Far East, and of the relations of the Great Powers to China, came about from an entirely unexpected quarter, from which world capitalism least expected an initiative possessing universal historical significance. This transformation occurred on the initiative of Japan.

As you know, Japan was drawn into world trade and world politics later than China. In 1853, Commodore Perry, the admiral of a small American squadron, demanded that Japan open its ports, in this way initiating Japan's relations with the outside world. In the years following, American, French, British and German flotillas again appeared off the shores of Japan, and in the face of this terrible danger, Japan's ruling class capitulated, opening entry to foreigners in the Land of the Rising Sun where they had been forbidden to live and trade since the seventeenth century – with the exception of the Dutch, who had the right to trade in one or two places on very humiliating conditions.[104] The capitulation of the Japanese ruling class was conditioned by the political and social decline which Japan had experienced in the preceding one hundred years. Rule

---

104   Japan was closed for foreign trade in 1639. Only the Dutch and Chinese could trade with Japan on a small artificial island, Dejima, in the bay of Nagasaki. The trade took place under strict humiliating inspection.

by the feudal aristocracy had long been an obstacle to the development of the forces of production; the population increased and famine struck with increasing frequency, owing not to natural catastrophes such as floods or drought, but to social conditions. Intellectual ferment was evident. The decline of the social stratum which ruled Japan during the Tokugawa period[105] was expressed in the creation of a mass of 'unemployed' petty nobles who had nowhere to turn to.[106] In the cities a social stratum emerged that understood the impossibility of Japan's isolation. Through the Dutch, these young Japanese became acquainted with European science, and bought books on anatomy and physics. If you read the biography of Marquis Ito,[107] you will find the story of how Japanese students dissected a corpse secretly at night (in Japan it was forbidden to do dissections) to ascertain whether the Dutch manuals were lying about anatomy. It was evident that the entire social system, which had been created over many centuries, beginning with Hideyoshi's attempt to conquer China,[108] was coming apart at the seams.

Little Japan came into contact with Europe and immediately manifested a greater ability than China to assimilate capitalism. You are aware that Japan's opening to the capitalist world was soon followed by the so-called 'Meiji Era', an era of political and social reforms carried out by the ruling class itself.[109] Why did this ruling class turn out to be capable of reforms while the ruling elements in China – the bloc of merchant capital, landlords, and the bureaucracy itself – turned out to be incapable? I think that two factors played a decisive role – geographic and social. Japan was a small country, and unlike China it could not hope that if the barbarians (the Japanese also viewed the Europeans as barbarians) burst into their islands, they could be overcome by the enormous size of their country. China is an enormous continental power; it occupies half of Asia,[110] and the Chinese ruling classes could suppose that the foreigners would be unable to conquer the empire. The small, spread out Japanese islands lay entirely within range of the cannons of the European warships. Furthermore, if one takes into account the enormous size of China and the number

---

105   This refers to the period of the Tokugawa shogunate (the rule of the generals from the Tokugawa family) that lasted from 1603 to 1868.
106   This refers to samurai, members of the nobel warrior class, who lost jobs after the pacification of Japan under Tokugawa. They were called ronin, i.e. masterless samurai.
107   It is not clear what biography of Marquis Ito Radek had in mind. By 1926, there had been published at least two biographies of this Japanese politician. See Palmer 1901 and Nakamura 1910.
108   This refers to the Japanese shogun Toyotomy Hideyoshi's plans to invade China.
109   The Meiji capitalist reforms took place in Japan in the period between 1868 and 1912.
110   Radek exaggerates. China occupies only 19 percent of Asia approximately.

of landlords, which we can establish approximately, then it is clear that the landlords in China must have drowned in the mass of peasants. Japan was fragmented into small principalities, and in these principalities the landlords were the real rulers of the regions; they still really held control of the peasants in their hands. Despite their fragmentation, the Japanese landlords functioned as a ruling class, confident in their power, and possessing a larger specific gravity in comparison to the other classes than the Chinese landlords. It is very revealing that the professions of trader and craftsman are much less respected in Japan than in China and rank lower in the social hierarchy, although handicrafts and trade play a very significant role in the economy. The strong landlord class, concentrated in a rather small territory, and connected with handicrafts and trade (Japanese peasants long since paid their taxes in cash), seeing the cannons that were trained upon them, understood that they would perish unless they quickly changed political course. Efforts to preserve this class were also dictated by the reforms of the Meiji Era. Their core was the centralisation of power, because for the struggle against foreign capitalism Japan had, first of all, to show its fist. The external sign of this centralisation was restoration of the role of the Emperor. For the time being, power remained in the hands of the same class which had ruled up till then, but from their own extended families the ruling feudal clans created a central organ of power – the *genro* – comprising the clan leaders.[111] This centralisation was bolstered by decisions to build railways, construct a fleet, and equip an army with modern weapons without delay. From Germany which, by virtue of its victory over France, gave the impression of being particularly accomplished in military affairs, Japan quickly recruited the Prussian General Merkel [Meckel], who immediately set to work organising the Japanese army. In order to compete against the foreign capital which was beginning to penetrate the country, Japan moved decisively to establish modern industries. We see here behaviour directly opposite to that which we observed in China. When in 1879, British and American merchants constructed a small railway from Shanghai to Wusong, ordinary people gladly made use of it, but the bureaucracy prohibited railway transportation and ordered the rails torn up on the pretext that laying rails involved driving nails into the ancestral spirits.

When Li Hongzhang, the future governor of Tianjin, constructed the first telegraph line from Tianjin to Beijing, then his officials, who had much to lose because they conducted the courier service, ripped off the wires and reported to Li Hongzhang that the spirit of feng shui had cut the telegraph wire. Li

---

111   *Genro* (the original elders) was a group of senior advisers to the Japanese Emperor in the late nineteenth through early twentieth century.

Hongzhang, who was a very wise and sober man, replied to these tricks that if the spirit cut the wires again, he had better not show up where Li Hongzhang could get hold of him. But Li Hongzhang was only one of a very few satraps who possessed such resoluteness. The Japanese immediately stopped worrying about spirits. They maintained the spirits only to keep the people obedient, but forbade them from interfering with technical progress. The development of industry in Japan in the years following the reforms indicates what great progress was made in the course of the next two decades.

I will cite several figures to demonstrate the tempo of Japan's economic development at the end of the last century. In 1885, Japan imported 800,000 pounds sterling of foreign cotton. It had only just begun to construct its own cotton textile industry. In 1894 it already imported 19.5 million pounds sterling worth of cotton, in other words, over a nine-year period it increased the importation of cotton twenty-four fold. In 1885, Japan had only nineteen cotton mills with 50,000 spindles. By 1893 it already had forty-six cotton mills with 600,000 spindles. The growth of the textile industry is also seen in the decline of imports of finished textile products. In the same period that cotton imports increased by a factor of twenty-four, imports of finished textiles from England declined by 40 percent and from India by 90 percent. In the 1890s, Japan not only supplied its own textiles from domestic production, but had already begun exporting them to China. Thus in 1893, it exported 4.5 million pounds sterling worth of textiles to China.

The textile industry reaped huge profits for Japanese capitalists whose ranks were recruited not only from the merchant class, but also from among wealthy landlords. In 1894, ninety-five Japanese textile mills paid dividends of 15–20 percent. In Lancashire in England at this same time, ninety-three companies operated at a profit. The government sheltered the industry by introducing a very high governmental tariff. This tariff protected not only the textile, but also the silk industry. We see how rapidly the latter grew notwithstanding the fact, which you know, that Japanese silk was lower in quality than silk from China. Export of Japanese silk goods increased from 54,500 pounds sterling in 1885 to 8.5 million pounds sterling in 1894.

The development of the coal-mining industry is shown by the fact that Japan not only supplied its own demand from domestic production, but also in its exports which rose from 2 million pounds sterling in 1885 to 6.5 million pounds sterling in 1894. Overall, Japan's foreign trade increased by 3.5 times in the decade. In 1885 it equalled 65.5 millions pounds sterling, and by 1894 it was already 230 million pounds sterling. These data on the development of Japanese trade paint an entirely different picture than the one given by Chinese trade. First of all, at this time China was still importing opium which was the main trade commodity; textile goods held second place. One can probably not even speak of the import of industrial raw materials for Chinese industry. In Japan, however, almost all imports were directed toward the development of domestic industry. Chinese exports were only of tea and silk. Japan was already beginning to export its own industrial items.

Japan is a small country with 40 million inhabitants; China is half of Asia with a population of 400 million; nevertheless, Japan began to overtake China in foreign trade turnover. Japan was developing along rails that led to an industrialised country. This was threatened by its shortage of coal, iron, and cotton, everything that it needed for production. All of these had to be brought in from abroad.

Therefore, in youthful capitalist Japan which had not yet become an industrialised country, Japan, which was still capital-poor, began to manifest warlike imperialist tendencies. At once it appeared on the scene with a powerful force, since this coincided with the interests of the nobility. The petty nobles were suffering from capitalist development; they were dissatisfied with the reforms of the Meiji Era, with government policy, and with the development of capitalism for the simple reason that in the capitalist system the possession of capital, rather than the possession of noble ancestors, was what counted.

The large landowners had been wealthy even before, and now they made money from the industrial development of the country, investing their capital in the newly established industries. The petty nobility found places only in the bureaucracy which could not grow as rapidly as the disintegration of the petty nobility which, therefore, became the source of the bellicose-nationalist current in Japanese politics. As early as 1874, at the height of the Meiji Era, these nobles pushed the government toward war with China, because of the murder on Formosa [Taiwan] by Chinese of several shipwrecked Japanese subjects (although it is still unclear whether they were really Japanese subjects).[112]

Even then China, figuring it was not in a condition to fight, bought off Japan by paying an indemnity, the American and British press observed that China was essentially a rich country that was able to pay a significant tribute, but unable to go to war. But Japan cast greedy looks at China, not only on account of the latter's weakness, but because the ruling circles were extremely well-versed regarding international affairs. They believed that the enormous growth

---

112   This refers to the so called Mudan Incident, i.e., the Japanese punitive expedition to Taiwan in May 1874 in retaliation for the decaptitation of 44 Japanese Ryukyu island aborigines by Taiwan aborigines in December 1871. These 44 victims landed on Taiwan because their ship sank near the southern tip of this island.

of industry starting in the 1890s, right after the depression, would provide a powerful impetus not only to Japan, but to the entire capitalist world to pursue expansionist policies, and that, therefore, they should not let the opportunity slip by; moreover, they were observing a new political factor in the Far East, namely, incipient Russian expansion in that quarter.

In 1891, Russia began to build a railroad from Vladivostok. The Siberian railroad was already far advanced. In its war with Turkey in 1878, Russia in fact had been smashed and its hopes disappointed.[113] Russia, which was involved in an endless struggle with England in Central Asia, and had gone as far as it could without resorting to war, began to move on the Far East in order to find another platform from which to pursue its global struggle against the British empire. But construction of the Siberian railroad alerted Japan to the danger that the tsarist government might seize Manchuria and Korea. In this lecture I will not delve into the particular sources of Russian expansion in the East. I will do that when we examine the negotiations between Li Hongzhang and Russian diplomats in 1896. Here I mention Russian expansion only to indicate why Japan was in a hurry, why it initiated a struggle against China, a struggle which in its first phase was a struggle for Korea. You know, of course, that Korea was not actually ruled by China. The power of the Great Khan was so weak in China itself that it was out of the question for China to exercise actual rule over Korea. But, formally, China considered Korea subject to its control, a subordinate vassal country. The Japanese did not recognise this; they sought to take over Korea by supporting those elements which they called the reform party, who were ready, under Japanese pressure, to transform this feudal country that was the most backward in the East. A silent struggle was going on between Japan and China. First Japan brought in its troops, a small garrison to defend its interests, then China did the same. The struggle for influence in Korea, rife with the possibility of clashes, concluded with Japan's decision to employ military force in order to repulse China's pretentions to control of Korea.

The German historian of Far Eastern affairs, the Sinologist Professor Franke, voiced the supposition that the reason China decided upon this war, decided to fight for Korea, should be sought in British policy. I think this is correct. Ever since it was opened to foreign influence with the aid of European cannons, China has pursued a very cautious policy. The Chinese bureaucracy was aware of its own weakness. It remembered that in a direct military struggle,

---

113 Russia waged a war against the Ottoman Empire in 1877–8. The war developed victoriously but England, Germany, and Austria-Hungary did not let Russia complete its victory.

China had to yield significant holdings in the south to France, and in its dispute with Russia over Kulja,[114] the Chinese government was forced to make enormous concessions. China's decision to go to war against Japan, therefore, would be incomprehensible if did not take into account England's interest in this war.

The British were observing Russian expansion in Siberia and the movement of Russians into the Amur region no less vigilantly than were the Japanese. Still earlier their attention was drawn to the movement of Russians into Turkestan and the clash over Kulja. Now England feared that if the Japanese seized Korea, then Russia would respond by seizing Manchuria, and thereby possess in the Far East not just Vladivostok, which was frozen for four months a year, but a more serious military base for its struggle against England. In light of this, England then supported the Chinese government. If we examine British political literature regarding the situation in the Far East in 1894, before the Sino-Japanese War and after it, we will see a complete about-face after Japan's victory. But prior to the war the British were firmly convinced that China would be victorious in the event of a clash with Japan. Prior to 1894, Britain was the number one trading power in the Far East, importing from China and exporting its goods to a greater extent than others, possessing Hong Kong, dominating Canton and Shanghai. It was the power that exerted the greatest influence over the Chinese ministry of foreign affairs and it tried to ensure that its position was unshakeable. The British understood very well that if Russia achieved a firm foothold on the Pacific Ocean, then in the event of continuing struggle between England and Russia over the strait, over Constantinople, and over India, Russia would also be in a position to deal a blow to England in the Far East. From all these considerations, I think that the supposition of Franke, this very well-informed German historian, that China decided upon war with Japan, acting under the influence of British advice[115] is correct. Probably had England known just how weak China was militarily, it is possible it would not have tendered such advice. From the book by the editor of *The Times*, Ignatius Valentine Chirol, published right after the Sino-Japanese War,[116] we learn that the British ministry of foreign affairs not only had no military expertise regarding China, but not even a military attaché who could correctly assess the military situation in the Far East. England knew that the Chinese government was buying cannons and outfitting its ships with modern artil-

---

114   Kulja (Ghulja, Gulja, Quilja, Ili, or Yining) is a city in northwestern Xinjiang.
115   See Franke 1923, pp. 26–7.
116   V. Chirol, *The Far Eastern Question*, London, 1896. Radek's note.

lery, but the British government did not suspect how weak China really was. Incidentally, no other power except, perhaps, Japan was aware of China's weakness.[117]

Europeans often make fun of how China had a poor understanding of Europe. The English author Chirol, whom I just mentioned, wrote about his conversations after the Sino-Japanese War in the ministry of foreign affairs in Beijing, and laughed at how the officials hopelessly confused Holland and Austria, and if they were able to distinguish between them, thought Holland stronger than Austria because it possessed colonies. But if we begin to leaf through the history of the Sino-Japanese War as it is reflected in the European press and literature, it will become perfectly clear that all of the European states likewise failed to understand the relation of forces in the East. Franke, whom I spoke about, writes that the start of the Sino-Japanese War provoked panic in all of the government cabinets, feelings of distrust in all the previous assessments because a new factor had appeared in the form of Japan which no one had previously considered. Up till then, Japan had been viewed as a toy-like nation of puppets. Just as puppets are made to look like adult people in top hats and women's gowns, so Japan copied real people – it developed all kinds of industry as well as railroads, but in essence this was a nation that would play no role at all. 'The situation', Franke says,

> was even more terrifying, so that everyone thought they were facing something new and unknown to which all previous standards and measures turned out not to apply, that in the struggle which had begun in late 1894,[118] a power was developing which no one knew and everyone feared. There were no leading figures in any of the ministries of foreign affairs that possessed even the slightest concept of Far Eastern nations, of their historical relations with the West or of their relations among themselves. In March 1895, the Russian minister of foreign affairs Prince Lobanov[-Rostovskii], in conversation with the German chargé d'affaires [Gustav Adolf Schenck zu Schweinsberg], complained that not a single person thoroughly understood the situation in Eastern Asia, and that among all the ambassadors in Peking [Beijing] there was not a single one upon whose opinions one could rely. In Paris, according to the French chargé d'affaires in Petersburg [Louis-Gustave Lannes de Montebello], the same view reigned. How things were in England is evident from the

---

117   Chirol 1896, pp. 3, 5, 65,66.
118   The words 'which had begun in late 1894' are not in Franke's text.

completely confused policies of the cabinet there. In Berlin, when they needed to make certain decisions, they resorted to an unheard of step which was not in accordance with either the customs or the normal practices of the German government: they called upon a retired official who had been the ambassador to China for many years, Mr. von Brandt, to give advice.[119]

The impressions from the clash in the Far East, as from something rife with the most diverse consequences, were evoked from the circumstance that contrary to all expectations, little capitalist Japan had summoned the power to defeat such an enormous power as China.

If you recall the history of the Opium Wars, you will see that in these wars the European states fought with very few forces and within a small territory. There were small Chinese armies along the seacoast, but in their hearts the Europeans were convinced that China was an enormous power, and that it would be extremely dangerous to get involved in a real war with it. Now they were struck by the fact that little Japan had embarked on such a war, fielded troops with every kind of weapons, and as a result the Chinese fleet was smashed, one after another large Chinese armies were defeated, Japan occupied Korea, the Liaodong peninsula, landed troops in Shandong, and had an open road to Beijing.

The young Chinese Emperor [Guangxu] ended the war, and addressed a manifesto to the nation, writing that he had spent sleepless nights, weeping over the misfortunes that had overtaken his army and fleet, over the incompetence and venality of his commanders, and over the fact that an enormous wave had destroyed the coastal fortifications (the Emperor's pride kept him from ascribing this to Japanese artillery), but that it was not all this which compelled him to refrain from an attempt to restore military good fortune to his army, but rather his debt to the Empress Dowager, the venerable woman [Cixi] who, if hostilities resumed and the Japanese should threaten Beijing, would have to flee from Beijing a second time, subjecting herself to all manner of inconveniences during a long and tiring journey.[120]

However, the capitalist powers of the whole world understood very well that it was not a question of the Empress Dowager, but rather that a new power had

---

119   O. Franke, 'Die Großmächte in Ostasien von 1894 bis 1914', Braunschweig und Hamburg, 1923, pp. 37–8. *Radek's note*. It refers to Franke 1923.

120   Cixi fled from Beijing (that time with Emperor Xianfeng) in 1860 during the second Opium war and in 1900 during the Allied intervention against the Boxers.

emerged in the Far East, a new power that was closer to China, which knew it very well, and which had taken the initiative into its own hands.

In Shimonoseki on 15 April 1896, China, defeated, concluded a treaty with Japan[121] which not only delivered Korea into the hands of Japan, but also gave it the Liaodong peninsula with Port Arthur and, therefore, control over all of North China. Moreover, China was obligated to pay an indemnity of 200 million *taels*. Japan's victory provoked an intervention by Russia, France, and Germany on the side of China and British support for Japan. In order to understand the underlying cause of the French, German, and Russian pressure on Japan and Britain's refusal to take part in this pressure, in the following lectures we need to focus on Russia's turn toward the Far East and on the emergence of German imperialism.

Here I only wish to consider the assessment of the events in the Far East that appeared in the contemporary literature and which was not without influence on policy. This assessment indicates how enormously important these events were. I will quote only two authors, persons who were very well-versed in international affairs – the editor of the *Times*, Valentin Chirol, and Lord Curzon. Shortly after the Sino-Japanese War, both of them published books devoted to surveying the overall situation in the Far East. What were their conclusions in these books? Chirol begins his book by quoting from a speech by Lord Rosebery, the former British prime minister, on the subject of the Sino-Japanese War:

> We have hitherto been favoured with one Eastern question, which we have always endeavoured to lull as something too portentous for our imagination, but of late a Far Eastern question has been superadded, which, I confess, to my apprehension is, in the dim vistas of futurity, infinitely graver than even that question of which we have hitherto known.[122]

Chirol observes that these misty distances of the future turned out to be very close to the time of Lord Rosebery's speech.

The Sino-Japanese War announced to the entire capitalist world the emergence of a huge new problem that was significantly more difficult than the Middle Eastern question which the capitalist world had been preoccupied with since the end of the nineteenth century. From his British point of view, what sort of assessment does our author provide about the situation in the Far East in connection with the 1894 war? He points out that from the moment when

---

121   Radek is mistaken. The treaty of Shimonoseki was concluded on 17 April 1895.
122   V. Chirol, *The Far Eastern Question*, London, 1896, p. 1. *Radek's note*.

Great Britain by force of arms first smashed the great wall of Chinese seclusion, over the course of fifty years it had enjoyed almost total influence in the Far East.

> Her prestige as a great Asiatic Empire, the splendid strategical positions which she holds at Singapore and Hong-kong [Hong Kong], the steady maintenance of a commanding naval force in the China seas, the overwhelming preponderancy of her trading fleet [flag], the magnitude of her commercial interests, of which an import and export trade of some forty millions sterling per annum conveys only a partial idea, the unrivalled prosperity of British colonies [her settlements] in the treaty ports of China and Japan, the widespread diffusion of her language [as *the lingua franca* of the East] – all combined to secure for her a paramount influence in these regions, which was almost openly recognised by the two leading Powers of the extreme Orient and tacitly admitted even by the great Powers of Europe.[123]

But in the course of some twelve months, the situation changed sharply. China and Japan had a bloody confrontation 'and the theory that China's latent resources as a fighting Power, upon which our Asiatic policy for some time past had been largely built up, was violently shattered'.[124] By its victory, Japan confirmed its right to respect among the great military and naval powers; Russia, France, and Germany here began to play an independent role. They came out against the Shimonoseki treaty and compelled Japan to renounce part of its gains.

> [A] dominant position in Peking [Beijing], are lost to us and transferred to political and commercial rivals who have already given us a taste of the spirit in which they intend to exercise their ascendancy over the decrepit Government of China.[125]

In his opinion, what conclusions should be drawn regarding China? He says,

> [I]f the Japanese victories have failed to rouse China from her lethargy, they have exposed the full measure of her weakness, and left her lying in the last extremity. A resolute hand might still, perhaps, galvanize China

---

123 Chirol 1896, pp. 2–3.
124 Ibid., p. 3.
125 Ibid., pp. 4–5.

[her] into fresh vitality. Otherwise China's [her] inheritance lies open, and the inexhaustible resources in the shape of raw material and labour with which nature has equipped her to become the great industrial country of the Orient, if not of the whole world, are at the mercy of the strongest and boldest.[126]

As for the future of China itself, Chirol speaks even more vividly about it in connection with the following episode. After Chirol returned from a trip to Tianjin from Beijing, Li Hongzhang asked him why he was staying in the Chinese capital much longer than he had originally intended. 'I replied', Chirol writes,

> that I had been looking for some sign of the awakening of China. 'I hope', rejoined the Viceroy with a grim smile, 'that your time has not been wasted'. In one sense certainly, as I assured his Excellency, my time had not been wasted, for I had at least satisfied myself that the search upon which I had been engaged was a futile one. Nowhere in Peking [Beijing] could the faintest indication be detected of a desire to apply, or even of a capacity to understand, the lessons of the recent war.[127]

Such was his assessment of the Chinese government – stupidity, impotence, and dullness. He said that the Chinese bureaucracy was a kind of parasite living at the expense of the country, stealing from the country, and thinking only of its own interests. As for the Chinese people, it did not even exist as far as he was concerned. He went on to say that it was impossible to expect a spontaneous uprising and it was even less likely now than before the war. In general, he characterised the situation as one in which China was going through a period of utter bankruptcy.

Lord Curzon, the future minister of foreign affairs of England, the viceroy of India, and one of the most important government figures in England, a specialist on Eastern questions, in his book titled *Problems of the Far East*[128] also tried to predict the future of China.

His prognosis was that the Chinese might preserve their existence as a race, they might preserve their culture, but that with regard to forming a Chinese nation capable of governing itself and able to adapt to international conditions, that was a complete mirage. Miracles don't occur, and therefore it would be absurd to suppose that China would be able to play an independent role in the

---

126   Ibid., p. 5. *Radek's note.*
127   Ibid., p. 9. *Radek's note.*
128   Karson. *Radek's note.* It refers to Curzon 1896.

future development of the Far East. These thoughts are not without practical application. If up until now England tried to conquer China for its trade, lacking the desire to annex it, but only to establish points along the broad coastline, then now: 1) it had arrived at the conviction that it was impossible to preserve the entirety of China as a market for England, and that China needed to be cut up; and 2) it understood it needed to form a partnership with Japan as a new power.[129]

Lecture Eight

In the last lecture we focused on the moment when, contrary to the provisions signed in Shimonoseki on 15 [17] April 1905 [1895], according to which China ceded the Liaodong peninsula with Port Arthur to Japan, promised to pay reparations, and conceded its industrial activity to foreigners, Russia, Germany, and France intervened in the negotiations despite the fact that the peace treaty had already been ratified, and demanded that Japan make concessions on a whole range of issues, in the first instance giving up Port Arthur and the Liaodong peninsula. What reasons compelled Russia, France, and Germany to step in as friends of China? We must study this question attentively.

When we spoke about the reasons that pushed England into the Opium War, it was clear we were dealing with the expansion of a powerful capitalist country which was striving to propel China into the whirlpool of world trade, fighting for the interests of its own industrial exports. In the first half of the nineteenth century, the interests of the English textile industry played a leading role in British Far Eastern policy. Although initially opium exports exceeded the export of textile goods, it was only because of the interests of the Indian Exchequer that the English bourgeoisie did not proceed to conquer China.

What economic interests propelled the Russian government toward the East? To answer this we must first explain the general character of tsarist Russia's expansion. This theme has already been well-explored in the Marxist literature. In an interesting article from the 1890s, Engels already pointed out that the driving force in the development of tsarist policy was the fact that its connections with capitalist countries was the source of its power.[130] The wars which Russia fought to acquire territory along the Baltic coast were commercial wars. Capitalist agriculture began to develop in Russia from the sixteenth cen-

---

129 See Curzon 1896, p. 342.
130 See Engels 1962 [1890], pp. 11–52.

tury, the estate owners in whose hands the economy of the country lay began to export Russian agricultural products abroad. They exported grain, timber, tar, and other products. Everything that Russian agriculture produced was in high demand abroad. At first the landowners traded with the West through German merchants organised into the hanse [merchant guild], and later only via Russian merchant capital which obtained from abroad that which the ruling classes required.

Overall this question was worked on by Russian Marxist historians. In his works Mikhail Pokrovskii, our leading historian, and in one of his works Riazanov studied this question in detail and pointed out that all the attempts to modernise Russia, to effect a transition from a feudal order to a landlords' economy in the sixteenth century under Ivan the Terrible, the attempt to transition from a gentry economy to a bourgeois-capitalist economy in a more contemporary sense of the term under Peter, was connected with Russia's exports overseas.[131] Since exports went via the Baltic sea, the core of the foreign policy of the tsarist government was a struggle for the Baltic coast. From the time tsarist Russia took control of Ukraine in the seventeenth century, and the centre of Russian agriculture shifted there, the role of the Black Sea began to grow for Russia's foreign trade. It suffices to say that between 1759 and 1769, the export of Russian grain via the Black Sea grew tenfold. This is why tsarism initiated a conflict with Turkey for control of Constantinople and the straits. War for the straits, war for a passage through the Black Sea for Russian grain was the core of tsarist policy from the seventeenth century up to the last imperialist war. To be sure, in the event of a war, the British fleet, which ruled the Mediterranean Sea, could attack Russian ships and render the export of Russian grain impossible. But as long as Constantinople remained in the hands of the Turks, not only an Anglo-Russian war could interfere with the grain trade; that was not something England would undertake lightly, but also a clash between England or another state with Turkey would suffice to hold up Russian grain in the Dardanelles. The conquest of Constantinople for tsarism would guarantee to some extent more freedom of movement than they would have at the time when there was a threat to close an exit out of the Black Sea even without a war with Russia.[132] It goes without saying that this was not the only reason for the struggle over the Dardanelles. Tsarism was guided not only by the economic interests of the Russian aristocracy, but also by the political interests of the aristocratic stratum. The aristocracy comprised the main mass

---

131 Radek must have assumed Pokrovskii 1924 and 1926, but it is not clear what work by Riazanov he had in mind.
132 Thus in text.

of Russian bureaucrats and militarists. To the greatest extent possible, it had to strive to develop the country, to conquer colonies, new territories, which would enable the aristocracy to fill new administrative and military posts. Just as pastoralists need to expand their pasture lands so they can feed their herds, so landlords are always seizing new territories to feed their aristocratic descendants.

In its striving to subdue Turkey, to conquer her, tsarism always encountered obstacles from the European powers, England most of all. In the Crimean War of 1853–6, Russia was defeated by French and British forces. In 1878 Turkey was victorious in the same goal; Russia was rebuffed again at the Congress of Berlin[133] thanks to the intervention of England. England would not countenance the seizure of Constantinople and Turkey's total subordination to tsarist Russia, because as the leading commercial power it sought itself to seize as many territories as possible in the East. Whoever held Constantinople would control one of the routes to Central Asia and Persia. The seizure of Constantinople would signify an intensification of Russia's drive toward the east, something that neither British merchants nor industrialists would permit in any form.

You may be asking what has this to do with Russia's expansion in the Far East? It is actually of great significance. We will see that tsarism turned to the Far East precisely because it was defeated in the Near East. As we know, Russia's expansion toward the east began as far back as the sixteenth century, when the Strogonov trading house (again a typical role for merchant capital) which financed the Cossack band of Yermak who seized the Urals, crossed the Ural mountain range, and began to conquer the khanates in Siberia.[134] At the same time, the armies of the Muscovite Tsar Ivan the Terrible conquered the remnants of the Mongol states along the Volga – Kazan and Astrakhan.[135] Thus, Russia at once entered the East from two directions – into Siberia and Central Asia. In the seventeenth and eighteenth centuries, Russia advanced step by step into Siberia and strengthened its position. The driving force was the desire to expand the territory for hunting fur-bearing animals. The fur trade occupied an important place in Russia's foreign trade and even English capital developed an interest in the seventeenth century and followed after the

---

133   The Congress of Berlin in 1878 was a convention of representatives of Russia, Great Britain, Germany, France, Austria-Hungary, Italy, the Ottoman Empire, Greece, Serbia, Romania, and Montenegro following the Russo-Turkish war of 1877–8. The great powers did not let Russia complete her victory over the Ottomans.
134   Yermak's Cossack troops began conquering Western Siberia in 1582. The Stroganov merchant family financed him.
135   Ivan the Terrible conquered Kazan in 1552 and Astrakhan in 1556.

Russian conquerors. They established a large Russian-English company which financed further conquests in Siberia and provided precious goods for world trade.

By the end of the eighteenth century, Russia had advanced to the shores of the Pacific Ocean. During the reign of Catherine II, all of Siberia and Kamchatka were in Russian hands, and even, on the other side of the Bering Strait, Alaska on the American continent. You probably never knew that in the eighteenth and nineteenth centuries Russia had one foot in America: Alaska, a wealthy land, was in Russian hands until 1867 when Russia sold it to the United States for seven million dollars, that is, an entirely insignificant sum.[136] Tsarist Russia was always a poor master; it did not understand that Alaska had gold, and during a period of financial difficulties it let the peninsula go for a song. That is how far Russia had sunk. But the development of expansion in this direction was more spontaneous; it followed the path of the beasts which it hunted. After the hunters came wagons with vodka for the local trappers and exiles whom tsarism sent to Siberia to die among the snows. The tsarist government could conceive of no better use for this richest of its colonies. The local governors, of course, were well aware of the enormous importance of Siberia. If you read the memoirs of the revolutionary Peter Kropotkin,[137] who in the 1860s served in the Amur Cossacks troops, or the biographical materials of another great Russian revolutionary Bakunin,[138] who also lived in Siberia in the 1860s, where the governor-general then was Muraviev[-Amurskii],[139] you will see that the Siberian governors, invoking the enormous size of the regions, tried to win over the Tsar to building a Siberian railroad, and first proposed such a project in 1858. But tsarism was occupied with the struggle for Constantinople, focused on Europe and the path from Ukraine via the Black Sea, and therefore saw no vital need for a Siberian railroad.

When tsarism was repulsed from Constantinople, it began to look for ways to administer blows to England. At first it expanded its holdings in Central Asia. Of course, after the failures in the Balkans, conquests in Central Asia represented not only a diversion against the English, but the conquests of General Skobelev were directly linked to preparations for a campaign in India. Russia completed its conquest of Turkestan, occupied Merv, and clashed with the English avant-poste – Afghanistan. It was only unfavourable geographical conditions that compelled it to refrain from striking a blow against England in this

---

136 In fact it was 7.2 million US dollars.
137 See Kropotkin 1902.
138 See Bakunin 1921.
139 Muraviev was the Governor-General of Eastern Sibiria from 1847–61.

direction. But it was not only India that England dominated; it held Singapore, and after 1844 it possessed Hong Kong.[140] It had long since become the leading commercial power in China, and part of its strength derived from its dominating position in the Far East. From the Central Asian side, England seemed almost invulnerable owing to the deserts and mountain ranges that separated India from Turkestan, but in the Far East, especially from the north, it was open to attacks, and understandably, after the conquest of Central Asia, Siberia acquired a completely different significance than it had before in the eyes of the tsarist government. When in 1887 the Irkutsk Governor-General Count Ignatiev again proposed the idea of building a railroad in eastern Siberia, Alexander II wrote that everything had to be done to implement this demand. Soon a commission was appointed to examine the question of building an enormous Siberian railroad, more than 4,600 miles in length (from Cheliabinsk), which would link Russia with the Pacific Ocean.

At the same time, the Black sea fleet was rebuilt as well as a 'volunteer fleet' which in peacetime would be used for commerce, but was built in such a way that it could be armed and used for military purposes.

Thus, Russia approached the China question from the perspective of its struggle with England. Behind the back of the Chinese people, a struggle began to unfold in relation to England's capitalist expansion and the expansion of tsarism which, having been defeated in the Near East, sought a detour via the Far East.

You are aware that relations between Russia and China began in the seventeenth century, the land border between them which takes place over the enormous distance made contact between Russians and Chinese unavoidable. We have descriptions of China in the seventeenth and eighteenth centuries even in the old Church Slavonic language, for example the descriptions by Spafarii.[141] Sometimes we also established official relations but only in the nineteenth century do these relations become no longer incidental or secondary but rather a regular part of the foreign policy of the tsarist government.

Here it is not without interest for us to examine how the tsarist government, which after the negotiations in Shimonoseki appeared in the role of a friend of China, dealt with China prior to the Shimonoseki peace treaty. To assess nineteenth-century tsarist policy toward China, we possess two important facts: the 1858 Aigun Treaty and the treaty regarding Kulja.[142] They demonstrate that with respect to China tsarism pursued the same policy of plunder

---

140   Radek is mistaken. England colonised Hong Kong (Victoria Island) in 1842.
141   See Spafarii 1910.
142   According to the 1858 treaty of Aigun, Russia occupied 231,660 sq mi of Chinese territory

that it followed in Central Asia and tried to follow in the Near East. By moving into Siberia, Russia became China's neighbour in Manchuria. It shared a common border where the Manchuria railway station is now located, where the Aigun river flows into the Amur. The entire region along the left bank of the Amur and further to the Ussuri river belonged to Russia. In 1858 the Russian Governor-General Muraviev occupied the district along the Amur. In the face of this threat, the Manchu officials agreed to the Treaty of Aigun according to which the left bank of the Amur would belong to the Russian and the right bank to the Chinese up to the place where the Ussuri flows into the Amur, and the entire district between the Ussuri and the sea, up to the Korean border, would be under the joint control of China and Russia. The Chinese government refused to ratify this treaty. However, during the Taiping Rebellion and the simultaneous war against England and France, when the French and the English occupied Beijing, the Russian diplomat, General Ignatiev (who was later the tsarist ambassador to Constantinople and known as the 'God of lies'), succeeded in getting the treaty approved. For the help he promised the Chinese government, in 1860 he not only received agreement to seizure of the district along the Amur River, but also the final transfer to Russia of the Maritime province and the city of Vladivostok. In this fashion, for the insignificant support rendered during the negotiations, the Chinese government had to cede an enormous region, one, to be sure, that was shorn of its Chinese population and, in general, thinly inhabited.

In the 1860s, in Kulja on the border of Chinese Turkestan, with Russian help, the Mohammedan population rose up against the Chinese governor. The Mohammedans put forward the slogan of self-rule, created a military organisation, and defeated Chinese troops. They were on the verge of establishing an independent khanate when Russian troops appeared on the scene in 1871 and occupied all of Kulja. China protested this seizure. Negotiations began which lasted about ten years and concluded with China ceding a part of the Kulja region that had strategic significance to Russia. Moreover, the Chinese government was obliged to pay nine million rubles and also grant significant privileges to Russian merchants.[143]

---

       on the left bank of Amur River. According to the treaty of Kulja signed in 1851, China had to open two cities including Kulja in Xinjiang for the trade with the Russian Empire.

143 This refers to the treaty of St.-Petersburg signed in 1881. Russia returned to China most of the Ili (Kulja) region that the Russian troops had conquered in 1871 during the Muslim uprising against Chinese rule. Not only did China have to pay the Russian government nine million rubles, but the Russian merchants also got the right to trade duty-free in Xinjiang and Mongolia.

These two facts demonstrate that tsarism pursued a policy of plunder with respect to China, seizing everything that lies not properly – even before it had given serious attention to the Far East. From the moment that the struggle with England arose, the tsarist government had to devise a broader and clearer plan with regard to the Far East as well. Such a plan was worked out by the government and the diplomats in connection with the question of building a Siberian railroad. The Siberian railroad had two major drawbacks. One was that Vladivostok, as the terminus of the railroad, was an inconvenient port since it was ice-bound four months of the year. Thus, the only Russia's naval base in the East was unsatisfactory because it did not provide warships sufficient freedom to manoeuvre. The question arose of where to find another harbour that would better serve as a military base. The second drawback was that the Siberian railroad, which would run along the left bank of the Amur River, would have to make a big arc, which would entail a loss of time in the event of war.

Tsarist diplomacy, the ministry of war in particular, concluded that it would also be necessary to construct a railroad on the other side of the Amur. The idea of the Chinese Eastern Railroad existed prior to the construction of the line along the Amur. This idea was implemented later when the eastern section of the Siberian main line which was started in Vladivostok in 1895 was built. But the construction of the CER still did not solve the problem since Russia still lacked an ice-free port. Initially, the tsarist government thought about finding one in Korea, but when, in the Shimonoseki Treaty, [the Japanese] who knew all the best ports in the Far East, demanded Port Arthur and the Liaodong peninsula, the Russian bureaucrats at once realised that Port Arthur should become Russia's outlet to the sea.

Why Port Arthur? To understand this it suffices to read how tsarist diplomats assessed the Japanese seizure of Port Arthur. When peace conditions in Shimonoseki became known, this is how the Russian minister of foreign affairs reported to the Tsar:

> There can be no doubt that the peace terms proposed by the Japanese, their sole occupation of the peninsula on which Port Arthur is located would evoke the greatest concern, as it would constitute a permanent threat not only to Peking [Beijing], but even to Korea, whose independence one assumes to declare, and, at the same time, from the point of view of our interests, it would be an extremely undesirable fact.[144]

---

144   See an ar[ticle] by M.N. Pokrovskii in a collection '1905: Istoria rev[oliutsionnogo] dv[izheniia]' v otdel'nykh ocherkakh'. V. 1. Predposylki revoliutsii, p. 525. *Radek's note*. See Pokrovskii 1925–6, Vol. 1, p. 525.

What this minister – Prince Lobanov[-Rostovskii] – said about the significance of Port Arthur to the Japanese, also applied, of course, to the Russians. If the Russians could hold Port Arthur in their hands, they would thereby be able to hold hostage the Chinese government.

This is the solution to the riddle of what goals tsarist diplomacy was pursuing. It concealed these goals with a number of economic arguments. You know that economists often exist to provide arguments to non-economists. If, for example, a feudal wants to rob, then he will easily find economists who will prove that this is not only necessary for his pockets but also generally from the perspective of economic development.

Three arguments were put forward for constructing the Siberian railroad as the basis for the aim of colonizing the Far East. The first argument was the economic significance of the Siberian railroad. But when motives for building the railroad were not being addressed to the general public, then the official point of view was different. Minister Witte explained the significance of the railroad as follows: 'The Siberian railroad will establish an uninterrupted rail connection between Europe and the Pacific Ocean and thus will open new horizons for trade, not only Russian, but also world-wide'.[145] This is clearly correct if one considers the long term. The Siberian railroad significantly shortened the route from Europe to the Far East. For example, if you go to China from London via the Suez canal, it takes 34 days, but it takes only 14 via the Siberian railroad. But tsarism did not spend two billion rubles and employ 7,000 labourers over a ten-year period to help English capital ship its goods to China.

In reality, that was not the point at all. At the very start of discussing the railroad project [in 1887], a 'special commission' of four ministers which was organised as a result of statements by the Priamur Governor-General and the commander of troops in the Irkutsk Military District [Ignatiev] on the need for a railroad extending at least from Tomsk to ports along the Amur, concluded that

> a continuation of the railroad across Siberia, requiring enormous expenditures by the treasury, did not promise any positive benefits in the near future in view of the limited commercial prospects in the region, and would only save on time. *But one cannot but acknowledge that from an overall state perspective, particularly from a strategic perspective, that acceleration of our communications with the distant East becomes ever more urgent by the year.* Therefore, without predetermining the means of

---

145   Ibid., 522–3. *Radek's note.*

construction, we must urgently survey those sections of the Siberian railroad *that are the most important strategically ... otherwise our main port on the Pacific Ocean will be cut off from convenient communication with the rest of Siberia* and will lose any base, and *in view of the primarily strategic significance of the projected line, it is desirable to have the most active participation of the War Department in the person of the governor-general in carrying out the survey.*[146]

Another argument was the significance that the railroad would supposedly have for Russian agriculture in Siberia. In this connection, the Amur district was accorded particular importance. But the description of this district, even in the official reference book, is unreliable:

> The beautiful soils that appear to be fertile, cannot compare in their productivity with the black earth of Russia ... But what especially complicates the development of cultivation in this district is the unfavourable climatic conditions and, in particular, the extremely uneven seasonal distribution of precipitation that renders agriculture impractical. Moreover, one cannot assume that grain from the Amur district will find markets in neighbouring countries, including China, Japan, and America, both because of its inferior quality and the lack of demand there for agricultural products. The same situation in the region holds with regard to cattle-raising ... Taking everything into account, the only thing that could increase the productivity of the district is *the development of manufacturing industry in it.*[147]

What this means is that the railroad had no real importance for the population of the Priamur district. The Russian grain there was of very poor quality, and neither China, Japan, nor Korea had any need whatsoever for it. Let us consider the same problem about the population of the district. In his memorandum of 1892, Witte spoke about construction of the Siberian railroad from the perspective of the interests of the Russian peasantry. He asserted, 'The peasants' shortage of land has long since been noted in many provinces of European Russia, and must undoubtedly be considered a negative feature of Russian life'. That the peasant had little land was not good. To be sure, the landlord had a

---

146 Ibid., pp. 519–20. *Radek's note and emphasis.*
147 Pokrovskii, 'Diplomatiia i voiny Rossii v XIX stoletii' ('Diplomacy and wars of Russia in the nineteenth century'). 1924. *Radek's note and emphasis.* This refers to Pokrovskii 1924, p. 357. The words 'the development of manufacturing industry in it' are emphasised in Pokrovskii's text.

great deal of land. It would have sufficed had Witte given the landlord's land to the peasants. Naturally, however, our minister was not about to do that:

> The most appropriate means of addressing the shortage of arable land is to allot to needy peasants public lands in Siberia, especially in its western part. The striving of the meagre farmers to resettle in new places is already observable, but is spontaneous in character; if the government directs the resettlement movement under more proper conditions, then we may suppose that the settlement of fertile Siberian wilderness lands will proceed very successfully, and with the arrival there of a sufficiently large work force, the fertile Siberian lands will doubtless also attract better-educated social strata who will bring capital, knowledge, and a civilizing influence to these environs. In this way, the Siberian railroad will provide some of the main conditions for the development of agricultural production in the wide area through which it passes, namely, markets and a labour force, opening the way for the state and solving one of the most difficult tasks – construction of a sound economic way of life for the land-poor peasant population of the interior provinces of European Russia.[148]

This was the third economic argument in favour of building the railroad.

Let us consider some statistics and see how resettlement went in reality, at least with respect to the Priamur district. In the entire Priamur district, seized from China, there were 100,000 Russian settlers in all in 1895. Concerning how these settlers lived, I found verses in a book on Russian colonisation in Siberia that circulated at the time. These verses speak better than a lengthy description to the question of how tsarism took care of the peasants it settled in Siberia.

> There were measles and scarlet fever,
> Diphtheria as well.
> Well then? You burn up for a week,
> Lie in bed, then it's over.
> Death in life, a malevolent God.
> Mistakes are all around
> And not a few of our own
> For which no reproach is due us.
> We have not learned to sow.

---

148   '1905: Istoria rev[oliutsionnogo] dv[izheniia] v otdel'nykh ocherkakh'[,] t. 1. 'Predposylki rev[oliutsii]' ('1905: A history of the revolutionary movement in separate essays': Volume 1. 'Preconditions of the rev[olution]'), pp. 520–2. *Radeks's note*.

So that no blame befall us
We put off reporting to the chief.
Here we exaggerate, there we smooth things out
And generally all goes well.
People take sick – they are treated,
Those who die are interred.
The percentage is such-and-such. It is nice, sounds well.
Everywhere we see fruits of labour,
There is one moral everywhere:
The land is almost settled,
We await further instructions.[149]

This was evidently written by a petty official, an intellectual who saw the suffering of the Russian peasants who had fled to Siberia from the knout of the landlord, and found nothing there but poverty and disease.

The tsarist government was very little concerned with settlers. The government did not think about the interests of the economic development of Russia, nor of the interests of the peasantry, nor even of the interests of trade. All Russian exports to China totalled six million rubles and that only in kerosene, while Russia bought 30 million rubles worth of tea from China. Even when Russia seized Manchuria, the industrial products in Manchuria were Japanese and British. The entire Far Eastern policy of Russian tsarism was a war policy, based on strategic considerations and directed, in the first instance, against England.

Lecture Nine

We turn now to Germany's role in mitigating the terms of the Shimonoseki peace. Since we will be dealing with Germany's role in the Far East in our continuing study of history when we will be speaking about the Boxer Rebellion,[150]

---

149 Volkhovitov, 'Kolonizatory Dal'nego Vostoka' ('Colonialists of the Far East'), Vel[ikaia]. Ross[ia] (Great Russia), 1910, p. 221. *Radeks's note.* Radek is mistaken. The author's name is L.M. Bolkhovitinov. See Bolkhovitinov 1910, p. 221.

150 The Boxer anti-foreign uprising (otherwise known as the *Yihetuan* uprising) took place in China in 1899–1901. As a result of its suppression by the armies of eight foreign powers in 1900–1, the Chinese government was forced to sign in Beijing a so-called Boxer Protocol with the representatives of these powers, a new unequal treaty, strengthening the privileged position of foreigners in China. The Boxer Protocol was signed on 7 September 1901 in Beijing by the Chinese representative Li Hongzhang with the representatives of the eight foreign powers which had taken part in the suppression of the Boxer Uprising.

of the battle for concessions, and so forth, I want to provide a brief sketch of Germany's development and explain its motive forces, because it is only on this foundation that you will be able to understand the growing significance of Germany in the Far East in the late nineteenth and early twentieth centuries. Despite the Versailles peace treaty Germany has not ceased to exist, and now we can see it gradually getting stronger. It is again beginning to play a role in international affairs, although for the present only economically. And this is another reason why you must take note of the outlines of Germany's development.

The first question you must ask is why we heard nothing about Germany in the period when capitalist powers, initially in the seventeenth century, and then in the nineteenth century, generally began to pursue colonial policies, and, in particular, struggle with China? Why did Germany not take any part in the Opium War? Why only in 1895, after the Sino-Japanese War, did it appear as a factor exercising any noticeable influence?

One must look for the answer to these questions in the general fate of Germany. Germany was of prime importance in the sixteenth century. I have already spoken about the role of the Hanse, the organisation of cities that was the main trading intermediary between northern and southern Europe in the fifteenth and sixteenth centuries. If you read the history of Russia, you will see that it was German merchants who linked the Russian market with the West European; from the history of England you will learn that, in a certain sense, German merchants dominated the English market in the fifteenth century; the history of Italy informs us that German merchants were the middlemen between Italy and all of Northern and Central Europe. Why, subsequently, did Germany stop playing this economic role? There are numerous reasons. The most important is what we call a *transformation of trade routes*.

In the twelfth and thirteenth centuries when Germany began to play the role of middleman, northern Italy was the most economically developed country. The Italians brought in all the goods which came from the East via Constantinople and Egypt. These Eastern goods were sent to India and Venice and from there, via Switzerland, to Germany on the Rhine river and further on to Holland where English merchants congregated. Thus, this commercial route inside Europe was in the hands of Germany. On this foundation the industry and trade of southern German cities like Nuremburg, Augsburg and others developed. At the same time, Hanse merchants travelled on the Baltic Sea to what is now Latvia, Estonia, and Russia; they travelled further to Pskov and then to Moscow and exported Russian goods – furs – one of the most important items of their trade, honey, wax, flax, and hemp.

When the Turks seized all of the Middle East, Egypt, and Constantinople, Italian trade began to decline. Direct contact with the East – with India, Persia, the Middle East, and China – was severed, and the Spanish and the Portuguese began searching for a path to India around Africa. Germany ceased playing the role of middleman between Italy and northern Europe, and this impacted all of its trade. Russia and Holland began direct trade with each other, and the English likewise began trading with Russia without Germany as middleman, and expelled the German merchants. With the unification of Holland, its merchants also freed themselves from the influence of German trade. The German economy declined more and more. The seventeenth and eighteenth centuries were the time of its economic nadir, and this led to its political decline. Germany was divided among a larger number of principalities than existed in China during the feudal age.[151]

Until Germany emerged from a state of economic decline, it could not establish a strong political authority, and it ceased playing any sort of serious role among the rising great powers in Europe. Owing to this, Germany did not take part in the colonial politics of the sixteenth century, in the plunder of the world by the colonial powers, and later when the struggle to open the Chinese market began, in the beginning and middle of the nineteenth century, the Germans were not involved. The development of industrial capitalism was just beginning in Germany, and it had barely begun to emerge from a state of political non-existence. During the second Opium War and the Taiping Rebellion, Germany was engaged in the decisive battles for its own unification. Its attention was fully absorbed with the process of domestic consolidation. Therefore, as before it was not at all involved in the development of Far Eastern events. Later, when the French and the British forced the Chinese to open ports, then the Germans, too, sent a fleet to China (consisting of unfit and outmoded vessels which had no military value) and also demanded for themselves the right to trade, which was granted. To grasp just how weak German interests in Chinese affairs were, it is enough to point out that the great German geographer Richthofen, who wrote a five-volume work on Chinese geography (which remains even today one of the outstanding books on China), lived and studied in China for many years on money from the Shanghai chamber of commerce, not from the German government. Part of his support came from the British. This is how little interest Germany had in Far Eastern affairs.

---

151   Radek is mistaken. Germany (The Holy Roman Empire) had already disintegrated in the High Middle Ages. In the early sixteenth century there were over 300 German states.

But the unification of Germany occurred during the course of the nineteenth century. How this happened you have already heard in lectures on the history of the West. I will remind you only of the key dates. In 1834 a Customs Union [*Zollverein*] was established. Prior to this a politically fragmented Germany was also fragmented economically. Every principality collected special duties. You know how, at present, foreign capitalists make a big fuss over *lijin* which in China are collected at the border between two provinces. In Germany prior to 1884, the same *lijin* existed, with the difference being that China was an enormous continent while Germany was a comparatively small country. If someone travelled from any one of the principalities to another for no more than three hours, he would already have to pay a customs duty. But starting from the first decades of the nineteenth century when the Industrial Revolution spread from England to other countries in Europe, agitation for the economic unification of Germany began. A struggle against the German *lijin* began in the interests of the German bourgeoisie which wanted to have a single market. German merchants from various cities – Hamburg, Bremen, or Köln – wanted to sell their goods throughout Germany without any obstacles, and they also wanted to organise politically as a class.

The creation of a customs union in 1834 was the first step in the unification of Germany. Several decades later this unification was accomplished by means of war – first in 1866 with Austria, and in 1870–1 with France.[152]

Why by means of war? It is worth pausing on this point in order to better understand current Chinese events.

In 1866, a war was going on between Prussia and Austria. Prussia was one of the strongest principalities of Germany. According to its constituent parts, Austria was partly German, partly Hungarian, and partly Slavic. The Hohenzollerns ruled in the first one; the Habsburgs in the second. It seemed that this was only a war between two dynasties as many still think now when Zhang Zuolin and Wu Peifu fight that it is only a war between two warlords who want to fight. One cannot explain this war by nationalist motives. The German bourgeoisie of Prussia supported the Hohenzollerns and the German bourgeoisie of Austria supported the Habsburgs. How can the war between these two states be explained? There is a very simple reason.

In 1848 the German people – the urban petty bourgeoisie, the peasantry, and workers – tried to unify the country from below and get rid of all fifty Kings and Princes.[153] But the revolution was crushed. The people were unable to unite the

---

152   There was also a 1864 war between Prussia and Austria, on the one side, and Denmark on the other, for Schleswig and Holstein.
153   Radek exaggerates. There were no fifty Kings and Princes in Germany at the time.

country from below. Therefore, unification had to come in some other form, if only by means of one of the Kings demonstrating that he was the most powerful and able to force the others to submit to him. There has not yet been a single instance in history when any nation has achieved unification solely by agitation and propaganda. The unification of a nation always takes place amidst great upheavals. Either revolution or counter-revolution may triumph on the road to unification, and future developments depend on which of these is victorious, but weapons are needed in either case.

If the Chinese revolution does not unify China from below via a revolutionary path, if the peasants, workers, and the working intelligentsia do not drive away the warlords by armed force, then in the future we will have a series of wars, and in these wars the strongest of the warlords will unify the country. If this fails to accomplish the tasks of the working masses, still it will satisfy the bourgeoisie, opening new opportunities for it to exploit the workers and peasants.

In 1866 the Prussian King defeated the Austrian King and threw him out of the union of German Kings once and for all. Eight million Germans were cut off from Germany. Thus, in order for the Prussian King to unify the nation, he had to sacrifice part of the Germans.

And what is it that brought about the other war – the war of 1871?

Here once again there is a very important precedent for you. While Germany was broken into pieces, split apart, it did not play any sort of independent international role. Almost all the wars from the seventeenth century were fought on German territory.[154] You know that in the Far East, when Russia fought with Japan, it fought in Manchuria, on Chinese territory, because China played no role, it was weak. So it was in Europe with Germany. But when Germany became unified, its international importance underwent a change. Instead of a country fragmented into pieces, of a mere geographical expression, a Great Power appeared, and France, which dominated Central Europe at the time, did not want to permit this. It wanted to keep Germany fragmented. Therefore, a unified Germany had to demonstrate its power with arms in hand, demonstrate its right to exist as an important power. If China unifies, then most likely it, too, will have to show with arms in hand that it is truly unified, so that others will take it into account, perhaps even the very process of unification will require a great war of China against the European powers, and in a certain sense we may say that this war has already begun. We know that Sun Chuanfang and Wu Peifu are waging war to a significant degree on British funds. In essence, they represent a British army which is interfering with the unification of China.

---

154 Radek might have assumed that these wars started with the Thirty Years War (1618–48).

For you the study of German history is important, because it can explain a lot that is not clear in your country's current situation. I was very pleased to read the article by a Chinese economist, published in the English-language book by Reber, who understood perfectly this comparison between the fate of Germany and the fate of China.[155]

Thus, in 1871, after its victory over France, Germany stepped onto the stage of history as a great power, as a single economic organism with more than 40 million people, as a significant factor both in the world market and in world politics. However, from 1870 to 1894, this great Germany still did not intervene in Chinese affairs. It was only after the Franco-Prussian War that Germany's amazing economic development began which subsequently made it the foremost industrial power in Europe. Yet Germany's economic development from the time of the Franco-Prussian War to 1894 was far from proceeding at the pace which it did in the 1890s, closer to the time of the Shimonoseki settlement. The years of 1893, 1894, and 1895 were the great economic turning point. Only from those years did the triumphal procession of German industry get underway.

Along the path of its development Germany had to overcome a variety of large obstacles. If you compare the conditions under which Germany and England developed, you will see a great difference. England is an island defended by the sea from attack by large land forces. Only an enemy with a large navy can fight against England, therefore, we see that from the beginning of England's capitalist development, England waged war, but no one waged war against England.

Germany was in a geographic position which placed it constantly under threat – on one side from France, on the other from Russia. France was a powerful, centralised state; Russia – like China – was a colossus in terms of territory, population, and natural resources. Between these two powerful states, and strategically between two rivers – the Rhine and the Wisła – lay Germany.

Russia can very easily endure any defeat, because in Russia there is a lot of space to retreat just as you have here in China. If, during the civil war of 1917–20, the Whites beat us, then we could retreat, we had space where we could retreat to. In 1918, each of us, looking at the map, saw how our Soviet Russia, first stretched out to one side, then contracted; in some places the front line bent toward the centre, and our territory became ever smaller, but then expanded again. This was always Russia's enormous advantage. China has this advantage, too, and like Russia, in the civil war in China it wholly favours the

---

155   It is not clear whom Radek had in mind.

revolutionary troops since it enables the revolution to survive any defeats and await a favourable relationship of forces which, in the final analysis, will always benefit the revolution. Without horses or the railroad, Cantonese forces have advanced more than 1,400 *verst* to the north, a truly remarkable campaign which, of course, must exhaust the troops.[156] But even if the battle taking place now along the Yangzi ends in the defeat of the Cantonese forces, this would not be a decisive victory for the counter-revolution – the Cantonese can withdraw to the south. The enemy will go after them, run out of steam, and then the Cantonese can advance once more. The Chinese revolution is able to take advantage of geographic conditions, and because of this we may rest easy. It is not for nothing that our [Soviet] military advisers in Canton have graduated from the school of the civil war in Russia.

Russia was able to take advantage in this way. It was not only the Red Army that possessed this advantage vis-a-vis the Whites, but also the tsarist army vis-a-vis the German. Germany had a small territory. A decisive defeat could set it back for a long time. Germany was broken into pieces for two hundred years, and when this ended in 1870, the main concern of the German bourgeoisie was not to blunder into war against Russia and France simultaneously, because this would spell disaster for Germany.

But in addition to political obstacles, Germany also had to overcome large-scale economic obstacles. If you look at England, you will see that before the railroads all the main economic centres were connected to each other. From London to Liverpool, Bristol, and Scotland, one could travel everywhere by sea. And sea transport is the cheapest. Germany lacked this advantage, and it had to establish an outstanding railroad network in order to link various parts of the country into a whole, to invest enormous capital in transport to make giant steps in the area of industrial development feasible.

Moreover, England had been accumulating capital continuously since the sixteenth and seventeenth centuries. It had been exploiting half of the world, and its constantly growing, enormous amount of capital very quickly developed the economy of the metropole. Germany was just beginning to accumulate capital and invest it in industry. If you read English novels written in the 1860s and 1870s, you will find the following picture everywhere. A German engineer travels to England, cap in hand, and humbly asks for a position in an English factory. There he can learn and find work. At home he can still not find appropriate employment.

---

156 This refers to the Northern expedition of the National Revolutionary army of the Guomindang.

To be sure, England had to import agricultural products, but here, too, Germany enjoyed no advantage. Germany is a country with many forests and mountainous areas. The land could not feed even half the population if technology and science had not improved German agriculture. It is said that the Chinese practice the most intensive agriculture. Europeans enjoy stories like the one which says that when a Chinese peasant shaves his head, then, as a French writer tells us, he takes the hair to fertilise his field, or when a guest comes and is well-fed, he is not allowed to go on his way until he returns to the earth that which he ate. But even though Chinese peasants work tremendously hard, carrying earth on their backs in order to improve their plots, the intensiveness of their agriculture still does not compare to the intensiveness of German agriculture. The difference is that in China in the literal sense of the words the peasant pours his sweat into the ground, the strength of his muscles, but the German bourgeoisie have adopted the greatest technical means to develop agriculture.

To whet your appetite for the future development of Chinese agriculture, I will pause to consider this question for a while.

In order to develop their agriculture, Germans focused on the question of artificial fertilisers. Where could they come from? German chemists created a new branch of science – the science of fertilisers. Potassium salts were used for the first time for this purpose in Germany. The Germans were also the first to use phosphates which were the residue from steel-making. They made wide use of nitrous substances and even, during wartime, when they were unable to import needed fertilizer from South America (from Chile) – they invented a method of extracting nitrogen from air in a form which plants could utilise.

Animal husbandry was no less serious a problem which the Germans confronted. With utmost attention they began learning how to feed domestic livestock, how to achieve the maximum amount of lard from swine, how to increase milk production from milk cows, etc. Such knowledge was already developed in England, but the Germans advanced it much further.

They next focused on developing knowledge that would enable them to substitute what they had for what they lacked. Sugar came from sugar cane which grew in Egypt and America, but not in Germany. They found a solution in the production of sugar from sugar-beets. This was primarily the result of the work of German chemists and German scientists.

What kind of results did these efforts produce? I will give you some figures. From 1885 to 1910, the population of Germany grew by 30 percent, and in the same period the grain harvest increased by 40 percent, from 18 million to 25 million tons, and this was not due to the expansion of land under cultivation, but due exclusively to improvement in agricultural methods. The production of potatoes increased by 55 percent. If you look at the production of sugar from beets, then in 1870 it took 11.5 kilograms of beets to produce one kilogram of sugar; thirty years later it took six kilograms. In other words, it took only half as many beets to produce the same quantity of sugar.

By developing its agriculture, Germany, first of all, reduced the amount of grain and other products needed for food which had to be imported from abroad and, second, created in the peasantry an enormous domestic market for its own industry. Before the start of the war, Germany exported almost 10 billion Deutschmarks – about five billion rubles – worth of goods. This is an enormous sum, but it represented an insignificant part of total German production, which was mainly directed toward satisfying the needs of the domestic market which was growing every year. Before the war, German industrialists began outdoing all other countries in the realm of technology. If we set aside diplomatic history (since very many people study diplomatic history), and focus on the economic history of the last decades before the war, then it will give us an amazing picture of how every year Germany outstripped one branch of British industry after another. Thus, for example, between 1890 and 1910, the German steel industry grew seven times faster than the British.

By 1893, the Germans, who earlier badly lagged behind the British in steel production, had already caught up with England, and then quickly overtook them not only in steel production, but also in the production of iron. Before the war, Germany outranked England in the production of steel and iron, in chemical and electro-technical industry. England rushed into war in 1914, because Germany had surpassed it in everything except the textile and coal industries. This development was achieved by means of enormous technological improvements. The following example will suffice: In England in the 1870s, the engineer Bessemer invented a method by which the process of smelting steel was reduced from one and a half hours to twenty minutes. At once this gave England an enormous advantage. England has very pure iron ore without phosphorus, and Bessemer's method was appropriate only for steel production from pure ores. But Germany does not have phosphorus-free ores, so it seemed that the German steel industry was condemned to death. However, in 1878, the English engineer Thomas perfected Bessemer's invention and found a method of smelting steel from ores containing phosphorus. His improvement was not adopted in England, but the Germans utilised it and learned to produce steel from inferior grades of ore.

And so it went in all branches of industry. Germany left England far behind in matters of technology. As far back as 1903, our comrade [Fedor Aronovich] Rothstein, who was living then in England, pointed out in a very interesting work based on debates at congresses of British scholars, just how deficient was the training of workers and engineers in England.[157] The German bourgeoisie defeated the English by developing their technology. They defeated them even more by developing their school system. The German bourgeoisie knew that if it wanted to win out over England, it had to learn how to extract the most from its workers. Therefore, no other country had so many schools, and such good schools as Germany. Despite the fact that the German bourgeoisie hated the working class, it also understood that it needed to provide the best living conditions in order to maximise labour productivity, and it was the first to provide insurance against sickness and disability. Of course, it did not do this voluntarily, but in response to pressure from the workers, but it yielded to such pressure understanding this was in its own interests.

The results of all this became perfectly clear only in the final years of the nineteenth century. The years 1893, 1894, and 1895, as I have already said, were the years of the great economic turning point when it became clear to the whole world that Germany was a great power which was entering upon the path of imperialism. Before 1895 there was a depression. Germany did not yet feel itself a victor in the world economy, and the German bourgeoisie was not yet thinking about a colonial policy. Its main concern, as before, was that the Russian Tsar not join together with the French bourgeois republic, so that by this means tsarist Russia and France, which had been defeated by Germany in 1871, would not strangle Germany. Count Shuvalov, the Russian minister of foreign affairs,[158] speaking of the leadership of the German politician Bismarck, said that even in his dreams he suffered from the nightmare of such a coalition: he dreamed that tsarist Russia and France together would strangle him. In the initial period after its victory over France, Germany's policy was entirely directed toward organising a defence against this future coalition. In 1879 Germany concluded an alliance with Austria, and then [1882] it dragged Italy into this union precisely in the event of a war with Russia and France.

Fear of such a coalition along with the youthfulness of the capitalist development of Germany were the reasons for Germany's late entry onto the path of a colonialist policy. Germany took the first step in this direction in 1884, fourteen years after its own unification. But just what could it get out of this? All of the colonies had already been distributed, and all it could seize were a few crumbs. Like a hungry dog roaming around the room looking for a bit of bone, Germany scoured the world to pick up whatever France, England, and Russia

---

157   See Rothstein 1903.
158   Radek is mistaken. Shuvalov was not a minister of foreign affairs, but head of The Third Department of His Imperial Majesty's Own Chancellery from 1866–74.

had not taken. If you look at Germany's colonies on a map, it is evident that Germany snatched the bones that the others had ignored. At first it went for parts of Africa that had not been seized. These were all pieces completely unconnected to each other; everywhere they had to station special forces, nowhere were conditions appropriate to maintain a large army or to build railroads. The German colonies in Africa could not even serve as significant sources of raw materials. These were all bits and pieces with neither strategic nor economic significance.

Later it began to grab whatever little islands in the Indian and Pacific oceans, strategically weak positions for the future. The German bourgeoisie did all of this despite the fact that they generally derived nothing economically useful from these seizures. It sensed that a new period of growth of imperialism had begun. After the 1871 war, France began to expand its holdings in Africa and seized Indochina. England everywhere rounded out its colonies and dominions; Russia advanced into Siberia, and the German bourgeoisie dimly sensed that it also needed to secure some bits and pieces. But where to go? It had no idea until China was defeated by Japan and it became clear that a time had come in the East not for tearing off small chunks, but for partitioning a great state, a process in which it could intervene. This was the first ray of Germany's broad colonial hopes.

Moreover, there were other reasons for Germany's efforts to take part in Far Eastern affairs.

Russia had taken the initiative to divide up China; Japan ripped it away, and Russia had to tell her 'Stop! Not one step further'. This she could not do alone. In its diplomacy every power tries to secure the diplomatic support of others. Every power seeks to avoid isolation. One of the most important tasks of every policy is precisely that. When you will be fighting in the future, always remember that the worst thing is a unified enemy. You have to find a fissure between your enemies through which you can pass in order to break them apart. That is why Russia was seeking support from other countries.

From whom could she find support? France was already sated: it had and was not directly interested in acting together with Russia in the Far East. It went along with Russia only because Russia was its ally. Defeated in 1871, France forged an alliance with Russia which was directed, in the first instance, against Germany, but which also obligated both powers to support each other in other cases. Russia sealed this alliance because the Russian Tsar needed money. He fought with England over Asia, and therefore could not get any money from her. At this time, France was the strongest banker and tsarism took out loans from her, promising to repay not only with funds, but also with the blood of Russian peasants.

When tsarism came out against Japan, an alliance with France alone was too little to guarantee success, and the Russian government turned for support to other powers. German diplomacy quickly promised support to Russia. It figured that if in the Far East not only France, but Germany as well went along with Russia, then the Franco-Russian alliance, directed against Germany, would lose some of its original significance. By joining with its enemies in the East, the German bourgeoisie hoped to diminish its contradictions with them in Europe.

Thus we can see that the German bourgeoisie intervened in Far Eastern affairs with two aims: first to tear chunks away from the teeth of the Japanese, second to form a bloc in the Far East to smooth over differences in Europe. The meaning of German policy towards France was the following:

> Messieurs Frenchmen, you want to quarrel with us because in Europe we took a small piece of land – Alsace-Lorraine. Why fight us over this trifle? Let's go together to China where we can tear off more than we tore from each other in Europe. It is an enormous country which we can cut into pieces and all have big shares.

As you all know, the intervention of the powers – France, Germany, and Russia – took place as follows. After these countries one fine day delivered a note to Japan in which they declared that they could not allow Japan to occupy the Liaodong peninsula, because this would enable Japan to dominate Beijing, the Germans declared they were prepared to prevent such an occupation by armed force.

Japan was forced to give up Port Arthur and the Liaodong peninsula because it faced the opposition of three great powers. England still stood aside. Disabused of the notion that China could repulse Japan, it had still not made a final decision to ally with Japan. You know that later, in 1902, such an alliance was concluded, but in politics not everything happens right away. Japan was still a very new world power, and England was still unsure how seriously to take its transformation into such a power, and owing to this the compact among France, Germany, and Russia wrenched part of Japan's spoils from its hands.

But China understood perfectly well that the greatest danger was just beginning, that those who had saved it from Japan would present a bill that could not be paid. In the following lecture we will see what form this danger assumed.

We have spoken a lot about German, British, and Russian policy, but the time which we have spent on this is justified as we will learn when we see the results of the development of the foreign policies of these states as they affected China. We will devote the next lecture to the struggle for concessions in China which flared up in the years immediately following the Shimonoseki peace.

Lecture Ten

The theme of today's lecture is the struggle for concessions which followed the Sino-Japanese War, and which, in essence, opened China to foreign capital.

You are aware that on the basis of the Shimonoseki Treaty and the Sino-Japanese Convention, China was obliged to pay 250 million *taels*. At the prevailing exchange rate that was about one billion marks or about 500 million gold rubles, an enormous sum which the Chinese government was unable to raise on the domestic market. The question of a foreign loan arose. Already during the negotiations between China and Japan, the *Birzhevye vedomosti* (Stock Exchange Gazette),[159] one of the leading newspapers of the Russian financial world, indicated that the powers which would give China money should receive control over it.

Tsarist Russia was the power that declared its readiness to help China receive money. Russia, as you know, was itself indebted to France for construction of railroads and for building up the tsarist army, and was far from able to finance China through its own means. The French bourgeoisie provided the funds, not to China, but to the Russian government. This is how tsarist policy in the Far East was financed. The agreement whereby the funds were received was signed on 6 July 1895 between a Franco-Russian banking consortium and the tsarist government. The signature of the Chinese government appeared only at the end of this agreement. According to the agreement, China received 400 million francs at a relatively low interest of four percent, but on the basis of a guarantee from the tsarist government. The tsarist government assumed the responsibility of ensuring that China would pay the interest on this loan. In this way, it became something like a trustee over China. England, which knew from its own experience what it meant to provide loans, since England had gained control of Egypt by this means – the khedive[160] of Egypt was taking such loans for a long time before he realised he had wound up in the pockets of the British – England understood that this meant nothing other than tsarist Russia grabbing China from the north and later seizing it. Therefore, British diplomacy made every effort to prevent the conclusion of the loan agreement. The British ambassador [Sir Nicholas Roderick] O'Conor literally threatened the minister of foreign affairs in Beijing. Taking advantage of this, the Germans offered their services to China. Their proposal was an indicator of how friendship and enmity are created in world politics. The Germans had just walked hand-in-hand with Russia

---

159 *Birzhevye vedomosti* (Stock Exchange Gazette) was published in St. Petersburg in 1861–79 and 1881–1917 (with an interruption).
160 Viceroy.

and France and pressured Japan with the aim of wresting the Liaodong peninsula from it. Now they were turning against Russia. Why? Because after France and Russia, along with Germany, had grabbed Japan by the scruff of the neck, they excluded Germany from all further actions. Now they no longer needed Germany, and Russia and France themselves laid hands on China. In order to show how dangerous it was to deal with Germany in this fashion, the Germans offered a loan to China. China (this was after the British threats) agreed to Germany's proposition, but on condition that the British financial market not take part in the loan.

The German historian Franke, in describing the situation in the Far East at this time, pointed out a very interesting fact: the Berlin government wanted German banks to deal with the question of a loan, but British banks did not want this, and the bankers of both countries met each other half-way. Franke complains that with regard to the China loan, German banks gave greater weight to the desires and views of their business friends than to the opinion of the government in Berlin.

Thus one way or another, China did not receive any loans from other countries and had to accept the Russian loan from the pockets of the French, although the Chinese government understood very well that this loan represented a mortal danger, that it opened the heart of China to tsarist Russia.

In 1896, the Chinese government sent Li Hongzhang to the festive coronation of Nicholas II in Moscow. He stayed as a guest at the home of the largest tea merchant – Perlov.[161] Since Russia had long been connected to China via the tea trade, this merchant was a very influential figure in Russia's Eastern policy, and it was not without an ulterior motive that Li Hongzhang had been housed with him. To comrades who read Russian, I recommend that you read the memoirs of Count Witte which give a splendid description of how they tried back then to suborn Li Hongzhang, to influence not only his mind and his heart, but also his purse. All of tsarism's subsequent Far Eastern policy was predicated on buying off Li Hongzhang. It was then that negotiations between the Russian and Chinese governments began about constructing a railroad which would connect Russian territory with Vladivostok via Manchuria, about constructing the Manchuria-Pogranichnaia line.[162] The Russo-Chinese Bank[163] was established

---

161 In fact the house belonged to the brothers, Ivan Semenovich and Nikolai Semenovich Perlov, co-owners of the Russian tea company Vasilii Perlov and Sons. It was located at no. 5 on the 1st Meshchanskaia St. in Moscow. Li Hongzhang arrived here on 5 May 1896.
162 See Witte 1922, Volume 1, pp. 37–55, 57.
163 The Russo-Chinese bank was established in 1895 in Paris from Russian and French capital. In two months it opened it Shanghai branch. Shortly thereafter China joined the bank. In

which, in turn, organised a society to construct the Chinese railroad in Manchuria itself. It was said aloud that this would be a *Chinese railroad*. But one of the British papers in China published a secret agreement which is known in diplomatic history as the Cassini convention which made it clear that tsarist Russia aimed at seizing Manchuria.[164] This agreement was supposed, first of all, to hand over the entire management of the railroad to the Russians since the chairman of the board – a Chinese – was simply a figurehead to liaise between the railroad and the Chinese government. Second, according to the agreement there would be a large zone running along both sides of the railroad in which the railroad, that is, the tsarist government, would possess the right to exploit the resources, the land, and the forests, so that it was not merely a matter of the railroad, but of a broad concessionary zone. Third, the agreement gave the tsarist government the right to station troops to guard the railroad.

This is how things stood in 1896.

At this time Germany began a fresh intervention in Far Eastern affairs. Germany tried to act independently in China.

Already at the time when Germany was trying to coordinate its actions with Russia, during the negotiations which were intended to undermine the Treaty of Shimonoseki, Wilhelm II addressed a series of letters to the Tsar devoted to the Far Eastern question. Thanks to the October Revolution in Russia and then the German Revolution, the contents of this secret correspondence between the Tsar and Wilhelm II are now known to us.[165]

It is worth pausing to consider some of these letters. First, it is very revealing what the German Emperor wrote to the Russian Tsar at a time when German diplomacy was posing as a defender of China and a friend of the Chinese people. Generally speaking, of course, it is not very important what the Emperor was or was not thinking, but on acquainting yourselves with it, you may be convinced of what, fifteen or twenty years from now, the revolution in America will publish – what the leaders of the American government, who now are not loathe to play at being friends of China, are writing and

---

1910 it was renamed Russo-Asiatic Bank and in 1926 it was closed. The bank financed the construction of the China Eastern Railway.

164 The so-called Cassini Convention was a secret agreement between the Russian Empire and China negotiated by the Russian ambassador to China Count Cassini in 1895. It gave Russia the right to build the Trans-Siberian Railway across northern Manchuria, lease the Jiaozhou bay on the southern coast of Shandong for 15 years and occupy Port-Arthur and Dalian on the Liaodong peninsula. The text was revealed on 28 October 1896 by *The North China Daily News*, a newspaper that was published in Shanghai from 1864–1951. See Anderson and Hershey 1918, pp. 251–2.

165 See William II 1918 and William II [1923].

wrote – what they said amongst themselves about China in the absence of witnesses – this will provide a very similar picture. The political significance of studying the correspondence consists in our training ourselves not to listen to the pleasant-sounding words, but asking what lies behind these pleasant-sounding words.

On 26 April 1893, Wilhelm wrote the following to the Tsar:

> I will definitely do everything in my power to preserve peace in Europe and to protect Russia's rear so that nobody will interfere with your actions in the Far East. It is clear that in the future Russia's great task will be to turn its attention to the Asiatic continent and defend Europe from the great yellow race. In this you will always find me on your side, ready to help you with all my strength.[166]

So Russia's task, in Wilhelm's opinion, is to defend European civilisation from the yellow race. We already know that for tsarism it was not a matter of the yellow race or the dangers which it allegedly posed to Europe, but rather a matter of tsarism preparing to strike a blow in the Far East against England, a blow in which German imperialism had an even greater interest than did the government of Nicholas II.

But Wilhelm, helping the Tsar 'protect Europe from the yellow race', immediately demanded that he be paid something for this. And in the same letter, the Emperor of great Germany, of the greatest industrial nation, writes to the Tsar, 'I hope that you will look kindly upon Germany in like fashion obtaining a harbour somewhere where it will not inconvenience you'.[167]

One defender of European civilisation says to another: You are going to the East 'to defend civilisation', but in defending it, you probably want to get something out of this. So please be so kind, if it doesn't bother you, please give me some sort of harbour, too, in a place you consider convenient.

When Wilhelm was in Peterhof in 1897, returning from a military parade together with the Tsar in one carriage, he asked him in conversation: 'Will you be discomfited if Germany takes Jiaozhou for itself?' The Tsar replied that he had no objections.[168] After this, the German chancellor, to confirm the Tsar's

---

166 Quoted from O. Franke *Die Grossmachte in Ostasien von 1894 bis 1914*. 1923, p. 117. *Radek's note*.
167 Ibid., p. 124. *Radek's note*. Radek is slightly mistaken regarding page numbers. This refers to Franke 1923, pp. 124–25.
168 Radek is not precise. Nicholas II did not say that he had no objections. According to Witte, he just 'could not refuse categorically, and the German Emperor could understand that the

words, when the Tsar was already in Petersburg, picked up the thread of the conversation: 'May Germany take Jiaozhou for itself?' In essence, the government made no reply, because at the time it still was unsure whether it would take this port itself. In the document known as the Cassini Convention, it was proposed to take not only the Liaodong peninsula, but Jiaozhou as well. Therefore, Germany decided to act. The newly appointed German ambassador received instructions to begin negotiations with the Chinese government to have the latter give Germany the port in exchange for Germany's support of China against Japan. Several times the German ambassador returned to this question, which was extremely delicate because it was impossible to say directly to the Chinese government: 'Since others will soon loot you, cut off your head, and slice you in pieces, please be so kind, and, in the name of friendship, cut off your leg and give it to us'.

The then head of the Chinese government, Prince Gong, replied very pleasantly but very firmly to the German ambassador, requesting that he not raise this question again.

Then a miracle occurred. You are aware that in politics, miracles are often helpful. In Shandong where Jiaozhou is located two German missionaries were killed. Needless to say, the German government swiftly demanded, as compensation for the murder of the German missionaries, not only that those who sent the 'Holy Fathers' to the other world be executed – (who killed them was not known) – but also that China cede Jiaozhou to Germany for 99 years. According to material from the German archives, it is evident that representatives from the German War Department had been declaring their intentions regarding Jiaozhou for two years already. They had been wavering till then as to whether they should seize Xiamen; but they were afraid of the English sphere of influence along the Yangzi. Two years prior to the 'martyrdom' of the missionaries the German military headquarters had already decided that they needed to take Jiaozhou. At first they thought they could achieve this via negotiations, but they had already firmly decided on the place. The missionaries, moved by the Holy Spirit, thus knew that for the development of German imperialism it was useful to be killed in Shandong and not in any other province.

I think that if at some time a more intimate correspondence is revealed, we will learn something on this score. Up till now we have German documents from the 1870s, and recently a volume appeared which gives us correspondence concerning a period of interest to us,[169] but in both cases we have only

---

Russian Tsar gave him, so to say, his blessing to do it'. Witte recalls that the Tsar was really upset. (Witte 1922, Volume 1, p. 112.)

169   It might refer to Radowitz 1926.

official materials. But it is clear that apart from official correspondence there was other correspondence, too, and I would not be surprised if upon their publication it turned out that these missionaries were killed by Chinese hired with German money. In 1898, Germany seized Jiaozhou.

Thus, Russia's move into Manchuria was one of the seizures [of territory] after changes in the terms of peace between Japan and China. Germany seized Shandong, because apart from the port of Jiaozhou, in the treaty granting concessions it also received the right to construct a railroad and exploit mines; this was the second region.

At the same time, the third of China's saviours went into action. This third one, as you know, was France. France was a neighbour of China adjoining it on the side of Tonkin. The first thing France did was to make minor corrections by smoothing out the former border. The second was obtaining a concession for a railroad to Yunnanfu [Kunming]. Moreover, it received a significant concession to exploit mineral wealth in Yunnan province. The French policy of intrusion into Yunnan aimed at extending to Sichuan, to the Yangzi and linking all of western China with its port in Haiphong, thereby shipping goods to Tonkin. By applying diplomatic pressure, France secured this concession. Then it became clear that Russia would no longer bide its time. Germany had seized Jiaozhou, France had received its payoff, for Russia northern Manchuria was exceedingly small, so then began the final stage of the struggle to build the Chinese Eastern Railroad, to push a line from Harbin south to Port Arthur which had just been ripped from the hands of the Japanese.

Still Port Arthur was a Chinese port and the CER was considered a Chinese railroad. In order actually to control both the railroad and the port it was necessary: 1) For Russia to conclude a loan for construction of the railroad; 2) For the Chinese 'to lease' Port Arthur to Russia. England staunchly opposed both of these. Moreover, there was considerable prejudice against this within the Chinese bureaucracy. However, the Russian ambassador Pavlov, a gentleman of the chamber, and an agent of the Ministry of Finance Pokotilov, succeeded in overcoming the resistance of the British and of the Chinese officials.

The methods by which Russia operated may be seen from documents of the tsarist ministry of foreign affairs which we have published in volume II of *Krasnyi arkhiv* (Red Archive), an organ of our Archive Administration, and, I think, of no little interest to you.[170]

I will read you several of these documents.

---

170   See Central Soviet Archive 1922. *Krasnyi arkhiv* (Red Archive) was a scholarly jornal published in Moscow in 1922–41 by the Soviet Central Archive.

Here, first of all, is a ciphered telegram from Beijing from the court counsellor Pokotilov to the minister of finance [Witte], dated 8/20 January 1898:

> The slowness of the Chinese in the matter of the loan may likely be ascribed to the intense intrigues against Li Hongzhang and the disinclination of other ministers to allow Li Hongzhang to arrange this matter. On the other hand, there are grounds for supposing that the British have promised a huge bribe to the ministers for arranging the loan. Among members of the Zongli yamen [Office for the Management of the Business of All Foreign Countries] there is a widespread conviction that we do not intend to clean up the matter of Port Arthur and Dalianwan [the bay of Dalian]. Pokotilov.[171]

On the very next day came a reply from Petersburg addressed to the Russian ambassador Pavlov:

> From the telegram received from Pokotilov, it is evident that the British have promised the minister a large bribe for arranging the loan. In view of this, it pleases His Majesty the Emperor that you, together with Pokotilov, arrange for a million rubles held in the Russo-Asiatic Bank, to be secretly disbursed as gifts to the high Chinese dignitaries in the event that you, based on local considerations, deem it necessary in order to arrange a loan from Russia.[172]

There was no delay in implementing this 'delicate' assignment. On 12 (24) January Pavlov reported:

> Yesterday evening I invited Li Hongzhang over and, in extreme secrecy, via Pokotilov, informed him that in case a loan was arranged from us, as soon as a contract and declaration was signed, 500,000 *liang* would be provided for his personal disposal to cover secret expenditures which he had to make in arranging this matter. Li Hongzhang promised full cooperation; he informed us that if we can arrange the loan at the current rate of exchange, then he can almost guarantee success. Today in the Zongli yamen I noted an obvious change in our favour on the part of Li Hongzhang and Weng Tonghe.[173]

---

171 Central Soviet Archive 1922, p. 288.
172 Ibid., p. 287.
173 Ibid., p. 288.

Since the agreement of the two ministers was still not enough, the 'softening up' of the Chinese cabinet continued. A telegram from 15 (27) January said:

> Yesterday, together with Pokotilov, I had a secret meeting with Zhang Yinhuan; I promised him 200,000 on the same conditions as Li Hongzhang. Zhang Yinhuan assured me that we may wholly depend upon him in this matter as in subsequent ones. The Minister of Finance Weng Tonghe declined a secret meeting, fearing it would arouse suspicion, since he generally has no personal dealings with foreigners, but I know that he had a secret talk with Li who will share with him.[174]

On the original of this document is a hand-written inscription by Nikolai Romanov [Nicholas II]:
'In the final analysis I very much hope that we will succeed in concluding a loan with China'. Very often the Tsar revealed his 'acumen' this way ...
The main difficulty, however, had to do with the lease of Port Arthur, and there is a sequel to the history of bribes. In March–April and later in September the Russian embassy in Beijing exchanged a series of new telegrams with Petersburg on the very same theme. In an urgent ciphered telegram of 9/21 March 1898, Pokotilov informed the minister of finance:

> By an agreement with the chargé d'affaires, today I had a confidential conversation with Li Hongzhang and Zhang Yinhuan, and promised them 500,000 *liang* if the matter of Port Arthur and Dalianwan is taken care within the time we have designated and without extraordinary measures on our part. Both ministers complained about the extreme difficulty of their position and the great excitement reigning among the class of officials. A mass of requests has been addressed to the Great Khan [the Emperor] not to yield in any way to our demands. The Chinese minister in London [Luo Fenglu] telegraphed the Zongli yamen, saying that the British minister of foreign affairs [Robert Gascoyne-Cecil] told him of his extreme lack of sympathy regarding our demands. Pokotilov.[175]

At the same time, the Russian ambassador Pavlov telegraphed:

---

174   Ibid., p. 289.
175   Ibid., p. 290.

Peking [Beijing], 9 March 1896.
In complete secrecy, Pokotilov and I promised Li Hongzhang and Zhang Yinhuan 500,000 *liang* each if the agreement is signed no later than 15 March without our having to resort to extreme measures.[176]

In the next telegram dated 12/24 March, Pavlov already states:

> The promised reward produced the desired action. Li Hongzhang and Zhang Yinhuan evidently got the other ministers and the princes themselves to take an interest in the matter. It is desirable that after the signing of the convention on 15 March, the promised funds be paid as soon as possible. I respectfully request instructions on this subject. Pokotilov.[177]

The tsarist government did not stint on such expenditures. On 9 March Minister of Finance Witte issued a clear directive on new bribes:

> It would be desirable if prior to 15 March our trusted agent were in Port Arthur with the required sums so that he can make arrangements on the spot to our benefit with the appropriate authorities and actors and, in addition, provide assistance to our landing. Proceed in agreement with Pavlov and telegraph the latter. (Signed) Witte.[178]

Pavlov telegraphed that 'for the gifts and financial assistance' to the authorities in Port Arthur and Dalianwan a total sum of from 250,000 to 300,000 *liang* was needed. The appropriate credit, of course, must be forthcoming without delay.

Li Hongzhang did not have to fret for long. He had provided the service and the account was settled on time. On 27 March (8 April), Pokotilov gave an accounting to the minister of finance:[179]

> Today I paid Li Hongzhang 500,000 *liang* by weight which in daily practice in Peking [Beijing] equals 486,500 *liang* gong-fa [?] in the banks. Li Hongzhang was very satisfied and expressed his profound gratitude to you. At the same time, I am telegraphing [Adolf Iulievich] Rothstein about this. I have not had the opportunity to transfer funds to Zhang Yinhuan who is acting very cautiously.[180]

---

176   Ibid.
177   Ibid., p. 291.
178   Ibid., p. 290.
179   Radek is mistaken. This ciphered telegram is dated 16/28 March 1898.
180   Ibid., p. 292.

HISTORY OF THE REVOLUTIONARY MOVEMENT IN CHINA 135

That same day, a few hours later, he supplemented this report:[181]

> I had a confidential conversation with Zhang Yinhuan regarding payment to him of 500,000 *liang*. He is very fearful of taking the money now, saying that there is already a mass of accusations against him for taking bribes, and he prefers to wait until the rumours cease. I told him that the promised sum, in any case, would remain at his disposal. Meanwhile, only 10,600 *liang* has been disbursed in Port Arthur, since the persons who were promised gifts have now gone away and payment of the funds will take place later. I intend to travel to Port Arthur at the first opportunity, probably on Sunday.[182]

It was not for nothing that Zhang Yinhuan displayed such caution. For several months he was within a hair's breadth of being arrested, and finally, in September, as is evident from a telegram by the very same Pokotilov (from 9/21 September), the inevitable occurred.

'As a consequence of denunciations against Zhang, his house was surrounded by soldiers and an inventory of his property compiled. I have still not paid him anything. Pokotilov'.[183]

Zhang was arrested, then released and sent into exile. Apparently the agents of the tsarist government did not leave him penniless, bestowing small gifts upon him, and toward the end, before going into exile, Zhang asked them to give him an additional 15,000 *liang*. 'I refrained from making any reply. I request instructions. He is departing for his place of exile and requested that a reply be sent to Baodingfu', Pokotilov reported.[184] The minister requested the opinion of Ambassador Pavlov who replied that he considered it desirable to fulfil the request of Zhang Yinhuan 'in light of the favourable impression this would create for us among the Chinese officials who had previously served under him which might prove useful to us'. (Telegr[am] from 28 September–10 October).[185]

The money was paid ...

I am convinced that when the secret archives of all the bourgeois governments of the world are opened, then you will see that not only in this period, but right up to the present day, Chinese policy is carried out, at least half of

---

181 Radek is mistaken. Since this ciphered telegram was indeed sent on 27 March (8 April), 1898, it was eleven days later.
182 Ibid.
183 Ibid.
184 Ibid., p. 293.
185 Ibid.

it, by persons who have been suborned by world imperialism, by persons who have sold out China, some for half a million, others for less – fifteen thousand – but if the turnover of goods in China in other areas has not achieved great successes, then the commodification of Chinese politics, the trade in the honour of Chinese ministers has achieved great success. We possess documents concerning the sell-out of their fatherland to Russia by Chinese ministers, because of the unexpected circumstance that the Russian revolution opened the archives. So far this has not occurred elsewhere. We can only guess how they are 'operating' in China. Tsarism was no worse and no better than them.

If this hurts your national pride, then I must say that, of course, Chinese officials were not total exceptions when it comes to venality. When concluding foreign loans, Russian ministers also doubtless took bribes. But imperialism introduced the greatest corruption into the most backward states. [Karl] Helferich, the German minister of finance who was the former director of the Baghdad Railroad and the Eastern Turko-German Bank, relates that when he signed an agreement for a loan with the Turkish government, around 1902, several ministers showed up quite openly to receive bribes.

Somewhat confused, because he had only recently been appointed, he asked the Turkish minister of war, who had come directly bearing a letter from another influential personage indicating that the minister, too, had to be given something, was he not embarrassed to take something from another government? The minister replied that he would be embarrassed if he had harmed his own fatherland, but building a railroad was useful for his fatherland, so why should he not receive a reward in such a case?

Imperialism is not just a policy of violence, plunder, and robbery, but at the same time it is a policy of bribery and demoralisation of weaker governments by imperialist governments. You, Chinese revolutionaries, have no cause to be ashamed of this past in your history, because we are dealing with a law of history. The epoch of depravity and bribery in China is the consequence of the imperialist policies of Western European states. We do not need to conceal these things; on the contrary they should serve two aims: First, to open the eyes of the masses to the essence of the politics of the governments which speak in the name of the Chinese people, but in essence reflects the policy of the imperialists; Second, so that you yourselves will learn to embody the most profound distrust in politics.

The period of bribery has not ended in China. You already know about Zhang Zuolin's relations with Japan and Wu Peifu's with England, but in the central Chinese government as well all the recent cabinets have been governments of bribed persons from start to finish. Now when there appears in China dangers for world imperialism that are ten times greater than before, because the masses are rising, it will suborn not individual persons with a half-million rubles; it will corrupt entire strata, bribe newspapers, establish political parties. From the history of your country learn to be profoundly mistrustful, since you will have to make temporary compromises with world imperialism more than once, in which complete transparency and the deepest mistrust are necessary guarantees against betrayal. Your revolution is young; it has no old traditions, it does not have a large cadre of persons who passed through the school of underground activity, whom the masses tested in action, whom you could be sure of on the basis of their proven long fidelity to the revolution, who are above suspicion, and therefore learn from this example that the first rule of a revolutionary engaged in struggle is to be deeply mistrustful not only of imperialism, but of any policies that may lead to rapprochement with it and which apart from the need to engage in tactical manoeuvres can be a source of the depravity, the corruption of the human souls which imperialism introduces into the system ...

If you look at the picture which came into focus in China after the struggle for concessions, you will see the following. Hong Kong and Shanghai are in the hands of the British. England is sitting on the Yangzi. There is almost nothing in this time that it has not seized; it already has in hand whatever it needs. However, after Germany seized Jiaozhou, England took Weihaiwei for itself.[186] The Germans crept into Shandong province to cut off a piece for themselves when China began to be divided up. France is advancing from the south with the goal of seizing the south. Guangdong and Yunnan provinces constitute the region through which French capital is advancing with the aim of breaking through to Sichuan and thereby taking in hand the entire trade and development of the south. Russia is advancing from the north. Tsarist Russia not only forces China to open the way through northern Manchuria, but also to permit the building of a railroad to the south to Port Arthur which they ripped from the hands of the Japanese. By holding Port Arthur and Manchuria in its hands, tsarist Russia dominates North China.

What constitutes the economic conquests of the imperialists in China during this period? First of all, in addition to the initial loan of 400 million contracted under Russian guarantee, China is bound by a second loan of 16 million pounds sterling from a German-English consortium. 160 million rubles, a five percent loan without state guarantee, but what is interesting in this connection is that China is obligated to pay the interest on this loan over a period of thirty-

---

186 England conquered the city of Weihaiwei on the northern coast of Shandong in 1898. It was leased by the British until 1930.

six years from its customs duties, which are collected by an administration run by the British, and until the entire loan is repaid, the Englishman who heads the Maritime Customs Service [Robert Hart] cannot be dismissed. In this way, China is deprived of the possibility of transitioning to an autonomous tariff. A third loan is likewise concluded, also for 160 million pounds sterling and from the same consortium. In this way, China suddenly turns out to be burdened with large state debts, from one side Russia's noose has been thrown over its neck, from the other side one from the German-English banking consortium.

China, which heretofore resisted constructing railroads, has now been forced to allow construction of the extension of the Siberian railroad, and in the south grant permission to France to build a railroad to Yunnanfu, and generally refrain in principle from resisting railroad construction. This means that international capital, which until this time lacked the means to move its goods into the interior of the country, now has begun to drive rails into the body of China.

So far the imperialist powers have not yet resolved to divide up China. They have only marked out the regions into which China should be broken up. They have four colonies in mind: a French colony which would comprise all of the western part of China, a British colony consisting of all the provinces along the Yangzi, a Russian colony comprising regions of North China, and a German colony so far limited to Shandong province. Moreover, Japan, which was the first to throw itself at China's throat, but was repulsed by other powers, is standing in reserve. 'We, the older powers, have stronger claws and went on the prowl first', such was the thought underlying their policy toward Japan, and Japan had to wait – won't it get some crumbs falling down from the imperialists' table? Japan lost Shandong and the Liaodong peninsula and was forced to make do with reforming Korea, where the Japanese ambassador arranged the assassination of the Queen [Min] who was pursuing an anti-Japanese policy.[187] (In the literature this is referred to as peaceful penetration.)

The entire Chinese nation feels that it has come to such a pass.

In the following lecture we will see how the reaction of the Chinese people began, starting on the one hand with the policy of reform emanating from Kang Youwei, head of the reform party, and on the other hand the spontaneous revolt of the masses which took the form of the Boxer Rebellion.

---

187   The Queen Min was murdered in October 1895.

Lecture Eleven

All of the political upheavals which China experienced beginning in 1894 had the greatest domestic political consequences for China, consequences which preceded their influence on China's social development. These upheavals included defeat in the war with Japan, the seizure of Jiaozhou, the agreement to construct the Manchurian railroad, and the negotiations of the powers to establish spheres of influence in China, that is, preparation for dividing up China, which historians call the period of the scramble for concessions. Therefore, before giving a picture of the development of the new China, the development of its industry and its impact upon agriculture, we need to devote two more lectures to political events. Today's lecture will be devoted to the attempt to save China by means of reform from above, a policy known in history as the Hundred Days of Reform.[188] In the following lecture we will look at the attempt to save China by means of a popular movement, the so-called Boxer Uprising. In both cases, we enter into a period when the sources allow us to clearly orient ourselves not only regarding the general outlines of development, but in the concrete history of the struggle among different groups in China. Regarding the Hundred Days of Reform, the attempt at reform from above, there exists a three-volume work in Chinese by one of the pupils of Kang Youwei, titled *History of the State Reform and Reaction* which I have not read in Chinese,[189] but on the basis of which another Chinese [Lim Boon Keng] has written a book in English with which I am familiar called *The Chinese Crisis from Within*.[190] Moreover, the German Sinologist Professor Franke translated all seven of Kang Youwei's memoranda into German.[191] Furthermore, we have a report based on memoranda by Kang Youwei translated into French by a certain Jesuit and published in Shanghai in 1891.[192] With the help of these works we can comprehend the profound content of the Hundred Days, which is very important to us as revolutionaries.

You know what a pessimistic assessment of the situation in China all the representatives of the capitalist world held after the Sino-Japanese War. I have

---

188 The 1898 reforms initiated by the Emperor Guangxu with the aim of stimulating the self-strengthening policy of China.

189 This might refer to Liang Qichao's famous book *Wuxu zhengbian ji* ('Notes on the Wuxu political reforms'), composed in 1898, i.e., Wuxu year according to the Chinese lunar calendar. However, Liang's book is in one volume.

190 See Wen 1901.

191 Franke 1902 and 1911, pp. 20–35.

192 This must refer to Tobar 1900. If so, Radek made a mistake in a date.

also quoted the view of Lord Curzon, later the minister of foreign affairs in England, who, on the basis of what he saw in China, and considering the influence of the defeat, arrived at the conviction that China would never stand on its feet as a nation. I also adduced the opinion of one of the main authors on foreign policy issues in England – Chirol – who, returning from the Far East, said there is no force in China capable of saving it.

E. Reclus, one of the greatest geographers of the world, an anarchist, not an imperialist, in 1900 in his book about China,[193] says that there was the following disagreement among Europeans regarding the future of China. Some said that China needed to be torn apart into pieces; others that China would be conquered by Japan which would transform it into a gigantic weapon to struggle against Europe, while a third group, when asked what should be done, thought that China needed to be itself, import a lot of opium, and let the Chinese poison themselves, let the poisoned and degenerate Chinese go quietly and peacefully out of existence.

It is perfectly understandable that those in China who generally thought about the future of the country could not calmly contemplate the prospect that their country of 400 million people should perish.

Even among the corrupt Chinese bureaucracy there was a significant number of persons who could not accept this. We know that soon after China's defeat a gathering of Chinese officials took place in Beijing at which several thousand unanimously adopted a resolution demanding a continuation of the struggle and protested against the government's capitulation.[194]

Among this stratum of more or less progressive Chinese bureaucrats there worked a small vanguard group of mostly young Cantonese and the Southerners in general, headed by Kang Youwei, who even prior to the defeat began striving for reform. In 1887, Kang Youwei submitted his first memorandum[195] in which he provided an assessment of the situation in China and tried to sketch out a path toward its salvation.

Kang Youwei's memoranda are very interesting. First in them Kang Youwei understood perfectly the menacing international situation which China faced. If one reads Kang Youwei's memoranda now, having already in hand the diplomatic documents and correspondence between the ambassadors of the great powers and their governments, one involuntarily is surprised at the clarity and perspicacity with which Kang Youwei assessed the situation of his country. This

---

193   See Reclus 1900.
194   In fact, on 15 and 30 April and 1 May 1895, there were three meetings of Chinese intellectuals who unanimously adopted a collective memorandum to the Emperor. All together more than 1,200 persons took part in these meetings.
195   Radek is mistaken. Kang Youwei submitted his first memorandum in 1888.

assessment, repeated in a number of his memoranda, pointed to the fact that he considered tsarist Russia the greatest threat to China in the immediate future. England, he said, was a commercial power, which feared war (this was correct at the time), it possessed 80 percent of Chinese trade, and as long as China remained whole, it could only be the winner. For both political and technical reasons, it was harder for England than for Russia to start a war. Russia was a neighbour of China, the Russian masses were bound hand and foot by tsarism, and the threat from tsarist Russia was many times larger and more dangerous. But Kang Youwei also understood that if tsarist Russia pursued a policy of seizing territory in China, neither England nor Japan would fight against it to save China. On the contrary, they would become convinced that once Russia was tearing chunks from China, the jig was up and they would have to take part in dividing China up. And so, in his first memorandum, Kang Youwei asks, 'What is to be done?' He provides a description of the domestic situation inside China and says literally the following: 'Official positions are for sale, there are no capable officials, all institutions are open to corruption, the law is wholly neglected in all respects'. Then he points to little Japan and says that thanks to the Meiji era reforms, Japan has become a modern power, and that China must take the path of reform. He indicates that reform cannot be carried out solely from above and he requests that the government allow anyone to address it with proposals for various reforms. This memorandum from 1887 produced no results whatsoever. The censors were frightened by its contents and did not even bring it to the attention of the government. Kang Youwei departed for the south and only after China's defeat in the war with Japan did he return to Beijing and resume his agitation for reform. The passage of several years of difficult experiences for China added a certain weight to his arguments and the importance of his views.

The shocks in China compelled Kang Youwei to focus on foreign relations, to study them, and include them in the memorandum which he submitted in 1895 as well as in the ensuing six memoranda which propounded an entire economic and political programme based on his study of other countries.

I will focus on just a few places in these memoranda in order to assess the social content of Kang Youwei's aspirations for reform, those which best of all indicate the bourgeois essence of the progressive tendency within the Chinese bureaucracy.

Kang Youwei says that in order to improve the welfare of the people it is necessary to adopt four means – aid to agriculture, support of handicrafts, assistance to commerce, and care of the poor. As for agriculture, in France and Italy the government provides support to sericulture. In Ceylon to tea which competes with China. The Chinese government should provide the same kind of support to the cultivation of tea and to sericulture in China. In Europe the support of handicrafts led to steam-powered machinery, to electricity, railroads, and armaments. Special schools were established for agriculture and handicrafts in all countries, and should be established in all Chinese provinces. Because our exports are neglected, they are not comparable at all with the export of foreign goods despite the wealth of our country. We need to found commercial schools, support the creation of commercial associations, and abolish *lijin*. Chinese consuls should study what is needed abroad; in China strong industries must be created. Owing to overpopulation and to the lack of industry in China there is enormous poverty among the masses. The Emperor is not even aware of its dimensions. To eliminate all of this we need to support emigration to Turkestan, Mongolia, and Manchuria. There the government should help establish settlements, and toward this goal construct railroads. We need to train the people for industry and handicrafts. We need to establish an educational school for persons unused to working and for the unemployed. We need to be concerned about the poor and orphans. Toward this end we need to reform the system of instruction. The examination system in China is obsolete. We need special schools and associations which can develop the level of knowledge among the masses. The knowledge of the masses indicates the power of the state. In China only twenty of a hundred people can read.[196]

In Kang Youwei's memorandum you have, in essence, the programme of the future Chinese bourgeoisie: the solution of the agrarian question by settlement of the enormous regions of Mongolia, Turkestan, and Manchuria, the development of handicrafts, industry, railroads and, as a condition for all of this, the dissemination of contemporary knowledge among the masses.

If several years earlier Li Hongzhang, building a telegraph line between Tianjin and Beijing, encountered outright sabotage on the part of officials, then Kang Youwei represented an entirely new type of bureaucrat, a type of official who was unafraid of technical progress and European innovations.

Kang Youwei did not break entirely with the past. In this same memorandum he provides an appreciation of Confucian teachings, indicating how strongly he was still tied to the past. The relations existing in China seemed to him the result of deviating from the teachings of Confucius in their ancient form, and the substitution of bureaucratic routine in place of pure Confucianism. He was convinced that the implementation of all the needed economic reforms in China would reinvigorate Confucianism.

---

196   Dr. O. Franke, 'Ostasiatische Neubildungen', 28–9. *Radek's note*.

'Just what is Confucianism?' he asked. And he replied, 'Confucianism gave the world two correct ideas – the idea of the unity of mankind and the idea of peace, which exists only when the entire world is unified on the basis of the teachings of Confucius'. Kang Youwei did not understand that the idea of the unity of mankind was typical of all great religions which strived to submit the world to themselves, and that all large medieval powers lived with the ideology that they could seize the whole world. For example, in the Middle Ages the German empire tried to construct such an all-embracing empire in Europe. The Roman Church defended this idea along with the German empire. It was far from being just a Chinese idea, and this is certainly not what Confucianism was.

Perhaps Kang Youwei himself failed to realise this clearly; perhaps in his discussion of Confucianism we have only a tactical means of avoiding the reproach that he was destroying the old. He presented the reforms as a return to the old, but in the same memorandum, speaking of China's needs, he writes, 'We need to arm China', we have a military fleet, but we don't know how to use it. We have embassies, but no knowledgeable ambassadors. We have troops who have been trained by foreigners, but our soldiers lack courage, we have arsenals and wharves, but there are no machines in them; we have a ministry of foreign affairs, but no ministers who know about foreign countries. We have a steamship company, but no steamships capable of sailing overseas.[197] He says the following about schools: 'They are not applying what people are learning, and they are learning what cannot be applied'.

In the next memorandum from 1897, Kang Youwei paints a vivid picture of the defeat of China, of the imperialist penetration of the country, and again focuses on the domestic situation. Here Kang Youwei appears as a modern bourgeois reformer. He says,

> I am afraid that the time will come when the Emperor and his top advisers who are ready to preserve peace at any price and who spend their time from morning till night in games and dances or enjoyment of nature, soon will no longer be able to live like that. I fear that the Emperor and his top advisers, who thirst for eternal peace and who delight in their ceremonial apparel, soon will no longer have them ...
>
> We must indicate to officials and the people that we must have done with old customs and introduce new ones instead. We must gather the best talents in the country so they may work out the best plans for reform.

---

197   O. Franke, p. 31. *Radek's note.*

From among the laws of all countries we should choose the best examples for state-sponsored and civil legislation. We need to vet all the officials in the country and see how suitable they are. All of the old and incapable ones should be dismissed, and the princes and the most capable young ones sent abroad. Those who are not abroad should be removed from government service. We need to introduce state control relying upon harvest statistics, statistics of work and the population, so that we may set up an annual budget. We need to study all of the waste – government income and expenditures – so we may take appropriate measures. We need to try and obtain loans abroad so we will be able to carry out these reforms. An imperial edict should be an appeal to the entire country which will stimulate the brains of educated people and evoke new efforts and hopes throughout the country. We need to put an end to the old ways of promoting officials in order to attract talent; we need to increase the salaries of officials so they can live in a manner appropriate to their positions. We need to eliminate the sale of official positions; we need to get rid of a massive number of useless officials; we need to create a cadre of specially trained officials; we need to pass new land laws; we need to protect the population; we need to implement humane administration, which is concerned about the people's health, about the poor, we have to reform our prisons; we have to eliminate barbaric forms of punishment; we need to raise taxes on opium; eliminate *lijin*; we need to build railroads and build warships to defend our country.[198]

Kang Youwei insists that there be at least 30,000 soldiers with modern training in each province.

This, as you see, is a completely defined programme of bourgeois reform.

In his large, fifth memorandum written in December 1897, soon after the Germans seized Jiaozhou,[199] Kang Youwei wrote the following in four discussion points which he chose from the *Shujing*:[200]

---

198 O. Franke, p. 33. *Radek's note.*
199 Radek is mistaken. The Germans conquered Jiaozhou in March 1898.
200 *Shujing* ('Book of documents') is an ancient Chinese historical record. Among other stories, it tells how Zhong Hui, a minister of Cheng Tang, the first King of the Shang/Yin Dynasty, advised his ruler to conquer the declining Xia dynasty: 'The weak should be enslaved, the fools should be punished, the desecrated should have their countries taken from them, the hopelessly lost should be eliminated'. Kang Youwei chose these words to express his fear and sorrow with regard to the situation in China of his days.

1. The great European powers have annual incomes in the billions, millions of trained troops, and hundreds of battleships. They possess modern knowledge and modern machines. Every year brings thousands of new inventions, and new books. Innumerable masses of peasants, craftsmen, merchants, soldiers, and scholars study their specialties. Women and girls, young people and children are all able to read and write. As for us? Our annual income is all of 70 million, including the war indemnity due to Japan after the 1894–5 war. This shows the weakness of our finances. We are untouched by modern knowledge and modern technology. This shows the weakness of our knowledge. Our military men are totally uneducated, and our educated men know nothing of military affairs. Our merchants have insufficient schooling, our peasants lack development. This is the weakness of our education. The masses are passive, the educated are listless. This shows our weakness of character. These are the anxieties which Zhong Hui's words inspire in me: The weak should be enslaved.

2. In the course of 4,000 years we have been untouched by any innovations. Life is changing in foreign states, but we always remain the same and learn nothing. Our highest officials stick by the principle: 'Honour the Emperor and keep the barbarians at a distance'. They cling to stupid scholasticism and obsolete ceremonies, but foreigners laugh at us because the officials are nothing but empty shells with nothing inside. We have not learned to adapt to the times, therefore we experienced a catastrophe in our wars with France and Japan, but even this did not make us better; therefore, now we are again reliving our past. [The occupation of Jiaozhou.] One hundred high officials and governors-general, none of whom have been abroad, rule over 400 million people and none of them knows the contemporary European constitutions. These gentlemen, burdened with years, who have attended only old-style schools, whose powers are already waning, and who are always occupied with affairs of state, have no opportunity whatsoever to study new discoveries and modern ideas or to learn about the situation in foreign states. Their eyes and ears are accustomed only to outmoded forms of speech and ways of thinking. They conduct their arguments in one and the same way and are familiar only with the usual peaceful situation. Even among the more important of them, all their feelings, thoughts, concepts, and concerns are expressed in the old framework of ideas; they are mediocrities full of arrogance and haughtiness, who think only of their own amusements and benefits or helping the mercenary plans of their relatives. On the other hand, foreign travellers and missionaries study the situ-

ation in China; they follow economic and financial issues in China in politico-economic works and handbooks. They write newspaper articles to enlighten the public or various official reports. Therefore, we need to eradicate the old ways and energetically put new ideas into practice. This is the fear I have with regard to Zhong Hui's words: The fools should be punished.

3. From the time we ceded Formosa [1895], everyone knows that our government does not deserve any respect. Our people lack strength. Every kind of riff-raff and barbarian is occupying our mountains and borders, and there is a quarrel between the people and the Christians in the interior provinces. The riff-raff are hostile toward the Christians and this is only leading to the uniting of the various sects and societies and now they are exerting greater pressure and coercion; disorder and rebellions are appearing. There is no strong authority able to suppress them. Thus, the Europeans make use of them as a pretext for military measures. Thus, the Russians have driven off the Mohammedans and occupied the province of Ili. This is the fear I feel in regard to Zhong Hui's words: The desecrated should have their counties taken from them.

4. Concerning the Europeans' plan to divide up China, we see how Africa was divided among several powers, Poland between Russia, Germany, and Austria, Annam taken over by France, India by England, but our officials sit patiently with folded hands, and with dull indifference await their fate. Thus it was in 1884 and 1894.[201] No one flared up with noble anger and heatedly took an oath to remain firm and save the nation. From ancient times there has not been such a spectacle. Our princes and high officials, our scholars and the masses cling to life and wait to become bond servants of Europe, to be slaughtered like dogs or sheep. There is nothing worse than withering away like this, no worse disease than consumption, no sadder spectacle than fragile leaves which blow away in a killing wind; there is no need to stretch out one's hand with difficulty toward half-dead flowers; they are dying and they are losing their shape. This is the sorrow I feel with regard to Zhong Hui's words: The hopelessly lost should be eliminated.

Perhaps there is an intention to call upon a stronger neighbouring country for assistance, and thereby preserve one's own independence. But the principle of the European military undertakings consists of being victorious whatever it takes on and completely destroys the country of

---

201   That is, on the eve of the war with France and Japan respectively.

their vanquished opponent. The military power of Russia and Germany are identical. How would they deploy their troops against each other on our behalf and thereby put at risk their own political existence?

With respect to the question of dividing Asia, we should remember the example of the ancient Turkish people. Their enormous territory quickly broke into pieces although Turkey still dragged out its doomed way of life, or Persia whose powerful position and influence were stripped from it although it still retained its old territories. China possesses enormous territories, but the process of dividing them up has been going on for a number of years without any resistance. The authoritative statesmen of China are old and decrepit. They await only death and their legacy – the loss of the future. The religion of the ancient Turkish people was Mohammedanism. They had a rough and firm character and caused the Europeans to fear them. The religion of our people is soft and yielding, sluggish and devitalized. The rulers of Persia travelled throughout the countries of Europe, but our princes and statesmen sit within their four walls and cultivate their virtues in solitude. A Swedish envoy who was traveling through our country declared to newspapers of all countries that in the course of the past years the ancient states of Asia are experiencing a decline, and that for them it is the beginning of the end. But we cover our ears so as not to hear the steps of our approaching doom. And we are such fools that we boast about how we deceive ourselves. We praise the man whose house has caught on fire and who instead of going to fetch water continually shouts for help and at the moment when his dwelling is engulfed in flames rushes there to save his valuables and loses his life along with all his valuables. Therefore, I say that our ministers are not faithful to the state and do not love their own country. They think exclusively of their own well-being. The Emperor should think about the fate of the Qin and Song dynasties in ancient times and the fate of the Turks and the Persians in recent times. The Empress Dowager alone cannot consider the fate of the entire country. She should remember Empress Xie (the Song dynasty).[202] After their sovereign was dishonored, even with their death the ministers could not stop the fall of the empire. Now they sit with heads empty and arms folded against the foreign pretensions and calmly await a new disgrace and ruin. The catastrophe in Jiaozhou is a sudden misfortune that has overtaken us only

---

202 Grand Empress Dowger Xie Daoqing was the last ruler of the Southern Song dynasty.

today, but is the result of our weakness and inertia during the course of the recent past. I don't want to escape from the blade of an ax, which I have reported on more than once. Right now I cannot set forth a plan on how to defend and preserve the empire. This requires calm work in peaceful times. In the face of the Jiaozhou catastrophe, I implore Your Majesty to muster all your strength and show the world your anger. Your Majesty's self-accusation should first move the heart of the people, then reveal our shame in order to arouse the fervor of the educated and the strength of the masses. I implore Your Majesty to seek the counsel of the people, so that the appeal of the Sovereign be known everywhere. Let everyone be invited to submit memorials so that You may know the mood of your subjects, so that empire may be strengthened, so that reforms may commence. The issues before the empire should be discussed throughout the empire.[203]

O. FRANKE, 'Ostasiatishe Neubildungen' Hamburg, 1911, pp. 41–6.

I will allow myself to cite just one more passage from Kang Youwei's speech which he delivered in 1897 on the occasion of the founding of the political club of supporters of reform. In this speech Kang Youwei demanded a parliament:

In parliament the will and mood of the nation is expressed; there the Emperor is of extremely little significance while the people do not have extremely little significance. The interests of the people are paramount. These principles are completely in line with the tendencies of our classics; that is why foreign countries which adopt these principles are so strong. Here the main state institutions do not take the needs of the people into account. We have no fundamental laws that protect us, move us forward, and instruct the people. There is no connection between the throne and the people; the former signifies everything, the latter nothing. This contradicts the teachings of our classics.[204]

It is perfectly clear that the reference to the classics is only a tactical device. There is no mention of parliament in Mencius or Confucius. Clearly, Kang Youwei is trying to cloak his reforms in modern dress to make them easier to carry out.

---

203   Thus in the text.
204   Ibid., p. 46. *Radek's note.*

There are several very interesting historical parallels and comparisons in the memoranda that show what an enormous amount of work the circle of Chinese reformers accomplished in a short time.

As is well-known, Kang Youwei was also the author of a series of historical works. Among them is a book about the reforms of Peter the Great.[205] Of course, he did not realise that these reforms were not a matter of the sole initiative of the Tsar. After all, he did not have the guidance of comrade Pokrovskii, whom every student is now familiar with, but the fact is that he studied the example of reforms in other countries. He also wrote a work on the reasons for the division of Poland,[206] a work on the reasons for the fall of the mighty Turks.[207] In a word, he studied examples of both the downfall of states and the rise of new powers to use them as examples to illustrate both breakdown and power for the Chinese people.

Kang Youwei's memoranda were circulated widely. (This was the beginning of modern public agitation.) They profoundly affected broad circles of bureaucratic public opinion and caused a split in its ranks. It was not only the ruling elements of the Manchu court princes and the governors who became opponents of these reforms, but also a large part of the middle- and lower-ranking Chinese officials. The reason for this split lies in the material interests of the opponents of reform. Even the bourgeois historian Franke understood this very well. He points out that when a demand to abolish the old-style exams was put forward at a meeting of literati, only a small minority supported the proposal of the reformers. The examination system, which is primarily based on a knowledge of literature and an ability to write, was introduced during the Han dynasty as an aggressive measure aimed against feudalism. In feudal times officials were those who had land, that is, landlords. The Han dynasty tried to attract merchants and even peasants to serve in the administration of the state, which is why they grounded their demands upon those who aspired to become officials in a knowledge of the classics, something that was not connected to the material position of the aspirants to bureaucratic positions. The classics back then were nearer in time to and more closely reflected the experience of the Chinese people. To be sure, one nineteenth-century American school reformer [John Dewey] was so enamoured with this system that he demanded it be introduced into America, but he did not see what had happened to this examination system since the Han dynasty. In reality, it was not those who

---

205   It refers to Kang Youwei's work *E Pide bianzheng ji* ('Notes on Russian Peter's reforms').
206   It refers to Kang Youwei's work *Bolan fenmie ji* ('Notes on the division of Poland'), 7 vols.
207   It refers to Kang Youwei's work *Tujue youji* ('Notes on a travel to Turkey').

qualified who received official posts, but those who pleased the ruling strata or who bribed the examiners. The examinations were a screen behind which official and unofficial commerce in positions took place. Now it was proposed that the method of awarding certificates via the old examination system to those wishing to obtain a position be abolished, and instead persons capable of reforming China be appointed as officials. The bureaucratic world should have renounced its own interests in order to follow after Kang Youwei and, needless to say, it did not do it. Only the most progressive, idealistic elements and youth who had been unable as yet to hold any of the best-paying positions, were followers of Kang Youwei.

Kang Youwei's memoranda made an enormous impression on the court.

Conservatives at the court immediately demanded the arrest of Kang Youwei. The young Emperor Guangxu, on the contrary, profoundly shaken by the picture of the approaching total parcelling out of China, under the influence of his old tutor [Weng Tonghe], chose the side of the reformer. Kang Youwei was appointed a member of the *Zongli yamen*.

He gained direct access to the Emperor, and after his audience with the Emperor on 11 June 1898, one imperial decree after another began pouring out as if from a cornucopia.[208] The Emperor tried to save the state with the help of decrees. New laws required reforms in the examination system, reform of schools, dismissal of redundant officials, and the establishment of newspapers everywhere. In the Emperor's mind, in this way the bureaucracy itself should enlighten the people and demonstrate how ill-suited it was ...

These decrees even dispensed with Kang Youwei's attempt to cloak the reforms with references to Confucius and, from the perspective of the old ideology of the ruling classes, demonstrated openly revolutionary views. In a decree of 13 September 1898, the Chinese Emperor declared in the most unequivocal way that the West, in possessing knowledge, stood higher than China, that the policies of the Western states saw their task as improving the condition of the masses, that it was far-sighted at the same time that the policies of China were deficient in knowledge.

We can no longer continue living as we have up till now ...

It is perfectly clear that the attempt at radical reform, relying on the Emperor who had been terrified by defeats, on his adviser, and on several reformers, could only end in a total catastrophe in the face of resistance from the ruling classes and the passivity of the masses.

---

208 In the period between 11 June and 21 September 1898, Emperor Guangxu issued sixty edicts.

As is well-known, the centre of resistance to the reformist policies of the Emperor was Empress Dowager Cixi, relying upon the old bureaucracy and elements at the court.

Obviously, Kang Youwei should have tried to smash the resistance manifested to the attempt at reform by means of a palace coup d'état. The main weapon in the hands of the Emperor was Ronglu, the governor of Zhili province, who commanded the only modern armed force which China had succeeded in forming over the course of several years with the help of German instructors. Kang Youwei demanded that the Emperor dismiss Ronglu and place the army under the control of Yuan Shikai, a protégé of Li Hongzhang who had expressed progressive views. Yuan was summoned by the Emperor and received an order to arrest and execute Ronglu, after which he should carry out a palace coup and arrest the Empress Dowager.

However, assuming responsibility for carrying out these orders, Yuan Shikai calculated the actual balance of forces, and preferred to inform Ronglu and the Empress Dowager of everything. The result was that the Emperor, the ministers, and the reformers were quickly arrested. Kang Youwei alone was saved. He had left Beijing several days earlier on order of the Emperor.

In a few words, one of the closest pupils of Kang Youwei conveyed the entire tragedy of the attempt of reform from above. He relates that when the Emperor was already under arrest and persons loyal to him proposed arranging his escape, he refused, pronouncing the famous words about the coup d'état which may serve as the 'motto' for the entire history of the Hundred Days. 'Although I know what China needs, I am unable to bring it about'.

The reformers were that part of the bureaucracy capable of understanding the entire tragedy of the situation, the full danger threatening China, and that envisioned a completely realistic programme of reform, but they found no forces in Chinese society with whose help they could carry out such a programme. The masses were downtrodden and expressed their dissatisfaction only in spontaneous movements against foreigners which arose in many places prior to the era of reform in the 1890s. The reformers were totally cut off from the masses and did not even dare to appeal to them. The bureaucracy itself could not carry out reforms since the reforms were directed against its own interests. This entire era was a brief episode which could only demonstrate that thoughts about the necessity of reform were ripening, and that as yet there were no social forces capable of bringing it about.

When friends suggested to Tan Sitong that he take flight, like the Emperor he refused, and expressed a thought which contemporary Chinese revolutionaries should bear in mind. He said, 'In no country can profound reforms be carried out without bloodshed; I have not heard that blood has been shed in China in the name of reform, therefore, the country is unfortunate'. This reformer along with his comrades wanted to present an example of steadfastness, and make sacrifices for the country. He wanted the bloodshed in this first battle for reform to help bring it about later on.

In assessing the era of reform, the bourgeois European historians have demonstrated a poorer understanding of the history of the Hundred Days than those who participated in it. For example, the French historian of China, Henri Cordier, author of a four-volume history of China, reproaches the reformers for wanting to achieve their goals too quickly, which is why they perished.[209] The reformers could not but wish to achieve their goals quickly, because China faced being divided up, and they perished not because they wanted to carry out reforms quickly, but because there was as yet no mass support to implement reforms.

How should we relate to, what should be our historical assessment of this attempt to reform China from above?

This profoundly tragic history greatly reminds one of the Decembrist Uprising in Russia.[210] In Russia, too, at that time, the necessity of reform became increasingly apparent, and there was likewise no mass public support capable of carrying it out. Within the ruling class, as in the Chinese bureaucracy, there was a group of people who understood the necessity of reform, but who did not yet dare to appeal to the masses. This group, like the group of Tan Sitong, could only stand on the square, facing the cannon trained on them and perish with steadfastness in the vaulted underground chambers of the fortresses. The progressive party of Kang Youwei was a more clearly defined group of reformers than the Decembrists. Only part of the Decembrists understood the need to emancipate the peasants and to destroy tsarism as clearly as the Chinese reformers understood what needed to be done in their times. The development of Europe in the time that has passed since the death of the Decembrists, helped the pupils and comrades of Kang Youwei to take their bearings more quickly and more accurately. But in essence both the Decembrists and the group of Kang Youwei were bourgeois reformers who did not come from the bourgeoisie and were unable as yet to depend upon bourgeois development which had yet to occur. Present-day Chinese revolutionaries, both communists and non-communists, should view the group of Kang Youwei and its attempt at reform as forerunners of the revolutionary movement in China. They must understand two extremely profound lessons expressed in the words

---

209 See Cordier 1920–21, Volume 4, p. 215.
210 Decembrists are Russian nobel revolutionaries who rose in uprising against serfdom and Absolutism on 14 December (new style December 26) 1825.

of the Emperor who was Kang Youwei's pupil, which I quoted. First, it is not enough to know what China needs, one must also be able to link one's demands with the popular masses who alone are in a position to carry them out. Second is the conduct of Tan Sitong. We must respect the revolutionary steadfastness of the reformers who were willing to die for their cause. We have a different understanding of the words of Tan Sitong than he himself. The bravery and blood of the group of intellectuals is not enough. What is needed as well is the struggle of the popular masses. This struggle will not come to fruition without a sea of blood. Of course, it will achieve its goal not because more blood will be spilled, but because it will be spilled not by solitary individuals to whom the masses failed to respond, but persons who are connected to the popular masses. The supporters of Kang Youwei had still not posed the question in that way, but we must respect the bravery with which this small group went to their deaths for their ideals.

Things are much easier for us than it was for them. When you have to fight, suffer, and make sacrifices, then you will already know very well that not a single drop of blood will be shed in vain, that standing behind you are the great popular masses. When Kang Youwei and his comrades looked death in the eye, they could not yet know this.

The fact that some thirty years after their death, China finds itself in the midst of the flames of a revolution in which vast numbers of the masses are taking part, speaks to the point that their actions were not fortuitous, but an historically necessary episode. Without it, all of the subsequent struggles of Chinese revolutionaries could not have become what they are at present.

When we come to the rise of the Guomindang, the rise of the revolutionary movement headed by Sun Yat-sen, a movement which, by the way, arose in conflict with the surviving followers of Kang Youwei, then you will see that, on the basis of the history of his fellow provincial Kang Youwei, Sun Yat-sen understood that the bureaucracy was unable to reform itself, that one had to appeal to other strata. The defeat of Kang Youwei was necessary so that a new generation of revolutionaries, standing on the backs of those who had fallen, could explore new paths.

Lecture Twelve

Following the coup d'état, the Manchu dynasty – Empress Dowager Cixi and the court – were in a very difficult position. First of all, a number of organisations which sympathised with Kang Youwei began to function in south China, and accused the court, saying that the coup d'état was aimed not only at reform, but generally against Chinese, that the Manchu dynasty was opposing the Chinese people. At the same time, news came in about popular movements directed against foreigners in a series of districts in China. On the basis of historical material, we now know that these movements had already begun back in 1891. That is the year organisations emerged which accused the Manchu dynasty of selling out to foreigners.

The court was afraid of being caught between two fires. On the one side was opposition from supporters of Kang Youwei who embodied the public opinion of the intelligentsia, an opposition pushing it toward reform. On the other side was opposition from the popular masses directed against the influence of foreigners. What was the nature of the people's movement? What was its social composition and objective significance? It had its roots in the disturbances, the destruction of the previous conditions of life which the penetration of capitalism into China brought about from the very start. It is very revealing that even diplomatic cables from that time (and you know that diplomats are remote from investigating the actual causes of phenomena, since they see only very superficial indicators) constantly pointed to the economic factors which brought about the movement. To be sure, their reports were very meagre and insufficient for our purposes. They spoke, first of all, of the series of droughts which brought ruin to the peasants. Especially in the north. Evidently the peasantry linked the droughts and defeats at the hands of foreigners with the conduct of the dynasty. And saw in them divine punishment for making concessions to foreigners. In Zhili province this link between natural disasters and the intrusion of foreigners was more evident to the people in that construction of the Beijing-Tianjin railroad led to the destruction of the cartage industry. Since traffic between these two cities was significant, this led to the ruin of large numbers of peasants who made their living from this industry. This was the second economic reason for the movement to which diplomats pointed. If we had access to more direct economic sources from this period, then probably we would find even more important economic reasons. But since the task of Marxism is not to invent things one doesn't know, I can only point out things which I found thus far in the sources.

The general background of the movement, its general mood was expressed in protests, in a struggle against permitting foreigners free rein. This protest against foreigners, naturally, was met with sympathy from reactionary circles in Chinese society and at the court which became increasingly inclined to support the movement. We possess an illuminating document which enables us to follow the internal history of the Boxer Uprising day-by-day. English soldiers found it after Beijing was seized and the plunder initiated. It is a diary that was kept during the entire preceding period by one of the old Chinese dignitaries (then seventy years old), the courtier Jing Shan, whose sons served at court, and who was close to seven ministers.[211] Incidentally, the old man was deaf, and he wrote in his diary, 'They say that Peking [Beijing] is undergoing bombardment, but I can't hear it'. Every day he recorded all the details that were reported to him, and we can see how the court's relationship to the Boxer movement was changing.

Moreover, we have a series of reports by opponents of the Boxer Rebellion. I also informed you in the last lecture about Ronglu, the governor-general of Zhili province, whose troops were the only modern forces in China. Ronglu was an opponent of the Boxer Rebellion, and in his reports he repeatedly expressed his negative opinion regarding the Boxer movement. There is more. For example, three memoranda from Minister of Foreign Affairs Yuan Chang who perfectly understood the danger threatening China from the foreign powers. These documents shed a lot of light on how the dynasty related to the Boxer movement.

I will quote from and expound upon them from *China under the Empress Dowager*, a book by two Englishmen, [John O.P.] Bland and [Edmund T.] Backhouse,[212] living in Beijing at the time, who were very close to the diplomats, and had many ties with bureaucratic circles.[213]

From the very beginning, Ronglu predicted what might happen. Empress Dowager Cixi was afraid that if the dynasty did not assume the leadership of the Boxer movement, the movement would turn against it. She feared a new Taiping movement, and, moreover, she herself hated foreigners. In all of this she was supported by those in her entourage. The most typical and eye-catching aspect of their conduct was that the court and the government took no notice of the actual balance of forces even after the war with Japan and after all the concessions made to European capitalism. They did not take into consideration that they would be dealing not with the small number of troops present in China during peacetime, but with powerful European capitalism. They were full of superstitions, for example, they said that it was impossible to kill Boxers. As is evident from these reports, Yuan Shikai decided to put this to the test. He ordered that a group of Boxers be brought into his presence and that his soldiers shoot at them. Since the Boxers turned out to be ordinary mortals in the very literal sense, Yuan Shikai immediately quieted down. The court, however,

---

211 See Ching-shan 1924. Today many scholars consider the Jing Shan diary as a fraud. See Trevor-Roper 1977 and Nathan and Link 2002, pp. 461–3.
212 See Bland and Backhouse 1910.
213 German translation, Bland und Backhouse, *China unter der Kaiseren Witwe*, Berlin, 1913. *Radek's note*. This refers to Bland and Backhouse 1913.

continued to be deeply convinced that the Boxers were immune to the effects of bayonets and bullets. The worldview of the courtiers was at the same level as those of the peasants. The diary of the high dignitary Jing Shan relates how, during the Boxers' siege of the Europeans in Beijing, he was informed that a large number of dead Boxers was seen next to the Foreign Quarter, and how badly shaken were those persons who had not believed that Boxers could be killed when they heard about it for the first time.[214] The Empress Dowager was convinced that the forces of the Boxer national movement would sweep away the foreigners. Therefore, she decided to support the Boxers. She instructed all the governors to establish national militias on the basis of the Boxers, and ordered the Manchu troops to support the Boxers.

After this government order, the military governor of Zhili province Ronglu wrote to the Empress Dowager: 'If we allow the growth of the Boxer movement, we will lose control over it and the only result will be chaos'.[215] (By chaos, of course, he meant revolution.)

He pointed out to the Manchu dynasty the danger of playing with such a mass movement. The popular movement, Ronglu predicted, would not have an enormous force even though the masses really hated the foreigners. But, he said, these forces would not be satisfied with driving out the foreigners; they might turn against the dynasty as well. He also pointed out that in the south there were many members of various secret societies and revolutionary clubs, smugglers and other desperate people who, given the opportunity, might rise up against the throne and order. To support the Boxer movement would be to light a spark in a cellar filled with explosives.

He even turned to governors who were close to him, imploring them not to listen to the decree of the Empress Dowager and not to support the Boxer movement.

The Empress [Dowager] and the court rejected all warnings and, in official state documents, proposed that governors should pay rewards to those who killed foreigners. The Boxer movement received leadership in the person of Prince Duan, and with the collaboration of the government and the help of local authorities, spread like a giant wave across all of northern and part of central China.

You all know what were the subsequent course of events. The Boxers surged into Beijing and there first killed an adviser to the secretary of the Japanese mission, Sugiyama,[216] and then the German envoy Ketteler when the latter set

---

214 See Ching-shan 1924, p. 70.
215 Radek rephrases Ronglu's words. See Ibid., p. 7.
216 In fact, Sugiyama Akira was the chancellor of the Japanese mission to China.

off for the Ministry of Foreign Affairs. The killer of Ketteler [En Hai], a sergeant of the Palace Guard, after his arrest and interrogation following the end of the movement, quite clearly and calmly declared that since there was a government order to kill foreigners, being on guard duty, upon encountering Ketteler, he killed him.

Characteristically, upon receiving news of the murder of the ambassador, the Empress Dowager was overjoyed. She did not even consider that the murder of a foreign ambassador would entail the most serious political consequences and that China would have to pay for this.

Prince Duan likewise displayed great joy on this score and petitioned for an extraordinary reward for the killer of Ketteler since, in his eyes, exterminating a famous foreigner was a greater service than getting rid of an ordinary barbarian. Ronglu and his entourage, more modern-minded bureaucrats, pointed out to the government that this was a more serious matter than the killing of any missionary, and that this might provoke all of capitalist Europe to move against China. But they were commanded to remain silent.

Then the Boxers mounted a real siege of all the diplomatic missions, but just how weak was their organisation, their weaponry, their military preparations etc. was evident from the fact that over the course of several weeks until the arrival of a more substantial number of troops, four hundred European soldiers who were guarding the foreign embassies were able to defend the diplomatic quarter. They suffered just one hundred casualties while tens of thousands were killed on the side of the Boxers. The Europeans were armed with modern weapons. Ronglu, who possessed European artillery, refused to provide cannons to the chief of the Boxers for the siege of the embassies. When the chief threatened retribution, Ronglu replied, 'Come with a rescript from the Empress Dowager to cut off my head, then you and she shall receive cannons'. He realised this was an international war, and if the Boxers killed all the ambassadors all possibility of coming to an agreement would be lost. The entire court clique of Manchu princes viewed opponents of the killing of the European ambassadors as Chinese who were traitors to the dynasty.

Such an apprehension on the part of the Manchus was expressed most clearly in the diary of Jing Shan, namely, that from the perspective of the Chinese bureaucrats the interests of the Manchu dynasty were not paramount, and that even Chinese occupying very high positions were not doing enough to defend these interests.

On the other hand, in Beijing the Boxers behaved as if they were masters of the situation. We see in Jing Shan's diary the constant fear that the movement might assume a different character. He says, for example, with great anxiety, that Prince Duan extended his hand to Boxer leaders, ordinary commoners, and that the Boxers who had come to Beijing acted very independently toward the Manchu officials. He describes how the Boxers came right into the court itself, and expresses his fear that they will pillage it, how the Boxers forced open the imperial gates in the very presence of the Empress Dowager.

It took all of the Empress Dowager's presence of mind and all of the palace guards loyal to her from among the troops of Ronglu to restrain them. Meanwhile, even the physician whom the Empress Dowager had summoned for the Emperor, was forbidden to lift his eyes to look at his patient, and he had to diagnose him from the sound of the Emperor's voice and the Empress Dowager's description while kneeling before her and the Emperor and staring at the ground. The Empress Dowager herself had to go out to the Boxer soldiers who had gained entrance into the court and order them to leave!

Thus, this young movement, reactionary in content inasmuch as it defended the old order, having overwhelmed the capital, eluded the control of the government and threatened to become a movement directed not only against foreigners, but also against the dynasty ...

By this time, foreign imperialism had already begun its rebuff of the Boxer movement.

Throughout capitalist Europe, the Boxer movement provoked a punitive mood vis-a-vis China. Until this time only very limited circles had taken an interest in the policies of the Great Powers toward China. In essence, economic relations between Europe and China were still quite small and did not affect the broad strata of the bourgeoisie. But now we see a complete change. The bourgeoisie is capable of solidarity in cases of uprisings against capitalism. The interests of the limited circles connected with the China trade, their striving to conquer China, was strongly supported by the entire European and American capitalist world.

The capitalist press presented the Boxer movement as the beginning of a rebellion by the yellow race. It depicted the situation not as one in which European capitalists had burst into China and were pillaging it, but as one in which China had suddenly risen against culture and civilisation and wanted to conquer the whole world.

The governments themselves probably knew full well how things stood; even the not very clever European governments understood this. You are aware that the Russian Tsar Nicholas II was by no means among the brightest heads of European capitalism. There is even an anecdote in Russia that if someone says, 'The Emperor is an idiot', and when put on trial he swears that he was thinking of the German Emperor, the court will not believe him. It is not for nothing that if you speak of an idiot, it can be none other than Nicholas. And here is Nicholas II writing in his own hand on the draft of a telegram from the [acting] minister of foreign affairs [Vladimir Nikolaevich Lamsdorf] to the Russian ambassador in Paris [Lev Pavlovich Urusov]:

> Completely approve. There is another extremely sensitive question – for France in particular – that of missionaries. In my opinion, these persons are the root of all evil. They, together with commercial oppression, are most responsible for stirring up Chinese hatred toward Europeans. Somehow we should refer to this for the purpose of limiting the shameless exploitation of the popular masses in China in the holy name of Christ.[217]

The Tsar understood splendidly that, on the one hand, the merchants were fleecing the Chinese people while, on the other hand, the missionaries were facilitating this under the pretext of the defence of Christianity.

But the broad masses of petty bourgeoisie were fed the slogan of defending Christianity, of defending European civilisation against the yellow barbarians who did not want to allow foreigners to exercise dominion in China however they pleased.

The greatest impression of the events in China took place in Germany. The *German* ambassador was killed, moreover – and of greater importance – Germany still possessed nothing substantial in China. German imperialism sought to become one of the leading powers in the Far East and, naturally, it wanted to get as much as it could from the killing of its ambassador. Kaiser Wilhelm II, the German Emperor, therefore took the lead in the campaign against the 'Yellow barbarians'. He appealed to all the Europe courts to engage in collective action and proposed the creation of a united army with overall command of European forces in China, a command which he offered to the German Field Marshall Count Waldersee. Thus, taking advantage of the Boxer movement, Germany strived to make its appearance in the Far East as a power whose command all the others would follow. The other powers were not very pleased with this, and soon, in the face of this same 'Yellow Peril' which they were making such a fuss about, the capitalist powers began squabbling among themselves.

Tsarist Russia took a more reasonable position. It had already seized Manchuria, and tsarism didn't want others to seize as much as it had. It was afraid that if a large-scale intervention began in China, the British would grab the Yangzi River valley. Therefore, Russian tsarism occupied a wait-and-see position with respect to this issue. It continually sent telegrams expressing sympathy and condolences; when it was pointed out that the Russian ambassador

---

217 Central Soviet Archive 1926, p. 31.

[Mikhail Nikolaevich Girs] was also in danger, it shed diplomatic tears, but did not hasten to dispatch a large number of troops to China, because it understood that the Tran-Siberian railroad was not yet completed, and if a large-scale war developed in China, the British would easily redeploy troops from India by sea, and would turn out to be much stronger than Russia which would have a hard time sending troops. In such an event, the British would grab more. It would be more advantageous to keep everything within the limits of a small war.

For their part the British quickly put forth a demand on Germany. They agreed to the appointment of Waldersee, but demanded recognition of the Yangzi valley as a British sphere of influence. Negotiations commenced concluding with a new Anglo-German agreement which is one of the important political documents of this period since Germany recognised Britain's special interests in the richest and most developed region of China.[218]

Finally the expeditionary forces arrived – Germans, Russians, and British. They landed at Tianjin, bombarded and destroyed the Dagu fortifications, then set out on their first march to Beijing which ended with a defeat along the road midway between Tianjin and Beijing. Subsequently, the European forces were beefed up, the siege of the foreign quarter in Beijing was lifted. Because the Empress Dowager took fright, seeing that the European powers were acting decisively, Chinese regular troops were ordered not to support the Boxers. Ronglu undertook an expedition against the Boxers. The Empress Dowager ordered that the archives be removed, that all the documents and edicts supporting the Boxers be destroyed, and that, on the one hand, all the blame be placed on the Boxers, and on the other, on a few high-placed officials.

Nevertheless, foreign troops entered Beijing.

You all know very well just how the representatives of the Christian West taught what they called 'culture' and 'civilisation' to the 'Yellow barbarians', how they pointed out to the Chinese just how backward China lagged behind enlightened Europe. In any case, the European powers did not resort to peaceful negotiations until after their troops demonstrated they could pillage better than the Boxers.

That they dealt with the Boxers as well as peaceful persons who had not taken part in the uprising with the cruelty of Genghis Khans cannot surprise us now that we know the even more vivid pages of the history of imperialism soaked in fresh, hot blood, but that they celebrated their victory with the most obscene looting and organised pillaging by their troops, the command of

---

218   It refers to the Anglo-German agreement of 16 October 1900, signed in London.

which was shared by all the governments, and the plunder of, what from the perspective of culture and civilisation, were the most valuable objects, was the distinguishing feature of this glorious campaign by the civilisers.

I will read to you several documents from these days which will forever remain a shameful, indelible stain on the history of capitalist civilisation.

On 17 August 1900, Pokhotilov [Pokotilov], the Russian financial agent in Beijing whom you know from the story of his bribing Li Hongzhang, telegraphed the minister of finance in Petersburg:

> The entire detachment consists of about 20,000. Of these, 4,000 Russians, 9,000 Japanese, 4,000 British as well as Americans and French. On the day after its arrival, the detachment resorted to bombarding and occupying the imperial city which they have almost finished doing now. The Chinese put up a strong resistance which greatly enraged the troops who engaged in large-scale violence, killing a mass of neutral, peaceful Chinese, and unrestrained pillaging. The Japanese distinguished themselves in this regard. They behaved in Peking [Beijing] like total masters, posting guards, seizing the treasury in which money was stored, but not much. The Japanese quickly took it for themselves. The Empress Dowager, the Bogdy Khan [Emperor], and the entire government fled from Peking, where they went is unknown.[219]

But the Tsar received reports not only about pillaging by Japanese soldiers, but also about the valiant Russian soldiers engaged in the same activity with equal success. We find this in a telegram from the Russian minister of war Kuropatkin to the Commander-in-Chief of Russian forces Linevich, dated 4 October 1900: 'Telegrams from English sources report that our troops in Beijing have removed property from one of the palaces. His Majesty expressed his indignation to me regarding these rumours'.[220]

To this General Linevich replied,

> I inform you that no objects were removed from the palaces. The disgraceful British slander accusing Russian soldiers of pillaging the palaces is not the first such slander; it is merely a new means of slandering Russians. From respect for allies, I have never allowed myself to refer unworthily to the British. Now I deem it my responsibility to report that I have seen

---

219 Central Soviet Archive 1926, p. 27.
220 Ibid., p. 36.

with my own eyes even commanding officers, British, with mountains of various sorts of stolen goods, bundles of new silk material, also mountains of silk dresses, furs, carpets, and other palace goods. Moreover, every British soldier had his own suitcase full of various things and furs. All of this was shipped off to India in a timely fashion, and those materials and things which they were too late to ship to India were auctioned off in Peking [Beijing] at the British embassy, daily over a period of three weeks. All the allies were informed of the unusual auctions. People from every country, including our Russian officers and soldiers, purchased things at these auctions. The Russians did nothing like this nor could they. Our Russian troops were even ordered to turn over silver ingots they found at various times.[221]

Although China is a very unusual country, General Linevich was undoubtedly carried away when he said that in China one could 'find' silver ingots in such quantities that they would later be turned over, moreover, by the *hundredweight*, as he writes further in this same telegram.

Thus, the Russians report that the Japanese engage in pillaging, the British say the Russians engage in pillaging, the Russians respond that the British pillage, and the Germans themselves do not hide that they are no fools.

The social democratic press printed a huge number of soldiers' letters which talked about this pillaging. Wilhelm Liebknecht, the father of Karl Liebknecht, gave a speech in the Reichstag on 28 July 1900, about the violent robberies which German soldiers had perpetrated. But it was not only soldiers and officers who pillaged, the governments did so as well. For example, from Beijing the Germans carried away ancient astronomical instruments which were only returned to China in 1919. All the libraries in European capitals are full of the treasures of ancient Chinese literature, and museums with palace treasures stolen in 1900. When we have more time and our Chinese comrades will help us, then our responsibility will be to examine Russian libraries, too, and I am sure we will find in them precious manuscripts and documents which were removed then by Russian soldiers ...

The Boxer movement was drowned in blood. Those who suppressed it stole whatever they wanted and were able to steal, and China must now seek repayment from the capitalist powers. In this case, the contradictions which existed among the imperialist powers again helped China. The hopes of those who counted upon a decisive division of China were dashed.

---

221 Ibid., pp. 37–8.

This was due to the Boxers' failure to seize the embassies, to the Beijing court, which at first was convinced of the weakness of the foreigners, now fearfully backtracking. To the fact that those elements in the Chinese bureaucracy who opposed the Boxer Uprising such as Li Hongzhang, Yuan Shikai, and Ronglu, got the upper hand, to the fact that the imperialist camp witnessed the triumph of those who thought the time for dividing up China had passed. Chinese diplomacy, taking advantage of disagreements among the imperialists, played upon the contradictory interests of the European powers.

In this connection, the telegram from the Empress Dowager to Britain's Queen Victoria proposing an end to the conflict is of interest. Greeting the Queen, Cixi expresses regret that her country is in a state of war and notes that a significant part of China's trade – 70 to 80 percent – is in England's hands. The British customs system is the most favourable in the world; it facilitates the development of commercial relations. Therefore, British merchants will always be treated in a friendly fashion in Chinese ports. In the event that a radical change in circumstances should occur, the Empress Dowager asked the Queen to consider that the loss of Chinese independence would also be unfavourable to Britain's position in the world. She pointed out directly that the British had the greatest interest in preserving an independent China. And this was true. Having received Germany's recognition of its interests on the Yangzi, England already had a mortgage on the future. Russia, likewise, was not yet interested in going forward (the railroad not having been built as yet), in throwing itself into a large adventure. Li Hongzhang, who was negotiating with the European representatives, was splendidly informed about all the inside squabbles taking place among the great powers, and there is no doubt that the Russians were informing him.

There are documents proving this. Tsarism was concerned that England and Germany not make any further territorial gains in China, and informed Li Hongzhang of the disagreements between them. Li Hongzhang himself played upon the contradictions among the powers; thus the Boxer Protocol – a political document that resulted from the negotiations – however onerous it was for China, did not bring it any further territorial losses.

China was obligated to pay the powers 500 million *taels*.[222] This Boxer Indemnity was secured by customs duties which were completely removed from the authority of the government, from its economic accounts and politics which, of course, entailed extremely onerous consequences and not only for state finances. The Boxer Indemnity is still being paid to this day. Amer-

---

222 Radek is mistaken. In fact it was 450 million taels, which was equal to US $333 million.

ica refused the indemnity on special conditions advantageous to imperialism; Germany and Austria were forced to decline the indemnity by the terms of the Versailles Treaty; Soviet Russia voluntarily declined the indemnity; France and England continue to receive it as before on the basis of the Boxer Protocol.

At the same time the [Chinese] government was obligated to execute the leaders of the Boxers. Thirteen high officials were executed, many were exiled, and many were forced to commit suicide.

Only members of the ruling house were accorded humane treatment. Prince Duan, the main culprit, insofar as one may speak of such historically, was saved by the diplomats, who considered it impossible to execute such a high-born person.

As for shooting tens of thousands of innocent persons, this, of course, did not offend their sensibilities.

And so, what were the consequences of the uprising?

The main result of the Boxer movement was that it wrapped up the matter of the Sino-Japanese War. If the Sino-Japanese War manifested China's weakness, then the defeat of the Boxers delivered China economically wholly into the hands of foreign imperialism. The Manchu dynasty, which was and remained a resolute opponent of reform, refused to resist the foreigners, at least with respect to the economic and technical consequences of the intrusion of imperialism.

Now a few words in principle assessing the Boxer Uprising.

In many ways it reminds us of the pogroms against Jews and Zubatovshchina well-known from the history of the Russian revolution.[223] In the face of a growing popular movement which might turn against it, tsarism often resorted to such methods, trying to take control of the movement into its own hands. During the period of 'Will of the People',[224] when terrorist acts threatened tsarism, it unleashed the first European pogroms. Since the Tsar feared that the people would join the revolutionary movement, he tried to turn the movement in a different direction. He did the same when a wave of revolutions arose.

Prior to the 1905 Revolution, tsarism fully unleashed a pogrom movement in Russia. In precisely the same way, when the workers' movement began to grow, the gendarmes tried to take it over. The Zubatov affair is a case in point.

---

223 This refers to the practices of Sergei Zubatov, the tsarist Russian police administrator, who set up government-run trade unions to divert workers' protest into harmless channels. *Trans.*

224 Will of the People (or People's Freedom) was a Russian terroiristic organisation in 1879–84.

Why was tsarism able to do this? It did not create pogroms artificially. Peasants were in a very difficult condition; they were exploited by landlords, but capitalists, too, were likewise ruining them. In the villages, capitalists appeared in the person of their agents – petty Jewish traders. Therefore, the anti-Jewish movement of the peasantry was a fragment of the gathering revolution. It was reactionary inasmuch as killing several thousand Jews would not improve the position of the peasantry, but the very fact that peasants came out against exploitation was a symptom of revolutionary movement within the peasantry. The Boxer movement was likewise a symptom of revolutionary ferment of the Chinese masses who felt that something had to be done. The Manchu nobility feared the growth of this movement, feared that it might turn against the dynasty, therefore, it turned the movement solely against foreigners. In Russia, the movement – both the anti-Jewish and the Zubatov movement – turned against tsarism. You know that the bloody events in January 1905, in Petersburg, were provoked by an organisation headed by a priest [George Gapon] who enjoyed the support of the police. This organisation, taking shape, ignited the movement in a certain direction, which led to what they did not want at all, namely, an uprising of the proletariat. In China, owing to the interference of foreigners in a bloodbath, which foreign capital arranged for the mass movement, it was crushed while it was still reactionary. Despite this, as Marxists and revolutionaries we cannot view this movement the way not only European, but also Chinese bourgeois scholars view it – as a bandit movement.

This peasant movement was the result of the breakdown of old China and a forerunner of the future Chinese revolution. Despite the fact that it was manipulated by the Manchu dynasty, it represented one of the waves, one of the domestic underground shocks, which indicated that old China had ceased to exist.

Lecture Thirteen

Strictly speaking the modern capitalist development of China began with the development of railroads. Until such time as European capital began to construct railroads, one could speak of the importation of a certain quantity of European goods and the export of goods from China, but not yet of the real influence of capitalism on the Chinese economy.

You are aware that even before the Boxer Uprising and even prior to the Sino-Japanese War, the first attempts were made to build railroads in China. A Shanghai firm which still exists to this day, one of the largest British firms in the East, Jardine, Matheson & Co.[225] attempted to secure a concession in 1865 for a railroad from Shanghai to Wusong. Since it was afraid the government would not permit it openly to build a railroad, it secured the concession through a subterfuge. It requested a concession for a road, but it did not specify whether it would be a railroad or some other sort of road. At first, in 1875, it built a horse-drawn tramway then it connected the wagons to a steam engine and began to operate. This provoked great consternation on the part of both the government and the people, and they forced the firm to sell the road back. The government bought up the concession, dismantled the entire railroad, and shipped the material off to Formosa. It tore down the stations and ripped up and destroyed the roadbed. Such was the first attempt.

The second attempt was intended to serve the Kaiping mines which were located not far from Tianjin. In the 1880s, the administration of the mines built a small, seven-mile long rail line. The main leader in constructing this railroad was Li Hongzhang. Construction began in 1881; Li Hongzhang was generally not concerned with railroad construction, but in connection with difficulties in transporting troops, every year he added to the original line, a piece in the north, a piece in the south, in this way building a railroad that became part of the later Beijing-Mukden [Shenyang] railroad. For now they were afraid to bring the railroad into Beijing lest it impair the dignity of the capital.

Thus, the first railroad was built by the Chinese themselves. Plans for other railroads were discussed in Beijing. But these were all weak efforts.

A decisive turning point in the construction of Chinese railroads came after the Sino-Japanese War. This was the period when the government was granting concessions. In general, the actual construction occurred only after the Boxer Uprising. If the years 1894–8 are known as the period of the struggle for concessions, then the period from 1900 to the 1911 Revolution was the period of railroad-building in China.

Which were the major railroad lines built? I will not give a chronological picture of railroad construction, instead I will depict the course of construction according to the main directions. I begin with the line which was intended to link Beijing, Hankou, and Canton. The idea was to create a main line which would cut through all of China from the north to the south. This line, as you know, has not been completed up to the present.

What was built and by whom? The concession for the northern line from Beijing to Hankou was granted in 1897, and the line was built in 1905; in the

---

225   Jardine, Matheson & Co. in the nineteenth century was the largest trading company operating in the Far East. It was founded in 1832 in Canton. In 1844 it moved to Hong Kong.

vicinity of Kaifeng an enormous three-kilometre-long bridge had to be built, which greatly complicated the construction of this line. This line was built mainly by Belgian and French capital. The southern line, which was supposed to have been built from Canton, has a very long history and has still not been completed as of the present. The Americans received the concession to build the line from Canton to Hankou. Up to this time the Americans had played a very minor role in the Far East, and capitalists from all the other countries objected to this concession. They argued that during the Boxer Uprising financial securities issued by the railway company fell in value, and under the leadership of the Belgian monarch, King Leopold, who was a first-class stock market swindler, they began to buy up these securities. The Chinese government, supported by the Hong Kong-Shanghai Bank,[226] began a struggle against this, offering funds to purchase the concession from the Franco-Belgian organisation. The Chinese received a loan of 22 million *marks* (10 million rubles) from the Hong Kong-Shanghai Bank and paid the group of concessionaires to return the concession. They had still not succeeded in building anything, but received an enormous sum. For the first time the Americans had received a concession, issued stocks, and 'earned' a lot from this; when the price of the stocks began to decline the Belgians bought them up cheaply, and having resold them to the government again made a killing. The government borrowed money from the British and the latter also made a killing. All of this was at the expense of the Chinese people. But there was still no sign of a railroad. You can see how the bourgeoisie can extract profit from building a railroad. In the south considerable agitation began for building a railroad with their own Chinese capabilities, but they succeeded in raising only twenty percent of the necessary capital. Finally, in 1909, the provincial government signed an agreement with Germany which promised to build a railroad to Hankou.[227] You are aware that then a disaster came from above – the imperialist war – and to this day the railroad has still not been built, only a small piece of it. Moreover, the branch from Canton to Kowloon, which cost 16 million Chinese dollars, is in the hands of the British. Thus, the Beijing-Canton mainline still does not exist.

---

226   The Hong Kong-Shanghai Bank was established by the British in 1865. In 1866, it was renamed The Hong Kong and Shanghai Banking Corporation. Since 1989 it has been The Hong Kong and Shanghai Banking Corporation Limited.
227   Radek must be assuming a draft loan agreement initiated by Minister of Military Affairs of the Qing government Zhang Zhidong, who supervised the constriction of the Canton-Hankou railway with German Deutsche Bank, the British Hong Kong and Shanghai Banking Corporation, and France's Banque Indosuez.

The second line, along which railroad development proceeded, was the Shandong railroad which the Germans built. This railroad was supposed to link Jiaozhou with Jinan. Its significance lay in that it not only provided a railway across Shandong, but that it was also supposed to give a boost to the development of the mining industry. Prior to the construction of the railroad the daily production of ore in the Fangzi mines was around 200 tons, but after the construction it was 450 tons. Just in the first years of its existence the railroad produced an income of two million marks (one million rubles), and in 1907 it annually transported about one million people, 35,000 head of livestock, and 409,000 tons of military loads. From the very beginning it was a profitable railroad and yielded high dividends. The Germans tried to extend the Shandong railroad to Tianjin and Beijing to have, in this way, a direct link with the capital. For this reason, there was a big struggle between Germany and England. On the basis of a 1900 treaty, known as the Yangzi Treaty, British and German capital divided up spheres of railway construction. The Germans were obligated not to intrude into the Yangzi River valley, and the British gave them free rein in Shandong province. In this connection, the British had to do a deal when they decided to link Beijing and Shanghai themselves. The deal was that the Germans were supposed to build the northern part of the line and a British syndicate would build the more southerly part. In this way, Shandong province was connected, on the one hand, with the central commercial-industrial region (the Shanghai region), and, on the other hand, with Beijing, and via Beijing, with the Manchurian railroad system. This construction, which required an enormous investment of capital, was jointly conducted by German and British capital.

As for the railroad linking Beijing with the Manchurian net, it was built by the Chinese under the leadership of British engineers. After the Sino-Japanese War or, more precisely, during the Boxer Uprising, it was seized by the Russians and became an object of a big dispute until, finally, it wound up again in the hands of the Chinese government.

It is very important to examine the conditions under which railroads were built in this period. These conditions were unbelievably onerous. The Russian author Kantorovich, who last year published a book on foreign capital and the railroads of China, describes the following major features of these agreements.[228] First, foreign capital reaps enormous profits from these agreements. The profit comes primarily from the fact that China receives less money from the loans than it nominally takes for construction. Usually it receives only ninety rubles per hundred, but it has to repay one hundred rubles, not ninety.

---

228 See Kantorovich 1926a.

Further, the Chinese government guarantees the annual interest on the loans; finally, the group of capitalists who build the railroad are granted the opportunity to purchase all the materials to construct the railroad. The bank which supplies the money, not only receives interest, but also 'earns' as a middleman in the purchase of construction materials. The bank is connected with foreign industrial enterprises and receives goods from them; the price is set in agreement with the Chinese bureaucracy which had a certain degree of control. It is easily understood that banking capital dealt with the Chinese bureaucracy by employing bribery and that, by this means, the prices received were significantly higher than when European capital procured railroad construction materials at home.

Second, the railroads essentially remained in the hands of foreigners. Although the government usually appointed the chief director as a figurehead, the actual leader who functioned as director was a foreign engineer. All the main positions, for example, accountant, chief engineers, etc. were in foreign hands; the majority of technical personnel were likewise foreigners.

Finally, a very revealing feature is the fact that in the event the government failed to pay interest, the railroads would pass into the hands of the builders. If the Chinese government was unable to pay the interest, then possession of the railroad itself would be the means of paying the interest. Only later did China secure a change so that interest payments would be guaranteed by certain state income, usually customs duties which were under the supervision of foreigners. China sought this change so that in the event it was unable to pay the interest on time, the railroads would not become the property of the construction firms.

Such were the conditions in the initial agreements China signed to construct railroads. It is no surprise that very early on, under the influence of these agreements, in China bourgeois circles began large-scale agitation to refuse foreign loans. The movement against foreign loans took the form of collecting funds, of subscription for domestic railroad loans, thereby providing the government an opportunity to liberate itself from the grip of foreign capitalism. In this period the Chinese bourgeoisie itself gave loans to build a whole series of provincial lines (for example, Nanjing-Shanghai). Foreign capital, viewing this movement, which, as you know, provided the final impetus for revolution in 1911, was very dissatisfied. Its interests in this case coincided with the interests of the central Manchu bureaucracy which looked askance on the creation of provincial railroads that were in the hands of the provincial administrations. It feared this, because it recognised the danger of the aspiration for autonomy in China itself. The government worked hand-in-glove with foreign capitalists in attempting to wrest the possibility of building railroads with their own means from the hands of the provincial bourgeoisie. One of the last decrees of the Manchu government unequivocally stated, 'We declare to the entire Empire that the construction of mainline railroads must be in the hands of the government'.

The entire period of railroad construction up to 1911 was marked by endless struggle among various capitalist countries. They fought literally like dogs over a bone.

When opposition to foreign loans and the government arose, fearing this opposition, an attempt to secure better conditions for loans, then the international banks understood the need to put an end to competition among themselves. Negotiations began to form a banking consortium to secure a monopoly on loans for China. The major European powers – England, France, Russia, and Germany – made an agreement binding them not to support any banking group which acted independently of the consortium in negotiating with the government. If the government gave a concession on terms more favourable to China to a group that was not part of the consortium, then international diplomacy, acting in unison, would apply pressure on the government. America also took part in the consortium. One of the chief initiators and defenders of the consortium was the American consul in Manchuria [Fred Douglas Fisher] who understood that since America had become involved in Chinese affairs later than other capitalist powers which already possessed concessions, then it would be to its advantage if all the concessions were held in common. Upon joining the consortium, Japan stipulated that Manchuria was excluded from the sphere of action of the consortium. Southern Manchuria was to be Japan's; northern Manchuria Russia's. This was a special region for exploitation, but construction everywhere else should be in the hands of the consortium.

Even prior to the war the consortium fell apart. America was the first to leave. Wilson covered the departure from the consortium with a very bombastic and high-sounding declaration that the consortium had been founded to exploit China, and that America did not want to take part. That this was only talk is best demonstrated by the fact that America itself suggested the internationalisation of the Manchurian railroads, and conducted lengthy negotiations about this between 1909 and 1913. America left the consortium, because, first of all, it was very unpopular, and as a power which came late to the exploitation of China, it had to play the role of a 'friend' of China, and, second, America's reputation was very soiled by its participation in this consortium, and the war greatly retarded railroad construction in China. The consortium did not build any railroads at all, and under growing pressure from the nationalist movement, the Chinese government could not accept its conditions.

An attempt to reestablish the consortium – again with American participation – essentially yielded no practical results. It was concluded for a five-year term, and last year the term was up. I don't know if it was extended or not, but, as you know, during the five years of its existence the second consortium also did not build any railroads.

The reason is clear. In order to construct more or less major lines more or less stable political conditions are necessary. Capitalists will not risk investing large amounts of capital when the terms which the central Chinese government accepted might not be recognised by provincial governments and when there is no guarantee that they will receive back the money they have invested. If Japan indeed gave a 'railway' loan to the Anfu clique, it was actually a purely political loan which the Anfu politicians spent on political purposes – they had no intention of building railroads.

The result of all this development is that China has only 11,000 kilometres of railroads, and lacks a mainline railroad that actually connects the north with the south and the west with the east. All of western China – Sichuan, Chinese Turkestan, etc. – has no rail connection with central China. In essence, everything that was done until our time was a means of economic mobilisation of the maritime regions. This was not construction which would have united China as a national organism. The best proof that railroads are still not in a position to become a powerful means of developing the commercial economy in China is demonstrated by the statistics – not very precise, to be sure – of railroad cargo. First place in the turnover of goods is occupied by products of the mining industry. Of total turnover, 46 percent of rail transport is coal, iron, and salt, with coal first, utilised in the iron industry of the central region. In second place is the export of agricultural products. But they constitute only 22 percent of cargo. What does this mean for an agricultural country? Even if one takes into account that part of the cargo goes by water transport, still this percentage is very low, and here one must bear in mind that this includes wheat which Manchuria exports, soybeans, tea, silk, and in part foreign agricultural products which are trans-shipped from Tianjin. You are aware that several regions of China receive grain from abroad. The railroads have not yet taken over mass agricultural transport. Industrial manufactures are a very low percentage, around 10 percent.

What does this signify? It means that products of heavy industry are not yet reaching the peasantry. Although the railroads are the real start of capitalist development, the weakness of the rail net still does not permit them to penetrate the economy of the country and become a factor wholly altering this economy. (The figures I cited were for 1923.) Other results of railroad construction, in addition to their direct impact on the economy, were necessary for them to be able to play the role of a really significant factor in transforming the economy. Thus far we can discern two such results:

1) The indebtedness of the state which compels China to raise taxes on the people and thereby forces the peasantry to sell part of the products of their production; 2) the development, albeit local in a few regions, of capitalist industry around the railroads and under their influence.

In subsequent lectures I will talk about these two consequences of railroad construction.

Today I want to say the following. When European capitalists constructed these railroads, it never occurred to them that this would provide a stimulus to the creation of Chinese industry itself. They thought as follows: We will build railroads and thanks to them we will be able to sell to China industrial products from the West, and we will pump agricultural products out from China. If you read imperialist propaganda from that period, you will always encounter this argument. When, for example, opportunists in the German social-democratic movement were persuading German workers not to oppose capitalist expansion, then they pointed out that Germany had a large population – more than sixty million – and that its agriculture was unable to feed all of these people. Therefore, Germany either had to export industrial goods to China and make use of Chinese agricultural products or Germany would have to export people.

They did not take into consideration that China itself would develop its own industry and that on the foundation of this industry modern classes would be created, and in this way the preconditions for revolution would arise, a revolution in which not only hungry peasants would take part, but the working class as well.

Richtofen, the scholar from the last century who wrote in the 1870s, understood that there were tremendous opportunities for the development of Chinese industry. Fifty years ago, the Russian Sinologist Vasiliev predicted that China would be the number one industrial nation in the world.[229] But when the struggle among imperialists heated up and class conflict in Europe intensified, then European bourgeois scholars no longer approached the study of conditions in China objectively and calmly. The bourgeoisie was attracted by the hope that it would be possible to build railroads in China without reconstructing Chinese life. This did not happen, as you know, nor could it happen.

---

229 See Vasiliev 1900, pp. 155–6.

Lecture Fourteen

The last lecture was devoted to railroad construction in China, and today I must turn to the question of debts which China must pay on the basis of these railroad agreements. But since then I have received several new works on the history of railroad construction in China and I have become convinced that we must supplement the last lecture and rework it so that you can receive a more vivid and accurate picture than I was able to give you on the basis of the materials I previously possessed.

I will begin at a very interesting place which I found in a work by the German engineer Strewe, a specialist in railroad construction in China.[230]

> Already in the late '90s, specialists in railroad construction asserted in Berlin that in the coming decades it would be impossible even to think of building railroads in China, because all of China is a huge cemetery. The Chinese consider the graves of their ancestors sacred and, therefore, will never allow railroads that pass through these graves to be constructed.

Moreover, these specialists, Strewe tells us, pointed out that China has a huge number of canals and, therefore, requires such a large number of bridges that railroads will be unable to pay for themselves. Finally, he says that Chinese generally do not consider it necessary to have railroads. This means that 30 years ago in the circles of German capitalists in Berlin, those who knew China predicted that decades would pass and the Chinese would not have any railroads. Now says Strewe (his book was written in 1919), it turned out that in a very short time the Chinese have become accustomed to railroads; railroads are very popular, and that fourth class, which is used the most, is the most profitable part of exploitation for the railroads. Thus, for example, the Shanghai-Nanjing railroad derives a big profit exclusively from passenger traffic, and fourth-class traffic at that, since cargo is transported by water along the Yangzi River. But the most interesting of his reports relates to the question of how much religious prejudices and respect for the graves of ancestors inhibited railroad construction. He says that religious prejudices turned out to be only occasions for speculation. Societies were established that bought up sections full of graves in places where railroad lines were projected and then sold them at inflated prices to the railroad companies. The religious prejudices of China inhibited the matter as

---

230   Radek might be thinking of Maria Theodor Strewe, but he was not an engineer. What book Radek had in mind is not clear either.

little as the prejudices of European capitalists regarding the special conditions and specific routes of development in China.

In essence, railroad construction, which began in earnest in the last years of the nineteenth century, was part of a grand crusade in China.

The American author Overlach, describing step-by-step the struggle for railroads, was entirely correct in saying that the period of railroad construction was a period of conquering China through railroads and banks.[231] It is very important to become acquainted with the overall assessment of railroad construction given by this American, because the Chinese revolution is a struggle not only against unequal treaties. Now we are speaking about extraterritoriality, about settlements, and so forth. But with the further development of the revolution the struggle against indebtedness, which lies like a heavy burden on China, will be at the fore. China's debt for railroads equals $500 million dollars, and it is perfectly obvious that when the struggle against this debt is the order of the day, foreign capitalists will resist and will put forward the argument that

> it's well and good that the Russians refused to pay their debt for conducting a war, but we lent you money for such a useful purpose as constructing railroads and, therefore, any attempt to cut this debt is a direct attack against the holiest of property rights.

Therefore, it is very important that we understand how the bourgeois scholar, who has studied the entire history of railroad construction from the documents, assesses the negotiations regarding railroads which culminated in a series of loans. He says the following in the introduction to his book:

> Though at first sight political, and fought by diplomacy, the struggle for foreign control in China was not less one of international financial interests, contending for the exploitation of new opportunities for investment. Foreign capital was attracted to China by the hope for large profits. With the help of diplomacy, the states and financial groups concluded agreements on policy, the goal of which was that the banks and syndicates would receive the railroads into their own hands, and that the loans which they extended to China would be supported by the government. The struggle for foreign control in China was a struggle to conquer China with the help of the railroads and the banks.[232]

---

231 See Overlach 1919.
232 Radek quotes incorrectly. After the words 'new opportunities for investment', the Overlach text continues: 'Foreign capital was attracted by the great profit to be gained from the

In his book, the bourgeois writer openly acknowledges that all the while it was not a matter of helping China or developing China, but rather that a series of capitalist banks in Europe were striving to enslave China by means of the railroads. He says further,

> It should be remembered that the concessions and loan agreements were received not in private negotiations among bankers, but rather that the bankers acted as political and financial agents of their own governments and were assisted by diplomacy.[233]

When, so to speak, you will be reckoning accounts in political struggle, and the matter has entered a serious phase, then acquaintance with the concrete history of the struggle for railroads in China will put into your hands a powerful political weapon, because one needs to know, first, by what means foreign capitalism received concessions for each railroad and, second, one needs to know on what terms each concession was received and to what degree these terms demonstrated the exploitation of China. If we examine the goals which each of the states pursued, you will see that railroads were built not only as economic enterprises, but as a means for conquering and dividing China.

In the tenth lecture I spoke of the history of the agreement whereby Russia received permission from China to build a railroad linking the Pogranichnaia and Manchuria stations, that is, bisecting the northern part of Manchuria (this was in 1896), and of the conditions under which China, in 1896, allowed Russia to build a railroad to the south, connecting the Siberian main line with Port Arthur. As we have seen, this, in reality, was the seizure of Manchuria by Rus-

---

impending industrial revolution of China. In order to eliminate financial competition of other nations or to counteract political moves on the part of other governments, if such were destined to be harmful to its own expansion, foreign finance often solicited, and freely received, diplomatic protection. With a protection and promotion of foreign enterprise several governments combined the furtherance of national ambitions of a more or less political character. All banks and syndicates in charge of the railways and loans became more and more generally recognised as indispensable means to serve the political and commercial ends of their respective governments. The struggle for foreign control in China has accordingly been marked by a most singular and distiguishing feature, namely, the closest possible cooperation between foreign finance and foreign policy. The period was one of "conquest by railroad and bank"' (Overlach 1919, pp. i–ii).

[233] Thus in the text. In Overlach's book this sentence is a bit different: 'It is important ... to bear in mind that concessions and loan contracts have been negotiated not only by bankers who acted as politico-financial agents of their governments but also by diplomats directly' (Overlach 1919, p. x).

sia, and the agreements with Russia served as the main stimulus followed by the frantic struggle for railroad concessions. But it would be a great mistake to think that the tsarist government, and even more the financial circles in France, which pulled the strings behind the back of the tsarist government, were satisfied with preparing to seize Manchuria. Tsarist Russia had much broader plans in mind at the time. I am referring to the plan to build a railroad from Beijing to Hankou which had been advanced by the so-called Belgian syndicate. You are aware that Belgium is a small country, but rich in capital. It was obvious that Belgium was not the main force, but that someone was hiding behind it. These were the very same circles which built the CER and seized Manchuria; behind the Belgian syndicate stood French and Russian capital, supported by the tsarist government. The tsarist government was pursuing such a plan. A glance at the map is enough to understand its significance. In the north, all of Manchuria was in Russian hands. A railroad from Beijing to Hankou was supposed to extend Russian influence to the very heart of China. If such a railroad was in Russian hands, this would raise the issue of a whole series of other lines. The railroad linking Beijing with Tianjin would be up for grabs, a plan to build a Beijing-Kalgan line with an extension to Mongolia would be bruited, the financial plan, hinted at, but not yet worked out precisely, to construct a line going through Chinese Turkestan to Kaifeng, would take clear shape and, in this way, all of North China could wind up within the grand system of Russian railroads.

But Russia was not alone; it was acting hand-in-hand with French capital. What was French capital aiming for? We know of two directions in which French policy in China was developing. One line went from French Indochina to Yunnanfu and was supposed to be extended further north to link up with the railroad going to Hankou. Thus, from the same region which financial plutocrats from the north, under the cover of Russia, were aiming, it would also go south. Moreover, when the Americans received a concession to build a Canton-Hankou railroad, during the Boxer Rebellion this concession was bought up by a group of Belgian syndicates linked to French and Russian interests.

You can see how all these individual, fragmented plans aggregate into one enormous plan.

One might say that this was a fantasy, that this necessitated enormous expenditures, billions of rubles, but France at that time was a country which supplied money to all the colonial powers. France was a country of wealthy peasants and rentiers who kept their money in their stockings and willingly invested it in foreign loans, resulting in the slow growth of French industry prior to the war. France itself was not strong enough to secure its advance in China by means of its own political influence and its own troops. But France was an ally of Russia, and if French capital invested billions of francs in Russia, then it was not at all utopian to devise a plan which would give French capital, supported by the bayonets of the tsarist government, the opportunity to take possession of half of China. It would be folly to think this was not a real possibility, just because it didn't actually happen. Just how much others took these plans into account is evident from the report of Brandt, the German envoy in China, issued in 1898. His report contains a geographical map on which almost all of these plans are traced out. Brandt composed the map on the basis of official British material published by the government for parliament.[234]

Now let us examine how, in their own interests, England and Germany tried to destroy this Franco-Russian plan.

You have seen by what means Russia secured its railroad concessions. It received concessions in Manchuria through pure deception. Li Hongzhang was seduced by the notion that Russia would defend China against Japan. A treaty of alliance was signed between Russia and China.[235] Witte related how, when during the Boxer Rebellion, Russian troops under the command of General Linevich seized the imperial palace, this treaty was found in a secret wardrobe in the room of the Empress Dowager, and stolen.[236] Subsequent railroad agreements regarding Manchuria were concluded by means of bribery and such actions that, in his memoirs, even the Russian minister Witte called perfidious treachery.[237] But these agreements, too, were cloaked in 'defending China'.

England also defended its interests and prepared its policy of seizing territory under this flag. Generally, not a single one of the powers forgot to say that everything it was doing was being done to 'defend China'. On 13 April 1898, Minister of Foreign Affairs Balfour sent instructions to the British ambassador in Beijing, Sir MacDonald, and in these instructions Balfour said,

> Inform the Min[istry] of For[eign] Aff[airs] in Peking [Beijing] that although it has not followed our advice, insofar as possible we will defend the unity of China and, therefore, we will not make any new territorial demands. But it is absolutely necessary if we are to follow this policy that China on its part first enter into negotiations with us about handing over the territory required for the defence of Hankou.[238]

---

234 See Bradt 1898.
235 See Witte 1922, p. 49.
236 See Ibid., pp. 167–8.
237 See Ibid., pp. 128–9.
238 Radek is mistaken: Balfour did not write about the defence of Hankou, but about the defence of Hong Kong. Here is what Balfour telegraphed to Sir MacDonald: 'Inform Yamen that, although they have not followed our advice, we are anxious to maintain, as far as pos-

They don't want any new territorial conquests, but they demand the territory needed to defend Hankou [Hong Kong]-Tiaolun [Jiulong, i.e. Kowloon] on the coast. 'After that Nanking [Nanjing] must be made a treaty port, China must give us a number of railroad concessions. Finally, China must promise not to cede either Kwangtung [Guangdong] or Yunnan province to the French'.[239]

England demands territorial concessions along the riverfront across from Hankou for the 'defence' of Hankou [Hong Kong]; England considers Guangdong and Yunnan provinces to be its sphere of influence and is concerned lest these provinces be transferred to France without its knowledge. England wants to have concessions. Balfour himself doesn't yet know which concessions are needed, but that concessions, of course, are of primary concern. And all of this is 'absolutely necessary' if England is 'to defend' the unity of China.

At the time when the Belgian syndicate, backed by the Russo-Chinese Bank, was conducting negotiations with the Chinese government, Lord Salisbury, the new minister of foreign affairs in England, learning of the negotiations, declared, '[A] concession of this nature is no longer a commercial or industrial enterprise and becomes a political movement against British interests in the region of the Yangtsze [Yangzi]'.[240]

It turns out that a central region of China – the Yangzi River valley – is not Chinese territory, but a 'sphere of British interests', and that when tsarism and the French are targeting it, they are not aiming at the heart of China, but at British pockets. Therefore, the British government instructs its representative:

> You should inform the minister of foreign affairs[241] [in Peking – *K.R.*] that the English [Her Majesty's] Government cannot possibly continue to cooperate in a friendly manner in matters of interest to China, if, while preferential advantages are conceded to Russia in Manchuria and to Germany in Shantung [Shandong] these or other foreign Powers should also be offered special openings or privileges in the region of the Yangtsze [Yangzi].[242]

---

sible, integrity of China, and will, therefore, not make new territorial demands upon them. It is, however, absolutely necessary if we are to pursue this policy, that they, on their side, should first immediately conclude negotiations – (a) for giving us all the land required for military defences of Hong Kong' (Overlach 1919, p. 29).

239   Radek quotes incorrectly. Here is what Balfour wrote: '([B]) to fulfill their promise to make Nanking [Nanjing] a Treaty port; (c) to give some railway concession; (d) an agreement as to the non-alienation of Kwangtung [Guangdong] and Yunnan' (ibid., p. 29).

240   Ibid., p. 31.

241   In the Overlach text: the Tsungli-Yamen [*Zongli yamen*].

242   Ibid.

When China will conduct a struggle around the question of debts – and you know that Chinese customs duties secure the payment of interest on debts – and the British press shouts that this is a kind of friendly agreement which provided China the opportunity to build railroads – then it is worth remembering this note in which Lord Salisbury declares that he will not continue a peaceful policy toward China if the Chinese government does not provide a guarantee to British capital of exclusive possession of the Yangzi valley. The Chinese government began to rush about and tried to assert that no French or Russian interests were behind the Belgian syndicate, although the ministry knew very well who stood there. Of course, one could not deceive British capital with such a subterfuge, and the British government ordered its warships to enter Chinese waters, and MacDonald received instructions to tell the Chinese government that if it did not submit on this question then England would consider the Beijing-Hankou railroad concession awarded to the Belgian syndicate a hostile step, consciously aimed against England, and would react accordingly. At the same time, Balfour gave the English ambassador the right to communicate with the English admiral commanding the English fleet in Chinese waters and to act as the situation demanded. In this way, the railroad concessions which England received in 1896 on the Yangzi and the agreements regarding loans for the construction of railroads were brought under the pressure of military force. China had old maritime tubs, not warships. It could not fight the British. When the English fleet appeared off the coast of China, the Chinese government had no other option than to grant the English the concessions they demanded. The American writer of whom I spoke, a defender of the international consortium, Overlach, say very simply, that the *Zongli yamen* 'being aware of the concentration of the (English. – K.R.) fleet, conceded to everything. Thus did Great Britain obtain her railway concessions'.[243]

England received the Tianjin-Pukou and Beijing-Hankou railroad concessions. The length of these railroads was 2,800 *verst*.[244] I will discuss the economic terms of these concessions later.

Now I will say a few words about the struggle which took place among the European powers themselves over the concessions. The European powers engaged in a ceaseless fight with each other over pieces of China, concluded agreements over demarcating spheres of influence not only with China, but among themselves as well. Thus, for example, England promised not to crawl

---

243 Ibid., p. 33.
244 This equals about 2,968 kilometers. *Trans*.

into Manchuria. When an English bank gave 16 million *taels* to the Chinese government for further construction of the Tianjin-Pukou line, Russia protested and England had to retract the agreement. In return, Russia promised not to crawl into the Yangzi region. A fight between the Germans and the English erupted over the Tianjin-Pukou railroad concession. The Germans said that the Tianjin-Pukou line passes through Shandong, the homeland of the German-Asiatic Bank, and neither that of the Shanghai-Hong Kong Bank nor the Indian Bank, therefore, German capitalists should build it. England was compelled to conclude an agreement with Germany according to which Germany would build the northern part of the Tianjin-Pukou line, and the British the southern part.

British capital is building the railroad from Shanghai running along the Yangzi.

Thus, the upshot of these quarrels is that Russia kept Manchuria for itself, but its attempt to go south from Beijing to Hankou, and link up with the French who were coming from the south, ended in defeat. The railroads going south from Beijing wound up in the hands of England and Germany. The lines in the Yangzi region are in British hands. France is building a railroad only in Yunnan. For a long time, because of the constant quarrels, no railroads were built at all from Canton. The large-scale overall plan of Franco-Russian capital to bisect China with central main lines in their hands alone did not come to pass because of the conflict of interests among the capitalist powers. Competition among the imperialist interests obstructed this aggressive plan.

Despite this mutual struggle, the imperialists achieved a lot. China was burdened with onerous terms inhibiting its further development. All of the agreements concluded by the foreign banking groups with China may be broken into two groups. One group of powers essentially seized territory and by this means ensured profits for themselves. Such were the agreements with the Germans and the Russians. Having received formally a concession for the Russo-Chinese Bank, the Russian government did not demand any guarantee of profits from the Chinese government; it did not demand any interest on the loans. It did guarantee to itself exploitation of all the natural resources and mineral wealth along both sides of the railroad; it had full control of management of the railroad. One of the directors of the railroad was a Chinese, but everyone knew, of course, that this was only for show. Moreover, the Russian government assumed responsibility for guarding the railroad; it received the right to deploy its own regular troops under the guise of a railroad militia. In this way, the Russian railroad lines were not a means only of economic exploitation of China, but also a means of seizing territory and wholly enslaving the local population. We see the same thing in relation to the agreements which the Germans concluded. The German railroad in Shandong was built as an openly German road under German administration. In it we have a type of territorial acquisition.

The English had to act differently because, even if, to a certain degree, China was reconciled to the fact that owing to its weakness, parts of its peripheral territories were detached, the Chinese government was unable to go so far as to give away territories located in the centre of the country. Moreover, English capital did not dare to demand this, because then it would have to deploy a huge number of troops. The English love to have others do their fighting for them, therefore their policy in China is that there is no need to cut off any part of China, but rather to exploit China as a whole while letting the Chinese government itself guard the English concessions. The English agreements on concessions are structured in such a way that the English bank which is lending money receives a guarantee from the Chinese government that interest will be paid. How? In certain agreements the guarantee stipulates that in case interest is not paid the railroad will become the property of the bank; the bank will receive the first mortgage on the road. A second kind of agreement was that regarding construction of the Tianjin-Pukou line. Here the guarantee was predicated on customs revenues and partly on the salt tax. In fact, the English retained administration of the railroad for themselves (the chief accountant was English as were the directors, the engineers, and so forth), but for the sake of appearances a Chinese administration existed, but without any real authority. In the Russian and German agreements we see a flagrant, barbaric system of overt seizure, but here is a more refined approach. The railroad is called Chinese, but if you do not pay your debt, it is not yours; the management of the railroad is Chinese, but the actual management of the road is in the hands of the English.

The railroads which were built in the period from 1898 to the Revolution of 1911 were, consequently, in one part of the imperialist world a direct means of seizure; in another part a means of economic enslavement and primary mortgage which, in the event of international complications, naturally, would provide the stimulus for political seizure. Therefore, these railroads became one of the primary sources for the growth of Chinese national consciousness. The Chinese bourgeoisie and the Chinese gentry understood perfectly well that the railroads threatened the independence of their country, and it was around the issue of utilisation of the railroads by Chinese that public opinion began to form in 1911.

Naturally, railroads were supposed to provide an enormous stimulus to the growth of industry. To be sure, there were plans to import railroad equipment and coal from abroad so that China, in this way, would not have its own industry, but it is clear that this was wholly utopian. It became necessary to restore, for example, long-established primitive coal and iron mines, because this would reduce the cost of building railroads and increase profits, but this in itself constituted a stimulus for the development of industry in general.

Lecture Fifteen

We will now be dealing with the history of the development of capitalist industry in China and questions arising from the creation of this industry by new social classes. Beginning the cycle of lectures dedicated to this topic, I must make the reservation that the statistics regarding the contemporary Chinese economy are in such a state that no two sources give identical numbers on any question whatsoever. For example, how many spindles and how many machine tools does the Chinese textile industry possess? Every source gives different answers to this for various years. Given the state of the statistics, it would be impossible to answer if it was a matter of precisely assessing the situation. With such statistics, not a single sphere of production in China can be precisely delineated. Even less can a picture of the influence of capitalist development on, let us say, Chinese handicrafts, be provided in the form of statistical tables. For this, there are absolutely no approximate but reliable figures. However, despite the statistical confusion the *trends* of development can be established.

I am making these preliminary remarks so that comrades who may find other figures in other books will not subsequently try to unmask me as a falsifier of the numbers. I will point out the sources, but I ask you to bear in mind that even such sources as the reports of English commercial agents are full of errors and numbers which contradict other data.

European literature has repeatedly posed the question of the possibility of capitalist development in China, but the European capitalist powers have not pondered this question. They have looked upon China as their raw materials base and as a country importing foreign goods. Therefore, if one looks at the economic literature from the '80s and '90s, China is depicted as a country which is incapable of capitalist development owing to its backwardness and stagnation. Among European writers and scholars of that period there were only a few exceptions to this rule, including the German geographer Richthofen and the Russian Sinologist Vasiliev, one of the best Sinologists who enjoyed international renown. In 1880, after the uprising in Chinese Turkestan, he wrote the following:

> Not ten years have passed since the restoration of peace in China … even less since the restoration of the dominion of the court in Peking

[Beijing] over all the lands belonging to it – I am referring to Turkestan and Dzungaria[245] – but just look what has already happened in this time. The Europeans compelled China to open access to trade with them in the coastal ports; they have even penetrated into the center of China – to Hankou; but in this time Chinese have succeeded in seizing control of the trade in European goods. Chinese shop assistants are already sitting in European offices. Chinese are not novices when it comes to commerce. They have been involved in it from the very beginning of their historical existence. The classical books speak of the miserly merchant Lao Xier. And the time may not be far off when China will have no need of European goods just as it reduced the importation of English opium and obtained it at home. European goods penetrated into China thanks to the cheapness of machine production, but who will deny the possibility that Chinese may set up their own factories and mills? They have a multitude of capitalists who possess millions, unprecedentedly cheap labour, and a people who are prepared to work at anything, and turn out to be capable at everything. The Europeans initially thought that their steamships would dominate all the waterways; the Chinese have their own steamships managed by their own local mechanics and have already beaten the Europeans at their own game. The cheapness of labour and the capability of the people are a big deal! It is easy for the Chinese to set up their own machine industry and build their own railroads, and all of this will be cheaper and better than in other countries. And the trade with the Europeans that was initially necessary may lead to a situation in which the very same goods which are now imported into China will be sent back to the foreigners from China. After all, cotton goods that were previously exported from China are now foisted upon it.[246]

To be sure, in these assertions written in 1880, Vasiliev was far ahead of his time. The first modern factory was founded in 1890, that is, thirty-five years ago, but prior to the victory of world imperialism in the Boxer War and before the start of railroad construction, the building of factories in China could only be an exotic fact or, in the best case, it was possible only in ports where European capital could easily deliver coal and where it operated under the protection of

---

245   Dzungaria (Zungharia or Beijiang) is a northern part of Xinjiang.
246   *'Otkrytie Kitaia' i drugie stat'i akademika V.P. Vasilieva* ('The opening of China' and other articles by academician V.P. Vasiliev), Saint Petersburg, 1900, pp. 155–6. *Radek's note*. This refers to Vasiliev 1900.

foreign arms. Actually, we see that factories began to be built in the port cities following the Sino-Japanese War. These were textile factories built by the English. In 1895 an English textile factory was built in Shanghai with 72,000 spindles and 700 machine tools. In 1896 a factory was built with 96,000 spindles and 960 machine tools and an initial capital of 5 million *taels*. In 1897 a Shanghai factory with 45,000 spindles and 446 machine tools was built with an initial capital of half a million *taels*. In 1898 the Oriental Factory was built with 52,000 spindles. Overall in this period we have the construction of five English factories with about 300,000 spindles and about 3,000 machine tools. This was the start of modern industry, affecting Shanghai in the first instance, which later on became a large centre of capitalist development. Instead of importing only finished cotton textiles as before, English capital established the first capitalist factories, utilising Chinese cotton to a significant extent and beginning to exploit cheap Chinese labour.

But when capitalism began to build railroads, it was compelled, as a matter of necessity, to begin to establish heavy industry as well. It had to look for coal near the railroad lines, and iron ore. The trend toward establishing heavy industry was facilitated by circulation of greatly exaggerated reports concerning China's mineral wealth. A few words about these reports. There were numerous estimates of China's natural wealth. These estimates varied from the assertion that China had sufficient iron and col – especially iron – to supply the entire world, to extremely modest reports (*China Yearbook*) that China had coal reserves equivalent to 79 percent of Germany's, 33 percent of England's, and 25 percent of the United States'. And ore reserves one-quarter that of the U.S., 80 percent of Great Britain, and one-third that of France and Germany. But we should not give much credence to these estimates. Very little geological exploration of China has taken place. If one even takes such investigations as the works of Richthofen – the basic investigations which mark the beginning of the modern study of China – then it is clear that this is nothing more than an initial, superficial reconnaissance, for it is impossible in several years of riding around China, with the help of only one geological hammer, to determine what deposits of coal and iron exist there. Not a single Chinese province has been explored using scientific methods, therefore Chinese comrades should neither swell with pride and think they will supply the whole world with iron in the future nor lose heart and courage in the conviction that China will run out of coal in three hundred years. Even if it turns out that China really does have very little coal, technology is advancing, and, generally speaking, coal no longer possesses its former importance.

In the last decade of the nineteenth century, however, this question was still a pressing question and exaggerations regarding Chinese resources played a definite role in the appearance of the breed of 'concession hunters' who had previously been unknown in China. An entire phalanx of foreign adventurers with ties to the capitalist world, and even representatives of serious capitalist firms threw themselves upon China, knocking on every door and demanding access to the development of the capitalist economy.

What were the results of this pursuit of concessions? There is a very good work by Collins, which was also published in Chinese,[247] and in it you will find a detailed answer to this. I will speak only briefly about these results which now are of merely historical interest.

At first, the Chinese government, without much consideration, granted foreigners permission to explore Chinese mineral deposits and open up mines and pits. Only later did it begin to have misgivings that this would lead to the total enslavement of China by foreign capital. As for the Chinese bourgeoisie itself, from the very beginning it resisted this penetration of foreign capitalism. The classic example of this was the history of the French capitalists who, having received a concession from the Beijing government, penetrated into Yunnan and Sichuan and there received a rebuff from the local bureaucracy and merchants. It reached the point that the local authorities destroyed the concessions and paid compensation to the foreign capitalists.

Foreign capital was unable to penetrate into heavy industry outside those zones which were under direct pressure from the Beijing government or those places where territory had been seized by foreign capital or was under pressure of its military forces – in Zhili province, in Shandong, in Shanxi, and along the Yangzi. The Fushan mines in Shandong, after Jiaozhou was seized by the Germans, were under direct threat from German armed force and German capital succeeded in intruding. The struggle between English capitalist interests and Chinese over the Kailan mines ended as follows. The mines established by Chinese capitalists were crushed by the cheapness of English production and were forced to strike a deal with the English to establish a syndicate and merge Chinese capital with English. This was possible because the mines were located along the Beijing-Mukden [Shenyang] railroad where foreign capital was easily able to apply pressure on the Chinese. The Hanyeping mines and the entire coal region comprising a local industrial complex including mines, pits, and iron foundries, established by Chinese capital with a great expenditure of material means, fell under the domination of the Japanese only because, after the fall of the Manchu dynasty, the Chinese government had insufficient means to support this industrial complex and the latter's financial difficulties

---

247 See Collins 1922b.

forced it initially to make commercial deals and go into debt to the Japanese and then surrender to them entirely.

What were the overall results of the development of the coal and metallurgical industries in China? I will give only a few figures by way of illustration. In 1900, in total the capitalist coal industry produced six million tons of coal, and this coal was extracted by primitive methods in small mines. In 1913, prior to the war, this industry already produced 13 million tons, and in 1924, 23 million tons of which 16 million tons were obtained from 37 large coal mines. I will speak later specifically about the significance of the war for the development of this industry, but what is striking here is that in 1900, China's coal industry did not exist as a large-scale capitalist industry, but in 1913 we already have a large-scale coal industry which has doubled in the past ten years. We should not overestimate the importance of this development. Considering China's needs and the possibilities for development, 23 million tons is still an extraordinarily low level of production. If one takes the United States of America, then in 1880, that is, almost half a century ago when the United States was not yet considered an industrialised country, it produced 60 million tons of coal.

Let us look at the development of iron ore production. In 1900, according to my data, China produced about 80,000 tons, a figure that is barely plausible. Since the ore is obtained from innumerable small mines, it is difficult to calculate, especially given the terrible state of Chinese statistics. But if we look at modern Chinese industry after the establishment of the Kailan and Fushan pits and the Hanyeping mines, then we have in 1916, 355,000 tons, in 1918, 500,000 tons, in 1920, 2 million tons. Some half million workers were working in the pits and mines. Let us compare this data again with America. In 1880, when the United States was still not an industrialised country, 3.5 million tons of iron ore were mined in the U.S.

The negligible progress of China's industrial development is even more striking if we shift our attention to the main branch of its manufacturing industry, namely, textiles. Here, incidentally, I was able to collect more comparative material, arranged also by year to a certain degree. The textile industry began to develop in 1890 when the first factory was built,[248] but by 1906 there were still only fourteen textile mills with 400,000 spindles. In 1910, China's entire textile industry had 800,000 spindles. The textile industry developed rapidly from the start of the war. In 1916 we have 42 mills and about 1,200,000 spindles, in 1923, 83 mills and more than 2.5 million spindles. Regarding the number of

---

248 Radek is mistaken. The first textile factory in China was built in 1882.

spindles in China at present, some sources give the figure of three million, others 3.5 million. On a world scale this is a minimal number. It suffices to point out that Czechoslovakia, with a population of 14 million, has the same number of spindles as all of China. It is even more telling that from the perspective of supplying the textile industry with raw materials, China is in a very favourable position: it is the number three country in the output of cotton. Although Chinese raw material is of a poorer quality than American cotton, this is not a hindrance to the development of the textile industry since only low-quality foreign goods go to China.

If we emphasise that the results achieved by China's industrial development are rather insignificant from the perspective of the global and European economies, then comparing China only with Asiatic countries produces a different picture: Japan in 1925 had five million spindles; India, 8 million; and China 3.5 million. This indicates that China has drawn very close to the standard of the most advanced countries in Asia.

If we examine the changing figures regarding the turnover of products of the textile industry, then we will also perceive large and very important changes which are expressed in the following facts. The import of textile goods which, according to Chinese statistics, occupied third place in 1914, are now in seventh place. Moreover, there has been a systematic decline in the import of foreign yarn. China produces yarn on its own. I will not stop to consider data on a whole series of other branches of manufacturing industry. Let us only look, for example, at the electricity industry in China. Prior to the war there were only 136 electric power plants in China; in 1925 the statistics show there were already 400. There are many such statistics, and they demonstrate that capitalist development had begun to penetrate all branches of production.

I would now like to turn to a series of generalisations which are of greater interest to us than numbers, which you can find for yourselves in Chinese sources. The questions which I now pose are the following: 1) Did imperialism retard the development of Chinese industry? 2) What role did foreign capital play in this development and what role did indigenous Chinese capital play? The answers to these two questions are very important in explaining the interests of the capitalist classes which are playing a leading role in the Chinese economy and politics.

The basic question which we must investigate before we turn to the social consequences of the development of capitalist industry in China is the question of whether imperialism developed and is developing the productive forces of China.

It would be quite absurd to assert that imperialism did not play a role in developing China. The construction of railroads and the equipping of mines and pits as a result of the first period of the penetration of capitalism in China prior to the World War are facts which it is impossible to deny with any theoretical sophistry.

Imperialism played an enormous role in awakening productive forces in China. But what does 'awakening productive forces in China' mean? Imperialism did not bring coal and iron to China; they were found in the Chinese earth. Imperialism also did not create the labour force. There were already millions among the mass of the Chinese peasantry who had no property and now there are tens of millions. To be sure, these propertyless working hands were not yet proletarians, because a person without property becomes a proletarian only when he is employed in a capitalist enterprise to create profit.

The role of imperialism was that of smashing the Chinese wall of social stagnation which separated China from the rest of the world. The railroads which forced their way into China brought it into contact with the world economy, and rendered possible the influence of the world economy. The investment of foreign capital helped to bring together surplus labour in the villages with the material elements existing in the country which, together, made up the capitalist economy, destroying the foundations of the old Chinese economy in the countryside and in this way playing a progressive role in the present as well.

The positive response to the question of the role of imperialism, acknowledgement that imperialism played an enormous progressive role in the development of China, is not a defence of imperialism or capitalism. We know that capitalism, while playing a progressive role, plays it at the expense of the masses, at the cost of the ruination and impoverishment of these masses, at the cost of disaster. Nowhere has capitalism taken another path; everywhere it has developed along the path of the suffering of the masses.

Is imperialism playing a progressive role in China now as well? This is quite a different question, and in order to answer it we must examine more attentively the fate of the development of capitalism in China over the past years. Let us look at railroad construction. Since 1912–13, China has not built any railroads, and this is one of the main reasons why Chinese industry has not developed at the pace which it might have developed. China has about 10,000 kilometres of railroads, but the minimal quantity of railroads China needs, according to the calculation of engineers and economists, is 50,000 kilometres. Why is foreign capital not building these railroads now? Here we encounter the change in the function of foreign capital in China. Foreign capital, penetrating into the Chinese economy, wanted to develop it under one condition: on the condition of the imperialist subjugation of China. From the time when the Chinese bourgeoisie was battling against the consortium in 1911–13, and refused to accept the terms of imperialism, a financial boycott of China actually commenced. Imperialism gave the Chinese people an ultimatum. Either you agree to my intrusion on the terms of enslavement or I will not develop the Chinese economy. Such was the political meaning of the financial approach of international imperialism.

Let us look at manufacturing industry. In all the time after the war the English have not only not built a single new textile factory, but they have managed to sell two of them to the Japanese and negotiations are ongoing to sell more. The French, the Americans, and the Germans have built no new factories in the past ten years. The reason for this is partly the war which diverted European capitalism away from the Far East, and partly the process of political disintegration which occurred in China after the war, and now the developing revolution. Only Japanese capital, which appeared on the Chinese market during the war, began feverishly constructing factories in China and purchasing existing enterprises, so that now about 30 percent of China's textile industry is already in the hands of Japanese capital. After the war, Japan is the only capitalist power which is developing Chinese industry. All the rest of development falls to the lot of the Chinese bourgeoisie itself which, taking advantage of the wartime situation and the diminished competition from cheap English, German, and other factory goods, itself began building factories, because high wartime prices enabled Chinese capitalists to compete. Thus, the social situation which came into being in China under the influence of imperialism hindered imperialism from further enslaving China, and since it was prepared to develop China only on condition of its own unchallenged monopoly, it then ceased taking part in the development of the country. But imperialism not only ceased being a powerful motor of China's economic development, it became a factor inhibiting that development. If foreign capital simply left the country, then China would probably find sufficient resources to tackle development on its own. No one can precisely calculate the amount of indigenous capital in China, but experts on the Chinese economy assert that on the basis of the slow accumulation in commerce, handicrafts, manufacturing, and agriculture in China, no less than a billion *taels* of available capital in silver has been formed. Data on the importation of precious metals from abroad into China, in the absence of significant export, suggests that this assertion is quite plausible. In any case, the development of Chinese industry, insofar as capital is involved, would not have encountered any insuperable obstacles.

Why has Chinese capital not squeezed out foreign capital more quickly than it has up till now? Because not only have the imperialists not left China, they are fighting for China and hindering its own development. How is this expressed? Above all, China does not have tariff autonomy. This is the greatest obstacle to China's industrial development. All countries in the world develop this way: when their industries are young, they defend these industries with tariffs and duties, not with tariffs and duties in the range of 2–5 percent, but 10–15 percent or more, depending upon the strength of a given branch of industry and the strength of the competition. The insane reality that China is subordinate to the customs tariff, which all branches of industry equally do not defend, leads to a situation in which the Chinese bourgeoisie are afraid to invest capital in Chinese industry. We know that the initial years of the development of capitalist industry in China led to an enormous number of bankruptcies. Capitalists got down to business not knowing enough about modern methods of industrial organisation; young Chinese engineers who had just finished studying abroad and had neither deep technical knowledge nor experience were in charge. Industry had to pay for its period of apprenticeship.

We in the Soviet Union built industry by relying on a much broader experience of capitalists which we received as an inheritance in the form of our engineers, bourgeois bookkeepers, directors and others whom we mobilised. And despite this, the high cost for industrial goods which Russian workers, peasants, and the urban poor pay is a result of the fact that we ourselves, without capitalists, are just learning how to do management and did not know enough about how to construct our state-run industries. How should we protect them from foreign competition? If we levied a five percent tariff, none of our branches of industry would have survived for two years. We protect our socialist construction via a monopoly of foreign trade. If we deem necessary a complete ban on the import of certain goods, we ban them or allow them in only at very high import duties. Chinese industry gets no protection from import tariffs. Imperialism, providing no means to develop industry, hinders Chinese capital from developing its own.

Let us look at other, no less important, facts. Let us look at the facts concerning the correlation between Chinese and foreign capital in the Chinese textile industry. There are 73 Chinese textile mills with 2,112,000 spindles and 13,500 machine tools; the English have five textile mills with 250,000 spindles and 2,863 machine tools; the Japanese have 41 textile mills with 1,208,000 spindles and about 6,000 machine tools. This means that more than 30 percent of the textile industry is in Japanese hands. How does this impact the Chinese economy? It does so in such a way that approximately 40 percent of the entire profits of the textile industry end up in Japanese hands. Are they fully invested in Chinese industry to promote its further development? We must put a big question mark over this. But at least there is no direct threat here.

Let us look at coal. If we look at extraction in millions of dollars, then in 1920, $50 million dollars of the coal industry was in the hands of foreigners:

$27 million in Japanese hands and $22 million in English hands. About 40 percent of the coal produced in Japanese mines is exported to Japan. And Chinese industry still imports foreign coal. Japan extracts coal for its own industry.

If we look at the production of iron and cast iron, we encounter the fact that Japanese capital of the Hanyeping mines is invested under the condition that for a period of many years a certain quantity of iron ore from the Hanyeping mines must be exported to Japan for the Japanese steel industry. Japanese mines in Manchuria export 90 percent of raw and semi-finished materials to Japan. This means that the bourgeoisie invest their capital in Chinese heavy industry in order to receive raw materials for themselves, and not for Chinese industry. And we see that the Chinese often need to import raw materials for themselves from abroad. Here we have a direct manifestation of exploitation of China in the simplest and most flagrant form. If the Japanese had been able to, they would have exported all the ore for themselves. In 1915, during the conflict between Japan and China over the so-called Twenty-One Demands, one of the conditions of the Japanese government was the subordination of China's heavy industry to Japan.[249] This demand was put forward by Japan with the intention of securing for itself the opportunity to exploit Chinese mines and collieries in the event of a war with America, mines and collieries which should be serving the development of Chinese industry.

In this way, imperialism began to be a factor inhibiting the development of Chinese capitalist industry. It does so in two ways: 1) Foreign capital refuses to take part in Chinese industry while simultaneously holding in its hands the mechanism of customs policy, and 2) The way Japanese capitalism functions by investing capital in Chinese industry, but trying to pour all the raw materials produced on Chinese soil into the development of Japanese rather than Chinese industry.

Thus, we arrive at the following theoretical conclusions. Chinese capitalism developed, in the first instance, owing to the influence of imperialism. Owing to the fact that imperialism smashed the wall of Chinese isolation from the world market. Notwithstanding its cruelty and contrary to its own will, it played the role of a progressive factor which awakened China. At the second stage, when, under the influence of all the consequences of this imperialist policy, the Chinese bourgeoisie arose and began to struggle against foreign imperialism, when the labouring masses then became involved in this struggle and a broad

---

249 The so-called Twenty-One Demands were an ultimatum to the Chinese government presented by Japan on 28 January 1915, acceptance of which would have turned China into a Japanese colony. Radek is mistaken. Nothing was said about China's heavy industry in this document.

nationalist movement was born, a change occurred in the policy of imperialism vis-a-vis China. Imperialism changed from a factor promoting development into a factor inhibiting the capitalist development of China.

Here we turn to an extraordinarily important theme which demands our special attention. After arousing modern production forces in China, capital then destroys the old Chinese system, ruins the countryside, and thereby creates conditions from which the demands of capitalist development in China find a revolutionary expression.

We will devote the next lecture not to the agrarian question, but to the Chinese banks and commerce as elements involved in the ruination of the countryside.

Lecture Sixteen

Before tackling the agrarian question, we need to examine the indirect ways by which capitalism broke down the Chinese countryside. There are basically two ways. One is the influence of capitalism, the influence of competition of industrial goods on peasant trade, on handicrafts, on the domestic labour of peasants, and the other is that of increasing taxes, increasing the exploitation of peasants by means of taxes.

Let us begin with the latter. What was the taxation system like in China prior to the beginning of the capitalist era? You are aware that prior to the war with Japan the Chinese central government had a very modest budget. The Chinese budget was equal to about 150 million rubles a year. The central administration received no more than 150 million rubles from the entire Chinese people in a year. Actual taxation was significantly higher. The English writer Chirol writes that local officials collected five times more than they sent to the central government.[250] Another English specialist on Chinese affairs, [H.B.] Morse,[251] thinks that officials collected only three times as much as they transmitted to the government.[252] How was this done? On the basis of a compromise in 1713 between the Manchu dynasty and local authorities, the amount of taxes the governor of a given province had to remit to the central government was precisely fixed, but how much tax he himself could levy was not established and, therefore, the governor tried to collect as much as he could.

---

250   See Chirol 1896.
251   Hosea Ballou Morse was actually an American. *Trasaltor's note*.
252   See Morse 1913.

Now let us consider what taxes were collected. Of the income of the Manchu government 35 percent comprised the land tax – the tax which peasants paid on land. Then came the salt tax: for each kilo of salt which a peasant bought, he paid a certain tax to the government. The third source of income was customs tariffs. All the other taxes played a rather small role. Thus, the land tax was 35 percent, customs and transit income was 35 percent, 10 percent local customs duties, and 10 percent the salt monopoly.

Was this tax burden heavy? One of the causes of the Taiping Rebellion was the extraordinarily heavy taxes, but these taxes grew even more from the moment imperialist states penetrated China following its defeat in the war with Japan. In 1894, China still had no external debt. The foreigners tried to thrust loans upon China, but the Chinese government was very much afraid of these foreign loans and when they had resort to loans during the Taiping Rebellion or during the expedition to Formosa,[253] the government quickly repaid them. But the war with Japan and the indemnities which had to be paid immediately created, in one fell swoop, a comparatively large indebtedness for China. At the end of the Sino-Japanese War, China wound up with a debt of 500 million rubles. The Boxer Indemnity of 450 million *taels*, that is, 700 million rubles, further increased this debt, so that in 1911 China's debt exceeded one billion rubles. But this was not the end of it. Simultaneously with the imposition of the indemnity in 1901, the imperialist powers decided to take control of the customs revenues in order to ensure payment of the indemnity. You know that during the Taiping Rebellion, administration of the customs revenues passed into the hands of foreigners, but at that time they only collected the customs revenues while the Chinese government disposed of them. In the Boxer Protocol of 1901, the imperialist powers stipulated that to ensure the regular payment of interest, the customs revenues received in the open ports would be handed over to the Inspector General of Customs (this inspector was the Englishman Sir Robert Hart) and to the English banks in China which paid the interest to the foreign powers. These duties constituted 35 percent of the total revenues of the Chinese government. Thus 35 percent of the revenues were wrested from the hands of the government and passed into the hands of foreign capitalists. This already created a large deficit in the Chinese budget. Moreover, the war with Japan, the Boxer Rebellion, and the Russo-Japanese War showed China that if it did not create a modern army, it would be divided into pieces. The Manchu government attempted to modernise the army. Yuan Shikai, while still the gov-

---

253   This refers to the Japanese expedition to Taiwan in 1874; see reference 112 to this chapter. The Qing government had to give to the Japanese an indemnity of 18.7 tonnes of silver.

ernor of Zhili, began to create a modern army, armed with modern weapons; he invited foreign instructors and this again demanded a lot of money. Owing to the fact that 35 percent of revenue was going directly into the hands of foreigners, that expenditures on the army were growing, and that the national movement, which grew by leaps and bounds after the Boxer Rebellion, demanded the opening of schools and sought the modernisation of administration, new expenditures were required and the Manchu government turned out to have a hole in its pocket. The budget was completely ruined and, to a certain degree, the fall of the Manchu government was the result of the budgetary disaster, the diminution of sources of taxation which had sustained the power of the Manchus.

The Manchu dynasty turned to foreign capital, requesting financial aid to reorganise the budget. The foreigners proposed that the dynasty also give them control over the land tax. In 1904 Sir Robert Hart addressed the Chinese government with a report in which he said that if the collection of the land tax was made the responsibility of foreigners then this land tax, which then yielded no more than 100 million *taels*, would be increased to 400 million.[254] But the mood in the country would not allow the government to do this. The English ambassador [Jordan] suggested to the English government that it give a loan, but the Shanghai-Hong Kong Bank cautioned that the south was so anti-Manchu that it might not acknowledge this loan. The English government then refused to extend a loan, and this was the immediate reason for the fall of the Manchu dynasty. Soldiers were not paid, and a soldiers' uprising began and, as you know, in Wuchang in 1911 these rebellious troops united and began to seize one province after another. The central problem of the 1911 Revolution was finding the means to cover the deficit. When the comprador bourgeoisie, after uniting with Yuan Shikai, triumphed over Sun Yat-sen, compelling him to give up power and step down from the presidency,[255] then the international financial markets, the financiers from all countries, offered Yuan Shikai a loan of 250 million rubles, that is, a reorganisation loan to cover the deficit. But to ensure payment on the interest of the loan, foreign capital also took control of the salt monopoly, the salt revenues. Thus, 45 percent of Chinese tax revenues wound up in the hands of foreigners. Almost half of all the revenues received by the Chinese government were in the hands of foreign capital and could not

---

254 Hart's report was published in *North China Herald* on 5 April 1904.
255 Sun Yat-sen, who was chosen provisional president of China by the Nanjing assembly of representatives from revolutionary provinces on 29 December 1911, stepped down in favour of Yuan Shikai on 13 February 1912. The Provisional Senate unanimously elected Yuan Shikai provisional president on 15 February.

be used for China's domestic needs: building schools, railroads, and creation of an army. This is the main reason why a strong central government could not be established after the fall of the Manchu dynasty.

The capitalist world mocks China's inability to become a strong power. It depicts the disintegration of the Chinese state, which we have witnessed over the past years, as some sort of unusual phenomenon. But if one deprived the King of England of half of his revenues which he uses to maintain his army and his bureaucratic apparatus, then the English government would collapse just like China. The collapse of the Chinese state is the result of the imperialist policies of the foreign powers in China. Why has it not been possible to create a unified central power in China from the death of Yuan Shikai right up to the present? If you approach this question from an economic perspective, from the perspective of establishing state power, you will find nothing secretive about this. The reason for the collapse of state power is very simple – the state had no money to maintain its armies and, therefore, these armies had to feed themselves. Each of the Chinese military chieftains who possessed their own army, seized a part of China in order to levy taxes for their own needs.

The final reason for the collapse of state power in China was the seizure by foreign capital of the financial sources of the Chinese government. Already in the past, the central authorities had a hard time compelling provincial officials to send money to Beijing. Needing to increase its revenue, the government now had to take more from the country than it had previously, but at the same time it was unable to provide for the bureaucracy and the military, so naturally each governor-general tried to extract as much revenue as he needed from his particular province and not hand it over to Beijing. In the final years of its existence, the Manchu government received no more than seven million in revenue per annum; it depended completely on what it was able to collect in Beijing and its environs. The collapse of the state resulted from the fact that foreign capital imposed enormous debts on China, and took half of China's revenues to secure these debts. On the other hand, the collapse of state power had larger consequences – namely that, since half of the revenues were in the hands of foreigners, each military governor at least had to double the revenue from his own province to support his provincial administration. The military governors did not limit themselves to this, however, but continued to raise taxes further, since after the collapse of the central authorities, a struggle commenced among various military cliques. Nowhere was it said how much land should belong to Zhang Zuolin and the Anfu Club, to the Zhili clique and Wu Peifu.[256] A

---

256 Anfu Club (named after Anfu hutong [alley] in Beijing) and Zhili military clique (named after Zhili province) were factions of warlords in the early republican China.

struggle between them for territory began, because each wanted to seize as many provinces as they could to increase their revenues. This led to an enormous increase in the size of armies. At present, China has no fewer than 1.5 to 2 million men under arms. During the Manchu dynasty, the Chinese army was very insignificant; now China has to spend enormous sums to maintain these armies which serve as the instrument with which the militarists retain their grip on provincial power. Thus, an indirect consequence of imperialist policy and of the collapse of state power in China is the enormous increase in taxation. Despite this collapse we know that China's trade turnover has increased in recent years and, therefore, customs revenues have grown, but simultaneously all other taxes have also grown due to the intensification of tax assessments by the provincial militarists.

What have been the consequences for the agricultural economy? The first consequence is the increase in tax assessments on the part of the provincial authorities. The provincial authorities are increasing the land tax. In addition to the general tax which they levied before, they have increased local surcharges and tried under various pretexts to collect this tax. First, they are engaged in constant warfare and because of wars they are in need right away of significant material means. Second, none of them knows how long he will be in charge of any given province and whether he will be crushed by any one of his neighbours. Therefore, every one of them says: Seize the day, for who knows what tomorrow will bring. There are no statistics which would enable us to calculate by how much taxes on the peasants have been raised. In the past China lacked a precise budget. Since 1909, there has been no overall Chinese budget; Yuan Shikai tried to compile an estimate of state tax receipts, but these were assumptions without precise calculations. *Dujun* [military governors] did not record how much they collected from the peasantry; they preferred that the peasants not know how much they had paid. There is no possibility of precisely establishing the size of the tax; nevertheless, we know very well on the basis of a multitude of information – newspaper accounts and complaints – just how the tax burden has grown in China. To a significant extent the peasant movement is a struggle against the inhuman exploitation of the peasant masses by means of raising taxes. Moreover, peasants pay a whole series of other levies, suffer other losses which they did not have before. Earlier the Chinese army was insignificant. Now in order to build up their armies, military governors arrange entire hunting parties in the villages. I recently had occasion to read a report which stated that in Beijing, the nation's capital, there were weeks when all the coolies vanished out of fear that Zhang Zuolin would take them into his army or draft them as labourers in the army. During the endless battles among militarists, often for months at a time peasants were forced to carry provisions and ammunition for their armies; thus, in addition to very high taxes, they also provided free labour to the militarists.

All of these changes must have caused a lot of destruction to the peasant economy. One of the consequences of the collapse of state power was general impoverishment, the ruination of the peasantry. This ruination was a general fact and when the imperialist powers pointed to this ruination, they only forgot to add that they themselves were complicit. This was the result of their financial policy in China which led to the collapse of state power, but these financial consequences of imperialism – the growth of taxes – were not the only means by which international capital destroyed the economy of the Chinese peasantry. The Chinese government debt, which did not yet exist in 1894, is now the equivalent of 2.5 billion rubles and is one of the most powerful instruments by which foreign capitalism destroys the Chinese peasant economy. Militarism, which did not exist in China prior to the world war, is now the second powerful instrument for destroying the peasant economy. The third instrument is competition from foreign capital. How is this manifested? If you consult works on the history of Chinese handicrafts, then you will see that in the period prior to imperialism, in a majority of cases handicraftsmen in the city only made luxury items. Objects of mass domestic use remained the product of domestic peasant labour. Not only in the winter, but in the summer as well, peasants were busy at home; they had hand-operated machines and produced items of mass consumption – working on leather goods, making silk and cotton textiles, tea, and specialised technical goods that were the products of household labour which served as a source of a significant part of peasant income. Now all of this production is under the constant blows of foreign competition. Why? The reasons are very simple. Foreign goods imported into China pay customs duties of only 2.5–5 percent and they substitute all provincial taxes. Foreign goods do not pay *lijin*, foreign textiles in Chinese territory do not pay any taxes except for municipal ones. In Shanghai, for example, foreign factories only pay taxes associated with municipal welfare; they do not pay state taxes. Because of this, no matter how hard he tries, the Chinese peasant is unable to compete with the products of foreign industry. The Chinese handicrafts industry will either collapse entirely or the peasants employed in these industries will have to work significantly more while earning significantly less than before. In an economic sense foreign competition is no less destructive than the militarists' tax increases in the way it impacts peasant production.

We know that we lack any statistics on this. We only have a mass of information that has made its way into the economic and daily press which shows that all of the handicraft industries are ruined except for those in which the Chinese produce cult objects, objects which foreign industry does not produce. All of this puts peasants in a condition in which they lose a significant part of the sources of income comprising their budget and this, along with increased taxes, is the reason for the growing neediness of the peasant masses. It is not difficult to imagine the consequences of such a situation. Peasants must pay more and earn significantly less and this has created a serious crisis in Chinese agriculture which, over the past twenty-five years, wholly changed the face of the Chinese countryside. Only by bearing in mind the overall situation in which this rural crisis has arisen are we able to understand what is happening in the countryside, why the Chinese countryside has wholly changed during the past twenty-five years, and why the Chinese countryside is now the greatest revolutionary factor.

How have all these factors influenced the distribution of land, how have they brought about changes in land ownership? How have they influenced the cultivation of land and the relations between the peasantry and usurer capital and commercial capital? We will see this next when we turn to analysing agrarian statistics. These agrarian statistics are very weak, like statistics in China in general, but despite all their defects they demonstrate that the assertion that there are no classes in China, that every peasant in China is equally wealthy and that, therefore, there is no class conflict in China, that such an assertion is divorced from reality. There are few countries on earth in which such a strong agrarian crisis rages and where the agrarian question, therefore, stands so starkly in the centre of all economics and politics as it does in China.

Lecture Seventeen

We now turn to an analysis of the influence of capitalism on the agrarian situation in China. Before beginning this analysis I would like to draw the attention of those comrades who know Russian to a work by comrade Volin (who has been working in China for several years already), 'Basic Problems of the Agricultural Economy in China', published at the end of last year in the journal *Na agrarnom fronte* (numbers 10 and 11–12).[257] I recommend this work to all comrades. I think this work poses the questions in the right way. It is based upon all of the literature which the author then had access to except for two new works which came out subsequently. Moreover, the author was

---

257   See Volin 1926.

able to study these phenomena on the spot, and all the other articles which have appeared in Russian on the agrarian question have been based upon this work.

My task is to supplement Volin's data, expand upon it, and point out several errors, but I think his article should be translated into Chinese. It is short – one and a half printed sheets [i.e., about 35 pages] – and serves as an excellent guide for posing the basic questions.

The first one requiring an answer given our approach to studying the agrarian question in China is the question of the forms of landholding – who holds the land in China at present? We analysed this question already in relationship to the past in the introductory lectures in this course when we posed the question of who owns land, and then I devoted an entire lecture to proving that all the stories concerning the nationalisation of land in China are legends. Nationalisation of land signifies in the first place prohibition on the sale of land. China entered the capitalist period with complete freedom to buy and sell land in the absence of nationalisation; all the agrarian development of capitalism in China has taken place on the basis of the free sale and purchase of land.

What groups exist in Chinese landholding? Chinese statistics in this area are lacking any scientific basis, but they do provide raw material which one may use with appropriate caution, and the regrouping of statistics from 1917 done by the Russian researcher Volin gives the following basic figures.

As much as possible I will try to give the most indispensable figures so as not to tire the comrades, hoping that they will work through Volin's article. He identifies four basic groups among Chinese landowners, the same groups which Lenin indicated in the resolution on the agrarian question at the Second Comintern Congress on the basis of agrarian relations.[258] A group of peasants with very small parcels of land, who are unable to feed themselves from the harvests they produce on these parcels of land, and then the groups of small, medium, and large peasants. What figures does Volin provide for each of these groups? Here we must bear in mind one thing: that one *mu* of land is not one and the same thing in Shandong province as in Canton, near Hankou or near Shanghai. Depending on whether the province is far from or close to the sea, far from or close to large cities, one *mu* of land will have different value. Near large cities, for example, land can be used for market-gardening, and someone who owns a few *mu* of land can live very well, raising produce which will fetch a high price in the city. But it is obvious that when we wish to examine agrarian relations in China generally, then we need to engage in abstractions, that is,

---

258 See Lenin 1971a [1920], pp. 170–5.

not consider the various prices and various significance of units of land in various parts of China, but we need to try and identify certain basic groups. We take the following as the basic groups: 1–20 *mu* peasants with very small parcels of land, 20–40 *mu* small peasants; 40–75 *mu* middle peasants; 75–100 *mu* well-off, rich peasants – kulaks. Following this division, we arrive at the following figures: 49 percent, that is, about half of all peasant households in China have less than 20 *mu* of land. This half of the peasantry comprises peasants who are unable by any means to live by working only on their own land. How much land does this half of the peasants possess? Half of the peasants have in their hands 24 million *mu* or 15 percent of the land. The next group are small peasants with 20–40 *mu*. We know that in some provinces 40 *mu* is no longer a small peasant, but if one takes figures from all of China, then we have 75 percent of the population who together have 35 percent of the land. This means that three-quarters of the peasants have just as much land as the top 11 percent of rich peasants. I must confess that when I read these figures in Volin, I thought that the Russian revolutionary, coming to China, saw everything more sharply than things were in reality. I was convinced that these figures exaggerated the sharpness of differentiation in the Chinese countryside. I thought the same when it was a question not of land ownership, but of land use, which I will speak about further. In a while I will give you some material which was not yet known to Volin – works by Americans and Germans that confirm these completely fantastic figures. What do these figures indicate? They speak, first of all, to the existence of a strong kulak stratum in the countryside – 11 percent, which owns 35 percent of the land. They speak to the great poverty of three-quarters of the entire countryside and, in this way, completely destroy the legend that social equality exists in China, that there are no huge class contradictions in the Chinese countryside. These figures themselves speak of very large class contradictions in the countryside. But perhaps these are general figures derived by means of general statistical calculations? If you take the works which Volin summarises here, namely, the works of Dittmer, Tayler and Nanjing University,[259] they will show you that these figures which Volin derived by means of investigating overall Chinese statistics are wholly confirmed in the investigations by Professors Dittmer and Tayler with regard to small regions. There is a work relating to Shandong and another work resulting from investigation of a number of villages in Jiangsu.[260] Both these works fully confirm the

---

259 See Dittmer 1918 and Tayler 1924. There is no reference to a work by Nanjing University in Volin's article.

260 It is not clear what works Radek had in mind.

general statistical data. I will not tire you with further statistical figures, but turn now to the question of land utilisation, not how the land was divided juridically, but how the land was worked and on what conditions.

The figures cited demonstrate that peasants belonging to the first two groups – peasants with very small parcels of land, and small peasants – were unable to live only from the land which they had in their own hands. They had to rent land, and we see that 28 percent of peasants were private renters. So the 28 percent were peasants who possessed no land of their own, but worked on land belonging to other persons. 22 percent were peasants who had some land of their own and partly rented land and only 50 percent of peasants worked only on their own land. Thus, to a greater or lesser degree, 50 percent worked on rented land. What was this group of peasants and what was their social profile? There is no doubt that among these peasants was a certain percentage of very rich peasants who had capital, lived near the cities, possessed the means [of production], and rented more land from which to receive a profit. It is impossible to determine statistically how large this group was, but the basic mass of peasant renters rented land not for profit, but because otherwise they could not survive. Who were these renters, who rented out land, and who took it?

I mentioned to you two new works on the agrarian question in China. The first work is by the German agronomist Wagner[261] who lived sixteen years in Shandong province and directed an agronomic experimental station. The work is devoted for the most part to the technology of agriculture in China. Everyone who wishes to study the agrarian question in China should familiarise themselves with Wagner's work. The second book is by the American Mallory, the former secretary of the China International Famine Relief Commission.[262] What we have here are not agitational brochures and casual investigations, but works whose contents deserves the most serious attention.

So, who is it that rents out land? What groups comprise the large proprietors-landlords in China? In his book, Wagner gives the following data on groups from which the landlord class in China derives: first of all, the descendants of the Manchu court, high-level bureaucrats who received land from the Manchu dynasty; they themselves did not work the land, but rented it out. He asserts that this group still exists in North China, plays the same role, and is the first stratum of the large landlords. The second stratum from which large landlords are recruited, says Wagner, are officials who invest capital which they wrested

---

261 Wagner, *Landwirtschaft in China*. Radek's note. This refers to Wagner 1926.
262 Mallory, *China the Land of Famine*. Radek's note. This refers to Mallory 1926.

from the peasants into land. They, too, do not work the land themselves, but rent the land to peasants. The third group are merchants. He says that this is the most widely-distributed group of landlords, that even ordinary merchants and even better-off craftsmen try to buy a bit of land in their village and then rent it out to peasants in need of land. What is the significance of these three groups that Wagner names? This material is of great importance to us because it poses the question of the nature of the landlord class. What is it? Are they feudalists or Chinese merchant large landowners? It is worth pondering this question, because a lot of current questions about the Chinese revolution follow from the answer to it. All of the material that Wagner presents demonstrates that it is not a matter of feudal large landlords, that commercial landowners predominate, merchants who rent out land for the simple reason that the interest which they receive from the capital they invest in land is at least 18 percent. Wagner presents a whole series of calculations demonstrating this. A merchant who fears risking his property in industry, who fears having his property confiscated by powerful militarists, rents out land, that is, he invests his capital in land because he receives a large rent. In what form do peasants pay this rent and how do peasants become dependent on the landlord? The answer to this question also provides very interesting material to illuminate the nature of the agrarian problem in China. How is it that 75 percent of the peasantry live in unbelievable poverty? How did it happen that 50 percent of the peasantry were compelled to rent land? Mallory supplies the answer in his book. First, he enumerates the taxes that peasants pay. Both Mallory and Wagner conclude that peasants in China pay higher taxes than peasants in any other country. Wagner gives the following calculations. He analyses three peasant households in various districts of Shandong province, comparing and analysing their budgets in the most detailed way possible, and comes to the following conclusion. Peasants pay fifteen times more taxes on a given unit of land than Prussian peasants paid in 1866. In another place, he supplies the following figures. In Prussia large landed tracts belong to the state which rents them out. The rent which peasants pay equals 3.5 percent of the value of the land. Wagner analyses a specific group of peasant estates in Shandong and comes to the conclusion that they pay 18.5 percent of the value of the land. Prussian peasants pay 3.5 percent rent to the Prussian state for the use of land in its formal estates, but in China peasants pay 18.5 percent. This simple fact, even without such misfortunes as drought etc., forces peasants to resort to loans and here we again have a series of data that cast very vivid light on the nature of renting. From whom do peasants borrow money when they find themselves in a difficult position? I will cite data provided by Wagner and Mallory. Mallory says the following: the state in China pays up to 25 percent annually for short-term loans. The peasant-trader, the well-off peasant, whom no one doubts will repay his debt, has to pay from three to five percent interest per month on loans he receives. Where can a small peasant get a loan? He will not go to a bank, because a bank will not give him a 10–20 ruble loan. He will either go to the merchant who purchases his grain and other agricultural products and get a loan from him or he will go to a pawnshop. In the American investigation attention is paid to the fact that pawnshops, which everywhere in the world are not considered respectable establishments (I consider pawnbrokers as petty swindlers) are greatly respected in China, because peasants cannot live without pawnshops. These establishments have social value. What percent interest do peasants pay? In the cities, they pay up to 100 percent; moreover, if disaster has gripped a large province then peasants have nothing they can pawn in a pawnshop, then they go to rich peasants and merchants who give them money which the peasants are unable to repay. Then the peasant often has to pay 200–300 percent interest if he does not wish to die.

Wagner gives the following data. He says there are no state credit establishments, but even in the smallest burg there is a pawnshop and private moneylenders, that in China the proprietor of a pawnshop is thought to occupy a very respectable position, and a pawnshop is seen as an enterprise producing the greatest profit. Moneylenders accept not only moveable property as security, but also land; moreover, they never give loans worth more than half the value of the given security. Who lends money to peasants? The merchant lends money as an advance against the harvest. These advances are the worst disease of the Chinese peasantry, because the peasant constantly falls into debt, and winds up losing his land. Wagner talks about 10 percent monthly interest and adds that nowhere in the world are peasants able to pay such rates; everywhere such rates lead to the total ruination of peasants.

What do these data tell us? They tell us that peasants, ruined by an aggregation of disasters – oppression by militarism, competition from foreign goods, famine and other disasters brought about by the absence of concern on the part of the state regarding restoration of the timber industry and the regulation of rivers, are driven into penury, fall into the hands of merchant capital, and that this merchant capital is the primary factor in the destruction of the peasant economy, a parasite growing at the expense of the total pauperisation of the peasantry. We have in China the remains of a feudal economy in several regions – Manchuria and others. We have in China not only feudal forms of rent, but even slave forms of rent. We know not only of peasants who come to the land with only a whip, who receive land from the landlord, receive tools, and become wholly dependent upon him, practically in serf-like dependence. We know that there are renters who are the private property of the landlord; slave labour exists. But these forms cannot conceal the fact that the class which employs these methods of exploiting the peasantry are not old feudal landlords, but landlords who came from the bourgeoisie, from the merchant stratum, from among the officials. When at the dawn of capitalist development, Venetian and Florentine merchants also used slave labour (all of the Near East was the region from which they received slaves) this form of exploitation still was not feudal, but capitalist.

English merchants from Liverpool traded in slaves for hundreds of years; they bought them in Africa and sold them in America. One cannot compare the merchants from Liverpool in the seventeenth and eighteenth centuries with the slaveowners of Africa who were unfamiliar with a money economy, and who sold slaves in order to receive gold and other ornaments which they used to buy beautiful women. Here it is a question of a capitalist economy. The political significance of this issue is the following: Because the landlord class came from the bourgeoisie, was closely tied to the merchant and industrial bourgeoisie, that the same capitalist who perhaps owned shares in some industrial enterprise simultaneously invested money in the countryside and was a landlord – owing to this the Chinese bourgeoisie cannot support the peasantry in its struggle against all the burdens which the payment of rent places upon it. The Chinese bourgeoisie cannot be the liberator of the peasantry. Everywhere throughout the world, generally speaking, the bourgeoisie has been a class with an interest in having the peasants liberated and no longer paying tribute to the feudalists, so they would have buyers for their goods. Naturally, in the eighteenth-century revolution, too, part of the petty bourgeoisie had some land. In the eighteenth century the French nobility sold part of their land to the grand bourgeoisie and various Parisian bankers were also interested in the liberation of the peasant. But the broad strata of the bourgeoisie were not concerned that the peasants were paying high rentals to landowners.

In China the bourgeoisie is a class with an interest in exploiting the peasantry, and therefore not the feudal, but the bourgeois nature of this parasitical stratum will result in the Chinese bourgeoisie struggling against the national liberation movement's efforts to free the peasantry from its unprecedentedly difficult position.

The next question worth considering is the material conditions of the peasantry that have come about from the loss of a significant part of their land, the accumulation of this land in the hands of merchant capital which has created a new landlord class on the foundation of high norms of rental payments. When I read in the works of our comrades that Chinese peasants pay 50, 60, 70 percent of their harvest to the landlord, I could not believe these figures. I considered this an exaggeration by the revolutionaries. The works by both of the authors I have cited fully confirm these data. Both Mallory and Wagner state that the minimal norm for rent is 50 percent. The historian of contemporary China Schüler, in a new work on the peasant movement in China[263] (and he knows Chinese, was recently in China, even in Canton) relates how, when conversing with merchants in Shanghai, he questioned them about the situation of peasants in that particular region. Wishing to say that the peasants were doing well, they replied that in that region peasants paid only half of their harvest. Wagner and Schüler fully confirm the figures of 60, 70, 80 percent which I thought were an exaggeration for propaganda purposes. Wagner says that three-fifths of the harvest goes for rent. This is a widespread phenomenon in China. It is perfectly clear that there is no need here and now to disabuse ourselves of the picture of the indigence of China's peasants. In the works of Volin and Mallory you will find a summary of English and American works in which peasant budgets are analysed. In Wagner's work there is an analysis of budgets in a whole series of districts in Shandong province. It is well-known that the peasants in Shandong are not in the most lamentable condition, and Wagner comes to the conclusion that if a peasant family did not exploit the unpaid labour of its own relatives, if it had to remunerate this labour, then the peasant would close his accounts not with the existing deficit, but would generally be unable to maintain his household. I will not repeat all the figures about peasant budgets provided by Volin and the American and German scholars whom I have mentioned. You know this better than we do. This is very important to us, because thanks to this we receive a realistic picture of how things are. Mallory presents the following basic figures. He cites the portion of food that an Englishman in prison receives. He says if you take one-third of this and consider it sufficient to feed a Chinese peasant, then we must recognise that 70 percent of Chinese peasants do not receive one-third of the food which an Englishman gets in prison. This is Mallory's conclusion from all the budgets which he examined. I will not go into all the details here, I will only give a summary.

The results are as follows. The capitalist development of China which created in China the beginnings of modern industry, awakened forces of production, and provided a stimulus to the construction of railroads, mines, pits, and the banking system, produced only a colossal amount of destruction in the countryside. Naturally, in the Chinese countryside as well there are small sprouts of new capitalist land-ownership and agriculture. First, in Manchuria where a capitalist type peasant is coming into being; second along the Yangzi

---

263   This refer to Schüler 1927.

River – the top layer of the peasantry. And this 11 percent of peasants who have begun to practice a capitalist economy – this is what is new, the positive side of what capitalism has brought to the countryside. But for the great mass of the peasantry, capitalism has brought ruin, destroyed their private property, and turned them into a class of renters. Those who own their own land labour under conditions which not only fail to give them a profit as small proprietors, but place them into a position considerably worse than that of the urban slaves of capitalism. Therefore, the agrarian question is the primary issue which has created a revolutionary situation in China. The agrarian question in China is sharper than it was in Russia. The Chinese revolution will be, above all, a peasant war. Having sketched in the last lecture the basic motive forces of development, the chief centres of contradiction, having examined the development of industry, the development of finances, and the ruination of the countryside, let us now turn, therefore, to what interests us most of all, namely, the contemporary revolutionary movement, its development and its problems. Now we will be dealing not so much with history, as with answers to very current questions of Chinese development. The lectures on the economic history of China from the time of its conquest showed us the following phases. The first stage was the stage when capitalism entered China, and opened China with the help of arms. This period reached its high point in the Boxer Uprising when China surrendered to foreign capitalism. The second stage of this development was the social changes that capitalism brought about in China. These social changes directly brought about, first, the construction of modern industry, the creation of the modern bourgeoisie and the working class and, second, the destruction of the old way of life in the countryside. These are the two main centres, the two main foci of the Chinese conditions of the Chinese revolution.

In the next lecture we must examine the development of the Chinese revolutionary movement after the Boxer Uprising, the development of Sunyatsenism, the experience of the 1911 Revolution, the rise of the Guomindang, the rise of the modern workers' and peasants' movement in China. These will comprise the next set of lectures, after which we will turn to the decisive questions of what should be the programme of the Chinese revolution, how should we build the state in China, how should we develop the economy in China, what should be the economic programme for the revolution of workers and peasants, and by what means should China fight against foreign imperialism? All these questions will require that we return constantly to economic problems. I think that even the superficial survey which we have been able to give in this course has already provided you with basic material so that our political judgements may be grounded not in our desires, but in facts.

RGASPI. F. 326. Op. 2. D. 33. Ll. 1–160.
Typescript, memograph, unsigned.

Published in Russian: *Istoriia revoliutsionnogo dvizheniia v Kitae: Kurs lektsii 1926–27 goda* ('History of the Revolutionary Movement in China: The 1926–27 Lecture Course'). Moscow: UTK im. Sun Yat-sena, 1926–1927.

Published in Chinese: *Zhongguo geming yundong shi* (History of the revolutionary movement in China), Translated by Keren (Liu Renjing), Shanghai: Xin yuzhou shudian, 1929; Second ed. Shanghai: Xin yuzhou shudian, 1931; Third ed. Shanghai: Xinken shudian, 1932; Fouth ed. Shanghai: Xinken shudian, 1933.

CHAPTER 3

Controversial Questions of Chinese History: Lecture to the Society of Marxist Historians
26 November 1926, Stenographic Report

The development of the Chinese revolution confronts the young Chinese Communist Party with the necessity of determining the social relations of the forces in the country and the direction of the development of the country.[1] The whole question of the Chinese economy, the relations of classes ⟨...⟩ [question], arising from the capitalist development of China, depends at the same time on China's past. The simple fact is that contemporary capitalism only annexed the maritime regions of China, that in a considerable part of China there are social relations which have nothing in common with that which we call contemporary capitalism, or which arise from contemporary capitalist industry. All this demonstrates that a scientific orientation is impossible without a study of China, as a precondition of the political [activity] of the Chinese Communist Party. It goes without saying that a Party does not begin by considering how things were earlier, but all the same a historical party is bound to try and orientate its policies towards the study of those processes which it leads, and therefore it is no accident, that with the rise of the workers' movement with us in Russia, the proletariat as hegemon of the revolution tried to establish its hegemony by studying and offering its point of view on the country's past. The Chinese Communist Party is young throughout, not educated in Marxism and too inexperienced to be in a position to deal with this task. The intelligentsia in its ranks, to whom this task falls, is in a position to radically reject [?], but not in a position to provide a map of the development of China corresponding to Marxist methods. How many times have we spoken with the most enlightened representatives of the Chinese revolution, but, when it came to dealing with such a simple fact as the restoration of a dynasty, they simply replied to us that that was a legend of the Chinese mandarinate, but that this is a developing movement.[2]

---

1 In connection with several stylistic errors in the stenographic record of the lecture, the document is published with minor abbreviations.
2 Thus in the text. The sense of the phrase given is not fully comprehensible. It is not clear, for example, what Radek had in mind in the words 'a legend of the Chinese mandarinate'.

The revolutionaries heading the Chinese movement today have no material and no revolutionary point of view worked out, even in relation to such a movement as the Beijing revolution in the first half of the nineteenth century, which embraced tens of millions of the population.[3] We were too remote from Chinese affairs to be in a position to deal with this question, and therefore the grandiose development of the revolution in China caught us out completely. We are not in a position to give Chinese comrades a fully worked out picture of the development of socio-political relations in China. This has implications for the most practical questions: in relation to the agrarian question, to the evaluation of such phenomena as military warlordships against which the struggle is now directed. The foundation of the University by Sun Yat-sen[4] set us this task. It was clear that it was impossible to teach Chinese revolutionaries Marxism and Leninism without being in a position to apply them to Chinese realities, or without responding to the past of the Chinese people.

I had the good or bad fortune to listen to Professor Conrady for several semesters during the first revolution[5] (a Chinese was appointed for Chinese history) but now, after only two years of work, I would not have dared to appear before you with the working hypothesis which I have developed on the basis of my work, for I must say (and I will justify this), that my hypothesis arises to a large extent from insufficiently studied material. The fact is that history does not allow us to wait until everything has been thoroughly studied. We must cast light [on history], but our understanding of Chinese history is such that it entirely coincides with a Confucian understanding, though this question at least should be clear for us, even if only on the basis that Confucianism is two thousand years old and it cannot aspire to the heights of the Marxist world view.

I will provide just two concrete examples so as to demonstrate how great our illiteracy is in this field. One of the few who know the Chinese language in our Party of Bolsheviks is comrade Ivanov, who is sitting in Beijing learning the language. He has expressed the opinion that Chinese peasants are private landowners.[6] To which another comrade, an author of fat tomes, called him an ignoramus and said that private landownership does not exist in China.[7] I am not going to speak about the curiosity that the first of the authors quoted

---

3   It is not clear which Beijing revolution in the first half of the 19th century is meant. Most likely, Radek has in mind the Boxer Uprising of the end of the 19th and the beginning of the 20th century, during which the rebels occupied Beijing for a short period.
4   Thus in the text. It should be: the foundation of the Sun Yat-sen University.
5   This refers to the Russian Revolution of 1905–7, but Radek is mistaken. He attended Professor Conrady's lectures after the revolution, in 1908–9, when he lived in Leipzig.
6   See Ivin [Ivanov] 1925, p. 110.
7   See Khodorov 1925, pp. 88–91.

expressly proves that private landownership exists in China. Such an oddity does not belong to the field of literary criticism, but [there is] a well-known reference to authors, which they had not read. But the very possibility of a dispute about whether there is in a country of 400 million population, with 11 [thousand] kilometres of railways, nationalised property, assuming the existence of state nationalisation, [speaks for itself]. There must be state power, and this strong power is already possible. This presentation of the question already demonstrates the dimensions of the ABC space which exist in this field.

But this is not just a matter of illiteracy, but of the fact that we have not thought about this question. I will permit myself to cite here an essay by a highly literate Marxist from whom everyone can learn something, an essay by comrade Varga in the November and December issues of *Planovoe khoziaistvo* of last year, in which comrade Varga tries to give a general formulation of the regime in China.[8] He asks himself: what the Chinese state is, what class rules in China, and to that question he gives a completely astonishing reply. He writes as follows: 'It seems to us that the reasons for the absence of a native Chinese capitalism are as follows: firstly, there did not exist a strong state organisation based on compulsion, which might have enslaved the workers in the service of the capitalists. Secondly, central and local state power originated in China from the necessity of regulating water supply, defence from floods and guaranteeing the irrigation of land. Its power originated from deeply peaceful objectives, and not as in Europe, in the struggle of royal power with the feudalists and the militarily equipped urban bourgeoisie. As a result, apart from the gigantic dimensions of the state, especially after the building of the Great Wall, significant areas of China remained desertified as a result of foreign wars, so state power took on a purely pacific character. As a result, a state power of a totally special type was formed, unknown in each of the areas of European culture, namely the power of the literati'.

And so, the state grew in a struggle with water, secondly, state power did not conduct wars. Thirdly, state power did not have the means of compulsion in respect of the working class, and fourthly, state power was not connected with any class, but was connected solely with literacy.

Comrades, I do not want to abuse your attention, otherwise I would have read you a quotation from Mencius. He was a student of Confucius,[9] one of the greatest writers, in whose book we find such clear reflections of feudalism as scarcely exist in a single work of European literature. And in the work of this

---

8 See Varga 1925, pp. 165–83.
9 Radek is inaccurate. Mencius was a student of a student of Confucius.

ancient wise man, who was not a Marxist, you will find the same – from first to last – an explanation of the origins of the Chinese state two thousand years ago. If comrades are interested, I can read it out. This must be the most ancient explanation of the theory of a non-class state, [the theory of] the intelligentsia as the ruling class. He is a direct ancestor not only of comrade Varga, but also of Miliukov.

(*Voices: 'Please read it out'.*)

In the third chapter of Mencius he relates that in the reign of Tang, a scholar arrived (*quotation*).[10]

In this case, it means that only an imperial administration is compatible with agriculture. The great men have their affairs, the small ones their own. But one cannot demand that each man prepares for himself all that he needs without the help of craftsmen. This would have the consequence that the whole people would live without any rest. Therefore, it is said that one will work with his mind and the other with his muscles. The worker of the mind administers people, but the worker with muscles is ruled by other people. The ruled feed the rest and the rulers are fed by others.

And further he relates how all were equally supplied with bread, arms and everything. But comrade Varga did not obtain this from Mencius. He took it from a book, which represents the weakest point of generalisation of bourgeois science about China. This is Weber's [work] devoted to Confucius,[11] which presents a compilation of materials from a purely bourgeois point of view, in which the author responds to all the basic questions, which lead to such thoughts as we see in Varga. So long as we see the absence of even an attempt at a Marxist approach, even in a comrade who is a specialist in Chinese history, so [the same] may [be] seen, when comrades read in the recently issued number of *Vestnik*[12] an article by comrade Kantorovich, devoted to the system of social relations in China in the pre-capitalist epoch.[13]

C[om.] Kantorovich is a highly literate person. [But] with regard to materials and historical facts, this article of his shows that we still have to undertake a massive amount of work, that bourgeois science and its conclusions about Chinese history are still accepted as true by us, and therefore, we cut ourselves off from the possibility of a scientific approach to contemporary issues also.

---

10   The quotation in the record of the lecture is missing but it is definitely the same as in Radek's 'Lecture Three'. See reference 40 to Chapter 2.
11   In all probability this refers to Weber 1922.
12   This refers to the journal *Novyi Vostok* ('The New East'), which was the journal of the Academic Association of Soviet Orientalists.
13   See Kantorovich 1926b, pp. 67–93.

The next obstacle to this work consists in the simple fact that only a minimal number of Chinese sources are accessible to us. In Russia, knowledge of the Chinese language is very limited. You can count on the fingers of one hand our Sinologists who know the language, and in addition, nine tenths of these Sinologists are linguists, who at best became interested purely in the culture and religion of China, who naturally approach [China], from the point of view of a member of the Russian intelligentsia, but not from a historical, nor from a materialist point of view. Even using them in the capacity of interpreters is very difficult for the simple reason that people who are not educated in the humanities do not understand the sources. It often happens that a comparison [of their] translations with [translations] of Chinese sources, [carried out] by such major Sinologists as the Englishman Legge or the German Professor Wilhelm demonstrates a complete difference in translation, arising from the fact that these [our] translator linguists possess absolutely no understanding not merely of the concrete social relations, and for whom the social question simply does not exist. As a direct source, with which we can try to sketch a picture of Chinese relations, there are the translations of a small number of Chinese books.

We have translations of the [Chinese] classics ⟨...⟩ of the feudal epoch, we have translations of Sima Qian.[14] New translations are now appearing. Recently, two weeks ago, a Chinese chronicle was received.[15] Overall, these are very meagre resources. What about bourgeois historical literature? Let us take, for example, the Granat encyclopaedia. There is an essay on the history of China by one of the most distinguished, and not only of the Russian, Sinologists, Professor Ivanov,[16] a man who knows Chinese, author of most interesting monographs on the reforms of Wang Anshi,[17] another source is the Brockhaus & Efron encyclopaedia, where there is also an essay, it seems, if I am not mistaken, by Georgievskii,[18] also a very literate Russian Sinologist. There's no point in reading this essay. It is a list of dynasties, which march in rows, no one knows where they came from or where they went. These essays fully reflect the condition of European history of the old China. One might say: there is not a single book on the history of China, which one could pick up, even if only as we would take in our hands the books of the most mediocre of European historians, not to mention Kareev, at best Ilovaiskii. With the exception of the work of Professor

---

14 This probably refers to Chavannes 1895–1905.
15 It is not clear which chronicle this refers to.
16 See Ivanov 1914, pp. 186–231.
17 In reality this refers to one monograph by the Russian historian A.I. Ivanov. See Ivanov 1909.
18 Radek is in error. This essay was written by A.O. Ivanovskii. See Ivanovskii 1895, pp. 172–221.

Conrady, who was the first to try to apply some kind of scientific method[19] [to] the periods of Chinese history ⟨...⟩ there is not a single work which escapes beyond the limits of chronology, and then uncritically and simply by retelling, giving information about the culture and the history of warfare. Such works, as the works of Boulger and Cordier[20] are the most inferior science of Europe. I do not know Chinese literature. I know only a book written in English by a Chinese who stands high above the European experts because he knows concrete facts better, and therefore tries to establish for himself a very primitive preliminary conception of Chinese history.[21] It is time to set out along the road, not of elaborating a guide [to] Chinese history, but through developing a whole series of monographs, which will give us in fragments the possibility of the first scientific hypothesis.

There exist works on the agricultural history of China, works which were the basis of my orientation. The first work, to which I shall return, is the work of the Russian author Zakharov, published in [18]56 by the religious mission in Beijing.[22] The second work, a chronological one, is a work published by the Royal Geographical Society,[23] [the work] of Jamieson, which gives a survey of 15 provinces, with a description of the Chinese provinces.[24] The third work, by a German Professor Franke, was translated into Russian and is devoted to juridical agrarian law in China.[25] Furthermore there is a work in the field of the development of agrarian relations. In the field of crafts and industry a series of monographs exist. There is a recently published work on the history of the development of typographical art. There exists a history of coal and iron mining. There are works on the history of art by Münsterberg, who is obliged to discuss the material as a pioneer.[26] Thus we possess only weak material on Chinese history. Finally, one must consider the descriptions of travellers as one of these sources, the older the better. Marco Polo is the first major source, which has not yet been fully used.[27] Obviously, people have approached [his] reports out of curiosity, but at the same time he presents a picture of social relations

---

19   See Conrady 1910.
20   Judging by documents from Radek's personal papers preserved in RGASPI, this refers to the following works: Boulger 1898; Boulger 1900; Cordier 1920–21.
21   Judging by documents from Radek's personal papers, this refers to the following work: Li Ung Bing 1914.
22   This refers to the work of Zakharov 1853, pp. 1–96.
23   This refers to the British Royal Asiatic Society.
24   See Jamieson 1888, pp. 59–174.
25   See Franke 1908.
26   See Münsterberg 1910–12.
27   See Minaev 1902 [1298].

at the time of the Mongol rule. Works on the history of trade go further, giving a series of information on which we can base ourselves. From the end of the eighteenth century they have begun to accumulate more extensive information.[28] A scientific hypothesis, a working hypothesis is absolutely essential, in approaching the first schools,[29] which we Marxists create in this field. We must not direct young Chinese comrades to study a question without indicating what to look for, where to go, what questions arise before us. Therefore I say that irrespective of the fact that the material is still very limited, [despite the fact that] every scientific hypothesis in future ⟨...⟩ will be exposed as fallacious in many ways, we must formulate one. During the existence of the university I had to work with the assistance of this hypothesis, as a teacher of history of old China and new China. And I would like to share the results with comrades, not so as to claim the title of an expert mandarin (I fear [this] entering this high cathedra), but so as to interest a small group of historians, and perhaps I shall succeed. We have a small group which is working in this direction, and we will beg our Chinese comrades studying Russian to help us in this work.

C[om.] Mif, who is smiling at me, is probably already circulating a paper asking for the signatures of those comrades who would like to participate in this academic work.

After this introduction, which I had to provide in excusing my boldness in making such a peremptory approach to the attempt at generalising about Chinese history (and this is a history of four thousand years; I have given in all my life no more than four years to it, which is one year per each millennium; a very short time), permit me to pose the questions which arose before us when we took on this work.

The first question, is the question of the exceptionality of Chinese development: does the history of the development of China fit the general framework of historical development, is our scheme of history appropriate for Chinese history, or is it a question here of a case of completely different forms, which develop on the basis of some other kinds of laws. For us this is a strange question, but this question arises in [reading] all the books on Chinese history which we consult, for there the history of China is regarded, with a few exceptions, as miraculous, as something that has nothing in common with our history. Apart from that, the Chinese students travelling to us, educated in Chinese schools, arrive with a conviction of the total uniqueness of Chinese development.

---

28 Thus in the text. It should read 'circumstantial information'.
29 Thus in the text. It should read 'steps'.

I think that we must answer this question like this. The scheme of the development of society, which Marxism provides on the basis of the existence of the history of European humanity fully corresponds to Chinese history. However, a series of exceptions will exist, about which we must speak further on. We can already establish the existence of tribal society in China. Chinese classical literature has been very little examined from this point of view and even the examination which we were in a position to conduct on the basis of English translations shows us what follows. But these books come from the period of Chinese feudalism. They say that a communal system and a matriarchy existed, – this unhappy matriarchy which is a stumbling block even for many Marxists. In connection with matriarchy the most bitter battles took place among the academic colleagues in our university, but this matriarchy can be fully established on the basis of Chinese religious ceremonies, wedding ceremonies and on the bases of the study of these earliest sources. The non-Marxist Prof. Conrady also does exactly this in his work, a very valuable work. After the appearance of this work by Prof. Conrady, another academic, Kvintor, also a non-Marxist, undertook the re-examination of this question and the question is already clarified in part.[30]

We are treading on very firm ground when we set about the study of the feudal period. I already said that I know of few world literatures in which feudalism could have found such a reflection not only in juridical documents but also in literary documents. An analysis of Confucius and Mencius gives us a picture of economic relations, social relations, the organisation of state power and its world view. So, on the basis of Mencius alone, one of our teachers, com. Zhakov, got to work and was able to deliver a fine book.[31] But in this work he was not yet in a position to consider ⟨...⟩ massive further material which introduces us with complete clarity to the scheme of relations in Chinese feudalism. In the field of the study of the period of feudalism, there will not be any major hurdles. This literature introduces us to fundamentals that we must know. The first attempts to overcome feudalism as a social as well as a political system occur in the third century BCE. But here, so to speak, the obstacles begin. More distant times are considerably easier to study than the most recent – [for example,] the eighteenth century, which ought to be closer is significantly more difficult to study. The whole period of the foundation of a money economy, the consolidation of mercantile capital, the influence of the ruling mercantile cap-

---

30   This evidently refers to Harold Scott Quigley, who published several works about the situation in China in the 1920s.
31   See Zhakov 1927.

ital on the development of Chinese history, this period is the most difficult. The difficulty of this period consists in the fact that we do not have a single dominant line of development for the whole extent of the eighteenth century. The line is disrupted at a number of points, which I shall speak about. But there is a line for the third period of this history, that moment when European capital began to alter social relations in China.

We must characterise the period after the fall of feudalism as the period of the domination of a money economy and mercantile capital. Between the feudal period, a period in which the landholding feudal class was consolidated, and the period of mercantile capital there lie a number of centuries, and in the succession of these centuries in the first few centuries CE, we see a period of a struggle by the defeated feudal princes for a return to power, a period of the struggle of the nobility or the magnates, deprived of power in appanage principalities, for land [and also] of a struggle of the peasantry for the return to the so-called well-field system, which seems to be all that remained of the tribal commune under feudalism. This reminds us of the German marks in the period of the existence of feudalism as a basis of organisation in the early feudal period. This struggle is reflected in a rich literature. Fortunately, we know about this reflection only from the work of Zakharov, that same Zakharov, who wrote about agrarian reform in Russia,[32] and despite the fact that he was a Sinologist, and even a linguist, he had a very sharp sensitivity for an understanding of the agrarian question. He cited a whole series of passages from Chinese sources and strengthened his citations with the assertion that for the whole period until the ninth century all Chinese literature had been full of the struggle for and against this well-field system, that is a system which gave the landholders the possibility of taking from the peasants a land tax or labour service. At one time this was a social system embracing the peasantry, guaranteeing them land, and they struggled against its usurpation. Comrade Zakharov, remote from Marxism, says that this question was determined by force and that the section of the bureaucracy, which was in favour of the well-field system [all the same] feared to create this system. But the peasants themselves were responsible for this victory. Over the whole extent of Chinese history until the nineteenth century, we have not a single century without massive peasant uprisings, which in the first part of this period, in the period of the [birth] of the money economy, set themselves the task of a return to the past, to the peasant commune. But who even then, when the given money economy was well developed, [and when, it seems, they] could not accomplish this task, [all the same] rose in

---

32 Thus in the text. It should read: 'in China'.

rebellion, [having an interest] in the administrative limitation of the amount of land per person.[33] [This was] a struggle of the peasantry against the differentiation of the peasantry and the emergence of large-scale landowning. But did they [landowners] emerge? In his article, comrade Kantorovich asserts that in the whole period after the fall of feudalism, China was a country of small-scale landholding, and that in China there were no large-scale landowners. The insufficient accuracy of his article pays witness to the fact that this is his fantasy. He relates that the whole history is full of the struggle of the peasants against the expropriation of land. But if there were no landowners, then why were the peasants rebelling and who had taken their land? For the duration of the existence of the money economy, we observe the struggle of the peasantry against the differentiation of the peasantry and against the emergence of landowners and at the same time we have the constant rebirth of feudal or non-feudal large-scale landowners. We have, on the one hand the invasions of Tatars, Mongols, Manchus, which, as nomad tribes, have military organisation, and in conquering China, they divide up a significant part of the land. They do not simply transfer it to [the feudalists], but at the same time provide their soldiers with land on a large scale. We see this in a whole series of invasions in the first century CE. We see in the thirteenth century the attack of the Mongols and Manchus,[34] landowners who emerge on the basis of a money economy, but who do business with the well-field system of feudalism. If you read Marco Polo, you will find a description of the country, as a land in the hands of the Emperor ⟨...⟩ In the space of 20–30 miles he sees castles of feudal knights (we will see further on that he does not only see knights), but [the main thing is that] this invasion reveals the process of struggle of the peasantry against the domination of the major landowners. But the most interesting thing is the invasion. The most interesting thing is that [the invasion] leads [to] the establishment [between the Chinese landowners and the external enemies] ⟨...⟩ of a general common defence [against the rebellious peasants] ⟨...⟩ That's a fact.

The victory of peasant rebellions [leads] through whole long intervals of time [to] the establishment of peasant dynasties ⟨...⟩ A consideration of this question leads us to the causes, and in particular to the role and the fate of mercantile capital in China. The struggle of the peasantry against feudalism existed in Europe, but with the exception of the Khilsudsii [?] war,[35] we do not know

---

33 Thus in the text. It should read: 'striving for the administrative limitation of the quantity of land in the hands of a single person'.
34 Radek is mistaken. The Manchus attacked China in the seventeenth century.
35 Which war is referred to is unknown.

of any period in which the peasants in a great country were able to seize power for themselves, and therefore this period, the beginning of the Ming dynasty, is very interesting from a sociological point of view.

We have before us facts. The Han dynasty comes to power. Qin Shi Huangdi, who was the first in China to try to do away with appanage princes and feudalism, played a large role. Qin Shi Huangdi relied on mercantile capital in this struggle. [There exists] a source in which this is clearly described in a reference to Lü Buwei, a major merchant, who supported him: but for a merchant to support a King a class must exist. This merchant was needed to complement the forces that Qin Shi Huangdi possessed. At the same time a centralised monarchy was founded, which began to build the Wall against the nomads. It was necessary to mobilise a peasant labour army to exploit its labour. This is apart from the question as to whether the Chinese had enough labour. According to Rezen Kr.'s[36] calculation, more than 300,000 men were at work. The fall of Qin Shi Huangdi occurred thanks to the rebellion, which was headed by peasants and artisans, of these peasant labour armies. At the same time, a link was established between these rebellious peasants and the appanage princes, who were trying to utilise the rising for the seizure of power. The old gentry bureaucrats, which Qin Shi Huangdi had replaced by a bureaucracy of various ranks, overcome the peasants and in the Han dynasty they try to undertake a turn of the well-field system.[37] The Han dynasty finishes as a feudal dynasty.

If we take the Ming dynasty, which overthrew the Mongol yoke, also relying on massive peasant uprisings, then the Ming dynasty in the second half of its domination in the seventeenth century, emerges as the most exploitative of the peasants. A question arises here. At first I answered simply enough – the degeneration of a peasant dynasty. These peasant dynasties, having come to power, cut themselves off from the peasantry and this was for me, after an initial examination, the cause of the transformation of these peasant dynasties into the foundation of a social class of landowners etc. But when I began to study the agrarian reforms of the non-peasant dynasties, the reforms of Wang Mang and the reforms of Wang Anshi, it became clear that the issue goes significantly deeper. If you exclude that which concerns the individual attempts of Wang Mang and Wang Anshi, all these reforms add up to the following.

A money economy leads to the disaggregation of the peasantry. The rich peasants, peasant-merchants, peasant-officials, who exploit the peasants,

---

36 Whom this refers to is unknown.
37 Thus in the text. It should read 'to put an end to the well-field system'.

handing over to the state only part of the taxes, buy up the land from the peasants and a considerable part of the peasants are left without land. Peasant movements begin, and against this [Wang Mang and Wang Anshi] attempt to propose reforms, consisting in a prohibition of land purchases beyond a limited amount, for the salvation of small-scale economy by means of limiting the influence of the money economy [on it]. All these reforms finish with nothing at all. There is a very concrete description of how the merchants and landowners purchase land using the family names of their servants. The law operating against the tendencies of historical development is evaded. And that which concerns the purely personal transformation of the elements of the peasantry which have cut themselves off from their class, in the light of a study of the reforms of Wang Anshi and ot[hers], turns out to be a deeper phenomenon. The peasant dynasties are not in a position to defend the interests of the peasantry from differentiation in the context of a money economy. And they degenerate not because the dynasty has torn itself away from its class, since even a feudal dynasty fears ⟨...⟩ the peasant, but it conducts an anti-peasant policy, or is not in a position to conduct a pro-peasant policy, because it cannot historically resolve the task of defending the peasantry on the basis of a money economy. If we are dealing here with degeneration and decline, it is because we see before us an historical attempt of these peasant dynasties to resolve an irresolvable task.

This question, which we will have to study in the most intensive way, leads us to the following question. I have pointed to the fact that, taking our basic periodization of history as fully applicable to Chinese history, I see the first difference: there is the enormous number of peasant uprisings, with the arrival in power of peasant dynasties and their bankruptcy, which cannot be compared with what we know in Europe. This question leads us on to two new questions. The first of these new problems is one of cause: why does the peasantry demonstrate such enormous power in the struggle not only with the feudalists, but also with the major landowning class? I am not in a position to give an answer to this question on the basis of the material available to me. The material does not yet permit an answer apart from a very superficial hypothesis, it does not give any explanation at all. But before us another question arises, a question about another difference in Chinese history.

We see the fall of feudalism, we see the money economy, we see concrete facts of the development of arts and crafts, the development of commodity capital, and we see an enormous landless rural proletariat, the poor, who escape into banditry, which plays a considerable role in Chinese history. Understandably, those peasants who have nothing to eat become bandits, and they are not in the tens of thousands but in millions. They rob on the streets, overthrow the authorities etc. All the elements are present: commodity capital, artisans, and a landless proletariat. Why then did a contemporary bourgeoisie not develop in China? How far did China go in the development of a money economy on the way to capitalism? I must here establish the following facts:

If you take the rule of the Mongols in the thirteenth century, we find a stunning picture of it in Marco Polo. If we take this picture as a starting point, then we are obliged to say that China in the thirteenth century stood head and shoulders above any European country. Marco Polo, arriving from Northern Italy, which was then the first capitalist country in Europe, recognised no bounds to his astonishment. He describes Chinese crafts as crafts producing the things which Italy produced but better and more beautifully. He sees for the first time in his life the use of coal as a fuel. He describes the Chinese financial system, where Chinese banknotes [exist], guaranteed in gold, which were accepted from the Pacific Ocean to the Caspian Sea. He describes a wealthy Chinese merchant class. In other words, if we compare this picture with European history, then we can see that China in the thirteenth-fourteenth centuries knew not only crafts and artisan shops, but knew manufacture, knew a developed class of merchants.

Some words on the reasons for this dawn under the rule of the Mongols. Here I must approach a fundamental question – on the reasons for the deceleration of this development. The Mongol dynasty did not only conquer China. The Mongols subjected the whole of Asia to their rule, contemporary Persia, Turkestan and India – all this was in the hands of the huge markets of the Mongols, markets to which the products of the Near East, Syria, contemporary Turkey, and Persia were taken. On the other hand, there were Chinese products, Chinese production. An enormous trading exchange, which raised the prosperity of the whole of Asia. The decline of Mongol sovereignty signified the decline of Asia. The decline of this enormous market of trading routes also gave a stimulus to the regressive movement in China. Mercantile capital, which then existed in China, was the result of the development of a money economy for manufacture. What surprises us in the backwardness of China at that time is the question of why China did not independently move towards contemporary industry. It is not appropriate to disparage China in this connection. Apart from the English not a single people crossed this brink, they all followed England. On the basis of the industrial revolution in England and comparing the conditions of the development of capitalism in Europe with Chinese conditions, we receive a clue: why Chinese mercantile capital, – which was a great organiser of the Chinese economy and state and of the Han dynasty, – does not demonstrate a simple transition from feudalism [?] in China, but presents a bloc of landowners with mercantile capital.[38] One can only understand these causes, if we move from an abstract history of capitalism to a concrete history of capitalism.

Capitalism developed in its metropolitan countries – Holland, England and Italy. What distinguishes these three maritime countries? And what unites these three countries in the sequel? They all make the transition from crafts and the beginnings of manufacture towards higher forms of economy thanks to capital accumulation through colonial policies. We can see how the northern Italian cities, having enriched themselves in trade with the Levant and the sack of the Levant, approach a resolution of the problem of a transition from manufacture to industry. It was no accident that Leonardo da Vinci sought a solution to such great tasks. In Holland we see in the seventeenth century an attempt to resolve the problem of motor power, attempts to move towards the machine. This attempt is finally successful in England. Both India[39] and England can approach this task solely because of primitive accumulation, which they have received not by means of the exploitation of the hired labour of the workers of the country concerned, but in the first place by means of accumulation in colonial policy, by means of primitive accumulation. England resolved this question, having – in addition to those conditions which Italy and Holland also enjoyed – a larger internal market and an insular location, which gave it the possibility of greater economic development than Italy and Holland. And [here it is important] the very fact that China, had lost massive opportunities for expansion after the fall of the Mongols, it lost [them] because India established the rule of the Great Mughals,[40] which was stronger. In Persia, we see a revival which strengthened Persia on the basis of its policies.[41] Having met rivals in the south and west of Asia, having lost that market, where was Chinese mercantile capital to turn? The Pacific Ocean did not unite, it divided. Given the marine technology of that period, typhoons provided greater practical obstacles. China built an enormous canal, because it could not compete with the tasks of overcoming the obstacles presented by the so-called Pacific Ocean, which is in fact very stormy.

And so began the withering away of Chinese mercantile capital. It was not in a position to advance beyond crafts and manufacture. But there are also

---

38 Thus in the text. Radek means that mercantile capital in China did not fully free itself from feudal remnants.
39 Thus in the text. Radek means 'Italy'.
40 The Empire of the Great Mughals existed in India in 1526–1858.
41 Radek refers to the formation in Persia at the beginning of the 16th century of the Safavid Empire.

other causes of this withering away. Thanks to the continual Christian wars, mercantile capital also lost part of its internal market. You know that until the appearance of bread as a mass object, trade was in the first place a trade in articles of luxury, which served the needs of feudal landholding courts. The Christian wars, ⟨...⟩ continually, century after century, raising a landowning economy, ⟨...⟩ undermined this internal market. Therefore China [was] only in a position to preserve that high level of development of crafts and manufacture, which it reached in the time of the rule of the Yuan dynasty. But when in the eighteenth century, the King of England sent his Ambassador Macartney to China, and Macartney brought a present from the King of England, the Chinese Emperor answered: 'We make better [things] than you so there is no cause for you to arrive with your goods. If you require our tea and silk, I will permit their sale to you'. And typically, until that time, while the Europeans were learning to produce opium, they paid in silver for goods. Only later, with the development of the textile industry, he [the European] would create a new mass product. It is typical also, that by the end of the nineteenth century, they are selling more opium than textile goods.

If we ignore contemporary history, China demonstrates the following. [This is] a country, which did not supersede the period of mercantile capital in its development and approached contemporary capitalism with its own independent forces, besides which the [cause] for this must be sought on the one hand in geographical conditions, the role of the Pacific Ocean, [but] on the other hand, [in] the decline of the Mongols, limiting Chinese capital to a role of merely providing for an internal market. And this withering away of Chinese mercantile capital leads to the fact, that it was not capable of providing the basis on which the Chinese bourgeoisie might have consolidated itself.

In this understanding of history the fall of the Ming dynasty and the origins of the Manchu dynasty are very typical. Our literati usually present the case that – all this has already clogged up my ears – the Manchus conquered China. But this is an absolutely mistaken view. The history of the fall of the Ming dynasty demonstrates a remarkable picture of class warfare.

It is interesting that Russia knew this in the eighteenth century. There exists in the Russian language a reworking of a French history of the fall of the Ming, in which even the surnames of the Chinese leaders of the revolution are Russified and Ukrainianised.[42] The history of this rebellion is typical for a characterisation of class relations in this period of the withering away ⟨...⟩ of mercantile

---

42   See Vauger de Bruyne 1788.

capital in China. In the course of 14 years the peasantry struggled against the Ming dynasty, and conquered the whole of Central and Northern China. Peasant risings rolled up to Beijing. Simultaneously, the Ming Emperor conducted a war with the Manchurians. The Manchus were then changing from the atomised life of nomads to unification, centralisation. The Manchu princes were struggling for an amplification of pasture. They decided to expel the Chinese peasantry from the present southern Manchurian provinces. The Ming Emperors went to war with them. And at that moment the uprising reached Beijing. The Commander-in-Chief of Chinese forces on the Manchurian front, Wu Sangui proposed to the Manchurians the conclusion of a peace and a joint suppression of the peasant uprising. And we find in the sources a brilliant, clear class picture. We have the proclamation of the leader of the Manchus, who turns to the Chinese people and says: 'I have not come as a conqueror, I come as the pacifier of the peasant rebellion'. All that mystification, which Professor Weber and o[ther] European historians throw over us, completely disappears. And we see further on that in this struggle the mercantile bourgeoisie is far too weak to be able to direct the peasantry. They fear that the cities will be drenched in blood; as a result of their decline they conduct negotiations and try to remain neutral. We no longer see the picture which we saw at the very beginning of the development of a money economy, [when] the uprisings against the Han dynasty were led by peasant-artisans. Perhaps a more detailed examination will show us these elements, but from what I have succeeded in comparing [it is evident] ⟨...⟩ that at this period of the withering away of the capitalist development of the Chinese mercantile bourgeoisie it did not have sufficient strength to attempt to take over the leadership of the peasant movement, and it was [ostensibly] beaten by the Manchus, who created an alliance with the remains of the Ming ruling dynasty. This uprising was defeated by the landowners of the Ming dynasty with the neutrality of the cities.

If you ask, how China appeared at the moment of its collision with and adaptation to capitalist Europe, then all the legends of the existence in China then of the nationalisation of land, of the supra-class character of the Chinese state – you will read [this] in comrade Kantorovich's article, which attempts to say to us Marxists that a supra-class state is possible, – all these legends are the result of the fact that we accept [as true] the results of bourgeois sciences, but have not yet initiated a Marxist analysis of the question.

In China private property in land exists. For the whole of this period, beginning with the first centuries, as early as the second century BCE, there are periods of a return to the well-field system, but the predominant form for all this historical time is private property in land. All the legends that the land belongs to the Emperor, all this is just a variation on a theme of titles. Just as the

Emperor of All Russia had a long list of titles, so in the title of the Chinese Emperor it is stated that all land and water belongs to the Emperor. This had nothing to do with reality. The law on buying and selling is not from the tenth or the thirteenth century, [but much earlier], it was retained and it still exists.

The second question: which was the ruling class? The history of China for this period is reduced to a sliver between two poles. When the peasants come to power we have rule by the peasants and the petty bourgeoisie. Peasants are owners of private property. They become bankrupt under the influence of the differentiation caused by the money economy. Who then comes to power? Then, the landowners, in an alliance with the merchants, find themselves in power.

The Russian monk Iakinf, who studied China at the beginning of the nineteenth century, left a superb work on Chinese history. There is more Marxism in it than in that written by comrades who found a state power representing no class at all. Iakinf very simply describes what went on. He says: *there they rob the people, re-sell the land, and the land is taken over by the speculators in salt, the merchants.* He gives a picture of the real power which existed in China. If you take such a simple fact as that England forced China to pay reparations, then [the question arises] who will pay, who will surrender this money? The merchants give the government the money. But you know, they don't give money for nothing.

The historical movement which held back the development of China did not permit a class of contemporary bourgeoisie to arise, which might have unified China on contemporary foundations. This is what distinguishes China from Western Europe, and there is no mystification here. There are major difficulties in studying Chinese history, thanks to the state of our unfamiliarity with the Chinese language, the absence of easy access to the sources. But, comrades, allow me to say at the conclusion of my lecture that helping the Chinese comrades in the study of this question belongs to the most important issues of the solidarity, which our Chinese comrades expect of us.

It is understandable that no one is going to ask them: 'Before you take power please take an examination in the Chinese department'. But without an understanding of the process that caused the present situation, without an understanding of those social complexes, which exist in the great majority of China, the CCP will not be in a position to lead a conscious policy, will not be in a position to find a conscious directive for those great battles which stand before it. I hope that comrades will not be afraid of the fundamentals of my report, and having seen that it [the Chinese issue] is not diabolic but quite humanitarian, will help us to establish its investigation.

I do not demand that everyone does this, but if even only ten men dedicated themselves to this I would be content, and if after five years you reject this hypothesis, then we won't quarrel about it.

ARAN. F. 377. Op. 2. D. 2a. Ll. 2–28.
Typescript, copy, unsigned.

CHAPTER 4

On the International Situation of China

11 March 1927, Stenographic Report

The Chinese revolution has entered into a period when, even for the broader masses of the population of the Soviet Union and for the rank and file Communist, it begins to assume a shape somewhat similar to what we have already lived through. Throughout the last few years whenever the rank and file Communist read information about the Chinese revolution, this information seemed very strange to him. It seemed as though it was not the classes that wage the struggle, but generals of some kind with very odd surnames. At all events, I must say first of all that the relationship of our Party masses to events in China was one of sympathy, as towards a people which is struggling for its intrinsic rights with our common enemy, British imperialism.

When speaking about events in China, questions arise; in the first place: what kind of revolution is the Chinese revolution, what class relations gave rise to it, what classes are struggling in it? To all these questions a clear response has not somehow or other been found, and therefore Chinese events have not called forth the response which they should have done. In addition, I must underline another fact: Russia has never lived through a national-liberation movement, despite the fact that the former Russia, the Russia of the tsarist period, was a prison of nations, where enormous, multi-million masses of people were tormented and yearned for their liberation from the iron yoke, in which human dignity and a feeling of individuality was stifled and lost and so on. Despite this, Russia, I repeat, never experienced a national-liberation movement, and in our schools we learnt in our young skulls to understand those classic bourgeois revolutions, in which the struggle took placed within the confines of one people. Such revolutions as the German revolution of [18]48, or the Italian liberation movement,[1] which had a national flavour and which were a national-liberation movement, thanks to the fact that Russia did not experience a national revolution, thanks to the fact that the domination of the Great Russian tribe over the others seemed to be taken for granted, they did not then receive the attention required and all this made the understanding of Chinese

---

1 The bourgeois-democratic revolutions of 1848–1849 in Germany and 1859–1861 in Italy were directed towards the overcoming of the fragmentation of these countries. The German revolution was defeated, the Italian revolution was crowned with success.

events much more difficult. But now it is clear to all, even on the basis of those disjointed bits of information, which appear in the press (it must be said that our press informs us very badly about Chinese events amongst other things), that now in China precisely that enormous class movement is taking place ... A movement of the peasants, clashes between peasants and landowners, great strikes; all this demonstrates that more could already be known on the basis of Marxist theory.

The national-revolutionary liberation movement, the national revolution is one of the forms of the bourgeois revolution, one of those special forms of class struggle in countries finding themselves in the given period dependent on other countries, dependent on imperialism. But this is insufficient, insufficient to take just one algebraic formula and content oneself with this definition. One must also ask oneself, first of all, what are the driving forces existing in the Chinese revolution, which classes are struggling within it, in the second place, which phase has this revolution reached, what does it now represent, and finally, a third question which deserves attention, that is of the prognosis of the further evolution of Chinese events. All these questions should stand at the centre of our attention.

First of all, I must say, that all this should already be, so to speak, 'the property of every Communist'. We ought to know this ... But, if we don't know it, then we have an excuse: we don't know it because our press has chosen a very strange policy: it is silent about the most important manifestations of class struggle in China, as though the fact that people are struggling there, as in all other classes,[2] as though this were something shameful ... It seems to be hypnotized.

I will start from the first question, with the question about the driving forces of the Chinese revolution. At its present phase this is a bourgeois revolution. What is a bourgeois revolution? What sort of bourgeoisie is struggling, which of its social strata is struggling and for what objectives? There is a bourgeoisie which is striving for a deal with tsarism, there is a bourgeoisie of the nobility, [there is] a petty bourgeoisie, which is full of all sorts of naïve republican and socialist illusions and which goes into battle with tsarism ... To say: 'the Chinese revolution is a bourgeois revolution', is not to give an exhaustive explanation of the question. To say it and not to clarify which social strata are struggling and why they are struggling, means to say nearly nothing. One might understand which strata are struggling and what they are struggling for, if one remembers if only in brief the history of the development of capitalism in China. This,

---

2   Thus in the text. It should read 'countries'.

essentially, is a brief history, which is counted in decades in all and does not involve more than 25 years of existence. It begins in [18]90, when the first large textile factory was built in China. Shortly after [18]90 (in [18]94) they began to construct railways on a large scale in China, which were extremely rare until then. Thence emerged capitalism. In essence one might say that capitalism in China only begins to flow in a massive wave after the Boxer Uprising, which is already at the beginning of the twentieth century. What sort of changes did it introduce in a petty bourgeois country, where until then, the land belonged to the peasants, who worked on tiny plots cultivating them, where there was no kind of industry in the contemporary meaning of the word, and where all the products of industry were the handwork of artisans or craftsmen ...? What changes did capitalism introduce in relation to the national economy?

First of all the implantation of capitalism demanded the construction of railways. This was the work of foreign capital. About 10,000 kilometres of railways were built, a quarter of the railway network of Russia. This required the working of coal seams and iron ore. Thus contemporary industry began to develop in China. It goes without saying that for the development of its activity, foreign capital needed to attach itself to someone in China, and in the first instance it attached itself to part of the merchant class. The Chinese merchants appeared to the foreign capitalists in the shape of guides so as to distribute their goods among the population. It is obvious that the foreign industrialists, not knowing the way of life of the country, not knowing its language and customs, were entirely at the mercy of Chinese merchants ... In this way a special stratum of the bourgeoisie was created, the first layer 'of merchant-intermediaries', tied to foreign capital. This means that the first layer of the Chinese bourgeoisie was created on the basis of the imperialist movement and was bound up with foreign imperialism. If we ask ourselves the question as to whether this bourgeoisie would struggle against foreign capitalism and against foreign imperialism, then the answer would be immediately clear: no, it would not struggle.

Now, how exactly was the first contemporary Chinese revolution [of 1911–12] defeated? Sun Yat-sen was beaten ... but capitalism in China could not reserve in its hands all the positions conquered up to the war. Thanks to the war, which distracted the attention of world capitalism, the importation of foreign wares was halted, as a result of which a situation was created, in which a part of the Chinese petty bourgeoisie, and even the comprador bourgeoisie, attempted to create its own industry. Germany, England and France stopped importing their cheap factory products into China, and a wave of American goods were directed mainly towards Europe. The petty bourgeoisie of China tried to create its own industry. This indicated that a new class was being born, a class of industrialists, already with an interest in the struggle against foreign capital. Why was that? For a very simple reason. Capitalism develops in all countries under the protection of a capitalist state. It defends young capitalist industry with protective customs dut[ies], corresponding to its tariff policy, by the construction of railways, the construction of a network of technical schools, in a word, by means of a series of measures, which we know from the history of capitalism in other countries, Germany, France, Russia, England.

The Chinese bourgeoisie could not command this assistance or this defence. Let us take, for example, such a question as the free exportation of their goods by the foreigners. Could the Chinese bourgeoisie defend itself from the competition of cheaper foreign goods? No, it could not. Since the West European states assumed for themselves the right to export their wares with a customs duty of no higher than five percent, and secondly, because the customs duty which China did levy in its customs system was located in the hands of foreign officials, who controlled the entire customs and excise administration.

This means that the struggle for a defensive tariff, which might have preserved young Chinese industry, pushed the Chinese bourgeoisie into a struggle with foreign imperialism.

But apart from that, there are thousands more reasons. Foreign capitalism appeared armed to the teeth with modern technology. But this was no longer the period when British imperialism was characterised by better quality goods than Chinese goods. Now Chinese industry and Chinese trade demanded that its development should be supported by the government with all available means. But was there such a government in China? There was not. And so the revolution of [1]911 went bankrupt. In China there were no distinct class groupings. The bourgeoisie was exclusively foreign, and only the merchant class was allied with it. There were few railways. Therefore no bourgeois government could be established.

But apart from that, there is another even more interesting reason for revolutionary struggle in China which hits you in the face. A capitalist government can only be established when there are specific material sources for it, if the taxation system in the hands of the state collects resources, with the help of which it favours capitalist development. But if this system is in fact in the hands of foreign capital, if China is burdened with reparations for the [18]94 war with Japan and for the Boxer Uprising to the sum of a billion rubles, if the customs income flows into the hands of foreign officials, who transfer it to foreign banks and they in turn pay them out to foreign states, you don't get far.

And the Chinese state is obliged to squeeze this money from the peasants. For that you need good shares, good railways. These did not exist. And that which was squeezed from the peasants in the localities remained there and did not reach the centre. And so we see during the past few years a complete collapse of the central government. And the Chinese bourgeoisie, the Chinese industrial bourgeoisie, is striving not only for the liberation of the customs receipts from the hands of foreign capital, corresponding to the economic policy of the state, but also for a stop to the collapse of the state and the establishment of a single strong capitalist government. And you can see all these objectives in the Chinese industrial bourgeoisie which has entered the fray.

It would be pointless to think that the Chinese bourgeoisie never had any progressive or even revolutionary will. If you remember the history of the struggle of imperialism for the railways, coal and other concessions in China, then you will see that the local landowners and the bourgeoisie struggled against the conquest of China by foreign capital. After the war, when this new class emerged on the scene, it entered the struggle, refusing to sign the Treaty of Versailles which was directed against China.[3] This was the beginning of a new Chinese movement. And the bourgeoisie played a big role in this movement: on the one hand there is the pre-war bourgeoisie, that is bound by its capitalist interests to imperialism which is hungry for new conquests. On the other hand there is the industrial bourgeoisie, which wanted to be master in its own house and wanted to exploit the peasants itself.

But this bourgeoisie is not very numerous, and it stands to reason that if it stood alone, it would not be able to achieve much. If you look at the masses marching under their leadership, then these masses do not belong essentially to the bourgeoisie. Who organized boycotts, who went to demonstrations etc.? This was the petty bourgeoisie, the students, for in [19]19–20 the student body emerged into the arena of revolutionary struggle. This student body is not a class, it is an unimportant group, tied to the bourgeoisie and in its majority had emerged from petty bourgeois strata. In the revolution, the student body emerged on the scene in the capacity of the petty bourgeois mass, but this petty bourgeois mass of the student body is merely a herald of the subsequent emergence on the historical stage of the basic petty bourgeois mass of the peasants.

In what follows, we shall see how it emerges.

---

3 The Versailles Peace Treaty, concluding the First World War, was signed on 28 June 1919 by twenty-six victorious powers, members of the Entente, with Germany. According to the treaty, and notwithstanding Chinese participation in the war on the side of the Entente, German possessions in China (the Qingdao district on the Shandong peninsula) were officially transferred to Japan, which along with Britain had seized them on 7 November 1914. The Chinese delegation refused to sign the treaty.

The beginning of a new wave of the national movement after the war, born by a new class, the industrial bourgeoisie, calls onto the scene a second class, born from the contemporary movement, the proletariat.

In [19]22 a German engineer who had lived in China for a long time, a specialist in the railway business, published a book which states that China is fortunate in that there is no worker problem, there is cheap labour and the labourer works peacefully ...[4] In actual fact, as we shall see, this is far from the truth.

Those same conditions which led to the creation of a Chinese industrial bourgeoisie during the war, also created the Chinese proletariat, which more or less doubled in size. They were only slightly fewer (proportionately) than those who made the October Revolution. The workers now enter the struggle under the flag of defending their communist ideals and their interests. The struggle is conducted everywhere ... Here an uprising explodes on the mines which belong to the English, there strikes are declared in Japanese factories, etc. Already in 1923 you see the first major bloody confrontations of the Chinese workers with the Chinese bourgeoisie. Strikes and struggle are conducted everywhere. You see strikes on the Beijing railway, which lead to the shooting of workers, the shootings of Chinese workers by Wu Peifu, a representative of the Chinese bourgeoisie.[5] But these shootings do not stop the movement: together with them you see a strong growth in the so-called strike wave: strikes occur now in Beijing, now in Tianjin, now in Shanghai ... This strike wave reaches the peak of its intensity, when in 1925 the Japanese factory guards fight with the workers, which leads to the murder of several thousand workers. For several days, Shanghai is actually in the hands of 200,000 workers, who not only strike but to be more specific, go onto the streets in the name of the class struggle for power. But they do not yet advance clear slogans, apart from the most minimal demands which can be reduced to the removal of the most savage forms of maltreatment over the working class. It is clear that they do not yet raise the question of state power, but they protest against foreign imperialism and demand an improvement in their situation. This struggle threw 200,000 working people out onto the streets, and demonstrated the massive power of the Chinese proletariat. The Chinese bourgeoisie did not dare to come out against this force. This strike, which was directed against the English and Japanese capitalists provoked sympathy on the part of the broadest masses of the poor urban population, artisans,

---

4 This refers to Harold Stringer, who in 1922 published in Shanghai the book *The Chinese Railway System*; see Stringer 1922. He was not German, but British.

5 This refers to events on the 7 February 1923 on the Beijing-Hankou railway. A workers' strike led by Communists was suppressed by the Hubei warlord Wu Peifu.

smaller scale merchants etc. All this enormous mass went on strike and the strike was transformed into a broad national movement against foreign capitalism.[6] The Chinese bourgeoisie, which had until then led the struggle against foreign capital, motivated by a desire to obtain the abrogation of the unequal treaties, was obliged given the situation to seek the protection of the workers and pay money for the strike. A situation occurred, as in 1905 in Russia, when the Russian bourgeoisie during the October days of 1905, paid for the strike and at the same time had to strike itself …[7] The Chinese industrial bourgeoisie was extremely frightened by this strike, but still told themselves by way of consolation that the strike was not to be feared. Thus, before our very eyes, there is another class which has emerged. And now a struggle for hegemony begins between them. Who leads the movement? To whom do the broad masses of the petty bourgeoisie listen? So far, the petty bourgeoisie is only emerging in the cities. The countryside is still silent and it is not clear what position it should take up. What position could the countryside take up? An answer to that can be gained by a quick glance at those changes which have been provoked by capitalism in the Chinese countryside. What exactly was the Chinese peasantry? They were small-scale proprietors who worked on minute plots of land. Prior to the origins of contemporary capitalism in China, handicrafts were widely profitable, textile raw materials were produced, cotton manufacture; buyers went into the countryside and bought up the wares of this peasant production. Such was the picture in the countryside. What has changed? First of all one must note here that cheap foreign wares begin to seriously damage the handicraft worker and to establish highly disadvantageous competition for him. In this competition of cheap wares from foreign factories owing to the importation of foreign goods, victory is naturally not on the side of the handicraft workers. The position of the peasantry sharply deteriorates.

The second change can be summed up in the statement that in so far as state debts rise (in [18]94 China still had no foreign debt, in [19]11 this debt had already reached a figure of 1 billion, and now it has already climbed to 2.5 billion), the government was obliged to resort to the raising of money taxes.

A third factor is the collapse of government power. China dissolves into a series of independent territories … Each territory has its own warlord, who conducts continual warfare with the others. Naturally, as might be expected

---

6 This refers to events in Shanghai on 30 May 1925, marking the beginning of the National Revolution of 1925–1927.
7 At the beginning of October 1905 an All-Russian political strike was organised, forcing Nicholas II to grant to the peoples of Russia a *Manifesto*, laying down the bases of a constitutional-monarchist regime.

this warfare imposes a heavy burden on the Chinese peasantry, whose back is already bent without that. So how do the warlords mobilise their forces? Each of them has a small group of mercenaries, which he drives into the countryside, to whom he hands it over. They collect the rural poor and forcibly press them into military service. For example, in a city like Beijing, suddenly one fine day, all the coolies disappear ... This means that Zhang Zuolin is conducting a recruiting drive. We see how the soldiery ravages the countryside, chases the mass of the peasantry and captures it, one part for military service while one part is forced to carry on their backs military equipment for 500–600 *verst*, all that is needed by the army. The position of the peasantry is extremely harsh in China. There is not a single province there in which the peasants have not paid taxes in advance for five to six, or even 10 years.

How does the peasantry live now? What is its income? 80 percent of the Chinese rural population has an income no greater than 60 rubles a year from its land. This is an appallingly low figure, but it has been verified by a whole series of statistical investigations. The Chinese peasant has an income below that level, which was established by American scientists as the minimum for human survival. They are dying out ... The death rate in China after each poor harvest reaches 1 million people. This occurrence of mortality has become more or less normal in China so that people have got used to it and no one is surprised by it any more. They react to this phenomenon as to something quite normal, so that it is only mentioned in small references in the newspapers.

What does the peasant do when he is forced to pay taxes? How can he extract himself from his difficult situation and where can he find salvation? He turns to the moneylender. He asks once, twice, a third time, and he finds himself completely in the moneylender's hands. He has become like a leaseholder and the merchant has become the owner. Willy nilly the question occurs, why does a peasant not leave his land? For the simple reason that he has nowhere to go. In recent times, industry has grown up in China comparatively quickly. But all the same one might say, this is a pathetic amount of industry for a country with such an enormous population as China. While China may have, let's say, a significantly well-developed textile industry, all the same the contemporary Chinese textile industry is no bigger than the industry which exists in Czechoslovakia, a country with a population of 14 million. But in China, there is a population of 400 million. We, with our sparse network of [Russian] railways, calculate its extent at 40, 000 *verst*, while they have only 10,000. What does that mean? It means an extraordinarily slow industrial development of the country. We see in the course of 20 years the foundation of an entirely new stratum of landowners. Some of our writers describe some kind of semi-feudal landholders. This is untrue. Maybe they existed before the birth of Christ, in the third, fifth, or even the thirteenth centuries, but they have long since disappeared. The mass phenomenon is commodity capital, the moneylender who enslaves the countryside.

If you saw in the Turkestan cotton industry unbelievable levels of exploitation by commodity capital, about which one of our comrades has written a book published by our Party School in Tashkent,[8] then in the rice, cotton and tea plantations in China you would see the same social picture, the same exploitation by commodity capital. And local capital goes into the countryside, because local industry is not developing sufficiently rapidly. The Chinese capitalist does not take the risk of building a factory, against which some American trust would defeat him by virtue of the cheapness of its wares. Therefore, he, like the moneylender directs his money into the countryside. So it is predetermined that the peasant appears on the historical scene and will fight against the landowner, who forms part of the capitalist class of China.

C[omrades], just two years ago and up to last year, when we spoke with our Chinese comrades, partisans of Sun Yat-sen, and predicted that the peasants would revolt, they disagreed with us. They told us that the peasants are too oppressed and are capable only of raising themselves up to the level of a bandit movement, but they would certainly not play a role in a mass revolutionary movement. For us as Marxists, however, it was clear that it is inevitable that the time has come for the peasantry to emerge on the stage of political struggle. I shall speak of that further on.

Thus, the capitalist enters the revolution so as to destroy imperialist privileges, which prevent him from exploiting the workers and peasants himself.

The worker enters the struggle against foreign capital and against Chinese capital.

The peasant enters the war against the landowner who exploits him, which is the Chinese bourgeoisie.

What relation has the workers' struggle to foreign imperialism? Why is the workers' struggle a national struggle at the same time? There is a very simple reason. It comes from the fact that 50 percent of Chinese coal, 80 percent of Chinese iron, 50 percent of the Chinese textile factories are in the hands of foreign capitalists, and the workers cannot struggle for the amelioration of their conditions, since Japanese, British, and American naval vessels rise in defence of these capitalists. Therefore, the peasant strikes at foreign capitalism in struggling with the landowner. Since foreign capitalism holds all China's income in its hands, it maximises the fiscal pressure on the people, giving them no respite.

---

8 Which book is referred to is unknown.

All these social questions exist in the struggle against foreign imperialism. But you can now see that if foreign imperialism, [if] the influence of foreign capitalism on the development of China is the major cause of revolution, then at the same time within this revolution very contradictory interests emerge. The capitalist struggles against foreign capital in order to be able to exploit the workers and peasants himself. However, the capitalist can only struggle against foreign capital until the moment when he reaches the conviction that the worker is more dangerous to him than foreign capitalism. On the other hand, the worker can accompany the bourgeoisie only so far as his interests do not conflict with the interests of this bourgeoisie, until the national bourgeoisie cries out: 'Guard, help! Chamberlain, help me against my own workers!' The bourgeoisie can only go along with the worker until it sees that the people who have gone against foreign capital, can also direct their rifles towards him [it] under the same banner.

Now I shall briefly touch on the historical perspectives of the movement. The history [of the revolutionary] movement of China since the very beginning has reflected two currents – the upper bourgeoisie and the petty bourgeoisie. At this time Sun Yat-sen appeared, about whom Lenin said that his ideology is the ideology of a great representative of a great revolutionary people.[9] Lenin did not spend much time on China, but he immediately recognized that he [Sun Yat-sen] represented the left bourgeoisie and the peasants, just as the SRs did in the Russian revolution, until they betrayed them. These groups do not want the development of the country for the benefit of large scale capital, and even then, at the time of the [1]911 Revolution, they struggled for liberation from foreign imperialism and ⟨...⟩ for the liberation of the peasant masses and full democracy.[10]

At the same time there was a peasant class in China. And Lenin then also said that the working class will support Sun Yat-sen in his struggle against the foreign bourgeoisie.[11]

---

9   See Lenin 1968a [1912], p. 401.
10 See Ibid., pp. 400–06; Lenin 1961a [1913], pp. 138–40.
11 Radek is mistaken. 'Then', i.e. in 1912–13, when Lenin wrote the above-mentioned works, he did not mention and could not have mentioned that the working class would support Sun Yat-sen 'in his struggle against the foreign bourgeoisie'. At that time, Sun Yat-sen had not proposed any anti-imperialist slogans. In his article 'Democracy and Narodism in China' published on 15 July 1912, Lenin merely mentioned that a Chinese Social Democratic party 'criticising petty-bourgeois utopias and the reactionary views of Sun Yat-sen, would probably carefully separate, conserve and develop the revolutionary-democratic kernel of his political and agrarian programmes'; see Lenin 1968a [1912], p. 406.

During the fifteen years which have passed since the [1]911 Revolution, significant shifts have occurred in Chinese development. Above all, they are characterised by the collapse of state power in China.

In 1921, Sun Yat-sen, relying on his connections, conquered what seemed like a small corner in South China for the development of his revolutionary struggle.[12] On the maps, this province in South China seemed very remote and small, equal to no more than a third of a typical Russian province. In actual fact this was a large territory with a population of thirty-eight million, that is approximately the same as our Ukraine.

In [19]21 at the very beginning of the national movement, Sun Yat-sen considered that he needed to create a corresponding military organisation to mobilise the revolutionary forces and embark on the Northern Expedition.

This Northern Expedition, which is unfolding before us, was the dream of old man Sun Yat-sen. Three times in recent years it came out to fight and was beaten.[13] In 1922 a connection was established between us and Sun Yat-sen: Comrade Borodin, arrived in China and began to assist the Chinese revolution.[14] In his final address[15] which will be published by us shortly, Sun Yat-sen reported to the members of the Chinese Guomindang with surprising candour and simplicity ...[16] Borodin explained to them why their military conspiracies, in which they won many victories, still ended in nothing in the last analysis. He said that the reason for this consisted in the fact that they had no party for a start. Secondly, that they had no policy connecting them with the popular masses, so that the whole thing was some kind of military adventure. It was necessary first of all to found a party which could organise the working class and the peasantry; it was necessary to formulate a system of demands; it was necessary to mobilise the popular masses, in which case success was guaranteed. Only then should they establish an army. Until then, according to

---

12 Sun Yat-sen arrived in Canton from Shanghai at the end of November 1920, after the army of Chen Jiongming, the Guangdong warlord, who then supported him, had inflicted a defeat on the armies of his enemies, the Guangxi warlords. On April 7, 1921 he was proclaimed the extraordinary president of the Chinese Republic in Canton. However, in June 1922, Chen Jiongming mutinied and Sun Yat-sen was obliged to escape to Shanghai.
13 Sun Yat-sen tried to organise a Northern Expedition three times, in 1917–18, in 1922 and in 1924.
14 The first contacts between the Soviet Government and Sun Yat-sen took place in 1919. In speaking of 1922, Radek apparently had in mind the conversations of Sun Yat-sen with the Comintern representative Hendricus Maring. As regards Borodin, he arrived in China at the end of October 1923.
15 This refers to the *Testament* of Sun Yat-sen.
16 The quotation is missing from the text.

Sun Yat-sen, it was only possible to use the military. According to Sun Yat-sen, Soviet Russia had taught them to establish their own army, after first creating a party. The first party, the seedling so to speak, was the Guomindang party. It was founded at exactly that time, during the years 1922–23. Before that it was not a party, but simply a well-known political tendency of the general ideology of the struggle of the petty bourgeoisie against imperialism. Only in 1922–23 and [19]24 did they begin to establish youth cadres, educated in the 'ABC' of the struggle against imperialism. In Guangdong it was impossible to do much. The province was full of guerrilla detachments, various generals, who paid lip service to Sun Yat-sen, but who themselves robbed the peasants. There was very little industry in Canton, it was growing very weakly, the majority of the local proletariat consisted of artisans (whose forces were feeble enough), from whom one could not create a significant force. A change occurred only at the moment of the Shanghai strike.[17] Then circumstances began to change a little in a more promising direction. In the first place, Canton received allies. Secondly, during the strike, a hundred thousand Chinese workers left Hong Kong island, blocking the way to Canton. One hundred thousand Canton workers were mobilised, from which workers' pickets were organised, which denied passage to goods, and a hundred thousand armed workers (albeit, naturally, poorly armed); that was already a significant force.[18] The military academy established in Whampoa[19] provided the first cadre of Chinese soldiers, and this situation led to the first major confrontation in Canton. What did the events in Canton amount to? What was the situation in the Guomindang in Canton up to that time? Sun Yat-sen had died and there remained a revolutionary programme, a programme for the liberation of the peasants, a programme of the socialist base in Canton and it was necessary to carry this programme out. But between this programme and reality there were many contradictions. What this reality was is demonstrated by the fact that with a population of thirty million, the government could only obtain less than five dollars a month

---

17 This refers to the Shanghai events of 30 May 1925, i.e. the demonstration by Shanghai citizens, including workers, under anti-imperialist (mainly anti-Japanese) slogans. These events marked the beginning of the National Revolution of 1925–1927.
18 This refers to the Hong Kong-Canton anti-imperialist strike, which took place on 19 June 1925 to 10 October 1926. It was organised by the CCP as a mark of solidarity with striking Shanghai workers. According to some accounts 250 thousand workers took part in the strike; see Akatova 1959, p. 5. The Hong Kong-Canton strike committee under the leadership of Su Zhaozheng headed the strike.
19 The military academy of the National Revolutionary Army of the Guomindang was founded on 1 May 1924 in the Whampoa district of Guangdong with the assistance of Soviet military advisers.

through the poll tax,[20] that means that they had no administration for tax collection in the countryside, this existed only in Canton. If you examine its financial policy, then it consisted in taxes on paper houses, taxes on beverages, etc., in other words these were indirect taxes. In the field of the workers' question, it was impossible to provide assistance to the small scale artisan proletariat; in the field of agrarian policy it was also impossible to do much. In the countryside the landowner, who often employed guerrilla detachments to tighten the noose around the peasant, carried on untouched. Such a situation could not last long. The peasants began to arm themselves against the landowners. [They] began to understand the national struggle, though after their own manner. The landowner took 80 percent of his harvest from the lease holding peasant. Therefore, the national movement signified a loss to the landowner, and the agrarian movement grew in the countryside, and at that time the first disagreements between the Guomindang and Canton began to be visible. The Guomindang published brochures in which it is argued that the revolution must be a bourgeois revolution and that therefore, there must be no *jacqueries*.[21] The Guomindang members are experienced politicians and an experienced politician is one who does not say what he thinks. The so-called centre emerges in the Guomindang. The Chinese revolutionaries declare: we will obey the Guomindang. But as Ilych said, ears don't grow from the forehead. The Russian revolution demonstrated that the revolution demands the dictatorship of one party, they said, and this party can only be the Guomindang, and it follows that one must obey the Guomindang alone. There can be no division between Communists and Guomindang members. At the head of the movement is the Guomindang, despite the fact that Marx and Lenin are great teachers.

They suggested an enumeration of the Communists. But usually people want to know something not just out of casual interest, but for some purpose or other, so that it may have significance at a certain moment in the future. They declare a quota for the Communists – one third, because, if you follow, just because we are a part of the world revolution but are an oppressed people, we will not allow ourselves to be oppressed by the Communists. Last year, there was an attempt to conduct something like a coup d'état. In Canton there were small Communist demonstrations. But the coup did not come to a conclusion. It provoked resistance in the Guomindang and suffered entirely predictably defeat.

---

20   Thus in the text.
21   *Jacquerie* is a peasant uprising in France in 1358.

I ought to say that the possibility of a British provocation cannot be excluded here. Chiang Kai-shek himself belongs to the most vacillating wing. They begin to scare him saying that the Communists want to exclude him etc. But it is not a question of personalities. It is typical that no sooner than the first reports of uprisings reach the papers, than they are embellished with information that 'a Russian has been arrested, Communists have been arrested' …

Usually, it comes down to the fact that ⟨…⟩ a group of Communists sat under house arrest for several hours. And the whole story is terminated. As comrade Kropotkin said, whoever studies the beginning of the revolution attentively, will find the whole structure of the future revolution in its very first days. The roles are determined. Chiang Kai-shek will struggle together with the workers and peasants, but the bourgeois right wing of the Guomindang will break away. This breach will create groups of Communists and Guomindang and grow until such time as the defeat of Feng Yuxiang leads to a strong Communist government in China.[22]

I ought to say that when we came to make speeches or talk in private conversations with our Chinese comrades, we were the most determined opponents of this approach until the last possible moment.[23] We considered that they were still weak through and through. But it turned out that the enemy was ten times more rotten than we had thought, but they were ten times more powerful. The enemy had ten-time better arms than the Canton people. Wu Peifu had the major metallurgical factories in China as his bases. The Chinese [Cantonese] had only a small arsenal, hardly any aeroplanes, and very little artillery. Worse still, the railways do not connect Canton with Hankou, and they had to march this route on foot. If the peasants had been against the Canton army, they could have made their movement impossible. It was impossible to take three-inch mortars through the rice paddies without the assistance of the local population. But behold the peasants met the Canton army with the deepest sympathy, helping it to advance. It turned out that Wu Peifu's army was destroyed. The struggle with it involved more bloodletting than any conflict up to the present time, since they controlled significant forces in the shape of good artillery, but still they could not stand up to the Canton bayonet. In the course of several months the Canton men marched through several thousand *verst*, and conquered the whole of southern China up to the Yangzi River.

---

22 Thus in the text. This refers to the defeat of Feng Yuxiang's army in battles with the Fengtian militarist clique in March 1926. Naturally this defeat could not lead to a strong Communist government in China.
23 This refers to the Northern Expedition.

What happened on this territory? Everywhere where the army marched, the peasants rose, and armed peasant bands rose against the landowners. The landowners recruited kulaks, which were about ten percent of the rural population. At the same time, the workers went on strike. The strikes were against foreign and Chinese capitalists. Now the Chinese revolution found itself at a turning point, from the point of view of the internal situation. Up to that time, the Chinese revolution represented an alliance of the industrial bourgeoisie, the petty bourgeoisie of the cities and countryside and the working class. Who would break way from this bloc? The landowners and the industrial proletariat ...[24] In what way did they break away? One part departed openly, and this was the least dangerous part. The other part, on the contrary, flowed into the Guomindang party and attempted to oppose ... slogans to the struggle of the popular masses ... and tried to terminate the victory of these masses. In the papers ... very characteristic material was printed: the government has changed and the merchants greet it with bread and salt. At the same time, tens of thousands of workers who had fought against Wu Peifu, enrolled. The merchants began negotiations with the government. 'We are prepared to support the government', they said, 'we are prepared to support it with all possible resources. You, of course, will issue new currency, and we will help you by distributing this currency. We have accumulated the money under Wu Peifu. If we lose it, then you will ruin us, i.e., those who support you. Pay us for our old money and we will distribute the new money'. Then there is also a demand concerning workers' disorders and strikes. How can we establish healthy finances if the workers are on strike? It is necessary to improve the position of the workers, wind up the strikes, and forbid them. The landowners declare that although they are against the national enemy, money is being taken from them because the rent is being reduced. Thus, you see pressure exercised against the Canton government, on the one hand, by the open breaking away of a part of the bourgeoisie, by the flight of part of the bourgeoisie, and on the other hand ... That which is being endured at the moment must be resolved in the course of weeks and months, during which the issue of a united Guomindang army must be resolved. The government raises the wages of the workers. The rate of pay in the most industrial district fluctuates between three and twenty-five rubles a month. The government almost doubles the pay ...

But the working class cannot accept compulsory arbitration even under a revolutionary, even under a coalition government, and not even under a

---

24 Thus in the text. It should read 'bourgeois class'.

workers' government.[25] Concerning the peasantry, the government decrees the reduction of leases by 25 percent. But if the peasant is giving up 80 percent of his harvest in the shape of lease payments, then he has too little left over.

In the army almost all of the commanders are the sons of landowners. The government is in a really tight relationship with this class. Sun Yat-sen's son is a merchant educated in America.[26] Such a situation is most dangerous, as there is nothing more dangerous than manoeuvring or sitting between two stools. This means not supporting the bourgeoisie and certainly losing the peasant, the peasantry. The Guomindang ranks understood this. 20 March of last year the then president of the Political Bureau of the Guomindang[27] was obliged to resign under the pressure of an attempted coup d'état. In Hankou, the workers arranged a sort of carnival, just as we in our time burned Vandervelde etc., so they burned a puppet ...[28] of the Guomindang.

Now the question arises of a reshuffle [within] the government, a reshuffle, which from the period of the deal [with the bourgeoisie] should have led to the period [of a bloc] of the peasants, workers and the petty poor. The fate of the Chinese revolution in the next few months will depend on the degree of strength, bravery and energy, with which this is conducted, for the centre of the issue is no longer Shanghai but Hankou. Let's think carefully about the question of the struggle with imperialism. The Hankou government is conducting negotiations with the British. When you are a young and growing force preparing for battle, you must win time. But even if you want to win time, you still need to march with small steps. In principle, these negotiations are correct, and the Chinese Communists do not object to them. But let us suppose that the Hankou government decides to orientate itself not towards the peasants and workers, but towards the capitalists and landowners. Then, these negotiations would signify a deal of the Chinese bourgeoisie with world imperialism.

Let's take another example. Now it may be irrational, and I personally think it is irrational, to throw oneself on imperialist bayonets. But suppose the Hankou government is forced to go and storm Shanghai. If this government attacks without co-ordination with revolutionary Canton, then a defeat in Shanghai could be a defeat lasting for many years.

---

25   At the beginning of December 1926 an arbitration commission was set up in Wuhan for the resolution of disputes between entrepreneurs and workers. The creation of this commission was endorsed by Zhang Guotao on behalf of the CC of the CCP.
26   Sun Fo.
27   Wang Jingwei.
28   In the text at first stood 'pra[vogo] Guomindanga' (rig[ht] Guomindang), but then 'pra' (rig) was struck out.

When the Poles smacked us in the face in 1920, and they gave us a bloody nose in that operation,[29] Vladimir Ilyich said, [that] if that had happened in 1918 we would have gone to pieces. But in the intervening period we had become so much stronger that after rolling away with the greatest elegance from Warsaw to the Berezina [River], we even found enough strength to suffocate Wrangel. And if we had not had a dictatorial government, linked to the masses, it would understandably have been routed and we would have withdrawn from the front as Kerensky did. Therefore this is the critical moment for the establishment of a revolutionary government. I would like to dwell for a minute on the question of perspectives. Many comrades are interested in the question of the so-called non-capitalist development of China. What sort of formula is that? Whenever I have spoken I have always received a heap of notes on the topic, asking what is the non-capitalist development of China? C[omrades], there is nothing to be afraid of. Nikolai Ivanovich [Bukharin] often uses academic words describing completely understandable things.[30] Look at the history of the Russian revolution for example. This is the transformation of a bourgeois revolution into a proletarian revolution. It was belated like the [1]905 Revolution and even more than the [1]905 Revolution. The motive forces are now the proletariat and the peasantry. The Chinese bourgeoisie is considerably weaker than it was in Russia, and this already indicates that the Chinese bourgeois revolution is only the first stage, the first step in the development of a coming revolutionary movement, which will go on to the struggle for socialism. Some comrades think that this is possible only after, let's say, the proletariat is victorious in England or Germany or after we have become much stronger. I think that is wrong. This revolutionary movement will develop on the basis of its own internal forces, and its final victory depends on the international conjuncture.

Can it proceed to a socialist revolution even given the present international situation? Of course it can.

Imagine, for example, the following. The English gentlemen decide that they must go on the offensive against the Chinese revolution. The English begin to intervene. What can the proletariat say then? 'I am a bourgeois revolution, so I will not harm the factories'. Of course not. It will throw itself into the con-

---

29 This refers to the defeat of the Bolsheviks in the war with Poland in 1920, as a result of which the Soviet Government was forced to conclude the humiliating Riga Treaty of 18 March 1921 with that country.
30 Radek is probably referring to Bukharin's declaration about the non-capitalist perspectives of development of countries underdeveloped in economic terms, made in his speech to the Seventh enlarged plenum of ECCI. See Comintern 1927b, Volume 1, p. 89.

fiscation of the English and Japanese factories, wherever there are no occupying forces yet. In the second case, how could it conduct the defence of China without taking into its hands railways and factories? Therefore even in the present situation, the proletariat can go over to a general offensive, and very possibly even we Communists would not be able to prevent the proletariat from trying to take over the factories. Here the question might arise as to whether there are enough factories so as to begin the struggle for socialism? Comrades, there is no book in the world, which determines how many factories you need to begin the struggle for socialism.

I remember the words of an old Party comrade, a good comrade, who said to me: 'We are disciples of Marx, but the proletariat is only 10 percent of the population. Can you struggle for socialism with that?' And I then replied to him: 'We shall try and then see how much socialism we can carry out'. Now we have ten years' experience. Socialism begins wherever the proletariat is in power, when it begins to control the national economy. If the industry of the country weakens, then one must make a significant concession to the petty bourgeoisie of the cities. Suppose we had had a strong co-operative movement. We would have exterminated private trade ... We establish co-operatives and as far as possible, we squeeze private trade. We have our successes and defeats, but this is the general tendency. If in the next period of the Chinese revolution the Chinese proletariat is forced by events to take power, it could do two things: build capitalism or build socialism. There is no neuter economy ... Hermaphrodites, if they exist, are an anomaly, an exception in nature, and they don't occur in history ... This word means, as Lenin said, that 'we are not cut off from revolution by the Great Wall of China' ... The proletarian revolution grows out of the bourgeois revolution which has been concluded. When we speak about the two-eyed character of the Chinese revolution, we do not mean that they have created capitalism. Such an idea is understandably unwelcome to the Chinese proletariat. This is a great danger, a danger consisting in the fact that the party did not want for tactical reasons, to jump over stages of development. In 1905, Lenin splendidly foresaw that October was approaching ... True, he did not think that this would come exactly in October. He might have thought that it would be in March, April, or whenever, but in any case he foresaw that the thing that occurred in October was approaching. When he struggled against the idea of permanent revolution, he did not do so because he thought the revolution should end. He very much wished it to be permanent, and he was convinced that that would be realised. But he wanted to show that before building socialism, it was necessary to stir up the peasant, to lead him to crush the landowners and then to develop the democratic dictatorship of the proletariat and peasantry. The actual struggle would lead to a transformation. If you look up the fifth volume of the *Leninskii sbornik*, you will find a small footnote relating to December 1905 'Perspektivy i etapy' ...[31] You will see that Lenin already considered that when the peasant and worker establish a dictatorial democratic government, then not only the bourgeoisie, not only the landowner, but also a significant part of the middle peasantry would secede. He said that then there would be a new period of the dictatorship of the proletariat, which, relying on Western Europe, would be able to repel the attacks of hostile forces of any kind. Lenin devised the 'stages' which would come ... The immediate task was the transition from a coalition of the bourgeoisie to a government coalition exclusively of the petty bourgeoisie of the cities and countryside. This would represent a dictatorship of the basic strata, which would provide the mass of partisans for the Chinese revolution. Only on that basis was victory possible. Of course there is a certain danger that the English will try to oppose ... but there is a thousand times greater danger that the peasant, after months of a national government in Canton, might say: 'But I remained just the same slave that I was already' ... Victories in the Chinese Revolution are very ephemeral things. The army of the provincial [militarists] flowed into the Canton army, and a change in military fortunes was still possible. The Chinese revolution, like the Russian revolution, can win only on the basis of an alliance of the working masses and the peasantry, besides which the petty bourgeois of the cities will play a major role, for they include an important stratum, the artisans. The idea of this alliance is what we are trying to get over to our Chinese comrades. At the same time, we are persuading them, we must persuade them, that to conclude an alliance, the working class must have its own strongly disciplined party, a party standing on its own feet.

As you know, Chinese workers have frequently been shot down. It is different with the generals. When this or that army captures a general, they organise a banquet for him. Then they ask him: 'Do you want to march with us?' If not then, please, depart ... One comrade who lives in China wrote to me: 'Do you know, there is one thing that worries me: the air does not smell of blood here' ... This was written by an extremely peaceable person, who has never harmed anything in his life, apart from fleas. (*Laughter*).

In any case it is clear that the struggle will end with the victory of the bloc of workers and peasants only given the maximum development of an independent Chinese Communist Party, for a peasant communist party should be led

---

31   This refers to Lenin 1926 [1905], pp. 451–52. See also Lenin 1968b [1906], pp. 154–57. This work is dated to the end of 1905-beginning of 1906.

to peasant communism. And only a communist working class, which creates a national movement and constitutes its backbone and which will conquer in the future can lead it.

Our Chinese comrades often ask us: 'Well then, does the Chinese working class exercise hegemony or not?' We answer: 'Obviously, not yet'. But one must not just shout about hegemony, but achieve it. Achieve [hegemony] for yourselves by your relation to the petty bourgeois masses, to the working masses and the peasant, so that they overthrow the present government and install you. Something is already being done in this field. Remember how the British concessions in Hankou were seized.[32] They were taken over by the trade unions without the knowledge of the alliance. The British began to protest. But it's always better when the other man is complaining.

Now a few more words about the relation of these events to us. What I have said shows that we have here a genuine popular revolution, which still finds itself with much in common with our [1]905 Revolution. It is typified by mass solidarity and at the same time has major world significance. If the hands of the coolies throw the British flag off from the buildings of the British concession, then that shows that this revolutionary movement comprises not just a protest against the English, but is also based on mistrust of their own government. Before us is a picture of a people bound hand and foot. And this picture of the Chinese revolution will have an influence on the whole Asian revolutionary movement. But, comrades, though this is a good thing, we might also pay dearly for it. If we want to help the Chinese Revolution, we must consider what serious consequences that this might have for us.

So should we help? This goes without saying.

It is quite possible that the English will declare an ultimatum. They will say: 'Renounce the Russians and we will make concessions to you'. In exactly the same way, the moment will come when they say to us: 'Let the Soviet government barricade the Soviet motherland, so that not a single Communist, nor a single Red Com[mander] can enter China, even via America'. This is all possible. For if we postpone the victory over British imperialism, if only for a few years, then after breaking the Chinese Revolution, they will embark on a direct assault on us, just as in trying to defeat us if the Chinese revolutionaries renounce us. Consequently, it would be in total contradiction with our own interests, if we refused to support the Chinese Revolution. So we can

---

32   At the beginning of January 1927, the workers of Hankou seized the British concession in that city. This took place without the preliminary endorsement of this action by the National government or the General Council of Trade Unions. The Communist Liu Shaoqi organised the workers' actions.

say to the English gentlemen: 'Take us as black sheep, which we are, with all our sympathy for the Chinese revolutionaries. Anyone can love us as white sheep'.

So what does this amount to? It could be a breach with England. Is this breach guaranteed? I don't think so. The English are a practical people, and as they say, it's not worth chasing two rabbits. For, if it comes to fighting with Hankou, then it's better not to be forced to fight on a second front. However, at the moment there are attempts to break off our trading relations with other countries around the world, to influence our logistics in that way etc. Comrades, it would be the height of frivolity to simply wave this aside. These are grave matters. But whoever wants to make revolution not for serious but as a joke, had better abstain from it entirely.

When we struggled for revolution ten years ago, we did not think of holding back. Ten years have passed. As you see, we held back. But now it is coming towards us from the Pacific Ocean. But if we approach this massive movement with petty measures we would not be worthy of the Russian revolution, and on the other hand, we would not consolidate the peace.

On the contrary, one might say that from the point of view of the development of the world revolution, a simultaneous offensive on both China and us would be the most favourable outcome! If the front extended from the Pacific Ocean to the Berezina [River], this would be the most advantageous for us. But they won't go that far. And then our task would consist in ensuring that the sectors under fire would be supported by the other sectors.

In any case, the Chinese events are only just starting to develop. It is impossible to forsee what will happen in three to six months time.

Events in China are very important, and we cannot predict them. It is impossible for us to predict them purely mathematically. Everything is in motion ... Imagine that suddenly a minor unpleasantness occurs tomorrow, and several thousand Englishmen are accidentally chopped to pieces in Hankou. (*Laughter amongst the listeners*).

However, comrades, I fear you have no humanitarian feelings.

(*Laughter*).

If that should happen, you can imagine the wave of hysteria which would greet it in London. They would begin to beat the tocsin, because they are not used to such treatment. The English have organised bloodbaths. Custom is a powerful thing. (*Laughter*).

A whole series of unexpected events might follow ... Events have essentially confirmed, as Lenin profoundly foresaw, when he said that we have in the East a great ally, even when there was as yet absolutely no mass movement. He was deeply convinced that such ideologies as that of Sun Yat-sen, would not arise in vain. Mr. Chamberlain complained not long ago that the English have not learnt much from our school of political literacy (the poor things). (*Stormy laughter*).

They do not understand that it was not the Bolsheviks who gave birth to the revolution, but trade, which first demanded the destruction of the old wall of China, then built Chinese roads and factories, created the contemporary proletariat, upset the peace of the countryside and pushed the peasant towards revolution ... They simply don't understand. Perhaps if they had read Bukharin's *Istoricheskii materializm*,[33] they would have orientated themselves better to these events. (*Laughter*).

[One author] in one of his books, *Progress in China*, predicted that China would become one of the most powerful industrial countries of the world.[34] This brilliant prophecy was not accidental then. The author analyses the economic and geographical conditions and comes to that conclusion. There are those who say that without the French Revolution no contemporary regime could exist. Vasiliev, a tsarist professor of Kazan University, says that it is better not to develop industry if you don't want to pass through a revolution. But this would not be the French Revolution, it would be the first classical proletarian revolution. It would be a revolution beginning with a Jacobin phase, but it would not be a revolution culminating with the execution of Gracchus Babeuf, it would be a revolution which would end with the victory of the international proletariat, which is growing with such speed, that we anticipate that it will soon be able to become the equal ally of the Russian proletariat.

RGASPI. F. 326. Op 2. D. 32. Ll. 46–72.
Typescript, original, unsigned.

---

33   See Bukharin 1921.
34   This may refer to Wang 1926.

CHAPTER 5

Driving Forces of the Chinese Revolution: Lecture to the Communist Academy

13 March 1927, Stenographic Report

Comrades! The second anniversary of the death of Sun Yat-sen coincides with a turning point in the history of the Chinese revolution, with a moment of major political crisis, which may well determine the fate of the Chinese revolution for a very long time to come. If until now we have had warfare in China, both of the military cliques between themselves, and the war of the Canton army, having everything ahead of it, or so it seemed, now there is a very specific kind of class war. If it was difficult for a Russian Communist to penetrate the meaning of this struggle, if you needed special skills to understand why Zhang Zuolin was struggling with Wu Peifu, now during the past six months we see before us a massive picture of unfolding class war in China, which rips down all the curtains, disperses all the clouds which had complicated an understanding of what the Chinese Revolution is, and what its driving forces are. All this time we defined the Chinese Revolution as a revolutionary national liberation movement. A revolutionary national liberation movement is one of the types of bourgeois revolution, it is a bourgeois revolution in countries in which the yoke of exploitation by the ruling classes is connected with the supremacy, direct or indirect, of the imperialist ruling classes in a period, let's say, of the industrial bourgeoisie, in a period of imperialism, of the financial bourgeoisie. But already in 1905, Lenin taught us that it is not sufficient to say bourgeois revolution. To make clear what kind of revolution it is, one must clarify here what strata of the bourgeoisie are struggling, one must clarify precisely which popular masses are taking part in this struggle, for which objectives; one must weigh up the international conjuncture and only then will the naked slogan, the naked definition of the 'bourgeois revolution' take flesh on its bones, will the character of the revolution and its tendencies become manifest. In 1905, in polemic with the Mensheviks, Lenin said that the bourgeois, Kadet, industrial landowner seeks a deal with tsarism in the revolution. The naïve republican peasant who was struggling against tsarism, attempted to eliminate the social basis of tsarist rule – feudal agriculture. Therefore, if we speak about the driving forces of the Chinese Revolution, we must here and now clarify, in broad brushstrokes in the first place, the peculiarities of the capitalist development of China. [We must] clarify the sources of the strange phenomenon that part [of the Chinese] bourgeoisie – that part which in other countries was closer to the corresponding period of the history of the bourgeois-national movement, for example, mercantile capital, from the very beginning [was] against revolution, while another part of the bourgeoisie – industrial – played a progressive role in certain periods, that the struggle of the landowning class played a progressive role in one field of the contemporary development of China. Only after clarifying this for ourselves can we understand what this turning point, which we must now overcome, consists of. And only then will it be possible to pose correctly the question of the so-called non-capitalist development of China. Understandably, I will not give any figures in my lecture: it is already late evening and this is only one lecture. But I will try in a short introductory section of my lecture to give a description of the peculiarities of Chinese capitalism. We have usually taken the view that the Opium War broke down the Chinese wall and opened China for world capitalism. But if we take figures for the ninety years of penetration of China by foreign capital, that is, since the beginning of the nineteenth century up to the [1894–95] Chinese-Japanese War, we shall see that during this period, during which we had two major wars,[1] a massive revolution[2] in whose battles millions of people perished, this period provided minimal fruits for the development of capitalism in China.

If we take just the figures for Chinese exports and imports for the period from 1803 to [18]94, then we shall obtain completely ludicrous figures. It is a matter of t[aels], that is units of 1 ruble and 60 kopecks. Exports from China were equivalent to 116 million t[aels]. What did these exports consist of? 58 percent tea, 28 percent silk. If you take exports for one hundred years, then they rose by only one million. 45 million consisted in the supply of cotton textiles, and seven million of metal goods. True, nothing goes into the category of machine production and the growth of this is explained not by the growth of the staples of foreign wares, but by the inclusion of a certain number of ports, an increase in the number of treaty ports. What do the imperialist wars signify? The two Opium Wars gave England the following gains. The capitalists seized military bases for further incursions in the shape of several treaty ports, and the capitalists were able to export into this huge country some of their textile products, plus opium, which went to the closest ports. What products did China export? Tea and silk, of which there was a surplus in the country, products which were the object of internal trade at all times.

---

1   This refers to the Opium Wars in China (1839–1842 and 1856–1860).
2   This refers to the Taiping Rebellion (1851–1864).

This introduced no changes in the process of production. Production in the countryside was in the hands of the peasant petty proprietor, industrial production was in the hands of the artisan in the city. This was in the main the production of articles of luxury. Mass industrial production was in the hands of peasants and craftsmen,[3] whose products were bought up by capitalists and trading buyers. This was the picture for ninety years and we see no change in it. Changes only begin after the Sino-Japanese War, between [18]94 and 1901.

[In the period] between the Sino-Japanese War and the Boxer Uprising, the levers by means of which foreign capital inserts itself in China were as follows. In the first place, the binding of China with a state foreign loan. Until 1894, China had no foreign debts. By the time of the 1911 Revolution it had already a foreign debt of more than a billion rubles, created by reparations to Japan and reparations for the Boxer Uprising.

The second means for the insertion of foreign capital into China was the construction of railways, binding China by the force of English, Russian, French and German capital. At the end of the nineteenth and beginning of the twentieth century, ten thousand kilometres of railways were created in this way.

A third element was the construction of capitalist enterprises by foreign imperialism. Stimulated by the construction of railways, the high tide of foreign capital permitted the foreigners to take into their own hands the mining of coal and the mining of iron ore and to build textile factories in China itself. If you take the figures for this period, then it appears that for the decade after the Boxer Uprising ⟨...⟩ before the First World War, the figures are pathetic.

Already before the war, a series of books appeared on industrialisation in China, but all this was just science fiction. World capital, having built the railways, could have raised the question of the industrial development of China. Until then, the class results of this development were as follows: under the influence of the war a very wide stratum of mercantile bourgeois emerged, tied with foreign capital, precisely a comprador bourgeoisie. Not knowing the language, not knowing the country, foreign capital needed an intermediary, which was in part hired, in part collaborated with it, and thus created a class of mercantile bourgeoisie, in contact with international imperialism and capitalism and tied up with them. There was no industrial bourgeoisie yet. The proletariat was scarcely emerging, the peasantry was hardly touched by this capitalist process.

---

3 Thus in the text.

What was the relationship of the old classes to the invasion of China by foreign capital? What was the relationship of the landowning class and the local merchant class living in the treaty ports? Part of the bureaucracy, but not all, begins a struggle against the penetration of foreign capital. The peasant masses rise up against foreign capital in the Boxer Uprising. The collapse ⟨...⟩ of this rising was to the benefit of the most reactionary part of the Chinese democracy, which dreamt of the penetration of China by foreign dividends. The massive defeat of this uprising and its consequences increased resistance to the penetration of capital altogether. A part of the most reactionary elements of old China tried to defend itself from the penetration of European capitalism on the basis of Chinese capitalism. Collins book, *The History of the Metallurgical and Coal Industries of China* draws a remarkable picture of the sabotage of the concession policy of the government in the provinces by the landowners, merchants and a progressive part of the bureaucracy.[4] They advance the slogan 'We ourselves will develop capitalism'. In this period, two tendencies emerge in the Chinese national liberation movement. One taking its beginning from Li Hongzhang, who was perhaps the first of all the Chinese bureaucrats to understand the impossibility of denying access to foreign capital and who built the first telegraph line between Tianjin and Beijing. And when officials tore down the telegraph lines and declared that this line attracts an [evil] spirit, he declared to them that if the line were torn down again, something evil would happen to their spirits.

This line of going along with capitalist development found its expression in Kang Youwei, who seeing the advancing imperialist threat, proposed in his memoranda the following programme: the establishment of a parliamentary government, the facilitation of industrial development, the support of the development of agricultural technical cultures as an export staple, the foundation of a contemporary army [and] etc., etc.[5]

The whole contemporary programme of Chinese liberalism can already be seen in this memorandum, and in this attempt at a coup d'état by revolutionary forces, at whose head stood ⟨...⟩[6] Now K[ang Youwei] and Yuan Shikai have continued to develop this programme. If Kang Youwei represents a left liberal

---

4   Radek is mistaken in the title of William F. Collins's book. See Collins 1918 and 1922a.
5   This refers to the memorandum submitted by Kang Youwei to the Emperor Guangxu in 1895.
6   It is difficult to say what exactly Radek had in mind. It is possible it refers to the so-called 'Hundred Days of Reform'. Radek may have regarded the activities of Guangxu as an 'attempted coup d'état' in the sense that their realization might have led to a strengthening of the power of the Emperor and a weakening of the position of the all-powerful Empress Dowager Cixi.

policy, then Yuan Shikai represents a policy, if one can use the expression, of the Octobrists[7] in the Chinese sense of the term. But simultaneously, another line begins, the line of the national-liberation movement, represented by Sun Yat-sen, who from the very beginning, from the very first steps of his activity begins to advance the line which Vladimir Ilyich calls populist,[8] the line of the dictatorship of the petty bourgeois revolution.

I am not in agreement with comrade RASKOL'NIKOV when he said, that Sun Yat-sen knew the Chinese economy well. A man who never read any economics, apart from the American popularist Henry George, could not know the Chinese economy well. He merely sensed it magnificently. Emerging from a poor peasant family with traditions of the Taiping Rebellion, Sun Yat-sen instinctively understood that capitalism was bringing ruination to the rural masses of the countryside and to the petty bourgeois in the cities. Understanding that, he began to search vaguely for means to adopt all the progressive things from the West while all the same avoiding the consequences of capitalism. When Lenin spoke about Sun Yat-sen's utopianism,[9] he meant exactly this aspiration of Sun Yat-sen: to evade the consequences of capitalist development on the basis of capitalism, of modern technology, given the domination of world capitalism. Already in the first works by Sun Yat-sen, and in his first speeches, a plan begins to take shape which, when we read it for the first time, appears so incomprehensible to us.

But I think that if we were to give an English liberal our polemic with the populists to read, it would seem rather savage to him. And when we read Sun Yat-sen for the first time, we cannot understand what he is talking about either, but then, after thinking about it, we see that this is a great ideology, whose brain had at its disposal neither the weapons of Marxism nor the generalisations of Chinese revolutionary theories, but which is aspiring to clarify the ideology of the petty bourgeoisie (the proletariat did not then exist), to find

---

7   Octobrists are members of the October 17 Union, the Russian conservative party of constitutional monarchists. The name is derived from the Julian calendar date of publication of the October Manifesto (the Russian Bill of Rights) by Nicholas II (October 17, 1905).

8   Populism is the populist tendency in the Russian revolutionary movement of the 1860s–1880s. Its followers acted against both the autocracy and also the capitalist transformation of Russia. They strove for the egalitarian redistribution of the land amongst the peasants, which they considered the main revolutionary force, and the strengthening of the *obshchinas* (peasant communes), which were, from their point of view, the initial form of socialism. The populists organised the so-called 'going to the people' movement so as to arouse the peasantry for the struggle against tsarism: they also employed methods of political terror.

9   See Lenin 1968a [1912], pp. 399–406.

a way out. He seeks an exit using two means; since there is as yet no capitalism in China then the main question is the agrarian question. It is necessary to avoid the disaggregation of the peasantry, to avoid the consequences of capitalism, which is possible by means of the nationalisation of land rent. As you can see again, utopianism. Lenin said that the nationalization of land is no obstacle to the development of capitalism,[10] on the contrary, it opens the door for the development of capitalism. But Sun Yat-sen tries to do this by means of a corresponding fiscal programme and at the same time, tries to seize all the levers, which will prevent the bourgeois democracy borrowed from the West, from having those consequences which bourgeois democracy has, as the organised weapon of capital in the West. For this purpose Sun Yat-sen finds in Chinese history two methods which emerged during the transition from feudalism to a money economy. One of these means was the examinations system, which was introduced by Qin Shi Huangdi in the third century CE,[11] a bit like the reforms of Ivan the Terrible, destroying the Chinese boyars. Its purpose was to tear the administration from the hands of the feudal bourgeoisie. He established the principle that anyone who could show an acquaintance with learning could become an official. Naturally, this principle must develop its own contradictions, so that with the help of money the examinees would buy the examiners, and in time this would not be any kind of barrier against bureaucratic corruption. Sun Yat-sen advanced this means, as we shall see, in one connection and at the same time he thought it necessary to establish an institute of censors, and I do not mean this in a sceptical sense, it would be supposed to play approximately the role which the Control Commission plays with us. There was a massive decentralisation of the country, it was necessary to prevent the officials having too close contact with the population. It was necessary to set up a state institute of censors which was not tied to the localities, which would travel about, would accept the petitions of the population, would defend the interests of the population and exercise control over the administration. Both these institutes [of state examinations and the censorate] were borrowed by Sun Yat-sen from Chinese history. He made them the levers for the military revolutionary dictatorship for the whole transitional period of the founding of the new state, which would stand over the parliament, over the democracy and which would exist as long as it would take to elevate the cultured masses and thus open up the road for further development.

---

10   See Ibid., pp. 404–05.
11   Radek is mistaken. Qin Shi Huangdi ruled China in 221–210 BCE.

Thus, Sun Yat-sen from the very beginning represented a populist strain, a petty bourgeois revolutionary strain as a counter-weight to the liberal-bourgeois. And for that reason, the struggle of these two currents is the struggle throughout the whole history of the Chinese Revolution. The first time after the polemic ⟨...⟩ in America, in London, in Paris, after the struggle between Sun Yat-sen and those people who shared Kang Youwei's point of view, this struggle assumed the sharpest character in the 1911 Revolution, which began in Wuchang. What were the sources of this revolution? The answer to that question would give us the possibility of advancing by another step our acquaintance with the driving forces of the Chinese revolution, for the answer to that question is an answer to the question why the attempt to create a single capitalist government in China failed, why present-day China appears to be a federation of territories struggling against one another, in which each one finds itself in the hands of one of the warlords. The international bourgeoisie, international imperialists now weep over the collapse of China. The present American Ambassador in Beijing Mr. Mon [John McMurray] ... several weeks before his nomination to this post wrote an article on the significance of railway construction in an American journal, in which he says: 'We could have found any amount of money for them, but who should we give it to? Instead of having a single firmly established government, to which we could give money, either they do not have it at all, or, which is worse, they have ten governments fighting among themselves'.

Austen Chamberlain declared recently: 'We', he said, 'are a nation of shopkeepers, we want to trade, we began to trade with China, but now there is such disorder that there is no government'.

What led to the fall of the Manchu dynasty, why did the founding of a new government fail, and what role did the revolutionary movement in China play in this struggle? We must show briefly that the gradual loss of the land in the hands of the Manchu aristocracy, of the Manchu Cossack regiments [banners],[12] which the state failed to counter, though it was obliged to repurchase almost three times over ⟨...⟩, with the result that the whole Manchu core of the dynasty was left without land. Of course this circumstance played a role, but this was not the decisive reason. We must search for the decisive reason in the Chinese budget. Before the Sino-Japanese War, the Chinese budget consisted of 150 million rubles. 35 percent of them consisted of customs duties, transit duties, and salt taxes. After the Boxer Uprising in the Boxer Protocol it was decided that the customs income, which until then was levied on foreigners,

---

12   This refers to the traditional Manchurian eight-banner forces.

but which was in the hands of the Chinese government, would be transferred into the hands of foreigners as a guarantee of the interest from the loans for the payment of the Boxer reparations.

In 1911 the salt monopoly was also handed over. In this way, 45 percent of the Chinese government's income was located outside its budget, in the hands of foreign capital. Meanwhile the expenditure requirements of the Chinese government rose to unheard of heights for the simple reason that the pressure of foreign imperialism forced China to create an army. We see how Yuan Shikai begins to build in Zhili Province ... We see how instructors are recruited from Europe, how ammunition is ordered from Europe. This massive expenditure comes at the same time as there is a reduction in government income and the disappearance of 45 percent of government income. I think that if the King of England were to find himself in this situation, that 45 percent of his income had been handed over to America, I doubt if he could command the loyalty of all the civil service. And the collapse of the Chinese government was provoked by the fact that every local administration tried to secure for itself those sources of income which it could gather in the localities. The Wuchang Rising itself began with the fact that while the peasant masses were silent, the army, whose wages had not been paid, mutinied and the revolutionaries used this opportunity, but, I must emphasise, in the absence of a broad mass peasant movement.

When Sun Yat-sen became head of the government in 1911,[13] he unveiled his programme. He wanted to carry out his populist programme. In the absence of a peasant movement, in the absence of a workers' movement, the intelligentsia, or that stratum of it, which could respond to this programme, understandably found itself to be an extremely weak base. Yuan Shi-kai prudently concluded a bloc with the compradors and advanced his own programme, in which it is stated that imperialism will give us a loan, we will set the national budget on a correct footing, we will reorganise the budget. We will found an army, capitalism will grow with us, even if only foreign for the time being, and then we shall see. And the capitulation of Sun Yat-sen,[14] which C[omrade] Raskol'nikov has described, suggests that his closest collaborators had lost faith in the populist programme. It was a mistake but not an accident. One might carry it out perhaps in other forms, but it was a capitulation of a petty bourgeois programme in

---

13   Sun Yat-sen was elected provisional president of the Chinese Republic on 29 December 1911 and began his term of office on 1 January 1912.
14   This refers to Sun Yat-sen's resignation on February 13, 1912 from the post of Provisional President of the Chinese Republic in favour of the most powerful warlord Yuan Shikai. Sun Yat-sen took this step so as to avoid civil war.

the face of the silence of the petty bourgeoisie and in the absence of the classes which might have organised the petty bourgeois and led it behind them.

In 1911, we also see the struggle of both tendencies, on the one hand, the mercantile bureaucracy, tied up with foreign capital, incapable of struggling against it since this mercantile bourgeoisie was ruining the countryside and could not lead the countryside behind it, incapable of struggling against it because it feared any kind of revolution, the old administration and the military went along with it. And, on the other hand, the petty bourgeoisie, of whom only the avant garde came out into battle in 1911. And we shall see later, how it is now not just the shadow of Sun Yat-sen that hangs in the air over Hankou, but also the shadow of his enemy, Yuan Shikai.

What did the world war add? It added the origins of a new class, the Chinese industrial bourgeoisie. Thanks to the fact that as a result of the war, the importation of goods to China from England, France and Germany was held up, the petty bourgeoisie, the mercantile bourgeoisie of China begins to accumulate money and invest it in industry. You can find a very characteristic picture of what was going on in China in the wonderful monograph of one of the best books on China in existence, in Professor [B]Lieu ... 's book.[15] He describes the whole social structure in China. He describes the origins of the Chinese textile factories during the war. We see the landowner giving three thousand, the merchant five thousand, and a certain capital is created, on which they tried to construct their own industry, which emerges in the absence of foreign wares, in the absence of competition, despite the inadequacy of capital, inadequate experience and maybe, the poor quality of their wares.

The war years establish a new bourgeoisie, they double the size of the proletariat, and establish, at least, the fact that China now has 3 million spindles in the textile industry. But when they speak about the massive development of Chinese capitalism, one must point out that Czechoslovakia with a population of fourteen million has the same number of spindles in its textile industry.

When they talk about the massive development of Chinese capitalism, one must point out that Czechoslovakia with its fourteen million population has just as many spindles in its textile industry as China with its 400 million population. We see the emergence of metallurgical industry, the coal industry etc. The industrial bourgeoisie of China proposes a new programme to world capitalism. If Yuan Shikai had reconciled himself to the fact that China would not be able to establish its own industry, because it could not nurture it with the help of protective tariffs etc., then that bourgeoisie, already feeling firm ground

---

15   This refers to the following publication: Lieu [1927].

under its feet, comes to world capitalism with a programme for the equality of relations between China and the world bourgeoisie, comes with a programme for the cancellation of all the imperialist privileges. That attempt would have created the conditions for the victory of capitalism by a liberal route, but it unravels thanks to the fact that world capitalism does not simply refuse to make any deals with it, but on the contrary, tears off Shandong Province and hands over its factories to the strongest capital investors in the Far East.

And here in 1919 begins the second wave of the national movement in China, the boycott of Japanese goods. The petty bourgeoisie is without its own programme and places itself at the disposal of the upper bourgeoisie. But thanks to the fact that for a while in these years the influx into China of foreign capital, apart from Japanese capital, is stopped, thanks to the fact that we have in practice a financial boycott of China by the international imperialists, the degeneration of the entire capitalist development in China begins. Imperialism developed the bourgeois and capitalist forces but slowed down the participation of the Chinese bourgeoisie in independent capitalist construction. But together with this, thanks to the upheavals of the war and the post-war crises, the importation of foreign goods into China was very limited. The simple fact that in the country there are no railways, the fact that the English sell the Japanese their textile factories is characteristic for an evaluation of what is going on there. We know, for example, of the wealth of America, but capital investment by America in China is insignificant in this period. By its policies, imperialism places China in conditions in which China can't exist. Why can't it? Who could exist in those conditions? The question is not in the interests of the industrial bourgeoisie. It is struggling for its advantages, but it is still a weak class, which has also suffered from revolution. Therefore, the central question of the revolution is its organisation as of a mass revolutionary movement given the weakness of the proletariat in the countryside. How do all these economic processes resonate in the countryside? In the first place, the competition of cheap foreign wares kills off the small craft industries, subjects them to unheard of heavy conditions, for the urban artisanate makes objects of luxury, but the peasantry with his canvas and his cotton textiles must compete with cheaper foreign wares. Apart from that the Chinese peasantry must compete on the world market with tea which the English produce in Ceylon, besides which they produce it with the use of all up-to-date technology. To no less a degree this relates to tobacco also. After exporting tobacco abroad, the peasantry of China were confronted there with cheaper varieties. It produces dearer tobacco, since it has no modern technology at its disposal and therefore cannot stand the competition. What is the result of this? Crafts, artisan crafts, the crafts of the Chinese workers, like domestic work, have either gone bankrupt or the circumstances of their work have deteriorated to such an extent, that the peasant does not receive from their crafts that part of their budgets, which they did previously.

In the second place, the fiscal yoke on the peasants grows to unheard of levels. The experts in Chinese finances, Girol [Chirol] ... and Lores ... write that at the present time the Chinese peasant pays four to five times more than he paid in 1910.[16] For a very simple reason. On the basis of the compromises of 1913 [1813 in the text] ... This was limited by the central government in so far as it strove to gouge out the maximum. That was one source. The Taiping Rebellion. Now the central bureaucracy has less income, but since it needs greater means to cover its expenditure, then these expenses are allocated by the central government in peasant provinces. The militarist is obliged to fight with the peasant in so far as ⟨...⟩ it is possible, since he does not know how long he will last, and he must use this time to gouge out the maximum. This is the first point. Secondly, since the peasant has become the object of struggle between the warlords as a source of tax revenue, this is where one must find an answer to the question, why did Zhang Zuolin drop out of Manchuria and poke his nose in Zh[ihli] and other provinces. For a very simple reason. Having occupied this province, he has in his hands a region in which tea and silk are produced, and in which there is iron and coal. Consequently, it is a region from which one can gouge out more than from other provinces. But since this situation creates a condition of permanent war, and warfare requires great armies, so now in China 1.5 million men or more are accounted as under arms. Such curiosities as the following often occur: travellers who previously discovered little towns, now discover entire armies. (*Laughter*). What does this figure mean – 1.5 million peasants under arms? This means the ruination of the whole mass of the peasantry both by means of taxes and by means of conscription. A couple of days ago I read a wonderful description of social life in Beijing, written by a teacher of the Sun Yat-sen Institute, com. ANDREEV.[17] He has studied Chinese social life thoroughly, as he lived in Beijing for several months, and what is especially important, he lived with a worker's family and with the family of a petty bourgeois. From Beijing he brought out a simple lecture, which says more about what is going on there, what the situation is, than ten books on China published by us, which are nothing more than reprints of Brockhaus and Efron, with a new sauce each time. (*Laughter*). In this lecture, c[omrade] ANDREEV relates that in Beijing, every now and then the coolies disappear, because they know that Zhang Zuolin is advancing; he will mobilise a labour force, so the coolies

---

16 Which work this refers to is unknown.
17 See Andreev 1927, pp. 198–213.

scatter. One must say that the Chinese peasantry does not only give the army conscript soldiers, but literally, and I use the term in the direct and not the figurative sense of the word, all the wars in China are conducted on the backs of the peasants. Given the [absence] of roads in China, when not even a canon can pass through a rice paddy, the peasants are obliged to carry everything on their backs, beginning with the Commander-in-Chief and ending with canons. (*Com.* BUBNOV: *'I must say that not a single canon will ever cross a rice paddy'*). Com. Bubnov is a great general in the name of God, but I have seen with my own eyes in a photograph how the Canton army carried canons on their backs during the relocation of a headquarters. I repeat, I myself have seen this photograph and can present it to the Military Revolutionary Council (*laughter, applause*), however I do not vouch for the fact that the field in question was a rice paddy. (*Laughter, applause*).

Comrades, the ruination of the Chinese peasantry on such a great scale, the ruination of the peasantry by military taxation and labour services is the main consequence of the influence of capitalism on China. The peasant countryside of China can no longer continue its life under these conditions. I say that in the literal sense of the word. Some years ago, we only had the works of American and English experts on the agrarian question in China. We had no books about how the Chinese live, how their work is rewarded, in what conditions are they obliged to work and so on. But we had works describing the customs of the Chinese, how they get married, pray and so on. Now we have several works by our comrades, which give us a full picture of social life in China. I refer, for example, to the work of com. VOLIN, printed in the 9th [and] 10–11th issues of the journal *Na agrarnom fronte*.[18] Several months ago, the work of the German agronomist Wagner appeared,[19] one must observe in passing that Wagner lived in China for around 16 years as the chief of an experimental agricultural station. Wagner's work removed those doubts which I had at that time when I read c[om]. VOLIN's work. One must say that while reading his work, I wondered whether he had not transferred several paragraphs from the 9–10th volumes of the works of Lenin on the Chinese question. In sum, the whole picture drawn by these authors shows that 70 percent of the Chinese peasants live on a budget on which they cannot continue to exist. The ruination of the countryside is taking giant strides. Half of the peasants are leaseholders or semi-leaseholders. And the lease is not, as we say, a semi-feudal lease, it is a new capitalist lease, where mercantile capital, a merchant or an official is the

---

18   See Volin 1926.
19   See Wagner 1926.

landowner, who puts his money into loans given to the countryside. Why? For the simple reason that the sluggish development of industry does not encourage them to invest their capital in industry. You know that the Chinese banks are bad, they are cannibalised, as Shchedrin says, industry is young, inexperienced, works without management, has no tariff protection, so it is dangerous to invest your money in industry. And here it is a simple business: the government takes taxes four years in advance from the peasant. The peasant has nowhere to turn. He goes to and gets in debt with the merchant. So the merchant soon becomes the proprietor of his land and he extorts 50-60-70 percent of the harvest from the peasant as payment for the lease.

The peasant has no escape to the city, because the whole capitalist development of China has been slowed down. There are no growing cities, industry grows feebly, so the mercantile capitalist invests money in the countryside at extortionate rates, and the peasant must accept them whatever the conditions. Such is the influence of capitalism in the countryside. That is why it appeared that the revolution ⟨...⟩ in 1894 had no basis in the popular masses, the peasant always remembers that the Boxer Uprising was ⟨...⟩ beaten, and will not now rise up in the face of continual famines, from which a million people a year die in China (it is worth noting in this connection that the Guomindang rightists say in their declarations: don't follow the Communists, because the peasants are dying of starvation in Russia). The peasant mass has shifted, and this is the new element which we could not demonstrate with such confidence earlier. We were theoretically convinced that it would move on the basis of what was becoming manifest about the Chinese countryside, but even last year I had to persuade comrade Hu Hanming several times that the peasant is on the move. He said: 'We have bandit movements, but the Chinese peasant will play no part'. The Guomindang rightists subscribed to the revolution, but in their heart of hearts they were convinced that only the workers would revolt, while the peasant would sit still. See how the peasant sat still. But the peasant was rebelling in China a hundred years before the birth of Christ. There is no other country where there have been so many peasant revolutions and on such a scale, but they were all suppressed. They were all defeated because the peasants themselves could not make a revolution. The peasant had no ally in the city. The emergence of the working class and its appearance on the historical scene gave the peasant movement leadership. We see the proletarian movement, three or four million industrial workers, there are no exact statistics, beginning with strikes on the Beijing rail[way] in 1922, and ending with the events of 1925 in Shanghai. Now we see, in the first place, the entire depth of the sources of the Chinese revolution. The sources of the Chinese revolution are no less profound than the sources of our 1905 Revolution. One can say with confidence that the alliance of the working class and the peasantry will be still stronger than it was with us in 1905 for the simple reason that they will not fight against two classes, but a single bourgeois class. And this development immediately rescues the national liberation movement from a dead end. If in 1919–20 the Guomindang's national liberation movement was bourgeois, the Communist party had just emerged, they looked at it as at a little group of revolutionary students, Communist fanatics, and no one then believed that the Chinese worker would rise. The German engineer Schtrecker [Stringer], w[ho], it appears, worked in railway construction for 20 years in China, declared in his work on the industrial development of China, that there is no labour problem in China, that the workers are very content. This book appeared in 1922.[20] The author wrote it in 1921 but in 1922 we see a heroic struggle of the Chinese railwaymen and we have a whole series of workers' strikes. When the workers' strikes extended to the grandiose Shanghai strike in 1925, and when the leadership went over spontaneously into the hands of the proletariat, the industrial bourgeoisie was forced to bow to the demands of the workers, to finance the strike to a considerable extent in the same hope which led our liberals to pay for the strike days of 1905. It considers that world imperialism, alarmed at the strike, will make concessions to it, and when it recovers its strength it will settle scores with the workers. The workers' movement stimulates the peasant movement across the country. The peasant sees that a leader has appeared at the very moment, when the mercantile bourgeoisie, bound up with foreign imperialism, is running away from the national movement, at that moment a new industrial bourgeoisie [appears], from which a part of the leadership emerges in the Canton government, for example, T.V. Soong [Song Ziwen], the owner of a large factory in Shanghai. He was obviously not yet an experienced capitalist constructor, because he went bankrupt and then attached himself to the national liberation movement. The Mayor of Canton City[21] is also the proprietor of large undertakings in Hong Kong. There was a whole series of them, who, perhaps sincerely, attached themselves to the movement, thinking that it would be a liberal movement for the liberation of China, for the revision of the unequal treaties and imperialist burdens. It is understandable that now it looks to these gentlemen a little on the difficult side, and how they will react to this remains to be seen. The fact is manifest that the dismemberment is beginning not just of the periphery of the Guomindang, which, like Dai Jitao, was connec-

---

20 In actual fact, as has already been said, this refers to a British engineer Harold Stringer; see Stringer 1922 and 1925.
21 Sun Fo.

ted with various mercantile industrial circles etc., but also of the leading group of the Guomindang. This represents nothing surprising historically speaking. After all, we know Sun Yat-sen's works. In 1911 [1912] all his so-called comrades in arms betrayed him, all his comrades renounced his programme, considering that his petty bourgeois populist programme was rubbish. Some demonstrated their politeness by calling it premature, and other said directly 'get lost' ⟨...⟩ Sun Yat-sen alone mobilised ⟨...⟩, all those who came to him. The students and the merchant diaspora ⟨...⟩ They obviously did not read Sun Yat-sen as we read Lenin, they did not break their heads about what he meant when he said 'censorate'. Let there be a censorate. They were for the liberation of China from the imperialist yoke slowly, step by step. These were liberals, who went with Sun Yat-sen until the time when he spoke and harangued them to follow his programme, but then these people deserted him.

When Sun Yat-sen appeared and broke up the central government, he arrived in Canton and took power, they surrounded him once more and once again recognised his three principles of the five branched constitution.[22] However, what could they do with Sun Yat-sen's principles? So that it will become clearer how they really related to Sun Yat-sen, let me quote for you a few words from the speech by the leader of the left-wing of the Guomindang Wang Jingwei, delivered by him after the death of Sun Yat-sen. 'I remember the autumn of the Chinese year 12' he said, 'that is in 1923,[23] the deceased president summoned his first military conference to the headquarters ...' (*Quotation*).[24]

So what did the power of Sun Yat-sen and the Canton government amount to in the national movement? We who read the declaration of this government in Moscow (and for many years I have had no information apart from the press), we read there of the declaration of the liberation of the peasants and workers. Last year, I wrote an article in *Pravda* about this government, calling it a 'peasant-worker' government. But comrades, the editors, corrected it to 'worker-peasant' government thinking I had made a mistake.[25] I did not protest

---

22 This refers to Sun Yat-sen's Three Principles of the People and his 'Five-Power Constitution'.
23 After the Xinhai revolution a new calendar was introduced in China, from the date of the proclamation of the Republic on 1 January 1912. Thus, 1923 was the 12th year of the Republic.
24 The quotation is absent from the text.
25 This refers to the following phrase: 'In China there is a worker-peasant government in Guangdong province' (Radek 1926). Radek is fibbing here. In actual fact, he had first expressed the thought that the Canton government is the 'first worker-peasant government' of China as early as August 1925; see Radek 1925b. It is true that he developed

and so it remained a worker-peasant government. But comrades, this worker-peasant government consisted from the beginning of the following: a series of generals who looted the provinces, Wu Peifu and Zhang Zuolin looted the provinces, especially Guangdong province, which had the reputation of being the socially developed South, from which the Taiping Rebellion emerged, the province which has a diaspora in America. This province did not permit such methods of crude looting to be used against her as took place in Manchuria. The generals needed a fig leaf and [they] regarded Sun Yat-sen as their fig leaf. But Sun Yat-sen regarded Guangdong province as his revolutionary base. Under the influence of the Russian revolution, under the influence of his personal contacts with the Russian revolutionaries he considered his objective as being to link up with the masses.

Perhaps you have read c[om.] Dalin's article, his letters, where he says that the main aim of Sun Yat-sen ⟨...⟩ was to win over the peasants and in the first place, the poor.[26] In his last, so far unpublished speech in Canton, Sun Yat-sen describes the course of his development. He says: '[W]e defeated the militarists 20 times ...' (*quotation*),[27] 'militarists, who pretended to be my followers. So why were we always beaten? Because we did not have slogans for the masses, we could not create a mass party, which would have been the backbone. We thought we could use the military. But they used us'. And Sun Yat-sen took up the task seriously, as a revolutionary, the task of reorganising the Guomindang in Canton, striving to make it into a popular revolutionary party, uniting the workers, the peasants and the urban poor, to create a military cadre, which would educate the people for war in the name of the revolution, but would not hand over the war and the revolution to people who regard revolution as nothing but war. Sun Yat-sen took on this great work in which he deeply believed, for Sun Yat-sen – comrade Raskol'nikov is absolutely right – he was no falsely inflated grandeur, he is a major historical figure, speaking of which com. Lenin said that the revolution in the East has a great future.[28] In reality during Sun Yat-sen's lifetime the Guangdong government was not what it is now represented as. We can see this most easily if we take the work of our Russian com. Vishniakovskii, devoted to the finances of Guangdong,[29] if we take the work on the position of the workers in Guangdong province, if we take the work of com.

Stalin's thesis of a 'worker-peasant' Guomindang, already enunciated in May 1925. For more detail see Pantsov 2000, pp. 86–87, 114; Pantsov 2001, p. 330.

26 See Dalin 1927.
27 The quotation is absent from the text.
28 See Lenin 1968a [1912].
29 Radek is mistaken in the name of the author. It refers to Vishniakov 1926.

Andreev about the peasant movements in Guangdong province.[30] We shall see what this real government does when it has a financial administration in its hands. What does it do? It does not liberate the poor from financing or direct taxes ... but [liberates them only from] some direct taxes such as the tax on playing cards and on ot[her] entertainments of an even baser kind. (*Laughter*). This epitomised its policy concerning the peasantry. The peasantry of Guangdong province belongs to the most exploited. Major landowners of a mercantile type ruled absolutely here. The working class was very weak, and there was nothing one could do with a few thousand workers. In essence, this was not just a worker-peasant government, but it was a government of progressive mercantile capital, which permitted the workers' organisations and the revolutionaries to campaign in public. This was the essence of its power. Until the moment when about 100,000 Hong Kong workers arrived in Canton from Hong Kong during the boycott of the English. The Hong Kong workers set up workers' pickets, the Hong Kong workers gave the Guangdong Communists strength for a continuation of their work [in] the organisation of the peasants, which had been started under Sun Yat-sen. For the *min*[*tuan*],[31] for the military organisation of the landowners and kulaks, if there had earlier been a major contradiction between the revolutionary platform and reality, now it begins to increase from both sides. It starts to develop from the revolutionary side. The physical fact of the appearance of the Hong Kong workers alters the picture by itself, since up to then the workers found themselves in the deepest ferment, they were dispersed, not representing any real force. On the other hand, the Guomindang centre, seeing what was in preparation, seeing that the Canton government threatened to move towards a really revolutionary path, tried from its situation to make a small correction. Comrades, what does the Guomindang centre represent? The Guomindang centre is nothing more than a diplomatic myth: The Guomindang centre does not exist in nature. The Guomindang centre is people of the right wing, who have not behaved as stupidly as the Guomindang rightists. The right-wing Guomindang have openly announced and said, 'One hand against imperialism and the other hand against Communism', demanding a breach with the Communists. But the Guomindang centre said as follows: 'The experience of the Russian revolution taught us that the revolution requires the dictatorship of one party'. What sort of party can impose a dictatorship if it consists of two parts? Therefore, you can be a Communist in your soul, but you must be a Guomindang man in your politics.

---

30   Radek is mistaken. M. Andreev did not write an article about the peasant movements in Guangdong. Radek may have had in mind Alskii 1926 or Volin 1927.

31   *Mintuan* is detachments for local self-defence.

We know that the Chinese Revolution is a part of the world revolution. Therefore, we subject ourselves to the Communist International, but the Comintern should not interfere in our affairs, but should secure the overall leadership ⟨...⟩

But it should not intervene in military affairs nor in politics. This is the special point of view of the leader of the centre, and the leader of the centre adopted appropriate conclusions from this point of view on 20 March of last year. We read a reference to this 20 March in our press, but I do not know whether the comrades know what this 20 March was. On the 20 March the [soon-to-be] Commander-in-Chief of the present Chinese Army Chiang Kai-shek tried to arrest several Comrades working there, to cordon them off. Later, it seemed as though this had been a misunderstanding. But essentially the Chinese Committee of the Central Party[32] was entirely right, when it declared in its theses, that this was an attempt at a coup d'état.[33] But it is absurd to say that this was just an attempt. It *was* a coup d'état, which only 50 percent matured, for, notwithstanding the release of the Communists from under 'a guard of honour', the Chairman of the Polit[ical] Bureau of the Canton government,[34] Wang Jingwei, a Guomindang leftist, was removed, and Chiang Kai-shek politely proposed to the Communists: if you want to remain within the Guomindang, register as Communists within the Guomindang, so that in case of necessity it will be known where to mount this 'guard of honour'. Secondly, the Communists were obliged not to criticise Sun Yat-sen, and thirdly, to be limited to a quota in the leading [organs] and the administration no higher than 30 percent.

This was a limited coup d'état. Why did the centre not go further? It went no further because, for one, this met with resistance from the lower ranks of the Guomindang. Secondly, it was weak internationally. The central committeemen of the centre could not go further without serious concessions on the part of imperialism, without an agreement with them, but imperialism was preparing not concessions, but an offensive. The help of Soviet Russia was needed, and so the centre did not go all the way.

Comrades, the Canton government in its concrete everyday activity was a government, which did not represent the revolutionary interests of the popular masses. But the simple fact that major revolutionary work was unfolding in

---

32 Thus in the text. It should read the CEC of the CCP.
33 This refers to the resolution of the July (1926) plenum of the CEC of the CCP on relations between the CCP and GMD. See CCP 1926a, pp. 16–24.
34 Of course, there was no Politburo of the Canton government. At that time, Wang Jingwei headed the Military and Political Councils of the CEC of the Guomindang.

Canton, that an army was established there, in which the revolutionary movement had taken root, despite all the obstacles, despite the contradictory tactics of the Chinese government – it played a massive revolutionising role. And this revolutionising role of the Canton government fully justified the assistance given to the Chinese government by our Russian Communist Party. It was only a hook for further advances, for the penetration of the masses. Not just [for] the defence of their economic interests, but to penetrate those strata, into which it was possible to make advances along the line of the national struggle. The Canton government went onto the offensive ⟨...⟩ after the events in Shanghai, there was an attempt to definitively smash Feng Yuxiang's army. Feng Yuxiang's army was born from that movement, for, although it was created by the imperialists, it fought free of them, it distinguished itself from them thanks to the influence of revolution in Russia and thanks to the revived revolutionary movement in China. But then, when they did not succeed in destroying Feng Yuxiang's army, when – and this is the most important fact – the customs conference which was supposed to reach a compromise with the imperialists,[35] collapsed, when it further appeared that Wu Peifu and Zhang Zuolin could not unite, that the Chinese bourgeoisie was too weak to force the militarists to subordinate their particular interests to the common interests, – bourgeois Chinese Canton entered the movement and the Canton Army moved north. But if, perhaps, someone or other among the Canton people thought that they were moving north for military laurels, that they would achieve a great victory for the bourgeois strata in the Chinese revolution, then history mocked them, for, wherever the Canton army appeared, everywhere the peasant masses arose and even the working masses appeared and entered the battle ahead of the Canton Army. The victory of the Canton army – it is not only a victory, as com. Stalin correctly said, of national pathos,[36] which knocked down the enemy, but it is the victory of the influence of the events in Shanghai on the army of the warlords, on the peasant and worker masses of the whole of China. And from that moment on, when the Canton government found itself in the central industrial region, in the Wuchang region, reached Hankou, and found itself under the pressure of the proletariat, the period in which the national movement was essentially a bloc of workers, peasants, the urban petty bourgeoisie and a significant part

---

35   This refers to the Washington Conference of the USA, Great Britain, China, Japan, France, Italy, Holland, Belgium and Portugal, which took place from 12 November 1921 to 6 February 1922 and was devoted to problems of limiting naval armaments and also the situation in the Pacific and the Far East. The main participants of the meeting refused to abrogate China's semi-colonial status.

36   See Stalin 1952c [1926], pp. 360–61.

of the industrial bourgeoisie came to an end, and we moved over to a turning point, a period of transition, which may well decide the question of the future of the Chinese revolution for many years.

I will now move on to what the Hankou government does, what sort of class policy it conducts, how does the crisis which it is living through develop, and what is the way out of this crisis. Only an accurate answer to this question will bring us nearer to the new historical phase. It is vain to talk now about the non-capitalist development of China as of something concrete, until we first determine the preliminary question of the period of the democratic dictatorship of the workers, peasants and the urban petty bourgeoisie. I will say more about this later, but I consider that the most important thing, which a Russian Communist and a member of the Communist International has the right to and must now know is the concrete material, exact material about this class policy, which the Hankou government is now conducting. If we don't know this, we can't even help the Chinese national movement with our sympathies, because if you go to the workers and begin to speak about the national liberation movement, then it seems primitive to the worker who has not lived through a period of national revolution, but has only lived through a socialist revolution. But when you place him on the ground of facts, who, what and for what is struggling in the Chinese revolution – it will immediately become clear, that there they are deciding questions, which affect us as representatives of the working class, as representatives of the Communist Party. I do not know what is happening, at what speed events are moving there in Hankou, in the near future the question will be decided, whether the spirit of Sun Yat-sen will come to the top, which at all events for us, even for Marxists, is not something alien, but which is in the given historical situation the spirit of the union of workers and peasants for the completion of the national revolution to the very end.

Comrades, the former Canton, but now national-revolutionary government of China, occupies areas including the most economically developed. And therefore, the arrival of Canton troops here faces the revolutionary government with basic questions of the revolution. Wherever the troops of Canton arrived, they met support on the part of the peasantry. Without this support the speed achieved by the Canton troops, would have been impossible. In the rear of the Canton army, an extraordinary strong peasant movement began. If last year, receiving figures of the organised peasantry of let's say, Guangdong province, I viewed them with a degree of scepticism because I asked myself how was it possible, given the presence of a million organised peasants in Guangdong province, that agrarian relations there remained without any alteration, when now there cannot be any doubt that this massive movement of the peasantry is a genuine reality. Because time is short, I cannot now read all those descriptions we have which illustrate the rise of the peasant movement which is taking place in China. The bourgeois press abroad and the capitalist press in China just confirm this information. Just days ago I received the work of a German Sinologist, the well-known Dr. Schüler, author of a history of China,[37] who provides an overview of this movement on the basis of Chinese materials, basically confirming this information.[38]

In whose name is this movement growing? It is understood that it would be a bad case of idealism to think that the peasant in the countryside is rising in the name of the national idea in the first place, that the national idea has deeply penetrated into the popular masses there where they have contact with Chinese and foreign capitalism in the heart of China. This foreign imperialism, as a reality, does not influence their lives. This is understood. The peasant rises in the name of his real immediate interests. But if you even allow that the peasant rises in the name of national liberation from foreign imperialism, then one must not for a minute think that the peasant is rising for the sake of one part of his existence – national consciousness, that he wants to liberate China from the foreigners, but does not want to liberate himself from the landowners, who make him an object of their exploitation, who demand interest from loans. We must not forget that the Chinese landowner also takes 50-60-70 percent for the lease. Therefore, it is understood that at the centre of the struggle of the Chinese peasant stands the struggle for land, for the reduction of the tax burden. How does the Guomindang relate to this struggle? We have a resolution of the Canton conference of the Guomindang, in this resolution the Guomindang conference says the following: our officials regard peasant movements as bandit movements, and it is necessary therefore to explain to them the fact that if the peasant struggles for an amelioration of his situation, that does not mean that he is a bandit. Propaganda is a very potent medium, but the question is why officials of the Canton government of Guangdong province for the duration of a whole series of years regarded the peasant movement as banditism [?] For the simple reason that power in the countryside is to be found in the hands of either the landowner or their protégés. But if this is how things stand, then clearly you will be hard put to explain to the landowner by means of propaganda, that if the peasant refuses to allow himself to be robbed that is not banditism.

What is the situation in those Chinese provinces, occupied by the Canton army? How is the situation there? One must say, that power in these provinces

---

37 See Schüler 1912.
38 See Schüler 1927.

was transferred to the hands of the Canton people without any fuss. In the best cases, the governor and some of his closest people ran away, but this was only in the best cases. In the majority of cases the governor remained in post and sent the new powers, the Canton army, against which he had so recently been fighting, their visiting cards. (*Laughter*). As far as the administration is concerned, it remained the old, landowner administration, an administration bound up with the merchants. The entire old government administration remained in place.

How did the new government relate to the agrarian question? How did it relate to it not in words, not in resolutions adopted by the party conference, but by means of an act of state. Such acts of state exist – the decree, which reduced by 25 percent the burden of peasant leases. But what does this reduction mean? Comrades, who know agrarian relations in China well, assert that since the merchant or landowner themselves directly lease out land, this is normally done via an intermediary, so that this 25 percent remains in the pocket of the intermediary. But let us allow for a best case, in which in the name of the national revolution, this intermediary really does reduce the cost of leases by 25 percent. Then that means that the national revolution has reduced by a quarter the burden of the peasants' leasehold payments. But if the national revolution does reduce the peasants' leasehold payments by a quarter, then I am very interested in the question as to how the Canton government will conduct war, because the merchant, the capitalist, even under government pressure, – and we shall see how this pressure appears, – will find a hundred ways of hiding his capital from this fiscal pressure. A significant number of the merchants in Hankou wound up their affairs as fast as they could, transferred their money to banks and moved house to Shanghai. There is information about this in a Shanghai newspaper. But even if the government squeezed with all its force, then it is clear that it would be difficult to grab this mobile capital by the collar. If we as revolutionaries are going to stare the truth in the eye, it is clear that the revolution will be conducted at the expense of the peasants, like all revolutions. Therefore, even given all the confiscations, the main burden falls on those classes which are the leaders of the revolution. By what miracle will the government be able to get from the peasant bread and rice for the conduct of the war? I am not even mentioning money, if it can be separated from the tribute given by the peasant to the landowner. The agrarian policy of the Canton government is so far a policy of liberal landowners, prepared under pressure to grant a concession of a quarter of its burden.

What policy is the Canton government carrying out in relation to the working class? It must be said that the Canton government decreed an increase in wage rates in a whole series of districts, but decreeing does not even compensate the workers for the reduction in wage rates, which have been observed in China in recent years. We have the investigations of our comrades in Canton about the position of the Canton workers, we have Chinese investigations in English about the position of the Beijing workers. As far as the central region is concerned, we have an official document – a proclamation by Chiang Kai-shek. In these investigations the wages of Wuhan workers are cited. They begin from three rubles a month to 25 rubles a month. Chiang Kai-shek says in his proclamation that inflation has left wages far behind where they were ten years ago. The Chinese workers find themselves in a most painful situation. The government, conceding to the demands of the workers for the raising of wage rates, at the same time publishes a decree, introducing compulsory conciliation, forbidding strikes on military establishments ⟨...⟩

Furthermore, armed demonstrations and armed workers' pickets are forbidden. Trade unions are recognised, but they must be registered, and so long as they are not registered, they may not act. But in such a revolutionary situation, you know what a spontaneous movement means, but how an official can hold things up, how can he slow down and drag out the registration, if he personifies the local administration while the government is somewhere far away.

The broad wave of the workers' movement, which seized Hankou led to a less ambiguous demonstration of a workers' policy, if not by the entire Canton government, then at least of part of it. Around Hong Kong there was a case when a factory was picketed off by the military during a strike by order of the Canton ⟨...⟩ region, and when for several days they did not allow the workers' wives in with food for the workers, but allowed representatives of the trade unions in so that they would force the workers to surrender. If this could happen near Hankou,[39] you can well imagine what might happen and what does happen in other more remote districts.

I will permit myself to read out to you several facts so as to acquaint you with the atmosphere of the situation. I have had one of these communications translated into Russian, and it will give you a clear picture of the situation. It says as follows:

'The shooting of workers in Wuzhou in Guangxi province showed that the government of Guangxi province does not relate sympathetically ...' (*Quotation*).[40]

I am not in a position to read all the other communications. I have about 12 of them. I will provide a summary of their information. In L ... province workers' pickets have been disarmed, a workers' demonstration dispersed. In Hun[an]

---

39   This in the text. It should read 'of Canton'.
40   The quotation is missing from the text.

province they relate that members of peasant organisations have been arrested, etc. In a word, we have a whole series of communications, telling us how they beat and wounded arrested workers, how they ban workers' pickets etc.

Comrades, it would be incorrect to think that this is the entire conduct of the government. The general course of the government, as it expresses itself in its programmatic announcements, is a course of manoeuvring between the classes. In official proclamations it says that the workers have the right to improve their situation, that the workers have the right to organise, but that they must take account of the situation, that without the capitalists it is impossible to save China, and that therefore the capitalists should give way to the workers, but the workers, in turn, must give way to the capitalists. Local provincial powers act according to their personnel and commanding staff. Where there are Guomindang leftists or military going hand in hand with the revolution, there the army assists the workers. Where at the head of the army and administration there are landowners, merchants and the old local bureaucracy, there things take place of which we know only a thousandth part. In a word, we have there a sharp picture of the struggle of the working class, the struggle of the peasantry against the landowners and the capitalists. However, if we take its administration as a whole, then the leadership of this administration is not yet to be found on the side of the worker-peasant elements. When Chiang Kai-shek spoke of the necessity of supporting the national movement in a proclamation to the merchants, they, the merchants, put the following question to him: firstly, does he consider strikes as a normal phenomenon, and secondly, how does he consider it possible to finance the government in the face of economic disturbances. How can the government be financed in the presence of economic disturbances ⟨...⟩ asked Minister of Finance T.V. Soong [Song Ziwen] whom (according to the British press so I do not yet regard this as confirmed) the railway workers of the city of Hankou carried around the city in a wheelbarrow, which I consider an entirely correct criticism of his financial policy. (*Laughter, applause*). Soong [Song] publish[ed] a decree about how to put the revolutionary government on its feet financially. This decree provides a key to an understanding of the social policy of one part of the Canton government. This decree establishes the following measures: in the first place, the old money issued by Wu Peifu and ot[her] militarists is accepted, because the money has been amassed in the hands of financiers, merchants and bankers. The peasant receives a reduction of 25 percent of his leasehold payments, but the merchant should not lose any of the money previously amassed. In the second place, we have the recognition of the debts of the Ministry of Foreign Affairs, the recognition of loans, which the merchants gave Wu Peifu in support of the struggle against the national revolution. These debts must be recognised. And the Guomindang organ *Canton Gazette* publishes the very interesting communication that the government has received the support of financial circles by these means. This regulation was very well received here. In foreign circles the plans of Minister of Finance Soong [Song] were also greeted with great satisfaction, for they represent the beginning of the restoration of trust in the government and this appears an 'indication' of the overall financial policy of the National government in relation to the financial obligations, which this government received as its inheritance, which provide world capital with two billion rubles of loans, to which China was bound in the past on fraudulent terms by military force. I do not know whether it would be common sense for the Chinese government to declare a default on these loans at the present time. The present situation of China, perhaps, requires a degree of manoeuvring, but in any case I consider that without a rescheduling, without a review of by whom and when this debt was contracted, it does not follow that it must be sanctioned. For ex[ample], the Boxer debts, to which the defeated country was bound [or] the debt of 230 million, which Yuan Shikai took out without the agreement of parliament, or the debt of more than 300 million, which Japan paid ⟨...⟩ to its own protégés, who betrayed China to Japan ... a revolutionary government is not in a position to recognise these loans without any attempt at rescheduling, without a struggle if it wants to be a revolutionary government. But a recognition of where the money is going, as it is stated in the *Canton Gazette* confirms the interview which Mr. Soong gave to the foreign correspondent. One can regard the English correspondent with scepticism as also the Japanese who have their interests here. But here is the *Frank[furter] Zeitung*[41] which prints the report of its old reporter Müller of a conversation with Soong [Ziwen], who, when they asked him how he wants to reform his finances, replied: 'How can we reform our finances? War, revolution. We must take what we can when and how we can'. Probably Mr. Soong [Ziwen] will not be in a position to raise this money for the conduct of war from the capitalists, and therefore his entire policy is a policy demonstrating the presence in the National government at present of a capitalist clique, which is not capable of either deciding the internal questions of the Chinese revolution, nor of conducting the struggle for national liberation.

Comrades, it would be a profound error, made by some Chinese comrades with whom I had an opportunity to speak, who consider it impermissible for Eugene Chen to conclude a treaty with the British, a treaty which does not exclude the possibility of the domination of capitalism. The following picture

---

41   *Frankfurter Zeitung* – a German newspaper published in Frankfurt/Main in 1856–1943.

is clear. If the National government is going to win, it will abolish the concessions as it abolished the Hankou concession, which, between ourselves, was seized by the trade unions without the knowledge of the Guomindang government. This is no shameful treaty. The English shot 200 peo[ple] in ... The English shoot whom and where they like and pay compensation to no one, but when Chinese workers demolished ... belonging to the English, then the Canton government committed itself to pay them compensation. The Chinese revolution is against this compensation because it rose against the English capitalists. This precedent is more important. The struggle which the Chinese revolution will have to conduct will require sensitive manoeuvring, resistance, bayonet charges, retreats, diplomatic negotiations, and it goes without question that all this will provoke economic disruption. The popular masses will suffer from the revolution as the popular masses have suffered in all revolutions. And if the government in this situation does not steer a sober course so as to extract from the landowners and capitalists the maximum and does not liberate the peasants from leasehold payments or raises the issue of the nationalisation of the land, which can be solved, evidently, only given the existence of a firm revolutionary government, then either the Guomindang will perish, as the SRs perished, – it was not inscribed on its cradle that it would be the party of the Russian counter-revolution –, or it will have to consolidate from itself detachments who will march with the peasant masses and will throw out what is in effect a Yuan Shi-kai clique, which to this very day sits in its leadership and directs the National government.

Comrades, what we are saying now, at which comrade Raskol'nikov has already hinted, and about which I was speaking, are not something completely unexpected. Already in October in the resolution of the enlarged plenum of the Executive Committee[42] [it was stated], judging by Chinese and foreign newspapers, and these are the only sources available to me [that] there [in China] a massive struggle is already taking place by the workers, who have understood very well what this means. The English press even identifies the leader guiding this struggle, the secretary of the trade unions, who studied here in the KUTV [Communist University of the Toilers of the East];[43] they even know that. I checked and confirmed it. But when I myself read in *The Times* an extract from the appeals of the Canton trade unions, I saw that this person already knew

---

42   This must refer to the resolution of the October (1925) enlarged plenum of the CEC of the CCP on a report of the CEC.
43   This refers to Liu Shaoqi, who studied at the KUTV (Communist University of the Toilers of the East). In May 1926 he was elected secretary of the Executive Committee of the All-China Federation of Trade Unions.

even the slogan 'Down with the Capitalist Ministers'. It does not say ten capitalist ministers, the number is not specified, they were too reticent to name them, but 'Down with the Capitalist Ministers' is explicit. In any case, the thing that most deeply concerns us here, which we are discussing here, concerns the popular masses there a hundred times more.

Comrades, the centre of the issue of the Chinese revolution is not in Shanghai now, not over whether Shanghai will be captured in the near future. The centre of the issue is now in Hankou. To take Shanghai is in general a very difficult matter. I am no military expert but I know roughly how the Canton army is equipped and how the English have armed Shanghai. If the English say that they are not intervening, then they will not intervene only until the battle is joined and if a battle takes place, then their heavy artillery and their technical equipment can only be paralysed by an uprising of the popular masses. I do not know whether they will succeed in taking Shanghai in the near future, but the revolution can move ahead even without being in a position to resolve this task in the near future, for Shanghai is the lungs of the whole Yangzi, just as Hankou is the heart of this region. Shanghai cannot exist without Hankou, and Hankou cannot exist without Shanghai. This contradiction must be resolved, but this contradiction does not require an immediate solution ⟨...⟩ The revolutionary movement is becoming stronger on the Yangzi, is establishing military positions there, from which they cannot be expelled. It is producing deep progress in the country, establishing a strong government and going into battle. If compromises are made with imperialism, [it] will be a non-revolutionary government, th[en] that which would be a necessary manoeuvre [?] for a revolutionary government, may serve as a bridge for the right wing of the Guomindang to the international bourgeoisie. There is another danger ⟨...⟩ in that this government would not be clarified in the sense of an understanding of the situation, of a concise plan etc., they could throw themselves into a frontal attack. A defeat which the government would suffer, a major military defeat during a frontal attack would force it to retreat a little, but if it develops a revolutionary policy, then it could go into battle with new forces. But if a major military defeat produced a deeply socially contradictory government, then it would open the road to the enemy, a road to appeals to the masses in the name of peace, in the name of rest, in the name of reconciliation. And finally, how long will the masses, who have risen for revolution celebrate a national revolution, from which they receive nothing or very little? I am very sceptical about whether such a situation can long endure. It is understood that the revolution has arrived at a moment when a transition from and to something is needed.

The Comintern has printed a very interesting essay, in which a whole series of elements of Chinese reality are presented. This is com. Martynov's essay.

This essay deals with the central question. In this essay it asks: who is now dominant in China, in Hankou? In the essay it is phrased as follows: 'Thanks to the yoke of the foreign imperialists,[44] from which not only the workers and peasants, but also the young industrial bourgeoisie suffers, for whom foreign capital blocks off the road to the development of Chinese industry, the revolutionary movement has embraced broad circles of the bourgeoisie in its first phase ... (*Quotation*)[45] up to the present stage'.[46]

Comrades, here we find a somewhat strange view. *If the generals are really closely linked to the bourgeoisie, then the dictatorship of these generals is not the dictatorship of the general staff, but the dictatorship of the bourgeoisie.* Now we can come to the conclusion that in the present moment one must not pose for oneself the fundamental task of a transition to the next stage. I would not screw up the courage to say, that now the moment has come when our comrades must go *onto the streets and overthrow the dictatorship of the general staff, closely bound up with the bourgeoisie.* This is a matter of a calculation of the concrete relations of forces, but one must say that the task is one of weakening dictatorial manners not by means of deepening democratic freedoms, but by means of an open struggle for the overthrow of the bourgeoisie. Comrade Martynov says that they should not take this as far as the seizure of power. One can only do this after power has already been seized. It is understood that when one has seized power, there is no point in going back onto the streets and seizing it again. (*Laughter, applause.* C[om]. MARTYNOV: '*Read further on*'.) C[om]. MARTYNOV would like me to read more of his essay. Well then, with great pleasure, since in that 'further' he raises fundamental questions of Leninism and decides them somewhat differently than they have been decided up to now. For example, he says: 'From this special feature[47] of the Chinese revolution ... (*Quotation*)[48] absolutely not of the kulak'.[49]

Comrades, if this is true, then how can we move from the dictatorship of the bourgeoisie to the dictatorship of the proletarian revolution, to the dictatorship of the peasantry without a second revolution, without even the decisive removal of the existing government. I do not understand that. I can imagine

---

44 According to Martynov, 'of foreign imperialism' (Martynov 1927, p. 15).
45 The quotation is missing from the text.
46 It is not possible to reconstruct the quotation involved, as the words 'up to the present stage' are missing from Martynov's article.
47 According to Martynov, 'from the same peculiarity' (Martynov 1927, pp. 15, 16).
48 The quotation is absent from the text.
49 It is not possible to reconstruct this quotation as the words 'from the same peculiarity of the Chinese revolution' occur twice in Martynov's text, and the words 'not at all of kulak' are absent.

that a certain small movement is possible, which will facilitate the solution of some tasks, so that Communists can enter the government without a change in the character of the government. This might be possible so that Communists could enter a government, which was a capitalist bourgeois government, – I leave aside the question how far this would be in agreement with a policy of Communism –, but it might be possible. But to replace a dictatorship of the bourgeoisie with a dictatorship of workers and peasants without a decisive struggle, this is unheard of, comrades. (*Laughter.*)

Comrades, when in 1923 we in Germany considered whether we should use the parliamentary majority in the Saxon Landtag together with the Social Democrats and the deputies of the workers' government, there wasn't a single comrade, who considered that this government could last for more than two weeks without a decisive armed battle. And when Brandler expressed it thus that we take democratic law as a springboard and then move from this bridgehead to civil war, then this was already considered a revision of Leninism. And if Martynov's statement is not a revision of Leninism then the word revision has absolutely no meaning. (*Laughter*).

I did not want to sharpen this question personally against com. Martynov. But I could not fail to dwell on it, as it expresses objective dangers of some kinds. In what does the danger consist? It is clear that the English battleships on the Yangzi are advancing on Shanghai, and the question is therefore, that without a revolutionary class one cannot conduct a struggle. But at the same time, the danger consists in that this struggle opens the fron[t] to imperialism. And here begins the petty bourgeois dream about how nice it would be if aunty was on wheels and moved like a tram. (*Laughter*). How nice it would be if it were possible to go from a dictatorship of generals representing the bourgeoisie, to move to a dictatorship of workers and peasants, to move towards it without a decisive struggle, because it is dangerous. From the fact that it is dangerous one can draw only one conclusion: the struggle must be better prepared, one must not be nervous, one must wait for the moment, one must calculate the mood of the masses and the relations of military forces. But the most dangerous thing in such a dangerous situation is to console oneself with the idea that one fine day this dictatorship of the bourgeoisie would become a dictatorship of the workers and peasants and (this is indispensable given the specific circumstances of the Chinese revolution) of the urban petty bourgeoisie.

But Chiang Kai-shek, who orders the shooting of workers. (MARTYNOV: 'Disgusting'.) You sent him a diplomatic note, but not your article.

Comrades, there is another consideration. Here it is not only a psychological reflection of the danger of the situation, here is also a reflection of the past of the CCP. How can you imagine a worker-peasant government without a strong, independent, Communist Party? The entry of the Communist into a government, even with the Guomindang leftists, which I consider necessary, represents a great danger without a strong Communist Party. Is the Communist Party armed for such a task?

As early as July 1926, the Chinese Communist Party adopted a resolution, informing the Chinese working class of the following matters: 'The amelioration of all these sufferings is the immediate demand of the Chinese people, this is not Bolshevism. One can say that this is Bolshevism in the name of our people, but not Bolshevism in the name of Communism [this is a resolution of a plenum of the Chinese C[E]C. – *K.R.*]. It [the bourgeoisie. – *K.R.*] does not understand that such a minimum of class struggle as is manifested in the organisation of the workers and in strikes, in no way weakens the militancy of anti-imperialist and anti-militarist forces. Besides this, they do not understand that the welfare of the Chinese bourgeoisie depends on the successes, together with the proletariat, in the war against the warlords and against the imperialists, and not at all on the continuation of the class struggle of the proletariat'.

I have just selected these small quotations. C[om.] Raskol'nikov has mentioned them. What does this mean? Communists, marching in unison with the petty bourgeoisie, as Lenin taught them, as the Comintern taught them, as is the duty of Communists, have become a bit frightened of frightened liberals and Communists have forgotten a little bit that in a bloc with the bourgeoisie, however revolutionary it may be, the most important thing is to tell the workers the complete and open truth about the existence of this bloc, about the character of this bloc, about the perspectives of the struggle ⟨...⟩ and if the Communist Party wants to calm down the bourgeoisie, then the creation of the proletariat is weakened as a result. This mistake was, as C[om] Raskol'nikov stated, corrected by a plenum of the Comintern. Comrades, you know that if such a mistake is possible, something was incorrect in the whole agitation and propaganda of the Party which created a situation in which Moscow alone was obliged, on reading this missive, to understand that something was not quite right here, but that the Party itself could not correct it. I argue that the organ of the CCP does not conduct a regular sustained critique of the vacillations of the Guomindang – vacillations, to put it mildly.

An enormous territory has now been conquered. A massive struggle by the trade unions is now going on. The trade unions now include millions of members. I claim that in the Chinese government there is not a single organ of the Party, in which Communists [do not] appear in meetings either as Guomindang members, or as trade unionists, but not as Communists. This creates an enormous danger in the moment of transition. This reflects a fear of this transition, which is entirely justified. Why? Because the Party might break its head and achieve not the democratic dictatorship of the proletariat and the peasantry and the petty bourgeoisie, but might obtain the isolation of the proletariat, might obtain the retreat of the petty bourgeoisie. All the strikes are taking place under the flag of the Guomindang, but on the other hand shootings are taking place under the flag of the Guomindang, while at the same time the Communists are not appearing before the broad masses as an independent Communist Party; all this demonstrates objectively that despite the enormous growth of the workers' movement, it has not been consolidated into a distinct force, making alliances with the bourgeoisie to a sufficient degree, and here is the central point of danger of the situation. Perhaps ... the situation will permit the Party to continue to stay with a direct struggle for alterations in the government, for the removal of the Ten Capitalist Ministers, for the foundation of a government, representing the workers, peasants and the urban petty bourgeoisie and the revolutionary army. Perhaps, though I don't know this, the time [has come] to hurry towards a strengthening of an independent Communist Party and towards its open appearance before the masses, there is not the slightest doubt of this. I hope, and I am convinced of it, that in the first place the attention of the Comintern and the attention of the CC of our Party as one of the leaders of the Comintern will be directed to this.

It remains to me, comrades, to cast light on several more prognoses. It is understood that it would be stupid to talk of prospects in the sense of a calculation of what will happen in the next few weeks. It is always better to predict what will happen in 100 years. The worst is to predict what will happen after 100 days, because it is easier to get it wrong, and most important – it is easier to be found out. So I won't get involved with that.

It is clear that the task of the moment which is maturing in China, is the transition from a bloc of the upper bourgeoisie, of the urban and rural petty bourgeoisie and of the working class to a bloc of the urban and rural petty bourgeoisie and the working class. This is a new phase in the revolution. It is clear that this is very critical, very serious. But, comrades, all our attention should be focused on this struggle.

In recent times the question has been posed about the non-capitalist development of the Chinese revolution.[50] This is a correct question, but it has been posed incorrectly in my view, not in a Leninist form. I think that here we have Trotskyism of 1905, not as it is represented in the books directed against

---

50   This refers to the resolution of the Seventh ECCI enlarged plenum on the Chinese revolution, Stalin's speeches in the Chinese commission of the plenum and Bukharin's report to the plenum. See Titarenko 1986, p. 94; Stalin 1952c [1926], p. 366; Comintern 1927b, Volume 1, p. 89.

Trotskyism, but historically, these are its weaknesses as they existed in historical reality. So what was wrong with com. Trotsky's views in 1905? Not that c[om.] Trotsky put forward the idea of permanent revolution, while Lenin did not want permanent revolution, but wanted to pause for a moment. It goes without saying that whoever reads the theses printed in the fifth volume of the *Leninskii sbornik* will see that Lenin established with total acuity that this was the permanent revolution of the proletariat in its struggle for power.[51]

In the first place, c[om.] Lenin fixed the tasks for the next phase, these tasks consisted in the necessity of creating a bloc of workers and peasants, and secondly according to him, without a revolution there would be no socialist revolution, since it was indispensable to attract the international proletariat also. From the solution of the tasks of the national democratic phase of the revolution, from the sharpening of struggle in this phase, the next phase will grow. According to him it will be a development of the democratic dictatorship of the proletariat into a socialist dictatorship. So what was the difference between Lenin and Trotsky in 1905 and what was the historical error of Trotsky's formulation of the question in 1905? What did he do, comrades? He said: the bourgeois revolution – this comes first. In this bourgeois revolution we will pose the question of a bloc of the workers and peasants. And if socialism triumphs in some country or other in the West or becomes stronger in Russia, then something will begin, we don't know what it means but not a capitalist course of development.

Comrades, we must get used to the idea once and for all, that there is no sexless economy. Just as people are divided into boys and girlies, (*laughter*) in every given period we either have a socialist phase or a bourgeois phase, or an economy striving towards the building of socialism. Therefore, we must throw out this meaningless term – non-capitalist, which just confuses people and whose very concept signifies nothing. This is the first point. Second, we must not, comrades, abandon the belief in the construction of socialism in one country. And in China, comrades, we must put the question like this: the struggle for socialism will grow from the resolution of the tasks of the national revolution by Jacobin means. If that struggle brings with it the liquidation of foreign imperialism in China, then will that consist in the fact that they judge capitalists in a foreign court, or in something else? No. It will mean that the commanding heights of imperialism, which consist in plants, factories, mines etc., will be taken from them, and then the question will arise for the Chinese proletariat: to whom shall we give them? To a private owner, a capitalist, or should

---

51   This refers to Lenin 1926.

the state retain them in its hands? In a state in which power is held by the worker with the participation of the peasantry, perhaps this question will come sooner, will come even with the resolution of the tasks of the national revolution. Imagine the English mounting an intervention against a dictatorship of the workers and peasants, a revolutionary-democratic dictatorship. But they wouldn't be able to get very far with intervention, because intervention is difficult, when cities are transferred from hand to hand. It will be necessary to struggle. it will be necessary to gather everyone into one fist. But it cannot be that in the resolution of this task, given an alteration in the international situation, when military measures have to be taken ... and that is all. And what will happen then, will [occur] from the sharpening of class struggle on an international scale. Does this mean that a sharpening of class struggle in the course of the revolution is possible, its outgrowth, could one build socialism completely with those forces which it commands without the support of the proletariat in other countries? No, of course not. This support will be necessary but [if] we start the socialist revolution, this metamorphosis [will] not necessarily co-exist with a scenario in which the international situation changes to the benefit of the Chinese revolution. It might be necessary even in view of the deterioration of this situation – I am speaking ironically of course.

The next mistake in this formulation of the question, is the question of civil war. This formulation is sharply expressed in Rafes' essay, published by him in *Kommunisticheskaia revoliutsiia*,[52] where it is expressed like this: cited in the words of the resolution of the Executive Committee of the Comintern [ECCI], 'that our main prospect is socialist revolution' – this is correct. Yes, socialism is our main objective in all countries. But c[om.] Rafes announces and proclaims: there are two alternatives – the capitalist road and the non-capitalist road. But these are not of equal value for us. Not of equal value, but what does this mean, comrades, what can our Chinese comrades make of this? I must say to you that though I reduced the beauty of this formulation by a single atom, I will cite it in all the meetings which I have to address. The content demonstrates the following: the history of the Chinese revolution is really at the present phase, making a transition from revolution to ... it now finds itself in a period of struggle for the democratic dictatorship of the workers and peasants. In its development this revolution will not only liberate the forces for the development of the bourgeoisie in China, but given another international situation, without the determined support of the world proletariat and a decisive victory of the international bourgeoisie, the revolution in China has in general ten

---

52   See Rafes 1927a, pp. 43–57.

times more chances that it will become more acute. Two facts vouch for that: the unheard seriousness of the agrarian question, and so as to give the peasant at least something at least ten billion rubles must be invested in the industrial development of China by the world bourgeoisie. I think that the prospect of the conversion of what should be ... for this will be a huge burden for the working class. They say: we must work so that the bourgeoisie can develop. The workers will find that very hard, just as hard as, perhaps the Communists will find it.

This is the perspective that is really loaded onto the fundamentals of the Chinese revolution, one must try and understand it. One must talk about it clearly, but not talk of it so as to console ourselves in respect of the repulsive reality [?]. We must in the first place, to put it bluntly, pose all those problems which arise during this phase of development of the Chinese revolution. It is vital to resolve these questions, however, not only on paper. After the resolution of these problems then other questions will arise in reality. There are not two perspectives: one major and one minor. There is only one perspective, that the petty bourgeois revolution will develop into a socialist revolution. When and at what speed no one knows. We must prepare the views of the Chinese workers for that. But the main objective – is not consolation in the future, but an improvement of today's tasks, their resolution on the stage reached by the Chinese revolution.

Comrades, I am finishing my report with the wish that you also may have the possibility of hearing from comrades better informed than I am, who have been in China themselves, so that they can describe their impressions of China for you, since they can give you ten times richer material than I have by employing press cuttings alone. But I have acquainted you with the basic question – that the Chinese revolution is not some kind of bourgeois revolution to which we are moving. We must give them assistance, since we have a common enemy – imperialism. The Chinese revolution is a revolution which deserves our concentrated attention, which demands that every Russian Communist relates with the most profound attention to its dilemmas, that every Russian Communist has the possibility of finding out about these questions to their full extent.

Comrades, I have had a whole series of disagreements with comrades about this question. But I read in terms of the resolution adopted by the Executive Committee of the Comintern, that a significant stride is possible, which would lead to a clarification, that maybe a group of comrades are not correct, on the one hand, but on the other hand towards a clarification of the organisational questions which we have posed. I did not pose them, but they now stand on the agenda, great questions which demand an answer.

In the first place, my lecture had only one objective – to get us to start talking about the class contradictions of this Chinese revolution. This will not weaken the attention of our workers towards it, but will strengthen it. This will not weaken the position of our Chinese comrades. The English bourgeois press is very well informed. We cannot say anything secret since it usually knows all secrets within 24 hours, if not 24 hours earlier than we do, and so there is no good reason why Communists, Marxists should not undertake to work through all of these questions, for whose analysis we already have sufficient material. This analysis has an enormous practical significance for our Chinese comrades. I assert that the young Chinese proletariat has a very small cadre of personnel, while the matter is one of the leadership of the Communists. It is a matter of questions of financial policy, questions of agrarian policy and so on. I would claim that the work that has already been done by a group of our modest comrades and a certain circle of volunteers, which already exists for a whole series of questions, has already given useful assistance to the Chinese revolution. We now have enough material, so as to get to work on the questions bound up with the Chinese revolution. We should attract broad circles: both our agricultural experts and our economists, and our other comrades, for whom the Chinese revolution, as for the whole international proletariat opens up grandiose perspectives. Moreover, it will fall to us to defend it to the Russian peasant, who is not an internationalist, who will at some time present us with the demand that he does not want to prolong the Chinese revolution, and to whom all this must be explained. And for that explanation we need a deep knowledge of the Chinese revolution. We don't have it yet, we are only approaching this question, and this task can be decided to the benefit of the Russian, Chinese and international revolution solely with the assistance of broad masses of Communists.

RGASPI. F. 326. Op. 2. D. 32. Ll. 101–89.
Typescript, copy, unsigned

CHAPTER 6

Concluding Word to the Lecture 'Driving Forces of the Chinese Revolution'
27 March 1927, Stenographic Report

Comrades, a series of comrades have spoken who have expressed general criticisms of my lecture. Com. Rafes concerned himself with an analysis of the firmness of my political views. He is fully entitled to do this. (*FROM THE AUDIENCE: 'Absolutely right, fully entitled'*). Comrade Rafes develops the same point of view on revolution, which he developed in 1905, as a Menshevik. As you can see, he has very firm views. (*VOICES: 'Correct'; laughter*). Then c[om.] Martynov spoke and directed my attention to a trifle, which I did not get round to in discussing questions of the Chinese revolution. Comrade Martynov devoted two thirds of his speech to a study of the role of imperialism in China, pointing out that in the past few days he has tirelessly read a number of pamphlets, which in his opinion are unknown to me. (*Laughter*). Finally, c[om.] Ioffe also taught me how to orientate myself critically towards the imperialist press. I, an inexperienced novice in this matter, accept with the greatest gratitude this recommendation from a man of experience. And finally, c[om.] Shumiatskii took the floor. He is my colleague and Rector of the Communist University of the Toilers of the East, who came out with a paean of praise in honour of our wonderful Marxist literature on China. I would be deeply indebted to c[om.] Shumiatskii, if he would present a list of this literature to our universities (*laughter, applause*), because until now I have not found books on the Chinese question which we could recommend to our Chinese comrades. True, there are several valuable pamphlets describing China at our disposal, but there is not a single book on the Chinese economy, in which the statistics do not contradict one another, and in which you do not find profound attacks on Marxism. (*Laughter*). Relying on this as his Marxist armament, com. Shumiatskii pointed to a series of supposedly untrue assertions by me and demanded that I justify them, but he made no attempt to demonstrate the incorrectness of my judgments. I would be grateful to him if he would develop his thoughts in the press. Then we could argue.

I will move on from my opponents to serious questions. I will start, comrades, from what has already been established here.

1) In the lecture it was established, and no one has tried to refute this, that *the old authorities have not yet been destroyed on all the territory of the national gov-*

ernment, and everywhere in the countryside the administration dominates, which previously served the merchants, landowners and militarists. This is a basic fact, and no one has attempted to refute it by a single word. Nowhere, apart from Shanghai, where the workers undertook to disarm the police, i.e. the apparatus of coercion, without waiting for the arrival of national troops, and began to arm themselves, *has the revolution yet arrived at the resolution of its first task – the disarming of the administration of the old government.* That is established and no one has tried to refute it.

2) A second fact, which I established was that *the National government has not yet even posed the question of the solution of the Chinese agrarian question.* It has only accepted the decree about the reduction of leasehold payments by 25 percent, and after it was issued the implementation of this decree met great resistance. It resolved to establish a commission, which would study ways of implementing the decree, which relieves the peasant of just a quarter part of the burden of his lease. Since the agrarian question is the central issue of the Chinese revolution, this means that the National *government has not yet embarked on the resolution of this fundamental question.* And understandably, it could not embark on it for if the administrative power remained in the hands of the defenders of traditional peasant exploitation, then it is clear that no decree can have any significance. If the government issued a decree for a 100 percent liberation of the peasants, that would not alter the administration and its relation towards the implementation of such a decree. And therefore, the peasant himself must implement this decree by means of class struggle etc.

3) The third fact, established by me in my lecture and not refuted by anyone, was that no measures have been taken to improve the position of the workers. We have just seen c[om.] Kantorovich's article in *Trud* ['Labour'], the organ of the ACUTU, which demonstrates that the rate of pay in the major industrial regions rose during last year by 25 percent at best, while items required for the survival of the masses, rice, rent etc. rose by 300 percent. This assertion is by a comrade who knows the Chinese economy better than any of us, although his conception of Chinese history is not Marxist. In this connection, the National government occupies a 'between class' line. On the one hand, it turns to the capitalists with a demand for concessions, and on the other, it adopts a law on compulsory arbitration, adopts laws which in a whole series of provinces are directed by reactionary authorities against the workers, the authorities which r[ule] in Canton, exploiting the return of the Hong Kong workers to Hong Kong and the absence [in the city] of the revolutionary soldiers, then breaks up the workers' organisations.

In the last months, Canton has seen a completely changed situation. If there were conflicts earlier, then the government there on the spot in Canton did not attack the workers, but now the Canton government of Li Jishen, who holds power, breaks up the workers' organisations. We see open attacks by the police on the workers, shots are exchanged with the workers, workers' organisations are smashed up. We have spoken here of the shootings in Guangxi. Then c[om.] Ioffe said that this is only in Guangxi, where Guomindang power has only existed for a few months.[1] But we know what is going on in Canton now. We don't know this from the Communists; we know it from the Guomindang newspapers! The smashing of workers' organisations is underway. The central organ of the Chinese Communist Party writes about it. And not only in Canton, but also under the nose of the government, in Hunan and Hubei provinces. We have a whole series of similar facts.

4) Next is the question of finances. At whose expense is the national struggle conducted? I assert that natgov [the National government] has not simply not embarked on the taxation of the upper bourgeoisie, but has bound itself to recognise loans, which this upper bourgeoisie gave to the enemies of the national movement – to Wu Peifu, and that it is buying up old money so as to issue new.

5) Finally, there is the question: what does the army represent? The main error, which one can make, consists in the fact that we think that a single national army exists. But there is not a single national army in China, despite the co-ordination of military activities. The Canton soldiers present themselves as a mercenary army, but a mercenary army, whose core is to be found under the constant influence of revolutionary work, an army which was all the same educated in the midst of revolutionary propaganda, an army which one must consider the beginning of a revolutionary army. The majority of this army accepts the whole burden of rev[olutionary] war ⟨...⟩ accepts the greatest losses. And all the other armies – they are the armies of military governor-generals, either defeated or having come over to the side of the revolution for fear of being defeated. I would point to the army of Tang Shengzhi. This is an army of the great landowners, which did not even sniff at revolutionary propaganda earlier. It goes without saying that the whole situation influences this army also. It is understood that it would be laughable to compare this army with the old militarist armies of Zhang Zuolin and others. The simple fact that they are now struggling against imperialism, that some kind of agitation takes place there, that meetings of hundreds of thousands take place there, affects that army.

---

1 This is not reflected in the stenogram. For Ioffe's speech see RGASPI, F.514, Op.1, D.253, Ll. 84–89c.

How is this army fed? Who finances it? Well, its administration is found in the hands of its old leaders, the military governors; and essentially the government, even the right-wing Guomindang government hangs by a thread in the air and is supported by a system of balances, confronting Tang Shengzhi with Chiang Kai-shek etc. *During all these months not a single attempt has been made to create new corps from revolutionary peasants* and workers. Not a single article which might have said something or other about this. Not even an attempt to pour into these armies new revolutionary elements in greater quantities which might have influenced the character of these armies. Therefore, these armies are still a very unreliable support for the national revolution, and from their point of view there is still the possibility of the most varied unexpected events.

6) Finally, comrades, how will this government conduct the struggle with imperialism?

It would be very good to really examine what slogans it advances in the struggle with imperialism, for these slogans indicate what ideas it broadcasts to the masses, what aims it pursues. In its agitation the accent is on the unequal treaties, which guarantee foreign capitalists that Chinese courts as opposed to their own courts, will not try them. The accent is on the fact that they have extra-territorial autonomy, but the stress does not fall on the *two billion debt*, imposed by the force of arms, a debt which is a stone around China's neck, a debt presented on ruinous terms. I do not want to say here that the government ought to begin with a declaration of a default from its debts. It is perhaps a question of tactics, demanding *the cancellation* or *the rescheduling* of the debts, but a question about whether they stress this debt in their agitation: are they preparing the masses that it is necessary to strike at this as one of the major levers of imperialism? No. What's more, when the decree on the recognition of loans given by the merchants to General Wu Peifu was adopted, the Guomindang pointed out in the *Canton Gazette* [of 15 January 1927?] that this recognition of imperialist loans is an '*indication*' [symbol], is an indication of how the Canton government will resolve the question of the debt.

Will the Canton government raise the question of an attack *on the commanding heights of imperialism*? Is it raising somewhere or other the idea that the national revolution cannot be victorious without the nationalisation of mineral and coal mines, factories, railways and banks, currently in the hands of the imperialists, with the aid of which the imperialists dominate China? I am not talking of immediate negotiations, the formulation of demands, but I am asking how should the popular masses be mobilised? Here in Moscow, at an enlarged plenum of the ECCI, in the China commission, c[om.] Stalin pointed out that the victory of the national revolution over imperialism should consist specifically in the nationalisation of all the commanding heights.² The imperialists totally understood the significance of this declaration and immediately there appeared in *The Times* an article by the chairman of holders of Russian debt, in which, extracting this point from c[om.] Stalin's speech, he said: look what the Russians are preparing in China – first of all they robbed us in Russia, and now they are urging the Chinese to rob us in China. The imperialists fully know what is the crux of the question. The Canton government only demands that the imperialists are deprived of diplomatic privileges, which even Zhang Zuolin demands, they demand customs autonomy, and this is the universal demand of the bourgeoisie, whose realisation would make possible the foundation of domestic industry in China.

If in this way we take the answer of the Nat[ional] government to all the basic questions of the revolution, one must come to the conclusion that the government which existed in China before the amplified plenum of the Guomindang, was a government ... (RAFES: 'Non-Communist'). You are already beginning to distinguish a Communist government from a bourgeois government? This was a *government of the mercantile-industrial bourgeoisie, which supported the national struggle as a road towards the achievement of compromises with foreign imperialism, on the basis of the recognition of the independence of China, that is the possibility of creating an independent Chinese industry, but which has not raised and cannot raise the aim of leading the struggle with imperialism to a conclusion.*

Comrades, when I established these facts, I ought to have born in mind that in our great press they have not written of this things yet. (FROM THE FLOOR: 'True'). Nothing is known about half of these facts up to the present day. Even about *such a question as the shooting of workers, we have said not a word.* Here a whole series of comrades have spoken, who have attacked me in every way, have shouted. C[om.] Rafes has even said: 'Radek, as usual, has stuck his finger in the air. *He talks about a crisis*, but *what kind of crisis*, where is this crisis? There were conflicts with Chiang Kai-shek, who wanted some kind of dictatorship but could not establish it. There was an amplified plenum of the Guomindang, but everything settled down. Chiang Kai-shek got into line'. Com. *Ioffe* spoke like a military man, coolly weighing up events, nothing can surprise him. A member of the Communist Party, AUCP, having heard in a meeting of Communists about the fact that one is shooting workers, about the fact that these workers, according to information printed in the Guomindang paper, shouted 'loudly and plaintively, that they are being shot for 30 kopeks' (*Min-*

---

2 Radek exaggerates. Stalin merely pointed out that it would be necessary to consider the perspectives for the nationalization of land, railways and the most significant factories and plants (Stalin 1952c [1926], pp. 369, 374).

guo ribao), a comrade who was born in our revolution, fought in the Red Army and who finished Military Academy in Soviet Russia, says literally that c[om.] Radek is telling 'atrocity stories' here. This speech was a pivotal speech on which we must evaluate the relation of some of the comrades to what is happening now in the great Chinese revolution. (*Com.* RAFES: *'Demagogy'*). When mister – I apologise – comrade Rafes speaks of demagogy I am not surprised. In Kiev in 1918 under Skoropadskii, com. Rafes called the attempts of com. Guralskii to withdraw elements of revolutionary workers from the Menshevik Bund demagogy. (*Laughter. Applause*). But when a young revolutionary born in our Party comes and denounces 'atrocity stories' in the face of such facts, then I say: 'Comrades, something is a bit rotten in the state of Denmark'. May I be guilty of ten left deviations, but I am convinced that every one of us who studied in our Party and who studied sincerely, would say that this is not the attitude of revolutionaries towards a revolution. And I am convinced that none of the comrades who were educated in the old underground, who were educated in the international workers' movement, would permit himself to respond in that way to the shooting of workers. (*Applause. Voices: 'Correct'. C[om.]* RAFES: *'Cheap, cheap, c[om.] Radek'*).

But there's another judgment: Radek shot in the air, because he said: the revolution is going through a critical moment. Why is there no crisis? Because there was a plenum of the C[E]C of the Guomindang, and Chiang Kai-shek got in line. At first he gave an interview, in which he said that they must throw the Communists out. But then he got in line completely and recognised his mistake. And there are Marxists speaking out in the role of urinologists, examining Chiang Kai-shek's urine, studying whether it is cloudy or clear etc. and, as a result, giving their judgment as to whether or not there is a crisis. And what does the *resolution of the Comintern* say on this matter? The resolution of the Comintern says that the essence of the present situation consists in the fact that *a significant part of the bourgeoisie is deserting the camp of the national movement for the camp of imperialism*. So, comrades, is it a crisis or not? And in the article of 18 March in the journal *Komintern*[3] I read: 'One must consider the present moment in the development of the Chinese revolution as critical.' [It is now that the general line for the further development of the Chinese revolution will be determined.

The national-liberation movement has been victorious in half the territory of China. The Southern National government is already at the present moment the government of an enormous state with a population of 200 million people.

---

3   Thus in the text. It should read: *'Kommunisticheskii Internatsional'*.

CONCLUDING WORD TO 'DRIVING FORCES OF THE CHINESE REVOLUTION' 289

An acute question demands to be answered: 'How should this state be organised, how must its government be organised, on what social forces should it rely'?[4]

Comrades, when the question is put before the revolution, *on what social forces must the government rely*, then that is exactly a crisis of the revolution. (*C[om.]* RAFES: *'In which direction is the crisis evolving?'*) Now we are going to talk about this. You are shouting too loud, c[om.] Rafes, you must be a little calmer. Has the Chinese revolution survived a crisis or not? Two days after we last sat here, i.e. 14 March, a meeting of 100,000 workers and poor people assembled in Changsha. And at that meeting, it was not I who spoke nor comrades from the Eas[tern] department of the Comintern, but Chinese Communists and Guomindang members who spoke. The meeting adopted a resolution with the following content: 'Down with the neomilitarist Chiang Kai-shek, who is conducting negotiations with Zhang Zuolin and the Japanese imperialists'. The meeting sent him a telegram with a warning, demanding of the government that it should carry out a worker-peasant policy and the alliance with the Communists. Comrades, I rate the intellectual capacities of all my opponents very highly and mine no less. (*Laughter. Applause*). But I must *say that 100,000 workers and poor in Changsha know better whether the Chinese revolution is or is not surviving a crisis*. Comrades, c[om.] Rafes has just shouted at me that I should tell him in what direction the crisis is developing. I will now give him his answer. Thanks to the fact that in Hankou and Nanjing there were too few Rafeses (*laughter, applause*) there were workers demonstrations and no one dared to come out in the name of the Comintern and say: 'Why are you making a racket, there is no crisis, go home', Chiang Kai-shek retreated. Com. Ioffe, an expert on the soul of Chiang Kai-shek, claims that he surrendered, but when I asked the Chinese Communists, who know China better than the comrade for special tasks in the Military Revolution Council, then they said to me, 'Chiang Kai-shek will fight on the right side of the barricades. [In the first place,] he has material and family links with the bourgeoisie, and secondly, he dreams, dreams – these are the literal words of a young member of the Party – of a monopoly of power, which the workers will not give him'.[5] But it is not a matter of Chiang Kai-shek, but of class relations.

---

4 Comintern 1927a, p. 3.
5 Until Radek's correction at this point in the stenographic record it read as follows: 'When I asked Chiang Kai-shek's son [Chiang Ching-kuo], a Communist, who knows his papa (*laughter*) better than the comrade for special missions of the RVS, then this comrade said to me: "My father will fight on the side of the barricades". Why? To which he answered

The crux of the question at this point in the Comintern resolution is where it says *that the bourgeoisie is moving to the right*. And we have seen immediately, comrades, where the crux is. When the Canton soldiers reached Shanghai, what did they see? By the way, as chance would have it, the head of the Canton troops was the same Guangxi General Bai Chongxi, a general from the province where they are shooting at the workers, chief of staff of Chiang Kai-shek, his right-hand man, a man who stands for a dictatorship of Chiang Kai-shek. But this general saw that *the workers met him with rifles*, confiscated from the police. Instead of greeting these patriots who could not be reconciled with imperialism, he reviewed a new detachment of the national army, he started to get wise: to whom would they subordinate themselves, would they take responsibility for the trade unions, and what would the English have to say? And this brave general has until the present day failed to come to an agreement with the armed workers. But when he arrived there, he saw something else: the Shanghai government. Comrades, Shanghai is not Kostroma, it is not Tsarevokokshaisk. Imagine the situation if the English had succeeded in capturing Petersburg during the Civil War, and the Soviet Red Army had succeeded in fighting off the enemy and seizing Petersburg, and the Petersburg workers met it as delegates of the Petersburg Soviet? Well then would our government have waited a single day for recognition by the Leningrad Soviet? And we have not yet obtained recognition for that government. What does that mean? That means that the turn in the line of the c[e]c of the Guomindang after the plenum is not decisive. The decision will depend from two things: Can we support the Shanghai workers in arms or not, but can we or can we not also *put them at the head of peasant regiments*, which will fight not for Chiang Kai-shek or Tang Shengzhi, but for the Chinese revolution. On this depends the question of whether we can break the old administration with the assistance of these poorer workers. It would be political nihilism not to understand the significance of this reshuffling in the government, in which, in the words of the Comintern resolution, until now five sixths of them were rightists; and of the rightists, the journal *Kommunisticheskii Internatsional* of the 18 March states that 'the Guomindang rightists include a series of major politicians, representing the bourgeois strata of China, who by their past, their present and all their social connections are inclined to make deals with imperialism, with the

---

me: "First of all he has material objectives and family ties with the bourgeoisie". I will naturally not go into these family ties. "Secondly, my father dreams" – those were the literal words of the young party member – "about a plenitude of power, which the workers will not grant him". Evidently, for some reason or other, when preparing to publish his speech, Radek deleted this from this text.

enemies of major social reform etc.'[6] Now a significant number of leftists and one Communist also followed. (*VOICE; 'Two'*). I only know of one. Maybe I am wrong, comrades, when you ask in which direction this is going. I say that if Rafes & Co. are representatives of the opinion of the Chinese proletariat – make the victory salute! – then these comrades in the government will do nothing, they will break their necks and compromise the revolution. Just think what Tan Pingshan may do? I consider it correct for Communists to enter the government, but with one condition: If com. Tan Pingshan has entered not to occupy himself in his ministry with agrarian reforms, which he will be unable to introduce, but to conduct a struggle in the government, and also, and in the first place, *he goes to the peasant and says: look, I am a representative of the working class and the Guomindang leftists, representatives of the petty bourgeoisie. We want to liberate you from the burdens from which you are collapsing, but the Guomindang rightists sabotages us*. But if Tan Pingshan gives an oath to tie himself to the cobweb of Guomindang solidarity, then Tan Pingshan will have the same significance as Skobelev, who promised to take a hundred percent of the capitalists' profits. The entry of Communists is correct if it is the beginning of work not just there, on the top, which is necessary, but if it is the beginning of an address with appeals to the masses, to the lower orders. We do not yet see this, on the basis of information about the mass movement which I have, but I am deeply convinced that these comrades will look upon themselves not as preservers of unity with the Guomindang rightists, but will look upon themselves as agitators, as organisers of the popular masses. (*RAFES: 'That is they will be Communists'*). That scares you terribly, but it does not frighten me. (*Appl[ause]*).

Comrades, but you will ask, how it happens that a series of our Party comrades, who as Communists or as the revolutionary youth, survived February and our transition for the struggle for October, say such things here that c[om.] Steklov, who was then observed close to the corridors of February and to c[om.] Sukhanov, says: '*The breath of Tsereteli wafts here*'. It does not waft, I say, *the breath of Tsereteli stinks here. (Laughter). Where is the source of these Tseretelian smells in the Com[munist] Academy?* It is understandable that they are talking about comrades, whose whole past is tied up with another, Menshevik conception, and this conception shines through all their speeches, which is rather

---

6 Radek is guilty of inaccurate quoting. This is what it says in this number of the journal: 'The Guomindang rightists include in their ranks major statesmen, representatives of the bourgeois layers of China etc. By their past, by their present, by their social and political ties the Guomindang rightists are inclined to make deals with the imperialists and are opponents of major social reforms'. (Comintern 1927a, p. 4).

uninteresting. This is a personal question – the difficulty of overcoming the old Adam, as they say in German. But we have heard here the speeches of a whole series of comrades. And I ask, where is this coming from? You will find a complete answer to that if you investigate a series of views expressed by these comrades. Com. Migulin says that *an anti-imperialist period exists in China now*, the period in which China is now living through is an anti-imperialist period.[7] Com. Migulin was not able to expound his theory of imperialism for us here, so I am not going to argue with him, but from what I heard it is quite enough to understand his point of view. Then com. Shchukar spoke and told us such things as: *all the blows must be directed at imperialism*. (*Com. Shchukar: 'Those who go into an alliance with imperialism will be cut off'*). When they go into an alliance with imperialism, they will cut us off, com. Shchukar. (*Laughter, applause*). C[om.] Shchukar, I cannot ascribe to you the view that you want to be in alliance with the allies of imperialism. I am a man, who long ago supported the etiquette that com. Polonskii defended here: love your brother, if he is not a scoundrel through and through. (*Applause, laughter*). Com. Shchukar says literally the following here: 'Part of the bourgeoisie will advance against the imperialists and the upper bourgeoisie', and after that, falling into a rage, he sai[d], I refer to his actual words, I wrote them down: *'The broad masses of the bourgeoisie'*. I wrote this down and I am convinced that the stenographic record will confirm it.[8] The comrades refer in this connection to a resolution of the Seventh enlarged plenum [of the Executive Committee] of the Comintern, holy, holy, holy, far from all. (*Laughter*). Comrades, I will not evade an explanation of that which I disagree with in this resolution. Com. Shchukar, the comrades who spoke in my defence and who wanted to protect me from several denunciations by telephone and other media, are not responsible for me. (*Laughter*). And I say they defended me unnecessarily. I will say what I want to say. I am a little man, but I consider it unnecessary to conceal my thoughts. I did the same under Lenin and when I wanted to speak against com. Stalin, I spoke from this platform. And in such a matter as the Chinese revolution, I don't know how to be diplomatic. Marx said that Communists must not conceal their aims even ... before com. Rafes.[9] (FROM THE AUDIENCE: *'Bravo'. Laughter, applause. Com.* RAFES: *'Com. Radek that is terribly cheap, that is farcical'*). I am with you, com. Rafes, about what is fitting and what is not, I will not argue. (C]om.] RAFES:

---

7 Migulin's speech is not in the stenogram.
8 The stenogram does not confirm this.
9 Radek re-phrases the famous words of Marx and Engels from the *Communist Manifesto*: 'The Communists disdain to conceal their views and aims'. (Marx and Engels 1969 [1848], p. 123).

'You are a scoundrel. I call on the Presidium to call c[om.] Radek to order'. CHAIR-MAN:[10] *'I call the comrades to order and I beg c[om.] Rafes to be silent'.*)

Comrades, what is the mistake of these comrades? This is the mistake of all mistakes. The Comintern speaks thus: *The departure of a whole class from the national revolution.* (*Com.* RAFES: *'Carry on in the same vein, com. Radek'. He leaves the hall. Calls: 'Goodbye, c[om.] Rafes, goodbye'. Com.* RAFES: *'Com. Radek you can now say whatever you like'*). I was mortally afraid of you and was just waiting for you to leave.

What then does the Comintern say, comrades? In its resolution, the Comintern says the following: the withdrawal of the bourgeoisie, the departure of a whole class, *of parts of a class which until then walked with the national movement, from the national revolution, does not happen overnight.* Communists, the working class in the unprecedentedly difficult position of the Chinese revolution are bound to use every vacillation of even a well-known small group of the bourgeoisie. For all who have brains, this means that *a class withdraws, but small fragments remain*, and one must use them. But what do our right-wing comrades say about this? They say that the broad masses of the bourgeoisie will remain and one must wager on them. The departure of a class disappears for them. They draw no conclusions from the departure of a class.

If, comrades, we could preserve Chiang Kai-shek, I would be bound hand and foot for it, because that might help us to avoid some of the upheavals, but the question is not about that, but about *whether or not there is a transfer onto new rails*. Is there something novel here or not? Is there anything *new* in the necessity of *a democratic* dictatorship of the workers and peasants or not? What will be the stages in this, we will talk about this. But at first answer the basic question. But from where do some of our comrades derive a transition *not to the head, but to the tail of the revolution,* where do they find a division between the national anti-imperialist revolution and the class struggle? The fugitive com. Rafes gave a speech like this: Radek says that the national revolution is a *corpse, and the class war is now beginning*. This gave him away. In 1905, there was a liberation movement. The revolution was a bourgeois revolution and Cherevanin wrote that it died because the workers began an independent class struggle. They struggled for the 8-hour day and thereby scared the bourgeoisie. The words ascribed to me by com. Rafes, indicate his meaning: *'If a class struggle of the proletariat begins, than the national revolution is a corpse'*. That means that he considers that *without the leadership of the bourgeoisie there is no national revolution*. All the words about the proletarian hegemony of the Chinese revolu-

---

10   Brinskii.

tion are quotations from Lenin, but the essence is old Menshevik views. And what do Shchukar's words mean, that we must concentrate the whole attack on imperialism and therefore not break with the bourgeoisie? What does it mean, comrades to strike against imperialism? Look how imperialism attacked. It captured and shot seven thousand people,[11] because it could, because imperialism is a *dictatorship, a single will*, but there, in the National government, a Contact Commission will sit, and today's revolutionary will be tomorrow's counter-revolutionary T.V. Soong [Song Ziwen] will tie Sun Fo up by the arms and legs,[12] and that will signify an attack on imperialism. Look, an attack on imperialism requires the destruction of the armies of the military governor-generals, their metamorphosis into *a single revolutionary army*. That means to bang the heads of various generals together. And how do you do that? *Arm the workers*, place them at the head of the peasant masses. And you imagine that Sun Fo, that T.V. Soong [Song Ziwen] and all those people tied up with the upper bourgeoisie will agree to the arming of the workers, will agree with the unification of the army in the hands of the workers? (VOICE: 'Never'). *If they never agree, then how can you attack imperialism, sitting with them in a single government*? And how are you going to feed the soldiers? For you are going to take crumbs from the peasant so as to feed the soldiers. That is indispensable. This means you must lighten the weight of the peasant's burdens, you must liberate him from the landowners, so that he can feed the rev[olutionary] army. A comrade from the East[ern] department, a great diplomat – he has not spoken here but he is a very intelligent comrade[13] – said this to me: a break with the bourgeoisie [must be] *after* a victory over imperialism. But I said to him: a breach is a *condition* of victory over imperialism. *And this is the crux of the matter*. Whoever has not understood this has understood nothing. The Chinese bourgeoisie cannot struggle with imperialism until the final victory for two reasons. The resolution of the Comintern[14] correctly indicates the first of them. I assert, however, that it means a turn to the left, which means that it is impossible to destroy imperialism without occupying the commanding heights of its economy. Imagine that the Chinese bourgeoisie would go that far? They could not. They need foreign loans, they cannot expropriate ⟨...⟩ the foreign imperialists.

---

11 This refers to the bombardment of Nanjing by American and British naval vessels on 24 March 1927 in retaliation for bloody pogroms of foreign residents by the NRA soldiers and local citizens.
12 Thus in the text.
13 It is not clear whom Radek had in mind.
14 This refers to the resolution of the 16 December 1926 by the Seventh enlarged plenum of the ECCI on the question of the situation in China. For the text of the resolution, see Titarenko 1986, pp. 89–105.

Secondly, to confiscate the factories from the foreign capitalists means posing the question: who should take them into their hands, Chinese private capital or ⟨...⟩ a Chinese worker-peasant government? The whole question consists in this. Therefore, they cannot enter the struggle with imperialism in China to the final victory. Therefore, the question of the *major, general line of the Comintern*, about the consequences of the departure of the basic masses of the upper bourgeoisie from the camp of the nat[ional] revolution is a thousand times more important than these petty questions about which part of the bourgeoisie still remains for a while in the nat[ional] camp. Little groups [of the bourgeoisie] can still remain, but the general line, is not for yesterday, but for tomorrow, the day of the democratic dictatorship of work[ers] and peasants.

Let's go over to the question of *the way out of the situation*. This question is tied up with the argument, which we have just had about whether there is a dictatorship of the bourgeoisie in China. A whole series of comrades spoke out here and in several other places, with the greatest aplomb, demanding not from me, old sinner, but from someone or other else: renounce the opinion that there is a dictatorship of the Chinese bourgeoisie, which offends the Chinese bourgeoisie. Comrades have beaten me with the same weapon. I quoted c[om.] Martynov's article. In this article it states (I am repeating it literally). Firstly, at the head of the soldiers stand the *generals, closely tied to the bourgeoisie*. Further on Martynov speaks of the '*present dictatorship of the general staff*'. As comrade N.I. Bukharin says it's as clear as an orange. In China there is a dictatorship of the general staff. After which Martynov asks: 'Can the Communists obtain participation in the government without a decisive conflict and sharp struggle for the existence of the old government, without a second revolution? *We consider that such a possibility is not excluded*'. Martynov poses a question about whether Communists can enter a dictatorial bourgeois government without a new revolution.[15] How did I answer c[om.] Martynov in my lecture? I said to him: 'If the general staff is really tightly bound up with the bourgeoisie, then the dictatorship of the generals is not a dictatorship of the general staff, but a dictatorship of the bourgeoisie'. (VOICES: 'True'). If this is a dictatorship of the bourgeoisie, then it is impossible to overthrow it without an uprising (VOICES: 'True'). But did I say that I agree that the National government is a dictatorship of the bourgeoisie? Excuse me, what did I say? I said two things about this government, I gave a picture of shootings and said: comrades, it would be incorrect to think that this is a general course of the government. The general course of the government, as it is expressed in its programmes and speeches, is one of

---

15   See Martynov 1927.

a *course of manoeuvring between the classes*. Furthermore, how did I define the government? I address this government and the Guomindang workers' party[16] and say that 'if the government does not take a firm course so as to liberate the peasants from leasehold payments, and raise the question of the nationalisation of the land, which can be resolved only given the existence of a firm revolutionary government, then either the Guomindang will perish, as the SRS did, or that a part of it will be consolidated, which goes with the peasant masses and throws out Chiang Kai-shek's clique etc.' In other words, I did not define the Nat[ional] gov[ernment] as a dictatorship. Why did I not say so? Here's why! Half of the Chin[ese] bourgeoisie is a bourgeoisie tied to compradors, enemies of the national movement. The industrial bourgeoisie is only partly with the national movement. *If the whole bourgeoisie in China cannot establish a Chinese bourgeois government*, then how could that part of this bourgeoisie establish a dictatorship over the nat[ional] movement? The National government presents itself as a weak bourgeois government, thrown up by a mass revolutionary movement. It strikes at this movement. So as to become a dictatorship it needs two things: *to suppress the worker-peasant movement and to do a deal with imperialism*. That hasn't happened yet and I hope it won't. And therefore, from my point of view, the possibility is not excluded that we can arrive at a government of workers and peasants, without destroying, without exploding the front of the anti-imperialist war ⟨...⟩ that we will succeed in coming to power by means of a partial modification of the present government, but after a revolutionary wave will throw the elements tied to the bourgeoisie out of this government.

Do you know, comrades, I am not an official for special tasks, and if I considered it necessary to overthrow the Canton National government,[17] then I would have said to the CC: take me away from university work, because I cannot teach Chinese Communists anything other than the slogan 'Down with the National government'. (*MARTYNOV*: *'That's basically what you are doing'*). I won't answer you, com. Martynov, because an argument with you is the last thing that interests me. I do not know where you learnt to hide your opinion before the Party. Rosa Luxemburg and after that com. Lenin taught me, that one must not hide one's opinions from the Party.

Comrades, what is the route to that which made itself the government by force of arms, which now recalls some well-known changes of the Provisional Government of 1918?[18] [But it recalls the Russian Provisional Government,] cer-

---

16   Thus in the text.
17   Thus in the text. This refers to the Wuhan National government.
18   Thus in the text. It should read: '1917'.

tainly with some significant changes, but all the same it recalls it in a certain sense, for a dual power is evident in China: already the Shanghai and Hankou workers are saying: in so far as ...! What is the road to a genuinely revolutionary power? Comrade Lenin said that even the Provisional Government which conducted an imperialist war, could not be *simply and directly* thrown out, for it relied on sincere defencists; he said that when these masses, who believed for so long in the government, ceased to support it, then, having the army and the soviets one could seize power. How does the situation in China remind us of our situation (after the Shanghai events)? The situation in China is similar in that when enormous layers of the popular masses come out, the popular masses are still for the Guomindang, they believe in the government and rush to join the army. Until September [1917], Lenin said to the Mensheviks and SRs: *take power and break with the Kadets*, and we will support you. He wrote an article about compromises,[19] and only then when that path appeared to be excluded, did he issue the slogan: 'Down with the Provisional Government!' It is exactly the same now in China, one must take account of it, and our slogan should not yet be the slogan 'Down with the Canton government', but our slogan should be a *slogan about changes*. We must formulate it a hundred percent openly: if it is not a matter of those formulations, which will be written on the placards in Hankou tomorrow, then I say the *idea of this formulation is down with the capitalist ministers, out with the upper bourgeoisie from the government*. This is the sense of the slogan in whose name we will rouse the masses. This means that we must aim at *a takeover of the government administration*, hopefully without much bloodshed, as they say in military jargon. But when Lenin advanced the idea of compromises, he well knew that the chances of success on such a peaceful road were few. Do I think that in China we also have as little a chance of success? I cannot answer that question, I don't know the concrete situation and in particular the military situation well enough to be able to say whether we will succeed in taking power with little bloodshed. *But Lenin never taught Communists, even given the existence of the soviets, that the working class road to power is guaranteed without another revolution*. He never taught us that and if we are going to teach the Chinese workers that they can remove the rightists and install the leftists using the Guomindang administration, [alternatively] you can cut off the dog's tail in instalments [and], comrades, the most harmless method would be that we disarm them.

For such a [non-revolutionary] method I would raise four legs and four hands. (*Laughter, laughter*). I repeat, that I would be a hundred percent for

---

19   See Lenin 1969 [1917], pp. 133–39.

this path, but c[omrades], I fear that *the dog won't go down that road*, that if you cut off its tail, it will naturally hurt and hurt badly. (*Laughter*). You may tell me that c[om.] Shchukar will hold her by the muzzle with his powerful hand (*laughter*), but if it is possible to do it, then I call upon him not as a university Rector and teacher, but as a humanitarian and say: 'Cut off its tail straightaway, why just prolong its suffering'. (C[om.] Shchukar: *'You need scissors for that'*).

Comrades, c[om.] Shchukar shouts at me now that one must have scissors beforehand, that is that one must have an army, the lower ranks. In speaking to us here he repeated the speech which I gave yesterday in his presence to my students at the Sun Yat-sen University,[20] but the repeat is unfortunately very unsuccessful. And this is why. He proposes ⟨...⟩ that *the foundation of an army and the development of an administration are military matters*, that one can do them without political preparation. He is deeply mistaken. For one thing, this demands a break with the militarists, a break with that situation in which *the Communists were afraid to tell the workers the truth about the shooting down of workers*. In China there is not yet a Chinese Party press, it must be established. For the Party directing the Chinese proletariat on Chinese territory does not yet have its own daily organ. It is vital to establish means by which the Chinese Party can tell the workers the truth, the truth about the fact that the upper bourgeoisie is deserting the national movement. It is vital that our press also tells our workers about this. Don't think that the Chin[ese] generals do not know what we write. When a representative of our university[21] went to Chiang Kai-shek, he found that he had on a table all our guidebooks published in Chinese. He even found lectures by com. Bukharin about a bloc with the opposition. And if we are silent about the shootings, then, comrades, the Chin[ese] generals will reach the conviction that we do *not* want to put pressure on them and that they will receive our assistance even despite the shooting of workers. But we think that we have the right to say to them that they *do not have our support in shooting the workers*. In the theses to the Second Congress of the Comintern, which comrades have quoted here, Lenin said: 'We will support the national-bourgeois movement if it does not prevent us from organising the workers and peasants'.[22] But that when they break up peasant organisations, when they

---

20   This speech by Radek has not been discovered.
21   S.A. Dalin.
22   Radek is mistaken. Lenin expressed this thought not in the theses, but in the 'Report of the Commission on national and colonial questions' to the Second Comintern Congress. This is what he said: 'We, as Communists, should only support bourgeois liberation movements in the colonial countries, when these movements are genuinely revolutionary, when their

CONCLUDING WORD TO 'DRIVING FORCES OF THE CHINESE REVOLUTION' 299

shoot down the workers, does this prevent ⟨...⟩ the organisation of workers and peasants? It seems to me that it prevents a little. And therefore, it seems to me that it is necessary that the comrades who direct our press knew that, otherwise the impression is given that we avert our glances from such things as the shootings of workers and the break up of peasant organisations.

Next is the second point: *there needs to be a campaign*, political campaigns, preparing for the seizure of power. They have begun everywhere, except we know nothing of this. They began in China. Look when Eugene Cheng conducted negotiations with O'Malley,[23] whose content was concealed from the workers, the Hankou workers came out on the streets with the slogan 'Down with secret diplomacy'. When there was a crisis in the c[e]c of the Guomindang, the workers also came onto the streets with placards against Chiang Kai-shek. This fact is known not from the imperialist press, against which this expert on the imperialist press, c[om.] Ioffe, warns; I know this fact from Guomindang newspapers. No, you can't seize power secretly, it is not a virgin, you can't rape her, you must seize power in open battle. But for that one can still prepare.

The third point means: preparing the organisation of the left wing of the Guomindang. Permit me to read what the resolution [of the seventh plenum of the Executive Committee] of the Comintern says: 'It is necessary to form a left wing and to strengthen close collaboration with it'.[24] Form a left wing of the Guomindang. And what does the article of the journal *Komintern*[25] No. 11 say on that account? It violently attacks a resolution of the c[e]c of the Communist Party which said that it is necessary that the left Guomindang binds itself to the urban petty bourgeoisie etc. To this the article in the journal *Kommunisticheskii Internatsional* replies: 'The task consist in organising some sort of new Guomindang or a new faction of the Guomindang so as to guarantee the whole Guomindang a leftist tendency'.[26]

---

representatives do not prevent us from educating and organizing the peasantry and the broad masses of the exploited in a revolutionary spirit'. (Lenin 1971c [1920], pp. 243–44).

23 This refers to negotiations by the Foreign Minister of the Wuhan government, Eugene Chen with Owen O'Malley, counsellor of the British mission in Beijing concerning the return to China of the British concession in Hankou. The agreement on returning the concession was signed on 19 February 1927.

24 Radek is inaccurate in his quotation. In the resolution of the Seventh enlarged plenum it mentions the necessity 'of forming a left wing [of the GMD] and the establishment of close collaboration with it'; see Titarenko 1986, p. 99.

25 Thus in the text. It should read: '*Kommunisticheskii Internatsional*'.

26 Radek distorts the quotation. This is what it says in this number of the journal *Kommunisticheskii Internatsional* ('Communist International'): 'The task consists not in organising some sort of new left Guomindang or a faction of the left Guomindang, but in guaranteeing the whole Guomindang a firm left-wing direction' (Comintern 1927a, p. 6).

Comrades, Durov could teach a dog, cat and mouse to eat from one plate. The editors of the journal *Kommunisticheskii Internatsional* want to demonstrate the same pedagogical skill in China in respect of different classes. But why should I be forced to think that our Party wants to occupy itself with such tricks? The resolution of the Comintern does not suggest such tricks. If I must choose between the resolution of the Comintern and that article, I will stick by the former, though I think that the resolution of the Comintern has been more thoroughly, more thoughtfully written even than that by the good authors of the article. The officials of the Comintern have led me to believe that there is a worker-peasant government in Canton. Now, knowing the facts, I don't even believe in a word of even a leader in the journal *Komintern*.[27]

If there was an argument between us about whether or not the workers and peasants should seize power in Hankou today, I would say that I will not take part in such an argument. When I was in Berlin,[28] but the leading comrades were here, I often regarded the situation [of things] differently than they did. And when I was here, but my closest comrades in Berlin, I also often thought differently. Circumstances decide there. It takes a telegram six days to reach Hankou. I have never taken part in an argument about whether to seize power there *now*. The argument is not about that. *If our official decision, as I hope, is that we tell the Chinese workers and peasants that they must seize power, that they must conquer a democratic dictatorship, but for that they must prepare the workers, then there is no disagreement between us.* But those who speak out here and who diminish the danger that exists, brings us to the consideration that they will not be for a seizure of power not only after a month, but not even after a year. The political and psychological attitude of a significant part of those taking part in the discussion was the attitude of people, *who are reconciled to a long period of bourgeois domination.* The greater the imperialist danger, the clearer that only an iron dictatorship, resting on the hands of the peasantry and the working class, but directed by the working class, can lead the national revolution to a conclusion. Now I must respond to two more questions, above all concerning the question of the *non-capitalist* road of the development of the Chinese revolution. I will say two words about this. The Comintern resolution says that China is not doomed to carry the chains of capitalism for ever.[29] Correct. What is not correct here? [Incorrect,] when people like Rafes declare and write: 'The Chinese *revolution* has perhaps only two roads [of development: 1] ⟨...⟩ in close alliance with the proletariat of the USSR and the whole world

---

27   Thus in the text. It should read: '*Kommunisticheskii Internatsional*'.
28   This refers to Radek's participation in the German Revolution of 1923.
29   See Titarenko 1986, p. 94.

(*reads*) [on the road of the socialist development of China, or 2) in close alliance with some or other group of the world imperialists – most likely the Americans – to remain a colony of this imperialism]'.[30]

Two paths of development: either the revolution will advance to socialism or to the status of a colony. These are the two paths of the revolution. It is all the same if someone says that there are two ways of life, one on Tverskaya, and the other in the grave. If China advances in conjunction with imperialism then that will be the path of counter-revolution but not revolution. Where did this nonsense come from? After 1905 Lenin said: *Russia* can either develop on an American path, this would be a victory for the revolution, or can develop along Prussian lines, this would be a victory for the counter-revolution.[31] But he did not say that these were the two paths for the Russian revolution. If capitalism wins in China, that will put a cap on the Chinese revolution until a future phase.

What do I still want to oppose now? Lenin spoke about a non-capitalist path of development.[32] This is known to me from the history of the Second Congress of the Comintern no less than to comrade Lentsner, the author of notes on world history. I will let you into a great secret: I was a member of this commission [of the Second Congress on national and colonial problems]. If you take the protocol of the Second Congress of the Comintern that you will see that apart from Lenin I, a sinner, also spoke at the 1920 congress about a non-capitalist path. But when we speak with the Chinese, then we must not use the naked term 'non-capitalist path'. For the whole of Sunyatsenism is built on that idea that there is capitalism and there is non-capitalism, which is not socialism. And Sunyatsenism reflects the whole Chinese revolutionary past. The whole Chinese peasantry struggled in twenty revolutions, destroyed the landowners, chased away the merchants, established small scale property and thought that this would be *non*-capitalism, but as a result received capitalism. And if I had not been deprived of the opportunity to take part in the [Seventh] plenum of the Executive Committee [of the Comintern], I would have said: comrades, don't talk about a non-capitalist path in China, talk openly and clearly about socialism, for in that way you will hold out a hand to Sunyatsenism. I consider Sun Yat-sen to be the most outstanding figure in the Chinese revolutionary movement, but he was a petty bourgeois revolutionary. We must establish a bloc with the left Guomindang people and the workers and peasants. In that sense c[om.] Dalin was entirely correct when he said that we will defend the legacy of Sun Yat-sen, in so far as he was for a bloc of workers and peasants.

---

30   Rafes 1927b, p. 105.
31   See Lenin 1961b [1907], p. 105; Lenin 1961c [1907], pp. 226–28; Lenin 1961d [1907], p. 340.
32   See Lenin 1971c [1920], pp. 245–46.

But, c[omrades], we are not Sunyatsenists and no one can make me proclaim myself a disciple of Sun Yat-sen and teach the Chin[ese] Communists that they are disciples of Sun and not of Marx and Lenin.

Now, comrades, I will address one secretive question, which disturbs all my opponents, this is the question of the *relations between the Communist Party and the Guomindang*. I have been asked many times here what I, my auntie and my old friends think about this etc., and so I think that despite the late hour, we are all interested in staying put for a while and introducing complete clarity to this question. Of course, if the meeting has another opinion, then as a democrat ... (VOICES: 'Please, please').

Comrades, I must say that this question about the Guomindang, this question takes on with us, I might say, for Marxists, comic forms. I repeat: this question assumes the most comic forms. It takes the form of a question: are you faithful to pretty Dulcinea or not, will you be true to her always? (*Laughter*). In his speech[33] to the Communist League in the [18]50s *Marx* said the following: (*Quotation*).[34]

In *1905* Lenin taught me that we see in an independent and irreconcilable party of the revolutionary proletariat the only guarantee of the victory of socialism, whose victory can be guaranteed solely by the revolutionary party of the proletariat. Lenin, finally, taught, saying this: 'Parvus is a thousand times correct then he says' (*Quotation*).[35]

Marx and Lenin taught us this. They taught us how to relate to the petty and the upper bourgeoisie. But in 1922 we, in agreement with Vladimir Ilyich, decided to enter the Guomindang. Why? Rafes says that then there were only 400 members of the Communist Party in China. Then they told us that the Communist Party of China counts one or two thousand members in its ranks. The Guomindang hardly existed as a party then. Sun Yat-sen sat [in] a palace in Canton, as he said in his speech, which Wang Jingwei cited ... having no power. What sort of Communists were in the Chin[ese] Communist Party? Comrades, a Chinese Communist[36] came to the Fourth Congress of the Comintern and said: we have no revolutionary-national movement yet, there will be no Guomindang, but there will be a socialist revolution. We were appalled, we said that in China instead of Confucianists, comrades have been born, who read Bukharin in English,[37] but who have no connection with the struggle of the

---

33   Thus in the text. It should read: 'address'.
34   The quotation is missing from the text.
35   The quotation is missing from the text.
36   Liu Rengjing.
37   This refers to Bukharin and Preobrazhenskii 1919.

popular masses of China. Then we wrote to Sun Yat-sen, advised him to rely on an alliance of workers and peasants, and showed him that it is vital for him to establish the Guomindang. But we, it must be said, dragged our resisting comrades by the collar and forced them into the Guomindang; they did not want to join and dug their arms and legs in. Then our party [i.e. the CCP] consisted one hundred percent of intellectuals. But we tied ourselves to the Guomindang administration, tied its work to the work of our party so as, in the first place, to establish a petty bourgeois revolutionary party, to help our future ally, and secondly, so as to show the Chinese Communists, suffering from left deviationism, that there would be a national revolution and that therefore it was necessary to go into an alliance with the bourgeoisie.

Such was the Guomindang in 1926 where General Chiang Kai-shek said to us: 'Messieurs, stop hugging us Guomindang; you want to suffocate us in your embrace. First of all give us your lists, so that I can arrest you in case of necessity, and secondly, go out of our main administration – 30 percent [of Communists in the Guomindang apparatus] is quite enough for an alliance'.[38] That was not so then, but since that time there have been a series of strikes by the Shanghai workers, 180,000 Hong Kong workers marched on Canton, we had a massive workers' movement, and the Guomindang began to become a mass party. A conflict of classes took place. Then a series of comrades proposed going over from membership in one party to an alliance of two parties. Why? As some comrades or other said today – maybe c[om.] Shumiatskii, my colleague, Rector of the KUTV, who was on diplomatic work in Persia at that time, and I do not know whence he obtained the very circumstantial information about the discussions, which were not published in the press at all, but even in quotations – he said that people who wanted to enter the Guomindang came so as to blow up the alliance with the petty bourgeoisie and isolate the proletariat. They wrote about it. Then we read something or other in the documents of the CCP, in which they say this: you need to consolidate the council of the Guomindang so that we can then found a strong administration.[39] Secondly, they beat them in our name, saying that they are Communists. Thirdly, we force a petty bourgeois party to adopt the pose of semi-Communists, instead of allowing them to remain a petty bourgeois revolutionary party. And further. We consider this as a powerful argument. The question was posed about an alteration in the relations – the party rejected it. We did not raise this. I said in my lecture that I would not raise this question. Why do I not raise it? Here's why, comrades. Not

---

38   This concerns the decision of the Third enlarged plenum of the CEC of the Guomindang in May 1926.
39   Thus in the text.

because I think that Lenin was wrong, not because I think that the situation in [19]22 would last for a hundred years, but because in historical sequence it is now time for a blow against the right Guomindang, an amputation of the upper bourgeoisie. I have learnt a bit about tactics not just from revolutionary Marxism, but also from British imperialism: it never decides two major tasks at the same time. An alteration of the form of our link with the petty bourgeoisie cannot march simultaneously with an alteration of class relations towards the upper bourgeoisie. Here the enemy may confuse the cards. Therefore, I will not pose this question. But will this question be raised by history? It will, comrades. If we throw out the upper bourgeoisie and stick alone with the left Guomindang, then, dear comrades, what will this left Guomindang be [?] It will be in terms of its historical potential, the party of the urban and rural petty bourgeoisie. So, comrades, do you think we can establish just a leadership of the revolution [on the part] of a worker-peasant party? Comrades, neither Marxism nor Lenin ever taught us about a worker-peasant party. We will strengthen and deepen the alliance with the petty bourgeoisie. But you have passed through the history of the Russian revolution, you have thought about it. Furmanov describes it. Everyone praises him, I also, but I wonder why he draws the petty bourgeoisie thus? Because we have an independent party, which openly determines questions itself, which taught them [Communists in Russia], where they should go, educated them in unconditional mutual confidence, as members of a party of two classes cannot be educated, and therefore they [Communists in Russia] dominate the storm, and the storm does not rage over them. In China peasant storms will be ten times stronger. If we take the history of China, there are five volumes about sects. Whoever has looked at the history of banditism in China understands that this is a whole sea of peasant *jacqueries*. Who is going to direct this storm? Communists. When? If, while preserving the former alliance they are going to decide its tasks independently, not to submit their decisions to any coalition party, and adapt their policy to reality. If at their meetings they will teach the whole proletarian mass, because, if simple workers command our armies, then simple weavers will command divisions. The proletariat is fewer there, but their solidarity in the party must be stronger, their independence must be stronger, their consciousness must be a hundred times stronger. And may as many blows as you like rain on me, poor Makar, for this because history will raise this question, and we are going to decide it not against our party, but together with our party. And now it is my deepest conviction that the thing which is the revolution has now moved into a period in which it needs one hundred percent support. We cannot give it military assistance, we can't because between us and there is Zhang Zuolin, which means Japan, and it is not only not in our interest to throw ourselves on

Japanese bayonets, but we must teach the Chinese revolution to avert the conclusion of an alliance of Japanese-British imperialism. Why don't we take the step, which would accelerate this alliance. But how could we help? We could help with our organisational experience, we could help with our knowledge, we could help by means of the fact that we consider this to be our revolution. Not a proletarian class revolution, as c[om.] Martynov says. Let him believe it, but I do not believe it because it will be a revolution, and we will come to this brother who turns to us for assistance, we will come not with cowardly formulations, but as Communists, who [find themselves] fully armed with our experience and fully armed with our Communist method of thinking things through to the end, and speak through to the end.

Comrades have made thousands of hints here. I find myself in a particularly difficult position, because I was placed by the Party in a post, which I deeply appreciate, of educating Chinese comrades, and I consider that I cannot diverge for a second from the directives of the Party in this post, even though I receive very few directives. But if there have been hints of my disagreement, then I will answer that I will never conceal my thoughts from the Party. And even then when I am not in agreement with the Party, I will carry out the directives of the Party and will carry them out in the deep conviction that history decides everything objectively. And this history poses a question first only in an embryonic form, but the second time in a more detailed form, and if I perceive my mistake I won't be afraid to say so. But for now I am convinced that the question will be posed by history, and not by malicious persons like us, who want not to take account of Party resolutions.[40]

RGASPI. F. 326. Op. 2. D. 32. Ll. 155–89.
Typescript with manuscript corrections, original, unsigned.

---

[40] Further on in the text it reads: 'Comrades, in this great work which awaits us, I would warn you of one thing: do not believe that a Marxist literature about China exists. You must create it, you must help us to create it so that we can help the Chinese revolution with it'. This final section, however, was removed by Radek while editing.

CHAPTER 7

The 'Betrayal' of the National Movement by the Chinese Upper Bourgeoisie

Early May 1927

12 April 1927 will go into the history of the Chinese revolution as the day signifying the most radical turn in its fate. On that day those sections of the Chinese upper bourgeoisie, which until then had gone along with the national-liberation movement, turned on the proletariat and the peasantry, turned against the national revolution and entered onto the path of deals with world imperialism. 12 April did not occur accidentally; the events of that day are the result of deep changes taking place in the class relations in the Chinese revolution. On that day the upper bourgeois section of the national revolution, facing a choice of struggle with imperialism or with the working class and the peasantry, chose the latter. Hundreds of workers stained the streets of Shanghai with their blood. This blood is destined to bear fruit to the working class only in the event that the Chinese and international proletariat draws up a clear unambiguous account of what has happened. In the first place one must get to know the facts which preceded Chiang Kai-shek's coup.

Rehearsal for the Coup

The Shanghai events of 1925 and the Hong Kong strike,[1] which displayed to the whole world the revolutionary energy and revolutionary strength of the Chinese proletariat, provoked a hullaballoo amongst the Chinese bourgeoisie. Until that time various factions of the bourgeoisie dominated the national movement; from 1919 the role of hegemon was occupied essentially by the industrial bourgeoisie. In 1925 a new claimant to the role of leader of the revolution appeared on the historical stage. The bourgeoisie limited their participation in the revolution to the fact that it organised student demonstrations and a boycott of English goods. The proletariat took the English bourgeoisie in Shanghai and Hong Kong by the throat. It drew after it the petty bourgeoisie, students,

---

1 This refers to the Shanghai events of 30 May 1925 and the Hong Kong-Canton strike of 1925–26.

shopkeepers, artisans. It created a powerful movement, which the bourgeoisie temporarily succeeded in mastering.

But the struggle of the proletariat was not only directed against the international bourgeoisie, but also against the Chinese bourgeoisie. The proletariat forced the domestic bourgeoisie to raise wages and shorten the working day. The bourgeoisie understood that it had to take measures against the growing influence of the working class in the national movement. It was not just the openly right wing of the Guomindang, which after the death of Sun Yat-sen had organised in the Western Hills near Beijing demanding a break with the Communists,[2] which rose in battle. The centrist elements, who had not yet decided to openly demand the expulsion of the Communists, also prepared for battle.

To the first group belonged the present minister of the National government, Sun Yat-sen's son, Sun Fo, to the second, Hu Hanming, whom the Guomindang leftists suspected of participation in the murder of the leader of the left Guomindang Liao Zhongkai. To them also belonged *Chiang Kai-shek*, who on the 20 March 1926 arrested workers in the Canton Communist army, removed the leader of the Government and leader of the left Guomindang, Wang Jingwei from his post and steered a course to the right. However, having met resistance on the part of lower party organisations, Chiang Kai-shek was, it's true, forced to stop the open attack on the left-wingers. But all the same, he achieved the outcome that the Communists entered the government and party administration of the Guomindang, only in such numbers as would not contest the leading role of the bourgeoisie. At the same time, Chiang Kai-shek demanded that the Communists renounce criticism of Sunyatsenism.

Chiang Kai-shek tried to camouflage the nature of his coup. After the arrests of the Communists he drove out several extreme rightists, such as C.C. Wu, a British agent, who had been a member of the Canton government until the events of the 20 March. Chiang Kai-shek swore on his loyalty to Sov[iet] Russia, demanded that the Guomindang be received into the Comintern[3] as sole

---

2 The Xishan (Western Hills) anti-Communist group in the Guomindang was formed in November 1925.

3 The Guomindang officially turned to the Presidium of the ECCI with a request for reception into the Comintern for the first time in February 1926, shortly after the Second Guomindang Congress, which took place during the dominance of the left Guomindang. In a letter sent by the CEC of the Guomindang in this connection, it stated, among other things: 'The Guomindang is striving to fulfill the task which has already confronted the Chinese revolutionary movement for 30 years – the transition from a national revolution to a socialist one'; Pantsov 2000, p. 90. The leaders of the CC of the AUCP(b) seriously examined this request, and a majority of the Politburo even expressed approval of accepting the Guomindang as a sympathetic party; RGASPI, F.514, Op.1, D.65, L. 21. True, then caution prevailed and on the basis of a pro-

leader of the Chinese Revolution. Obviously the whole idea and organisational camouflage which Chiang Kai-shek undertook could not conceal the essence of his policy. The Peasant Department of the C[E]C of the Guomindang in its report to the December Congress of the Guomindang of Guangdong province wrote the following about the consequences of the 20 March 1926:

> 20 March 1926 led to splits between various personalities in the Canton government. They found an echo in the countryside and *led to a hunt for the organised peasants*. The county heads changed their attitude to the peasant unions and distributed rumours that the government would take measures against the worker and peasant movement. In many districts they forbade peasant assemblies and began to call the peasant leaders bandits. The struggle against the peasants became sharper on the basis of internal party disputes at the [plenum] of the Executive Committee of the Guomindang of 15 May.[4] There were discussions about the dissolution of peasant unions and about the possibility that the Guomindang would turn away from the workers and peasants.

---

posal of the Presidium of ECCI and after Voitinskii's consultation with Stalin and Zinoviev, an evasive reply to the CEC of the GMD was drafted. After its adoption by the Presidium of the ECCI it was handed over on 25 February 1926 to the Guomindang representative, Hu Hanmin; Ibid, sheet 33. It was pointed out that although the Guomindang formal acceptance to the Comintern in the capacity of a 'sympathetic party', naturally did not meet any objections', all the same, the Comintern considers the moment for such acceptance inappropriate: attention was paid to the fact that the entry of the Guomindang into the Comintern 'would facilitate the formation of a united imperialist front against China', and would also give a new pretext to the internal Chinese counter-revolution to misrepresent the Guomindang as a 'party, which had lost its national character'. At the same time, the Presidium of the ECCI, underlining that it 'sees in the Guomindang party its direct ally in the struggle against world imperialism', expressed a promise that in the event that the CEC of the GMD insisted on its request, to include the question of the Guomindang's entry into the Comintern on the agenda of the forthcoming Sixth Congress of the Communist International; RGASPI, F.514, Op.1, D.171, Ll. 7–9. For the text of the reply, see also Titarenko 1994–96, Volume 2, pp. 131–32. However, the ECCI returned to the question of the acceptance of the Guomindang into the Comintern sooner. In September 1926, a new request from the CEC of the GMD was received in Moscow. On this occasion a corresponding letter was even signed by Chiang Kai-shek personally. In January 1927 the Presidium of the ECCI adopted a positive decision: The Comintern and the Guomindang exchanged representatives, and the representative of the CEC of the GMD (Shao Lizi) was co-opted onto the Presidium of the ECCI with no voting rights. Shortly afterwards a representative of the Comintern to the Guomindang, M.N. Roy, was sent to China; RGASPI, F.514, Op.1, D.233, Ll. 61–72; D.240, L. 1.

4 This refers to the Second plenum of the CEC of the GMD (15–22 May 1926).

This shows that the attempt at a coup from above, a turn to the right at the summit, immediately resulted down below, in the countryside, in counter-revolutionary pressure on the peasants.

The Northern Expedition

This policy of Chiang Kai-shek provoked unrest at the lower levels of the Guomindang and led to a significant fall in its authority. At that time, Wu Peifu advanced to the south for the liquidation of General Tang Shengzhi, who had tried to free himself from the leadership of Wu Peifu. Tang Shengzhi, though an ordinary militarist, turned for assistance to Canton. Chiang Kai-shek used the anxiety provoked by this advance in Canton for the purposes of raising his own authority and decided to give him assistance.

Two motives guided Chiang Kai-shek. First of all the material motive. The hundred thousand strong army recruited by the Canton government demanded ever growing expenditure. The peasantry, heavily exploited by the landowners and the moneylender-mercantile capitalists, could not give the government significant amounts; to make it capable of taxpaying an agrarian reform was necessary, or at least a reduction of the tribute paid by the peasant to the landowner. But Chiang Kai-shek was afraid of a struggle with the landowners, who formed part of the bourgeoisie. Therefore, he was forced to resort to an expansion of the territories subjected to the Canton government for the preservation of his army.

The second reason why the Canton government under the leadership of Chiang Kai-shek, decided on the Northern Expedition, was in the hope of consolidating by means of his military laurels his political prestige, which had collapsed among the masses as a result of the coup of the 20 March. All this was so clear that one of the participants in this expedition, the Communist *Sinani*, in an article of 7 August 1926 wrote: 'The Northern Expedition given the political characteristics which it now possesses, can *by the force of objective circumstances alone* be considered as pouring water not on the mill of militarism but on the wheels of the bourgeois revolution' (*Kanton*,[5] No. [8–]9).[6]

Com. *Chen Duxiu*, Secretary of the C[E]C of the Chin[ese] Communist Party, in an article of July 2, [19]26 relates the arguments, which were put forward, though very cautiously, by the Communists against the Northern Expedition:

---

5   *Kanton* ('Canton') was the journal of the group of Soviet advisers in Canton in 1926–7.
6   Sinani 1926, p. 12.

'In this question I disagree with the opinions of several comrades. They are naturally not against an advance to the north as such. Their point of view on this question is that they consider it necessary to *concentrate forces* for this expedition in Canton, rather than attacking to the north. One must not start by breaking one's head, without taking account of the dangers which may meet us on the journey'.[7] Many Chinese Communists understood that Chiang Kai-shek was getting ready for the expedition not from revolutionary, but from counter-revolutionary motives; they considered that a preliminary internal conflict in Canton itself was necessary, which would turn Canton into a really revolutionary base and would thereby predetermine the revolutionary character of the expedition. The majority of Russian comrades concerned with Chinese affairs maintained this point of view. (The arguments of the Chinese Communists prove the depth of understanding of the class context, demonstrated by com. Bukharin. He reprimanded me for demanding the preliminary unfurling of the struggle for the liberation of the peasants in Guangdong before launching a military Northern Expedition, while leaving power in the rear in the hands of the counter-revolution).

The following objective circumstances made the expedition, born in fear of a struggle with the landowner and searches for military force a revolutionary fact: the expedition exposed the complete rottenness of the militarist regime of Wu Peifu and in the passing of several months led to the collapse of his army. The expedition discovered the enormous strength of the national idea; finally, the Northern Expedition raised the workers and peasants onto their feet everywhere. The same objective conditions forced Chiang Kai-shek to use the Communists, whom he had arrested yesterday: half the force of the national army consists not in their bayonets, but in agitation, which Chiang Kai-shek could not develop without the Guomindang leftists and the Communists.

The strength of the national army consisted in the support which the peasantry extended to it in the course of the expedition. While hoping for assistance from the national army in their struggle with the landowners, the peasantry supplied the army with food, spies, and fell on the weaker detachments of the militarist soldiers, in a word, they gave complete collaboration to the national army.

---

7 Chen 1926a, p. 1584. Radek is in error. Chen Duxiu's article is dated 7 July 1926.

The Organisation of Power

Chiang Kai-shek understood the dangers concealed within the victories of the Canton army. Therefore, when he had gained control over the government, the Central [Executive] Committee and the military command, he concentrated all power in his hands. The main task of Chiang Kai-shek, around whom landowners and capitalists began to group themselves on a huge territory with two hundred million inhabitants, consisted in not allowing the collapse of the old administration, i.e. in saving the old apparatus of exploitation of the workers and peasants by the landowners and bourgeoisie. All revolutions begin with the destruction of the old government administration.

At home in Guangdong province the Canton government left the old power of landowners and merchants in place and untouched. The confirmation of the resolution of the Sixth enlarged plenum [of the ECCI], that 'the revolutionary government created by the Guomindang party in Canton *has already succeeded in connecting itself with the broadest masses of the workers, peasants and the urban democracy and, relying on them, has broken the counter-revolutionary bands supported by the imperialists, and carried out work on the radical democratisation of the whole political life of Guangdong province*' (see Protocols of the Sixth plenum, p. 71)[8] turned out to be a *total fantasy*. Therefore, one must consider as also a fantasy the further declaration that 'being in this form the avant-garde in the struggle of the Chinese people for independence, *the Canton government serves as an example for future revolutionary democratic construction in the country*'.[9] How this example appeared in reality was shown by com.

---

8 'Resolution on the Chinese question', Comintern 1927c, p. 71.
9 This complete *disinformation*, the whitewash of reality in Comintern reports, was the source of my mistaken evaluation of the class character of the Canton government. Relying on the reports of the Eastern workers of the Comintern, supported by appeals by the Guomindang, I thought that the Canton government really was 'an example of a genuinely rev[olutionary-] dem[ocratic] construction', i.e. a wor[ker-] peasant government. If *Pravda* (of 29 April) attacks me for that reason, then it is mocking itself. For, having convinced myself of the mistaken explanation by the Comintern of the situation in Canton, [I] spoke the truth about it, but *Pravda* of the 1 April 1927, twelve days before the shooting of the Shanghai workers, slagged off com. Alskii because in his book ['Canton is victorious'] on the basis of a study of the facts on the ground, characterised the Canton government as a 'liberal bourgeois government'. It attacked Alskii, reproaching him with a disagreement with the decisions of the Seventh enlarged plenum [of the ECCI] on the Chinese question: 'The Seventh plenum of the ECCI gave the CCP a directive to enter the National government. Obviously it would have been a turn to the right, opportunism of the purest water to propose to the CCP that it should take part in the National government if this government really were a 'liberal-merchant' government, only 'to a limited extent democratic', which would carry out a 'policy in the interests

Tarkhanov in his 'Essay on the Social-Economic Structure of Guangxi province', published in No. 10 of the journal *Kanton*. 'The description of the position of the peasantry [in Guangxi. – K.R.] would be, [however] incomplete, if we do not illuminate the political situation in the countryside,[10] – writes Tarkhanov. – In this connection there is no great difference between the Eastern and Western districts: in both districts the countryside is an *empire of the most profound[11] arbitrary rule by the local officials and the mintuans [people's militia] and the absolute political powerlessness of the peasant masses*. Neither the progressive destruction of the natural economy, nor the growth of towns, nor the victory of the nat[ional] army altered the regime in the countryside by one iota ... The county chiefs are nominated by the provincial government. Virtually all the county chiefs were already nominated by the revolutionary government. But, *all of them were former county chiefs or exercised other official positions before the coup*. Normally the government tries to nominate as chief in every country a native of that country which leads to the practice that *the chiefs are bound to the local landowners and gentry by links of kin and locality*.

The judicial administration is also completely staffed by the old officials. Naturally, they judge by the old laws, of which a number are of more than millennial old, for there are no other laws. Where there are government troops, the civil powers depend on them absolutely, but since the commanding cadres of these troops are a more reactionary mass than the old officials, that does not alter[12] the picture substantially, or only for the worse for the peasants. *At times of conflicts in the countryside, in all cases without exception the government*

---

only of the local mercantile-industrial bourgeoisie'. *The plenum of the ECCI regarded the National government as a provisional revolutionary-democratic government of a bloc of the workers, peasants, petty bourgeoisie and of the anti-imperialist part of the bourgeoisie.* Thus, *Pravda* of the 1 April 1927 insisted on and defended the opinion that the Canton government is a democratic dictatorship, i.e. is a worker-peasant government. If after that *Pravda* had the courage to launch against me a zealous youth, hiding behind the initials N.D. (*Nabityi Durak* [Obtuse Idiot]? How should we decipher it?), so as to break my back for my definition of the Canton government in the spring of [19]26 as a 'worker-peasant' government, a definition which it so energetically defended on the 1 April 1927. That just shows that for some graduates from Ostozhenka [evidently he has in mind graduates of the Institute of Red Professors, whose building was in Moscow on Ostozhenka Street], now making wind and weather in the public opinion of the Party, there is no limit to which they are not capable of going. These young people are evidently capable of anything, but not for anything useful. They will be very useful for someone, we just don't know who. *Radek's note.*

10   Tarkhanov gives: 'the situation in the countryside'.
11   Tarkhanov gives: 'crude'.
12   Tarkhanov gives: 'replaces'.

troops are found on the side of the enemies of the peasantry and support them with all their forces and means'. (Journal *Kanton*, No. 10, pp. 112–4. Underlined by me – *K.R.*).[13]

In each new province conquered in battle by the Canton army the nat[ional] army simply replaces the old administrative chief, substituting for him a new one from the military and the Guomindang rightists, who camouflage themselves with the label 'centrists'. Where the provinces went over onto the side of the Canton government without a struggle, they did not even bother to change the chief. The lowest level of administration, which previously served to extort taxes and leasehold payments from the peasants, remained untouched. Everywhere peasant organisations arose, which tried to expel the most hated exploiter-officials.

Chiang Kai-shek persecuted this intervention in matters of administration by the peasant organisations in the name of the National government. The Peasant Department of the Guomindang founded peasant organisations, often helped them financially, sent out instructors, acquired accommodation. But at the first conflict between the peasant organisations and the landowners' organisations or the government, the peasant organisations were declared bandits and their destruction commenced. *Already in September 1925 the organ of the Com[munist] Party, Guide Weekly*[14] *wrote*: 'One can say about the position of the Guangdong peasantry during the expedition that they were *surrounded by enemies on all four sides'*. The article relates that 'now the peasant organisations [by the way they have all conspired together. – *K.R.*] demand the exclusion from their programmes of these organisations of any politics ... In just the same way, the county chiefs received a certain *secret instruction* for their guidance'. The article closes with the words: 'From what we have written above, it is evident that the reactionary party is now strong and in connection with measures of administrative character, taken for the limitation of peasant organisations, this *will lead to a still greater dangers*' [emphasised by Radek].[15] In the cities Chiang Kai-shek's government has come out in exactly the same energetic way against any attempts by the workers to intervene in so-called administrative questions. In fact, in the total absence of any organisations of self-government, this means the *preservation of all power in the hands of the bourgeois-landowner administration*.

13　See Tarkhanov 1926.
14　*Guide Weekly* – an English translation of the title of the political journal of the CEC of the CCP, *Xiangdao zhoukan*. It was published in Shanghai from 13 September 1922 until 18 July 1927.
15　Radek is mistaken. This information was published in September 1926. See Luo 1926, pp. 1743, 1745.

The Army

The Army is the main organ of power; it undertook the Northern Expedition with a strength of sixty to seventy thousand bayonets. What is the Canton army? Officially, it consists of a mercenary army composed of déclassé peasant elements. It was created by means of the centralisation by the Canton government of guerrilla detachments of the various Guangdong generals. These generals, emerging from bourgeois circles, the landowners and the bourgeois intelligentsia gave Sun Yat-sen many difficulties earlier on. In his speech delivered after the death of Sun Yat-sen in Swatow, Wang Jingwei described how Sun Yat-sen dealt with these generals of his. He gathered them together in 1923 and said: 'You invited me to Canton to fight for my ideas. *You have dressed up in my hat and you shame my household. Therefore, I am leaving you*'.

All these generals struggling between each other for power eagerly submitted to Chiang Kai-shek; Chiang Kai-shek was a representative of the Guomindang, but the political work of the Guomindang in Guangdong province created a situation in which the generals could not any longer feed themselves in the old manner, without any ideological covering. They had to submit to the situation established, but they became unwilling 'revolutionaries'. Only the Whampoa academy began to put forward commanders going into the army in the name of revolutionary objectives, however these commanders belonged to both the right and left wings of the Guomindang.

Therefore, the Canton army was a *mercenary peasant army*, only recently subjected to the influence of revolutionary agitation. Its commanding staff was recruited in its majority from representatives of the officers of the old stamp, and in the minority from persons connected with Whampoa academy, which in the twenty two months (from April [19]24) graduated 1,700 officers, who had been through a certain revolutionary political preparation. Into this army flowed masses of defeated or voluntarily defected militarists who had come over to the victors' side. The soldiers of the militarist armies taken prisoner were at first used as coolies for the transportation of ammunition, food and all kinds of heavy manual work. Seeking salvation from forced labour, at the first suggestion of the National government, they transferred with enthusiasm to the ranks of the national army, which does not mean that they became revolutionaries. The matter was even worse there where whole armies with their counter-revolutionary officers went over to the side of the National government. The soldiers received a tricolour necktie[16] and were declared soldiers

---

16   This neckerchief was of blue-white-red colours, symbolizing the Guomindang administration of China.

of the National Revolutionary Army. Their old counter-revolutionary military commanders remained in charge.

A certain amount of political work was conducted in the army. But it stands to reason that given uninterrupted advances in heavy battle political education could be neither sufficiently broad, nor sufficiently profound. The situation in the big cities had greater influence on the army: [I mean] political meetings and demonstrations. The Chinese bourgeoisie kept their eyes peeled that Communist commanders and Communist propaganda were not urged on the army. They feared even more the creation of regiments of workers and revolutionary peasants. So Chiang Kai-shek in the name of the National government *banned all armed demonstrations, any arming of the workers*. According to an order issued in February 1927, trade unions, under the threat of dissolution, had to give up any arms and ammunition in their hands. On the basis of this order, the Canton workers were disarmed by Chiang Kai-shek's henchman, General Li Jishen, the Hankou workers received no arms at all, and the workers militias came out with nightsticks in their hands. The Shanghai workers captured arms by disarming the police before the arrival of the regular Canton army.

Chiang Kai-shek considered this growth of the genuinely revolutionary fighters of the national army as the main danger to the revolution. In disarming the Shanghai workers, he could cite the fact that he was acting in the capacity of head of the government on the basis of a decree which he had issued in February without any protest by this government.

Relations with the Workers

What policy did the Chiang Kai-shek government conduct with regard to the workers? When [in September 1926] the nat[ional] army arrived in Hankou in the heart of the central industrial region, the bourgeoisie forced Chiang Kai-shek to take a clear position. In his speech of 26 June 1926 he had declared that *there are no capitalists in China*, but there are just businessmen, and the victory over the imperialists depends on the collaboration of the workers, the bourgeoisie and the peasants. He demanded from the capitalists the recognition of the necessity of improving the conditions of the workers, from these same workers he demanded the submission of their class interests to universal national interests. In time of war there must not be strikes and therefore the government would itself assume the regulation of the worker question.

The government issued a law on *compulsory arbitration courts*, distributed not just in military establishments but also in undertakings of social significance. And since any undertaking could be drawn under this heading, so the local administration, which was to be found in the hands of the landowners and capitalists, turned to military force every time any kind of strike broke out. These conflicts, handed over to the courts of arbitration, dragged out for months.

The relationship of the government to the worker question provoked an *alteration in the tactics of the bourgeoisie in relation to the National government*. Before the arrival of the nat[ional] forces in Hankou the bourgeoisie escaped to Shanghai, removing money and storing all their valuables in English banks. From the moment when Chiang Kai-shek's policy was determined we see a complete change. The organ of the Com[munist] Party *Guide Weekly* writes in an article of 6 January 1927, that at the beginning in the central part of China and along the Yangzi River the capitalists and upper compradors abused the National government, saying that it must not help the workers, but suspecting that it had become 'red'. But later *'the capitalists suddenly woke up and gradually began to make up for lost time*. Wanting to protect their privileges at a time of revolution, *they began to enter its ranks, so as to preserve their position under it'* [emphasised by Radek].[17] The workers' organisations in Hankou immediately sussed out the policy of the bourgeoisie guided by the National government. Already in their proclamation of 2 October 1926, the Hankou trade unions declared that they would support the Nat[ional] government if the latter would help them in the struggle for freedom and rights of the working class. 'If the National government', declared the trade unions, 'will not help the workers then it is a matter of indifference to the trade unions what it calls itself'.

The struggle of the workers against attempts to tie them hand and foot and give them over powerless to the bourgeoisie unfolded all along the line. But in counting on the help of the military authorities, the bourgeoisie began to create *hooligan organisations* from lumpen proletarian layers of the urban petty bourgeoisie and from the least class conscious part of the working class as supposed trade unions. These organisations went into battle against the workers' trade unions, and organised pogroms of their buildings. In Canton alone, tens of workers died in the struggle with these hooligan organisations. Where the forces of the bourgeoisie were not enough the local administration intervened, relying on military force. At Chinese New Year in Canton there was a military struggle between the police and the workers, who besieged police stations and government buildings. Many dead and wounded resulted from this struggle.

---

17   Shu 1927, p. 1900. For the Russian translation of this article, used by Radek, see *Materialy po kitaiskomu voprosu*, 1927, No. 3, pp. 3–10.

THE 'BETRAYAL' OF THE NATIONAL MOVEMENT   317

In Wuzhou, in Guangxi province, three workers were arrested during a dockers' strike, and notwithstanding the protest of workers' organisations, they were shot by the commander of the 4th brigade.[18] The pretext for the conflict was the non-payment of wages of thirty kopecks a head. 'When they led them to the shooting, they shouted loudly and complained that *they were shooting them for the sake of thirty kopecks*', reported the Guomindang newspaper *Minguo ribao*.[19] Chiang Kai-shek attempted to unload the guilt for these events onto undisciplined generals in distinct provinces, but the government did not even think of dismissing these generals. But Li Jishen, commanding officer of the Guangdong forces, dissolved the local Guomindang committee and nominated another in its place, managing even to recruit a member of the Communist Party, Yang Pao'an, as cover.[20]

But military reprisals against the workers' movement were not restricted to the southern provinces. Shootings took place in *Hubei* province, whose centre is Hankou, i.e. *right under the nose of the government itself*. In December 1926 the first conflict took place between workers' pickets and soldiers of the 15th People's Army. In an attempted to bring an end to this first conflict, the leader of the workers' militia Chi Hu-zi[21] was wounded. On the 8 November 1926, with the intention of breaking a strike which had broken out, soldiers surrounded the cotton factory in Hankou and for a whole day did not let any workers out and did not allow their wives to bring them food. Even the representative of the trade union was not allowed into the factory. Obviously, the great majority of such demonstrations of the 'revolutionary activity' of Chiang Kai-shek are unknown to us unto the present day, for *the Chinese Communist Party does not possess a single daily newspaper*, and the Guomindang press prints such communications only under pressure from workers' organisations.

---

18   Thus in the text. It should read: '6th brigade'.
19   Thus in the text. In actual fact the organ of the Guangdong provincial committee of the Guomindang reported the shooting in the Canton edition of *Guomin xingmeng* (Flourishing of the Nation) of 24 September 1926.
20   Yang Pao'an was included in the Standing Committee of the Executive Committee of the Guangdong committee of the Guomindang; see *Canton Gazette*, 15 January 1927.
21   Thus in the text. Who was meant is unknown.

Relations with the Peasantry

Chiang Kai-shek's policy towards the peasantry has been no less hostile than his relationship to the working class. This is understandable. Every merchant and every industrialist invests part of his money in the land and enslaves the peasant through onerous loans, through pawnshops, through buyers of agrarian products and on the basis of these enslaving deals gains their land. For that reason the upper and middle national bourgeoisie fears the peasant movement. The government issued a decree on the lowering of leasehold payments, which in places amount to eighty percent of the value of the harvest, by 25 percent. Even this insignificant reduction of leasehold payments was not carried out in reality for the simple reason that the local administration, in the hands of capitalists and landowners, did not even think of carrying it out. The more energetically it took up the destruction of peasant organisations, which grew up like mushrooms over the whole of south China. In Guangdong province it forced the independent peasant armed militia to unite with the kulak-landowner militia and subordinated them to the police, i.e. in actuality they destroyed the independent peasant armed detachments.

The struggle of the peasantry for the improvement in their situation was declared a bandit movement by the officials. It went so far that a resolution of the Guomindang congress in Canton, adopted in December 1926 on the peasant question, was forced to acknowledge the following: 'In the course of these three years of the peasant movement, members of the party committed serious errors. If these errors continue they will create a *danger not only for the peasants, but also for the nat[ional] revolution*. These errors consist in the fact that the party and government officials regard *the peasant movement as something foreign, even inimical to the revolution*'. The struggle against the peasant organisation and the peasant movement is happening not just in the south. From Hubei province, where the government is established, we have the following information: in November 1926, soldiers of the 15th revol[utionary] army attacked the peasant union in Shiong-Pa-Ho [Xiongpahe?], wrecked it, looted and arrested members of the committee of the union. In Yingcheng [Yincheng?] a peasant organisation was wrecked by soldiers; its secretary was hanged. Officials justified the guilty; the river police attacked a worker-peasant demonstration and wounded more than ten people. In Kenyang [Gengyang?] the local administration wrecked a peasant worker union. In Hangyang soldiers of the 8th army whipped up by local officials, destroyed a peasant union. In Chi-Yang [Qiyang?] a peasant union was destroyed. We have a large quantity of information about cases of this kind.

C[om.] Tan Pingshan knew what he was talking about when he wrote in his report to the Comintern: '*When conflicts erupted between the major landowners and the peasant poor, the government always stood on the side of the former*' (p. 34) This was written in November 1926; unfortunately, this pamphlet only appeared in April [1927].[22]

The Masses against Chiang Kai-shek

The policy of the National government up until [...] the plenum of the C[E]C of the Guomindang, which took place in March 1927, – of six members of the government, as the resolution of the ECCI of December 1926 informs us, five belonged to the right wing, – provoked a widespread wave of mass protests. Indignation against the policy of the government was expressed by the departure of significant worker and peasant masses from the Guomindang and in a wave of meetings and workers' demonstrations, headed by trade unions, Communists, in part by left Guomindang with Xu Qian in the lead. The meeting of one hundred thousand which took place in Changsha on 13 March 1927 demanded the resignation of Chiang Kai-shek, calling him a neo-militarist and accusing him of a deal with Zhang Zuolin and Japan. During the whole of January, February and March we observed in Hankou a campaign of demonstrations and meetings, directed against Chiang Kai-shek. He is accused of profiting from the revolution, conducting secret negotiations with the Japanese and of attempting to become a dictator.

This movement forced the Secretary of the Chin[ese] Communist Party, c[om.] Chen Duxiu, who had until then defended the united front with the upper bourgeoisie with zeal deserving a better object, to print on 12 March in *Guide Weekly* an article under the characteristic headline '*Sadness on the occasion of the second anniversary of the death of Sun Yat-sen*'[23] Without deciding to name Chiang Kai-shek by name, he accused the 'hard party' of attempting to break the alliance with the working class, the peasantry and the USSR. He accuses them of attempting an alliance with Zhang Zuolin. From all these accusations he draws no practical conclusions, accompanying them with only the stereotypical slogan: 'Isn't this sad!' These tears and groans of the Secretary of the Chin[ese] Communist Party display a characteristic symptom of that indecisiveness which ruled in the leading circles of the Party. This indecisive-

---

22 See Tan-Pin-Sian (Tan Pingshang) 1927.
23 See Chen 1927.

ness did not permit the Party, even at the last moment, to adopt defensive measures against the counter-revolutionary coup that was in preparation. The March plenum of the Centr[al Executive] Committee [of the Guomindang] dissolved the dictatorial powers of Chiang Kai-shek, while leaving him the real power over the army. Chiang Kai-shek *verbally* submitted to the decision. He even greeted Wang Jingwei as his 'teacher'. But in reality he prepared the coup. The right wing of the Guomindang, representing the upper bourgeoisie came into conflict with the growing worker and peasant movement, decided on a split in the Guomindang, a split in the National government, i.e. they opened the front for the imperialist enemy.

The Betrayal by the Upper Bourgeoisie

The leading 'revolutionary' elements in the Guomindang feared a weakening of the anti-imperialist front. They hoped that together with the upper bourgeoisie they would succeed in uniting China, and that when they reached Beijing they could take the risk of a break with the upper bourgeoisie. But from the very beginning the upper bourgeoisie had no thought of a struggle to the death with imperialism. It aspired to the capitalist development of China, so it achieved a deal with imperialism; only a compromise with imperialism could give them the necessary loans. It was impossible to defeat imperialism without confiscating and nationalising the major capitalist industries and the banks, which in most cases belong to the foreign imperialists. But such nationalisation could have given the commanding heights of the economy *into the hands of a democratic dictatorship of the workers and peasants* and would have complicated the conditions for the development of private capitalist industry. The upper bourgeoisie could not therefore be anti-imperialist to the end, just as the European bourgeoisie could not be a partisan against feudalism to the end. Imperialism creams off from the capitalist exploitation of China, and therefore it appears as a rival of the Chinese nat[ional] bourgeoisie, but the working class aspires not just to a limitation of exploitation, but to socialism. Therefore, the Chinese upper bourgeoisie fears the Chinese proletariat more than imperialism.

The peasant aspires to the suppression of extortionate leases, which bring the bourgeoisie hundreds and hundreds of millions.

Therefore, for the upper bourgeoisie the opening of the front towards imperialism is a lesser evil than allowing power to fall into the hands of a democratic dictatorship of workers and peasants.

In destroying worker and peasant organisations, the upper bourgeoisie, under the leadership of Chiang Kai-shek, created the ground for a compromise with world imperialism. *The Daily Telegraph*,[24] organ of the British Ministry of For[eign] Affairs, said to Chiang Kai-shek: 'Until you restore order in Shanghai, you won't received a kopeck from the customs receipts'. *The Times*[25] of the 23 March, while explaining the transition from a policy of negotiations with the Guomindang government to a policy of shelling Nanjing, declared, that until the Guomindang rightists are victorious it is pointless to come to an agreement with Chiang Kai-shek. Chiang Kai-shek, in destroying the worker and peasant organisations, in disarming the workers, thereby declares to imperialism: 'Why are you keeping your troops in China, Messieurs? I can stand guard over your interests, if you make some concessions to me, if you conclude a deal with the Chinese bourgeoisie'.

Chiang Kai-shek's betrayal is not the betrayal of a personality, it is not the betrayal of a military clique, it is the betrayal of that part of the upper bourgeoisie, which previously went along with the national movement. *The national movement will be victorious as a movement of workers and peasants or it will perish.*

The Guomindang and the Communist Party in the Chinese Revolution

Is It Inevitable for the Proletariat to Be Taken Unawares?
Chiang Kai-shek's betrayal and the shooting of Chinese workers do not represent anything 'unexpected' for a Marxist, or so said those who until yesterday were still screeching about panic in answer to our warnings. Yes, Chiang Kai-shek's betrayal is 'natural'. Just as the Chinese revolution represents itself as a national-liberation kind of bourgeois-democratic revolution, just so the shootings of Chinese workers, the treason of the Chinese bourgeoisie towards the national movement correspond to a phenomenon which was found in all bourgeois revolutions.

In the English revolution of the seventeenth c[entury] the popular masses were first betrayed by the Presbyterian bourgeoisie, later by the Independents and finally ⟨...⟩ [after,] the mass movement was suppressed, the bourgeoisie proclaimed the dictatorship of Cromwell.[26] In the Great French Revolution

---

24 *The Daily Telegraph* – a British Conservative newspaper published since 1855.
25 *The Times* (of London) – a British Conservative newspaper published since 1785.
26 In 1640–48, the Presbyterians (conservative puritans) made up the ruling majority of the English Parliament. In 1649–60, after Independents (radical puritans) had excluded the Presbyterians, Independents only sat in the British Rump Parliament. In 1653–58, however,

the Girondins,[27] representing the trading bourgeoisie of the Midi, betrayed the revolution, and only by striding over their corpses could the revolution go further. Already at the dawn of the capitalist development of Europe in the struggle of the bourgeois Netherlands against feudal Spain, the Belgian bourgeoisie, frightened by the revolutionary struggle of the artisan proletariat in industrially more developed Belgium, raised a revolt against the small artisans, the lesser merchants and the minor artisan proletariat in Flanders and Brabant, seizing power under the leadership of Ryhove and Hembyze. They united with the feudal landowners and after overthrowing the revolutionary-democratic government, they concluded a peace with Phillip II on 17 May 1579, by which she [Belgium] broke with the Northern Netherlands and submitted completely to Spanish absolutism.[28] Phillip II was no Marxist, but all the same, he understood very well the reasons of this defection of the bourgeoisie from the national-liberation movement. While ratifying the peace with the landowners and capitalists of Belgium, he said that the reason for their return under the roof of absolutism was not just their love for the old Catholic Church, to which they referred, but '*a determination to escape the dangers threatening their property, provoked by the attempt to create a democratic tyranny over the clergy, the gentry and the honourable Bürgertum*'. The new hero of the Chinese bourgeoisie, Chiang Kai-shek, can refer to that example and contradict Struve's old assertion, that the further East one goes, the more disreputable the bourgeoisie.

Parliament did not have real political power, since the country was then ruled by the military dictator Oliver Cromwell. Marxist historiography regards the Presbyterians as representatives of the wealthy merchants and bankers of London, and also the bourgeois section of the landowners. The Independents, including Cromwell, are described as representatives of the liberal section of the English bourgeoisie.

27 The Girondins were the moderate democratic faction of the Jacobin political party in the National Convention of revolutionary France. Its leaders were natives of the department of Gironde, in the south-western region of the country. In the National Convention the radical Jacobins and other left-wing extremists opposed this faction. After the radical Jacobin coup on 31 May to 2 June 1793, the majority of the leaders of the Girondins were executed in October 1793. However, after the Thermidorian (July 1794) coup in the National Convention and the execution of the radical Jacobin leaders (Robespierre etc.) the surviving Girondins returned to power. Marxist historiography regards the Girondins as representatives of the French mercantile-industrial bourgeoisie, which tried to prevent the radicalisation of the Revolution.

28 This refers to the so-called Union of Arras, concluded by representatives of the Catholic nobility and the bourgeoisie of Belgium with Spain at a time of the Calvinist revolution in the Netherlands.

The Chinese upper bourgeoisie, in going over onto the side of the counter-revolution, has not betrayed itself, but only the cause of the national revolution. Its class interests are profit. Under the wing of imperialism it developed, for better or worse, until the present. The developing worker-peasant movement threatened to deprive the bourgeoisie of these profits. They hope to do a deal with imperialism. The betrayal of the revolution, even of a bourgeois revolution, on the part of the bourgeoisie is understandable; one must forsee and take account of this in good time. But is the fact also 'understandable' that *Chiang Kai-shek caught the workers and peasants of China unawares*? In all previous bourgeois revolutions, the upper bourgeoisie betrayed, *but its betrayal did not always catch the revolutionary masses unawares*. Robespierre warned of the betrayal of the Girondins, executing them in good time. Under the leadership of the Jacobins, the French petty bourgeoisie was able to protect itself against betrayal. In 1848 the working masses were caught unawares by Cavaignac.[29] The unpreparedness of the Fre[nch] proletariat was explained by the fact *that the young workers' movement had not yet finally separated itself ideologically from the bourgeoisie, that it did not possess its own strong political party, armed with the methods of Marxism, adapting itself to the environment, understanding all the mainsprings of the movement of the opponent.*

Marx drew all the conclusions from this experience. In the address of the *Communist League* in March 1850, he brilliantly described the tactics of the upper and petty bourgeoisie in the revolution. He provided a picture of the defection of the liberal upper bourgeoisie and predicted the treacherous role of the democratic petty bourgeoisie, in a few pages gave the proletariat exhaustive instructions on *how to defend themselves against this betrayal.* These few pages give not only a general presentation of the question of the tactics of the proletariat in a bourgeois revolution, but also sketch a concrete *practical* programme of action. Marx showed the proletariat how, while supporting the petty bourgeoisie while it was revolutionary, the proletariat must defend its independent party and its independent policy with both hands; how it must create mass organisations to rebuff future betrayals by the petty bourgeoisie, and arm itself for the struggle when it turns against it. The entire historical development since Marx's death completely confirmed the accuracy of his warnings, completely exposed the rottenness of liberalism and of the petty bourgeoisie in the capitalist countries of the West. If the role of the upper bourgeoisie *in the East* is the same as in the West, then this question will appear before the sharp-

---

29   In June 1848, the Paris workers organised an armed uprising, which was suppressed by General Cavaignac.

shooters of the proletarian struggle at the very beginning of the development of the revolution in the East.

The Comintern Warned, The Chin[ese] Com[munist] P[arty] Knew the Danger

In the resolutions of the Second Congress of the Comintern, *Lenin* adapted Marx's teaching to the new circumstances created by imperialism in the epoch of world revolution. [He] underlined: 'The Communist International must support the bourgeois-democratic national movement[30] in the colonies and backward countries *only on condition that elements of the future proletarian parties, Communist not just by name, must be organised and educated in an awareness of their special tasks in the struggle with the bourgeois-democratic movements within their nations*; the Communist International must go along in a *temporary* alliance with the bourgeois democracy of the colonies and backward countries, but *not merging with them, and must unconditionally preserve the independence of the workers' movement even in the most embryonic form*'[31] [emphasised by Radek].[32]

He complemented his thesis by pointing out that 'between the bourgeoisie of the exploited and colonial countries a certain rapprochement has occurred, so that very often – perhaps even in a majority of cases – *the bourgeoisie of the oppressed countries, even though it supports the national movement, at the same time and in agreement with the imperialist bourgeoisie, i.e. together with it, struggles against all revolutionary movements of all revolutionary classes.* As Communists, we should and will support the bourgeois-liberation movement in the colonial countries only *in those cases*, where the movement is *really revolutionary*, when its representatives *do not prevent* us from educating and organising the peasantry and the broad masses of the exploited' (V.I. Lenin, *Collected Works*, Vol. XVII, p. 275)[33] [emphasised by Radek.]

---

30 According to Lenin: 'bourgeois-democratic national movements'.
31 According to Lenin: 'his uniform'.
32 Lenin 1971b [1920], p. 167.
33 Radek is guilty of slightly distorting the quotation. In Lenin's version this passage reads as follows: 'Between the bourgeoisie of the exploiting and the colonial countries a certain accommodation took place as so often, even in the majority of cases, the bourgeoisie of the exploited countries, although it supports the national movement, it simultaneously, in agreement with the imperialist bourgeoisie, i.e. together with it, struggles against all revolutionary movements of all revolutionary classes ... We, as Communists, must and will support bourgeois liberation movements in colonial countries, but only when these movements are really revolutionary, when their representatives do not prevent us from educating and organising the peasantry and the broad masses of the exploited in a revolutionary spirit' (Lenin 1971c [1920], pp. 243–44).

In the spring of 1922, the Communist International decided that to support the national-revolutionary movement in China, the young Chin[ese] Communist Party must enter the Guomindang, so that while struggling in the vanguard of the national revolution it would conquer the trust of the broad masses for itself so that it would subsequently take the leadership of the revolution into its own hands.[34] The Fourth Congress of the Comintern in its resolution on the Eastern question[35] pointed out that 'a refusal by the Communists of the colonies to take part in the struggle against imperialist coercion under the pretext of the defence of independent class interests would be opportunism of the worst kind, which could only compromise the proletarian revolution in the East. But no *less harmful* [...] *would be an attempt to put off the struggle for the everyday and most vital interests of the working class in favour of 'national unity' or 'a civil truce' with bourgeois democracy'*.

The resolution of the Fourth Congress of the Comintern pointed out: 'There exists *the danger of an agreement between bourgeois nationalism and one of the imperialist powers* or many of them, which are involved in struggle for the semi-colonial countries (China, Persia)' and drew the conclusion: 'The revolutionary movement in *the backward countries of the East cannot be victorious unless it relies on the movement of the broad masses of the peasantry. Therefore, the revolutionary parties of the Eastern countries must work out a clear revolutionary programme. It is essential that they force the bourgeois-national parties to accept this programme in its entirety'*[36] [emphasised by Radek].

---

34 Radek is mistaken. In actual fact the ECCI took the decision on the entry of the CCP into the Guomindang at the end of July 1922. The text of the decision was written by Radek himself; see RGASPI, F.326, Op.2, D.24, L.1.

35 This refers to 'General theses on the Eastern question', adopted by the Fourth Congress of the Comintern on 5 December 1922.

36 Radek quotes inaccurately. The first two quotations, which he employs, actually read as follows: 'The refusal of the Communists of the colonies to participate in the struggle with imperialist coercion, under the pretext of the supposed "defence" of independent class interests, is opportunism of the worst kind, which can only discredit the proletarian revolution in the East. The attempt to withdraw from the struggle for the vital and everyday interests of the working class in the name of "national unity" or "social peace" with the bourgeois democrats must also be recognised as no less harmful ... The danger of a deal between bourgeois nationalism and one or several of the mutually hostile imperialist powers in the semi-colonial countries (China, Persia) ... is much greater than in the colonies'. The third quotation also reads slightly differently: 'The revolutionary movement in the backward countries of the East cannot be successful if it is not based on the activities of the broad peasant masses. Therefore, the revolutionary parties of all oriental countries must formulate their agrarian programme clearly ... It is essential also to force the bourgeois-national parties to accept this revolutionary agrarian programme to the greatest extent possible'. (Titarenko 1986, pp. 32, 34, 30).

At the Fifth Congress of the Comintern in 1924 c[om.] Manuilskii said in his report on the national and colonial question:

> A double danger arises before our sections: either the danger *of a nihilist know-nothingness of such new phenomena, revolutionising the East, or the danger of a deviation from a proletarian footing* onto a path of *vulgar collaboration with the petty bourgeoisie and the loss of our independent class profile* [emphasis by Radek].[37]

Already at the Sixth enlarged plenum of the Executive Committee of the Comintern, which took place between *17 February and 18 March 1926*, i.e. just a few days before Chiang Kai-shek's coup d'état, a resolution adopted on the Chinese question said:

> The Chinese Communist Party can fulfil the historical tasks of the leader of the working masses of China in their struggle against imperialism, [the tasks,] which stand before it, only in the event that along the whole line of the struggle it will *constantly strengthen its organisation and its influence as the class party of the Chinese proletariat* and as a section of the Communist International. The process of self-determination of the Chinese Communist Party over the last year has moved forward substantially as a result of the widespread economic and political strikes, which took place under the leadership of the party, but all the same, the organised formation of the party is very far from complete. The political self-determination of the Chinese Communists will develop in the struggle against one of two equally harmful deviations: *against right-wing liquidationism, which ignores the independent class tasks of the Chinese proletariat and leads to the amorphous merging with the general democratic and national movement, and against the extreme leftist tendencies*, striving to jump over the revolutionary-democratic stage of the movement directly towards the tasks of proletarian dictatorship and Sov[iet] power, *forgetting the peasantry*, this fundamental and determining factor of the Chinese national-liberation movement. *The tactical problems of the Chinese national-liberation movement despite all the specifics of the situation are very close to the problems standing before the Russian proletariat in the period of the first revolution of 1905. The assimilation by the Chinese Communist Party of the lessons of this revolution, as formulated by*

---

37   RGASPI, F 492, D. 1, D. 73, L. 15.

Leninism, and the political and organisational strengthening of the party help considerably towards the outgrowing of, and the forewarning against the deviations from the correct tactical line indicated here.

In the same resolution it states: 'A fundamental task of the Chinese Communists in the Guomindang is to explain to the mass of the peasantry in the whole of China, *that only the formation of an independent revolutionary-democratic government on the basis of an alliance of the working class and the peasantry* can radically improve the material and political position of the peasantry, attract the mass of the peasantry into an active struggle under militant slogans, uniting understandable and immediate political and economic demands with the general political tasks of the struggle against the imperialists and militarists'[38] [emphasised by Radek].

The Communist Party of China was persuaded to enter the Guomindang only after a very bitter struggle. All its leaders were at first against entering the Guomindang. This expressed not the guild interests of the Chinese proletariat (the party was in general still only tenuously connected with the working masses), but a mistrust of the Guomindang, provoked by a series of actions by the Canton government directed against the working class – the suppression of strikes etc. Only the authority of the Communist International forced the conference of the Chin[ese] Communist Party in Canton in the summer of 1922 to submit and to enter the Guomindang.[39]

At the Fourth Congress of the Comintern in November 1922, the representative of the Chinese Communist Party com. *Liu Renjing* said:

> The Guomindang, the national-revolutionary party in China, has pursued its plans for a military revolution for the duration of the last few years. *It did not conduct mass propaganda in the country, it did not organise the masses. It attempted to reach its goal using solely military methods.* Even before Guangdong province was conquered, the Guomindang had organised a government.[40] It wanted to use all the resources of this province for an expedition to the North, against the governments of the feudal militarists and the agents of world imperialism. At first this plan

---

38 Titarenko 1986, pp. 60–61, 62.
39 In actual fact the decision on entry into the Guomindang was endorsed by a small group of leaders of the CCP at a conference with the representative of the Comintern, Hendricus Sneevliet (Maring) on 30–31 August 1922 on Xihu lake in Hangzhou.
40 Liu Renjing had in mind the organisation of a Guomindang military government in Canton in August 1917.

seemed attainable, since all members of the party were publicly in agreement. But when they conquered Guangdong province, the military governor, a member of the Guomindang,[41] refused these plans, becoming every day more conservative and inclined to make do with the province and to pay no attention to anything outside it. There were many such members in the Guomindang. *Until they have conquered power they are revolutionaries. Afterwards they become conservatives. This general, who demolished the Canton government, was one of many elements of this kind, belonging to the Guomindang.* The majority of the Guomindang consists of *essentially reactionary* people [emphasised by Radek].

Having given such a testimonial to the Guomindang, the representative of the Chin[ese] Communist Party declared that

> our Party is for a united front with the Guomindang. The form of that united front consists in the fact that *we enter the Guomindang as separate people under our own name.* Thereby we can achieve two objectives: firstly, we want to conduct agitation amongst the workers belonging to the Guomindang, so as to conquer them; secondly, we want to struggle with imperialism only by *uniting the forces of the proletariat and the petty bourgeoisie. We want to compete with this party in the organisation and propagandistic embrace of the masses.* If we do not enter this party and remain isolated we will propagandise communism, but the masses will not follow us ... The masses will follow the petty bourgeois party which is using them for its own ends. *If we enter the party, then we are showing the masses that we are also for revolutionary democracy, but for us it is just a means to an end.* We will have the opportunity to show the masses that, in advancing more distant aims, we do not forget the daily needs of the mass. *Thus we will unite the masses and split the Guomindang* [emphasised by Radek].[42]

At the Fifth Congress of the Comintern in 1924, the representative of the Chin[ese] Communist Party c[om.] Qinhua [Li Dazhao] declared:

> In accordance with the instructions of the Executive Committee of the Comintern the members of our party and members of the Young Com-

---

41 This refers to General Chen Jiongming.
42 Comintern 1922, p. 5.

munist League entered *as individuals* into the Guomindang with the objective of reorganising it, changing its programme and setting things up so that it could gain close contact with the masses. Sun Yat-sen and the 'left' wing of the Guomindang decided to reorganise the party on the basis of our proposals [...] In conclusion [I] want to point out that the main objective of our work within the Guomindang is *to rouse the revolutionary spirit of the masses and to direct it against the international imperialists and the domestic militarists.* Within the Guomindang we are attracting to our side the *left* wing and thereby accelerating the growth of the revolutionary wave [emphasised by Radek].[43]

Having entered the Guomindang, our party *directed the proletarian movement independently,* beginning with the strike on the Hankou-Beijing Railway, advancing *under our own flag* or that of the trade unions. In Canton the Communists who had entered the Guomindang, conducted their work in the spirit of Communism, *infiltrating the Guomindang apparatus and through it trying to organise the peasants and the petty bourgeoisie for their struggle.* This strengthening of the Communists on the basis of the rise of the workers' movement and use of the Guomindang led precisely to the organisation of a consciously bourgeois *right wing* of the Guomindang, Sunyatsenism[44] and other organisations, whose goal was to exclude the Communists, if possible to throw them out of the Guomindang. As is well known *Chiang Kai-shek's attempted coup d'état of 20 March 1926* was born from these aspirations.

The Attack of the Guomindang Bourgeoisie on the Communist Party
The aim of this coup was to *bring an end to the use of the Guomindang* by the Communists and to turn against the workers and peasants. Chiang Kai-shek, meeting opposition from the lower ranks of the party, from several of its leaders and part of Whampoa military academy, contented himself, as is well known, with the partial realisation of his objectives. This is what the resolution of the plenum of the Guomindang of 15 May 1926 has to say:

---

43   Comintern 1925, pp. 670, 672.
44   It refers to the Society for the Study of Sunyatsenism which was founded on 24 April 1924 in the Whampoa military academy by the right-wing Guomindang members. One of its founders was Dai Jitao. From September 1925 until April 1926 the society issued the journal *Guomin geming* ('National revolution'), which propagandized the political ideas of Sun Yat-sen and Dai Jitao and campaigned against the CCP. On 20 April 1926 the society dissolved itself.

1. The other political party [the Communist Party⁴⁵] *must instruct* its members entering the Guomindang so that they understand that *the basis of the Guomindang is the three principles, therefore they must not allow criticism of it [the Guomindang] or of Sun Yat-sen, as the founder of the three principles.*
2. The other party must hand over a list of its members who have entered the Guomindang to the chairman of the c[e]c of the Guomindang.
3. Members of another party entering the Guomindang can be members of the Executive Committee and various high organisations of the Guomindang, but the proportion of such members must not exceed ⅓ of the whole membership of the given Executive Committee.
4. Members entering [the Guomindang] from another party cannot be chairmen of departments of the c[e]c of the Guomindang.
5. No one belonging to the Guomindang *has the right to call a party meeting without the permission of a par[ty] organ.*
6. No member of the Guomindang is permitted to organise *any kind of organisation* and develop its activity *without the permission* of a higher organ.
7. *All circular instructions* of the other party to its members entering the Guomindang must be handed over for the agreement of a united committee. In the event of a delay in agreement, the circular must be handed over for [recognition – literal translation⁴⁶] to be confirmed [emphasized by Radek].⁴⁷

In justifying these decisions in his speech delivered on the 25 [22] May 1926 before closing the plenum of the c[e]c of the Guomindang, Chiang Kai-shek declared:

> It should be known that the Chinese revolution is a part of the world revolution. The world revolution must be united and the Chinese revolution must also be united. The world revolution has a *single leadership of the Third International. The Guomindang has the leadership of the Chinese national revolution.* During this leadership of the national revolution, on the one hand, we must concentrate the revolutionary elements, we must

---

45 Radek's insertion in brackets.
46 Radek's insertion in brackets. It is unclear what Radek means.
47 In general, Radek correctly transmits the content of this decision of the GMD plenum. These demands were introduced by Chiang Kai-shek on the 15 May 1926; Tan Yankai and Sun Fo spoke in their favour, after which they were adopted on 17 May 1926. (For the text of the document see Guomindang 1986, pp. 714–15; RGASPI, collection of unsorted documents.)

unite; on the other hand, in view of the fact that the Chinese revolution is part of the world revolution, we must unite with the Third International; at the same time we must recognise that what has been said about a united leadership *does not mean intervention in military or political affairs. We must recognise the leadership of the Third International only in general objectives* – the overthrowing of imperialism, in tactics. In this one must have a single plan. But this does not mean such assistance as England and Japan give Wu Peifu and Zhang Zuolin. However, *we must be very vigilant to avoid entering imperceptibly on the road* leading to destruction like Wu Peifu, of imperialism and militarism.

We must also know that the Communist Party is the party representing the proletariat, a party which cannot not exist. Even if the Communist Party perished the proletariat cannot perish. *And so long as such a class exists, it must have its own political party*, which will represent it. As far as the opinion of the Communists about class struggle is concerned, the Guomindang is not obliged to oppose it. If there are classes, then struggle is inevitable. There are those who say that in China there is no bourgeoisie. However, the bourgeoisie is a class which opposes the proletariat, and one cannot say that there is no proletariat in China. If there is a proletariat then, naturally, there is a bourgeoisie. However, at the present time that class struggle must be limited. In general, class struggle is not an obstacle to the national revolution. Why unite the worker and peasant movements? By what means should they be united? And at the same time how to act so that *the worker and peasant movement can prove really useful and not destroy the united* front in the framework of a single revolutionary leadership? All this is very important. In general, in so far as the plenum has already confirmed the decisions and has rejected incorrect methods, all that now remains is so that our party can really grow stronger and develop [emphasised by Radek].

Chiang Kai-shek verbally agreed therefore to subordinate the Guomindang to the Comintern, warning only that the Guomindang should not fall into the kind of dependence on the international proletarian organisation, on which Zhang Zuolin depended on Japan and Wu Peifu on England. At the same time, he recognised the inevitability of the existence of a Communist Party and of class struggle, but demanded that class struggle did not destroy the united national front. But as is well known, the appetite grows from eating. Having observed the complete panic of the Communists (not only Chinese), on 7 June Chiang Kai-shek delivered a speech in Whampoa academy, in which while repeating that the Chinese national revolution is a part of the world revolution, that the Comintern is the leader of the international revolution, to which the Guomindang must submit, *demands the destruction of the Communist Party*:

> The Russian revolution was able to be victorious so quickly because the Social Democratic party tore power from the hands of the Kerensky government, seized the capital, made itself the basic centre of the revolution, gave instructions to the whole state. All revolutions come from *one party*, and a revolution is a revolution, which can be called really successful. We, Chinese, desiring revolutions and having recognised the necessity of a concentration of all our forces, must learn by the example of the Russian revolution. *A revolution without the dictatorship of one party will not succeed*. If a revolution does not have a dictatorship of one party, such a revolution is doomed to defeat [emphasised by Radek].

What kind of party should lead the Chinese revolution?

> The Guomindang can already count nearly thirty years of activity, while the Chinese Communist Party does not even have a decade of history behind it. There must have been more than thirty years of struggles and efforts so as to gather contemporary Chinese society under the leadership of the three principles. This has been achieved, and by now the Guomindang cannot perish. *There is no one else who could substitute it* and therefore, in trying to achieve the unity of our revolutionary forces, we must carry out in action the point of view I have raised. That is: *within the party we must unite our revolutionary forces, and create a single* revolutionary spirit.

Therefore, Chiang Kai-shek advances the demand:

> *It is necessary for members of our party to be **only** members of the Guomindang*. Only in avoiding all enmity and all suspicions can the intellectual forces unite and the strengths of the party destroy our enemies, and if we cannot do that, [and] within one party there are elements of two groups, we will not only fail to defeat our external enemies, but even between ourselves we will not avoid conflicts and reciprocal disaster. Therefore, I now stand on the point of view that *Communist comrades, within the Guomindang must temporarily leave the Communist Party and become simple members of the Guomindang*. Thereby, we shall avoid those illnesses of suspicion and enmity, which are observed at the moment amongst members of the Guomindang.

In consoling the Communists, Chiang Kai-shek turned their attention to the fact that

> we must understand why in the end members of the Communist Party joined the Guomindang. So as to achieve the successful completion of the Chinese national revolution, so as to concentrate the revolutionary forces ... we must help the Guomindang to become stronger and therefore *our minority parties must temporarily sacrifice themselves so as to achieve the successful accomplishment of our objectives*, without going into other matters [emphasised by Radek].

Chiang Kai-shek's programme was unambiguous. He demands the subordination of the Communist Party to the Guomindang in deed, that is, the *subordination in deed of the Chinese proletariat to the Chinese bourgeoisie*.

The Communists entered the Guomindang so as to conquer hegemony in the national movement. But the bourgeoisie, in the person of Chiang Kai-shek answered them: bow down to me and recognise my hegemony. How did the Communists reply?

The Submission of the Chin[ese] Communist Party to the Guomindang

The moment arrived when it was necessary to take a decision: should the Chin[ese] Communist Party remain within the Guomindang, submitting to the representatives of the upper bourgeoisie, which demanded from her a renunciation of an independent policy and who strove to convert her into a weapon of their bourgeois policy or leave the Guomindang organisation and try by defending the interests not only of the workers, but also the interests of the peasantry and of the urban petty bourgeoisie, to conquer its [of the petty bourgeoisie] trust, to tear it from the influence of the upper bourgeoisie; in this case to divide the Guomindang and conclude an alliance with its left wing – a bloc of two independent parties for the achievement of mutual aims. On the basis of a decision of the Comintern the Chin[ese] Communist Party submitted to Chiang Kai-shek's demands, *though it fully recognised that this meant a coup by Chiang Kai-shek and the class tendencies he represents*.

In the resolution [on the question of the relations between the CCP and the Guomindang], adopted by the plenum of the Central [Executive] Committee of the Chin[ese] Communist Party[48] it states quite openly that

---

48 This refers to the July (1926) plenum of the CEC of the CCP.

events of the 20 March in Canton, the Guomindang plenum of 15 May, Chiang Kai-shek's proposals on the Communists of 7 June at Whampoa academy amount to *a consequential chain of attacks against the Communists on the part of the military group of Guomindang centrists, who have taken power in the party, and also on the part of the rightists in the whole country*.[49]

In the report on the peasant movement, presented by the C[E]C of the Chin[ese] Communist Party to the Comintern we read:

> In the Guomindang resolution it states: 'The Chinese national revolution is a *peasant revolution* in character. Our party must above all liberate the peasantry to fortify the basis of the nat[ional] revolution. Any political or economic movement must make the peasant movement its basis. The policy of the Party should above all examine the interests of the peasantry, the conduct of the government should also be based on the interests of the peasantry and its liberation. However, can the Guomindang carry this out? The Guomindang is a party embracing all classes and by its nature cannot base itself on the peasantry. Apart from that, starting from 30 April of last year (since the Shanghai events) *the objective situation in China is such that a demarcation of classes has become more and more evident.* This enormous division began in the organisation of *the Guomindang. The Guomindang is getting closer to the capitalists with every passing day.* This deviation becomes clearer with every step. At the moment *part of the compradors and the major landowners* are still in the Guomindang. *As a result, the Guomindang and the National government can obviously not oppose the compradors and the major landowners with determination.* On the contrary, there is a possibility for them to press the peasantry in alliance with the major landowners. Such is, for instance, the incident connected with the attack of the Guangdong *mintuans* on the peasant unions. The military and the government often avert their eyes and do not resort to decisive measures to defend the peasantry. The Congress of the C[E]C[50] of 15 May, among other things, published a resolution *on the limitation of the worker-peasant movement: amongst the Dongjiang peasants*[51]

---

49 The words 'on the part of the rightists in the whole country' are absent from the resolution and instead of the words 'Chiang Kai-shek's proposals on the Communists of 7 June at Whampoa academy' it says: '[A]nd also the fact that the Whampoa military academy has again raised the question of relations with the communists'; see CCP 1926a, p. 16.
50 Thus in the text. It refers to a plenum of the CEC.
51 Dongjiang (Eastern River) flows in Guangdong province.

suspicions are already growing in connection with the conduct of the Guomindang and the Nat[ional] government. Therefore, we say firmly that ***the Guomindang cannot guide the struggle of the peasantry any more. In future class antagonism will be even clearer, and then this deviation will be even clearer.*** However, now we do not yet believe that the peasantry must break with the Guomindang, it is only necessary for the peasants to enter the Guomindang as a monolithic group and not as individuals. Or to put it another way, it is necessary to found in the Guomindang a peasant party which could unite with or leave the united front of various classes.

The disturbances in the Guomindang, which took place on 20 March and 15 May were in fact class conflicts, specifically: the representative of bourgeois ideology, Chiang Kai-shek on the one hand wanted to subordinate the petty bourgeoisie to himself and to exploit the proletariat, and on the other he was discontented with the compradors, and so he attacked them at the same time. The resolution for the regulation of part[y] affairs is directed against the leftists. If we now actively struggle against *Chiang* [Kai-shek] then we thereby force him willy nilly to come to an agreement with the compradors and the major landowners and intensify exploitation. Therefore, we must now *make a concession to Chiang [Kai-shek], i.e. unite with the bourgeoisie*, so as to defeat the compradors and the major landowners. Only this can meet [positively] the needs of our peasant movement.

The Chin[ese] Communist Party takes account of the victory of the upper bourgeois elements in the Guomindang. It takes account of the fact that the Guomindang is not in a position to guide the peasant movement by virtue of its class structure. But having started on the road of submission to the Guomindang, for the sake of avoiding a split with them, it is beginning to work out a justification for its policy, a justification which can be summarised thus: that it is necessary not to frighten the upper bourgeoisie so as not to thrust it into a union with more reactionary landowners. The Chin[ese] Communist Party is losing an understanding of that basic fact which has nowhere been clearer than in Guangdong province in particular, where the landowners and bourgeoisie are either one class or are connected between themselves by thousands of networks. Having submitted to the Guomindang with the permission of the Comintern, the C[E]C of the Communist Party is starting to talk to the proletariat *in the vulgar language of Menshevism*. In the appeal of the plenum of the C[E]C of the Chin[ese] Communist Party, published with the knowledge of the Far Eastern bureau of the Comintern, we read cheap, vulgar words, unworthy of Communism:

> The alleviation of all these sufferings is the everyday demand of the Chinese people. This *is not Bolshevism*. Please, *one might say that this is Bolshevism in the name of our people, but **not Bolshevism in the name of Communism** [...]*
>
> They (the bourgeoisie) do not understand that ***this minimum of class struggle***, as shown in the organisation of the workers and strikes, in no way reduces the military preparedness of the anti-imperialist or anti-militarist forces. Apart from that, they do not understand *that the welfare of the Chinese bourgeoisie depends on the success of its common war with the proletariat against the imperialists and the militarists, and in no way on the continuation of the class struggle of the proletariat'* [emphasised by Radek].[52]

What is this, accidental phrases of frightened and lost people? No. The founder of the Party, the secretary of its c[e]c, c[om.] *Chen Duxiu*, addressed himself to Chiang Kai-shek in an open letter of July 4, 1926 which represents *a capitulation in principle of the leadership of the Chin[ese] Communist Party to the Guomindang*:[53]

> I am certainly not against the opinion of Dai Jitao that the party must have a 'distinct faith'. *Sanminzhuyi* (the Three Principles)[54] are precisely such a common faith of the Guomindang. However, the Guomindang is in the last analysis a *party of class collaboration of all classes*, and is not a party of one class. Therefore, *apart from the 'common faith' it is necessary to recognise that there are other 'faiths', faiths of each class*. Exactly those, there also exist *particular* principles, which are produced by the special interests of each class in particular, apart from the common principles created by the general interests of all classes. *For example, one cannot forbid a worker entering the Guomindang, apart from that fact that he believes in Sanminzhuyi, to believe at the same time in Communism; to the industrialist or trader, entering the Guomindang apart from a belief in Sanminzhuyi in the same way* one cannot forbid him to believe in capitalism. From each member of the Guomindang it is necessary to demand only that

---

52 See CCP 1926b, pp. 1616–17. This declaration was adopted by an enlarged plenum of the CEC of the CCP on 12 July 1926 and published in *Xiangdao zhoukan* ('Guide weekly') on 14 July 1926.

53 Radek is mistaken. Chen Dixiu's letter to Chiang Kai-shek was written on 4 June 1926; See Chen 1926b, pp. 1526–29.

54 It refers to Sun Yat-sen's Three Principles of the People.

he believes in *Sanminzhuyi*, that he carries out *Sanminzhuyi* and that is enough. And naturally if you do not allow him to have another faith, or to have other principles, if you forbid him from *having a particular faith* apart from his *basic faith*, if within one organisation it is forbidden to have two principles, then that is almost impossible, and also non obligatory.

In so far as you are saying: 'Communist work is secretly carried on under the guise of *Sanminzhuyi* [Three Principles of the People] in the Guomindang' – this is the slogan of the right wing, one of the accusations against Communist elements in the Guomindang, which we have heard often enough![55] [emphasised by Radek].

Com. Chen Duxiu declares in public *that the Chin[ese] Communist Party stands on the ground of the petty bourgeois ideas of Sun Yat-sen*, ideas which may be a step forward for the oppressed petty bourgeoisie, but which for the Chinese workers on strike for months in Shanghai [in May–June 1925], or conducting a sixteen month boycott in Hong Kong [in 1925–6] would represent a shameful step backwards. He asks only that the future hegemon of the revolution in China is permitted to preserve his 'particular faith' in Communism in a corner of his heart. Chen Duxiu, leader of the Party, standing under the flag of Marx and Lenin declares, further, that

> *the Communist Party knows no other leader than Sun Yat-sen*. May a glorious leader appear in future who can lead our work, *but, as before, the theoretical leader, the spiritual leader will remain Sun Yat-sen*, and no one can doubt this at all. This is beyond argument and I do not understand why it was necessary for you, com. Chiang Kai-shek, to raise this question. I do not believe that a man can be found in the Guomindang (let alone in the Communist Party), who recognises a second leader like Sun Yat-sen. If they say that Communist elements in the Guomindang insult Sun Yat-sen as a person and diminish his significance as an historical personality then it is very easy to decide this question. One should *test* them as members of the Guomindang. *Communist elements are not those who are not subjected to summons and condemnation* [emphasised by Radek].

Com. Chen Duxiu goes further, having recognised Sun Yat-sen as the *sole* leader of the Chinese proletariat and having bowed his head before the three prin-

---

55 Chen 1926b, p. 1528.

ciples, he bows it before Chiang Kai-shek, before the man who has just tried to carry out a coup in the interests of the bourgeoisie, and who has demanded the elimination of the Communist Party. He presents him with a testimonial to his revolutionary reliability in the name of the c[e]c of the Chin[ese] Communist Party, in the name of the Chinese proletariat.[56] 'Of course, the foundation of a worker-peasant government is not a bad cause. However, its fulfilment now in practice would be a big mistake', writes Chen Duxiu.

> To remove Chiang Kai-shek it is undoubtedly necessary to possess *the precondition that he would have committed really counter-revolutionary deeds of some kind*. However, from the moment of the establishment of Whampoa academy and up to the events of 20 *March you cannot detect a single counter-revolutionary action on the part of Chiang Kai-shek*. Therefore, to talk about the overthrow of Chiang Kai-shek, particularly at a time when the counter-revolutionary forces of England and Japan, Zhang Zuolin and Wu Peifu, have united and are attacking the northern people's armies,[57] and when in Canton also, a conspiracy whose aim was the overthrow of Chiang Kai-shek ⟨...⟩ would have been to *render assistance to counter-revolutionary forces*. Com. Chiang Kai-shek, if the Chinese Communist Party is a counter-revolutionary party, you must destroy it, so that the world revolution would lose a counter-revolutionary organisation. If there is such a member of the Communist Party who is implicated in a counter-revolutionary conspiracy, you must *shoot* him. In such matters there must not be the slightest inhibition [emphasised by Radek].[58]

Many comrades, reading this declaration, consoled themselves that this was just a tactical manoeuvre. After all in entering the Guomindang we also recognised the three principles. But even on the basis of the miserable material which I have in my hands, it is clear that these were not manoeuvres and that the leadership [of the Communist] Party *broke its own back. In its* **practical work**, the Party **began to distort the revolutionary line**, *to roll up the revolutionary flag*. In the report which we have cited above, a report giving a picture of the peasant movement and explaining the tactics of the Chin[ese] Communist Party in the countryside, we find the following shattering point:

---

56 Ibid.
57 This refers to Feng Yuxiang's army.
58 Chen 1926b, pp. 1526–27.

> The Sichuan comrades advanced the slogan *'Down with the landowners'* and thereby forced those *notables, landowners and the best of the gentry capable of working with us to fear us and avoid us. All these are signs of inexperience* in our work.
>
> The slogan 'down with the landowners' can easily give rise to misunderstandings. In foreign literature those are called 'landowners' who do not just possess land, but those who have political rights in addition. In Chinese literature anyone can be called a 'landowner' who *has an income from leasehold payments. If he sees the slogan 'down with the landowners' he will naturally be frightened to death and will oppose us. For that reason we are definitely obliged to use all possibilities to alter these slogans, which can easily weaken the revolutionary forces we have, and only raise the slogan 'down with the notables' etc.* [emphasised by Radek].

The slogan 'down with the landowners' is a left-Communist slogan, because there are revolutionary landowners. Who are they, these revolutionary landowners, whom the Chin[ese] Communist Party ought to spare? Evidently, these are landowners belonging to the Guomindang. These landowners do not just enter the Guomindang, they even join peasant organisations, to disrupt them from within and break them up. *In coming out against the slogan 'down with the landowners', the Chin[ese] Communist Party not only weakens the whole breadth of the peasant movement, but hands it over into the hands of the landowners in practice.*

How they have amputated our work among the proletariat is evident from the fact that the Party has submitted to a decree of the government, *prohibiting strikes for even up to one thousand verst from the front during the Northern Expedition*. Not only strikes in arms factories were subjected to compulsory courts of arbitration, but in any factories with social significance. On the basis of this prohibition the local administration began to destroy workers' organisations in many places. The workers struggled against this with all their forces, but the Party, as an organised whole, submitted.

For the sake of avoiding conflicts with the leaders of the Guomindang, the Party has not raised the *slogan of arming* the workers and the revolutionary peasants *and is not taking any measures* for arming them. The Canton army went on the Northern Expedition with 70,000 bayonets. It expanded during this expedition to 250,000 bayonets. It expanded in this way at the expense of the armies of Wu Peifu, Sun Chuanfang, that it defeated in battle, and at the expense of the armies of Tang Shengzhi, the military governor of Hunan, who came over to the side of Canton. The mercenary soldier who has never heard a revolutionary word, who only yesterday burnt and looted the peasants, received a tricolour neckerchief and a rifle in his hand. Thus under the leadership of old counter-revolutionary commanders new 'revolutionary armies' were formed. The proletariat, who had carried the whole burden of revolutionary mass struggle on their backs, had shattered the foundations of imperialism in China, the revolutionary peasant, who had in the literal sense of the word carried on his back canons and ammunition from Canton to Shanghai, they were not honoured to be called to the colours. The national bourgeoisie with Chiang Kai-shek in the lead, looked at the proletariat and at the revolutionary peasantry, as at a wild beast, which might break its chains. The national bourgeoisie feared the proletariat and the revolutionary peasantry, the leaders of the Chin[ese] Communist Party feared to 'upset' the bourgeoisie. The Chinese proletariat and the peasantry snatched at arms. The Canton workers collected pennies to buy arms from the National government. The Hankou workers set up workers' pickets, dressed in hats with red stars, but they had only nightsticks in their hands. Only the Shanghai workers managed to seize 2,000 rifles from Sun Chuanfang's police.

These 2,000 rifles were up against 300,000 rifles of the national army: that was the outcome of the direction of the Chin[ese] Communist Party in the period since 20 March 1926.

The Comintern and the Capitulation of the Chin[ese] Communist Party

All the documents which we have drawn on here appeared in the press in Chinese or they were sent to the Comintern before the November–December Seventh enlarged plenum of the Executive Committee. All of them warned of the enormous danger, the danger that the Chin[ese] Communist Party would break its own neck. Only one thing could save it – *a decisive correction, a sharp, open turn by the Comintern*. Such a turn could not be done behind closed doors. It could not consist in the adoption of a resolution with a new general line without a sharp public criticism and a decisive attack on the men guilty of this liquidationism – whoever these guilty men might be, wherever they may be found. This turn could not be accomplished without a clear, practical, concrete programme.

We do not know what happened behind the closed doors of the Comintern. The resolution adopted by the enlarged Executive Committee is evidence *that the Executive Committee of the Comintern undertook no decisive turn*.[59] For even

---

59 This refers to the resolution of the Seventh enlarged ECCI plenum 'On the question of the situation in China' (For its text see Titarenko 1986, pp. 89–105).

if one accepts that *not all* the decisions of the Comintern have been published, the general character of the published resolution excludes the supposition that the unpublished decisions contain a correction of the mistakes made. It establishes that after the fact that in the first stage of the revolution 'one of the driving forces was the national bourgeoisie, seeking support in the ranks of the proletariat and the petty bourgeoisie',[60] at the second stage 'the working class appeared in the Chinese arena in the capacity of a first class political factor', which 'formed *a bloc with the peasantry,* actively entering the struggle for its interests, *with the urban petty bourgeoisie and a part of the capitalist bourgeoisie'.* This combination of forces was expressed in the Guomindang and the Chinese government. Now, says the resolution, 'the movement is *on the threshold* [of] *a third stage on the eve of a new re-distribution of classes.* At this stage the development of the basic forces of the movement is[61] a bloc of an even more revolutionary character, *a bloc of the proletariat, the peasantry and the urban petty bourgeoisie, with the removal of the majority of the upper capitalist bourgeoisie.* This bloc would create *a government of the democratic dictatorship of the proletariat, the peasantry and the other exploited classes'.*[62] In advancing this correct perspective, the resolution *would moderate its radicalism* by declaring that

> this does not mean *that all the bourgeoisie as a class is removed* (!) from the arena of the national liberation struggle (!). Besides the petty [and] middle bourgeoisie even *some forces* (!) *of the upper bourgeoisie can* (!) *still go along with the revolution for a certain* (!) *time* ... In the transitional moment, when *the gradual* (!) *departure from the revolution of the upper bourgeoisie* is historically inevitable the proletariat must of course *make widespread use of all those layers of the bourgeoisie* who at the given moment are conducting revolutionary struggle against imperialism and militarism in action[63] [emphasised by Radek].[64]

60　Radek quotes inaccurately. In the resolution it says: 'One of the most important driving forces was the national bourgeoisie and the bourgeois intelligentsia, seeking support in the ranks of the proletariat and the petty bourgeoisie' (Ibid., p. 92).

61　In the text of the resolution: 'will be'.

62　The final phrase in the text of the resolution is missing.

63　Titarenko 1986, pp. 93, 94.

64　On the resolution of the enlarged plenum of the Comintern, predicting the 'departure of the bourgeoisie' but not drawing any conclusions from this prediction it is necessary to repeat what Lenin said about the *resolution of the Menshevik conference of 1905* [this conference took place in Geneva, in parallel with the Bolshevik Third Congress of the RSDLP], devoted to the question of a provisional revolutionary government. He said that it

The democratic dictatorship of the workers and peasants in the country, which imperialism had previously dominated through the military cliques of the Chinese landowners and capitalists, is such a major social and political change of course that in holding up this perspective not as a perspective of the *remote* future but as a *real immediate perspective*, the Comintern is obliged to transfer the centre of gravity of the revolution to the *preparation for this transition*. If in reality certain layers of the upper bourgeoisie have remained in the ranks of the national movement, then in that case the central task will not consist in teaching the proletariat to use these layers, which may 'for a certain period still' not sell out, but in the political and organisational preparation for the *conquest of power. After all, if the bourgeoisie is leaving, it will not send a farewell letter by post, but will send canon shells and will say farewell with machine guns*. All power in the Guomindang and in the National government was held in the hands of *the bourgeois military group*, which kept the army and the government administration in its own hands. Let us allow that the leaders of the Comintern had some grounds for trusting Chiang Kai-shek, but it should have reasons not to trust him if only out of minimal caution. But you won't split the world with the wedge of Chiang Kai-shek. In the national army, there are a dozen more right-wing generals than Chiang Kai-shek and it was clear that *the departure of the bourgeoisie from the revolution meant an inevitable attempt at a rising by the parts of the army commanded by these generals*. Where is the press founded by the Comintern for agitation amongst the soldiers, where are the soldiers' committees in this army? Where is there agitation and the preparation for the arming of the workers and peasants? Nothing of that kind existed.

How could a democratic dictatorship be created? By means of a victory by majority vote in the Central [Executive] Committee of the Guomindang, an organisation similar, in the words of com. *Bukharin* to the soviets, and in com. *Stalin's* words, to a revolutionary parliament.[65] Soviets are mass lower level

---

expressed the psychology of *'passive observation', 'it expires in loquacious descriptions'*. This absence of conclusions from the 'predictions', this references to 'processes' makes Lenin indignant and he says: 'This is not the language of politicians, but the language of some kind of archivists!' [emphasised by Radek] (Lenin, *Sobr. soch.* 'Dve taktiti', Vol. 6, p. 322. [Lenin 1960a [1905], pp. 26–7, 28.]) When Lenin launched such an attack on the Martynovs, it would hardly have entered his head that this same Martynov would take part in the cooking up of new 'descriptions', new 'processes' but now under the *flag of the Comintern* and entrusted by the Central organs of the AUCP, at the sharpest moment of the revolutionary struggle. *Radek's note*.

65 On the 4 April 1927 at a closed meeting of the activists of the Moscow party organisation in the Hall of Columns of the House of the Unions, Bukharin declared that the Guomindang is something 'between a party and soviets'. On the following day at the same meeting,

organisations. They simply don't exist in the Guomindang. Neither the trade unions nor the peasant organisations provide a base for the Guomindang. In many places 'the Guomindang', i.e. its army, the organs of power struggled with this 'base'. The Guomindang is as much like the soviets as a fist is like a nose. Even if we accept the Stalinist comparison of the Guomindang with a revolutionary parliament, then never in a single revolutionary parliament were decisive revolutionary changes made without pressure from the masses, without lower level organisations exerting pressure on the parliament, without the existence of armed revolutionary masses. The Convention[66] sent the Girondins to the guillotine under the pressure of the armed Parisian sections. To speak of the approaching stage of the democratic dictatorship and not to say a single word about *the foundation of lower* centres of the movement is really to forget all the lessons of revolutions. Only in the presence of mass organisations of the proletariat, the peasantry and the urban poor, *connected with each other* could the foundation of a democratic dictatorship be achieved without a complete collapse of the army, without great losses. Only these organisations could prepare over a period of dual power the destruction of the power of the landowners and the merchants, which exists until the present day in the localities of the entire territory of the National government. Without the destruction of this local power, any democratic dictatorship of the workers and peasants is an empty phrase. The Comintern has not proposed the slogan of the foundation of such mass lower level organisations, which by their characteristics would be, naturally, a Chinese version of the *soviets*.

All this organisational preparation is conceivable only given the presence of the *most widespread political campaigns* directed against the policy of the upper bourgeois wing of the national movement, against the policy of the group which holds the National government in its hands. Their complete refusal to carry out even an agrarian reform, their policy of hunting down worker and peasant organisations, all this should be the object of the widest possible political campaigns of *exposure*. Nothing of the kind has occurred. The small weekly papers published by the Chin[ese] Communist Party whimpered in corners about the persecutions. They poured their misery into the organs of the Chin[ese] Communist Party in respect of Chiang Kai-shek's preparations for a coup, without even having the courage to say the workers *how to defend themselves*, but (see c[om.] Chen Duxiu's article in *Guide Weekly* of 12 March

---

Stalin compared the Guomindang with a 'revolutionary parliament' (RGASPI, F.324, Op.1, D.353, L.5; F.495, Op.166, D.191, L. 31; Stalin 2001 [1927], pp. 152–58).

66 This refers to the National Convention, the French parliament in 1792–5.

1927, which we cited in the first chapter of this pamphlet) did not have the courage to say to the workers *against whom* they must defend themselves. They wept into the waistcoat of the National government. As far as we know, only the Hankou trade unions conducted a campaign of revolutionary exposure, to the great displeasure of responsible persons, who accused them of – horror of horrors – Trotskyism. Several trade unions did this in other localities also.

We have a confirmation of how the Comintern related to Chinese events, *here* on the spot in Moscow. This confirmation is the central press of the AUCP and speeches by the leaders of the Comintern. The AUCP press systematically concealed all the activities of the National government directed against the worker and peasant movement. Either the reactions of our organs knew nothing about these events, in which case the entire reality of China was concealed from them by the Comintern, or they knew these facts and received an instruction to remain silent before Soviet public opinion.[67]

---

67 Some of these facts became known to me only at the moment when com. Dalin, a teacher in the Sun Yat-sen University returned from China. [This refers to Dalin's return from China at the beginning of 1927. He was in China since August 1926 in accordance with a decision of the Orgburo of the CC of the AUCP(b) to control the recruitment of new students for the UTC; see RGASPI, F.530, Op.1, D.9, L.11]. Several days before his return, I, as head of the university which sent him to China, received a formal reprimand from the Politburo of the CC of the AUCP for sending him, despite the fact that it was agreed with the relevant institutions. It was clear that someone in China was displeased by the presence of com. Dalin there, whom they regarded as my 'personal agent'. After com. Dalin's return I learnt that letters sent by him to my address were not only concealed but one was confiscated by the Comintern agent Rafes. [In the letter Dalin criticised the attitude of the Far [Eastern] bureau of the ECCI towards the recruitment of new students for the UTC. He also recalled that Rafes did not treat him in a comradely manner. In his explanation, Rafes observed that he considered Dalin's letter to be of an anti-party character. The incident was considered by party colleagues of the CCC, which on 13 May 1927 issued a reprimand against Rafes; see RGASPI, F.17, Op.85, D.233, L.44]. What was concealed behind these machinations of a former outspoken Menshevik became apparent when com. Dalin, after his return gave a report on the situation in China in the Eastern department of the Comintern and at a meeting of Communist teachers of the UTC. [The text of the report is not found. For a reference to it, see also Dalin 1975, p. 260]. For every Marxist, for every Leninist, it was clear on the basis of the materials provided by com. Dalin, that we stood before the preparation of a counter-revolutionary coup by Chiang Kai-shek, that the Chin[ese] Communist Party, as an organisational whole, leading the masses behind it, did not exist, despite the massive activity of the revolutionary peasant worker masses. It was apparent it considered the avoidance of any kind of conflict with the GMD to be the supreme law of the revolution. The Eastern department of the Comintern censored com. Dalin's article which sounded the alarm. In order to make public just a few of the facts, which should have upset any revolutionary, com. Dalin was forced to resort to the form of a leaflet, where amongst advertisements he managed to surreptitiously publish some material.

Then I decided to break through the conspiracy of silence and openly delivered a report on the anniversary of the death of Sun Yat-sen, 12 March 1927, at the Chinese university,[68] but on the following day, 13 March in the Communist Academy literally everyone was mobilised against me, beginning with the leader of the East Secretariat of the ECCI c[om.] Petrov and finishing with the economics expert of the OGPU. C[om]. *Petrov, Rafes*, one of the editors of the journal *Komintern Martynov, Shumiatskii*, Rector of the KUTV, Ioffe, secretary of People's Commissar of Defence Voroshilov for foreign affairs – all of them spoke in a united front: 'There is no crisis; everything is just fine. Whoever says otherwise is panic mongering, he is an extreme leftist who has no faith in the strength of the Chinese proletariat.'[69] Com. Bukharin calmed the Moscow Party activists on the 4 April by saying that the shooting of workers and peasants is explained by the enormous expanse of China which makes it difficult for the government to control the authorities in the localities and by an absence of discipline in the Guomindang. The shootings caused by geography, the lack of discipline, which predetermines the direction taken by bullets, all this was the result of a complacent policy of hiding one's head in the sand, avoiding reality. This effort found its most extreme example on parade in com. *Stalin's* speech.[70] Just seven days before General Chiang Kai-shek's mutiny, this comrade, who prides himself on his realism, declared before 3,000 members of the party: Com. Radek is wrong; there's no need to break with the bourgeoisie; the capitalist ministers are listening to us. They are helping us to disrupt the rear of

---

[This refers to Dalin 1927]. The report by com. Geller, an expert of the Executive Committee of the Trade Union International on Far Eastern questions, was refused by *Pravda*. [This refers to Geller's report on the situation in China, delivered at a session of the Executive Committee of the Trade Union International on 15 April 1927; see RGASPI, F.534. Op.3. D.220. The head of the Eastern Secretariat [Raskol'nikov] considered all these warnings to be panic-mongering. *Radek's note*.

68   Radek's report of 12 March 1927 at the Sun Yat-sen University of the Toilers of China is not found.

69   This is no joke: warning the proletariat that the bourgeoisie is preparing a strike against it and calling for its defence, were declared liquidationism in the newly cooked up strategy of the revolution by Martynov in *Pravda* of 10 Apr[il] (yes, in *Pravda*, dear reader). 'What is concealed behind the leftist line of our oppositionists? – An obviously liquidationist mood, a lack of confidence that the Chinese proletarat is capable of conquering hegemony' etc. The Martynovs are always disarming the proletariat in the face of the enemy, which is preparing its physical disarmament, out of their faith in it. It is just sad that it is enough for them to get hold of a Party card so as to conduct this vile work on the pages of our press. *Radek's note*.

70   This refers to Stalin's speech at the closed meeting of the activists of the Moscow Party organisation in the Hall of Columns of the House of the Unions on 5 April 1927. See Stalin 2001 [1927], pp. 152–58.

the enemy. No peasant will refuse a mare even though she is not up to much. We will squeeze them like lemons and then, if they do not listen to us, we will throw them away. Defending the silence in the press on the most important information about events in China, com. Stalin declared that 'Borodin is not asleep', that the matter is in safe hands. In respect of Chiang Kai-shek, he declared that Chiang Kai-shek is ten heads taller than Tsereteli and Kerensky, because Chiang Kai-shek is struggling with imperialism, while Kerensky conducted an imperialist war. Further, com. Stalin declared that Chiang Kai-shek may still be useful in the struggle with imperialism. All the warnings of the massive sharpening of class contradictions, relying on facts from Chinese reality, com. Stalin qualified as 'revolutionism'.[71] Com. Stalin's speech created an overwhelming impression on all his listeners by his decisiveness, by the fact that he left absolutely no doubt about his confidence in the solidity of the situation, which is the *most spectacular* example *of the bankruptcy* of a political orientation. Never in the whole history of the Comintern has one of its leaders ever erred to such a degree in the evaluation of a situation, as com. Stalin did. None of this would have happened if only the Executive Committee of the Comintern had taken up *not* in words but *in deed* a directive regarding the approaching transition in China from a government of the bourgeoisie towards a democratic dictatorship of the workers and peasants. However, the ECCI did not adopt such a directive. Com. *Martynov* recognised this openly in his article of 10 April in *Pravda* two days before Chiang Kai-shek's coup, printed with the note that the article is for discussion and does not reflect the views of the editors. Com. Martynov wrote thus:

> It is understood that if we adopt com. Radek's premise that the present National government in China is a 'government of the capitalist bourgeoisie' (*and not a government of a bloc of four classes*), then the answer to the question is clear. Communists have no place in such a government. Moreover, Communists should now begin the struggle against such a government, and he is ready indeed to advance against the Chinese National government, which is conducting a revolutionary-anti-imperialist war the slogan '*down with the ten capitalist ministers*', which the Bolsheviks advanced against Kerensky, who was conducting an imperialist war in 1917.[72] That which for *a plenum of the ECCI should appear* (!) *only in per-*

---

71   From my notes. I was unable to receive the stenograms. *Radek's note.*
72   This slogan was first raised by the Bolsheviks in June 1917 during the sessions of the First All-Russian Congress of Soviets. 'Ten capitalist ministers' were the bourgeois ministers of the Russian Provisional Government.

spective as a result of the conquest by the proletariat of hegemony in the revolution (the departure of the industrial bourgeoisie), for c[om.] Radek is the starting point – the overthrow of a capitalist government.

I will not touch on the fact here that Martynov's not just Menshevik, but outright Kadet view of the National government as a supra-class government (*a government of four classes*), which *Pravda*, the organ founded by Lenin, published without blushing. I will just establish that c[om.] Martynov pays witness to a directive for a democratic dictatorship as a *perspective* having nothing in common with the present *moment*. I repeat that this was printed in *Pravda* two days before Chiang Kai-shek's coup.

Only thanks to the fact that this perspective of the 'departure of the bourgeoisie' was for the leaders of the Comintern *something very remote, while the current task became the 'utilisation of the bourgeoisie' the leaders of the Comintern did not set up as an immediate objective the task of accelerating the political and organisational preparation of the masses for the approaching withdrawal of the bourgeoisie*. No references to one or another directive on the development of the movement, on the arming of the workers change the issue. I speak precisely: *in reality no reports by leaders of the Comintern exist which might testify about preparations for the withdrawal of the bourgeoisie; such reports cannot be presented for the simple reason that no such preparation was conducted*. Every, repeat, *every* attempt to offload responsibility onto poor subordinates cannot be motivated by anything else apart from an effort to evade the recognition of their own mistakes. Many subordinates were really straw men, but *the defeat of the Chinese revolution is a result not of a poor execution of the line of the Comintern by its representatives, but on the basis of an incorrect line by the Comintern*. Even more absurd, than pouring the guilt on bad Comintern subordinates is the *demonization of the Chin[ese] Communist Party*, the pouring of all the guilt over it. We have already presented in the second chapter documents bearing witness to the fact that the leadership of the Chin[ese] Communist Party not only did not prepare the party for its proper role, but how it capitulated before the Guomindang from 20 March 1926, and tied the party hands and feet preparing its bankruptcy. But the leadership of the Chin[ese] Communist Party is itself *more a victim than a culprit*. You cannot demand from a young party, which has a mere six years since its foundation, a party which has only just emerged from student circles, that it must be at the top of its game; you cannot load the responsibility for the errors committed in the C[E]C of the Party, a significant part of which consist of former anarchists used to looking on the Comintern as an infallible guiding organ. The leadership of the Chin[ese] Communist Party can prove in documents that a whole series of capitulationist documents published under its signature were prepared with the closest participation of the representative of the Comintern. It can refer to the fact that a policy of controlling the scale of the workers' movement was begun with the approval of representatives of the Comintern. It can refer to the fact that it received no directives pointing out any incorrectness in the fundamentals of its line.

As far as the masses of the rank and file members of the Party are concerned, as far as the working masses, who follow the Chin[ese] Communist Party, they stood at a height beyond the reach of the official leaders of the Comintern. The Chinese working class, – the Chinese worker Communists – demonstrated themselves as fighters for the revolution, full of mistrust for the bourgeoisie, expecting its betrayal, as activists striving to arm themselves, full of self-sacrifice. The leaders of the Comintern, *who now say,* that the Chinese Party turned out to be 'Trotskyist', that it wanted to jump over stages, to go into the battle for power prematurely, just repeated the old songs of *Cherevanin*, who demonstrated that the tactics of the Mensheviks were excellent, correct, and only the masses were bad, they could not understand these tactics. The leaders of the Comintern worked out a superb plan for a transition to the third stage of the revolution. The bourgeoisie should depart slowly and in small groups: its certain layers should continue to help us for a while in the peaceful reconstruction of the administrative apparatus of the bourgeoisie and the landowners into an administrative apparatus of the workers and peasants. The workers and peasants should be peaceful, and should calmly develop their forces, and organise themselves, without talking about what was happening so as not to frighten the bourgeoisie. The plan was superb, scientifically justified by Martynov and Bukharin. The misfortune consisted solely in that neither the Chinese bourgeoisie nor the Chinese workers and peasants played the role assigned to them by the authors of the ingenious military plan and did not develop their positions at the pace which was indicated to them from above. This farcical theory demonstrates that there is no folly, which even intelligent people cannot repeat, when they defend an incorrect line, a bankrupt line, when they do not want to or cannot recognise their mistakes. Com. Bukharin, repeating Cherevanin twenty years later, Bukharin embraced by the author of *Dve diktatury*,[73] who could have foreseen such a spectacle! But this is the spectacle of Bukharin, *printing Martynov's articles on the pre-capitalist character of China with the hegemony of the proletariat,* and of Martynov, praising Bukharin's tactics as realistic and healthy – this is no accident.

---

73   *Dve diktatury* ('Two Dictatorships') was a work by A.S. Martynov. See Martynov 1905.

The defeat of the Chinese revolution has its basis in just this ideological mixture of Bukharin and Martynov, a Bolshevik policy in words, but a Menshevik policy in deed.

He, who does not understand this policy, for which the Shanghai workers perished, has learnt nothing from the lessons of the Shanghai events. Therefore, this report would not have been complete without a chapter dedicated to the philosophy of history of Martynov and Bukharin.

The Menshevik Theory of the Chinese Revolution

Obviously, it was com. Bukharin who gave the Comintern its theory of the Chinese revolution. Bukharin developed his theory for the first time at the Fifteenth Conference of the AUCP,[74] for the second time at the [Seventh] enlarged plenum of the [Executive Committee] of the Comintern,[75] for the third time at the January report at the KUTV,[76] and for the fourth at a Moscow Party workers meeting on 4 April.

The theory of the Chinese revolution, expounded by Bukharin at our conference on the 26 October, and in a report to the plenum of the Comintern and in January to the KUTV, is *distinguished* fundamentally from the *theory*, which he developed at the Moscow Party activists' meeting of the 4 April and published in a new (also in a very much reworked edition) in the form of the pamphlet *Problemy kitaiskoi revoliutsii*, reworked after his entire theory had succeeded in specular fashion in going one hundred per cent *bankrupt*. I will permit myself in the first place to demonstrate in which respect Bukharin's views of November–January differ from Bukharin's views in April, so as to demonstrate later that, despite these differences, Bukharin's theory in both phases has nothing to do with Bolshevism, but is a repetition of Menshevik views in 1905, a repetition, in which, as is always the case in such transitions, there are many layers of old Bolshevik views, expressed in the form of all sorts of catch-alls 'on the one hand', 'on the other hand'.

---

74 See AUCP(b) 1927a, pp. 23–29.
75 Comintern 1927b, Volume 1, pp. 48–49, 83–91. At the beginning of 1927 Bukharin's report and concluding word at the Seventh ECCI plenum was also published as a separate pamphlet; see Bukharin 1927a.
76 See Bukharin 1927b, pp. 3–21.

Two Theories of the Chinese Revolution: With Feudalism and Without

From the point of view of the *internal combination of class forces in* China, the situation is like this: a weak *bourgeoisie*, a colossal *peasantry*, a substantial layer of *artisans* and petty *traders*, a *working* class, not very numerous, but already presenting itself as a sufficiently consolidated force and playing a considerable political role to a high degree. The antagonism towards foreign capital is so strong that *a significant part of the bourgeoisie is still marching in a united front with the broad masses*, which finds its original political expression in the leading role of the Guomindang[77] [emphasised by Radek].

You read and you don't believe your eyes. *Where has feudalism gone to?* Feudalism, which in Bukharin's report of the 4 April plays a decisive role in the determination of the character of the Chinese revolution. 'From among the various features which in combination provide the unique face of the Chinese revolution, it is necessary to linger in more detail on the relations between imperialism, feudalism and the revolution in China', said Bukharin at the Moscow Party activists' meeting of the 4 April. And he adds that '*the basic sense of any bourgeoisie revolution*, whether it is conducted under the hegemony of the working class or of the revolutionary petty bourgeoisie, *consists in the destruction of some or other remains of feudalism*. According to com. Radek, there is no feudalism in China. *How in that case can a bourgeois revolution take place. Against whom within the country is it directed*'? He characterises *the struggle of Canton against Wu Peifu, Sun Chuanfang and Zhang Zuolin as a struggle of bourgeois democracy against feudalism*.

> The so-called militarists, sitting in their provinces, are nothing more than *the remains of the feudal principalities* … If we pose the question like that we will receive the following picture: *the war on the internal front is going on against the northern militarists. The bourgeois revolution has directed its sharp edge against those feudal looters, against the landowner feudalists*, some of whom own their land legally, while others do not own land legally, but own it in fact by virtue of disposing of an enormous percentage of the income from land. For this reason, the *argument is between the so-called militarists, who represent feudal fetters, the fetters of historical development*,

---

77 Comintern 1927b, Volume 1, p. 89.

against which the national bourgeoisie can come out and do come out from time to time. This is the essence *of the basic content of the bourgeois revolution in China*, in so far as it is a matter of internal class forces. ([N.] Bukharin, *Problemy kitaiskoi revoliutsii*, pp. 23–4) [emphasised by Radek].

During the course of three months, com. Bukharin therefore discovered the fundamental content of the Chinese revolution, *which was absent from the report of c[om.] Bukharin at the Comintern plenum* in justifying a resolution, which was supposed to guide the Chinese Communists in revolutionary struggle. Since the enlarged plenum of the Comintern com. Bukharin has sent them into revolutionary battle *in ignorance of what they are fighting for*. Understandably, both in the resolution and in Bukharin's report the word 'feudalism' is mentioned; it is said that the feudal regime is fated to destruction, but there was and there could be *no theory, explaining the struggle between the national revolution and the militarists, as a struggle of the bourgeoisie with feudalism*. And this is the reason. Both at the Party conference and at the plenum [of the Executive Committee of the Comintern, Bukharin related a fact capsizing his entire theory of the struggle of the bourgeois south against the feudal north. In his report he said the following:

> It must be underlined that *since large-scale landowning is more developed in Guangdong province than in the other Chinese provinces, eighty-five percent of all the land in the valleys of Northern, Western and Eastern Han rivers*[78] *belongs to the major landowners* (N.[I.] Bukharin, *Capitalist Stabilisation [and the Proletarian Revolution]*. p. 147) [emphasised by Radek].

In this way, Bukharin explained in his speech both at the Party conference and at the Comintern plenum, *that the Canton government did not liquidate large-scale landowning*, which ruthlessly exploits the Guangdong peasantry and that *therefore, in starting out on the Northern Expedition, it could not do this for the sake of a struggle with feudalism*. Only by striking this out of his memory could Bukharin suddenly jump away from his theory of feudalism in April. Even worse, at the Fifteenth Party conference he gave a *diametrically opposed theory*. We will permit ourselves to cite the whole passage in Bukharin's report to the Party conference which refers to the link between the agrarian question

---

78   Correct: Jiang, i.e. of the rivers Beijiang, Xijiang and Dongjiang (of the Northern, Western and Eastern rivers).

and the national revolution. It does not just expose Bukharin's entire *superficial theoretical construction*, but it also shows us something even more important.

Now, comrades, in what do the fundamental difficulties and problems of the Chinese revolution at the present stage of its development consist. These difficulties consist in the fact that on the one hand, it is completely clear that it is now necessary for the Chinese people, the Guomindang and the Chinese Communist Party that the central blow must be concentrated on the struggle with the foreign imperialists. This is the central task, the struggle for the independent existence of China, for its national liberation. For the resolution of this task it is vital to *maintain a united national-liberation front*. This front now consists not just of *peasants*, not just of *workers*, not just of *artisans*, not just of the *democratic and radical intelligentsia*, but also of the *mercantile-industrial bourgeoisie*, of *merchants* and *industrialists*, not all of them of course, but of those who are not directly tied to foreign capital and who can [not] be accounted as compradors, as they are called, i.e. those who are mediators between foreign capital and China. But *that mercantile-industrial bourgeoisie, who are currently playing an objectively revolutionary role and with which at the present stage of development of the revolutionary movement a bloc is necessary, so that a numerical maximum of forces can be directed against the foreign imperialists, that bourgeoisie is tied through the government with those semi-gentry and kulak elements, who rule in the countryside.*

I must tell you that in China there is also a system of sub-leasing in which some kind of *powerful limited company* leases land, so as to lease this land out again, the new leaseholders give the land for leasing again, and so *the chain goes on ... If you touch it, if you start to destabilise this property in land, – then a wave will rush from here to the mercantile-industrial circles*. It is characteristic to observe that in Guangdong province, this fundamental base of the Chinese government, *a significant proportion of the land is in the hands of major landowning proprietors tied to the mercantile-industrial bourgeoisie, which supports the Canton government. If you touch them vacillations begin. In this lies one of the major difficulties of the entire Chinese revolution at the moment.* The very relationship of forces within the Guomindang is such that there are three wings in the Guomindang: right, centre and left. *The right wing of the Guomindang expresses exactly the class interests of this same bourgeoisie, even in its most right-wing directions. On the other hand the development of the revolution inevitably involves the need to attract the peasantry* (*!*) One must not steer against the peasantry now, and one cannot organise the revolutionary forces without putting a peasant foundation under this revolution. We can't do that. In this consists the *fundamental difficulty* of the present situation of things in China. In this consists the *basic problem* of the Chinese revolution as it appears to me now. The situation is now such that the Chinese Communist Party must decisively embark on a struggle for the carrying out of an *agrarian reform*. Despite the fact that the central task remains the expulsion of the foreign imperialists, despite the massive importance of the preservation of a united national revolutionary front, all the same it is necessary to set out on the implementation of agrarian reforms and the organisation of the peasantry. Assembling this immense reserve on the scene is demanded by the immediate interests of the Chinese revolution, which is only beginning to enter a much deeper phase of the differentiation in the class struggle. Obviously, this will be tied up with *several more unpleasant phenomena, in the sense of the further vacillations of the right wing of the Guomindang*. Obviously this way of posing the question may be tied up with the danger of a certain leftism, against which we must struggle, i.e. with tendencies to prematurely jump onto another theme and to prematurely break up the all-national cause. We must struggle against this. There the situation is extremely complex and one might formulate it as follows: *while standing on the basis of the struggle as a united national-revolutionary front against foreign imperialism, it is necessary at the same time to carry out an agrarian reform, thereby putting a broad peasant base under the Chinese revolution* (pp. 27–9. Protocols of the Fifteenth Party conference)[79] [emphasised by Radek].

What does Bukharin say in this long quotation? In the first place: the landowner is tied up with the mercantile-industrial circles in the tightest way, i.e. in December[80] Bukharin noticed no opposition by the feudal landowner to the bourgeoisie. There is no division in this quotation into a bourgeois south and a feudal north, fighting against one another, *the whole philosophy of the national revolution* has disappeared. No one knows why both sides are struggling against one another, but look how beautiful com. Bukharin's April concept was! Secondly, the conjunction of the landowners [and] the bourgeoisie also takes place in *the economy and in the Canton government*. Thirdly, the strike against

---

79 AUCP(b) 1927a, pp. 27–29.
80 I.e. at the Seventh enlarged ECCI plenum, which took place from 22 November to 16 December 1926.

the landowner will provoke the vacillation of the right-wing Guomindang and 'several unpleasant things'. Finally, despite the necessity of the united anti-imperialist front, Bukharin decides to dive headfirst ... He decides to demand *reforms*, i.e. he *leaves untouched* the *landowners, but simply reduces the leasehold payments*, otherwise he would not have spoken about reforms but would have spoken about revolution. All this he does since 'the development of the revolution has come up against the need to attract the peasantry'. *Not that the revolution is developing, that the peasantry is rising against the landowners, but that the revolution is coming up against the need for peasants to be the gunpowder against imperialism, and therefore* that great fighter against feudalism N.I. Bukharin (he is a Bolshevik after all) proposes to award the peasants reforms. *Thus did Bukharin direct the Chinese Communists, who feared to advance the slogan 'down with the landowners' in a revolutionary war, which he described in April as a war for the destruction of feudalism in China.*

The Comintern Resolution and Bukharin's Theory

In order that the reader should not think that we are dealing here with just an individual creation of Bukharin, it is worth remembering that in the resolution adopted by the Seventh enlarged plenum of the Executive Committee of the Comintern in the question *of the relation between the agrarian order and the revolution, fundamentally, Bukharin's conception rests on the foundation of the Bukharin of November–December and not on the basis of the Bukharin of April*. It says: 'The organisational particularity of the present situation (!) is its transitional character, when the proletariat *must choose between the perspective of a bloc with significant layers of the bourgeoisie and the perspective of further consolidation of its alliance with the peasantry*'[81] [emphasised by Radek]. What does that mean? Given the basically anti-feudal nature of the revolution, which Bukharin began to talk about in April, why should the consolidation of the alliance with the peasantry provoke an immediate break with significant layers of the bourgeoisie? This means that although in the resolution the words 'feudal, semi-colonial, remains of feudalism' are repeated, then essentially the resolution *does not regard the struggle of South and North as a struggle of the bourgeoisie with feudalism* but vaguely understands that despite the remains of feudalism in China, *the agrarian question is basically at a completely different phase in China.*

---

81   Titarenko 1986, p. 96.

Even worse, the resolution does not regard the militarists as representatives of feudalism. It speaks of them: '*A distinguishing feature* of Chinese militarism is the fact that it, while being a *military organisation, simultaneously represents one of the basic channels [of primitive] capital* accumulation in China relying on a whole system of state organs of a semi-feudal character'[82] [emphasised by Radek]. Given all the theoretical confusion, typical of this resolution from beginning to end, the following thought shines through its strokes, that *although in China many remains of feudal forms are still preserved, essentially, however, the landowner belongs to the bourgeoisie, the militarists are basically a channel for capitalist accumulation and that therefore a strike against the landowners is a strike against the bourgeoisie*. But typically, both then at the Party conference and at the plenum of the Executive Committee, when Bukharin was closer to the truth in his evaluation of the agrarian question, than in his April speech, and now when frightened by the developing Chinese revolution and its transformation into a plebeian revolution, he has thought up Chinese feudalism as the dominant form in China; and in both cases *he approaches the agrarian question not as a Bolshevik, but as a Menshevik, or Kadet. He talks only of reforms, but not of an agrarian revolution*. And this point of view makes its imprint on the *Comintern resolution*. This resolution speaks only of the '*maximum* reduction of leasehold payments', i.e. it leaves untouched leasehold payments themselves.

The Key to Bukharin's Position

In his speech to the [Seventh] enlarged plenum of the Executive Committee of the Comintern we find the following passage, which gives a key to understanding his entire policy. We have already quoted it but it is worth repeating it:

> *The principal and foremost task is of victory over foreign imperialism, a victory, of which the united national-revolutionary front serves as guarantor in its turn*. This front now consists not just of *peasants*, not just of *workers*, not just of *artisans*, not just of the radical and democratic *intelligentsia*, but also of the *mercantile-industrial bourgeoisie*, of merchants and industrialists, not all of them of course, but of these of them who are not directly tied up with foreign capital and cannot be accounted compradors, as they are called, i.e. those who are mediators between foreign capital

---

82   Ibid, p. 92.

and China. (N.[I.] Bukharin, *Capitalist Stabilisation [and the Proletarian Revolution]*, p. 156) [emphasised by Radek].

This formulation demands the most thorough analysis, because it is the very *heart of* Bukharin's *false* position. From it proceed all the characteristics of Comintern policy in China. To take the bull by the horns one must say that *there is not and has never been in the history of humanity a revolution directed exclusively against an external enemy.* The current enemy, occupying the given territory for a prolonged period of time always dominates, it is connected with one or other of the local classes exploiting the population. The popular masses cannot arise in struggle with the foreign exploiter without at the same time struggling with those who oppress them on a daily basis, whom they see at home in the countryside and in the small towns. *The united front of the exploited, i.e. the workers, the peasants and the urban petty bourgeoisie, is the guarantor of the victory of the Chinese revolution.* But so that the peasant shall arise at the summit of the national struggle, he must struggle with the landowner; the worker must struggle with the capitalist, the petty bourgeois of the city must struggle with the capitalist, all of them must struggle with the landowner-capitalist regime. *Therefore, the fall of a joint united front of these classes with the bourgeoisie and the landowners is a condition of the formation of a united front of the exploited classes.* Why did we enter the Guomindang, despite the fact that we knew that the merchant, the landowner, the factory owner, the moneylender and the tax broker were in it? We entered it *so as to win the petty bourgeoisie and the peasant who were still plodding along behind these layers away from* them. The representative of the Chin[ese] Communist Party understood this brilliantly, when he said at the Fourth Congress of the Comintern that *we are entering the Guomindang in order to split it.* This was not understood by or was forgotten by Bukharin and so he has slid into the marsh of Menshevism, where Martynov, the John the Baptist of Menshevism has picked him up and slobbered all over him.

Having accepted a Menshevik view that the preservation of a united bloc with the bourgeoisie is the guarantor of the victory of the revolution, Bukharin started to quake before the face of the peasant movement, and turned to the slogan of agrarian reform, i.e. to a renunciation of the slogan 'down with the landowners'; all this forced him to diminish and go vague over class contradictions in China, and finally led him to the *nonsensical theory of Chinese feudalism.* What connection is there between this theory and Bukharin's fundamental views, and the basis of his political attitude? Very simple. It becomes completely clear if you think through Martynov's article 'The problem of the Chinese revolution', which appeared in *Pravda* just two days before Chiang

Kai-shek's coup. In this article Martynov celebrated the fact that Chiang Kai-shek greeted a peasant conference in Nanjing and that he submitted to the Hankou government, and that the Shanghai workers 'had arms in their hands after the arrival of the national troops also' (this was written two days before the disarming of the Shanghai workers). Martynov did not develop any theory of feudalism. But he, tying himself to a single word of Lenin's, demonstrated that in China *pre-capitalist relations* predominate. Understanding the absurdity of such an assertion about a country with four million industrial workers, Martynov corrected himself and said that 'pre-capitalist relations predominate, *or to be more accurate, relations proceeding the epoch of industrial capitalism'.* What does that mean? From a factual point of view it is nonsense. In a country's economy, the factor dominates which has the greatest influence over it. The Chinese economy is characterised by the fact that factory merchandise of domestic or foreign production destroys the handicraft trades of the peasant artisan, that imperialism has destroyed the financial system of China and brought about its territorial collapse, the rule of militarism, which destroys the countryside by high taxes and the continual mutual bloodletting by the militarists, who are the propagators of its influence. In the village economy of China that fact dominates that *the moneylenders and mercantile capital, having destroyed feudalism,* now destroy the peasant economy; to call this multicoloured disorder in which a *period of mercantile capital overlaps with a period of industrial capitalism and* imperialism pre-capitalist is a complete theoretical absurdity, for the regime of a country is determined by the *dominant economic basis of the country.* Why did Martynov employ this nonsense? He used it so as to say to the proletariat: in the name of all the holy saints, don't break up with the bourgeoisie. *How could you seriously think about the real leadership of the revolution in a pre-capitalist country?* The contradictions of the conception of the pre-capitalist character of China and the hegemony of the proletariat are simple: the hegemony of the proletariat is a bow before a Bolshevik icon, to which Martynov committed himself in a certain hall in 1922,[83] but the pre-capitalist character of China, this is an argument of renunciation of hegemony, an argument so as to hang on to the tail of the bourgeoisie, the tail of the Guomindang, as Martynov clung to the tail of the Kadets all his life.

The same need which was born in unhappy Martynov, who became a Bolshevik in the 55th year of his life, the conception of pre-capitalist China, was born in Bukharin, who after a left radical youth, had metamorphosed himself on the threshold of the emergence of a statesman into opportunism, the theory of

---

83   This refers to Martynov's entry into the Bolshevik party. However, Radek is mistaken about the date. Martynov joined the RCP(b) in 1923.

the anti-feudal character of the Chinese revolution. Frightened by the developing class struggle, which threatened to destroy the united front with the bourgeoisie, which threatened to provoke a massive earthquake in that international conjuncture, from which Bukharin wanted to 'retreat', so as to continue to believe in the building of socialism in one country, he sought new means to consolidate the united front of the revolution which was falling apart in China. And therefore, this man, who knows magnificently that Marx, analysing the influence of money-lending capital on rural relations, demonstrated that '*money-lending [...] destroys* ancient *feudal* wealth and ancient *feudal property*' (*Kapital*, Vol. 3, part 2, p. 133),[84] that Marx said that the 'moneylender[85] plays a revolutionary role [...] only *in so far as* he breaks up and destroys [feudal. – K.R.] forms of property', has thought out feudalism as the dominant form of the Chinese economy now. All this work and all this sweat is poured no one knows why so that even if the content of the struggle in China were a struggle with feudalism, even then it would not follow that this struggle must take place in union with the upper bourgeoisie. Nowhere in the world has the upper bourgeoisie been the hegemon in the struggle for the liquidation of feudalism. Everywhere, it went for a deal with feudalism and the peasant liquidated feudalism in a bloc with the plebeian masses of the city. But Bukharin forgot the ABC of Leninism. The whole acuity of the Chinese agrarian crisis consists in the fact that money-lending 'does not alter the means of production, but clings onto it, like a parasite, and which exhausts it to complete collapse. It sucks out its juice, sucks its blood and forces production to take place under *ever more pathetic conditions*. Hence popular hatred of moneylenders'[86] (Marx) [emphasised by Radek]. See that the centre of the agrarian question in China is not in feudalism, although remains of it still exist, and although the forms of lease holding, thanks to the complete collapse of the monetary system in China, bear with them a character of natural exchange in many places. *The domination of money-lending and agrarian mercantile capital in the countryside, i.e. of the most influential faction of the Chinese bourgeoisie, will have an agrarian revolution as a consequence, directed against the bourgeoisie, which will give the Chinese revolution a massive scale.* Fearing 'several unpleasant things' in the Guomindang, Bukharin has emitted a smokescreen around his theory of feudalism and from behind the smokescreen he asks me, 'if there is no feudalism there, then in what way is the revolution bourgeoisie at the present stage? Isn't the struggle of the peasantry for its bit of property, ruined by the moneylender a

---

84   Radek is quoting from the following edition: Marx 1923 [1894].
85   Radek quotes inaccurately. According to Marx this is 'money-lending'.
86   Marx 1923 [1894], pp. 597, 596.

struggle for bourgeois private property? Isn't the struggle for the unity of China a struggle for the conditions *also* of the capitalist development of China'?

In another place I shall try to give a picture of agrarian relations, on the basis of the existing literary material, in which I shall try to explain what I have said here in detail.[87] But even what I have said is sufficient for it to be clear that all Bukharin's theories with feudalism and without feudalism served just one objective, *to prove the necessity of the preservation at all costs of a united front with the bourgeoisie*. This desire cost the Chinese revolution a major defeat and broke the back of the present leadership of the Chin[ese] Communist Party. *A radical break with this mixture of Bolshevik memoirs and Menshevik policy is the condition of the correct leadership of the Chinese revolution.* A renunciation of Bukharin's theory of the Chinese revolution is the immediate, practical task of all who want to help the Chinese proletariat recover from the strikes directed at them by the Chinese bourgeoisie.

> In general one must observe that before the Comintern stands the task of the worldwide popularisation of the Chinese movement, an acquaintance with it by the working masses of western Europe and the task of a *thorough study of the original economic and political conditions in Eastern countries. Without this study it is impossible to determine policy in extraordinarily difficult conditions*, where the particularity of the economic and political interrelations within the country are combined with the greatest possible diversity of the criss-crossing, often mutually contradictory influences of the most varied imperialist groupings with all their diplomatic games,

says Bukharin in his report to the plenum of the Comintern (N.[I.] Bukharin, *Kapitalisticheskaia stabilizatsia*, p. 140) [emphasised by Radek].

> But after this speech, recalling better times of the Comintern, when we all together, under Lenin's leadership, studied all questions with the greatest caution and thoroughness before giving responsible advice to the international proletariat. Bukharin is left as the sole ideological leader of the Comintern, has concocted on the run, on the basis of scraps of facts in a series of theories, related to one another by just one desire, not to see the great and terrible reality, so as not to have to draw revolutionary conclusions.[88]

---

87   Radek failed to do this.
88   This pamphlet was already written, when I received the May Day number of *Pravda*, in

The Lessons of Defeat

1 *The Meaning of the Defeat*

1) The Chinese revolution has suffered a major defeat. It has for the time been released from its hands the majority of the territory, conquered by it during the Northern Expedition. The army on which it relied, is broken into two camps. A significant part of the commanding staff of the revolution has gone over to the side of the counter-revolution. The main proletarian centre in China is practically lost. The working class is smashed in significant areas which previ-

---

which side by side with the article by General Svechin, a former theoretic star of the Tsar's army, I found an article by c[om.] John Pepper [see Pepper 1927], a star journalist of the wartime Austrian general staff, who demonstrates that in China a *family and clan regime* still existed [exists], that there are still many remains of primitive communism etc. etc. I awaited with horror that c[om.] Pepper would demand from the Chinese Communists, together with the progressive feudalists, the liquidation of the remains of primitive communism and with deepest horror I awaited which people he would classify as feudalists and which as the chiefs of primitive clans. My deepest fear was the thought that c[om.] Bukharin, as leader of the Comintern would be nominated as chief of a feudal horde or he would have to bear a name such as 'Pale Face' or 'Sharp Pen' as the Leader of clans heroically perishing in the struggle for their old way of life. It turned out that in China 'there is no large scale landowning and no serfdom', it turns out in addition that already before the arrival of Pepper 'an analysis of Eastern countries' made by Marx and Engels (what fine ancestors Pepperism has), has shown that the fundamental particularity of the Asiatic mode of production is encapsulated in exactly the fact that they never developed feudal agriculture. [The term 'the Asiatic mode of production' was introduced by Marx in his *Introduction to a Critique of Political Economy*.] I breathed a sigh of relief, it means 'I am thereby absolved' and it means that I am not guilty of the sin of denying the remains of feudalism, since it was never there. I read joyfully further and discovered that the system of *lijin* and *dujun* [a military governor of a Chinese province until 1923, when the term was replaced by *duban*] *are not remnants of feudalism*, but *beginnings of 'new* feudal formations'. This may be all fantasy from a mental hospital but I am not guilty before the remnants of feudalism. But I rejoiced in vain, and when I began to re-read the article again, so as to thoroughly imbibe the scent of the new teaching, I found alas, at the very beginning that 'the assertion by c[om.] Radek and other comrades that "there are no more existing remnants of feudalism" contradicts the facts in the sharpest way'. I drop my weapons. I am obliged to recognise that my mistake consisted in that I thought that people, divided into classes, but not monkeys exist in China, for I sense that in a few weeks the latter will be demonstrated by one of the serial Marxists from *Pravda*. I am obliged in the name of Party discipline to submit to this new application of Marxism, which in our epoch of absolute freedom of thought should be called 'Popperism'. If you've got to go, go like this said the parrot, when the cat dragged him by the tail. Marx spoke of the kinship of prostitution with the institute of bourgeois professors [perhaps, Radek assumes Marx's statement that prostitutes, lawyers and politicians are all equally workers in the service industries. See Marx 1962, p. 151]. Nowadays for such comparisons you don't even need the title acquired by heavy physical labour, you just need a will for the profession. *Radek's note.*

ously belonged to the National government. Trade unions have been smashed in Zhejiang, Fujian, Guangdong, Guangxi. A significant part of the organisers of the working class have perished or are in prison. The struggle continues now in the first place for the preservation of Hubei and Henan provinces as bases for the further organisation of the revolution with the assistance of a revolutionary state, from which further offensives of the revolution can take place, on the basis of greater experience obtained at such a high price.

2) The defeat of the Chinese revolution was provoked by the transfer to the side of the counter-revolution of that part of the Chinese upper bourgeoisie, which up to that time went more or less with the national movement (the local industrial bourgeoisie and the mercantile bourgeoisie tied up in the first instance with the internal market). This transfer means that it is now going along with a deal with world imperialism and the militarists, who are their weapons. No one can deny this anymore. The Chinese upper bourgeoisie has finally become counter-revolutionary in all its decisive layers.

3) The Chinese bourgeoisie cannot in future play the role of leader of the militarist cliques, which act in its name. It cannot unite China even on a capitalist basis. The militarists, the weapons of such a unification, will continue to conduct struggles between themselves for predominant influence. They are pushed in this direction not just by their thirst for gain, but by the aspiration of the bourgeoisie of the various parts of China to subject the other parts to themselves. Without serious economic assistance on the part of imperialism, without significant concessions on its part, the Chinese bourgeoisie cannot stabilise its situation, cannot create a firm bourgeois regime in China. Only the provision of work for significant masses in the countryside, those who have lost their land and who cannot find refuge anywhere, would reduce the sharpness of the agrarian question, only the growth of Chinese industry could create a social situation for the temporary resolution of the revolutionary crisis in the countryside. But it is very improbable that imperialism will make serious concessions to the Chinese bourgeoisie and that in the condition of collapse in which China is now, that imperialism would decide to invest substantial material means in the economic development of China. It is equally improbable that the imperialist powers will act in concert with the aim of founding a single bourgeois government. Having contradictory interests, they will in future doubtless wager on the various militarists, will ignite their mutual struggles and while permitting temporary agreements between them, will attempt in future to weaken and divide China. Therefore, one must assume that *the social situation in China will become even sharper in future, and that the fundamental forces of the revolution, which have now suffered a defeat, will grow and get stronger*. The Chinese revolution, having suffered a cruel defeat as a bloc of the proletariat,

of the peasantry, of the urban petty bourgeoisie and of the upper bourgeoisie, as a bloc directed by the latter, will comprehend and will win as *a revolutionary bloc of workers, peasants and of the urban poor under the leadership of the proletariat*.

A study of the mistakes made by the Chin[ese] Communist Party and the Comintern has enormous practical significance. Without taking account of the essence of these mistakes one cannot construct a correct policy in the new circumstances created by the defeat.

2   *Sources of the Defeat*

1) The fundamental mistake of the Comintern consisted in *an underestimation of the degree of the development of class contradictions between the proletariat and the bourgeoisie in China, and in an overestimation of the contradictions existing between imperialism and the Chinese bourgeoisie*. By theorising that in China the struggle is in the first place between feudalism and the bourgeoisie, when in reality the Chinese countryside is already exploited by the city, i.e. the bourgeoisie, and the Chinese landowning class either coincides with the Chinese middle and upper bourgeoisie or is tied to it by close links; not seeing the dominant role of mercantile capital in the Chinese countryside and the sharpness of contradictions between the bourgeoisie on the one hand, and the proletariat and peasantry on the other, only in embarking from these mistaken assumption could the Comintern think about a slow and partial departure of various layers of the bourgeoisie from the national revolution and hope for the extension of the period of its participation in the national movement, maybe right up to the unification of the whole of China. Only by understanding that even the industrial bourgeoisie, which took part in the national movement (without speaking of the comprador bourgeoisie), is not in a position to struggle to the end with imperialism, the Comintern could have hoped, in view of the anti-imperialist character of the national liberation movement, for a prolonged participation in it by the bourgeoisie. The industrial bourgeoisie struggles only for the fully achievable concessions on the part of imperialism, as for example, for protective tariffs, which to a significant degree the British colony of India achieved. The complete infatuation with the theory of a united national movement against imperialism did not allow the Comintern to take account of such a simple fact that even in Guomindang propaganda the slogan of the nationalisation of foreign owned mines, harbours and banks, without which the final victory over imperialism is impossible, played no role.

2) By exaggerating the activity of the participation of the bourgeoisie in the national movement and in consequence of this the forces of a united anti-imperialist front, while closing its eyes to the anti-peasant policy of the

Canton government, which is a consequence of the close ties between the landowners and the bourgeoisie, closing its eyes to the growing antagonism of the National government towards the growing worker and peasant movement, closing its eyes to the increasing evidence of the departure of the Chinese bourgeoisie from the revolution, the Comintern placed in the centre of its tactics *the avoidance of a breach with the Guomindang*. Therefore, in 1926 the Comintern ordered the Chin[ese] Communist Party to remain in the Guomindang, despite the fact that the Guomindang placed it in circumstances inconsistent with its independent political line. Therefore, the Comintern did not react to the fact that the C[E]C of the Chin[ese] Communist Party did not develop either the workers' nor the peasants' movements in sufficient strength, that the C[E]C of the Chin[ese] Communist Party, so as to find a common language with the Guomindang, began to speak the language of national Bolshevism. The whole policy of the Comintern in the Chinese question since the spring of 1926 meant *the liquidation of an independent Chinese Communist Party and a reduction of its role to that of an appendage to the Guomindang.*

3) The most striking expression of the policy of subjecting the Chinese Communist Party, the Chinese worker and peasant masses to the Chinese bourgeoisie is the complete failure of the Comintern to *prepare the Communist Party for battles*, which were inevitable once the bourgeois seceded from the national movement. The Comintern did not help the Communist Party to create organs without which it was impossible to educate the masses in a revolutionary spirit. *Without a daily press*, exposing every day the policy of the Chinese bourgeoisie, mobilising the popular masses against the right wing of the Guomindang, conversations about an approaching new phase of the democratic dictatorship of the workers and peasants were simply hot air. The Guomindang bourgeoisie left local power in the hands of the landowners and merchants everywhere. The Comintern, did not raise the slogan of the foundation of *soviets of workers, peasants, soldiers and the urban poor. Thereby* it left the worker and peasant movement in a condition of total dissolution and renounced the carrying out of the foremost task of the revolution, the destruction of the old apparatus of exploitation and oppression. The army was entirely in the hands of commanders who were counter-revolutionary in the great majority. The Party did not establish either secret or legal revolutionary organisations in the army, did not try to obtain an institution of commissars attached to the military commanders, i.e. it allowed the bourgeoisie to keep the army as a weapon of the counter-revolution in its hands. The Party permitted all arms to be concentrated in the hands of a déclassé army, which only yesterday had served the counter-revolution, so that the working class remained without any kind of armament and was not even conscripted for military service. The proletariat, the hegemon of the national

movement, was in practice excluded from the army, which was supposed to conduct the national war to a victorious conclusion.

4) Even then, when the working masses in Hankou, Changsha etc. went into battle independently with the right wing of the Guomindang, in battle against Chiang Kai-shek and in so doing forced the leaders of the Communist Party and of the left Guomindang to begin the battle from above, the leaders of the Comintern declared against 'a forcing of events', contenting themselves with the misleading explanations and promises of Chiang Kai-shek, dispersing the vigilance of the masses and awakening their hopes for a compromise. The resolution of the Seventh enlarged plenum of the Executive Committee of the Comintern, which speaks about the forthcoming departure of the bourgeoisie, was represented as a prospective resolution at a time when the centre of attention was concentrated on the possibility that the bourgeoisie would depart in groups, that it was vital to use the remainder. Ideologically disarmed, the working mass was caught unawares and disarmed, even there in Shanghai where it had collected an insignificant number of weapons at the cost of heavy sacrifices.

5) The April defeat of the Chin[ese] Communist Party is therefore *the result of the radically incorrect policy of the Comintern for the whole of last year, a policy which instead of using the Guomindang allowed itself to be used by the Guomindang, which instead of a conscious aspiration for hegemony of the proletariat in the national revolution actually submitted to the hegemony of the bourgeoisie.*

Against Lenin's teaching of the relationship of the proletariat towards the democratic revolution, against the theses of the Second Congress of the Comintern, against the decisions of the Fourth Congress, against the decisions of the Sixth enlarged plenum of the ECCI of March 1926, the Comintern conducted a *Menshevik policy* in practice in China, and it is therefore no accident that the old Mensheviks *Rafes and Martynov* have made themselves the propagators of this policy, having learnt and forgotten nothing. This could only take place because our own line began to move onto the Menshevik one.

3   What Is to Be Done?

1) The situation at the present moment amounts to the fact that the National government depends to a significant extent on the rightist general-landowner Tang Shengzhi, whose troops occupy Hunan and Hubei provinces. If it turns out that part of the Canton forces which are at the front stands on the side of the National government, then the National government will have a chance to oppose another military force to Gen[eral] Tang Shengzhi for a certain period, though it does not seem a completely reliable support. This would give the National government a chance to arm the workers and peasants.

2) That part of the government which has remained in Hankou still retains in its ranks *upper bourgeois* elements such as the speculator Sun Fo, characterised in com. Tan Pingshan's report[89] as an extreme right-wing representative of the landowners and compradors, and the Minister of Finance T.V. Soong [Song Ziwen]. The old local authority of landowners and merchants has not been destroyed. Therefore, the government still consists of representatives of the workers, the petty and *the upper bourgeoisie*. Com. Bukharin's assertion that it is now a 'government of the left bloc' (*Problemy kitaiskoi revoliutsii*, p. 59) is a simple self-delusion. Even if the Hankou government has already excluded from its ranks representatives of the upper bourgeoisie, it would not yet be a government of the democratic dictatorship of the workers and peasants, for there can be no talk of a dictatorship, if the government hangs in the air, if the old power still exists in the localities, if the government cannot count on the arms of those social forces which it aspires to represent. Without an understanding of this fact, the Hankou government will go bankrupt once and for all.

3) The first task of the Chin[ese] Communist Party and of the left Guomindang is the arming *by all available methods of the workers of Hubei and Hunan and the immediate disarming of the old local authorities*. They must be opposed by the power of the workers, the peasants and the urban petty bourgeoisie, *the organs of revolutionary self-government, from which the landowner, the upper and middle bourgeoisie, the old officials have been excluded*. Such organs of self-government can only be *local soviets* of workers and peasants, soldiers, petty traders, artisans. To oppose the slogan of the soviets, the slogan of strike committees, trade unions, peasant committees, means a *complete dispersal of the masses at a time when we must gather them into one military striking fist*. Moreover, if the old power is not destroyed, the peasant strike committees and the trade unions will be under the constant threat of destruction by the local landowner-capitalist administration.

C[om.] Stalin's assertion that the foundation of soviets would mean '*to issue a slogan of struggle against the existing power in this area*'[90] misses its target. In Wuhan district, the government exists in the Hankou palaces, though it is not a really left-wing government. It is not necessary to throw it out, one must merely cut off the right-wing elements. But this government still hangs, as we said before, in the air. A bourgeois-landowner power exists in the localities. It is not just necessary to publish a slogan of overthrowing the latter, *but it must*

---

89 This refers to Tan Pingshan's speech at the Seventh plenum of the ECCI.
90 Stalin 1952d [1927], p. 229.

be overthrown with the assistance of soviets. Only after overthrowing this local power will one be able to say that in Wuhan district there is a left-wing government. Stalin opposed the slogan '*all power to the revolutionary Guomindang*' to the slogan for soviets. Com. Stalin compares the Guomindang to a revolutionary parliament. Thereby he opposes the slogan of the power of the popular rank and file, of the workers and peasants and the urban poor to the slogan of the *power of a parliament*. The *opportunist* character of the Stalinist presentation of the question goes rotten directly from this formulation. C[om.] Stalin's fear that the slogan will hand a weapon to those who talk about 'Muscovite sovietisation',[91] indicates the illusion that the degree of antagonism of the Chinese bourgeoisie and imperialism does not depend on what the Chinese revolution does, but on how it calls its institutions. If it calls its power a parliamentary power, then that will work on the landowner, from whom land must be taken, as cocaine works on extracting a tooth. If you follow this argument to its conclusion, then the first conclusion which c[om.] Stalin must draw is that the Russian Communists, who have been sent as volunteers to China, must refuse to assist the Chinese revolution, for they have already been evidence of a Muscovite 'sovietisation' in the eyes of the Chinese and world bourgeoisie for a long time.

The renunciation of soviets in China is a renunciation of the position of Lenin, who said at the Second Congress of the Comintern in 1920:

> It is entirely understandable that the peasants in semi-feudal dependence can perfectly assimilate the idea of soviet organisation and *its realisation in deed*. It is also clear that the oppressed masses, exploited not just by mercantile[92] capital but also by feudalists and a state based on feudalism, *can apply this weapon, this form of organisation in their conditions also. The idea of soviet organisation is simple and may be applied not just to the proletarian but also to the peasant feudal and semi-feudal relations. Our experience in this field is not yet very great, but the debates in the commission in which several representatives of colonial countries took part, showed us with complete certainty that we must point out in the theses of the Communist International that the peasant soviets, soviets of the exploited, are a means suitable not just for capitalist countries but also for countries with pre-capitalist relations and that the propaganda of the idea of peasant soviets, soviets of the toilers everywhere, in backward countries and in colonies, is the unconditional duty of Communist*

---

91 Ibid.
92 According to Lenin: 'commercial'.

parties and of all elements which side with them; and there in so far as circumstances permit, to found soviets of the toiling people. (Lenin. Collected Works, Vol. XVII, [pp. 276–7])[93] [emphasised by Radek].

Thus spoke Lenin with regard to countries in which *'there is hardly any industrial proletariat'*[94] [emphasised by Radek]. What doubt should there be about the duty of Communists in a country like China where there are millions of industrial workers?

4) The Hankou government must immediately commit itself to the implementation of a series of social reforms, concerning the working class, the urban petty bourgeoisie and the peasantry. The ban on the payment of leasehold payments to the landowners and merchants, must be decreed immediately and all attempts to extort it must be pursued with the force of the democratic dictatorship. The eight-hour day, the raising of wages, the realisation of the security of employment must be immediately implemented. Measures must be taken for the creation of a credit fund for small traders and artisans. The latter must be organised for deliveries to the army. The simple fact that Chiang Kai-shek can hope to reduce the acuity of his relations with the Shanghai workers by means of promises of social reforms shows us that in this field nothing has been done by the Hankou government up to the present and that haste is essential.

5) Wuhan region can be a district in the capacity of a bridgehead of the national revolution only under the condition of *the preservation of the bloc of Communists with the left Guomindang*. The preservation of this bloc is possible only with the *expulsion of the right Guomindang* from the whole of the Guomindang from top to bottom. The sole serious *evidence* as to who is a rightist and who is a leftist Guomindang member must be the slogans: 'abolition of leasehold payments, the introduction of the eight-hour working day, the arming of the workers and the peasants, the creation of soviets'. Whoever is against these slogans has no place in the Guomindang. This position is known to com. Stalin. If he, in calling me by name, says that I am proposing a departure from the Guomindang now,[95] then he knows that he speaks a conscious *falsehood*.

---

93 Radek does not quote entirely correctly. This is what Lenin said: '[A]n unconditional obligation of the Communist parties and of those elements, which are ready to found Communist parties, is propaganda of the idea of peasant soviets, soviets of the toilers wherever and whenever possible, in both the backward countries and the colonies; and there where circumstances allow, they must immediately make attempts to found soviets of the toiling people' (Lenin 1971c, p. 245).
94 Ibid, p. 243.
95 See Stalin 1952d, p. 229.

He read my lectures to the Com[munist] Academy, was present at my speech at the Moscow Party meeting, where I precisely and clearly said that I do not demand the departure from the Guomindang at this stage of development of the revolution, if the Guomindang excludes representatives of the right-wing bourgeoisie. The comrades who defended the very same point of view as I did did not propose the slogan of withdrawal from the left Guomindang, either in c[om.] Zinoviev's theses,[96] or in the resolution of Six Central Committee members,[97] or in the speeches of c[om.] Zinoviev and Trotsky at the [April (1927)] plenum of the CC. In inventing a non-existent demand, com. Stalin *is concealing the real object of the argument. The object of the argument is the independence of the policy of the Communist party of China.* Com. Stalin does not say a single word about whether it is necessary even now, with a delay which led to an enormous defeat for the revolution, to create a Communist daily press. Should the Communists come out openly under the banner of Communism, should they strengthen the bloc with the left Guomindang and criticise all the vacillations of its petty bourgeois leaders? This question demands an answer. Com. Stalin isn't giving it. If this conceals the maintenance of the old policy of subjection to the Guomindang, then the Chinese proletariat will be betrayed by Wang Jingwei and Xu Qian as they were by Chiang Kai-shek.

4 The International Situation and the Chinese Revolution

1) Chiang Kai-sheks' going over into the camp of the counter-revolution, the schism in the national army, all this has increased to an unprecedented degree the danger threatening the Chinese revolution. International imperialism will not abstain from using the situation. Perhaps it will assume the role of butcher in relation to the Hankou government, so as not to compromise Chiang Kai-shek entirely. The change of government in Japan[98] does not seem a good omen. The situation is exceptionally serious, but it is clear that precisely this demands Bolshevik determination and courage. The centre of gravity in this situation consists not in manoeuvres, but in revolutionary determination. It must consist in the energetic implementation of measures to defend the Wuhan district and the undermining of the rear of the enemy by raising the workers and peasants in rebellion.

---

96 This refers to Zinoviev's 'Theses on the Chinese Revolution', presented to the April (1927) plenum of the CC of the AUCP(b).

97 This refers to the letter by Trotsky, Kamenev, Zinoviev, Sokol'nikov, Piatakov, and Evdokimov to the leaders of the Party of 4 October 1926.

98 On 17 April 1927, the Wakatsuki government, which had been in power since January 1926, resigned. It was replaced by the government of general Baron Tanaka.

2) The defeat of the Chinese revolution sharpens our international situation. It increases the threat of war, more than it was back in winter. But it would be childish naiveté to think that we can evade war by wrapping up our China policy. On the contrary, [we can evade war] only by helping with all the means available to us; unfortunately this does *not* include military assistance to the Chinese revolution. In defending ourselves, in preserving Wuhan district we will inculcate the enemy with a conviction of our determination and we can preserve the Chinese revolution as an ally.

3) The first condition of assistance to the Chinese revolution is a taking stock of the lessons of the defeat, the familiarising of the international proletariat with the class struggle proceeding in China, an approach to its understanding of the Chinese revolution not only as a national-liberation movement, but as a class struggle of workers and peasants. Therefore, we must finally break with the policy of hiding in the corner of the Menshevik theory of the Chinese revolution the facts of the class struggle, the hiding of defeats. Only in knowing what has happened in China, what the Chinese workers and peasants are struggling for, can the workers of Europe help to defend the Chinese revolution. After the depression provoked amongst the international proletariat by the betrayal of Chiang Kai-shek, who was just yesterday proclaimed a hero of the liberation struggle by the entire international Communist press, only complete glasnost about tactical questions in the Chinese revolution can establish a basis for the mobilisation of the forces of the international proletariat for the defence of the Chinese revolution.

RGASPI. Collection of unsorted documents.
Typescript text with manuscript corrections, copy.

Published in Iu.G. Felshtinskii and G.I. Cherniavskii (eds), *Arkhiv Trotskogo* ('Trotsky Archive'), Vol. 1, Kharkov: OKO, 1999, pp. 80–142. (The Kharkov publication was accomplished on the basis of a document preserved in the Trotsky Archive in the Houghton Library of Harvard University under the title 'Defeat of the Chinese Revolution').

CHAPTER 8

Speech at the Institute of World Economy and World Politics of the Communist Academy during the Discussion of the Lecture by L.N. Geller on the Chinese Workers' Movement

17 May 1927, Stenographic Report

Comrades! I have listened to c[om.] Geller's lecture with the greatest astonishment. Com. Geller is one of the most well informed of our comrades on Chinese affairs, a competent comrade, but his heated optimism amazes me. We have heard here [in the Communist Academy] in the discussion in March, 20 March, a speech saying that there is no crisis, that all is well. Chiang Kai-shek has submitted and so there are the most joyful perspectives. Today, after the events in Shanghai we hear again that thanks to the Bolshevik god the crisis turned out relatively mildly and everything now stands positively as it should. Imperialism is not as savage as we thought, the role of the bourgeoisie is not so great. Chiang Kai-shek has already been exposed, the left bloc continues to grow stronger, is being founded and growing stronger. The sole question is that of building Party and economic organisations, their organisational backbones etc.

Comrades! A month has not passed since the events in Shanghai and I thought that that was a thoroughly violent shock and that we would speak of perspectives accordingly. Before passing over to the perspectives, I will permit myself to summarise something of our experience. Facts are obstinate things: they teach.

It is necessary at first to establish – and that was essentially the first task of the lecturer – what the facts of the last month teach us.

If we regard the workers' movement in broad perspective, it is not sufficient to note how the strikes went, which forces got organised, but if we approach it as Marxists – and our lecturer tried to do this, – then the strength of the working class is not determined just by its numbers or its organisation, but by its relationship to other classes and to the tasks which are historically presented to it. And it is exactly from this point of view we must summarise the experience which the Chinese workers' movement has gained. What does this experience tell us? It says the following: firstly, concerning the desertion of the bourgeoisie, we have heard a theory here that the bourgeoisie deserts in groups and it is vital to use those groups which remain for the democratic dictatorship in future. On

Sunday, I had occasion to read in *Pravda* an abbreviated report by the Secretary of the Chinese Communist Party, c[om.] Chen Duxiu, in which he states that actually 99 percent of the upper bourgeoisie has deserted.[1] Therefore, from a formal point of view one percent remains, that is also a part. But it is understandable to say the least that the Trade Union International also said in its declaration that the upper bourgeoisie had departed. This is the first point. Second, how did it desert? When they considered the bourgeoisie, they said that it would desert, but they did not pose a question if it would leave a visiting card with the inscription 'farewell, my dear, I am leaving, I am tired of making the national revolution with you', or it would depart with machine gun and canon fire, in a civil war. The left wing of the national revolutionary movement feared that it would break up the national front; the bourgeoisie did not fear breaking up the national front, the bourgeoisie was not afraid and left with machine gun and canon fire, leaving hundreds of corpses in Shanghai.

The second fact, the greatest fact, the major fact is that the proletariat was caught unawares, that the proletariat was completely unprepared. Comrades, the bourgeoisie deserted during all bourgeois revolutions, and that which is taking place in China now is also a bourgeois revolution so far. But it seems that from the revolutions of [18]48, or, let's say, from the desertion of the Girondins from the revolution it took many decades, during which Marx, Engels and Lenin wrote and acted, a republic existed, a Comintern exists. We wrote throughout the course of ten years of revolution. How could it happen that the bourgeoisie was perfectly prepared for its departure, but the proletariat was in such a condition that only two thousand rifles were in their hands against 300,000 rifles on the side of the bourgeoisie? In the army in whose foundation we took an active part, which conquered by the strength of its national ideology represented by the left wing of the national movement, and therefore, [if] we speak of the perspectives of the Chinese workers' movement, without pausing over the reason why the bourgeoisie departed in a different way than we had anticipated, and why the proletariat seemed completely unprepared, this means to explain everything by statistical articles on strikes, but not to give an analysis of those enormous events which are unfolding before our very eyes.

Thus, the first question is why it was not understood that the bourgeoisie would desert not in groups and not peacefully, but would desert in a civil war, a civil war with the proletariat? Where is the source of the failure to understand this? The source of the failure to understand this is the incorrect, non-Marxist,

---

1 Radek is mistaken. Chen Duxiu declared that Chiang Kai-shek's 'betrayal' (this refers to the coup of 12 April 1927) expresses the 'departure from the revolution of 99% of the upper and middle bourgeoisie'; *Pravda*, 15 May 1927.

non-Leninist theory of the national revolution. I will read out one passage which I consider the central political and theoretical mistake, allowing that this desertion, this mass desertion in the form in which it occurred was not detected in time. Permit me to read this passage: 'The most important and first task is the victory over foreign imperialism, a victory for which the united national revolutionary front [in its turn] serves as guarantor'.[2]

This front now consists of not only of workers, not only of peasants, not only of artisans, not only of the rank and file democratic intelligentsia and the mercantile-industrial bourgeoisie, of merchants and industrialists, but [also from] those who are directly linked with foreign capital ... who may be compradors, i.e. from among those who are mediators between foreign capital in China.

The national revolution, the guarantor of her victory over imperialism is the united front into which the bourgeoisie entered. C[om.] Bukharin said this at the [Seventh] enlarged plenum of the Comintern at the end of November. One must distinguish some landowners from others. Did this theory flowing from the first one find sufficient resistance on the part of the leadership. It did not. If you read c[om.] Bukharin's report at the Fifteenth Party conference and at the enlarged plenum of the Comintern,[3] in that report you will find the following formulation. He says that we have to give the peasant something because the revolution is affecting him. For the revolution to grow it must give something to the peasant, and therefore, he says, we must demand agrarian reform. But if you pick up c[om.] Chen Duxiu's pamphlet, his report to the Comintern,[4] then you will find factual things there. When I bought it in the State Publishing House and read it through on the way to the Kremlin, I wanted to take up 50 copies of this pamphlet to convince myself that this was written in each copy.

Com. Chen Duxiu, developing the programme of the Communist Party before the Comintern, says: peasant taxes must be reduced, the peasants should not pay more than 50 percent of their income as taxes. The Chinese peasant must pay 50 percent of his miserable income to the government. This is from the Communist programme. And after that he says: we must reduce what he pays to the landowner. If he pays 60 percent of his harvest to the landowner, and receives 40 percent himself, then he should receive 55 percent and give the landowner 45 percent.[5] Comrades! I am not very strong in maths, and when I

---

2   Comintern 1927b, Volume 1, p. 90.
3   See AUCP(b) 1927a, pp. 25, 28–29; Comintern 1927b, Volume 1, p. 90.
4   Radek is mistaken. Here and further on he is referring not to Chen Duxiu's report, but to Tan Pingshan's speech at the Seventh plenum of the ECCI.
5   See Tan-Pin-Sian [Tan Pingshan] 1927, pp. 40, 42.

am forced to count beyond ten then I take my boots off, but I understand that c[om.] Chen Duxiu wanted to give the government and the landowner more than the peasant's entire income. Obviously it is an absurdity trying to rouse the peasant with such an agrarian policy. That is the first consequence.

A second consequence follows. The government bans strikes, and implements a law on compulsory arbitration;[6] so as not to break with the bourgeoisie, the Party submits to this law. Com. Geller shakes his head, and says no, but I assert as follows. Firstly, in one of the official documents it is stated that arbitration derives from c[om.] Borodin, and the second fact is that c[om.] Geller presents not a single document of the Chinese Communist Party against arbitration, not a single document showing that the trade unions rejected arbitration and that for this they were labelled not leftists, but I won't use such a terrible word as 'Trotskyism', as a result of which maybe someone might suffer.

How was this line developed further? This line was expressed in the fact that there is not a single document, in which the Party demanded the arming of the workers. There is not a single document that could have resulted in this. The Canton people came out with 70,000 bayonets, and they then had 300,000 bayonets until the schism with Chiang Kai-shek. Where did these 200,000–300,000 bayonets come from. Here are Sun Chuanfang's bands ...[7] were beaten. At first they disarmed [them], then for a month or two they forced them to act as coolies, and when they sent them into battle, they gave them tricoloured neckerchiefs and said: 'You are troops of the national army'. But they would not let the workers into the army, they did not arm the workers, they were subjected to the party. They had a headquarters but were not recruited into the army. When workers' pickets appeared in Hankou and when on 3 January the working class seized the concessions, without the knowledge of the C[E]C of the Guomindang, without the knowledge of the C[E]C of our Party, this is a fact which has been officially established, and when the workers' guard appeared with cudgels in this concession, then shouts rang out, that we know what that means: they are preparing a 'putsch'; these are not industrial workers but something else entirely.

So from a basically incorrect theory a tactic emerged which in practice meant that in a scattered million-and-a-half strong trade union movement not a single trade union had a newspaper, there was no political campaign which

---

6 The law forbidding strikes and the introduction of compulsory arbitration was announced by the Guomindang National government in connection with the decision of the CEC of the GMD of 5 January 1927. The Soviet readership found out about this in February 1927; see Martynov 1927, p. 11.
7 I.e. the armed bands of Sun Chuanfang.

might have prepared the masses for the desertion of the bourgeoisie, for such a preparation would mean vacillations, the shooting of the workers, the destruction of peasant organisations, an indication as to who the enemy was.

12 March on that very day on which I spoke out here for the first time,[8] the first, slightly sharper article appeared in our Communist press by c[om.] Chen Duxiu, dedicated to the second anniversary of the death of Sun Yat-sen.[9] Without mentioning anyone by name, he said in this article that there is a party which wants to struggle against the workers, against the peasantry and against soviet organs. He asked how that was possible on the second anniversary of the death of Sun Yat-sen? Why not wait for the third! An article followed in which no names were named, in which no one was called to do anything. And it turned out that it was all very sad. And this was the line of the summit of the Party in China, against which, it must be said, a brutal struggle was conducted amongst the working masses, not just in the form of resolutions (the Chinese rank and file are even worse than our workers, they write resolutions: to write a resolution there you need to know three thousand characters), but what it came down to was that the workers did what they thought necessary. The workers came out against Chiang Kai-shek, they went on strike, workers in Shanghai seized arms. The leadership of the Party, embarking from a fear of a split with the upper bourgeoisie, was no guide for such a policy. This was what experience said, experience from which the conclusion was that it was vital to break with the upper bourgeoisie in good time and conduct a split with the Guomindang. The united front of the workers, the peasants and the petty bourgeoisie is the guarantor of the victory of the national revolution. But the united front of the workers, the peasants and the petty bourgeoisie can only be created on the basis of a split with the upper bourgeoisie for the simple reason that the peasant cannot struggle merely for the national revolution. He must struggle for something or other more tangible for himself. That means he must struggle against the landowners, and if the bourgeoisie does not want to break with the landowners, then he cannot really be drawn into a struggle together with the bourgeoisie. And the fact that the workers cannot be drawn into a struggle together with the bourgeoisie is understood by everyone because the first act of such a struggle is a strike.

Comrades! These are the lessons of the past. Now let us see what is happening now. The most dangerous, the most short sighted is the officially broadcast message based exclusively on the fact that we know very little about what is

---

8 Radek's speech to the Communist Academy of 12 March 1927 is not found. It is possible Radek had in mind his report of 13 March.
9 See Chen 1927, pp. 2054–55.

now going on in Hankou. In the final chapter of his pamphlet, written after the events involving Chiang Kai-shek, com. Bukharin said that there is present in Hankou a left-wing government, a bloc of workers and peasants. This is stated on page 59.[10]

On Sunday an article was published, an abbreviated version of c[om.] Chen Duxiu's article. It has a double merit, apart from the establishment of the facts. He says: there is nothing more dangerous than confusing oneself about the fact that a left-wing government of a bloc of workers and peasants exists in Hankou. Why does such a government not exist; what does a left-wing government of the bloc of workers and peasants mean? If we call it by its name the left-wing government of the bloc of workers and peasants in China, then this will still not be a left-wing government. For that it is necessary for us to develop local government, which until the present moment has been in the hands of the landowners, of the old officials and of the merchants. This is the first condition of a left-wing government, the first condition, which is the liquidation of the old authorities, the liquidation of this old government. The Hankou government is an elite bloc of Communists and left Guomindang, it knows that although the peasant in the localities wants and is already beginning to disperse this old power itself, but it still exists at the present time in Wuhan [Hubei] and Henan, in both the main provinces of the old National government. This is the first point. Second, the left-wing government of workers, peasants and the petty bourgeoisie means that in this left-wing government there are no representatives of the upper bourgeoisie. Comrades, representatives of the upper bourgeoisie do sit in the Hankou government. You have presumably just read the interview with Mr. Sun Fo.[11] Who is this Mr. Sun Fo? He had the good fortune to be born the son of the well-known Sun Yat-sen. Here as chance would have it is a remainder of that same clannish feudalism, which Pepper could not find in China. He is also bound up with a very strong family network, which exists in China, and in which if the son is caught out, then the father and uncle pay for him, and if papa does good business, then the son must make money on it, must earn his living in this business. Meanwhile, this same Sun Fo was the organiser of a conference of the Guomindang rightists, which was summoned in Sichuan after his father's death. In this pamphlet this Chinese Communist,[12] whom I consider a right-wing representative of the compradors and landowners, this revolutionary who was Mayor of Canton, sold allotments of land and put the money into his own pocket. This fact is well-known to every political novice in

---

10   See Bukharin 1927c, p. 59.
11   See Sun 1927.
12   Thus in the text.

China. If Sun Fo takes me to court for libel, I will refer to articles on these matters. Meanwhile, Sun Fo remains in the government. Why does he remain in the government? Theoretically speaking there is the fact that the right wing of the Guomindang contains two orientations: one orientation is toward the militarists and Japan, and the other orientation is toward the upper bourgeoisie and America. Sun Fo is an American businessman, and Sun Fo sits in the Hankou government as a representative of a deal with America in which, – among other things which our press has not reported, – he assumed the guarantee of the emissions of a Canton bank, which is a government bank of America and ... he guaranteed ten million to be assigned to this bank. T.V. Soong [Song Ziwen] is in the Guomindang. T.V. Soong also comes from Sun Yat-sen's family,[13] and represents that golden network, which connects the dictatorial left-wing government with American capital, and therefore he remains in the organs of the old authorities of the upper bourgeoisie, which now connects America with the bourgeoisie which sits there.

Therefore, the first task of the Comintern and all the other friends of the Chinese revolution is to explain the role of that revolutionary hero Wang Jingwei in the shooting of the Shanghai workers. In the Shanghai newspaper [*Zhongyang ribao*[14]] of 8 April the following official communiqué appeared: it says that on the first days of April a meeting took place in Chiang Kai-shek's headquarters between General Chiang Kai-shek with Wang Jingwei and T.V. Soong [Song Ziwen],[15] who, between ourselves, laughed and sat in the French concession under the protection of the imperialists, so as not to fall into the hands, the Lord protect us, of their own government in Hankou. But up to the present day Chiang continues to consider himself as a member of the government. We have not heard that T.V. Soong [Ziwen] has left the government, he remains a saint of the revolution. So Wang Jingwei, T.V. Soong [Ziwen] and Chiang Kai-shek made a deal as follows: it is vital to reconcile this grow-

---

13   Song Ziwen [T.V. Soong] was the brother of Sun Yat-sen's widow, Song Qingling.
14   *Zhongyang ribao* ('Central newspaper') – the official organ of the Guomindang. From March 1927 to February 1928 it was published in Wuhan, thereafter in Shanghai. In 1929 the editorial office moved to Nanjing. In 1937 the newspaper was closed, but in 1938 it was re-established in Chongqing. In 1945 the editorial office returned to Nanjing, but in January 1949 it was transferred to Taiwan.
15   Wang Jingwei arrived in Shanghai from Europe on 3 April 1927. After a meeting with Chiang Kai-shek, Song Ziwen and other leaders of the GMD and NRA he sent a telegram to the CEC of the GMD in Wuhan, demanding 'changes' in the activity of the trade unions, peasant unions and militarised peasant organisations. On his part, Chiang Kai-shek also sent a telegram to Wuhan, in which he declared that the entire activity of the GMD would be conducted under the leadership of Wang Jingwei.

ing conflict by peaceful means. Wang Jingwei promises to convene a meeting of the c[e]c of the Guomindang and the government in Nanjing on 15 April. Until that moment, he will assume the responsibility of communicating to the Secretary of the Chinese Communist Party c[om.] Chen Duxiu, that the Communist Party is obliged to call off its activity until the decisions of the Nanjing conference. First of all that all armed workers' organisations or those who serve military purposes, as for example pickets with cudgels, must be subordinated to Chiang Kai-shek, and those who do not submit must be dissolved. Secondly, in view of the fact that agitation against the government is going on in the Guomindang, the trade unions and the Party, such activity by mass organisations must be stopped. The leadership of local organisations is subjected to the high command, which speaks in [their] name. And finally, in view of the fact that the Hankou government and the c[e]c of the Guomindang has recently found itself under the control of certain persons, all mandates issued by the Hankou government are declared null and void until their examination by a control commission in Nanjing. When I received this document, I said that if this is true then Wang Jingwei has played that role in the shooting of the Shanghai workers, which Kerensky and Savinkov played in the Kornilov coup.[16] I asked comrades about this. They told me that we do not know this document, we do not know but [it] may be false, because it is published in a right-wing Guomindang newspaper. But, comrades, I would remind you that when we tried to work it out, when we exposed the role of Kerensky in the Kornilov affair, we also did not have the sworn statements of Kornilov himself, but we judged only on the basis of what trickled into the right-wing White press. I gave a commission to comrades who can directly follow the Chinese press, to examine the entire left Guomindang press up to the 12 [April], since there was no shooting, no split until the 12th, if there could be a confirmation of this, but it was nowhere. And here in this hall I discover that the following communiqué appeared in a Hankou newspaper of 15 April, in which Wang Jingwei informs us that he left Canton in 1927 [1926] because he was convinced that Chiang Kai-shek was going wrong, that he had hoped that Chiang Kai-shek would improve, but on his return he became convinced that he had not corrected himself and that

---

16 The Kornilov mutiny in August 1917 pursued the objective of creating a military dictatorship in Russia. The mutiny was originally prepared by the Provisional Government, whose head, Kerensky, aimed at becoming a military dictator. Savinkov, a commissar of the Provisional Government, played the role of intermediary between Kerensky and Kornilov. Kornilov, however, sent troops to Petrograd so as to establish his own dictatorship. In reply to this, Kerensky declared him a mutineer, and troops loyal to the Provisional Government suppressed the attempted coup. Kornilov was arrested, but was shortly after released.

therefore he was against Chiang Kai-shek. I repeat that there is no confirmation of this fantastic document, fantastic not from the factual point of view, but regarding the role of Wang Jingwei. Moreover, you will nowhere find a single telegram about the speech of Wang Jingwei as head of the government. Wang Jingwei sits in an agrarian commission, maybe he has gone out there to sort out the agrarian question?

Why do I say all this? Obviously not for a testimonial to Wang Jingwei's personal role, but I say this because I consider that the policy needs verification; a policy has not only rights but also obligations. Such a document demands verification. I am speaking so as to state that this group of left-wing Guomindang to which Wang Jingwei belongs gives no guarantees that it represents a responsible revolutionary group tied up with the mass movement. I do not know if any Communists have joined this government[17] and if so how many.

According to our information we have had the fortune for a week and a half since 16 March to have, as far as we know, two Communists in the Chinese revolutionary government, two Communist-ministers in the most responsible posts in the revolution, but we have not read a single speech, nor a single decree of theirs, we know nothing about what they are doing, even though if they go bankrupt, dear comrades, I hope that this will not happen, but it is possible that they will go bankrupt not just on their account but they can go bankrupt on our account also. And we have a legitimate right to know what they are doing. But maybe there are more of them now, because Chiang Kai-shek has left, with him the whole bourgeoisie has left, and this must be reflected in the composition of the government. Who is sitting there and what they are doing, we know nothing, but we know a series of objective facts. The government which is still sitting in Hankou, where the Hankou workers supported, helped and defended it.

Are they armed? Today in *Pravda* there is a joyful telegram, a joyful telegram about a demonstration, that at the demonstration the peasant section was armed with nightsticks.[18] But we must know that one of the most enormous arsenals of China, the Hanyang Arsenal is there. This is the largest arsenal. Some of the pickets are armed, this is excellent. What more do we know?

Who is the boss of the province over 70,000 bayonets, in the military sense. There we have General T[ang Shengzhi]. A major landowner, a remnant of feudalism, who possesses 6,000 mu of land. General T[ang Shengzhi] is a general of the Japanese school, a mundane militarist, the most commonplace,

---

17 Thus in the text.
18 Radek is mistaken. The TASS telegram from Hankou, published on 17 May 1927 in *Pravda*, spoke about a partial arming of the urban trade union organisations.

most mediocre militarist, who until last year followed in the footsteps of Wu Peifu. He is the military boss of this province. Why did he not chase the government away? For the simple reason that the peasant is starting to beat up the landowners, and secondly, he fears an attack from Wu Peifu. He needs a banner for struggle. Should our Party use this militarist or should it say as follows: today, since Monday with the blessing of Chiang Kai-shek a new era has begun, an era of the democratic dictatorship and we from today will rely only on our own soldiers. But for that, firstly we need to have some and we need to be able to lead them. It will be good if the Hankou government is successful in attracting some of the troops, which are vacillating between Canton and T[ang Shengzhi]. If this information about the arming of part of the workers is correct, then the fact that they seem to be starting to move forward to the arming of the workers, we must welcome them, on condition that this will be a manoeuvre with the aim of winning time for the arming of all the workers. This is entirely permissible and legitimate.

Here we come over to the most important question. In c[om.] Chen Duxiu's speech there is a passage which must make a murderous impression on every thoughtful, serious Marxist. Com. Chen Duxiu says: the peasant question is the main question; without an agrarian revolution there is nothing to be done. But how to do it? We must chase away the major landowners, but it is not necessary to chase away the petty proprietors. The peasant who has the misfortune to have a petty landowner, will probably not be very pleased with this. But c[om.] Chen Duxiu goes further. He proposes a typical Menshevik formula, though he does not know what prose he is talking. He is a man who was an anarchist six years ago, he never completed a school of Marxism-Leninism. He cites the words of the Menshevik Iordanskii at the London Congress of 1906,[19] without ever having read them before. He says that one must broaden the revolution from the beginning and only after that deepen it.[20] He says further on that it will be time to cut the knot of agrarian relations only after the unification of China. After the peasant has paid Chiang Kai-shek generously and given General T[ang Shengzhi] bread, rice, his strength, his blood on credit for the unification of China, without receiving anything.

---

19   Radek is mistaken. The London (Fifth) Congress of the RSDLP took place in 1907, and Iordanskii did not take part in it. In 1906 the Stockholm (Forth, Unification) Congress of the RSDLP took place. Iordanskii took part with no voting rights.
20   Iordanskii did not say that at the 1906 congress. It is possible that Radek assumes Iordanskii's declaration about the erroneousness of the Bolshevik tactic of boycotting the First State Duma, made at the eighteenth session of the Fourth Congress; see RSDLP 1959 [1906], pp. 307–08.

This was the position of Kerensky in [19]17: victory first and then the agrarian question. This contradicts everything that we learned in the experience of the Russian revolution and of revolutions in every country.

Furthermore, comrades, how do relations appear between the Hankou government and the workers? I have just read out one amazing telegram in *Pravda*. The telegram carries the heading: 'Collaboration of the Wuhan government with the trade unions'.[21] I was glad. In what does this collaboration consist? The Wuhan trade unions committed themselves not to strike in foreign factories without the permission of the government. Chiang Kai-shek called this compulsory arbitration. Compulsory arbitration consists in the fact that one cannot strike without the permission of an official, who sits there. This is now called collaboration of the trade unions with the Wuhan government. But it is an unthinkable thing to hold back a strike movement in foreign factories and to allow it in one's own, because it flows from one to the other, therefore this makes me fear that we have there an obstacle, a brake on the workers' movement at the moment.

If we take the English papers, what do we see there? You remember that Ioffe from the Rev[olutionary] Mil[itary] Com[mittee] warned me here that I should not trust the imperialist papers and said that they all lie in saying that Chiang Kai-shek is preparing a coup d'état, but that c[om.] Ioffe knew on the basis of many sources that Chiang Kai-shek was not doing so.[22] Now they can also tell me: don't trust imperialist papers. But I have already tested some information in the imperialist papers. What do they say? They are laughing. They say that there is no any other place in China now, where they treat foreigners more cautiously than in Hankou. The English, who had begun to play lawn tennis with the coolies in the concession, now play by themselves, and American sailors are beginning to beat up Chinese workers.

All this, comrades, places the most serious questions before us. Before us arises the question about whether we are just at the very beginning of the crisis, because to understand during the sharpening crisis the role of the Communist Party, the role of the proletariat in the national revolution is to know your ABC. I beg you, comrades, to re-read Lenin in your free time, 'Victory of the Kadets', the chapter on Blanc.[23] I have just read it and I must say that it is the obligation of a revolutionary to apply it to the Chinese Communists.

---

21   This refers to TASS 1927.
22   See RGASPI, F.514, Op.1, D.253, L. 84.
23   This refers to chapter V, headed 'A Sample of Cadet Smugness' (Lenin 1968b [1906], pp. 312–46).

The first question, which arises here, is whether one can save the revolution by means of slowing it down or solely by means of accelerating it. There is such a theory. C[om.] Geller says that there is no united front of imperialism, and I agree with him. Other comrades say that imperialism does have a united front, or that in any case imperialism is very strong. So what do you want? To give up the peasant revolution under the noses of those Englishmen, whose naval vessels patrol the ⟨...⟩ Yangzi. The thought that one cannot move events forward in the face of the imperialist danger is a ruinous thought. If you follow that thought to the end, what does it mean? It means that one must wait until such time as the English, the Japanese and the Americans agree to a peasant revolution. This is the first point.

The second point is what does the recent history of China, of the last thirty years demonstrate? That the bourgeoisie is not in a position to unite China.

The role of the proletariat and the peasantry in the national revolution consists in this, that as soon as the peasantry, under the leadership of the huge masses of the city, is able to throw off this feudalism from themselves, so soon will it be able to unite China under the leadership of the proletariat. I consider that a peasant revolution is impossible under the noses of the English, but national unification on a national basis is also impossible under the noses of the English. So what is possible? I consider that the collapse of China is possible, that's what is possible, but for that there is no need to make a revolution.

Comrades, this question must be thought through thoroughly, for we are playing in this game not just about the head of the Chinese revolution, it is a matter of our own heads. It is harder to survive two revolutions than one. Who does not understand this, who thinks that we can hide our heads in the sand at the sight of danger, at the sight of these events, is blind. The questions of the development of the Chinese revolution are questions of the defence of the Soviet republic, one can defend it by unleashing the Chinese revolution. The facts tell us that there is no turning point yet. The turning point consists in the fact that Chiang Kai-shek deserted. But we did not achieve this, it wasn't us who made him depart, he left of his own accord. I ask whether the Chinese Communist Party has a daily paper? No. One and a half million trade unionists do not have their own paper. Have the relations between the Chinese Communist Party and the Guomindang been altered at all? Cannot we call it an alteration if only the right wing deserted, but in the sense of that independence which is so necessary, in that sense everything stays the same? After all, if the leader of the Party Chen Duxiu says that there will be a deepening, not a broadening of the revolution, then this is a form of the Northern Expedition.

I consider, comrades, that c[om.] Geller approached the question of whether the bourgeoisie in China is weak incorrectly. He says that it is weak since it can do nothing without foreign imperialism. But I say that the Chinese bourgeoisie is very strong because it can come to an agreement with foreign imperialism, can act as its umbrella. And there is nothing more dangerous for the proletariat than to underestimate its enemy. It is so weak, and we are so strong; it is so weak, but we helped it create an army of 300,000 bayonets. This army united half of China, we received just 2,000 bayonets from this army, by the way, the workers themselves were forced to come and take them. Of course, the Chinese bourgeoisie is not so weak, for this weakness is not just a physical factor but a political one; Chiang Kai-shek was able to lead us by the nose until 12 March,[24] but we, left-wing China, the Guomindang leftists are so strong. To reason like this is politically short-sighted. Undoubtedly, one must take the Chinese bourgeoisie seriously as a class. The policy of the Chinese bourgeoisie is so far more serious than the policy of the Chinese workers and peasants. The Chinese bourgeoisie has shown this not by rhetoric, they do not write resolutions, but they showed it with machine gun fire.

Now the following question: can the bourgeoisie unite China and what are the perspectives in this connection? I agree with c[om.] Geller that our chief danger lies not in the fact that [imperialism] represents a powerful force, thanks to the fact that imperialism is not united, that it will wager on various groups of imperialists and militarists, so as to unite China. In the first place, the bourgeoisie will need massive loans to resolve the agrarian crisis, so that they can give work to a million peasants in railway construction. Comrades, we have lost a battle, but we have not lost the revolution. The perspectives of the revolution, its strength, its breadth, its scale are enormous, after a year, after half a year of silence it can develop further. But a precondition for this must be a political line by a Chinese Communist Party that knows that for this it needs the peasant, for this it needs the worker. It is necessary to move and not hold up this movement, not to put off necessary change until the unification of China. There is no need to pose the question as though one must first broaden and then deepen without thinking through the lessons of the Northern Expedition, when the remnants of the counter-revolution were left in the rear in Canton, and the counter-revolution began to walk with its head up. Therefore, it does not all depend on whether there will be a turning point or not. All that we picked up, all the information from there, both theoretical and not theoretical, but which arrived from there, does not show that a course ahead has been chosen. The main evidence for this is the question of the form of power. If you want to break up the old local authorities, in the Wuhan government they sit

---

24   Thus in the text. It should read: 12 April 1927.

only at the summit, then obviously you will not create a new power. Throw out the bourgeois, throw out the old officials, the major merchants, create a local power of workers and peasants and the petty bourgeoisie. Fine, but what kind of power will that be? Will it be a power based on universal elections? Some comrades say that you can get a majority in the revolution by means of ballot papers. Yes, it's possible. But do you think that those gangs who seized power and who extort from the peasant will renounce their power when you show them a ballot paper. They must be broken up and destroyed, and this can be done only by a dictatorial organisation of the workers, the peasants and the petty bourgeoisie, and which will be a local soviet, as you call it. The devil may take it what it will be called in Chinese it is better not to say, it will be necessary to select a name.[25]

Comrades, this question is the crucial question. It is neither here nor there that there are those who say that it is a matter of ⟨...⟩ whether to leave the left Guomindang or not. There is no such proposal. This is on the one hand. On the other, who would now demand a departure from the left Guomindang, a split with them? The struggle is now about the question of whether the Chinese Communist Party is connected with the workers' movement, the question is about the decisive policy which the petty bourgeoisie now conducts and the organisation of parties which are now running after the bourgeoisie.

Finally, two theoretical words. We argue and create a mystique around the Guomindang and what it is. One comrade says it is like the soviets,[26] and another says that it is nothing more than an authentic revolutionary parliament.[27] I pose the question like this: if it is like soviets, then why be against soviets, and if it is like a revolutionary parliament, then dear comrades, not a single revolutionary parliament has ever taken decisive measures without mass rank and file organisations, which dispersed it. History knows a single great example of a revolutionary parliament, the Convention. But a Convention without the Parisian sections, which were soviets of the poor, would have been quite different. Therefore, if it is true that it is a revolutionary parliament then everything speaks for the foundation of sections, i.e. local soviets. So why this mystification? All literate people who have read Marx know the history of the French Revolution of 1848. The Guomindang is also the party which exists at the beginning of every revolution, the leading bourgeois party, then hand in hand with the growth of revolutionary events, this bourgeoisie deserts it. The

---

25 Radek is referring to the fact that the character *hui* in the Chinese expression *sovetskii komitet* (*suweiai weiyuanhui*) sounds obscene in Russian.
26 Bukharin.
27 Stalin.

very same thing happened in China also, at first the upper bourgeoisie entered this party, having united the proletariat with itself, but then it left, deserting the proletariat. But this proletariat remained in 1927, when the whole experience of the world war stood behind them, so that here the question arose about who would lead. Would the proletariat lead the petty bourgeoisie, or vice versa? But for us Marxists it was clear that the petty bourgeoisie has never led the revolution to the end, and could not do so in a single revolution. And so the crucial question consists in whether, after the 1848 revolution, according to Marx and Engels, the proletariat should be a hanger-on of the bourgeoisie or it should rule itself.

It is vital to found a party corresponding to the proportional weight of the proletariat, with a clear programme, with a universal organisation, not a skeleton organisation, this is very important, but there must be a central brain. You can create a good skeleton, respected comrades, for example, the German Social Democrats. [They] had a beautiful skeleton, but the brain led the masses in not quite the direction they should have done.

The question which now stands before us, is about the brain of a proletariat party, about the direction of its policy. And therefore, however instructive c[om.] Geller's lecture was, I consider that he circumvented the basic questions, which one must never do. We are in a situation, comrades, that our interest in the Chinese revolution is not a nationally limited Chinese interest, my interest as a former Rector of a Chinese university, or your interest, and that is the interest of every Communist, who is involved somehow or other with the world situation and understands that there on the Yangzi our fates will also be decided.

(*Appl*[*ause*].)

ARAN. F. 350. Op. 2. D. 150. Ll. 45–65.
Typescript, copy unsigned.

CHAPTER 9

A New Stage in the Chinese Revolution: From Chiang Kai-shek to Wang Jingwei

2 July 1927, G.E. Evdokimov, G.E. Zinoviev, K.B. Radek, G.I. Safarov, L.D. Trotsky

Recent events in China have such an enormous significance for the fate of the Chinese revolution and the entire Comintern that we consider it our duty to turn to you again, despite everything. The Eighth plenum of the Comintern, at the insistence of Stalin-Bukharin, endorsed and left in force the old conciliationist policy line on China.[1] It has not taken a single step forward in practical questions. A verification has not been slow in following. The Plenum had hardly dispersed when events in Changsha turned all the questions over again, having revealed that the Plenum directives were not up to strength for even a few weeks. It is always this way with the opportunist line in the epoch of the revolution.

The coup in Changsha, accompanied by a bloody massacre of workers and peasants, the events in the so-called 'left' Guomindang in Wuhan, the development of events at the front, the agreement of Feng Yuxiang, and apparently also Wang Jingwei with Chiang Kai-shek,[2] all this again entirely and completely justified and confirmed the analysis and those prognoses which we made in a series of documents, addressed to the CC of our Party and to the Comintern. Unfortunately (for all this is playing out on the spine of the Chinese working class), the lessons earned at the price of monstrous mistakes and losses will cost the Comintern unbearably dear.

---

1 Heading on the document: 'V Pravdu' (To Pravda).
2 On 19–21 June 1927 in Xuzhou Feng Yuxiang held a meeting with Chiang Kai-shek and other members of the Nanjing leadership. The result of these meetings was a joint declaration of Chiang and Feng. Feng Yuxiang telegraphed to Wuhan, demanding that the left-Guomindang government conduct joint activities with Chiang Kai-shek. Soon after this Feng conducted a purge of Communists in his army. As regards Wang Jingwei, he organised an anti-Communist coup just three weeks later.

1   What Happened in China after Chiang Kai-shek's Coup

As *Pravda* reports on 16 June 1927 the counter-revolutionary coup in Changsha already began on the *19 May*,³ meanwhile the Party and Comintern first knew of this highly important event from the *Pravda* telegram only a month later. A telegram reporting that Feng Yuxiang had been elected a member of the Nanjing government assembly (i.e. Chiang Kai-shek's white guard government), was received promptly by TASS on *24 May* (see TASS bulletin 'Not for the press.') This has become a system. If you can't hide, then at least you can procrastinate, 'having prepared' the Party for a new attack on the opposition. Isn't it clear that a *correct* policy would not require such methods?

What happened in Changsha and other places in Hunan province?

The union of officers of the local garrison, with several hundred soldiers, undoubtedly with the knowledge and authority of Tang Shengzhi, i.e. the current boss of the 'left' Guomindang, set out on 19 May to *disarm* worker and peasant pickets. On 21 May sections of the 35th Corps surrounded and dispersed worker and peasant unions. 500 men were disarmed and 12 killed. Around 20 leaders of the unions were arrested. At news of the coup peasants of the adjoining districts quickly organised detachments and went into the attack on Changsha. However, they were badly armed and they were fought off by machine gun fire and retreated. The commander of the 3rd National corps⁴ decided to withdraw the 'leftists' from the army. On his order the Communist political commissars were sent away from the corps. As is well known, the coup in Changsha was preceded by the rising of Xia Douyin and still earlier of Yang Sen. This is a brief chronicle of events. The 'union of officers' emerges as the principal active personality in them. There is no soviet of soldiers' deputies. Is that because it is not possible? No, but because the opposition has demanded it for a long time, but Stalin-Bukharin forbade it.

Tang Shengzhi followed Chiang Kai-shek almost photographically. Beginning with oaths and declarations, he finishes by shooting the workers and peasants and seizing power. It is absolutely obvious that he [Tang] disguised the preparations for a counter-revolutionary coup in the rear of his own 'leftist' government, whose whole policy facilitated his simple work, with his Northern 'Expedition'.⁵ On 10 May (TASS) a member of the Wuhan government Sun Fo

---

3   On 16 June 1927, *Pravda* carried a communication about the first clashes of the workers' pickets with the troops of Xu Kexiang.
4   This refers to Zhu Peide, who organised an anti-Communist coup in Nanchang, capital of the province of Jiangxi.
5   The National-Revolutionary Army of the GMD under the command of Tang Shengzhi con-

swore (in an interview) to his belief in the non-capitalist road of Chinese development.[6] The reactionary Sun Fo is surely not a pessimist, not one of little faith! On 19 May, nine days later, the first conflicts of the Wuhan troops with the pickets in Changsha began. Tang Shengzhi, de facto commander of the National-Revolutionary Army, endorsed the coup in Changsha. In the meantime, Feng Yuxiang did his deal with Chiang Kai-shek.

TASS communicates from Shanghai on the 11 June: 'The peasant movement in Wuhan has partly overflowed in a series of *excesses* (!). Thus there was observed a ban on the export of rice from some districts, the seizure of shops, the looting of property'. Which one of the Avksentievs wrote this reactionary stupid vileness? How could that have been published? Didn't they notice? The ability not to observe such pearls is no accident: it is implicit in Martynov's approach.

Another correspondent of the very same TASS, having added to his despatch as much butter and sugar as possible, was still obliged to recognise that on the territory of the Wuhan government 'in the steps of military victories a new reaction is on the march, depriving the peasantry and the working class of fundamental conquests of the revolution. This is taking place not only in the South and the South-West, but also in Henan province and in parts of Hubei province' (*Pravda*, 16 June). Events are developing almost automatically. The Stalin-Bukharin tactics are not going to stop them.

On 17 February 1927, *Pravda* printed an 'order of the Military Council of the Wuhan government' in which it states: 'It is possible, that inexperienced (!) peasant organisations have committed mistakes here and there. The Executive Committee of the Guomindang has already taken measures and *has forbidden the confiscation of the property* of soldiers (!) and *commanders*. Breaches of this directive will be punished with all possible severity. Widespread lying rumours, calculated to provoke antagonism between the peasants and the troops, will be punished with equal severity'. Everything is turning out as though by a timetable.

The Chinese Kerenskys are misleading the people, telling tall stories, as though someone is confiscating the land of *soldiers*. In actual fact it is a question of the land of the landowners, of generals, officers etc. Precisely the same deceit was practised in Russia by the Shingarevs and Avksentievs. But *Pravda* passes this on as sterling currency. The Minister of Agriculture, the Communist Tan Pingshan is silent. But Stalin-Bukharin are slagging off the opposition.

---

tinued the Northern Expedition to the end of April 1927. At the beginning of June it seized Henan province.

6 See Sun 1927.

The Wuhan officer corps consists of bourgeoisie and landowners. The government decrees, evidently with the agreement of the Communist Party, not to touch the land of the officers. The army is turned into an organisation for mutual insurance for the landowners. A revolutionary party should at least seize on a diametrically opposed course: for the confiscation of officers' land, for the involvement in this matter not just of the peasants, but also of the soldiers, for the expulsion of the landowning officer caste from the army, for the extermination of counter-revolutionary commanders. This or that military 'expedition' could hold back from that, but on the other hand an expedition of the oppressed against the oppressors would only gain immeasurably. To liberate and also unite China, i.e. to complete the national revolution is possible not by means of Tang Shengzhi's Northern Expedition in alliance with Chiang Kai-shek, but by means of a revolutionary expedition of workers and peasants against the oppressors, both domestic and foreign.

11   The Left Guomindang and the Agrarian Revolution

Who personifies the Chinese revolution? What is the national movement after Chiang Kai-shek's coup? These are the questions which we must decide first of all after Chiang Kai-shek's coup. Stalin-Bukharin have embarked on the point of view that the 'left' Guomindang should leave Chiang Kai-shek in peace for a while and send their troops North. 'It's better to let Chiang Kai-shek flounder about in the Shanghai district for a while, getting mixed up with the imperialists', said c[om.] Stalin at the Sun Yat-sen University on 13 May. (J. Stalin, *Revoliutsiia v Kitae i oshibki oppozitsii*, p. 17).[7] What happened in fact? It is not Chiang Kai-shek who is 'floundering', it is Stalin with his mistaken policy who is 'floundering'. Chiang Kai-shek has won himself time, has to a significant degree disrupted and has in fact won over to his side the C[E]C of the 'left' Guomindang and its 'revolutionary' generals, has made direct contact with the Japanese and English imperialists. At the same time, we have continued to console ourselves with the idea that 'our', 'revolutionary' generals are attacking the North, we have deceived ourselves and others, in forgetting that in fact these *are not ours* and *are not revolutionary* generals, and that in Beijing they are going *just because of an agreement with the English and Japanese and for a 'peaceful' division of power with Chiang Kai-shek and maybe with Zhang Zuolin also.*

---

7   The authors are mistaken over the page number. See Stalin 1927, p. 19.

The TASS telegram of 3 June provides the unexpectedly happy news that *'The National government has decided to struggle energetically with Nanjing'*.[8] Doubtless this is a *new deceit*. Whoever wants to struggle with Nanjing, would first of all settle with the Nanjingites in their own ranks.

If an expedition to Shanghai and Nanjing was good enough for Chiang Kai-shek to provide himself time for the preparation of the coup, if for Tang Sheng-zhi an expedition into Henan province is sufficient for a coup in the rear of a 'leftist' government, then the declaration of an expedition on Nanjing must obviously serve for the masking of the ultimate approaching coup: the expulsion or shooting of the unfortunate Communist ministers and the CC of the Communist Party in Hankou.

Events are developing in that direction practically automatically. The Toho Agency (TASS, 31 May) informs us that the 'compromise between both groups (Wuhan and Chiang Kai-shek), is apparently gradually taking on real forms'.[9] The 'nub' of the situation lies in the complete impossibility of countering the real strength of the revolution to the forces of the counter-revolution: the whole previous policy led to the fact that the *workers and peasants are not armed*.

The events in Changsha are no incident, as the 'optimists' of the falsifying workshop again attempt to represent the situation. The coup has embraced the whole of Hunan province and part of Hubei province. In the course of a series of weeks a white terror rages. Hunan is the centre of the peasant movement. Changsha is the centre of the revolution with its one-and-a-half million population. The attack was well aimed. Bukharin-Stalin's policy won't turn it away.

The essence of the matter is that the second-class Wuhan Chiang Kai-sheks 'departed' and 'betrayed', as we are used to say. The essence of the matter is in the *betrayal and bankruptcy of the 'left' Guomindang and of Wuhan*.

In order to smear the pessimists, *Pravda* of the 18 June informs us from Hankou: 'Despite the white terror reigning in Changsha and other important points in Hunan province, the peasant uprisings are growing and many districts are, as before, in the hands of the peasants. An armed struggle is going on in the villages between the peasants and the gentry'.

The more massive the dimensions of the movement, the clearer becomes the criminal opportunism of the leadership. The power in the hands of the peasants is after all directed against the Wuhan government. That means that Wang Jingwei will break up these peasants again and again. What sort of advice do we

---

8 *Pravda*, 10 June 1927.
9 This information was not published in the Soviet press.

give them? Maybe to broaden the movement? Fraternise with the urban workers? Found their own soviets? Or do we say to the peasants that after chasing away the landowners and seizing power, that they are jumping over a Stalinist 'step' in the most impermissible way? The opportunist leadership drives the revolutionary movement into a cul-de-sac at every new step. The peasantry can seize land, expel the landowner, kill the loan shark and the local governor. But it is not convenient for the scattered peasantry to strengthen the agrarian revolution by methods of statecraft. For that they need leadership. The Guomindang (the real existing Guomindang, and not Stalin's 'idea' of the Guomindang) will not give such leadership. The Guomindang fights against the agrarian movement. And if the proletarian avant guarde does not head the countryside, the peasant uprising will inevitably be smashed, as it has always been over many centuries.

For a long time the opposition has been bombarded with accusations of 'underestimating' the Wuhan centre as the hearth of the peasant revolution? And what happened in fact? Instead of a broadening of the base in the worker and peasant masses, the left Guomindang, and together with it, its weak-willed appendix the Communists, set out on the road of the 'Northern Expedition', that is, they went to meet the militarist generals, striving to broaden their military influence, so as draw a military sum under the territorial expansion of the revolution. The authentic mass people's revolution found itself once again, as with Chiang Kai-shek, a 'rear', limited by the needs of the front and subjected to it. The new Northern Expedition cannot be dictated by revolutionary objectives, for the further the troops advance to the North, the more they lose contact with the revolutionary base, the stronger the commanding generals become, the easier becomes the task of Feng Yuxiang, Tang Shengzhi and the other militarists to find a common language with Chiang Kai-shek, so as to do a deal with him and the imperialists. The real mechanism of events has been concealed from our Party. On the other hand, all the counter-revolutionary and conciliationist chaos, born in the new Northern Expedition, has bombarded the head of the Party as though it were an 'unforeseen' catastrophe. But meanwhile there is nothing unexpected in these events: you reap what you sow.

The 'leftist' Wang Jingwei helped Chiang Kai-shek to convene the Nanjing conference.[10] In an appeal signed by him and Chen Duxiu, he reassured the workers on the eve of a massacre.[11] Wang Jingwei clearly played a two-faced

---

10 The authors are mistaken. Wang Jingwei did not help Chiang Kai-shek.
11 The joint declaration of Wang Jingwei and Chen Duxiu was published in the Shanghai newspaper *Shishi xinbao* ('New paper of facts') on 5 April 1927. In the declaration it stated that China was not ready for a dictatorship of the proletariat.

role before the disarming of the Shanghai workers by Chiang Kai-shek's gangs. In agreement with the 'leftist' Wang Jingwei, the General Secretary of the Chin[ese] Communist Party wrote several days before the Shanghai massacre that 'the Chinese Communist Party loves peace and order, like all the other parties'.

The Policy of the 'left' Guomindang after Chiang Kai-shek's coup exposed itself, so to speak, as a continuation of the policy of the right Guomindang, applicable to a new phase in the revolutionary struggle on the territory of the southern armies. The 'left' Hankou government, exactly the same as the right-wing one, threw itself around the neck of a counter-revolutionary general, hiring out to him the flag of the Guomindang, dishonoured in Shanghai. It did not allow the workers and peasants to approach this flag, leaving them only to submit, to follow after the general. In the C[E]C of the 'left' Guomindang and in the 'leftist' Wuhan government only openly right-wing leaders remained, sympathisers with Chiang Kai-shek, like T.V. Soong [Song Ziwen], Sun Fo, Eugene Chen and others. They gave military matters to Feng Yuxiang and Tang Shengzhi, of which the former cannot be distinguished from Chiang Kai-shek, while the latter is only distinguished by being even more reactionary. No re-organisation of the armed forces has taken place. The conference in Zhengzhou[12] presented exactly the same picture as the previous conferences, at which Chiang Kai-shek was boss. The 'unity' of the C[E]C of the 'left' Guomindang, its 'discipline' was entirely directed *against the working class, against the agrarian revolution*. Its policies, comprising hypocritical zigzags, entirely serves the development of the forces of the counter-revolution, which climbs out from under the Guomindang umbrella, as it ripens. But the CC of the Chinese Communist Party plays the role of appendage to the C[E]C of the 'left' Guomindang, the role of hostage in the camp of the left-Guomindang bourgeoisie. The peasant movement, like the revolutionary workers' movement, remains dispersed, driven back, hunted into the underground, by the furious enmity of the army and state institutions, while the Communist Party impotently waits.

Already on 24 April news came from Hankou that the 'leftist' government bound the workers to compulsory arbitration in all cases of conflict between the workers and the entrepreneurs in foreign enterprises.[13] In fact this amounted to a general ban on strikes, for it is impossible to distinguish the foreign enterprises neatly from the undertakings of Chinese capitalists.

---

12   The secret conference in Zhengzhou took place on the 10 June 1927. Feng Yuxiang along with Wang Jingwei and other members of the Wuhan government took part. Wang Jingwei agreed to concede Henan province to the control of Feng Yuxiang.
13   This information was not published in the Soviet press.

After the coup in Changsha, the C[E]C of the 'left' Guomindang published a communiqué about the measures it had taken in connection with the situation in Hunan province:

1) temporarily (!) preserve the present (i.e. counter-revolutionary) Hunan government for the duration of the conduct of further investigations:
2) re-organise the organisations of the Guomindang and the worker-peasant organisations in Hunan province (It is not difficult to guess in which direction 'to re-organise');
3) All troops in Hunan province are to be subordinated to General Zhou Liang, to his special delegate, who is commanded in Hunan province by the C[E]C of the Guomindang;
4) All armed conflicts between the worker-peasant alliances, on the one hand, and the military on the other, must be stopped (i.e. the workers and peasants must remain silent when they are shot). Otherwise the most severe measures will be taken, in accordance with revolutionary discipline;
5) A special commission is nominated for the determination of the question of the situation in Hunan.[14]

Pravda calls these decisions 'half-hearted'. In reality they are *treacherous*. But *Pravda* has only mild words for the Guomindang reactionaries while it expends its entire vocabulary of insults on the opposition. In reality, the 'decisions' of the left Guomindang are copied from those written by the Kerenskys and the Shingarevs, when they covered up the Kornilovs and the Alekseevs.[15]

On 8 June 1927, *Pravda* printed a 'ceremonial' declaration by the vilest reactionary Tang Shengzhi, a major landowner, which repeated virtually word for word Chiang Kai-shek's famous oath of loyalty to the 'principles of Sun Yat-sen', to the Guomindang, to the alliance with the Communists etc. And once again

---

14 This declaration was made on 3 June 1927. A special commission consisted of five persons, including ministers of the Wuhan government Tan Pingshan (chairman) and Chen Gongbo. Borodin also took part in their work. At the beginning of June, members of the commission left for Changsha, however Xu Kexiang allowed only Chen Gongbo to enter the city. The other members of the committee were obliged to return to Wuhan.

15 This refers to the uncertainty, from the Bolshevik point of view, of the policy of the Provisional Government at the time of General Kornilov's mutiny against it in August 1917. General Alekseev sympathized with the mutiny even though he arrested Kornilov at Kerensky's request on 1 September.

the central organ of our Party reprinted Tang Shengzhi's vulgar conjuring tricks at face value, without a single word of criticism. Where *Pravda* shows critical acumen, then it only acts to suppress it! On 9 May 1927 in reply to Zinoviev's theses, c[om.] Stalin wrote:

> In practice two Guomindangs *have been created*, a revolutionary (!) *Guomindang* and a counter-revolutionary Guomindang, a Guomindang in Wuhan and a Guomindang in Nanjing ... The Guomindang has split into two Guomindangs and the developing agrarian revolution has thereby *received* (!) a centre in the form of the revolutionary (!!) Guomindang in Wuhan, cleansed (!!) of the right-wing Guomindangists.[16]

C[om.] Stalin said approximately the same thing at the recently concluded session of the Executive Committee of the Comintern.[17]

Under pressure from Stalin-Bukharin, it was decided by the Executive Committee of the Comintern to decisively reject the slogan of soviets for Wuhan. Stalin has even demonstrated to the Executive Committee of the Comintern that in 1905, we had *'only' two Soviets*: in St. Petersburg and Moscow (see *Bolshevik*, No. 10, p. 22). This is however a naked lie. In 1905, we had at least 30 soviets, including in such cities as Ivanovo-Voznesensk, Odessa, Nikolaev, Kostroma, Saratov, Orekhovo-Zuevo, Ekaterinburg, the Nadezhdinskii and Votkinskii factories, Kiev, Ekaterinoslav, Yuzovka, Rostov-on-Don, Taganrog, Baku, Krasnoyarsk, Irkustsk, Chita, Libava, Revel etc. (*1905*, edited by Pokrovskii).[18] C[om.] Stalin does not even stop before the appalling distortion of the factual history of 1905, just so long as he achieves the rejection of the slogan of soviets for Wuhan, where the agrarian revolution has already 'received' a ready-made centre in the shape of Tang Shengzhi and Wang Jingwei.

But confirmation was not long in coming. The Stalinist 'centre of the revolution' ('our' Guomindang) followed in its military section (and that is now its only real force) in the steps of 'our' Chiang Kai-shek, i.e. with the right Guomindang.

From a Marxist-Leninist point of view this fact is entirely explicable. But not from a Bukharinite.

In the left Guomindang, says c[om.] Bukharin, the petty bourgeoisie, the workers, the peasants and several small groups of the bourgeois-radical intel-

---

16 The authors are mistaken about the dating of the Stalinist reply, which was actually prepared on 7 May 1927; see RGASPI, F.17, Op.2, D.284, L.31.
17 This refers to the Eighth ECCI Plenum.
18 See Pokrovskii 1925, p. 12.

ligentsia have remained, with several *hangers-on* (!) playing a relatively *secondary* (!) role, of the *radical (?!) layers of the upper bourgeoisie*. (See 'Doklad ob itogakh plenuma IKKI', *Pravda*, 18 June [1927]) [emphasised by the authors].

So it turns out that there are still 'radical (!) layers of the upper bourgeoisie', who are ready to content themselves with the role of hangers on, so as to give pleasure to Bukharin. The essence, however, lies in the fact that these 'radicals' are playing not a 'secondary' role, but a *principal* role. Bukharin even now thinks that the *'left GMD is under the influence (?) of the Communist Party'*. The facts insistently assert the contrary: it is not Tan Pingshan and Chen Duxiu who influence Sun Fo, T.V. Soong [Song Ziwen], and Eugene Chen, but the opposite. Therefore, Wang Jingwei goes along (has already gone) along not with Tan Pingshan, but with Sun Fo, Tang Shengzhi and even Chiang Kaishek.

The Chinese Party of 'all classes' again *revealed itself* in deed *as a bourgeois* party with hangers on from the Communists. Bukharin again showed that he does not distinguish the tail from the head.

The test arrived and demonstrated that the Stalin-Bukharin policy in China systematically weakened the positions of the Communist Party and the proletariat, subjected its interests to the interests of the upper bourgeoisie and the conciliationist leadership of the petty bourgeoisie. The Chinese bourgeoisie on the other hand has conducted a precise class policy: while masking itself with the false policy of Moscow, it used the workers and peasants up to the point when it was *convenient to it*. The bourgeoisie shot them down when it perceived the threat of a growing popular revolution. 1848 repeated itself and still repeats itself, as if neither 1905, nor 1917, nor Marxist theory, nor the experience of Bolshevism had ever existed.

III   The Chin[ese] Communist Party and the 'Left' Guomindang

The agrarian revolution is pushing from below, striving to lay down a road. But from 'above' the 'left' Hankou government frantically opposes it. What should the Communist Party do at this time? Upon taking up his responsibilities, the Communist Minister of Agriculture Tan Pingshan developed a programme that can only be called a programme of craven ingratiation before the bourgeoisie, tied by blood with the officials, the landowners and the moneylenders. The General Secretary of the Chinese Communist Party, c[om.] Chen Duxiu declared, at the Congress of the Communist Party in Hankou (on 3 May), that 'for the confiscation of major and medium agricultural property it is necessary to await (!) the further development of military activities'.[19] An equivalent subordination of the interests and tasks of the peasant revolution to 'military considerations' of the counter-revolutionary generals was also in fact created as a precondition for Chiang Kai-shek's coup, and then for the coup in Changsha, for Xia Douyin's rising, as for all the future counter-revolutionary coups. It goes without saying that our central organ printed Chen Duxiu's speech without a single word of criticism. It was a different matter with the opposition, which had warned of the consequences in good time.

At the time when 'a new (Hankou) reaction is marching in the footsteps of the military victories', after Xia Douyin's rising and the coup in Changsha, the CC of the Chin[ese] Communist Party addressed the C[E]C of the Guomindang in a courteously appealing letter. The Chinese Bolsheviks (?) urge the Chinese SR-Kadets in this letter that the time has come to reconsider 'how to realise some (?) measures (!) of agrarian reform(!)'. These are the same days when the Guomindang *reformers* are shooting at, or do not prevent the shooting of peasants accomplishing the agrarian *revolution*!

'The future of the revolution', the letter urges, 'depends on decisive measures on the part of the Guomindang'. Not on the risings of the peasants, not from the leadership on the part of the workers and the Communist Party itself, but on the C[E]C of the Guomindang, which has taken up a counter-revolutionary position in relation to the peasant uprising.

The CC of the Communist Party does not demand the arming of the workers in the letter, but merely a return of weapons seized from them. It also proposes such a 'revolutionary demand' as to 'immediately nominate a punishment expedition for the suppression of uprisings and to give *Tang Shengzhi full powers* (!!) to send troops for the suppression of counter-revolutionaries'. To send Tang Shengzhi to pacify counter-revolutionaries in Changsha is equal to sending Gen[eral] Alekseev to 'pacify' Kornilov, as Kerensky did in his time.

The letter from the CC of the Communist Party complains about the fact that feudal and military elements have taken up arms against the peasantry, and that this 'provoked vacillations in leading revolutionary circles (i.e. in the C[E]C of the Guomindang itself)'. From this it drew the unctuous conclusion: 'the army must support the Guomindang and the National government in the realisation of agrarian reform'. Instead of a revolution, a reform. Will a National government that does not want it accomplish it? The army under the leadership of reactionary officers who smash up the peasants is supposed to support reform. Tang Shengzhi, their father and protector is supposed to pacify them.

---

19   *Pravda*, 15 May 1927.

What then followed this persuasive letter? A telegram in *Pravda* of 16 June reports in a highly diplomatic style: 'According to information it is considered impossible for the C[E]C of the Guomindang to accept the proposals made by the Communist Party'.

And even if it had accepted them verbally, would that have altered the situation by a hair's breadth in reality? The C[E]C of the Guomindang knows that it is the 'sole' leading revolutionary party; that the Communist Party is subordinate to it; that the Comintern will not permit even the thought of the departure of the Communist Party from the Guomindang; that a Communist Party fated to subordination to a bourgeoisie party cannot be independent, is not accustomed to showing independence and is therefore incapable of it. The mutual relations of the Guomindang and the Chin[ese] Communist Party, are as expressed in the letter from the CC of the Communist Party quoted, but where is the answer?[20] Who is concealing the answer? They remain the most reliable guarantor of the victory of the bourgeoisie over the rebellious masses of workers and peasants. Who does not want to understand this even now is not worth the time of day for a Bolshevik.

How disruptively the 'Martynov' line affects the Chin[ese] Communist Party is visible from the declaration of the Chin[ese] Communist Party of 23 May 1927 (printed in the Hankou paper *Minguo ribao* of 23 May of th[is] y[ear]). At the time when Chiang Kai-shek, the generals and officers under the umbrella of the 'left' leaders of the Guomindang are shooting down rebellious peasant, the Chinese Communist (!?) Party writes literally as follows:

> The thoughtless (!) actions of the peasants, especially in Hunan, provoked discontent amongst the troops. Xia Douyin wants to use this discontent among the troops so as to achieve his counter-revolutionary aims. The programme of the Chin[ese] Communist Party in relation to the petty landowners is already clear. *Thoughtless actions of the peasants totally contradict the actions of the Communist Party* ... The Communist Party is against the confiscation of petty landowners' land and *the lands of the commanders* ... If the petty landowners accept with satisfaction (!) the certain norms of lease holding, defended by the National government, then they will not be against the peasant movement that is a foundation of the revolution ... Only if the peasant masses unite around the National

---

20 The reply by the CEC of the GMD to the 'Open Letter' of the CC of the CCP was published on 15 June 1927. The leaders of the left Guomindang demanded from the CCP that they put a stop to the worker-peasant movement; see Roy 1929, pp. 200–01.

government [which is shooting them down. *Auth*.], can the foundations of the revolution be strengthened.[21]

This is the language of Mensheviks, not Bolsheviks. The language of the liberdans[22] and of the Avksentievs, who defended the Kerensky government against 'thoughtless' actions by the peasants, whom the Kornilovite generals had suppressed. A false policy does not only bring defeat, it disrupts the only weapon of victory, the Communist Party.

That is the picture as a whole. Despite the brutal April destruction of workers' organisations, the peasants rose, though deprived of leadership. The Hankou military suppressed them. The Hankou government, in vacillating, supported the military. The Communist Party begged the Kerensky-Kornilov bloc to take up an agrarian reform at last. Martynov rationalises all this theoretically. Stalin and Bukharin slag off the opposition for its lack of faith in the left Guomindang. Not a single Marxist conclusion in relation to China. All sorts of 'organisational consequences' in relation to the opposition!

Several comrades (especially, for example, Voroshilov) explain the entire defeat and the false conclusions of the Chinese proletariat by a 'lack of revolutionary cadres'. As if revolutionary cadres can educate themselves in the face of a non-revolutionary political line! The Bolshevik line was the precondition of the education of Bolshevik cadres, with whose growth it became deeper and stronger.

If only the Communist Party, relying on its modest young cadres, had conducted an independent struggle for influence over the proletariat from its first steps, had directed strikes, had conquered a leading role in the trade unions; if only it had mercilessly exposed the claims of the bourgeoisie for leadership of the national revolution and had fearlessly intervened in all signs of discontent by the oppressed masses of the city and countryside; if only it had tirelessly explained to the proletarian avant guarde its great historical mission in relation to its class and to all the oppressed masses of the Chinese people, the Communist Party, in conditions of the rapid unfolding of the revolution, would not only have created stronger revolutionary cadres on the basis of this work, but would have conquered incomparably greater influence over the proletariat and the peasantry.

---

21   The authors are mistaken in their dating of the document. It refers to the CCP statement on the attitude to the petty bourgeoisie, published on 18 May 1927; see ibid. pp. 129–32.
22   This refers to the leaders of the Russian Mensheviks, M.I. Liber and F.I. Dan.

∴

But was it possible to struggle simultaneously against Chiang Kai-shek and Zhang Zuolin, having the military warships of the imperialists on our flank (at sea and in the rear – on the Yangzi)? This is how the numerous disciples of the Matrynov school now pose the question. After all, they say, they've got regular armies with capable commanders, high-class technology, open assistance from the sea. What have we got?

We've got the revolution. Under Martynov's garbage everything is forgotten. The lessons of all the great revolutions, and especially the revolution of 1917 have been laid to rest. The enemy has generals, therefore, we must also adapt the 'revolutionary' armies to the generals. One must not harm the generals, otherwise the army will dissolve, and it will be impossible to complete the 'Northern Expedition'. Better not to harm Chiang Kai-shek, to get around him sideways, otherwise 'our' generals may cling to him. No need to provoke the landowners, bankers, property owners in general against ourselves too much, we must 'manoeuvre' with them (i.e. cling tightly to their tail), otherwise the foreign ships will smash up Wuhan and the other revolutionary centres in twenty minutes. That is the true background to the whole present Martynovite line.

This line is fatal. The revolution will never win along that path. To point the difficulties out with your finger and then 'get around' them, means to get around the revolution, i.e. to renounce the very thing that comprises our strength.

Fearlessly conducted, the worker-peasant revolution is the most terrifying of our artillery, which simultaneously strikes at Chiang Kai-shek, and also Zhang Zuolin, and at the imperialists, and in the first place, at Tang Shengzhi and at the whole entire pack of Wuhan reactionaries. The destruction of the landowners and the counter-revolutionary officers in Wuhan, a brave, decisive, massive destruction would exert a direct, infectious influence on the troops of Chiang Kai-shek and Zhang Zuolin and on the peasant masses in the rear of these troops. We can only create a real revolutionary army from the bowels of the agrarian revolution, conducted under the leadership of the workers. Neither Tang Shengzhi, nor Chiang Kai-shek, nor Zhang Zuolin can create strong and resilient military forces in these conditions, never mind all their technology and surplus of officers. The foreign imperialists in their turn will turn out to be weaker and more powerless, the less we play with their internal agents, persuading these latter, tying ourselves to them and leaving them, at the same time, with an empty battlefield. The soldiers and sailors of imperialism will be subjected to the influence of the Chinese revolution all the more strongly:

the deeper that latter excites the masses, the more mercilessly it settles with the enemies of the people.

'But aren't we against the agrarian revolution?' (the voice of Bukharin etc.)

Whoever makes revolution hand in hand, at first with Chiang Kai-shek, then with Tang Shengzhi, and now with Wang Jingwei; whoever subjects the Communist Party at first to Chiang Kai-shek, then Wang Jingwei; whoever rejects soviets as impermissible in the rear of the armies of the generals, he will show himself as an opponent in deed of the agrarian revolution or, at least, as the greatest obstacle on its path.

IV Once More on the Nature of the Chinese Revolution

What was the point of departure for the opportunist, Stalin-Bukharin line in the Chinese question?

The starting point consisted in the idea that the essence of the Chinese revolution, an essence which the opposition supposedly misunderstands, consists in a struggle against foreign imperialism. From that elementary and incontrovertible proposition, however, a radically false conclusion was drawn. The pressure of foreign imperialism, according to the thoughts of Stalin-Bukharin-Martynov, supposedly consolidates the various classes in China, creating the possibility of a 'bloc of four classes' and even of a special non-capitalist government of the four classes (Martynov, Rudzutak, Kalinin, etc.)

As a direct consequence of the fact that internal political contradictions are (supposedly) softened by imperialism and are subjected to the needs of the struggle with 'external' aggression, in actual fact imperialism sharpens the basic antagonisms. A miracle has occurred: Martynov's old theory, which collapsed so shamefully in 1905–1917, turned out to be cut according to a Chinese pattern. Martynov was pleased to discover that he had always been a Bolshevik in essence, just not for Russia but for China.

In so far as the workers' and peasants' (agrarian) questions are concerned, then Martynov recommended in *Kommunisticheskii Internatsional* to decide all social conflicts by means of arbitration commissions in the interests of the economy of the national revolutionary forces. This right-Menshevik idiocy has been given out as Bolshevism with impunity.

The 'classic' course of the old bourgeois revolutions consisted in the fact that the proletariat helped the bourgeoisie into its stirrups, and then the bourgeoisie got rid of it with a kick in its head. Precisely that was and still remains the course of the Chinese revolution. So as to provide this classic course, correspondingly new methods were needed to cope with the new epoch. In this an enormous help to the bourgeoisie was the theory and practice of Stalin-Bukharin-Martynov, which unintentionally helped and still helps the bourgeoisie to conceal the class character of its leading party. The Chin[ese] Communist Party was obliged and is still obliged to submit to the Guomindang, right up to a renunciation on its part of a criticism of Sunyatsenism, i.e. a petty bourgeois theory, which became a powerful counter-revolutionary weapon in the hands of the upper bourgeoisie against the proletariat.

The class struggle has become an abstraction. The inevitability of the betrayal of the bourgeoisie in the national revolution was converted into an empty phrase, having no relation to the politics carried out in practice. With all its forces and means they helped the Chinese bourgeoisie to subject the proletariat to themselves, to use them to mount the stirrups and then to kick the proletariat away with its boots. But when that happened, Bukharin had the pathetic courage to declare: 'We always foresaw that'.[23] Don't slander yourself. You never foresaw anything of the kind! You hoped that by means of intrigue you would 'use' the bourgeoisie and throw it out like a 'squeezed lemon'.[24] Your real foresight was smashed to smithereens in the class struggle.

To attempt to justify the Martynov policy by reference to the *Northern Expedition*,[25] which was supposed to awaken the workers and peasants, meant simply to emphasise their insolvency, to underline their bankruptcy. Capitalist development in general 'awakens' the masses, from which however, a bloc with the bourgeoisie does not follow for a revolutionary. The classic bourgeois revolutions always awakened the masses, so as later to destroy and enslave them. A Communist, who after the Shanghai and Canton destruction of the workers continues to pride himself on the fact that Chiang Kai-shek's expedition awakens the masses, is acting like an apologist of the bourgeoisie, and not like a proletarian revolutionary. We helped the bourgeoisie – in their way, i.e. in a bourgeois way – to awaken the masses; but we did nothing to prevent them from smashing them up. Such was the role of the petty bourgeois radicals in all the classic bourgeois revolutions. Martynovism is petty bourgeois radicalism, simply belated and rotten, for we live in an imperialist epoch.

---

23   See Bukharin 1927e.
24   Stalin spoke about the idea that one must 'exploit to the bottom' the right Guomindang and 'later throw them away, like a squeezed lemon' on 5 April 1927 at the meeting of the Moscow Party activists in the Hall of Columns of the House of Unions. See Stalin 2001 [1927], p. 156.
25   It is relevant to note that Stalin and Bukharin throughout – i.e. until the great victories – spoke out determinedly against the Northern Expedition, but when the victories began, they forgot by whom and where the expedition was leading. *Authors' note.*

The agrarian movement, which suffered less directly from Chiang Kai-shek's coup, which in the first place smashed up the proletariat, and continued to grow, despite the Stalinist theory of the superiority of national over class coinage and of the 'bloc of four classes', and despite Martynov's generous promise to resolve the agrarian question by means of arbitration commissions after the joint victory over Imperialism. It is now time at last to convince ourselves and recognise the facts: yes, the peasants are conducting a civil war against the landowners, the officials, the officers and the moneylenders, without concerning themselves with whether the gentlemen in the Guomindang have given their permission.

After its hopeless vacillations here and there the opportunist Stalin-Bukharin line draws a sharp zigzag around this issue: the struggle with imperialism is disappearing; the struggle with feudalism is taking its place. The agrarian movement is proclaimed the basic content of the revolution. The entire 'particularity' of the Chinese revolution is thereby immediately scattered to dust. The new zigzag signals panic and confusion. But as we now see, this zigzag is well within the bounds of opportunism.

In his speech at the Executive Committee of the Comintern c[om.] Stalin hopelessly tries to mock the fact that the opposition sees in the customs problem one of the basic tasks of the Chinese revolution. This is, don't you see, a bureaucratic point of view. It would be interesting to know what Stalin himself understands by the yoke of imperialism in China? It is very similar to that which he uses in ready-made phrases, without thinking through their content.

Under the protection of military power imperialism introduces itself into China in the form of finished goods, capital invested in railways and industry, in the form of banks, it celebrates money lending, in the form of state loans, guaranteeing the extortion of a massive part of the national income. The basis of the semi-colonial situation of China is its economic backwardness. In marching into China, foreign capital pushes the development of the country forward to a certain extent. In the period of the imperialist war [The First World War] major results were achieved in this direction, which even make possible the very question of the hegemony of the proletariat in the national revolution. But foreign capital influences the Chinese economy unequally. Pushing one branch forward at a certain moment, it consciously freezes others. In squeezing out massive profits, it holds back internal capital accumulation. In general imperialism is now freezing and disorganising the development of the productive forces of China, using for that purpose a combination of economic, political and military measures. The customs administration is the most important weapon in their hands. The semi-colonial character of China is expressed not least by the fact that the Chinese people or its possessing classes are deprived of the opportunity to protect the industrial development of their country by means of corresponding customs duties, without which a backward country cannot break out from its backwardness. It is a matter of the *economic sovereignty* of China. Through low customs duties, fixed from abroad, world capitalism forcibly opens China's door for its wares. The independent industrial development of the country is frozen, artisan trades are ruined. This leads, in turn, to the rotting of the agricultural rear, to the rise of surplus population and poverty. The most malevolent expression of this rotting is universal money lending. Exactly on this basis, slave-serf relationships are maintained, re-emerge and grow again. The sources of them for the majority of the country are not remnants of feudalism in the strict sense, but economic relationships, born of the military support for capitalist development. The customs problem is fundamental in the line of struggle with imperialism. Stalin understood none of this. He takes the customs question as a departmental-bureaucratic question and not as a question of the mutual relations of the Chinese economy with world imperialism. 'Down with the unequal treaties!' Above all, this means down with the customs dependence of China.

Does this mean that we reject or minimise the significance of the agrarian question? Such absurd accusations have even got into the resolution of the Leningrad Party activists. This example, to tell the truth, bears witness more than anything, to what murderous confusion the present system of permanent discussion introduces, which is led exclusively against absentees and those condemned to silence. In actual fact, it was the opposition which contraposed the slogan of the economic offensive of the proletariat and the agrarian revolution of the peasantry to Martynov's theory of a bloc of classes and the prescription of arbitration commissions. Only through an agrarian revolution can we attract the peasantry in reality to the struggle with imperialism, to bind the peasants to the workers and create a genuinely revolutionary army.

The massive role occupied by the money-lending-enslaving, serf and semi-serf relationships in the Chinese countryside, between the country and the city, but also in part even in the city, is absolutely beyond dispute. But mercantile-capitalist relations already play an indisputably leading role in China. This is exactly what creates the possibility of the leading role of the proletariat in all revolutions, including agrarian ones. Bukharin needs the dominance of 'feudalism' so as to minimise the possible political role of the proletariat and justify its present subordination to the bourgeoisie or petty bourgeois conciliators.

In connection with what has been said, it is completely untrue to summarise the entire Chinese revolution as an agrarian coup. The most radical reshuffle of agrarian relations (they must carry this out whatever may happen) will not, however, provide a way out from the economic cul-de-sac without the general development of productive forces, i.e. without industrialisation. But the development of industry is inconceivable without China's customs independence. This question has no less importance for the Chinese economy, as is our monopoly of foreign trade for us. Whatever path the development of productive forces takes in China in the immediate epoch, capitalist or socialist, China must in any case re-conquer its economic sovereignty. In this consists the *economic* content of the struggle with imperialism, i.e. of the national revolution. Without the conquest of power by the proletariat and the peasantry this question will not be resolved any more than the agrarian question.

Having made a detour from an abstract understanding of the 'national' revolution to an equally abstract understanding of the agrarian, Stalin and Bukharin have preserved their opportunist standpoint in full. The national revolution must be led by the Guomindang under Chiang Kai-shek's command. The 'left' Guomindang headed by Wang Jingwei must stand at the head of the agrarian revolution. Soviets are rejected by Stalin precisely because the *left Guomindang is entirely sufficient (supposedly) for the agrarian revolution.* This new prognosis turned out to be as deep and true as the old prognosis concerning Chiang Kai-shek.

The ban on forming soviets is motivated by the necessity of preserving a bloc with the petty bourgeoisie, represented by the Guomindang. Here a falsity long since exposed and condemned by the Bolsheviks is repeated: under the petty bourgeoisie, with whom it is vital to march in close alliance, they understood not just the most oppressed and revolutionary masses of the urban and rural poor but the conciliationist bourgeois-intelligentsia elite, who played the same role in the Chinese revolution that the SR-Menshevik committees in the army, *Vikzhel*[26] and the whole Kerensky business did with us. Precisely because the agrarian revolution has developed widely, *the enslaving bloc of the Communist Party with the Wang Jingwei Guomindang is the main obstacle on the road to the alliance of workers and peasants.*

The desertion by the bourgeoisie is stained with the blood of the Shanghai workers. After that it became, at least in words, an officially recognised fact. If so, then in any event only the proletariat together with the toilers and the exploited masses of the countryside and cities can be bearers of the revolution now. In the meantime, they tell us that the foundation of worker-peasant sovi-

---

26 Vikzhel – the All-Russian Executive Committee of the Union of Railway Workers from August 1917 to January 1918. On 29 October 1917 they threatened a general strike of railway workers, demanded from the Bolsheviks the creation of a 'monocoloured socialist government' of representatives of all the parties represented in the soviets and also the replacement of Lenin as chairman of the Sovnarkom (Council of People's Commissars).

ets would signify a rising against the Wuhan government, and that precisely therefore it is impermissible to create soviets. Which class is represented by the Wuhan government? Stalin and Bukharin do not reply to this question. A serious class analysis cannot be reconciled with opportunism in any case. Stalin and Bukharin are obliged to support the disguise of the Wuhan government as not a bourgeois, but also as not a worker-peasant government, as earlier they supported the disguise of the Canton government as a supra-class one (the non-capitalist government of four classes.)

What does the Wuhan government represent in a social sense? What is its relation to the basic classes of China? Despite all the 'peculiarity' of Chinese conditions, it is impossible not to see that the Wuhan government is a Chinese Kerenskism. The relation of Wang Jingwei to Chiang Kai-shek is approximately the same as the relation of Kerensky to Miliukov-Kornilov. Miliukov directly represented the bourgeoisie. Kerensky was its temporary salesman in a difficult historical moment. The conciliatonist, *Vikzhel*, the elite of the petty bourgeoisie, represented for a certain period and at the cost of secondary concessions to the masses the only possible bourgeois power, which could save the main thing: the property rights of the property-owners. The struggle between Wang Jingwei and Chiang Kai-shek has *basically* the same character as the conflict of Kerensky with Kornilov; these episodes, however stormy they may be, do not alter the fact that both groups fulfil the very same counter-revolutionary mission by means of a division of labour.

In what does the role of a revolutionary party consist under these circumstances? In counterposing not just the proletariat, but also the revolutionary petty bourgeois lower classes to the conciliationist elites, carrying out the role of a government of the propertied classes. To inculcate in the masses trust in the Chinese Kerensky is a clear crime against the revolution. All those are guilty of this crime who assert that the 'left' Guomindang is capable of carrying out an agrarian revolution, as though the workers and peasants do not need soviets. This is Stalin's position. Com. Stalin has transferred all their illusions concerning the 'utilisation' of the bourgeoisie and of the 'squeezed lemon' from the master to the salesman, from the bourgeoisie to its conciliationist assistants.

Does that mean that it is necessary to overthrow the Wuhan government immediately? Stalin-Bukharin object. For them there exist either the immediately overthrow of the Wuhan government or the assumption of full responsibility for it before the masses, participation in it, a renunciation of soviets in favour of a Wang Jingwei government, the renunciation of an independent party in favour of a Wang Jingwei Guomindang. Amongst other things a genuinely independent policy should consist in the mobilisation of the working masses under their own flag *against* a bourgeois-conciliationist government and thereby to *prepare* its overthrow. To support Wang Jingwei before the masses and at the same time to insure his revolutionary reputation with the jingle 'we know in advance that he will betray us' means to show in the clearest fashion what a Menshevik degeneration of Marxism looks like. We must prepare the destruction of the bourgeoisie and its conciliationist salesmen by the workers and peasants *in deed*. Bukharin is just preparing for himself a verbal loophole for the event of a new massacre of the workers and peasants by the Wuhan salesmen of the bourgeoisie, as foretold by the opposition. In the new phase these are the irreconcilable lines: Leninist or Martynovite.

v The Communist Party Must Leave the Guomindang!

The present leadership of the Party has succeeded in releasing a thick cloud and making a knot of confusions and contradictions around the question of the relations of the Communist Party with the Guomindang. The relationship to the Guomindang is fundamentally the relationship of proletarian democracy towards the bourgeoisie. All comparisons either with the soviets (Bukharin), or with a revolutionary parliament (Stalin) simply serve to paint over this question, in which there is no lack of clarity at all for a Marxist-Leninist.

It is therefore vital to summarise here the result of the arguments about the question of departure and of the term of the departure from the Guomindang, about relations with the Guomindang elite and with its 'rank and file'.

That the entry of Communists into the Guomindang was permissible only for a time, for a short time! while a genuine mass workers' movement emerged from elements of the workers' movement, – and only on specific conditions, – this was clear to us from the very beginning. The most important of these conditions were *the genuine independence of the Chin[ese] Communist Party, of its uncensored Marxist programme, independent organisational and agitational work.*

The admittance of the Guomindang into the Comintern (in the capacity of a 'sympathising' party) was also permissible only as a short-term political manoeuvre, with the intention of posing the leadership of the Guomindang with a series of hard and fast conditions, to expose its anti-revolutionary nature, to remove it from the Comintern in the eyes of the Chinese working masses and to transfer the whole force of our support to the Chinese Communist Party for the development and consolidation of its alliance with the Guomindang rank and file, and with the peasantry in general. The presence at first of the Chiang Kai-shek, and now of the Wang Jingwei Guomindang in the Comintern, signifies nothing other than our direct assistance to the Chinese bourgeoisie in the disguise of its party, against the workers and peasants.

As far as we are concerned, immediately after the development of mass workers' movements in 1925, we posed the question of the conduct of the continued presence of the Chin[ese] Communist Party in the Guomindang, concerning the absence of its organisational independence and of consequential revolutionary slogans. We did not for a moment trust the Guomindang elite. It became ever clearer that it was a bourgeois elite, from which we *needed to break*, while approaching the 'rank and file', i.e. the workers and peasants, who had entered the Guomindang. Already at the end of 1925, one of us demanded an organisational split with the Guomindang elite, replacing a bloc inside the Guomindang with a bloc outside it. Others proposed the slogan of the arming of the workers immediately after the Shanghai strike of 1925, and at the beginning of 1926, of a series of conditions to the C[E]C of the Guomindang, which would inevitably have led to the organisational liberation of the Communist Party, to its breach with the GMD elite and to an approach to its 'rank and file'. The Chin[ese] Communist Party itself at the plenum of its C[E]C (June 1926) came to the same conclusion, to a departure from the Guomindang. But Stalin and Bukharin cancelled their resolution.

Suffering defeat after defeat, Stalin & Co. maximised their hounding of us. They did not print our articles. Our declarations (for example c[om.] Zinoviev's declaration on the Chinese question at the July 1926 plenum of the CC) were not attached to the record. And at the same time, they misrepresented our position, as though we wanted a split not just with the bourgeois GMD elite, but also with its worker-peasant 'rank and file', the isolation of the Communist Party, its departure from the revolution etc. This crude falsification has continued for more than eighteen months. They told the workers that we were enemies of the Chinese revolution and of the Chinese revolutionary armies, that we were against the unity of the revolutionary ranks of China, that we were liquidationists. We did not even have the opportunity to call a lie a lie, and a slander a slander.

After Chiang Kai-shek's coup, it became even more necessary to break with the C[E]C of the Guomindang, opposing to it a tight alliance of an independent Chin[ese] Communist Party with the worker-peasant 'rank and file' of the Guomindang. We again proposed a *series of conditions*, which arose from the situation which had come about and with whose real observation we still might just have allowed the Chin[ese] Communist Party to remain in the

Guomindang for a short time, so as to gather our forces and attract the maximum number of workers and peasants behind us.

It became clear to us that the 'left' conciliators, like Wang Jingwei, would also betray the workers and peasants. So we proposed such conditions for the further presence of the Communists in the Wuhan 'left' Guomindang, as to be able to expose these 'left-wing' leaders with the minimum delay.

Instead of taking that path, Stalin, Bukharin & Co. Continued to hold our real views under lock and key, insisting at the same time that we wanted to break not just with Wang Jingwei's clique, but with the left Guomindang minded workers and peasants. They continued to represent Wang Jingwei himself & Co., including Feng Yuxiang, as reliable revolutionaries, allies of the proletariat etc.

We turned out to be correct right along the whole line. Stalin & Co., objectively turned out to be assistants of Feng Yuxiang, Tang Shengzhi and Wang Jingwei.

To remain in a continuing relationship with the Wang Jingwei C[E]C now means to remain openly in alliance with the shooters of the workers and peasants. *We must immediately withdraw from the 'left' Guomindang and its treacherous government.* We must liberate the Chin[ese] Communist Party from the bourgeois path, guaranteeing its independence and helping it enter an honest coalition with the worker-peasant 'rank and file' of the Guomindang against the Kerensky-Kornilovite elite.

The assertion that an exit from the Guomindang means the 'isolation' of the Communist Party is direct mockery of the theory and the experience of Bolshevism. The Communist Party is now isolated from the agrarian movement. The main isolator is the C[E]C of the Guomindang. Just in 1917 we mocked when they frightened us with isolation from the SR-Menshevik army committees, from *Vikzhel* and from all the rest of the Russian Wang Jingweism. By supporting Chiang Kai-shek we substantially isolated ourselves from the Shanghai workers. By our support of Wang Jingwei, we are now isolating ourselves from the peasants. Only an independent Communist Party can head the trade unions and *dominate the agrarian movement* through the workers. There is no need to chase after an alien blue flag, rather unfurl our own red one. Only the independent struggle of the Communist Party for the workers and peasants will introduce a *really revolutionary differentiation in the Guomindang*, will drive in a wedge of a split between the present ruling conciliationists, salesmen of the possessing classes and the revolutionaries, the rank and file, those capable of an alliance with the Communist Party. This alliance should be realised by methods of open political agreement in the view of the masses. The foundation of the alliance, the longer it lasts, should become the soviets of workers', peasants' and soldiers' deputies.

The exit from the Guomindang signifies the immediate resignation of the Communists from the Wuhan government and the exposure of the latter's counter-revolutionary role in relation to the agrarian movement and workers' organisations.

The withdrawal of the Chin[ese] Communist Party means the exclusion of the Guomindang from membership of the Comintern, in view of the non-revolutionary worker-peasant, but bourgeois-conciliationist character of the entire policy of the Guomindang.

The departure from the Guomindang means a condemnation of the line of Chen Duxiu and Tan Pingshan in the agrarian and other questions of the revolution, since the line of the comrades named it nothing other than a political expression of the dependence of the Communist Party on the Guomindang.

∴

In Lenin's time the Comintern proclaimed the slogan 'Proletarians of all countries and oppressed peoples of the earth, unite!' In Stalin-Bukharin's time this slogan was turned into a weapon for subordinating the colonial proletariat to the 'national' bourgeoisie.

In Lenin's time the Comintern attracted the popular-revolutionary organisations (the Congress of the peoples of the East in Baku,[27] the Congress of the peoples of the Far East in Moscow),[28] setting itself the aim of raising up and *leading after the working class* the peasant (and all the petty bourgeois) organisations of the oppressed peoples. In Stalin-Bukharin's time the Comintern in practice handed over the leading role to the Central [Executive] Committee of the Guomindang, in other words to the bourgeois-oppressor elite of the oppressed people.

They taught the Chin[ese] Communist Party itself not the lessons of Leninism but the lessons of Martynovism. This explains the fact that its elite now conducts a Menshevik policy.

---

27 This refers to the Second All-Russian Congress of Communist organisations of the peoples of the East, which took place in Baku in November 1919.

28 The Congress of the peoples of the Far East opened in Moscow on 21 January 1922, but the concluding session took place in Petrograd on 2 February. 131 delegates with voting rights and seventeen with no voting rights attended, mainly representatives of China, Korea, India, Japan, Java and Mongolia. Delegates of the peoples of the Soviet East (Buryats, Kalmyks, Yakuts) took part in its work. The Chinese delegation was one of the most numerous: it included more than forty persons.

We struggled for the independence of the Chin[ese] Communist Party. Stalin slandered us. We can only accuse ourselves of one thing: we did not struggle hard enough against Stalin's fatal line in China. The Stalinist regime within the Party prevented such a struggle, distorted our position, slandered us to the workers of the USSR, China and the whole Comintern. Our guilt lies merely in the fact that we did not succeed in preventing Stalin and Bukharin from turning the elite of the Chin[ese] Communist Party into an appendix to the bourgeois elite of the Guomindang.

The independence of the Communist Party is the principal, the most elementary condition of success, the principal revolutionary lever of the Chinese working class. Stalin and Bukharin betrayed this fundamental principle of Leninism. Thereby they undertook political responsibility for all the consequences.

So as to justify the mistakes they have made, for which there is no justification, Stalin-Bukharin must now minimise the degree of capitalist development in China, reduce the economic and political role of the proletariat, exaggerate the omnipotence of imperialism (its soldiers, its canons), – in a word, demonstrate that the Chinese revolution in general cannot achieve victory – by reason of the inadequacy of resilient cadres, by reason of the absence of experienced revolutionary commanders etc., etc. This always finishes with opportunism: to justify their half-heartedness, flabbiness and cowardice, it exaggerates the forces of the enemy and minimises the forces of the revolution.

VI To Save the Revolution It Is Vital to Drastically Alter the Entire Course of the Leadership

The Chinese revolution is defeated, but not conquered. Its tasks remain unresolved, its forces are not exhausted. The Chinese revolution has enormous reserves: the young working class, pouring its strength into the leading role of new technology and capitalist methods of production; the multi-million pauperised peasantry, forced by their entire situation to rise in struggle as a more and more consolidated mass. The working class and peasantry of China, given its readiness for self-sacrifice, with its ability to renounce everything and rise in greater and greater masses against the imperialists and their own bourgeoisie, landowners and moneylenders, represent an invincible force, with correct leadership.

On the road to victory the main obstacle is the present Stalino-Bukharinite line of leadership. We must finish with it whatever happens.

What is required for that?

1) Communist members of the Wuhan government must immediately leave it. To remain as Communists in the Wuhan government now means to bear

responsibility for the shooting of workers and peasants. Their resignation must assume a sharply demonstrative form. We must accuse the Wuhan government of crimes against the workers and peasants, building a widespread agitational campaign in the country on the basis of that accusation.

2) The Communist Party leaves the Guomindang, develops an entirely independent revolutionary line, creates its own Communist press, organises – legally wherever possible, illegally where not – scourges the traitors of the 'left' Guomindang and criticises the vacillators. In raising the 'rank and file' (workers and peasants) against the treacherous and shaky leaders of the Guomindang, the Chin[ese] Communist Party explains that it is willing to enter into a tight alliance for mutual defence on the basis of a revolutionary programme with the genuinely revolutionary part of the left-Guomindang masses.

3) The Communist International immediately excludes the 'left' Guomindang from the list of 'sympathising' parties. It openly explains that the international proletarian avant-garde can have nothing in common with those who bear responsibility for the shooting of workers and peasants in Changsha and for scores of other crimes.

4) The Chin[ese] Communist Party immediately begins, wherever possible, the open organisation of soviets of workers, peasants, soldiers and the urban poor. Concentrating around itself the revolutionary masses, the soviets direct their struggle against the counter-revolution, against the authorities favouring the landowners, the counter-revolutionary officers and the bourgeoisie. In all the soviets, Communist factions are organised aspiring to leadership of the soviets.

5) The Communist Party begins systematic oral and printed propaganda of the idea of soviets on the entire territory of China.

6) The Communist Party not only propagandises the arming of the workers and the poor peasantry, but undertakes wherever possible practical steps for the seizure of arms with the aim of creating armed detachments of workers and peasants.

7) The Communist Party develops determinedly and on a widespread basis propaganda among the soldiers of the Wuhan armies, the armies of their allies and their enemies, calling on the soldiers to settle with counter-revolutionaries and to support the peasant struggle for land. The soldiers should be granted an allotment of land from a state fund. The soldiers' soviets must nominate revolutionary commissars, controlling the activities of the officers.

8) The unifying slogan is the struggle for a revolutionary-democratic dictatorship of the proletariat and the peasantry, achieved through the soviets and directed against the foreign imperialists, the Chinese bourgeoisie, the landowners, the militarists, moneylenders, gentry.

9) The Comintern immediately addresses the Chin[ese] Communist Party in an open letter in the spirit of the proposals indicated. The Comintern must demand of the Chin[ese] Communist Party a decisive break with those Communists who remain in alliance with the present Wuhan government or who oppose the struggle with it.

10) The Politburo immediately cancels the ban on the discussion of the questions of the Chinese revolution in our press. The very idea that in the present situation one can suppress questions that are matters of life or death for the entire Comintern is utter madness.

∴

The time has come to recognise honestly, in a Bolshevik spirit, the massive errors made. It is time to stop speaking the official phrases that we foresaw everything and that the betrayal of our 'allies' simply strengthens us. No one believes this 'optimistic' nonsense. The Chinese revolution is in great danger. The Chinese revolution may win given correct tactics. The Chinese revolution *may* conquer, if the line is drastically corrected.

A hellish amount of time has been wasted. The workers and peasants of China are not obliged to rise up twice or three times in a row, just to force us finally to break up the reactionary blocs and correct the mistakes committed. In a sketchy form[29] freezing the revolution from above, one can reduce it to nothing for a long period. We must not waste another hour. The fundamental level of revolutionary activity is the Party. We must liberate the Chinese Communist Party organisationally, so that it can stand on its own feet, can feel independence and responsibility and can take its own course in the face of the masses. It is time, finally, to stop chasing after – in the Stalin-Bukharin style – the stained flag of the Guomindang, and criminally tarnishing our own flag!

The direct responsibility for the further development of events now rests on us. The decisions which we propose to adopt have a huge practical significance not only from the point of view of the development of the Chinese revolution, but also from the point of view of the defence of our country. Experience has shown that the false Stalin-Bukharin line holds back the revolutionary struggle, strengthens the enemy and inevitably leads *to a sharpening* [*of the possibility*] *of an attack by British imperialism on the USSR*. Unfolding the Chinese revolution along Bolshevik lines will show even the 'thick-headed' that it is more difficult to struggle with two revolutions than with one.

---

29 Thus in the text. It should read: 'systematically'.

This is not a matter of the naked prestige of the leading group in the CC here, but about the fate of the revolution at a most difficult historical turning point. As far as 'prestige' is concerned then it can be guaranteed seriously by one thing only: the correct revolutionary line.

2 July 1927
Evdokimov, Zinoviev, Radek, Safarov, Trotsky

Afterword: Bukharin Continues to Mislead the Chinese Communists

In his latest article 'The present moment in the Chinese revolution' (*Pravda* 30 June 1927) c[om.] Bukharin demonstrates that he does not want to and is not capable of learning.[30] By the whole cast of his thoughts Bukharin is not a Marxist but a scholastic commentator.[31] He always adapts his scholastic schemes to the policies of others, like Kautsky with the 'practicians'. In the first phase of the revolution he creates schemes *to the left* of the facts. Now he creates them *to the right*. It seems to him at the same time that he is correcting his previous mistakes. In actual fact Bukharin has never got so hopelessly lost as now.

Let's look in note form at the confusion of Bukharin's evaluation of the 'present moment of the Chinese revolution'.

1) 'The remarkable originality of the situation consists in the fact that three socio-class camps ... have three organised state centres' (Mukden [Shenyang], Nanjing, Wuhan). 'The remarkable originality' consists merely in Bukharin's historical ignorance: in almost all great revolutions there were three state centres. In our country the monarchists replaced the Committee of the Constituent Assembly on the Eastern front.[32] Alongside Wrangel's monarchist-

---

30 This section was written by Trotsky.
31 This refers to Lenin's description of Bukharin from his 'Letter to the Congress': 'His [Bukharin's] theoretical views can only with the greatest caution be considered fully Marxist, for there is something scholastic in them (he never studied, and, I think, never fully understood dialectics)' (Lenin 1964 [1923], p. 345).
32 The Eastern front was organised on 13 June 1918 by a decision of the CPC. In June–November 1918, the Red Army on the Eastern front conducted battles with the White Czechs, and also with the army loyal to the Committee of members of the Constituent Assembly. This committee was organised on 8 June 1918 in Samara on the Volga from members of the Constituent Assembly dispersed by the Bolsheviks on 6 (19) January 1918. From September 1918 it called itself the Congress of members of the Constituent Assembly. The majority of both, the committee and the congress, was composed of SRs. On 19 November 1918, members of the congress were arrested by the monarchist Admiral Kolchak, who had

landowning centre, petty bourgeois Georgia also fought against us, etc. Once upon a time Bukharin knew these phenomena in a Leninist light. They look new in the light of Martynovism so he failed to recognise them.

2) 'Class distinction gave birth to Chiang Kai-shek. Chiang Kai-shek 'gave birth to' Feng [Yuxiang]. Feng, in all likelihood will give birth in his turn to the betrayal of other generals, creating *the greatest possible* threat to Wuhan'. This evangelical word is really brilliant. Chiang Kai-shek 'gave birth to' Feng [Yuxiang]. But who was then the midwife? You haven't guessed? Take a look in the mirror sweetheart.

3) 'The strength of this *liberal-counter-revolutionary camp* (Chiang Kai-shek, Feng [Yuxiang]) consists in the first place of the numerical superiority of its armed military detachments; secondly in its political position ...'.

And who exactly assisted the liberal counter-revolutionaries and guaranteed their military superiority? Who demanded of the Communists their actual subordination to Chiang Kai-shek? Who supported and advertised Feng Yuxiang? Who forbade the Communists to call for the organisation of soldiers' soviets?

The matter of the 'political position' of the liberal counter-revolutionaries is even worse. They employ (Bukharin half teaches, half complains) 'the traditions of the national-liberation struggle'. Once more: who armed the liberals with these traditions? Who constructed especially for them the abstract theory of a national revolution, accomplished with the assistance of a bloc of four classes? Who made a fetish out of the flag of Chiang Kai-shek's Guomindang? Who prevented, or rather forbade the Communists, from the first phases of the revolution from laying down their own Bolshevik traditions? Bukharin should look in the mirror again and not reproach himself that he has a crooked face.

4) The feudal camp, according to Bukharin, is Zhang Zuolin. The bourgeois-liberal camp is Chiang Kai-shek and Feng [Yuxiang] (the latter rapidly stricken out of the 'worker-peasant' camp). The third camp is Wuhan. The class nature of the third camp has not been determined. This is simply 'our' camp, with some slight imperfections. As the Guomindang is 'almost' a soviet, so Wuhan is 'almost' a worker-peasant government. 'It's true', the Wuhan generals betray and will continue to betray, but, o sweet hope, messenger of the heavens! 'Wang Jingwei holds on more firmly than the others'. Everything is in order: The 'firm man' of the third day was Chiang Kai-shek, yesterday it was Feng Yuxiang, today Wang Jingwei. Sufficient unto the day is the evil thereof.[33] The bill for Wang

---

occupied Samara, and in December the majority of them were executed. From that time right up to January 1920, the Red Army on the Eastern front fought against Kolchak and his White army.

33   Matthew 6:34.

Jingwei's affairs will be presented only tomorrow. Then maybe even this upstart will rapidly be exiled to the camp of the liberal counter-revolution. All the more so as this has been once and for all 'foreseen' in Bukharin's resolutions, which are good for everything, except for helping the Chinese proletariat achieve victory.

5) The third camp is Wuhan. But, alas, 'this camp ... does not possess sufficiently reliable military forces. *Its army is hiding*'. But after all the entire Stalin-Bukharin policy was directed to not frightening the generals and not driving them into the camp of reaction. It was after all Stalin who considered it inappropriate to create soviets 'in the rear of the revolutionary armies'. The whole revolution was declared to be just the rear of the generals.

The whole authority of Moscow was directed to not permitting soviets. And there are actually no soviets. But, alas! There are therefore no revolutionary armies. There are armies under the control of counter-revolutionaries, who smash up the workers and peasants. By all our policy we prevented the foundation of worker-peasant armed forces. The representatives of the Comintern in China, in full agreement with the spirit of Martynov and Dan, preached: the minimum arming of the workers! Long live arbitration commissions between the classes! Borodin demanded the transfer of dictatorial powers to Chiang Kai-shek (see c[om.] Chen Duxiu's article). And at a meeting of the Moscow activists on 5 April 1927, Stalin reassured them: The cause is in good hands, Borodin is awake! That's how the Bukharin line 'gave birth to' Wuhan, which was good in all respects, though it turned out to be a weapon of the counter-revolution.

6) '*If only*', Bukharin mourns, 'the Comintern directives had been carried out in practice; *if only* the matter of the agrarian revolution had not been frozen; *if only* the arming of the workers and peasants had been energetically conducted; *if only* reliable military units had been concentrated; *if only* there had been a political line that was clear to the masses; *if only* they had carried out as they should have the directive on the democratisation of the Guomindang etc., etc. *then* the situation would not be as dangerous for Wuhan'. If only, if only ... this is no parody but word for word from Bukharin's article. If Bukharin would move a little closer to Marxism, then he would not have slid down into an opinion of such scandalous farcicality. Who are they who failed to carry out the holy directives? And why did they not fulfil them? And why were they issued? The famed Stalinist formula: the line is correct but the actors are bad. Isn't Bukharin now trying to offload onto the Chinese Communist Party responsibility for his own blindness? Nonsense! *The correctness of the line consists in the fact that it finds its own actors*. Bukharin's directives were not carried out for the simple reason that they were good for nothing, and in so far as they were carried out, they did not serve the class for whom they were designed.

Under the leadership of Chiang Kai-shek it was impossible to 'concentrate reliable military units', but Stalin-Bukharin demanded the preservation of Chiang Kai-shek's leadership. And who was supposed to concentrate them? The Communist Party? But we forced it to subordinate itself to the discipline of Chiang Kai-shek. To arm reliable units would only have been possible in open struggle, yesterday with Chiang Kai-shek, today with Tang Shengzhi. For this it was necessary to appeal not to the bloc of four classes, but to the social hatred of the masses against the elites. It is necessary to purge the army and the administration from the bottom up, through the soldiers, through the peasants, through the workers, without fearing 'anarchy' and 'excesses'. It is necessary to exterminate the turncoat generals on the spot; to seize the land of the landowning officers and redistribute it to the soldiers, to unite the soldiers with the peasants and workers through soviets of deputies.

'If only the political line had been clear to the masses', Bukharin laments. There you are: alas, if only it had been clearer in the head of the current composer of lines of all sorts.

'If only the directive on the democratisation of the Guomindang had been carried out as it should have been' (!). Why wasn't this remarkable directive carried out after all? They didn't want to? They couldn't? And to whom, in fact was the directive addressed? Sing, little angel, don't be shy! First of all they persuaded Chiang Kai-shek 'to get a worker image', now they persuade the 'reliable' Wang Jingwei. The Chinese Communist Party has been specially assigned to the task of persuading the Guomindang elites. That's what it has been trained for. In a word, the masses rise, the Guomindang shoots them, the Communist Party persuades, Bukharin writes directives which are not carried out.

7) After all that has been done (and everything possible has been done to undermine the revolution) Bukharin has now thought up the following fundamental slogans. 'Workers and peasants, rely only on your own forces! Don't trust the generals and officers! Organise your own armed detachments!'

This all sounds very decisive. The pity lies in the fact that Bukharin does not take his own decisiveness seriously. And he is essentially correct not to do so. So that the workers and peasants rely only on their own forces, these forces must first be organised: there need to be soviets of workers and peasants' deputies. There needs to be a Party, which could direct the foundation of soviets in outright struggle with the Wuhan counter-revolutionaries. There needs to be an independent Communist Party.

'Don't trust the generals and officers!' This sounds frightfully brave. But it is the generals who command, these generals have rifles and canons. Or do the soldiers have rifles and canons? Then it is necessary to oppose the solder to the generals. Then it is necessary to expel and exterminate the reactionary generals.

But who could do this? The rebellious peasants, hand in hand with the soldiers, under the leadership of the workers. But for that soviets of workers, peasants and soldiers' deputies are needed.

'Organise your own armed detachments!' Excellent advice. But how can the unfortunate Chinese actors carry out this Bukharinite directive? Under the leadership of the Wuhan government? With the permission of the 'reliable' Wang Jingwei? Or, maybe, in direct struggle against them? But for the leadership of this struggle, even for a mere call to arms, an independent Communist Party is needed.

8) Meanwhile, Bukharin accepts not a single one of these elementary, fundamental, unconditional, incontrovertible demands. For him the Communist Party is not in reality a class party of the proletariat, struggling for a democratic worker-peasant dictatorship in the bourgeois revolution. For him the Communist Party was and remains just the left wing of the Guomindang, which the liberal bourgeois directed yesterday, and today is ruled by the conciliationist salesmen of the bourgeoisie. Even now, when class relations have been written in blood, Bukharin stands for the subordination of the Communist Party to the Guomindang, which means politically the continued subordination of the proletariat to the bourgeoisie, and thereby to the final liquidation of the worker-peasant revolution.

9) But it is 'well-known that the influence of the Communist Party in the Guomindang grows continuously'. But something else is also well-known: under Bukharin's leadership the Chinese Communist Party, as its entire policy in fundamental problems demonstrates, has developed into a petty bourgeois-conciliationist party just like the left wing of the Guomindang and no more (see the declaration quoted above against 'thoughtless actions' of the peasants). The growth of the influence of this left wing testifies to the strength of pressure from the masses. But in order to organise this pressure for victory, we must lead the Communist Party from out of the Guomindang, we must purge the Communist Party of Guomindang spirit, we must liberate it from its false leadership, we must help it to drastically re-orientate itself on the basis of a Bolshevik line. The more we postpone this work of salvation, the sicker the forms it will take and the more belated it will seem in relation to the needs of the Chinese revolution.

10) But don't the Wuhan rightists also demand the expulsion of the Communists from the Guomindang? Should we really – Bukharin uses irony – go 'to meet this platform'? I'm ashamed to have to reply to such a mouldy Menshevik argument. The Guomindang rightists want to expel the Communists so as to destroy them. But the Communists should liberate themselves from the grip of the Guomindang so as to conquer the masses and destroy their enemies. This is a struggle decided not for life, but for death. Hindenburg is undoubtedly

Leon Trotsky (*second from left in the second raw*) and Karl Radek (*next to him*)
RGASPI, F.326, OP.1, D.4 L.1

against a bloc of bourgeois parties with the Social Democrats and even more against the amalgamation of the Social Democrats with the Communists. Does it flow from this that we are for the unification with the Social Democrats and a bloc with the bourgeois parties? And to defend the necessity of the continued political enslavement of a workers' party by the party of the bourgeoisie with such vulgarities in Lenin's Party ten years after October! We must burn this shameful line out of the Comintern with molten steel.

∴

A turning point in the fate of the Chinese revolution will begin when the genuine Chinese revolutionaries understand the ruinous nature of Bukharin's directives. It is the clear obligation of the Opposition to assist the Chinese revolutionaries and the Comintern as a whole in this matter.

2 July 1927
Evdokimov, Zinoviev, Radek, Safarov, Trotsky

RGASPI. F. 17. Op. 71. D. 88. Ll. 1–29.
Typescript, copy

APPENDIX 1

Letter from L.D. Trotsky to K.B. Radek
26 June 1926

To com. Radek.

It seems to me that it would be appropriate to develop in more detail two thoughts concerning the Guomindang, which you have expressed in passing.[1]

In the first place, the necessity of the existence of a united democratic-Communist party is based on the national yoke. It is easy to accept this argument, because it liberates people from the necessity of thinking through the mechanism of national oppression. This mechanism is a class mechanism through and through.

There was a time when the European Social Democrats told us that we should 'all' work together against autocracy. Now we are inclined to repeat the very same thing to the Chinese. Of course, there is a difference between foreign imperialism and tsarism, but it is not necessary to exaggerate this difference. Naturally, it would be important to demonstrate the concrete mechanism of the imperialist yoke in relation to the various classes in China.

Secondly, it seems to me that it would be vital to show more sharply that China's political evolution has entered a new phase, which commences from the independent emergence of their workers' organisations, the trade unions.

The organisational cohabitation of the Guomindang and the Communist Party was correct and progressive for a specific epoch, which, however, has now come to an end. In the current epoch, this cohabitation has become more and more of an obstacle. The chronological moment is not put forward in the theses.

The remainder seems correct to me.

L. Trotsky
26 June 1926
RGASPI. F. 326. Op. 2. D. 10. Ll. 108–108 reverse.
Typescript, original. Signature – facsimile.

---

[1] This letter was written in response to Radek's theses 'On the Fundamentals of Communist Policy in China'; see document 1 in this collection.

APPENDIX 2

Letter from L.D. Trotsky to K.B. Radek

14 May 1927

1) Underestimation of imperialism.[1] It would be appropriate to add that in general the pressure of imperialism does not soften class contradictions, but sharpens them, on the one hand, and on the other, that the struggle against all powerful imperialism demands the greatest possible revolutionary concentration of the worker and peasant masses, and this is indissolubly connected with their struggle for the alteration of their own economic and political situation in the country.

2) To page 38. The question of the seizure of concessions, railways, banks, etc. I think that there is a lot of vagueness and disagreement even among us in the presentation of this question. The revolution is being conducted against foreign imperialism. Its main outposts are the banks, the railways, industrial concessions, etc. The seizure of these enterprises is conceivable in a double sense: as the socialist expropriation of the expropriators, and as a military-revolutionary measure in the struggle with imperialism. In China, this means the second and not the first sense. Here the difference is very substantial, not just in the sense of the historical perspective, but also in the sense of a direct revolutionary policy. From the point of view of the socialist revolution, such seizures must be guided by the economic importance of the enterprise, its role in the economy. From the point of view of the struggle against imperialism, the 'nationality' of the enterprise may have decisive importance, its military significance, etc. The military-revolutionary seizure of foreign enterprises does not predetermine their future economic fate.

I think in general that we need to speak more accurately and carefully about socialist perspectives in China: without a victory of the proletariat of the advanced countries, there cannot be even a mention of the transition of China to socialism by its own forces, even with the assistance of the USSR. If we fail to say this, we risk feeding China with populist, maximalist[2] instead of Marxist theories.

---

1 This letter was written in response to Radek's essay 'The "Betrayal" of the National Movement by the Chinese Upper Bourgeoisie'; see document 6 in this collection. A manuscript note by Sermuks is attached to the document: 'To comrade Radek from comrade Trotsky. Sermuks. 14 May 1927'.
2 The Maximalists: the name of one of the factions of the SR Party, founded in 1904. From 1906, it was a separate party. The aim of the Maximalists was the socialisation of land and industrial undertakings, and their tactic was individual terror. The party collapsed in 1919. In 1920, one of its groups joined the RCP(b).

It is understood that if soviets are created in China and they win, the task of policy would consist in giving them the possibility to hold out as long as possible, carrying out all that 'purgative' and preliminary work, so as to later to catch the towrope of proletarian England, Germany, the USSR, etc. I say all this not for inclusion in your reply, but with the aim of 'mutual clarification'.

3) I have made minor observations in the text.

14 May 1927

∴

4) The chapter 'The Comintern warned, the Chinese Communist Party knew the danger', in my view, understates what took place. The Comintern essentially gave no warning about anything, and the Communist Party did not know the danger. Otherwise, how do we explain what happened? The so-called 'warnings' of the Comintern are cheap general points, of which one can find a surplus in Dan's *Sotsialisticheskii vestnik*. In his last article, he defends the 'desirability' of the preservation of a united front with the bourgeoisie, but also warns that a united front with the bourgeoisie is 'not eternal'. You even quote Manuilskii's speech about the danger of 'a deviation from a proletarian footing'. Even in your dictionary there are no such remarkable expressions! ... You seem to take all these considerations seriously, i.e. load them with a content which they lack. Meanwhile, in the mouths of their authors these are traditional reminiscences that carry no obligations. In my opinion, it is necessary to recast or completely omit this chapter.

It seems to me that the chapter on feudalism (the polemic with Bukharin) in its current form is capable of giving rise to misunderstandings.

5) It concludes that if there were powerful elements of serfdom in agriculture, then Bukharin's political line would be correct. However, it is not so. In Russian agrarian relations, serfdom played a major role, and tsarism was fundamentally a landowning-serf organisation. Even so, the policy of a bloc with the bourgeoisie was of no use even in 1905. Bourgeois property was intermingled with feudal property. The movement of the masses, directed in the first instance against feudal property, cut into the property of the bourgeoisie, and pushed capitalist profit into the embrace of land rent.

6) Money lending disrupts feudal economic relations, without making way for new ones. But just as a kidney infected with cancer is still a kidney, so feudalism corroded by money lending is still feudalism. That's how Bukharin answered you at that point in the argument which is devoted to feudalism.

7) In what does the bourgeois character of the revolution consist?, c[om.] Bukharin asks. You talk of the defence of private peasant property from money lending, and nothing more. This casts very little light on the question. It seems to me that we must

approach it from the point of view of the characteristics of the economy of a colonial country, in its mutual relations with the imperialist countries. The bourgeois character of the revolution consists in the first place in the removal of those complex and multiple obstacles, which overripe capitalism presents to the young capitalism of a colonial country. These hindrances support ever more backward forms of relations in a colonial country, advance to the first place the disruptive tendencies of capitalism and link them with all the remnants of the past. In such concrete, numerical and qualitative relations, remnants of feudalism are mixed with various transitional and purely capitalist forms, about which I will not bother to judge. Of course, these relations have great political significance, determining the potential scale of the agrarian revolution, as bourgeois but not as anti-bourgeois. It is entirely possible that the bourgeois character of the Chinese revolution consists to a considerable extent in the struggle with the more backward forms, which cannot themselves be consigned to the feudal or the serf. This needs concrete analysis. But Bukharin's tactics are incorrect, however the matter stands over the proportions of feudalism and capitalism. It seems to me, therefore, that you pose the fundamental struggle against the Menshevik policy in too direct a dependence on the resolution of a very important but still only partial question.

These are my notes. I am fully in agreement with all the rest.

RGASPI. F. 326. Op. 2. D. 25. Ll. 94–98.
Typescript, first part: unsigned copy, second: original.

APPENDIX 3

Facts and Documents Which Should Be Available for Verification by Every Member of the AUCP(b) and the Whole Comintern: Chronological Information

21 May 1927, G.E. Zinoviev and L.D. Trotsky

1. To members of the plenum of the ECCI.
2. Copy: to the Secretariat of the CC of the AUCP(b) – with a request to forward it to all members of the Central Committee.
3. Copy: to the Presidium of the CCC – with a request to forward it to all members of the CCC.

Respected comrades!

The Politburo of the CC of the AUCP(b) has forwarded you a declaration of 19 May 1927, containing a series of accusations against us. We consider it our duty to present you in this connection with our explanations – *of a purely factual* character. We will conduct our exposition in *chronological order*. In the appendix we offer a series of documents,[1] every one of the facts provided may, and should be, verified by you. Our exposition will be quite detailed in view of the fact that the matter is not over personal questions of any kind, but about a most important field in the life of the AUCP and of the whole Comintern, connected in the closest possible way with the fate of the Chinese revolution.

1. Our first disagreements over the Chinese question with the leading group of the present Politburo of the CC of the AUCP(b) go back to the beginning of 1926. This question already played a major role at the July (1926) plenum of the CC. We did not succeed at drawing the attention of the Party and the Comintern to the real kernel of these disagreements. Com. Zinoviev, for exa[ample], was not even permitted to attach his written declaration, dealing with disagreements on the Chinese question, to the protocol of the July plenum. At the same time, a series of unjustified accusations appeared in the press and at meetings.

2. In March 1927, c[om.] Radek succeeded in publishing his first articles in *Izvestiia* half-opening the curtain on Chinese events. In the course of a whole year not a word

---

[1] The documents attached to the 'Chronological Information' are missing.

was communicated about Chiang Kai-shek's first counter-revolutionary coup in Canton in March 1926, neither in the Party press nor in the Comintern press as a whole. Until c[om.] Radek's articles not a single word appeared about the shooting of workers and peasants by the Canton government, which had taken place in the autumn of 1926. (Nothing was said about this either in the resolution of the Seventh enlarg[ed] plenum of the ECCI.) It was impossible to print anything about the repression of workers' strikes by the Guomindang government in Canton, about the protection by this government of strike breaking organisations, hired militias of the employers, about the suppression by Canton of the peasant movement etc. All this was a forbidden zone both for the AUCP press and the press of the whole Comintern. All this was passed over in silence from an incorrectly understood tactic of a united 'nationwide front'.

In the second half of March 1927 interest in Chinese events grew exponentially and despite all the obstacles, c[om.] Radek succeeded in giving several lectures about Chinese events at the Communist Academy and several other party cells. In Moscow they started to talk about disagreements. Then even the core of the CC was obliged to react to c[om.] Radek's articles.

3. On the 4–5 April 1927 a meeting of the activists of the Moscow organisation took place in the Hall of Columns (after three postponements). At this meeting c[omrades] Bukharin and Stalin appeared as reporters and c[om.] Radek succeeded in getting a hearing. C[omrades] Bukharin and Stalin argued that the situation in China was entirely satisfactory, that Chiang Kai-shek had submitted to the plenum of the C[E]C of the Guomindang, that we are continuing to use the right Guomindang successfully, and that in general the cause is proceeding with unconditional success.

C[om.] Stalin's speech was especially noteworthy. He declared that Chiang Kai-shek stood several heads higher than Kerensky and Tsereteli, for he conducts a war against imperialism, that the right Guomindang had capitulated to the left Guomindang, that we can and must calmly continue to use the right Guomindang, as a peasant uses even a raddled nag, that these right-wing Guomindang are disorganising the rear of the northerners, that Chiang Kai-shek's declaration of submission to the Guomindang is our 'victory' etc.

Com. Stalin mocked com. Radek for 'panic', 'pessimism', 'revolutionism', 'ultra-leftism' etc.

C[om.] Bukharin's speech appeared in the press, drastically re-edited, and with some delay, only after Chiang Kai-shek's coup. C[om.] Stalin's speech has not appeared anywhere right up to now. They answer in silence our demands to give us, as members of the CC, the stenogram of c[om.] Stalin's speech so that we can get to know it. We are convinced that you members of the Executive Committee of the Comintern will not succeed in receiving it either, because it illustrates more clearly than anything the entire incorrectness of the Stalinist line on the Chinese question. Facts are obstinate things. The facts totally refute c[om.] Stalin's entire line.

At that meeting, com. Radek basically defended that line which we are defending now in the series of documents presented to you. Com. Radek warned in good time that Chiang Kai-shek is a traitor and demanded corresponding measures. His proposals were rejected. His speech was not printed. On the other hand, c[om.] Radek was removed the very day afterwards (6 April 1927) from his work in the Chinese Sun Yat-sen University.

4. On the 10 April 1927 in the Central Organ of our Party, in *Pravda*, appeared the 'notable' (notable in the sense of Herostratus) article by c[om.] A. Martynov on the notorious government of the 'bloc of four classes' etc. Before that in the ECCI organ *Kommunisticheskii Internatsional* several other such articles appeared by the same author.

Two words about c[om.] Martynov himself. A. Martynov is a former theoretician of Menshevism, who distinguished himself once and for all by the fact that he 'took' especially exotically 'to its logical conclusion' the counter-revolutionary Menshevik theory of the role of the bourgeoisie in a 'nationwide' revolution. After the introduction of NEP in 1922, c[om.] Martynov begged to enter our Party. Like all of us Lenin initially replied to this application with mockery. Later on the Politburo decided all the same to accept c[om.] Martynov into the Party, bearing in mind that c[om.] Martynov is an honest man and that his open departure from the Mensheviks would be useful to disrupt the ranks of the Mensheviks. With this aim c[om.] Martynov was then also sent into Georgia.

Now, three years after Lenin's death, Martynov disrupts not the ranks of the Mensheviks, but the ranks of the Bolsheviks. Martynov publishes with immunity in *Pravda* Menshevik filth in defence of a government of a 'bloc of four classes', an article, which is a straightforward distortion: a) of the facts of Chinese life and class struggle, b) of the theory of the state as we know it from the works of Marx and Lenin.

Until the present day, no one has been allowed to answer this purely Menshevik article by Martynov either in *Pravda*, nor in *Bolshevik*, nor at Party meetings. Martynov's article was honoured with direct praise in *Sots[ialisticheskii] vestnik* (Central Organ of the Russian Mensheviks, published in Berlin under the sponsorship of the German Social Democrats).

5. On the 13 April 1927 a plenum of the CC of the AUCP opened. At this plenum com. Zinoviev proposed theses about the Chinese revolution, *written at the beginning of April 1927 even before Chiang Kai-shek's coup*. These theses have been distributed to you. On the recommendation of the Secretariat of the CC they were not distributed to the members of the plenum of the CC of the AUCP. They were sent to the members of the CC only after three weeks with c[om.] Stalin's reply, confirmed by the Politburo. We are attaching the 'extorted answer' of c[om.] Zinoviev to this reply to the present document.

Meanwhile Chiang Kai-shek's coup was completed.

At the CC plenum itself the consideration of the Chinese question lasted just two to three hours and without stenograms either. A two-line resolution was carried, merely a confirmation of the actions of the Politburo *in the past*. Not a word was said by the resolution of the CC plenum about the new situation which has been created in China. The real consideration of the Chinese question, apparently took place at private (i.e. fractional) meetings of com. Stalin's fellow-thinkers, for it cannot be that such a question was not discussed in detail anywhere. And (as a result of these sessions) four days *after* the closure of the plenum of the CC c[om.] Stalin's theses for propagandists, confirmed by the CC of the AUCP, and which are known to you, appeared. We members of the CC became acquainted with these theses only from the newspapers. These deeply incorrect theses continue to distort the point of view of the opposition, ascribing to them among other things, a demand for the withdrawal of the Communists from the left Guomindang, which, as you already know from the documents distributed to you is a lie.

The stenograms of the April plenum of the CC on other matters (the Anglo-Russian Committee,[2] preparations for the Part[y] congress etc.) have not appeared up to now (nearly one and a half months have passed), since c[om.] Stalin evidently considers that now even some of the stenograms of the CC plenum are dangerous for his political line. For the information of members of the ECCI: stenograms of the CC plenum are distributed according to special lists of the Secretariat of the CC, mainly among comrades standing on the point of view of the majority of the CC.

6. During the CC plenum a letter from three Russian comrades, c[om.] Nasonov, Fokin, and Albrekht[3] (who are partisans of the views of the majority of the CC) reached the Comintern delegation of the AUCP from Shanghai. This letter describes the observations of these comrades in the field of action over several months. The facts adduced by this letter, one hundred percent confirm *our* position against the positions of c[om.] Stalin, Bukharin and Martynov. This letter is an extremely persuasive and weighty document. It refers to absolutely brazen facts, illustrating the incorrectness of the actions of the official representatives of the Comintern in China, and also the serious rightist errors of several leaders of the CC of the Chinese Communist Party. This letter was not distributed to members of the CC of the [Soviet] Party. This letter was also not transmitted to you, comrades from the Executive Committee of the Comintern. Despite this it has *primary* importance for an understanding of what has happened in China. We recommend you, comrades, to demand this letter for yourselves and to *study* it, as *one of the most important documents*.

On the other hand, the phrase in the letter has been torn out, in which before the coup, Chiang Kai-shek, pretending to be a 'leftist' for a moment, is supposed to have mentioned in conversation with one of his divisional commanders his faked 'solidar-

---

2   The Anglo-Russian Trade Union Committee was formed in 1925 on the basis of an agreement between the AUCCTU and the British TUC for the co-ordination of activities by the trade union movements of both countries. It was dissolved in September 1927.

3   Amongst the authors of this letter was also T. Mandalian.

ity' with the Russian opposition. This passage, torn out of context and distorted was printed in *Bolshevik*. The document itself, fatally exposing the complete incorrectness of the entire policy of c[om.] Stalin and Bukharin in China, was not even drawn to the attention of the ECCI. Can one accept as legitimate such handling of documents in Bolshevik circles?

7. At the April plenum of the CC we introduced a special proposal concerning the imminent Fifteenth Party Congress (the question of the congress was placed on the agenda of the plenum by the Secretariat of the CC) and of methods of liquidating inner-party conflict.[4] We also recommend this proposal for your attention. The essence of our proposal amounted to the following (we quote from the draft of our resolution):

1) To convene a special plenum of the CC, not later than three months before the Fifteenth Congress, for the *preliminary* consideration of all questions for the Fifteenth Congress.
2) This plenum must set itself the task doing everything possible to facilitate *unanimous* decisions, which would guarantee better than anything the maximum unity and a real liquidation of inner-party struggle.
3) This same plenum must entrust to the AUCP representation at the Comintern its adoption of the initiative of carrying out in the ECCI a series of measures for the return to the Party of those of the expelled c[om]rades, who beg the Comintern for it and who stand on firm Comintern ground, and for the creation of complete unity in fraternal parties (naturally, this does *not* refer to elements such as Katz and Korsch).
4) If however within this special plenum of the CC differences of principle are discovered, they must be formulated and published in good time. Every c[omra]de must receive an opportunity to defend his point of view before the Party, in the press and at meetings, as was always the case in Lenin's time.
5) Polemics must be conducted within strictly comradely functional limits, without aggravation or exaggeration.
6) Draft theses of the CCs of local organisations, of particular m[embers] of the Party and of groups of members of the Party must be published in *Pravda* (or as appen[dices] to *Pravda*), and also in local Part[y] newspapers, beginning roughly two to three months before the Fifteenth Congress.
7) Party publishers must also guarantee the timely publication of pamphlets, books, anthologies etc. and to those members of the Party, who would like to develop their views before the Party, but who do not yet have a majority in the Party.
8) The main slogan for all the preparations for the Fifteenth Congress must be the slogan of *unity*, the genuine Leninist unity of the AUCP.

---

4 This proposal was introduced by Zinoviev; see RGASPI, F.17, Op.2, D.284, Ll. 11–12 reverse.

All Opposition members of the CC voted for this proposal. The majority of the CC resolved to transmit this proposal as material for the Politburo. Up to now this proposal has not been drawn to the attention of the party. Meanwhile, it says clearly that the Opposition is not asking for the moon, just what existed in Lenin's time, even in the most difficult days for Soviet power, that the Opposition stands fully on the ground of party unity, that it alone introduced an exact, clear, practical proposal, *precisely so as to overcome differences*.

8. On 20 April CC members c[om.] Zinoviev and Trotsky addressed the members of the Politburo and members of the Presidium of the CCC with a proposal to convene a *closed session of the plenum of the CC and of the Presidium of the CCC* (i.e. without stenograms) for a discussion of the international situation, which has recently become worse and worse. This letter was written not only in a completely loyal, but even in a conciliatory tone (we offer you this letter in draft). All members of the Plenum of the CC and the Presidium of the CCC were then still in Moscow (at the Congress of Soviets).

So what happened? The Secretariat of the CC did not distribute this letter to the members of the CC, which was its direct responsibility, and only *three weeks later*, on 9 May, a reply to us was composed in the name of the Politburo and the Presidium of the CCC, however in the most compromising tone. They did not only refuse to convene a closed plenum of the CC, but announced accusations against us that we are 'disrupting the rear' etc. This accusation has an extremely specific flavour and is calculated to heat up the inner-party atmosphere.

9. On 7 May c[om.] Bukharin, the editor of *Pravda*, wrote to c[om.] Zinoviev, that he is not agreeable to print the latter's article, directed against Martynov, in *Pravda*, but is prepared to print it in *Bolshevik* as an item for discussion.[5] Several days later the Politburo resolved not to print *either* this article by c[om.] Zinoviev against Martynov, nor any article at all by Zinoviev or Trotsky on the Chinese question. At the same time, a one-sided 'discussion' continued on the pages of *Pravda*, distorting our views at every step.

10. On 9 May c[om.] Zinoviev's speech took place in the Hall of Columns at a Party meeting devoted to the fifteenth anniversary of *Pravda*, to which c[om.] Zinoviev was invited in the capacity of an 'old Pravdist'. The meeting was convoked by the CC and the CCC of our Party. Tickets were issued only by central Party organisations. On every ticket there was a special stamp of the Moscow Committee of the AUCP(b). The Presidium of the meeting consisted of members of the Bureau of the Mosc[ow] Committee. The report by the representative of the CC c[om.] Gusev was strictly in a Party spirit and informative. A resolution of the same character was adopted. (It may be that a certain number of non-Party people were present, but only those who were

---

5 Letter not found.

invited by the Central Committee and the Moscow Committee of the AUCP(b), i.e. people very close to the Party. This happens at many of our Party meetings, even those of a secret character.)

This meeting was retrospectively declared 'non-Party' and c[om.] Zinoviev was accused of speaking at a 'non-Party meeting'. C[om.] Zinoviev's speech contained, in a restrained and absolutely loyal form, a critique of the articles of A. Martynov and Svechin (a non-Party military expert) and an incorrect interpretation of the Chinese question. This was declared to be 'an attack on the Comintern, on the AUCP' etc. They do not print the letter to the editor sent by c[om.] Zinoviev (we attach this for you)[6]; they do not print c[om.] Zinoviev's speech in the Hall of Columns (this is attached for you)[7] – if it had been printed not a single Party cell would have adopted resolutions of protest against c[om.] Zinoviev. At the same time as they 'judge' c[om.] Zinoviev, without calling him to the Politburo nor to the Presidium of the CCC, they organise a newspaper campaign, following a directive of the Politburo, which leads the entire Party and the Comintern into confusion.

From all that is set out above it is clear that c[om.] Zinoviev's speech in the Hall of Columns served merely as the first 'appropriate' pretext for such a campaign. This very campaign was *predetermined*, as is evident from the letter under the signature of the Politburo and the Presidium of the CCC of 9 May, a letter written *before* c[om.] Zinoviev's speech.

The aim of the unheard campaign launched against c[om.] Zinoviev is evidently an attempt to remove him from the CC without the Fifteenth Congress and before the Fifteenth Congress, so as to have one opponent of the incorrect line less in the preparatory period of the Congress and at the Congress itself. Tomorrow, the same thing can be done with the rest of the oppositional members of the CC and in general, with workers defending the Leninist against the Stalinist Party line to the end.

11. The declaration concerning the 'ruin' of the Chinese revolution, ascribed to us in the letter of the Politburo of 19 May 1927 is a clear *fake*. In none of our documents (we attach all of our documents for the information of the ECCI) or speeches did we say that or could we have said that. We are *convinced* that the Chinese revolution will not perish, if, of course, the Communist International corrects the incorrect line that has been permitted. The Chinese revolution has suffered a major reverse, *but the situation can be corrected if the Comintern firmly carries out the line which was set out in the decisions of our five universal congresses and in the works of Lenin.*

12. We are not demanding any kind of special all-Union discussion in the sense of the term ascribed to us by the declaration of the Politburo of 19 May [19]27. We have

---

6   Letter not found.
7   Document not found.

already presented you with the eight points submitted by us to the April [19]27 plenum of the CC of our Party. *We still stand by those eight points*. They contain the most elementary demands, which a Bolshevik Party cannot renounce. This is how our Party *always* decided controversial questions in Lenin's time.

In the declaration of 19 May [19]27 distributed to us, the Politburo says that first of all any discussion would damage the Chinese Communist Party. Naturally we do not have the right to take a single step which might somehow or other make the work of the Chin[ese] Communist Party, which now stands at a critically responsible post, more difficult. But we assert that the real harm to the Chin[ese] Communist Party is done precisely by the present one-sided 'discussion', which distorts the real views of the Leninists, concealing the incorrect views of c[om.] Stalin, Bukharin, Martynov.

Why, in fact, should there be in the Party organ for theoretical discussion, *Bolshevik*, in the special anthologies, pamphlets, in the journal *Kommunisticheskii Internatsional* no place for an objective consideration of the problems of the Chinese revolution? Why is a monopoly of the consideration of the problems of the Chinese revolution given to the Martynovites? Why is it impossible to defend the views of Lenin, the views of the Second and Fourth World Congresses of the Comintern on the problems of the Chinese revolution in the Bolshevik Party press? Why in actual fact, can the entire international press (including the bourgeois and the SD press) declare that c[om.] Tomskii and ot[her] representatives of the CC of the AUCUTU have reached 'a cordial agreement' with Purcell, Hicks and ot[her] leaders of the TUC,[8] who are clearly agents of British imperialism? Why can they not permit in our organs, even if only in the theoretical ones, a discussion of this question which concerns the *fate of the whole Comintern*?

Why does the Secretariat of the CC of the AUCP, in breach of their obligations, not send out our declarations on the Chinese question even to members of the CC?

Because c[om.] Stalin has nothing with which to answer our documents. Because for c[om.] Stalin's radically incorrect positions it would be dangerous now, if even a narrow circle of Party c[omrades], who are not even oppositionists, were to get to know our documents, or would find out the essence of the dispute, the real facts.

13. It is untrue that in coming out with a defence of our point of view (which is a *Leninist* point of view) in questions about the Chinese events, or about the Anglo-Russian conference, we are supposedly breaking our declaration of 16 October [19]26.[9] In that

---

8 This refers to the British TUC.
9 This refers to the so-called 'Peaceful declaration' of the Left Opposition, sent to the Politburo of the CC. The declaration was signed by Trotsky and aimed at achieving a compromise with the leadership of the CC. The oppositionists recognised their mistakes in the question of sectarianism and declared that they would cease all fractional activity. In the words of the distinguished French historian Pierre Broué, Trotsky wrote this declaration 'before Zinoviev and many other oppositionists gave way to a mood of panic, fearing expulsion' (Broué 1996).

declaration we said then clearly and precisely that we do *not* renounce the defence of our views within the Party and *will* defend these views within the limits of the Party rulebook. This is what we are now doing, at an extremely responsible moment for our Party and for the entire Comintern.

14. It is untrue that we have distributed any of our documents to anyone at all without drawing this to the attention of the Politburo of the CC of the AUCP. *This never happened. Not a single fact* in the declaration of the Politburo of 19 May has been introduced or could have been introduced.

15. These are the facts and documents which should be available for verification by every member of the AUCP(b) and the whole Comintern. Not a single one of these documents contains anything conspiratorial, and if there were, it would be possible to omit that part. To leave the AUCP(b) and the whole Comintern in complete ignorance of these facts and documents is useful only to those whose political position is deeply incorrect.

∴

The international position of the USSR, and it follows, of the entire world proletariat, is deteriorating. The threat of war is becoming ever more real. This is the most important aspect of our present situation. *From this it follows that it is vital at all costs to consolidate the ranks of the AUCP and of the whole Comintern*, so as to defend together the cause of Lenin, the cause of peace, the cause of the construction of socialism, the cause of the USSR, the cause of the international revolution.

Several months ago already, at the first serious signs of a deterioration in the international situation, we sent (over the signatures of c[om.] Trotsky, Kamenev, Zinoviev) a declaration to the Politburo of our Party of our readiness to present ourselves for the entire disposal of the CC for whatever work the CC assigns against the growing dangers of war.[10] In the course of a whole year comrades belonging to the opposition have tirelessly demonstrated in the Central Committee (and when possible in the press) the growing danger of war, the necessity to *prevent* war by any means necessary, or at the very least, *to postpone it*. More than once we have proposed a consideration of a whole system of measures for this aim. But the more the international dangers have grown, the more determinedly c[om.] Stalin and his closest fellow thinkers have set alight the struggle within the Party and are trying to create (which is now quite clear) as situation in which joint work has become impossible. And the more in recent times the whole incorrectness of c[om.] Stalin's opportunist line on the Chinese question and the question of the Anglo-Russian Committee is exposed, the more clearly a line is conduc-

---

10   This refers to the 'Peaceful declaration'.

ted, whose aim is to *cut off* any possibility of joint work. The greatest problems of the Chinese question and of the dangers of war, on whose resolution unquestionably all Bolsheviks, all the workers of international Communism, would actually have worked together in Lenin's time, are now determined within the four walls of the Secretariat and are 'theoretically' formulated by Martynov.

If in normal times the success of the administration seems firm, then at the first serious crisis things may not work out so. It is one thing to vote, even if against one's wishes, for the Party administration when it is a question of 'working over' one or other of the opposition. It is another matter voting, if tomorrow it becomes necessary to go to the front and give up your life. In the latter case it is necessary for the rank and file members of the Party to have a really firm faith in the leadership. It is necessary for the ordinary members of the Party to express their true opinions, to possess a clear idea of the competing views within the Party, to get to know the arguments over principle from all sides and essentially. *Of course, iron discipline is demanded of us. But inner Party democracy is also necessary.* So Lenin taught. So Lenin did, even in the most tense moments of the struggle of Soviet power for its survival.

Comrades, if we have not bankrupted ourselves to the last degree, then we must understand that serious times are approaching, that we cannot be content with an official unity, but must aspire to a genuinely Leninist unity. There is no point in hurling haughty, sulky, officious, bureaucratic phrases claiming that the opposition is a little clique. It is well known to all of you that the real relationship of forces in our Party is not at all as it appears on the surface. The state of affairs in the whole Comintern is well known to all of you. Now is not the time for bureaucratic arrogance, it is not too late to take serious measures to put an end to a period which has already cost the Communist International dear.

We also ask you, the International Committee of the Communist International, to convene a closed session of the ECCI to consider collectively and in a comradely spirit which measures must be taken immediately, in this difficult situation to liquidate internal struggle and guarantee the line of the Comintern and the AUCP(b) in all their work. We will support any effective measure for the cessation of factional struggle.

We must preserve our unity whatever happens. We must unite on the basis of Lenin's views.

With Communist greetings,

G. Zinoniev
L. Trotsky
21 May [19]27

Appendices

1) Resolution on the Fifteenth Party Congress adopted at the April plenum.
2) Letter of c[om.] Zinoviev and Trotsky of 20 April to the Politburo and the Presidium of the CCC.[11]
3) C[om.] Zinoviev's speech of 9 May in the Hall of Columns.[12]
4) C[om.] Zinoviev's letter to the editor on the same question.[13]
5) C[om.] Zinoviev's article against c[om.] Martynov.[14]
6) The same about Tan Pingshan's book.[15]
7) 'An extorted response'.[16]
8) Letter from Shanghai over the signatures of c[om.] Nasonov, Fokin and Albrekht.
9) C[om.] Trotsky's article on c[om.] Stalin's theses.[17]
10) His article for *Pravda*.[18]

(Some of these materials have already been distributed, so we are not attaching them a second time).

RGASPI. F. 495. Op. 166. D. 189. Ll. 2–7.
Typescript, copy.

---

11 See Felshtinskii 1988, Volume 2, p. 234.
12 The text of the speech has not been discovered.
13 The text of the letter has not been discovered.
14 See Zinoviev, 'K urokam kitaiskoi revoliutsii. Po povodu stat'i tov. A. Martynova', RGASPI, F. 495, Op. 166, D. 188, Ll. 2–20.
15 See Zinoviev, 'Eshche k urokam kitaiskoi revoliutsii. Potriasaiushchii dokument', RGASPI, F. 324, Op. 1, D. 436, Ll. 3–25.
16 RGASPI, F.508, Op.1, D.107, Ll. 35–79.
17 This article was first published in English in 1932; see Trotsky 1932, pp. 158–98. It first saw the light of day in Russian in 1999; see Felshtinskii and Cherniavskii 1999, Volume 1, pp. 142–82.
18 This may refer to the article 'Class relations in the Chinese Revolution'; see Evans 1976, pp. 136–48. It was first published in Russian in 1999; see Felshtinskii and Cherniavskii 1999, Volume 1, pp. 44–57.

Biographical Dictionary

Albrekht, Alexander Emelianovich (alias Arno, Vudro, Max, Khaber, original name Abramovich) (1888–1972). Member of the RSDLP(b) from 1908. Until April 1917 in emigration. Successively member of the Petrograd, Odessa and Sevastopol Committees of the Bolshevik Party, member of the Presidium of the Odessa Soviet in 1917–18. Worked in ECCI from 1919. Representative of the Comintern in China in 1926–30 (with intervals).

Alekseev, Nikolai Dmitrievich (1857–1918). Infantry general. Participant in the Russo-Japanese and in the First World wars. Commander-in-Chief of forces on the North-Western, and later the Western fronts in 1915. From August 1915 to March 1917 Chief-of-Staff of the Supreme Commander-in-Chief. From March to May 1917 Commander-in-Chief, and subsequently military adviser to the Provisional government and Chief-of-Staff of the Supreme Commander-in-Chief. Took part in the suppression of the Kornilov mutiny against the Provisional government in August–September 1917, though he sympathized with General L.G. Kornilov. After the October (1917) revolution the supreme commander of the Volunteer Army.

Alskii, M. (original name Victor Moritsevich Shtein) (1890–1964). Member of the RSDLP(b) from 1917. Soviet Sinologist. Financial adviser to the National government of the GMD in 1926–27. Member of the Trotskyist opposition. Expelled from the Party in 1927. Arrested, later released. Research fellow at the Institute of Oriental Studies in 1935–64.

Andreev, Mikhail Georgievich (1888–1945). Russian and Soviet Sinologist. Studied and worked in China in 1913 and 1925–27 (with intervals). Taught at the UTK-KUTK in 1925–26 and 1927–30. Taught at the Institute of Oriental Studies in 1925–31 and M.V. Frunze Military Academy from 1928. Served in the WPRA in 1928–45. Research fellow at the IWE&WP from 1933.

Avksentiev, Nikolai Dmitrievich (1878–1943). PhD. One of the organisers and ideologues of the SR Party. Member of its CC since 1907. Chairman of the Executive Committee of the All-Russian Soviet of peasants' deputies in 1917. Minister of Internal Affairs in the government of A.F. Kerensky from 24 July until 2 September 1917. Between September and November 1918 was Chairman of the anti-Soviet All-Russian government (the Directory) in Ufa. Arrested by admiral Alexander V. Kolchak and exiled to China. From 1919 to 1940 lived in Paris, later in New York, where he worked as a journalist.

Babeuf, Gracchus (original name François Noël) (1760–1797). French Communist. In 1795–96 one of the leaders of the 'Conspiracy of the Equals' movement. In 1796 headed an insurgent Secret Directory, preparing an uprising against the corrupt government. Executed.

Backhouse, Edmund T. (1873–1944). 2nd Baronet, British Sinologist.

Bai Chongxi (alias Bai Jiansheng) (1893–1966). Chinese general, one of the leaders of the Guangxi militarist clique. Member of the GMD from 1924. During the Northern Expedition of 1926–27 Deputy Chief of the General Staff of the NRA. In April 1927 actively took part in the anti-Communist coup inspired by Chiang Kai-shek. Later occupied various military and political posts in Guangxi province. After the fall of the GMD government in 1949, he fled to Taiwan.

Bagnall, Benjamin (alias Bei Ge) (1844–1900). American protestant missionary in China from 1873. Murdered in the city of Baoding.

Bakunin, Michael Aleksandrovich (1814–1876). Russian revolutionary, anarchist.

Balfour, Arthur James (1848–1930). British Prime Minister from 1902–05 and Secretary of State for Foreign Affairs from 1916–19.

Baldwin, Stanley (1867–1947). British Prime Minster in 1923–24, 1924–29, and 1935–37.

Bessemer, Henry (1813–1898). English engineer, who improved a steelmaking process.

Bismarck, Otto Eduard Leopold von (1815–1898). Prince. Prussian and German (from 1871) Chancellor who played a leading role in the unification of Germany.

Bland, John O.P. (1863–1945). British Sinologist.

Blank, Ruvim Mordkovich (alias R.B.) (1866–1954). Journalist, employee of the Kadet journal *Osvobozhdenie* until 1905. Then a member of the editorial board of the Kadet newspaper, *Nasha zhizn'* and writer for the left-Kadet newspaper *Tovarishch*. In 1909–12 took part in the publication of the Kadet journal *Zaprosy zhizni*.

Boguslavskii, Mikhail Solomonovich (1886–1937). Member of the Jewish Socialist Workers Party in 1905–17. Member of the RSDLP(b) from 1917. Worked in Ukraine until October 1917. In 1918–19 Chairman of the Executive Committee of the Voronezh City Soviet. From the end of 1919 he was successively a Secretary of the AUkCEC, Secretary of the Political Administration of the WPRA, Secretary of the Kharkov Gubernia Committee of the CP(b)Uk, Chairman of the Union of Typographers, Deputy Chairman of the Moscow Soviet. Chairman of the Lesser CPC of the RSFSR in 1924–27. Member of the Trotskyist opposition. Expelled from the Party in 1927. Capitulated to Stalin in 1930. Director of Sibmashstroi in Novosibirsk in 1932–36. Arrested on 5 August 1936. Shot on 1 February 1937.

Boden, Frederick (?–?). American Protestant missionary in China.

Borodin, Mikhail Markovich (alias Anglichanin [Englishman], Bankir, Alexander Greenberg, Alexander Humberg, Michael Berg, Georg Braun, M. Braun, Jakob, Nikiforov, original name Gruzenberg) (1884–1951). Member of the RSDLP(b) since 1903. Worked with the ECCI from 1919. Main political advisor to the CEC of the GMD and ECCI representative in China in 1923–27. Deputy People's Commissar of Labour, deputy head of TASS, Editor-in-Chief of the Sovinformburo in 1927–32. Editor-in-Chief of the newspaper *Moscow News* from 1932. Arrested on 28 February 1949. Shot on 29 May 1951.

Boulger, Dimetrius Charles de Kavanagh (1853–1928). British Sinologist.

Brandler, Heinrich (1881–1967). Member of the SPD in 1901–16. Member of the KPD and its CC from 1919. Chairman of the KPD from 1921, member of the Presidium of the ECCI since 1922. One of the organisers of the October (1923) revolution in Germany. After the collapse of the Communist putsch he was withdrawn from leading posts. In 1924–28 worked in the central apparatus of the Comintern. From 1928 headed the opposition in the KPD. At the beginning of 1929 expelled from the Party. In 1933 he emigrated to France and in 1940 to Cuba. In 1948 he returned to Western Germany.

Broido, Grigorii Isaakovich (1885–1956). Member of the Bolshevik Party from 1903 to 1906, in 1918–41 and since 1955. Deputy People's Commissar for Nationalities in 1921–23. Rector of the KUTV in 1921–26. Chairman of the Gosizdat of the RSFSR in 1926–33. Secretary of the CC of the CP of Tajikistan in 1933–34. Deputy People's Commissar of Education of the RSFSR in 1934–41. Director of Partizdat in 1936–41 and of Medgiz from 1938.

Bubnov, Andrei Sergeevich (alias Ivanovskii) (1884–1938). Member of the RSDLP(b) since 1903. Candidate member of the CC in 1917, 1919–20 and 1922–23. Member of the CC in 1917–18 and 1924–37. Secretary of the CC in 1925. Head of the Department of Agitation and Propaganda of the CC of the RCP(b) in 1922–24. Chief of the Political Administration of the WPRA in 1924–29. Head of the inspection commission of the Politburo of the

CC of the AUCP(b) in Canton in 1926. People's Commissar of Education of the RSFSR in 1929–37. Arrested on 17 October 1937. Shot on 1 August 1938.

Bücher, Karl Wilhelm (1847–1930). German economist.

Bukharin, Nikolai Ivanovich (1888–1938). Member of the RSDLP(b) since 1906. Member of the CC in 1917–34. Candidate member of the CC in 1934–37. Candidate member of the Politburo in 1919–24. Member of the Politburo in 1924–29. Member of the Presidium of ECCI in 1919–29. Editor-in-Chief of the newspaper *Pravda* in 1917–29. Member of the Presidium of the SSNE in 1929–32. Editor of the newspaper *Izvestiia* in 1934–37. Arrested on 27 February 1937. Shot on 15 March 1938.

Brandt, Max August Scipio von (1835–1920). German ambassador to China in 1873–93.

Cassini, Arthur (alias Arturo Paul Nicholas Cassini) (1836–1919). Marquis and Count. Russian ambassador to China from 1891–96.

Catherine the Great (alias Catherine II) (1729–1796). Russian Empress from 1762–96.

Cavaignac, Louis Eugène (1802–1857). French general. In 1848 Minister of War and President of the Council of Ministers of the French Republic. Suppressed a workers' uprising in Paris in June 1848. Candidate for the Presidency of the French Republic in December 1848.

Gascoyne-Cecil, Robert Arthur Talbot (1830–1903). 3rd Marquess of Salisbury. British Foreign Secretary in 1878–80, 1885–86, 1887–92, and 1895–1900. Prime Minister in 1895–02.

Chamberlain, Austen (1863–1937). Member of the British House of Commons from 1892. Postmaster-General in 1902. Chancellor of the Exchequer in 1903–05 and 1919–21. Secretary of State for India in 1915–17. Member of the Imperial War Cabinet in 1918–19. Head of the Conservative Party in 1921–22. Secretary of State for Foreign Affairs in 1924–29. First Lord of the Admiralty from August to October 1931. Laureate of the Nobel Peace Prize in 1925.

Chen Duxiu (alias Old man, original name Chen Qiansheng) (1879–1942). Leader of the New Culture movement in China. Editor of the journal *Xin qingnian* from 1915. One of the leaders of the May 4th movement in 1919. Founder of the CCP. Leader of the CCP from 1921–27. Expelled from the Party in 1929. Leader of the Chinese Trotskyists in 1929–32. Arrested by the GMD police in 1932. Paroled in 1937.

Chen Gongbo (1892–1946). One of the founders of the CCP in 1921. Left the Party in 1922. Member of the Political Council of the CEC of the GMD from 1925. Collaborated with Japanese invaders in 1938–45. Shot for treason.

Chen Jiongming (1878–1933). Guangdong militarist. Collaborated with Sun Yat-sen in 1920–22. Governor of Guangdong in 1920–22. In June 1922 revolted against Sun Yat-sen. Defeated by the NRA in 1925.

Chen Sheng (alias Chen She) (?–208 BCE). Captain, the leader of the first rebellion against the Qin dynasty.

Chen Youren (alias Eugene Chen) (1879–1944). Member of the CEC of the Guomindang from 1926. Advisor to Sun Yat-sen in 1917–25. Acting Minister of Foreign Affairs in the GMD National government in 1926–27, Minister of Foreign Affairs in the Wuhan government in 1927. From 1927 in opposition to Chiang Kai-shek. In 1942 arrested by the Japanese in Hong Kong and transferred to Shanghai. Despite pressure from the Japanese to collaborate, he refused.

Cheng Tang (alias Tang of Shang, Da Yi) (1675–1646 BCE). The first King of the Shang/Yin Dynasty in China.

Cherevanin, Fedor Andreevich (original surname Lipkin) (1869–1938). Member of the RSDLP from 1900. Menshevik. Member of the CC of the RSDLP from 1917. Member of the Executive Committee of the Petrograd Soviet of workers' and soldiers' deputies and member of the ARCEC in 1917. After 1922 suffered repeated repression. Shot on 8 March 1938.

Chernov, Viktor Mikhailovich (alias Gardenin, Yu. Tuchkin, Ia. Vechin, V. Lenuar, B. Olenin, B. Iuriev) (1873–1952). Participant in the Russian revolutionary movement from the 1880s. One of the organisers and the major theoretician of the SR Party from 1901–02. Member of its CC from 1902. Member of the Presidium of the Executive Committee of the Petrograd Soviet of workers' and soldiers' deputies and member of the Executive Committee of the Soviet of peasants' deputies in 1917. Minister of Agriculture in the Provisional government in May–August 1917. Chairman of the Constituent Assembly in January 1918. Head of the Congress of Members of the Constituent Assembly in September–November 1918. Arrested by admiral Alexander V. Kolchak, but soon released under pressure from the White Czechs. Went into exile in 1920.

Chiang Ching-kuo (alias Jiang Jingguo, Nikolai Vladimirovich Elizarov) (1910–1988). Son of Chiang Kai-shek. Member of the CYLC from 1925. Member of the Soviet Youth

League from 1926. Candidate member of the AUCP(b) in 1930–41. Student of the KUTK in 1925–27. Student of the Special Military School and N.G. Tolmachev Military-Political Academy in 1927–30. Metalworker in the Moscow 'Dynamo' plant in 1930–31. Chairman of the October Revolution Collective Farm in Korovino village, Moscow Province from May to November 1931. Post-graduate student of the International Lenin School from November 1931 to the end of October 1932. Assistant chief of a shop in the Uralmash plant in Sverdlovsk in 1932–34. Deputy editor of Uralmash newspaper *Za tiazheloe mashinostroenie* in 1934–37. Deputy head of the Organisational Department of the Sverdlovsk City Soviet in 1937. On Stalin's orders he was sent back to China in 1937. Departed for Taiwan in 1949. In 1976 became President of the Republic of China (Taiwan).

Chiang Kai-shek (alias Jiang Jieshi, Jiang Zhongzheng) (1887–1975). Member of Sun Yat-sen's 'Revolutionary Alliance' from 1908. Member of the CEC of the GMD from 1926. Head of the Whampoa Military Academy from 1924. Commander-in-Chief of the NRA of the GMD from 1926. Head of the GMD regime from 1928.

Chirol, Valentine (1852–1929). British journalist, historian, and diplomat.

Cixi (original name Yehenara) (1835–1908). Concubine of the Emperor Xianfeng of the Qing dynasty until 1861. Empress Dowager and de facto ruler of China from 1861.

Cobden, Emma Jane Catherine (1851–1947). A member of the British Liberal Party, a famous suffragist.

Collins, William Frederick (1882–1956). American Sinologist.

Confucius (alias Kongzi, Kong Fuzi, original name Kong Qiu) (551–479 BCE). Chinese philosopher.

Conrady, Auguste (1864–1925). German Sinologist. Professor of Leipzig University from 1897.

Cordier, Henri (1849–1925). French expert on Japan and China.

Dai Jitao (alias Tianchou, Xiaoyuan) (1891–1949). Member of the GMD from 1911. Secretary of Sun Yat-sen from 1911. Member of the CEC of the GMD since 1924. Ideologue of the 'right' Guomindang. Rector of Sun Yat-sen University in Canton in 1926–27. Head of the Examination Yuan (chamber) in 1928–48. Committed suicide.

Dalin, Sergei Alekseevich (original name Rabinovich) (1902–1985). Member of the RCP(b) from 1919. Worked for the CYI in 1921–24. Member of the Presidium of the Far Eastern Secretariat of the Comintern in 1921–22. Representative of the CYI in China in 1922 and 1924. Taught at the UTK in 1925–26. Representative of the Moscow Sun Yat-sen University in China in 1926–27. Member of the Trotskyist opposition in 1927. Chief of the Department of Internal Information of the newspaper *Izvestiia* in 1928. TASS correspondent in Scandinavia in 1929–30. Deputy head of the Foreign Department of TASS in 1930–31. Deputy Chairman of the Krasnoiarsk Soviet Regional Committee in 1936. Arrested on 5 September 1936, sentenced to ten years' deprivation of liberty on 21 April 1937. Served his term in Norilsk, worked as a senior engineer-economist. Released on 5 September 1946, remained in Norilsk. Arrested again on 23 December 1950. Sentenced to exile in Krasnoiarsk region. Released on 16 December 1954.

Dan, Fedor Ilyich (original name Gurvich) (1871–1947). Member of the RSDLP since 1898. Member of the CC since 1905. One of the Menshevik leaders. After the February (1917) revolution a member of the Bureau of the Executive Committee of the Petrograd Soviet. Arrested by the Bolsheviks in 1921. Deported in 1922. Editor of *Sotsialisticheskii vestnik* in 1922–42.

Dewey, John (1859–1952). American philosopher and educational reformer.

Dittmer, Clarence Gus (1885–?). A doctoral student at the University of Wisconsin and an American teacher of Economics at Tsinghua College in Beijing in late 1910s.

Drobnis, Iakov Naumovich (1891–1937). Member of the Bund in 1904–05. Menshevik in 1905–06. Member of the RSDLP(b) from 1907 and of the CC of the CP(b)Uk from 1918. From 1919, successively Chairman of the Poltava and Odessa Soviets, commissar of the WPRA. From 1922 worked in the Lesser CPC of the RSFSR. Member of the Trotskyist opposition. Expelled from the Party in 1927. Capitulated to Stalin in 1929. Deputy Director of the Kemerovo Khimkombinatstroi from 1934. Arrested on 6 August 1936. Shot on 1 February 1937.

Duan (1856–1922). Manchu prince and politician.

Dulcinea del Toboso. Character in the novel *Don Quixote de La Mancha* by the Spanish writer Miguel de Cervantes Saavedra.

Durov, Vladimir Leonidovich (1863–1934). Equestrian. Honoured artist of the RSFSR from 1927.

En Hai (?–1900). *Zhangjing* (a sergeant or a low-rank officer) in a Qing dynasty firearms regiment who assassinated the German ambassador to China, Baron Ketteler. Executed.

Engels, Friedrich (1820–1895). German philosopher and revolutionary. One of the founders of Marxism.

Evdokimov, Grigorii Eremeevich (1884–1936). Member of the RSDLP(b) since 1903. Member of the CC in 1919–25. Chairman of the Petrograd Soviet of Trade Unions, secretary of the Leningrad Gubernia Committee of the Party in 1920–25. Secretary of the CC and member of the Orgburo of the CC in 1925–27. Member of the Zinovievist opposition. Expelled from the Party in 1927. Capitulated to Stalin in 1928. Chairman of the Samara Regional Union of Agricultural Co-operation from 1929, thereafter Director of the Chief Administration for the Milk Industry of the People's Commissariat of the Food Industry of the USSR. Arrested on 8 December 1934. Shot on 25 August 1938.

Feng Yuxiang (1882–1948). Chinese marshal, Commander-in-Chief of the Nationalist Army from 1924. Member of the GMD from 1926. Chairman of the Political Council of the CC of the Revolutionary Committee of the GMD in 1948.

Fisher, Fred Douglas (1874–?). US Consul-General in Shenyang in 1909–14 and Tianjin in 1914–15.

Fokin, Nikolai Alekseevich (alias Molodoi [Young]) (1899–1938). Member of the RCP(b) from 1919. General Secretary of the CC of the CYL of Turkestan and of the Central Asian Bureau of the CC of the CYL until 1924. Secretary of the ECCYI from 1924. Representative of the ECCYI in China in 1926–27. Head of the Eastern Department of the ECCYI in July 1927–30. Deputy head of the Eastern Department of the Trade Union International in 1930–1933. Then worked in the Political Department of the Transcaucasian railways. Repressed.

Franke, Otto (1863–1946). German Sinologist.

Frederick II the Great (1712–1786). King of Prussia from 1740.

Fridliand, Grigorii Samoilovich (1897–1937). Soviet historian. Repressed.

Furmanov, Dmitrii Andreevich (1891–1926). Soviet writer.

Gapon, Georgii Apollonovich (1870–1906). Russian Orthodox priest who was very popular among the workers in St. Petersburg, organized a workers' demonstration on January 9/22, 1905 that turned into a bloody massacre and precipitated the first Russian Revolution of 1905–07. Murdered by members of Social-Revolutionary Party for allegedly being a police provocateur.

Geller, Lev Naumovich (alias Professor, Professional, Tarasov) (1875–1942). Member of the RSDLP(b) from 1904. Chairman of the Council of International Propaganda in 1920. Head of the Eastern Department of the Trade Union International in 1922–30. Representative of the Trade Union International in China in June–July 1926. Taught at the International Lenin School in 1930–33. Repressed.

Genghis Khan (alias Temuchin) (1155–1227). Unifier of Mongolia and the great conqueror who subjugated North China (Kingdoms Xi Xia and Jin) and Central Asia.

George, Henry (1839–1897). American economist.

Georgievskii, Sergei Mikhailovich (1851–1893). Russian Sinologist. Professor of St. Petersburg University from 1890.

Gingorn, Semen Vladimirovich (alias Gingor) (1896–1937). Member of the RCP(b) from 1919. Taught history of Western revolutionary movement at the UTK from February 1926 to 1 September 1927. Member of the Trotskyist opposition. Arrested. Shot on 17 March 1937.

Girs, Mikhail Nikolaevich (1856–1932). Russian ambassador to China in 1898–1901.

Gong (1830–1898). Prince, a half-brother of the Chinese Emperor Xianfeng (reigned 1850–61) and a lover of the Empress Dowager Cixi. In 1861, along with Cixi initiated the Self-Strengthening policy. Head of *Zongli yamen* (Office for the Management of the Business of All Foreign Countries).

Gorev, Boris Isaakovich (original surname Goldman) (1874–1937). Soviet historian.

Guangxu (original name Zaitian) (1871–1908). The Chinese Emperor of the Qing dynasty from 1874.

Guralskii, Abram (Boris) Iakovlevich (alias Rustitko, Lepeti, Kleine, Iakov, Dupont, original surname Kheifets) (1890–1960). Member of the Bund from 1906. Member of the Federal Committee of the Social-Democratic Party of the Latvian region from

1907. Member of the RSDLP(b) from 1918. Vice-Chairman of the Kiev Gubernia Executive Committee, member of the All-Ukrainian CEC in 1919. Representative of the ECCI in Germany from the end of 1919 to 1920 and in 1921–23. Member of the CC of the KPD, Chairman of the Revcom of Germany in 1923. Delegate to the Fifth Congress of the Comintern from the KPD in 1924. Representative of the ECCI in France in 1924–1925. Head of a Department of the Marx-Engels Institute in 1926–28. Member of the Zinovievist opposition. Expelled from the Party in 1927. Capitulated to Stalin in 1928. Member of a delegation of ECCI to South America in 1930–34. Repressed.

Gusev, Sergei Ivanovich (alias Travin, P. Grin, original name Iakov Davidovich Drabkin) (1874–1933). Member of the Petersburg 'Union of Struggle for the Emancipation of the Working Class' in 1896. Member of the RSDLP from 1898. Member of the RSDLP(b) from 1903. In 1904–05 secretary of the Petersburg Committee of the RSDLP(b). Secretary of the MRC of Petrograd in 1917. During the Civil War was successively member of the RMC of the 5th and 2nd Armies, member of the RMC of the Eastern front, member of the RMCR, member of the RMC of the South-Eastern front, member of the RMC of the Southern front. In 1921–23 chief of the Political Administration of the WPRA. Secretary of the CCC of the RCP(b) and member of the Collegium of the People's Commissariat of the Worker-Peasant Inspection from 1923. Representative of the ECCI to the CP USA in 1925–27. Chief of the Press Department of the CC of the AUCP(b) in 1926–28, Head of the Central European Secretariat of the ECCI in 1928–1932 and the Anglo-American Secretariat of the ECCI since 1932. Candidate member of ECCI in 1928–29. Member of the Presidium of the ECCI in 1929–31. Candidate member of the Presidium of ECCI since 1931.

Hart, Robert (1835–1911). 1st Baronet. British diplomat and Inspector-General of China's Maritime Customs from 1863.

Helfferich, Karl (1872–1924). German politician and financier, Secretary for the Treasury in 1915–16 and Secretary of the Interior of German Empire in 1916–17.

Hembyze, Jan von (1513–1584). One of the Calvinist leaders in Gent (Flanders). Headed a rebellion against the Spanish monarchy in 1577. Executed.

Hicks, Ernest George (1879–1954). General Secretary of the Amalgamated Union of Building Trade Workers in Great Britain. Member of the General Council of the TUC in 1924–41, President 1927–28. Labour Member of Parliament, 1931–50.

Hindenburg, Paul von (1847–1934). Field Marshall, Supreme Commander-in-Chief of the German Army in 1916–17. President of Germany in 1925–34.

Horn, Robert (1871–1940). Viscount, President of the British Board of Trade in 1920–21.

Hu Hanmin (1879–1936). Member of Sun Yat-sen's 'Revolutionary Alliance' from 1905. Member of the CEC of the GMD from 1924. Governor of Guangdong province and Minister of Foreign Affairs in the Canton government in 1925. Head of a GMD delegation in the USSR in 1925–26. After 12 April 1927, Chairman of the Political Council of the CEC of the GMD in 1925 and in 1927–28, head of the Legislative Yuan (chamber) from 1928–31.

Huc, Évariste Régus (1813–1860). French Catholic missionary in China, Mongolia and Tibet.

Hus, Jan (1369–1415). The Czech priest and Christian reformer. Burnt at the stake.

Iakinf (secular name Nikita Iakovlevich Bichurin) (1777–1853). Russian Sinologist. Head of the ninth Russian Religious Mission in Beijing in 1807–22. In 1823–26, monk of the Valaam Monastery. From 1826 interpreter in the Ministry of Foreign Affairs of Russia.

Ignatiev, Nikolai Pavlovich (1832–1908). Count, Russian general and diplomat, plenipotentiary to China from 1859–60 and ambassador to the Ottoman Empire from 1864–77.

Ilovaiskii, Dmitrii Ivanovich (1832–1920). Russian historian, publicist, author of a *History of Russia* in 5 volumes.

Ioffe, Semen Samoilovich (1895–1938). Member of the RSDLP(b) from July 1916. One of the leaders of the Bolshevik movement in Smolensk in 1917. Voroshilov's secretary for foreign political affairs in 1927. Arrested. Shot on 10 June 1938.

Iordanskii, Nikolai Ivanovich (alias Negorev, N. Nadov) (1876–1928). Member of the RSDLP since 1899. Menshevik from 1903. From 1905 editor of the journal *Mir Bozhii* (from 1906 *Sovremenny Mir*). In 1905 member of the Executive Committee of the Petersburg Soviet of workers' deputies. Collaborator with the Bolshevik journal *Zvezda* in 1910–12. Member of the RCP(b) from 1921. Soviet ambassador to Italy in 1923–24.

Ito Hirobumi (1841–1909). Marquis from 1895–1907 and prince from 1907. Prime Minister of Japan in 1885–88, 1892–96, 1898, and 1900–01.

Ivan the Terrible (alias Ivan IV) (1530–1584.) Russian Tsar of the Rurik Dynasty from 1553–84.

Ivanov, Aleksei Alekseevich (alias Ivin) (1885–1942). Russian and Soviet Sinologist. Professor of Beijing University in 1917–27. Correspondent of the newspaper *Pravda* in China in 1927–30. Research fellow at the IWE&WP in 1932–42. Repressed.

Ivanov, Aleksei Ivanovich (1878–1937). Russian and Soviet Sinologist. Professor from 1915. Worked in the Soviet embassy in Beijing from 1922–27. Later taught at various colleges. Repressed.

Jamieson, George (1843–1920). British Sinologist.

John the Baptist. In Christianity the final prophet of the coming of the Messiah, the predecessor of Jesus Christ.

Jordan, John Newell (1852–1925). British envoy extraordinary and minister plenipotentiary to China in 1910–20.

Kalinin, Mikhail Ivanovich (1875–1946). Member of the RSDLP since 1898. Member of the RSDLP(b) since 1903. Member of the CC since 1919. Candidate member of the Politburo in 1919–26. Member of the Politburo since 1926. Chairman of the AUCEC since 1922 and of the Presidium of the Supreme Soviet of the USSR since 1938.

Kamenev, Lev Borisovich (original name Rozenfeld) (1883–1936). Member of the RSDLP since 1901. Member of the RSDLP(b) since 1903. Member of the CC in 1917–18 and 1919–27. Member of the Politburo in 1919–25. Candidate member of the Politburo in 1926. Chairman of the All-Russian CEC in 1917. Chairman of the Moscow Soviet in 1918–26. Deputy Chairman of the CPC of the RSFSR (USSR) in 1922–26. Director of the Lenin Institute in 1923–26. People's Commissar for Internal and Foreign Trade in 1926. Soviet ambassador to Italy in 1926–27. Member of the Zinovievist opposition. Expelled from the Party in 1927. Capitulated to Stalin in 1928. Director of the 'Academia' publishing house in 1933. Director of the M. Gorky Institute for World Literature of the AN of the USSR in 1934. Arrested on 16 December 1934. Shot on 25 August 1936.

Kamkov, Boris Davidovich (original name Kats) (1885–1938). Member of the SR Party in 1902–17. Member of its CC in 1917. Head of the Petrograd organisation of the SR Party in 1917. One of the organisers and leaders of the Party of Left-SRs (Internationalists). Member of the Presidium of the ARCEC in 1917–18. One of the organisers of the plot against the Bolshevik government on 6 July 1918. Subsequently one of the leaders of the Ukrainian Party of Left-SRs. Repeatedly arrested. Shot on 29 August 1938.

Kang Youwei (1858–1927). Chinese reformer, monarchist.

Kantorovich, Anatolii Iakovlevich (alias N. Terentiev) (1896–1937). Soviet Sinologist. In the 1920s worked in the People's Commissariat of Foreign Affairs. In 1924–28 in China. Research fellow at the IWE&WP from 1932.

Kareev, Nikolai Ivanovich (1850–1931). Russian historian and expert on France. Corresponding Member of the St. Petersburg Academy of Sciences from 1910, of the Russian Academy of Sciences from 1917, of the Academy of Sciences of the USSR from 1925. Honorary member of the Academy of Sciences of the USSR from 1929.

Katz, Ivan (1889–1956). Member of the SPD since 1906. Member of the Independent Social Democratic Party of Germany in 1919. Member of the KPD from 1920. In 1924 member of the Politburo of the CC of the KPD. In 1925 representative of the KPD in ECCI. Returned to Germany in the summer of 1925. At the beginning of 1926 broke with the Communist Party and organized the New 'Spartacus' League. Arrested by the Nazis in 1933, 1941 and 1944.

Kautsky, Karl (1854–1938). One of the leaders and theoreticians of German Social Democracy and of the Second International. Editor of the SPD theoretical journal *Neue Zeit* in 1883–1917.

Kerensky, Alexander Fedorovich (1881–1970). Russian Socialist Revolutionary. Minister of Justice in the Provisional government in March–May 1917. Minister of the Army & Navy in May–September 1917. Prime Minister in July–November 1917. Supreme C-in-C of the Russian Army in August–November 1917. Went into exile after the October (1917) revolution.

Ketteler, Clemens August Freiherr von (1853–1900). Baron, German plenipotentiary to China from 1899–1900.

Kitchener, Herbert (1850–1916). Count, British Field Marshal, Secretary of State for War from 1914–16.

Kornilov, Lavr Georgievich (1870–1918). General. Participant in the Russo-Japanese and the First World wars. In 1907–11 Russian military attaché in China. In March–April 1917, Commander-in-Chief of the Petrograd military district. In July 1917 successively Commander-in-Chief of the South Western front and Supreme Commander-in-Chief. At the end of August attempted to carry out a military coup, but at the beginning of September arrested. In November escaped. From December Commander-in-Chief of the Volunteer Army. Perished during the attack on Ekaterinodar.

Korsch, Karl (1886–1961). Member of the Independent Social Democratic Party of Germany in 1919. Member of the KPD from 1920. Minister of Education in the coalition government in Thuringia in the autumn of 1923. In 1925 broke with the Communist movement, and after 1928 abandoned political activity. Emigrated in 1933. In USA after 1936.

Krause, Friedrich Ernst August (1879–1942). German historian.

Kropotkin, Petr Alekseevich (1842–1921). Prince. Russian revolutionary, geographer, geologist, sociologist and historian. Theoretician of anarchism.

Krusenstern, Ivan Fedorovich (alias Adam Johann von Krusenstern) (1770–1846). Russian admiral and explorer.

Ku Sui-lu (?–?). Chinese scholar who in 1924 in Hamburg defended his Ph.D. dissertation on the banking transactions in China and in 1926 published it in German.

Kuropatkin, Aleksei Nikolaevich (1848–1925). Russian Imperial Minister of War from 1888–1904.

Legge, James (1815–1897). British Sinologist, translator of works of classical Chinese philosophy.

Lamsdorf, Vladimir Nikolaevich (1845–1907). Minister of Foreign Affairs of the Russian Empire from 1901–06.

Lannes de Montebello, Louis-Gustave (1838–1907). Marquis. French ambassador to Russia in 1891–1902.

Lenin, Vladimir Ilyich (alias Nikolai Lenin, original name Ulianov) (1870–1924). One of the organisers of the Petersburg 'Union of Struggle for the Emancipation of the Working Class' in 1895. Member of the RSDLP from 1898. Founder of the RSDLP(b). Member of the CC since 1903. Member of the Politburo since 1919. One of the organisers of the October (1917) revolution. Chairman of the Council of People's Commissars of the RSFSR (USSR) from 1917 and of the CLD since 1922. Leader and theoretician of Bolshevism.

Lentsner, Naum Mikhailovich (1902–1936). Member of the RSDLP(b) since 1918. Secretary of the Far Eastern Bureau of the CC of the CYI in 1920–21. Editor of the third volume of L.D. Trotsky's works in 1924. In 1927 chief of a sub-section of the Section for

Agitation and Propaganda of ECCI. In the 1920s member of the Trotskyist opposition. Expelled from the Party in 1927. Capitulated to Stalin. Part-time worker in the Central European Länder Secretariat of ECCI until 1931. In 1936 Deputy Chief of the Regional Plant Administration in Dnepropetrovsk city. Arrested on 1 April 1936, and shot soon after.

Leonardo da Vinci (1452–1519). Italian painter, sculptor, architect, scientist, engineer.

Leopold II (1835–1909). King of the Belgians from 1865.

Li Dazhao (alias Li Shouchang, Qinhua) (1889–1927). One of the first Chinese Communists. Founder of a Beijing Marxist circle in 1920. Member of the CCP from 1921. Member of the CEC from 1922. Leader of the North China Bureau of the CEC from 1921. Executed by Zhang Zuolin's police.

Li Hongzhang (alias Li Shaoquan) (1823–1901). Major Chinese politician, diplomat and businessman of the Qing dynasty. Commander of the Anhui Army. From the late 1860s successively Governor-General of Hunan and Hubei, Zhili, Guangdong and Guangxi provinces. Viceroy, Chief Secretary of the Imperial government, Imperial Mentor and Superintendent controlling trade in the North of the country.

Li Jishen (alias Li Renchao) (1885–1959). Chinese general. Member of the GMD from 1920 and candidate member of the Political Council of the CEC of the GMD from 1926. In 1925 commander of the 4th Army. In the period of the Northern Expedition of 1926–27 Chief of Staff of the NRA and of the logistical administration of the NRA High Command, governor of Guangdong province. On 15 April 1927 carried out an anti-Communist coup in Canton, and in December of the same year repressed a Communist uprising in the same city. Subsequently in various capacities in the government and army of the GMD. In January 1948 co-founded the Revolutionary Committee of the GMD in Hong Kong. After the fall of the GMD regime in 1949, Chairman of the National Committee of the CPPCC, Deputy Chairman of the Central People's Government of the PRC and Vice-Chairman of the Standing Committee of the NPC.

Liang Qichao (alias Zhuoru, Rengong) (1873–1929). Chinese philosopher, reformist, and journalist, Kang Youwei's student, one of leading activists on the Hundred Days of Reforms movement of 1898.

Liao Zhongkai (1877–1925). Member of Sun Yat-sen's 'Revolutionary Alliance' from 1905. Member of the CEC of the GMD from 1924. Well-known activist of the 'left' GMD.

Minister of Finance in the Canton government from 1923 and Political Commissar of the Whampoa Military Academy from 1924. Killed as a result of an attempted assassination.

Lieber, Mikhail Isaakovich (alias Ber, GLDM, Lipin, Lipov, original surname Goldman) (1880–1937). Member of the Social Democratic Party of Lithuania since 1896. One of the leaders of the Bund since 1897. Menshevik since 1903. Member of the CC of the Bund since 1904. Member of the CC of the RSDLP. Member of the Bureau of the Executive Committee of the Petrograd Soviet of workers' and soldiers' deputies in 1917. During the Civil War (1918–20) adopted sharply anti-Bolshevik positions. After 1923 repeatedly arrested. Shot on 4 October 1937.

Liebknecht, Karl (1871–1919). Member of the SPD since 1900. One of the leaders of the leftist tendency of German Social Democracy. Chairman of the Socialist Youth International in 1907–10. Member of the Reichstag in 1912–16. In 1916–18 one of the organisers and leaders of the left-radical group (league) 'Spartacus'. In 1916–18 imprisoned. Took an active part in the November (1918) revolution in Germany. Chairman of the KPD from early 1919. Murdered on 15 January 1919.

Liebknecht, Wilhelm Martin Philipp Christian Ludwig (1826–1900). Father of Karl Liebknecht. Co-founder of the KPD.

Lim Boon Keng (alias Lin Wenqing, Wen Ching) (1869–1957). Chinese physician and the president of Amoy (Xiamen) University from 1921–37.

Linevich, Nikolai Petrovich (1839–1908). General, Commander-in-Chief of the Russian military forces in Manchuria, 1905.

Liu Shaoqi (1898–1969). Member of the CCP from 1921. Student of the KUTV in 1921. One of the organisers of the Chinese workers' movement from 1921. Deputy Chairman and Secretary of the Executive Committee of the All-China Federation of Trade Unions in 1925–27. Member of the CC of the CCP since 1927. Member of the Politburo since 1928. Secretary of the Secretariat of the CC and Deputy Chairman of the Revolutionary Military Committee from 1943. Deputy Chairman of the Central People's Government of the PRC from 1949. Chairman of the Standing Committee of the National People's Congress from 1954. Member of the Standing Committee of the Politburo and Deputy Chairman of the CC of the CCP from 1956. Chairman of the PRC from 1959. Expelled from the Party in 1968. Repressed.

Liu Renjing (alias Lenskii, Niel Shih, Nelsi, Liu Ruoshui, Keren) (1902–1987). One of the founders of the CCP in 1921. Head of the CEC of the CYLC in 1923–25. Student of the International Lenin School in 1926–29. Member of the Chinese Trotskyist opposition. Expelled from the Party in 1929. One of the theoreticians of the Chinese Left Opposition. Arrested by the GMD police in 1935. Paroled in 1937. Arrested by the Communists in 1952. Capitulated to Mao Zedong in 1972. Killed falling under a bus.

Livshits, Iakov Abramovich (1896–1937). Member of the SR Party in 1913–15. Member of the RSDLP(b) from 1917. From 1919 worked in the GPU of Ukraine. From 1924 on economic work, Deputy Director of the Kharkov trust 'Donugol'. Member of the Trotskyist opposition. Expelled from the Party in 1928. Capitulated to Stalin in 1929. From 1939 successively Director of the Southern, North Caucasian and Moscow-Kursk railways. Deputy People's Commissar of the NKPS since 1935. Arrested on 16 March 1936. Shot on 1 February 1937.

Liu Bang (alias Han Gaozu) (256–195 BCE). The first Emperor of the Han dynasty in China from 202 BC.

Lobanov-Rostovskii, Alexei Borisovich (1824–1896). Prince. Minister of Foreign Affairs of Russian Empire in 1895–96.

Lorentz, Hendrik Antoon (1853–1928). A Dutch physicist.

Lozovskii, A. (original name Solomon Abramovich Dridzo) (1878–1952). Member of the RSDLP since 1901. Candidate member of the CC of the AUCP(b) in 1927–39. Member of the CC in 1939–49. General Secretary of the Trade Union International and member of ECCI in 1921–37. Deputy People's Commissar of Foreign Affairs in 1939–46. Deputy head of the Sovinformburo in 1941–45. Head of the Sovinformburo in 1945–48. Chairman of the Department of History of International Relations and Foreign Policy at the Higher Party School of the CC of the AUCP(b) in 1940–49. Arrested on 26 January 1949. Shot on 12 August 1952.

Lü Buwei (290?–235 BCE). Merchant from the Chinese kingdom of Zhou. Chief Minister of the kingdom of Qin until 246 BCE. According to legend, father of the Emperor Qin Shi Huangdi.

Luo Fenglu (1850–1901). The Chinese ambassador to the United Kingdom from 1896–1901.

Luxemburg, Rosa (1871–1919). Member of the SPD since 1898. One of the leaders of the left-wing tendency in German Social Democracy. Participant in the Russian Revolution of 1905–07. In 1916–18 one of the organisers and leaders of the left-radical 'Spartacus' group (league). Imprisoned in 1916–18. Took an active part in the November (1918) revolution in Germany. One of the founders of the KPD at the end of 1918 and the beginning of 1919. Murdered on 15 January 1919.

Macartney, George (1737–1806). First Earl. British Ambassador to Russia in 1764–69. Governor of Madras (Chennai) in 1780–86. Head of a British diplomatic mission to China in 1792–93, Governor of Cape Colony in 1796–98.

MacDonald, Claude Maxwell (1852–1915). Colonel, British diplomat, minister to China in 1896–1900.

MacMurray, John van Antwerp (1881–1960). US Ambassador to China in 1925–29, Estonia, Latvia and Lithuania in 1933–36, and Turkey in 1936–41.

Mandalian, Tates (Tateos) Gega(mo)vich (alias Sergei Georgievich Marchenko, Cherniak, Professional) (1901–1941). Member of the RSDLP(b) from 1917. In trade union work in Trans-Caucasia in 1920–23. Worked in the Trade Union International from 1923. Representative of the Trade Union International in China in 1926–27. Chairman of the Voronezh Council of Trade Unions in 1927–36. Political advisor of the General Secretary of ECCI G.M. Dimitrov in 1936–37. Soviet chargé d'affaires in Spain from 1937. Arrested on 22 August 1939. Shot on 28 July 1941.

Manuilskii, Dmitrii Zakharovich (1883–1959). Member of the RSDLP since 1903. Member of the RSDLP(b) from July 1917. Member of the CC in 1923–52. Secretary of the CC of the CP(b)Uk in 1921. Member of the Presidium of ECCI in 1924–28. Secretary of ECCI in 1928–43. Deputy Chairman of the CPC (Council of Ministers) and People's Commissar (Minister) of Foreign Affairs of Ukraine in 1944–53.

Margary, Augustus Raymond (1846–1875). The British diplomat and traveller.

Maring, Hendricus (alias Andreson, Martin Ivanovich Bergman, H. Brouwer, Mander, Philipp, Sentot, Simons, Joh van Son, original name Hendricus Josephus Franciscus Marie Sneevliet) (1883–1942). Activist of the Communist movement on Java and in the Netherlands. Secretary of the commission of the Second Congress of the Comintern on National and Colonial Questions in 1920. Member of ECCI in 1920–21. Representative of ECCI in China in 1921–23. Participant in the Communist movement in Germany, Austria, Holland, Norway, Sweden, France. Expelled from the Comintern in 1928. Murdered by the Nazis.

Martynov, Alexander Samoilovich (alias Miner, Poliakov, original name Saul Samuilovich Piker) (1865–1935). Member of the Populist terrorist organisation 'People's Will' since 1885. Member of the RSDLP since 1899. One of the theoreticians of Menshevism. Member of the RCP(b) since 1923. Editor of the journals *Kommunisticheskii Internatsional* and *Unter dem Banner des Marxismus* from 1924.

Marx, Karl (1818–1883). German philosopher and revolutionary. One of the founders of Marxism.

Meckel, Jacob (1842–1905). German officer who in 1885–88 served as a military adviser to the Japanese Imperial government. Later was major general and Deputy Chief of Staff of the German army.

Medhurst, Walter Henry (alias Mai Dusi) (1796–1857). English Congregationalist missionary to China.

Meiji (alias Mutsuhito) (1852–1912). Emperor of Japan from 1867.

Mencius (original name Meng Ke) (372–289 BCE). Chinese philosopher, follower of Confucius.

Mif, Pavel (original name Mikhail Alexandrovich Fortus) (1901–1938). Member of the RSDLP(b) from 1917. Pro-Rector of the UTK in 1925–27. Rector of the UTK-KUTK in 1927–29. Deputy head of the Eastern Secretariat of ECCI in 1928–35. Political assistant of the General Secretary of the ECCI G.M. Dimitrov in 1935. Rector of the KUTV in 1936. Director of SRINCP in 1937. Arrested on 11 December 1937. Shot on 28 July 1938.

Miliukov, Pavel Nikolaevich (1859–1943). Russian historian. Founder and ideologist of the Kadets from 1905. Chairman of the Kadet Party from 1907. Deputy of the State Duma in 1907–17. Leader of the 'Progressive Bloc' in the Duma from 1915. Minister of Foreign Affairs in the Provisional government in March–May 1917. After the October (1917) revolution one of the organisers of the White movement. Author of the Declaration of the Volunteer Army. In exile from the end of 1918. Editor-in-Chief of the newspaper *Poslednie Novosti* in 1921–41.

Min (1851–1895). Queen of Korea, assassinated.

Morse, Hosea Ballou (1855–1934). An American who served in the Chinese Imperial Maritime Custom Service for over thirty years and became a British subject late in life.

Muralov, Nikolai Ivanovich (1877–1937). Member of the RSDLP(b) since 1903. Member of the CCC in 1925–27. Commander-in-Chief of the Moscow military district in 1921–24. Commander-in-Chief of the North Caucasian military district in 1924–25. Member of the State Planning Committee of the RSFSR, Rector of the Agricultural Academy in 1925–27. Member of the Trotskyist opposition. Expelled from the Party in 1927. Capitulated to Stalin in 1930. Subsequently Chief of the Agricultural Department of Kuzbasstroi. Arrested on 18 April 1936. Shot on 1 February 1937.

Muraviev-Amurskii, Nikolai Nikolaevich (1809–81). Count. Governor-general of Eastern Siberia from 1847–61. Concluded an unequal Aigun treaty with China in 1858.

Münsterberg, Oskar von (1865–1920). German art expert and Orientalist.

Napoleon I Bonaparte (1769–1821). First Consul of the French Republic from 1799–1804 and Emperor of the French from 1804–14 and in 1815.

Nasonov, Nikolai Mikhailovich (alias Nazonov, Charlie, Iunosha [Youngster]) (1902–1938). Member of the RCP(b) from 1919. Secretary of the Tambov Gubernia Committee of the Komsomol in 1921–22. Member of the Far Eastern Bureau of the CC of the Komsomol in 1922–23. Secretary of the Vladivostok Gubernia Committee of the Komsomol in 1923–24. Secretary of the Central Asian Bureau of the CC of the Komsomol in 1924–25. Representative of the CYI in China in 1925–27 and the USA in 1927–28. Head of the Negro Section of the Eastern Department of the ECCI in 1932–33. Repressed.

Natanson, Mark Andreevich (1850–1919). Participant in the Russian revolutionary movement since 1869. One of the organisers of the 'Land and Freedom' group in 1876. Organiser of the 'People's Rights' Party in 1893. Member of the Party of SRs in 1902–17. One of the organisers and leaders of the Party of Left SRs (Internationalists). Condemned the plot against the Bolshevik government on 6 July 1918. One of the organisers of the Party of Revolutionary Communists in 1918.

Nicholas II (1868–1918). The Russian Emperor of the Romanov dynasty from 1894–1917.

O'Conor, Nicholas Roderick (1843–1908). British chargé d'affaires to China in 1892 and envoy extraordinary and minister plenipotentiary from 1892–95.

O'Malley, Owen (1887–1974). Counsellor of the British Mission in Beijing in 1925–27.

Oxenham, Edward Lavington (1843–1896). British consul in Zhenjiang (Jiangsu Province) from 1880–88, Qiongzhou (Haikou, Guangdong Province) from 1888–90, and Yichang (Hubei Province) in 1890.

Parvus, Alexander Lvovich (original name Israel Lazarevich Gelfand) (1867–1924). Activist of the Russian and German Social Democratic movements. Abandoned political activity in 1918.

Paul I (1754–1801). The Russian Emperor of the Romanov dynasty from 1796.

Pavlov Alexander Ivanovich (1860–1923), Russian acting plenipotentiary in China from 1896–98 and ambassador to China from 1898–1904.

Pepper, John (alias József Pogány, original name József Schwartz) (1886–1938). Member of the Hungarian SDP from 1905. Member of the CP of Hungary from 1919. People's Commissar for Military Affairs of the Hungarian Soviet Republic in 1919. Worked for the administration of ECCI from 1919. Head of the ECCI Information Department in 1924–26, and the Agitation and Propaganda Department from 1926. Candidate member of the Orgburo and the Secretariat of ECCI from 1926. Expelled from the Comintern in 1929. Worked in Gosplan. Repressed.

Perlov, Ivan Semenovich (1843–1900). Co-owner of the Russian tea company 'Vasilii Perlov and sons' after the death of his father in 1879.

Perlov, Nikolai Semenovich (1849–1911). Younger brother of Ivan Semenovich Perlov. Co-owner of the Russian tea company 'Vasilii Perlov and sons' after the death of his father in 1879.

Perry, Matthew C. (1794–1858). American commodore who forced the Japanese to sign the first unequal treaty of Kanagawa in 1854.

Peter the Great (alias Peter I) (1672–1725). The Russian Tsar of the Romanov dynasty from 1682–1721 and the Russian Emperor from 1721.

Philip II (1527–1598). Spanish King of the Habsburg dynasty from 1556.

Piatakov, Iuri (Georgii) Leonidovich (1890–1937). Member of the RSDLP(b) since 1910. Candidate member of the CC in 1921–22. Member of the CC in 1922–27 and 1930–36. Chairman of the Kiev MRC in 1917. Chief Commissar of Gosbank at the end of 1917-early 1918. Chairman of the Provisional worker-peasant government of Ukraine in 1918. During the Civil War (1918–20), successively member of the RMC of the 13th, 16th and 6th Army. In 1920–23 Deputy Chairman of SSNE. In 1927 Soviet trade representative in France. Member of the Trotskyist opposition. Expelled from the Party in 1927. Capitulated to Stalin in 1928. In 1928 Deputy Chairman, in 1929 Chairman of the Administration of Gosbank of the USSR. In 1931–32 Deputy People's Commissar for Heavy Industry. Arrested on 14 September 1936. Shot on 1 February 1937.

Pokotilov, Dmitrii Dmitrievich (1865–1908). Russian Imperial Minister to China from 1905–08.

Pokrovskii, Mikhail Nikolaevich (1868–1932). Soviet historian. Member of the RSDLP(b) since 1905. Chairman of the Moscow Soviet of workers' and soldiers' deputies at the end of 1917. Chairman of the Council of People's Commissars of Moscow and the Moscow region in 1918. Deputy People's Commissar of Education from 1918. Head of the Communist Academy (1918–36) and the Institute of Red Professors (1921–30), Academician of the AN of the USSR from 1929.

Polo, Marco (1254–1324). Venetian merchant and traveller. Author of a book about his travels in China, in which, according to him, he lived 17 years (from 1275 to 1292).

Polonskii, Vladimir Ivanovich (1893–1937). Member of the RSDLP(b) since 1912. Member of the Central Administration of the Petersburg Union of Metalworkers. In 1915–17 in exile in Tobolsk. Secretary of the Central Administration of the Moscow Union of Metalworkers from March 1917. During the Civil War (1918–20) commissar of divisions of the WPRA on the Western and Southern fronts, military commissar of the South-Western railway, Chairman of the Southern Bureau of the AUCUTU. In 1920–24 on trade union work. Secretary of the Rogozhsk-Simonovsk District Committee of the Moscow Committee of the AUCP(b) in 1925–28. Second secretary of the Moscow Committee in 1928–30. First secretary of the CC of the CP(b) of Azerbaijan and secretary of the Transcaucasian Regional Committee of the AUCP(b) in 1930–33. Head of the Organisation Department of the CC of the AUCP(b) in 1933. Head of the Political Administration and Deputy People's Commissar of the NKPS in August 1933–35. Secretary of the AUCUTU from 1935. Deputy People's Commissar for Communications. Arrested on 21 June 1937, shot on 20 October 1937.

Preobrazhenskii, Evgenii Alekseevich (1886–1937). Member of the RSDLP(b) since 1903. Candidate member of the CC in 1917–18. Member of the CC in 1920–21. Member of the ARCEC in 1917. Deputy Chairman of the Chita Soviet of workers' and soldiers' deputies in 1917. Chairman of the Presidium of the Urals Regional Committee of the RCP(b) in 1918. Secretary and member of the Orgburo of the CC of the RCP(b) in 1920–21. From 1921 Chairman of the Financial Committee of the CC of the RKP(b) and of the Council of People's Commissars of the RSFSR, Chairman of the Chief Administration for Professional Education of the People's Commissariat of Education of the RSFSR. In 1924–27 Deputy Chairman of the Chief Committee on Concessions. Member of the

Trotskyist opposition. Expelled from the Party in 1927. Capitulated to Stalin in 1929. Deputy Chairman of the Nizhny Novgorod Regional Planning Committee in 1930–32. Member of the Collegium of the People's Commissariat for Light Industry of the USSR in 1932–33. Arrested on 20 December 1936. Shot on 13 July 1937.

Prigozhin, Abram Grigorievich (1896–1937). Member of the RSDLP(b) since 1918. Taught at the Urals-Siberian Communist University in 1925–26. Taught history of Western revolutionary movement at the UTK from September 1926 until 1 June 1927. Member of the Trotskyist opposition. Arrested on 5 August 1936. Shot on 8 March 1937.

Proudhon, Pierre-Joseph (1809–1865). French politician and philosopher, founder of anarchism.

Purcell, Albert Arthur (1872–1935). British trade unionist and politician. Labour member of Parliament in 1922–24, 1925–29. Chairman of the Strike Organising Committee of the General Council of the TUC at the time of the 1926 General Strike. President of the International Federation of Trade Unions, one of the founders of the Anglo-Russian Committee for Trade Union unity in 1925–27.

Quigley, Harold Scott (1889–1968). Sinologist, specialist on the history and jurisprudence of China.

Qin Shi Huangdi (original name Ying Zheng) (259–210 BCE). First Emperor of China from 221 BCE, founder of the Qin dynasty.

Radek, Andrzej. Hero of the novel *Syzyfowe prace* by the Polish writer Stefan Żeromski.

Rafes Moisei Grigorievich (alias Max, Borisov) (1883–1942). Member of the Bund from 1900. Member of the RSDLP(b) from 1919. Worked in the Department of Agitation and Propaganda of ECCI from 1920. Secretary of the Far Eastern Bureau of ECCI from June to October 1926. Head of the Foreign Department of TASS since 1927. Arrested on 11 May 1938. Sentenced to ten years' deprivation of liberty on 2 June 1940.

Primrose, 5th Earl of Rosebery, Archibald Philip (1847–1929). British Secretary of State for Foreign Affairs in 1886 and 1892–94 and Prime Minister in 1894–95.

Raskol'nikov, Fedor Fedorovich (alias Petrov, original surname Ilyin) (1892–1939). Member of the RSDLP(b) since 1910. Deputy People's Commissar for Naval Affairs and successively Commander of the Volga and Caspian flotillas and also the Baltic Fleet in 1918–21. Soviet ambassador to Afghanistan in 1921–23. Head of the Eastern Department of the ECCI from March 1924 to February 1926. Soviet ambassador to Estonia, Denmark and Bulgaria in 1930–38. Emigrated in 1938. Expelled from the Party *in absentia* and declared an 'enemy of the people' in 1938. Assassinated.

Riazanov, David Borisovich (original surname Goldendakh) (1870–1938). Russian and Soviet revolutionary, historian and Marxist theoretician, Director of the Marx-Engels Institute from 1921–31.

Richthofen, Ferdinand, Freiherr von (1833–1905). A German traveller, professor of geology and geography.

Robespierre, Maximilien (1758–1794). French revolutionary, one of the leaders of the Jacobin Club. Head of the Committee of Public Safety in 1793–94. Executed.

Ronglu (1836–1903). The Qing governor-general of Zhili Province.

Ross, John (1842–1915). British Protestant missionary in Manchuria.

Rothstein, Adolf Iulievich (1857–1904). Co-founder of the Russo-Chinese bank in 1896 and a member of its Directorate from 1896–1904.

Rothstein, Feodor Aronovich (alias Theodor) (1871–1953). Russian and British revolutionary, diplomat and scholar, the first Soviet ambassador to Persia from 1921–22, the first Director of the Institute of World Economy and World Politics from 1924–25.

Roy, Manabendra Nath (alias Johnson, original name Bhattacharya Narendra Nath) (1887–1954). Activist of the Indian and Mexican Communist movements. Worked for ECCI since 1920. Candidate member of ECCI in 1922–24. Member of ECCI in 1924–27. Representative of ECCI in China in 1927. Expelled from the Comintern in 1929. General Secretary of the Radical Democratic Party of India from September 1940.

Rubach, Mikhail Abramovich (original name Rubanovich) (1899–1980). Soviet historian.

Rudzutak, Yan Ernestovich (1887–1938). Member of the RSDLP(b) from 1915. Member of the CC in 1920–37. Secretary of the CC of the RCP(b) in 1921–22. Member of the Politburo in 1926–32 and 1934–37. People's Commissar for Transport in 1924–30. Deputy Chairman of CPC and CLD of the USSR in 1926–37. Chairman of the CCC and People's Commissar for the Worker-Peasant Inspection in 1931–1934. Arrested on 24 May 1937. Shot on 29 September 1938.

Ryhove, François de la Kethulle van (1531–1585). One of the leaders of the Calvinists in the city of Gent (Flanders). Headed an uprising against the Spanish monarchy in 1577. Executed.

Safarov, Georgii Ivanovich (alias Volodin, Egorov, Samovarchik) (1891–1942). Member of the RSDLP(b) since 1908. Candidate member of the CC in 1921–23 and 1924–25. Secretary and head of the Eastern Department of ECCI from August 1921 to May 1922. Editor of the newspaper *Petrogradskaia (Leningradskaia) pravda* in 1922–26. First Secretary of the Soviet Embassy in China in 1926–27. Member of the Zinovievist opposition. Expelled from the Party in 1927. Capitulated to Stalin in 1928. Deputy head of the Eastern Länder secretariat of ECCI in 1929–34. Repressed.

Salisbury, Robert Talbot Gascoyne-Cecil, 3rd Marquess of (1830–1903). British conservative politician, prime-minister in 1885–86, 1886–92, 1895–1902.

Saltykov-Shchedrin, Mikhail Evgrafovich (original surname Saltykov, pen name N. Shchedrin) (1826–1889). Russian satirical writer, journalist.

Savinkov, Boris Viktorovich (alias V. Ropshin, Veniamin, James Galley, Kseshinsky, Pavel Ivanovich, D.E. Subbotin, Leon Rodé, Konstantin Chernetsky) (1879–1925). Member of the RSDLP in 1898–1903. Member of the SR Party in 1903–17. Deputy head of its Military organisation. In 1917 successively Commissar of the Provisional government in the 8th Army and Commissar of the South-Western front, Deputy War Minister, military governor of Petrograd, and Deputy Commander of the Petrograd military district. At the time of the Kornilov mutiny in August–September 1917 sympathised with L.G. Kornilov, but fell out with him over methods and timing. One of the organisers of the White movement. Founded the League for the Defence of the Motherland and Liberty in Paris. Published the newspaper *Za svobodu*. In 1924 persuaded by secret agents of OGPU to return illegally to the USSR and was arrested crossing the frontier. Killed or committed suicide in jail on 7 May 1925.

Schenck zu Schweinsberg, Gustav Adolf (1843–1909). German minister in China from 1893–96.

Schüler, Wilhelm (1869–1935). German missionary and Sinologist.

Shao Lizi (1882–1967). Member of Sun Yat-sen's 'Revolutionary Alliance' from 1905. Member of the CCP in 1921–26. Head of the Secretariat of Whampoa Military Academy in 1925. Representative of the CEC of the GMD in ECCI in 1926–27. After July 1927, successively head of the Department of Propaganda of the CEC of the GMD, Chinese ambassador to the USSR, and secretary of the CPPCC. Resigned in 1949.

Serebriakov, Leonid Petrovich (1888–1937). Member of the RSDLP(b) from 1905. Member of the CC and Orgburo of the CC of the RCP(b) in 1919–1921. Secretary of the CC of the RCP(b) in 1920–21. Member of Kostroma Soviet of workers' and soldiers' deputies in 1917. Member of the Presidium of the Moscow Soviet, secretary of the Regional Bureau of the RCP(b), member and secretary of the Presidium of the AUCEC, member of the RMC of the Southern front in 1918–20. Commissar of the Chief Administration of Communications from 1921. Deputy People's Commissar of Communications in 1922–24. In 1926–27 on diplomatic work in China. In 1927–29 in the USA. Member of the Trotskyist opposition. Expelled from the Party in 1927. Capitulated to Stalin in 1928. On economic work from 1929. Arrested on 17 August 1936. Shot on 1 February 1937.

Sermuks, Nikolai Martynovich (1896–1937). L.D. Trotsky's secretary. Repressed.

Shingarev, Andrei Ivanovich (1869–1918). Member of the Kadet Party from 1905. Member of its CC from 1908. Editor of the Kadet newspaper *Voronezhskoe slovo* in 1905–07. Deputy of the State Duma in 1906–17. Minister of Finance in the Provisional government in May–July 1917. Arrested by the Bolsheviks in November 1917. Murdered by Red Guards.

Shchukar, Maxim Ilyich (1897–?). Soviet Sinologist. Taught at the UTK-KUTK. Repressed.

Shumiatskii, Boris Zakharovich (alias Andrei Chervonii) (1886–1938). Member of the RSDLP(b) from 1903. Deputy Chairman of the Krasnoiarsk Soviet, Chairman of the CEC of the Soviets of Siberia in 1917. Deputy chairman of the Siberian Revcom in 1919. Chairman of the Council of Ministers of the Far Eastern Republic and Plenipotentiary of the People's Commissariat of Foreign Affairs for Siberia and Mongolia in 1920–22. Ambassador and trade attaché of the RSFSR (USSR) to Iran in 1922–25. Rector of the KUTV in 1926–1928. Head of the Department of Agitation and Propaganda of the Central Asian Bureau of the CC of the AUCP(b) in 1928–30. Chairman of the All-Union Cinema and Photo Corporation in 1930–33. Head of the Main Management of Cinema and Photo Production from 1933. Arrested on 18 January 1938. Shot on 28 July 1938.

Shuvalov, Petr Andreevich (1827–1889). Count. Head of the Third Department of His Imperial Majesty's Own Chancellery from 1866–74.

Sima Qian (145–86 BCE). Chinese historian of the Han dynasty, author of multi-volume 'Records of the Grand Historian' (*Shiji*).

Skalov, Georgii Borisovich (alias Sinani) (1896–1940?). Member of the RSDLP since 1916. Menshevik until 1918. Participant in the White movement in 1918. At the end of 1918 renounced anti-Soviet struggle. In 1919–20 in the Red Army. Member of RCP(b) since 1919. Member of the RMC of the Fergana army group in 1920. Member of the CC of the CP(b) of Turkestan since 1920. In 1921–22 successively Chairman of the Extraordinary Commission of Turkestan and secretary of the Semirechensk Gubernia Committee of the CP(b) of Turkestan. Rector of the Moscow Institute of Oriental Studies in 1922–23. Commissar of the 5th division of the WPRA in 1923. Member of the RMC of the 13th Corps in 1924–25. In 1925–27 military advisor in China. In 1927–28 was enrolled in the Oriental department of the M.V. Frunze Military Academy. In 1929–30 member of a USSR government delegation to Mongolia. From 1930, instructor, deputy head and acting head of the Länder secretariat for South and Central America of ECCI. Repressed, sentenced to ten years' deprivation of liberty on 27 July 1935.

Skobelev, Matvei Ivanovich (1885–1938). Member of the RSDLP since 1903. Candidate member of its CC in 1917. Menshevik. In 1912 collaborated with L.D. Trotsky. Deputy of the State Duma in 1912–17. Deputy Chairman of the Executive Committee of the Petrograd Soviet of workers' and soldiers' deputies in 1917. Minister of Labour in the Provisional government in May–September 1917. During the Civil War (1918–20) in Transcaucasia. In 1920–22 in exile. Member of the RCP(b) from 1922. From 1925 on Soviet work. Repressed.

Skobelev, Mikhail Dmitrievich (1843–1882). Russian general who conquered Central Asia and played a leading role in the Russo-Turkish war of 1877–78.

Skoropadskii, Pavel Petrovich (1873–1945). Lieutenant-General. Participant in the Russo-Japanese and First World wars. In 1917 commander of the 34th (1st Ukrainian) Army Corps. Head of the officers' organisation of the Ukrainian People's Assembly in 1918. Hetman of the Ukrainian State from 29 April until 14 December 1918. In Germany from the end of 1918. Collaborated with the Nazis.

Sokol'nikov, Grigorii Iakovlevich (original surname Briliant) (1888–1939). Member of the RSDLP(b) since 1905. Member of the CC in 1917–19, 1922–30. Candidate member of the CC in 1930–36. Candidate member of the Politburo of the CC in 1924–25. Member of the ARCEC in 1917. During the Civil War (1918–20) successively member of the RMC of a series of armies, commander of the 8th Army of the Southern front, the Turkestan front, Chairman of the Turkic Commission of the ARCEC and of the CPC of the RSFSR. People's Commissar of Finance in 1922–26. Deputy chairman of Gosplan of the USSR in 1926–28. Chairman of the Oil Syndicate in 1928–29. USSR Ambassador to Great Britain in 1929–34. Deputy People's Commissar of Foreign Affairs in 1934. First Deputy People's

Commissar of the Forestry Industry from 1935. Arrested on 26 July 1936, sentenced to ten years' deprivation of liberty on 30 January 1937. Murdered by fellow prisoners in the Verkhneuralsk prison on 21 May 1939.

Song Qingling (alias Madam Suzi, Liya) (1893–1981). Sun Yat-sen's secretary since 1913 and his wife since 1915. One of the leaders of the left wing of the GMD from 1925. In 1927–31 Honorary Chairwoman of the Anti-Imperialist League. In the 1930s worked with agents of the Comintern in China, participated in the transfer of financial aid from ECCI to the CCP. Honorary Chairwoman of the Revolutionary Committee of the GMD since 1948. After the fall of the GMD regime in 1949, Vice-Chairperson of the Central People's Government of the PRC. In 1954–59 and 1975–81 Vice-Chairperson of the Standing Committee of the NPC of the PRC. In 1959–75 Vice-Chairperson of the PRC. Member of the CCP since 1981. Honorary Chairwoman of the PRC since 1981.

Song Ziwen (alias T.V. Soong) (1894–1971). Member of the CEC of the GMD since 1927. Minister of Finance in the Canton and Wuhan governments in 1925–27. From 1928 occupied successively the posts of Chinese Minister of Finance, Deputy Chairman, then Chairman of the Executive Yuan (chamber), Chairman of the Central Bank, Minister of Foreign Affairs, ambassador to the USA, Chairman of the All-China Higher Economic Committee, Chairman of the Guangdong provincial government. Left China for France in 1949. Later lived in the USA.

Spafarii-Milesku, Nikolai Gavrilovich (alias Nicholas Spathary) (1636–1708). Russian diplomat and scholar, head of the Russian embassy to Beijing from 1675–78.

Spiridonova, Maria Aleksandrovna (1884–1941). Member of the SR Party since 1902. Member of its Military Organisation since 1905. Member of the Petrograd City Committee of the SR Party in 1917. One of the organizers and leaders of the Party of Left SRs (Internationalists). Member of the Presidium of the ARCEC in 1917–18. Honorary Chairwoman of the Petrograd Soviet of peasants' deputies in 1917–18. One of the organizers of the plot against the Bolshevik government on 6 July 1918. From 1918 repeatedly arrested. Shot on 11 September 1941.

Stalin, Joseph Vissarionovich (alias Koba, Vasilii, Vasiliev, K. St., Filippov, Feng Xi, original surname Dzhugashvili) (1878–1953). Member of the RSDLP since 1898. Member of the RSDLP(b) since 1903. Member of the CC since 1917. Member of the Politburo since 1919. People's Commissar for Nationalities in 1917–22. General Secretary of the CC from 1922. Chairman of the CPC from 1941.

Steklov, Iuri Mikhailovich (original name Ovshii Moiseevich Nakhamkis) (1873–1941). Participant in the Social Democratic movement since 1893. Member of the RSDLP since 1898. Menshevik. Member of the RSDLP(b) since 1917. Member of the Executive Committee of the Petrograd Soviet of workers' and soldiers' deputies. Editor of the newspaper *Izvestiia* in February–May 1917 and from October 1917 to June 1925. From 1929 Deputy Chairman of an Academic Committee of the CEC of the USSR. Arrested in February 1938. Died in prison on 15 September 1941.

Strewe, Maria Theodor (?–?). German journalist in China in the late 1910s. Later worked for *Deutsche Allgemeine Zeitung* and was General Secretary of the China Study Society.

Stringer, Harold (1883–1935). British engineer and expert on railway construction in China and Portuguese West Africa.

Stroganov, Semen Anikeevich (1540?–1586). Russian wealthy merchant. Financed Yermak's expedition.

Stroganov, Maxim Iakovlevich (1557–1624). Nephew of S.A. Stroganov. Russian wealthy merchant. Financed Yermak's expedition.

Stroganov, Nikita Grigorievich (1560–1616). Nephew of S.A. Stroganov. Russian wealthy merchant. Financed Yermak's expedition.

Struve, Petr Bernhardovich (1870–1944). Russian economist and publicist. Participant in the Russian Social Democratic movement from the 1880s. Author of the 1898 *Manifesto of the RSDLP*. From the end of the 1890s a liberal. From 1905 member of the CC of the Kadet Party. Deputy of the State Duma in 1906–07. Academician of the Russian AN in 1917–28. During the Civil War (1918–20) active participant in the White movement. From 1920 in exile.

Su Zhaozheng (1885–1929). Member of Sun Yat-sen's 'Revolutionary Alliance' from 1908. Participant in the Xinhai revolution of 1911–12. Organiser of the All-China United Sailors' Association in 1921. Member of the CCP from 1925 and of its CC from 1927. Candidate member of the Politburo of the CC of the CCP in 1927–28. Chairman of the Strike Committee of the Hong Kong-Canton strike of 1925–26. Member of the Executive Committee of the All-China Federation of Trade Unions in 1925–26 and Chairman of the EC of the ACCTU in 1926–28. Minister of Labour in the Wuhan government in 1927. Member of ECCI and of the EC of the Trade Union International in 1928–29.

Sugiyama Akira (?–1900). The chancellor of the Japanese mission to China.

Sukhanov, Nikolai Nikolaevich (original surname Gimmer) (1882–1940). Member of the SR Party from 1903. Member of the EC of the Petrograd Soviet of workers' and soldiers' deputies in 1917. Member of the RSDLP from May 1917 to 1920. Menshevik. Member of the ARCEC in 1918. From June 1918 on economic work. From 1931 repeatedly arrested. Shot on 29 June 1940.

Sun Chuanfang (1885–1935). Chinese warlord. Military governor of Fujian province in 1923–24. Controlled the provinces of Fujian, Zhejiang, Jiangsu, Anhui and Jiangxi from 1925. Defeated by the NRA in 1927. Resigned in 1929. Assassinated.

Sun Fo (alias Sun Ke) (1891–1973). Son of Sun Yat-sen. Member of the CEC of the GMD from 1924. Mayor of Canton city in 1921–22, 1923–24 and 1925–27. Chairman of the Guangdong provincial government in 1925–27. Member of the Wuhan government in 1927. Minister of Finance in the Nanjing government from September 1927. Head of the Legislative Yuan (chamber) in 1932–48. Left China for France in 1949. Arrived in Taiwan and became head of the Examination Yuan in 1965.

Sun Yat-sen (alias Sun Zhongshan, Sun Yixian, original name Sun Wen) (1866–1925). Chinese Revolutionary. Founder of the Guomindang. Provisional President of the Chinese Republic in 1912. President of the Military government of South China in 1917, 1920–22 and 1923–25.

Tan Pingshan (1886–1956). Member of the CCP from 1921. Member of the CEC (CC) and Politburo in 1926–27. Minister of Agriculture in the Wuhan government from March to June 1927. After the revolution of 1925–27 withdrew from the CCP. One of the organizers of the Chinese Revolutionary (later – Peasant-Worker Democratic) party in 1928. Worked for the PRC in state service from 1949.

Tan Sitong (alias Fusheng, Zhuangfei) (1865–1898). Chinese reformer, member of the Chinese Grand Council in 1898. Executed.

Tan Yankai (1880–1930). Member of the GMD in 1912–13 and from 1922. Governor of Hunan province in 1911–13, 1916–17 and 1918–20. Member of the CEC of the GMD from 1924. Acting Chairman of the National government of the GMD in 1926–27, 1928 and 1929.

Tanaka Giichi (1864–1929). Baron, Japanese Prime Minister in 1927–29.

Tang Wang (ca. 1700 BCE). Founder of the Chinese Shang/Yin dynasty.

Tang Shengzhi (alias Tang Mengxiao) (1889–1970). Chinese general. Governor of Hunan province in 1926. Member of the GMD from 1926. Member of the Political Council of the CEC of the GMD in 1927. Chairman of the government of Hunan province in 1927. Commander of the 8th Corps of the NRA. Member of the Military council of the Wuhan government in 1927. Later occupied various state and military posts. After the fall of the GMD regime in 1949 deputy chairman of the Hunan provincial government, member of the Standing Committee of the CC of the Revolutionary Committee of the GMD.

Tarkhanov, Oskar Sergeevich (alias S.P. Razumov, O. Tanin, O. Taube, O. Erdberg, Karrio, Yang Zhulai, original name Sergei Petrovich Razumov) (1901–1938). Soviet Sinologist, activist of the Communist youth movement, journalist. Member of the RSDLP(b) since 1917. One of the leaders of the young Communist underground in Odessa and Crimea in 1918–20. Secretary of the CC of the RCYL, member of the Executive Committee and secretary of the CYI in 1921–24. Political advisor in China in 1925–27. Member of the Trotskyist opposition. Expelled from the Party in 1927. Capitulated to Stalin in 1928. In 1932–34 on political work in the Special Far Eastern Red Flag Army. Advisor to the Soviet Embassy in the MPR from 1935. Arrested. Shot on 8 February 1938.

Tayler, John Bernard (1878–1951). British missionary from 1906 and professor of economics at Yenching University in Beijing from 1917.

Thomas, Sidney Gilchrist (1850–1885). English engineer.

Tomskii, Mikhail Petrovich (alias M.T., original surname Efremov) (1880–1936). Member of the RSDLP(b) after 1904. Member of the CC in 1919–34. Member of the Politburo in 1922–30. Candidate member of the CC from 1934. Chairman of the Moscow Council of Trade Unions in 1917–18. Chairman of the All-Russian (All-Union) Council of Trade Unions in 1918–21 and 1922–29. Deputy Chairman of the SSNE in 1929–30. Director of Gosizdat from 1932. Committed suicide.

Toyotomi Hideyoshi (1537–1598). Japanese shogun, a unifier of Japan in 1591.

Trotsky, Leon [Lev Davidovich] (alias Pero, Nikolai Trotsky, original surname Bronshtein) (1879–1940). Member of the RSDLP since 1898. Member of the RSDLP(b) from July 1917. Member of the CC in 1917–27. Member of the Politburo in 1919–26. One of the organisers of the October (1917) revolution. People's Commissar of Foreign Affairs in 1917–18. Chairman of the RMC and People's Commissar for Military and Naval Affairs of the RSFSR (USSR) in 1918–25. Chairman of the Main Concession Committee in 1925–27. Leader of the Trotskyist opposition. Expelled from the Party in 1927. Exiled from the USSR in 1929. Assassinated.

Tsereteli, Iraklii Georgievich (1881–1959). Chairman of the Executive Committee of student organisations of Moscow in 1901. Member of the RSDLP from 1903. Menshevik. Member of the CC of the RSDLP from 1917. Deputy of the State Duma in 1906–07. Member of the Executive Committee of the Petrograd Soviet of workers' and soldiers' deputies in 1917. Minister of Posts & Telegraphs of the Provisional government in May–July 1917 and simultaneously Acting Minister of Internal Affairs in July 1917. On the advice of V.I. Lenin, he left for Georgia in 1918. Member of the Executive Committee of the National Council of Georgia in 1918–20. Abroad from 1919.

Urusov, Lev Pavlovich (1839–1928). Prince, Russian ambassador to France from 1897–1904.

Varga, Evgenii Samuilovich (alias Evgenii Pavlovskii, original name Jenö) (1879–1964). Member of the Hungarian SDP since 1906. Member of the CP of Hungary since 1919. People's Commissar of Finance of the Hungarian Soviet Republic in 1919. Candidate member of ECCI in 1920–43. Head of a department of the journal *Kommunisticheskii Internatsional* in 1920. Director of the Information-Statistical Institute of ECCI in Berlin (alias the Information Bureau or 'Varga Bureau') in 1921–28. Director of the IWE&WP in 1927–47. Academician of the AN of the USSR since 1939.

Vasiliev, Vasilii Pavlovich (1818–1900). Russian Sinologist. Until 1851 worked in Kazan, thereafter in St. Petersburg. Academician of the St. Petersburg Academy of Sciences since 1886.

Victoria (alias Alexandrina Victoria) (1819–1901). Queen of the United Kingdom from 1837.

Voitinskii, Grigorii Naumovich (alias Grigorii, Grigoriev, Sergei, Sergeev, Steven(son), Tarasov, original surname Zarkhin) (1893–1953). Member of the RSDLP(b) since 1918. Chairman of the Revcom in the town of Alexandrovsk (Sakhalin) in 1920. Representative of the Vladivostok Department of the Far Eastern Bureau of the RCP(b) in China in 1920–21. Head of the Far Eastern Department, deputy head of the Eastern Department of the ECCI since 1922. Representative of ECCI in China in 1925. Head of the Far Eastern Bureau of ECCI in Shanghai in 1926–27. Deputy Chairman of the Fruit and Vegetable Centre of the All-Russian Agricultural Co-operation in 1927–1929. Secretary of the Pacific Ocean Secretariat of the Trade Union International in 1932–34. Taught at various colleges since 1934.

Volin, Mikhail (original name Semen Natanovich Belenkii) (1896–1938). Soviet Sinologist. Director of the Scientific Research Institute on China at the KUTK in 1928–30.

Voroshilov, Kliment Efremovich (1881–1969). Member of the RSDLP(b) since 1903. Member of the CC in 1921–61 and from 1966. Member of the Politburo (Presidium) of the CC in 1926–60. Chairman of the RMC and People's Commissar for Military and Naval Affairs of the USSR since 1925. People's Commissar for Defence of the USSR in 1934–40. Vice-Chairman of the CPC of the USSR since 1940. Chairman of the Supreme Soviet of the USSR in 1953–60.

Wagner, Wilhelm (1884–?). German agronomist and Sinologist.

Wakatsuki Reijiro (1866–1949). Japanese Prime Minister in 1926–27 and 1931.

Waldersee, Alfred Ludwig Heinrich Karl von (1832–1904). Count, Field Marshal, Chief of German General Staff in 1888–91 and Supreme Commander of Allied forces in China in 1900–01. Suppressed the Boxer Rebellion.

Wang Anshi (1021–1086). Chinese official and reformer of the Song Dynasty.

Wang Jingwei (alias Wang Zhaoming) (1883–1944). Member of Sun Yat-sen's 'Revolutionary Alliance' from 1905. Leader of the 'left' Guomindang, chief of the National government of the GMD, Chairman of the Military and Political Councils of the CEC of the GMD from July 1925 to May 1926. Chief of the Wuhan government in April–September 1927. Leader of the GMD Reorganisationists faction. Collaborated with Japanese invaders from 1938. Head of the pro-Japanese puppet regime in Nanjing from 1940.

Wang Mang (45 BCE–23 CE). Emperor of the Xin Dynasty in 9–23 CE. Killed as a result of the rebellion of the 'Red Eyebrow' peasants.

Weber, Max (1864–1920). German sociologist, historian, economist and jurist.

Weng Tonghe (alias Shengjie, Renfu, Shengfu) (1830–1904). Tutor of two Manchu Emperors, Tongzhi and Guangxu. Chinese Minister of Revenue from 1886–98.

Wilhelm, Richard (1873–1930). German Sinologist.

Wilhelm II (1859–1941). German Emperor of the Hohenzollern dynasty from 1888–1918.

Wilson, Woodrow (1856–1924). The 28th President of the United States from 1913–21.

Witte, Sergei Iulievich (1849–1915). Finance Minister from 1892–1903 and Prime Minister of the Russian Empire from 1903–06.

Wrangel, Petr Nikolaevich (1878–1928). Baron. Lieutenant-General. One of the leaders of the White Movement in South Russia during the Civil War. In 1920 Commander-in-Chief of the Russian Army. From 1920 in exile. In 1928 organised and headed the Russian All-Military Union.

Wu Chaoshu (alias C.C. Wu) (1887–1934). Member of the CEC of the GMD from 1926. Secretary of the Political Council of the GMD in 1924. Minister of Foreign Affairs of the Canton government in 1925–1926. Later on diplomatic work.

Wu Peifu (1874–1939). Chinese general. Head of the Zhili militarist clique, who controlled Hubei and Henan provinces. Defeated by the NRA in 1926. Escaped to Sichuan. In 1931 moved to Beiping (Beijing).

Wu Sangui (alias Changbai and Changbo) (1612–1678). Chinese general at the end of the Ming dynasty. In 1644 concluded an alliance with the Manchus with the aim of suppressing a peasant uprising in China. Governor of Yunnan province at the beginning of the reign of the Qing dynasty until 1674. Rose against the Manchus in 1674. Self-proclaimed Emperor of the Zhou dynasty in Yunnan province from 1675.

Xia Douyin (1885–1951). Chinese general. Member of the 'Revolutionary Alliance' from 1906. Participant in the Xinhai revolution of 1911–12. Commander of the 1st division of the NRA in 1926. Commander of the 14th special division of the NRA, member of the Administrative Council of Hubei province, member of the Executive Committee of the GMD of Hubei province in 1927. In May 1927 mutinied against the Wuhan government. Later occupied various state and military posts. After the fall of the GMD regime in 1949 he escaped to Hong Kong.

Xie Daoqing (1210–1283). Grand Empress Dowager of the Southern Song dynasty.

Xu Kexiang (1889–1964). Chinese general. Member of the 'Revolutionary Alliance' from 1906. Participant in the Xinhai revolution of 1911–12. Commander of the 19th regiment of the 6th brigade of provincial troops in Hunan in 1920–25. Commander of a separate brigade in 1925–26. In 1926 came over to the GMD. Commander of the 33rd regiment of the 35th Corps of the NRA from the spring of 1927. On 21 May 1927 carried out an anti-Communist coup in Changsha, the capital of Hunan. Commander of the 2nd Field

Army of the NRA from December 1929. Commander of the 24th division in 1930–33. Deputy Commander of the 37th Army in 1933–37. From 1937 until 1953 in Macao. Since 1953 worked in the administration of the President of the ROC (Taiwan).

Xu Qian (alias Xu Jilong, Qiao Zhi, George Xu) (1871–1940). Member of the GMD from 1912. Member of the CEC in 1926–27. Member of the Political Council of the CEC in 1927. Head of Sun Yat-sen's secretariat in 1917. Minister of Justice in the Canton government in 1920. Chairman of the Supreme Court in Canton in 1921–22. Leader of the Beijing Committee of the GMD from 1924. Head of the Political Department of the Nationalist Army of Feng Yuxiang in 1925. Member of the Military Council and Minister of Justice in the Wuhan government in 1927. In the autumn of 1927 withdrew from politics.

Yang Pao'an (1896–1931). Member of the CCP from 1921. Secretary of the Organisation Department of the CEC of the GMD in 1924–27. One of the organisers of the Hong Kong-Canton strike in 1925–26. Member of the CC of the CCP in 1927–28.

Yang Sen (alias Yang Zihui, Shu Zi) (1884–1977). Chinese general. Civil governor of Sichuan in 1924–25. Military governor of Sichuan in 1926. Commander of the 20th Corps of the NRA in 1926–27. Later occupied various leading military posts. After the fall of the GMD regime in 1949, fled to Taiwan.

Yermak Timofeevich (alias Vasilii Timofeevich Alenin) (1532 or 1542–1585). A Cossack warrior who started the Russian conquest of Western Siberia.

Yuan Shikai (alias Yuan Weiting) (1859–1916). Chinese general. Commander of the Beiyang Army. Prime Minister of the Qing government in 1911–12. Provisional President of the Republic of China in 1912–13. President from 1913.

Yu the Great (2200–2101 BCE). Legendary ruler of Ancient China credited with the founding of the Xia dynasty and the creation of the irrigation system.

Yuan Chang (alias Zhenchan, Shuangqiu, Zhongli) (1846–1900). The Qing Minister of Ceremonies who dealt with foreign affairs. Executed by Cixi for his opposition to the Boxer Rebellion.

Zakharov, Ivan Ilyich (1814–1885). Russian Sinologist. Professor of St. Petersburg University from 1875.

Żeromski, Stefan (1864–1925). Polish writer.

Zhakov, Mikhail Petrovich (?–?). Member of the RCP(b) from 1923. Taught at the UTK until the middle of 1927. Leader of the Trotskyist opposition of the Khamovniki district of Moscow. Repressed.

Zhang Guotao (alias Amosov, Popov, Spiridonov, Kotel'nikov) (1897–1979). One of the founders of the CCP in 1921. Member of the CEC (CC) of the CCP in 1921–23, 1925–38. Candidate member of the CEC of the CCP in 1923–25. Member of the Politburo in 1928–38. Secretary of the Jiangxi and Hubei Provincial Committees of the Party in 1926–27. Member of a delegation of the CCP to ECCI in 1928–30. Deputy Chairman of the Chinese Soviet Government in 1931–36. Expelled from the Party in 1938. Went into exile in 1949.

Zhang Yinhuan (1837–1900). Qing diplomat, China's minister in U.S.A., Spain, Peru, England, France, Germany, and Russia from 1886–89. Assisted Li Hongzhang during negotiations with Russians in 1898 in regard to Port Arthur concession.

Zhang Zuolin (1875–1928). Head of the Fengtian (Shenyang) military clique, which controlled the Beijing Government in 1920–22 and 1924–28. Defeated by the NRA in 1928. Assassinated by Japanese.

Zhong Hui (alias Lai Zhu) (?–?). Minister and adviser of Cheng Tang, the first King of the Shang/Yin dynasty who urged his ruler to conquer the declining Xia dynasty.

Zhou Dawen (alias Zhou Daming, Di Yi, Luo Fu, Vladimir Vasilievich Chugunov) (1903–1938). Member of the CCP from 1923. Chairman of the All-China Student Union in 1924. Studied and worked at the UTK and the International Lenin School in 1925–30. Instructor of political economy in the International Lenin School in 1930–32. Editor-in-Chief of the Khabarovsk regional newspaper *Gongren zhi lu* from 1932. Accused of 'Trotskyism' and arrested in 1937. Executed.

Zhou Liang (?–?). Chinese general. Deputy commander of the 36th Corps of the NRA in 1927. Special representative of the CEC of the GMD in Hunan in June 1927.

Zhu Peide (alias Zhu Yizhi) (1888–1937). General. Member of the GMD from 1920. Member of the CEC and of the Political Council of the CEC of the GMD in 1926–27. In 1925–26 member of the Canton government. In the period of the Northern Expedition of 1926–27 commander of the 3rd Corps of the NRA. Member of the Wuhan government, Chairman of the Jiangxi Provincial government in 1927. Later occupied various political posts.

Zhu Yuanzhang (alias Hongwu) (1328–1398). The first Emperor of the Ming dynasty from 1368.

Zinoviev, Grigorii Evseevich (original name Ovsei-Hersh Aronovich Radomyslskii) (1883–1936). Member of the RSDLP since 1901. Member of the RSDLP(b) from 1903. Member of the CC in 1907–17. Candidate member of the Politburo in 1919–21. Member of the Politburo in 1921–26. Chairman of the Petrograd (Leningrad) Soviet in 1917–26. Chairman of the Comintern in 1919–1926. Leader of the Zinovievist opposition. Expelled from the Party in 1927. Capitulated to Stalin in 1928. Rector of Kazan University from 1928. From 1933 worked in the Tsentrosoiuz. Arrested on 16 December 1934. Shot on 25 August 1936.

Zubatov, Sergei Vasilievich (1864–1917). Head of Moscow Security Bureau from 1896–1902 and head of the Special Section of the Police Department from 1902–03.

Works Cited

Akatova, T.N. 1959, *Sianggang-Guangzhouskaia zabastovka*, Moscow: Nauka.

Alskii, M. 1926, 'Krestianskoie dvizheniie v Guandune', *Bol'shevik*, 12: 40–51; 13: 50–72.

Andreev, M. 1927, 'V Pekine: Bytovoi ocherk', *Krasnaia nov'*, 5: 198–213.

Anderson, Frank Maloy and Amos Shartle Hershey 1918, *Handbook for the Diplomatic History of Europe, Asia, and Africa 1870–1914*, Washington: Goverment printing office.

Artemov, V.A. 2000, *Karl Radek: Ideia i sud'ba*, Voronezh: TsChKI.

AUCP(b) 1927a, *XV konferentsiia Vsesoiuznoi Kommunisticheskoi partii (b), 26 oktiabria–3 noiabria 1926. Stenograficheskii otchet*, Moscow-Leningrad: Gosizdat.

AUCP(b) 1927b, *Plenum TsK VKP(b) 13–16 aprelia 1927 g. Stenograficheskii otchet*. Moscow-Leningrad: Gosizdat.

AUCP(b) 1928, *XV s"ezd Vsesoiuznoi Kommunisticheskoi partii (b)*, Moscow-Leningrad: Gosizdat.

Bakunin, M.A. 1921, *Ispoved' i ps'mo Aleksandru II*, Moscow: Gosizdat.

Balabanoff, A. [1938], *My Life as a Rebel*, New York: Harper & brothers.

Bergère, M.-C. 2009, *The Golden Age of the Chinese Bourgeoisie 1911–1937*, New York: Cambridge University Press.

Boiarchikov, A.I. 2003, *Vospomonaniya*, Moscow: AST.

Bolkhovitinov, L.M. 1910, 'Kolonizatory Dal'nego Vostoka', in *Velikaia Rossia: Sbornik statei po voennym i obshchestvennym voprosam*, edited by V.P. Riabushinskii, (Volume 1), Moscow: Izd. V.P. Riabushinskii.

Boulger, D. 1898, *The History of China*, (2 volumes), London: Thacker & Co.

Boulger, D. 1900, *A Short History of China: An Account for the General Reader of an Ancient Empire and People*, New York: Harper.

Bland, J.O.P. and E.T. Backhouse 1910, *China under the Empress Dowager: Being The History of the Life and Times of Tsŭ Hsi, Compiled from State Papers and the Private Diary of the Comptroller of Her Household*, London: W. Heinemann.

Bland, J.O.P. and E.T. Backhouse 1913, *China unter der Kaiseren Witwe*, Berlin: Karl Siegismund.

Blumenberg, W. 1960, *Karl Kautskys literarisches werk: Eine bibliographische übersicht*, 's-Gravenhage: Mouton.

Brandt, C. 1958, *Stalin's Failure in China*, Cambridge, MA: Harvard University Press.

Bradt, M. von 1898, *Die politische und Commerzielle Entwicklung Ostasiens Während der Jüngsten Zeit (Vortrag)*, Leipzig: Verlag von Gedorg Wegand.

Broué, P. 1996, A Letter to A.V. Pantsov, 29 November 1996.

Broué, P. 1997, *Histoire de l'Internationale Communiste. 1919–1943*, Paris: Fayard.

Bücher, Karl 1896, *Arbeit und rhythmus*. Leipzig: B.G. Teubner.

Bücher, Karl 1899. *Trud i ritm: Rabochie pesni, ikh proiskhozhdenie i ekonomicheskoe znachenie*, St. Petersburg: Kantora izdanii i knizhnyi magazin O.I. Popovoi.
Bücher, Karl 1923, *Trud i ritm: Rabochie pesni, ikh proiskhozhdenie i ekonomicheskoe znachenie*, Moscow: Novaia Moskva.
Bukharin, N.I. 1921, *Teoriia istoricheskogo materializma: Popularnyi uchebnik marksistskoi sotsiologii*, Moscow: Gosudarstvennoe izdatel'stvo.
Bukharin, N.I. 1927a, *Kapitalisticheskaia stabilizatsiia i proletarskaia revoliutsiia*, Moscow-Leningrad: Gosizdat.
Bukharin, N.I. 1927b, 'Perspektivyi kitaiskoi revoliutsii', *Revoliutsionnyi Vostok*, 1: 3–21.
Bukharin, N.I. 1927c, *Problemy kitaiskoi revoliutsii*, Moscow: 'Pravda' and 'Bednota'.
Bukharin, N.I. 1927d, 'Problemy kitaiskoi revoliutsii', in *Voprosy kitaiskoi revoliutsii*, Moscow-Leningrad: Giz.
Bukharin, N.I. 1927e, 'Tekushchii moment kitaiskoi revoliutsii', *Pravda*, 30 June.
Bukharin, N.[I.] and E.[A.] Preobrazhenskii 1919, *Azbuka kommunizma: Populiarnoe obiasnenie programmy Rossiiskoi kommunisticheskoi partii (Bolshevikov)*, Petrograd: Izdatel'stvo Petrogradskogo Soveta rabochikh i krasnoarmeiskikh deputatov.
Carlson, O. 1977, 'Recollections of American Trotskyist Leaders', *Studies in Comparative Communism*, 10, 1/2: 161–66.
Carr, E.H. and R.W. Davies 1969–1978, *A History of Soviet Russia: Foundations of a Planned Economy: 1926–1929*, (3 volumes), London: Macmillan.
CCP 1926a, *Zhongguo gongchangdang di sanci zhongyang kuoda zhixing weiyuanhui jueyi*, no place.
CCP 1926b, 'Zhongguo gongchangdang duiyu shijude zhuzhang', *Xiangdao zhoukan*, 163: 1616–17.
CCP 1927, 'Rabochii vopros: Uhan: O khode zabastovki v Han-kou: Guide Weekly (Organ TsK Kitkompartii). No. 181 ot 6-go ianvaria 1927 g.', *Materialy po kitaiskomu voprosu*, 3: 3–10.
Central Soviet Archive 1922, 'Perepiska o podkupe kitaiskikh sanovnikov Li-Khunzhchana i Zhchan-yin-Huana', *Krasnyi arkhiv: Istoricheskii zhurnal*, 2: 287–93.
Central Soviet Archive 1926, 'Bokserskoe vosstanie', *Krasnyi arkhiv: Istoricheskii zhurnal*, 1 (14): 1–49.
Chang Kuo-t'ao 1972, *The Rise of the Chinese Communist Party. Volumes One & Two of Autobiography of Chang Kuo-t'ao*. Lawrence, KS: University Press of Kansas.
Chavannes, E. 1895–1905, *Les Memoires Historiques de Se-Ma Tsien*, (5 volumes), Paris: E. Leroux.
Chen Duxiu 1926a, 'Lun guomin zhengfu zhi beifa,' *Xiangdao zhoukan*, 161: 1584.
Chen Duxiu 1926b, 'Gei Jiang Jieshi de yifengxin', *Xiangdao zhoukan*, 157: 1526–29.
Chen Duxiu 1927, 'Sun Zhongshan xiansheng shishi er zhounian jinianzhong zhi beifen,' *Xiangdao zhoukan*, 191: 2054–55.

Ching-Shan (Jing Shan) 1924, *The Diary of His Excellency Ching-shan; Being a Chinese Account of the Boxer Troubles*, published and translated by J.J.L. Duyvendak, Lugduni Batavorum: E.J. Brill.
Chirol, V. 1896, *The Far Eastern Question*, London: Macmillan.
Collins, W.F. 1918, *Mineral Enterprise in China*, New York: Macmillan.
Collins, W.F. 1922a, *Mineral Enterprise in China*, Revised ed., Tientsin: Tientsin Press, 1922.
Collins, W.F. 1922b, *Zhongguo de caikuang qiye*, Tianjin: n. p.
Comintern 1922, *Bulletin des IV Kongresses der Kommunistischen Internationale*, 20.
Comintern 1925, *Piatyi Vsemirnyi kongress Kommunisticheskogo Internatsionala: 17 iunia–8 iulia 1924 g.: Stenograficheskii otchet*, (2 parts), Moscow-Leningrad: Gosizdat.
Comintern 1927a, 'Piatyi s"ezd Kompartii Kitaia i Guomindang', *Kommunisticheskii Internatsional*, 11: 3–8.
Comintern 1927b, *Puti mirovoi revoliutsii: Sed'moi rasshirennyi plenum Ispolnitel'nogo komiteta Kommunisticheskogo Internatsionala: 22 noiabria–16 dekabria 1926 g.: Stenograficheskii otchet*, (2 volumes), Moscow-Leningrad, Gospolitizdat.
Comintern 1927c, *Shestoi rasshirennyi plenum Ispolkoma Kominterna (17 fevralia–15 marta 1926 g.) Stenograficheskii otchet*, Moscow-Leningrad: Gospolitizdat.
Conrady, A. 1910, *China*, Berlin: Ullstein.
Cordier, Henri 1920–21, *Histoire Générale de la Chine et de ses Relations Avec les Pays Étrangers Depuis le Temps les Plus Anciens Jusqu'à la Chute de la Dynastie Manchoue*, (4 volumes), Paris: P. Geuthner.
Curzon, G.N., *Problems of the Far East: Japan-Korea-China*, Westminester: A. Constable.
Dalin, S. 1975, *Kitaiskie memuary, 1921–1927*, Moscow: Nauka.
Dalin, S. 1927, 'Sun Yat-sen: Ko 2-i godovshchine ego smerti (12 marta 1925 g.)', *Pravda*, 12 March 1927.
Degras, J. (ed) 1960, *The Communist International: 1919–1943: Documents*, (3 volumes), London: F. Cass.
Deutscher, I. 1989, *The Prophet Unarmed: Trotsky: 1921–1929*, New York: Oxford University Press.
Dittmer, C.G. 1918, 'An Estimate of the Standard of Living in China', *Quarterly Journal of Economics*, 33: 107–128.
Engels, F. 1962 [1890], 'Vneshniia politika russkogo tsarizma', *Sochineniia*, (Volume 22), Moscow: Gospolitizdat.
Eudin, X.J. and R.C. North, 1957, *Soviet Russia and the East: 1920–1927: A Documentary Survey*, Stanford, CA: Stanford University Press.
Evans, L. et al. (eds) 1976, *Leon Trotsky on China*, New York: Monad Press.
Fayet, J.-F. 2004, *Karl Radek (1885–1939): Biographie politique*, Bern: Peter Lang.
Felshtinskii Iu. (ed.) 1988, *Kommunisticheskaia oppozitsiia v SSSR: 1923–1927: Iz archiva L'va Trotskogo v chetyrekh tomakh*, (4 volumes) Benson, VT: Chalidze Press.

Felshtinskii, Iu. and G. Cherniavskii 1999, *Arkhiv Trotskogo*, (2 volumes), Kharkov: OKO.

Frank, P. 1979, *Histoire de l'Internationale Communiste: 1919–1943*, (2 volumes), Paris: Brèche.

Franke, O. 1902, 'Die wichtigsten Chinesischen Reformschriften vom Ende des neunzehnten Jahrhunderts', *Bulletin de lacadémie Impeériale des scences de St.-Pétersbourg*, 17, 3: pp. 47–58.

Franke, O. 1908, *Zemel'nye pravootnoshiiia v Kitae: Razreshennyi avtorom perevod s nemetskogo pod redaktsiei i [s] dopolneniiami N.I. Kokhanovskogo*, Vladivostok: Tipolit. pri Vostochnom institute.

Franke, O. 1911, *Ostasiatische Neubildungen: Beiträge zum Verständnis der politischen und kulturellen Entwicklung-Vorgänge im Fernen Osten: mit einem Anhange: Die sinologischen Studien in Deutschland*, Hamburg: C. Boysen.

Franke, O. 1923, *Die Großmächte in Ostasien von 1894 bis 1914: Ein Beitrag zur Vorgeschichte des Krieges*, Braunschweig und Hamburg: Verlag Georg Westermann.

Getty, A.J. and O.V. Naumov 1999, *The Road to Terror: Stalin and the Self-Destruction of the Bolsheviks, 1932–1939*, New Haven, CT: Yale University Press.

Grigor'ev, A.M. 1993, 'Bor'ba v VKP(b) i Kominterne po voprosam politiki v Kitae (1926–1927)', *Problemy Dal'nego Vostoka*, 2: 123–34; 3: 112–28.

Guomindang 1986, *Zhongguo guomindang di yici, di erci quanguo daibiaodahui huiyi shiliao*, (2 volumes), Nanjing: Jiangsu guji chubanshe.

Huc, M. (Évariste-Régis) 1854, *L'Empire Chinois: faisant suite a l'ouvrage intitulé souvenirs d'un voyage dans la Tartarie et le Thibet*, Second edition, (2 volumes), Paris: Librairie de Gaume Frères.

Huc, M. (Évariste-Régis) 1855, *The Chinese Empire: Forming a Sequel to the Work Entitled 'Recollections of a Journey through Tartary and Thibet'*, (2 volumes), London: Longman, Brown, Green, and Longmans.

Iakinf (Bichurin N.Ia.) 1827, *Otvety na voprosy, kotorye g. Virst predlozhil g. Kruzenshternu otnositel'no Kitaia*, St.-Petersburg: Tip. Imp. vospitatel'nogo doma.

Iakinf (Bichurin N.Ia) 1840, *Kitai, ego zhiteli, nravy, obychai, prosveshchenie*, St.-Petersburg: Tip. Imp. Akademii nauk.

Ivanov, A.I. 1909, *Van Anshi i ego reformy XI v.*, St. Petersburg: Moscow: Tip. Stasiulevicha.

Ivanov, A.I. 1914, 'Kitai', *Entsiklopedicheskii slovar' bibliograficheskogo instituta Granat*, (Volume 24), 172–221.

Ivanovskii, A.O. 1895, 'Kitai', *Entsiklopedicheskii slovar'*, St. Petersburg, (Volume 15), 172–221.

Ivin [Ivanov], A. 1925, 'Review: A.E. Khodorov and M.P. Pavlovich, 'Kitai v bor'be za nezavisimost'', *Bol'shevik*, 11–12: 110.

Jamieson, G. 1888, 'Tenure of Land in China and the Condition of the Rural Population', *Journal of the China Branch of the Royal Asiatic Society for the year 1888*, 23: 59–174.

Kantorovich, A.Ia. 1926a, *Inostrannyi kapital i zheleznie dorogi Kitaia*, edited by K. Radek, Moscow-Leningrad: Gosplan SSSR.

Kantorovich, A.Ia. 1926b, 'Sistema obshchestvennykh otnoshenii v Kitae dokapitalisticheskoi epokhi: (V poriadke gipotezy)', *Novyi Vostok*, 15: 67–93.

Kautsky, K. 1886, 'Die chinesischen eisenbahnen und das europäische proletariat', *Die Neue Zeit*, 4: 515–25, 529–49.

Khazanov, B.Ia. 1993, 'Radek, Karl Berngardovich', *Politicheskie deiateli Rossii. 1917: Biograficheskii slovar'*, Moscow: Nauchnoye izd-vo 'Bol'shaia rossiiskaia entsiklopoedia'.

Khodorov, A.E. 1925, 'K otsenke kitaiskikh sobytii (po povodu retsenzii A. Ivina)', *Bol'shevik*, 15: 88–91.

Krause, Friedrich Ernst August 1924a, 'Chinesische Geschichte', in *Orientalistische Literaturzeitung*, 27: 119–125.

Krause, Friedrich Ernst August 1924b, 'Die Epoche der Mongolen: Ein Kapitel aus der Geschichte und Kultur Asiens', *Mitteilungen des Seminars für Orientalische Sprachen*, 26–27: 1–60.

Krause, Friedrich Ernst August 1925, *Geschichte Ostasiens*, (2 volumes), Göttingen: Vandenhoeck und Ruprecht.

Kropotkin, P.A. 1902, *Zapiski revoliutsionera*, London: Izd. Fonda Volnoi Russkoi Pressy.

Ku Sui-lu 1926, *Die form bankmäßiger transaktionen in innern chinesischen verkehr*, Hamburg: Kommessions verlag L. Friederchsen & co.

Legge, J. 1960 [1870], *The Chinese Classics*; with a translation, critical and exegetical notes, prolegomena, and copious indexes, by James Legge, (5 volumes), Hong Kong: Hong Kong University Press.

Lenin, V.I. 1926 [1905], 'Etapy, napravleniie i perspektivy revoliutsii', *Leninskii Sbornik*, (Volume v), Moscow: Gosizdat.

Lenin, V.I. 1960a [1905], 'Dve taktiki sotsial-demokratii v demokraticheskoi revoliutsii', *Polnoe sobraniie sochinenii*, (Volume 11), Moscow: Politizdat.

Lenin, V.I. 1960b [1905], 'Etapy, napravleniie i perspektivy revoliutsii', *Polnoe sobraniie sochinenii*, (Volume 12), Moscow: Politizdat.

Lenin, V.I. 1961a [1913], 'Bor'ba partii v Kitae', *Polnoe sobranie sochinenii*, (Volume 23), Moscow: Politizdat.

Lenin, V.I. 1961b [1907], 'Kak ne sleduet pisat' rezoliutsiy', *Polnoe sobraniie sochinenii*, (Volume 15), Moscow: Politizdat.

Lenin, V.I. 1961c [1907], 'Piatyi s"ezd RSDRP 30 aprelia–19 maia (13 maia–1 iunia) 1907 g.: Doklad ob otnoshenii k burzhuaznym partiiam 12 (25 maia)', *Polnoe sobraniie sochineni*, (Volume 15), Moscow: Politizdat.

Lenin, V.I. 1961d [1907], 'Sila i slabost' russkoi revoliutsii', *Polnoe sobraniie sochinenii*, (Volume 15), Moscow: Politizdat.

Lenin, V.I. 1964 [1923], 'Pis'mo k s"ezdu', *Polnoe sobraniie sochinenii*, (Volume 45), Moscow: Politizdat.

Lenin, V.I. 1968a [1912], 'Demokratiia i narodnichestvo v Kitae', *Polnoe sobraniie sochinenii*, (Volume 21), Moscow: Politizdat.
Lenin, V.I. 1968b [1906], 'Pobeda kadetov i zadachi rabochei partii', *Polnoe sobraniie sochinenii*, (Volume 12), Moscow: Politizdat.
Lenin, V.I. 1969 [1917], 'O kompromissakh', *Polnoe sobraniie sochinenii*, (Volume 34), Moscow: Politizdat.
Lenin, V.I. 1970 [1922], 'XI c"ezd PKP(b) 27 marta–2 aprelia 1922 g.: Rech' po voprosu o pechatanii ob"iavlenii v "Pravde" 2 aprelia', *Polnoe sobraniie sochinenii*, (Volume 45), Moscow: Politizdat.
Lenin, V.I. 1971a [1920], 'Pervonachal'nyi nabrosok tezisov po agrarnomu voprosu (dlia Vtorogo s'ezda Kommunisticheskogo Internatsionala)', *Polnoe sobraniie sochineni*, (Volume 41), Moscow: Politizdat.
Lenin, V.I. 1971b [1920], 'Pervonachal'nyi nabrosok tezisov po natsional'nomu i kolonial'nomu voprosam (dlia Vtorogo s"ezda Kommunisticheskogo Internatsionala)', *Polnoe sobraniie sochinenii*, (Volume 41), Moscow: Politizdat.
Lenin, V.I. 1971c [1920], 'II congress Kommunisticheskogo Internatsionala. 18 iulia–7 avgusta 1920 g.: Doklad po natsional'nomu i kolonial'nomu voprosam. 26 iulia', *Polnoe sobranie sochinenii*, (Volume 41), Moscow: Politizdat.
Lerner, W. 1970, *Karl Radek: The Last Internationalist*, Stanford, CA: Stanford University Press.
Li Ung Bing 1914, *Outlines of Chinese History*, Shanghai: Commercial Press.
Lieu, D.K. (Liu Dajun) [1927], *China's Industries and Finance: Being a Series of Studies in Chinese Industrial & Financial Questions*, Beijing: The Chinese government bureau of economic information.
Leviné-Meyer, Rosa 1977, 'Radek', in *Inside German Communism: Memoirs of Party Life in the Weimar Republic*, by Rosa Leviné-Meyer, London: Pluto Press.
Luo Fu 1926, 'Beifa zhenzhong Guangdongzhi nongmin zhuangkuang (baiyue wuri Guangzhou tongxin)', *Xiangdao zhoukan*, 171: 1743–45.
Mallory, W.H. 1926, *China: Land of Famine*, New York: American Geographical Society.
Martynov, A. 1905, *Dve diktatury*, Geneva: Tip. Partii.
Martynov, A. 1927, 'K peregruppirovke sil kitaiskoi revoliutsii', *Kommunisticheskii Internatsional*, 8: 9–18.
Marx, K. 1923 [1894], *Kapital: Kritika politicheskoi ekonomii*, (Volume 3), Moscow-Petrograd: Gosizdat.
Marx, K. 1962 [1863] 'Teorii pribavochnoi stoimosti (IV tom "Kapitala")', *Sochineniia*, (Volume 26, part 1). Second ed., Moscow: Gospolitizdat.
Marx, K. and F. Engels 1969 [1848], 'Manifesto of the Communist party', in *Marx and Engels Selected Works in Three Volumes*, (Volume 1), Moscow: Progress Publishers.

Matthew, 6:34.
Mencius 1970, *The Works of Meng-Tsu*, translated by James Legge, New York: Dover Publications.
Meng Qingshu 2011, *Chen Shaoyu – Van Min: Biografiia: Vospominaniia*, translated and edited by Wang Danzhi. Moscow: BF 'Ontopsikhologiia'.
Minaev, I.P. 1902 [1298], *Puteshestvie Marko Polo*, translated by I.P. Minaev, edited by V.V. Bartold, St.-Petersburg: Tip. M.M. Stasiulevicha.
Morse, H.B. 1913, *The Trade and Administration of China*, Revised ed., London: Longmans, Green & Co.
Münsterberg, O. 1910–12, *Chinesische Kunstgeschichte*, (2 volumes), Essingen a/N: P. Nef.
Nakamura Kaju 1910, *Prince Ito, the man and the statesman, a brief history of his life*, New York: Japanese-American commercial weekly and Anraku Publ. Co.
Nathan, A.J. and P. Link (eds) 2002, *The Tiananmen Papers*, compiled by Zhang Liang, New York: PublicAffairs.
Nikiforov, V.N. 1970, *Sovetskie istoriki o problemakh Kitaia*, Moscow: Nauka.
North, R.C. 1953, *Moscow and the Chinese Communists*, Stanford, CA: Stanford University Press.
Overlach, Th.W. 1919, *Foreign Financial Control in China*, New York: The Macmillan.
Palmer, F. 1901, 'Marquis Ito: the great man of Japan', *Scribner's magazine* 30: 613–21.
Pantsov, A. 2000, *The Bolsheviks and the Chinese Revolution 1919–1927*, Richmond, Surrey: Curzon Press.
Pantsov, A. 2001, *Tainaia istoriia sovetsko-kitaiskikh otnoshenii: Bol'shevikii i kitaiskaia revoliutsiia (1919–1927)*, Moscow: Muravei-Guide.
Pantsov, A. and G. Benton 1994, 'Did Trotsky Oppose Entering the Guomindang 'From the First'?' *Republican China*, 19, 2: 61–63.
Pepper, D. 1927, 'Evroamerikanskii imperialism i kitaiskaia revoliutsiia', *Pravda*, 1 May.
Pis'ma I.V. Stalina V.M. Molotovu 1925–1936 gg.: Sbornik dokumentov 1995, compiled by L. Kosheleva et al., Moscow: 'Rossiia molodaia'.
Pokrovskii, M.N. 1924, *Diplomatiia i voiny Rossii v XIX stoletii: Sborni statei*, Moscow: 'Krasnaia nov''.
Pokrovskii, M.N. 1925, *1905: Materialy i dokumenty*, Moscow-Leningrad: Gosizdat.
Pokrovskii, M.N. 1925–1926, *1905: Istoria revoliutsionnogo dvizheniia v otdel'nykh ocherkakh* (Volume 1), Moscow: Gosizdat.
Pokrovskii, M.N. 1926, *Vneshniia politika Rossii v XX veke: Populiarnyi ocherk*, Petrograd: 'Priboi'.
Radek, K.B. 1924a, 'Imperialisticheskaia interventsiia i grazhdanskaia voina v Kitae. Doklad t. Radeka v Bol'shom teatre', In *Kitai v ogne voiny*, Moscow: Rabochaia Moskva.
Radek, K.B. 1924b, 'Rech' t. Radeka', *Ruki proch' ot Kitaia!*, Moscow: Gosizdat.
Radek, K.B. 1925a, *Ruki proch' ot Kitaia*, Simferopol: Krymgosizdat.

Radek, K.B. 1925b, 'Voprosy kitaiskoi revoliutsii', *Krasnyi Internatsional Profsoiuzov*, 10: 26–42.

Radek, K.B. 1926, 'God kitaiskoi revoliutsii', *Pravda*, 30 May.

Radek, K.B. 1927a, 'Novyi etap v kitaiskoi revoliutsii', *Novyi mir*, 3: 146–59.

Radek, K.B. 1927b, 'Vo vtoruiu godovshchinu smerti Sun Yat-sena', *Izvestiia*, 11 and 15 March.

Radek, K.B. 1930, 'Zadachi kitaiskoi revoliutsii i bor'ba s likvidatorstvom', *Problemy Kitaia*, 3.

Radek, K.B. 1989 [1927], 'Avtobiografiia', in *Deiateli SSSR i revoliutsionnogo dvizheniia Rossii: Entsiklopedicheskii slovar' Granat*, Moscow: 'Sovetskaia entsiklopediia'.

Radek, K.B. 1991 [1922], 'Instructions for the Representative of IKKI [ECCI] in South China', in Tony Saich, *The Origins of the First United Front in China: The Role of Sneevliet (alias Maring)*, (Volume 1), Leiden: E.J. Brill.

Radowitz, J.M.F.W.L. von 1926, *Briefe aus Ostasien*, Stuttgart, Berlin: Deutsche Verlags-Anstalt.

Rafes, M. 1927a, 'Kitaiskaia revoliutsiia i zadachi kommunistov (Kitaiskii vopros na plenume IKKI)', *Kommunisticheskaia revoliutsiia*, 1: 43–57.

Rafes, M. 1927b, *Revoliutsiia v Kitae*, Moscow-Leningrad: Gospolitizdat.

Reclus, Élisée 1900, *La Chine et La Diplomatie Européenne*, Paris: Éditions de l' Humanité Nouvelle.

Reclus, Élisée and Onésime 1902, *L'Emire du milieu: Le climat, le sol, les races, les richesses de la Chine*, Paris: Librairie Hachette.

Renard, Léon 1863, 'Les Européens en Chine: Les explorations anglaises du Yang-tsze-kiang', *Revue contemporaine*, 34: 515–41.

Richthofen, F.F. von 1907, *Tagebucher aus China*, (2 volumes), Berlin: Dietrich Reimer (Ernst Vohsen).

Richthofen, F.F. von 1877–1912, *China: Ergebnisse eigener Reisen und darauf gegründeter Studien*, (5 volumes), Berlin: Dietrich Reimer.

Rothstein, Th. 1903, *The Decline of British Industry: Its Cause and Remedy: Being an Essay on a Neglected Aspect of the Fiscal Question*, London: The Twentieth Century Press.

Roy, M.N. 1929, *Kitaiskaia revoliutsiia i Kommunisticheskii Internatsional: Sbornik stat'ei i materialov*, Moscow-Leningrad: Gosizdat.

RSDLP 1959 [1906], *Chetvertyi (Ob"edinitel'nyi) s"ezd RSDRP: Aprel' – mai 1906 goda: Protokoly*, Moscow: Gospolitizdat.

Schüler, Wilhelm 1912, *Abriss der neueren Geschichte Chinas: Unter besonderer Berücksichtigung der Provinz Schantung*, Berlin: Verlag von Karl Curtius.

Schüler, Wilhelm 1927, 'Die Kräfte der chinesischen Südpartei,' *Zeitschrift für Geopolitik*, 4: 325–33.

Sheng Yueh 1971, *Sun Yat-sen University in Moscow and the Chinese Revolution: A Personal Account*, Lawrence, KS: University of Kansas.

Shu Ying 1927, 'Lun Hangkouzhi bagun chao', *Xiangdao zhoukan*, 81: 1900.

Sinani, G. 1926, 'Bor'ba klassov v kitaiskoi natsional'noi revoliutsii i severnyi pokhod', *Kanton*, 8–9: 1–17.

Sinitsin, E.P. 1974, 'Konfutsianstvo v epoku Tsin', in *Istoria i kul'tura Kitaia: Sbornik pamiati akademika V. Pa. Vasilieva*, Moscow: Nauka.

Spafarii, N.G. 1910, *Opisaniie pervyia chasti vselennyia, imenuiemoi Azii, v nei zhe sostoit Kitaiskoe gosudarstvo s prochimi ego gorody i provintsii*, Kazan': tip. Imperatorskogo universiteta.

Stalin, J.V. 1927, *Revoliutsiia v Kitae i oshibki oppozitsii*, Moscow-Leningrad: Gosizdat.

Stalin, J.V. 1952a [1927], 'Beseda so studentami Universiteta Sun Yat-sena', *Sochineniia*, (Volume 9), Moscow: Gospolitizdat.

Stalin, J.V. 1952b [1927], 'K voprosam kitaiskoi revoliutsii: Otvet t. Marchulinu', *Sochineniia*, (Volume 9), Moscow: Gospolitizdat.

Stalin, J.V. 1952c [1926], 'O perspektivakh revoliutsii v Kitaie', *Sochinenia*, (Volume 8), Moscow: Gospoliizdat.

Stalin, J.V. 1952d [1927], 'Voprosy kitaiskoi revoliutsii: Tezisy dlia propagandistov, odobrennye TsK VKP(b)', *Sochineniia*, (Volume 9), Moscow: Gospolitizdat.

Stalin, J.V. 2001 [1927] 'Ne publikovavshaiasia rech' I.V. Stalina o Kitae', *Problemy Dal'nego Vostoka*, 1: 149–59.

Stringer, Harold 1922, *The Chinese Railway System*, Shanghai: Kelly & Walsh.

Stringer, Harold 1925, *The Chinese Railway System*, Second edition, Tianjin, n.p.

Sun Fo 1927, 'Sun Fo o zadachakh natsional'noi revoliutsii', *Pravda*, 12 May.

Szuma Chien [Sima Qian] 1974 [91 BC], *Records of the historian*, Hong Kong: The Commertial Press.

Tan-Pin-Sian [Tan Pingshang] 1927, *Puti razvitiia kitaiskoi revoliutsii*, Moscow-Leningrad: Gosizdat.

TASS 1927, 'Sotrudnichestvo profsoiuzov i Wuhanskogo pravitel'stva', *Pravda*, 29 April.

Tarkhanov, O. 1926, 'Ocherk sotsial'no-ekonomicheskoi struktury prov. Guansi', *Kanton*, 10: 79–160.

Tayler, J.B. 1924, 'The Study of Chinese Rural Economy: II. The Results of the Famine Commission's Investigations', *Chinese Social and Political Science Review*, 8: 196–226, 230–258.

Titarenko, M.L. (ed) 1986, *Kommunisticheskii Internatsional i kitaiskaia revoliutsiia. Dokumenty i Materialy*, Moscow: Nauka.

Titarenko, M.L. et al. (eds) 1994–96, *VKP(b), Komintern i natsional'no-revoliutsionnoe dvizheniie v Kitae. Dokumenty* (2 volumes), Moscow: AO 'Buklet'.

Tobar, J. 1900, *Koang-sin et T'se-hi, Empereur de Chine et Impératrice-Douairière: Décrets Impériaux 1898*, Shanghai: Imprimerie de la presse orientale.

Trevor-Roper, H.R. 1977, *Hermit of Peking: The Hidden Life of Sir Edmund Backhouse*, New York: Alfred A. Knopf.

Trotsky, Leon 1932, *Problems of the Chinese Revolution*, edited by Max Shachtman, New York: Pioneers Publ.

Trotsky, Leon 1980, *The Challenge of the Left Opposition: 1926–27*, New York: Pathfinder Press.

Trotsky, Leon 1995, *Pis'ma iz ssylki: 1928*, edited by Iu.G. Fel'shtinskii, Moscow: Izdatel'stvo gumanitarnoi literatury.

Trotsky, Leon 1988, 'Pochemu my ne trebovali do sikh por vykhoda iz gomindana?', *Kommunisticheskaia oppozitsiia v SSSR: 1923–1927: Iz archiva L'va Trotskogo v chetyrekh tomakh*, edited by Iu. Felshtinskii, (Volume 1), Benson, VT: Chalidze Press.

Trotzki, Leo [Leon Trotsky] 1990, *Schriften*, (Volume 2), [Hamburg]: Rasch und Röhring, 2 parts.

Vasiliev, V.P. 1900, *'Otkrytie Kitaia' i drugie stat'i akademika V.P. Vasilieva s portretom avtora*, Saint Petersburg: Izd. Zhurnala 'Vestnik vsemirnoi istorii'.

Varga, E. 1925, 'Ekonomicheskie problemy revoliutsii v Kitae', *Planovoe khoziaistvo*, 12: 165–83.

Vauger de Bruyne, B. et P.D.M. 1788, *Istoriia o zavoevanii Kitaia manchurskimi tatarami, sostoiashchaia v 5 knigakh, sochinennaia g. Vauger de Bruyne B. et P.D.M.[,] perevel s frantsuzskogo A P.*, Moscow: V tip. Kompanii tipografskoi s Ukaznogo dozvoleniia.

Vishniakov, A. 1926, 'Nekotorye dannye o finansovom polozhenii Guangduna', *Kanton*, 8–9: 60–78.

Volin, M. 1926, 'Osnovnye voprosy ekonomiki sel'skogo khoziaistva Kitaia', *Na agrarnom fronte*, 10: 57–68; 11–12: 89–96.

Volin, M. 1927, 'Kratkii ocherk istorii krestianskogo dvizheniia v Kitaie', *Kanton*, 10: 207–48.

Wagner, Wilhelm 1926, *Die Chinesische Landwirtschaft*, Berlin: Paul Parey.

Wang, Chengting T. 1926, 'Industrial Progress in China', *The Chinese Social and Political Science Review*, 10: 1–12.

Weber, Max 1922, 'Die Wirtschaftsethik der weilreligionen. I. Konfuzianismus und Taoismus', in Max Weber, *Gesammelte Aufsätze zur Religionssoziologie*, (Volume 1), Tübingen: J.C.B. Mohr (Paul Siebeck).

Wen Ching 1901, *The Chinese Crisis from Within*, edited by Rev. G.M. Reith, M.A., London: Grant Richards.

Werner, A, T. 1973. *Stillborn Revolution: The Communist Bid for Power in Germany 1919–1923*, (2 volumes), Princeton, NJ: Princeton University Press.

William II 1918, *The Willi-Nicky Correspondance: Being the Secret and Intimate Telegrams Exchanged Between the Kaiser and the Tsar*, edited by Herman Bernstein, New York: Alfred A. Knopf.

William II [1923], *Perepiska Vil'gel'ma II s Nikolaem II, 1894–1914 gg.*, Moscow-Petrograd: Gosizdat.

Witte, S.Iu., graf 1922, *Vospominania: Tsarstvovanie Nikolaia II*, (Volume 1), Berlin: 'Slovo'.
Wood, F. 1995, *Did Marco Polo Go to China?* London: Secker & Warburg.
Yakovlev, A.N. (ed.) 1991, *Reabilitatsiia. Politicheskie protsessy 30–50kh godov*, Moscow: Izdatel'stvo politicheskoi literatury.
Zakharov, I. 1853, 'Pozemel'naia sobstvennost'' v Kitae', *Trudy chlenov Rossiiskoi dukhovnoi missii v Pekine*, (Volume 2), Bejing: Izdanie Pekinskoi Dukhovnoi Missii.
Zhakov, M. 1927, *Otrazheniie feudalizma v 'Men-tsy'*, Moscow: UTK Press.

Bibliography of the Published Works of K.B. Radek on China and Literature about K.B. Radek

Published Works of K.B. Radek on China

- 1924, 'Angliiskoe rabochee pravitel'stvo i interventsiia v Kitae', *Imperializm v Kitae*, Leningrad.
- 1924, 'Bor'ba za vlast'' v Kitae', *Pravda*, 1 September.
- 1924, 'Imperialisticheskaia interventsiia i grazhdanskaia voina v Kitae. Doklad t. Radeka v Bol'shom teatre', *Kitai v ogne voiny*, Moscow-Leningrad.
- 1924, 'Rech'' t. Radeka', *Ruki proch' ot Kitaia!*, Moscow.
- 1924, 'Interventsiia v Kitae i ee tseli', *Pravda*, 27 July.
- 1924, 'Kantonskaia pobeda', *Pravda*, 30 August.
- 1924, 'Predislovie', in G.N. Voitinskii, *Chto proiskhodit v Kitae?*, Moscow-Leningrad.
- 1925, 'Chto nado govorit'' krest'ianstvu o kitaiskoi revoliutsii', *Sputnik agitatora (dlia derevni)*, 2(21): 19–24.
- 1925, 'Czhan-Tszo-Lin', *Izvestiia*, December 10.
- 1925, 'Fragen der chinesischen Revolution', in *Arbeiterbewegung und Revolution in China*, Berlin.
- 1925, 'Garantiinyi pakt', *Izvestiia*, October 25.
- 1925, 'Mezhdunarodnoe obozreniie. Itogi shangkhaiskikh sobytii', *Izvestiia*, 11 October.
- 1925, 'Novoe imperialisticheskoe nastuplenie na Vostoke', *Kommunisticheskii Internatsional*, 1(38): 60–9.
- 1925, 'Predislovie' in A.D. Popov, *Kitai*, Moscow.
- 1925, *Ruki proch' ot Kitaia*, Simferopol.
- 1925, *Sun Yat-sen i kitaiskoe revoliutsionnoe dvizhenie*, Moscow.
- 1925, 'Sun Yat-sen i kitaiskoe revoliutsionnoe dvizhenie', *Ogonek*, 21: 12–14.
- 1925, 'Taktika mirovogo imperializma v bor'be s kitaiskoi revoliutsiei', *Pravda*, July 29.
- 1925, 'Voprosy kitaiskoi revoliutsii', *Krasnyi Internatsional Profsoiuzov*, 10: 26–42.
- 1925, 'Vozhd' kitaiskogo naroda', *Pravda*, 14 March.
- 1925, 'Vstupitel'naia stat'ia', in Shpil'man, *Krest'ianskaia revoliutsiia v Kitae: Vosstaniie taipinov (1850–1860)*, Moscow.
- 1926, 'God kitaiskoi revoliutsii', *Pravda*, 30 May.
- 1926, 'Eshche o Kitaisko-Vostochnoi zh.d.', *Pravda*, 2 February.
- 1926, 'Imperialisticheskoe nastupleniie na Kitai', *Pravda*, 14 March; *Leningradskaia pravda*, 14 March.
- 1926, 'Interventsiia v Kitae i ee tseli' *Pravda*, 27 July.

- 1926, 'Istoricheskoe znachenie shangkhaiskikh sobytii. (Vmesto predisloviia)', in Pavel Mif, *Uroki Shankhaiskikh sobytii*, edited by K. Radek, Moscow.
- 1926, 'K otsenke poslednikh sobytii v Kitae', *Pravda*, 30 January.
- 1926, 'Porazhenie narodnykh armii v Kitae', *Pravda*, 26 March.
- 1926, 'Predislovie' in A.Ia. Kantorovich, *Inostrannyi kapital i zheleznye dorogi Kitaia*, Moscow-Leningrad.
- 1926, 'Rasstrely v Pekine', *Leningradskaia Pravda*, 19 March.
- 1926, 'Sotsial'no-politicheskie idei Sun Yat-sena', *Pravda*, 12 March.
- 1926, 'Zhizn' i delo Sun Yat-sena', in S. Dalin, *V riadakh kitaiskoi revoliutsii*, Moscow-Leningrad.
- 1927, 'Kitaiskaia revoliutsiia i anglo-kitaiskie otnosheniia', *Izvestiia*, 30 January.
- 1927, 'Kitaiskaia revoliutsiia i politika angliiskogo imperializma', *Mirovoe khoziaistvo i mirovaia politika*, 1: 8–16.
- 1927, 'Lenin i kitaiskaia revoliutsiia', *Pravda*, 21 January.
- 1927, 'Novyi etap v kitaiskoi revoliutsii', *Novyi Mir*, 3: 146–59.
- 1927, 'Osnovnye voprosy kitaiskoi istorii', *Novyi Vostok*, 16–17: 1–53.
- 1927, 'Shanghai pal', *Izvestiia*, 22 March.
- 1927, 'Sun Yat-sen', *Portrety i pamflety*, Moscow-Leningrad.
- 1927, 'V Shanghae i Nankine', *Izvestiia*, 21 March.
- 1927, 'Vo vtoruiu godovshchinu smerti Sun Yat-sena', *Izvestiia*, 11 and 15 March.
- 1927, 'Vstupleniie', in *Voprosy kitaiskoi revoliutsii*, (Volume 1), edited by K. Radek, Moscow-Leningrad.
- 1927, 'Voprosy kitaiskoi revoliutsii', in *Voprosy kitaiskoi revoliutsii*, (Volume 1), edited by K. Radek, Moscow-Leningrad.
- 1930, 'Revoliutsiia v Kitae i ugroza imperialisticheskoi interventsii', *Izvestiia*, 4 July.
- 1930, 'Voprosy kitaiskoi revoliutsii', *Izvestiia*, 10 June.
- 1930, 'Zadachi kitaiskoi revoliutsii i bor'ba s likvidatorstvom', *Problemy Kitaia*, 3: 10–20.
- 1932, *Doklad komissii Littona*, Moscow.
- 1932, 'The War in the Far East: A Soviet View', *Foreign Affairs*, 10, 4: 541–57.
- 1933, 'Predislovie' in O. Tanin i K. Iogan, *Voenno-fashistskoe dvizhenie v Iaponii*, Moscow.
- [1934], 'Japanese and International Fascism', in O. Tanin and E. Yohan, *Militarism and Fascism in Japan*, New York.
- 1988 [1927], 'Tezisy po kitaiskomu voprosu', *Kommunisticheskaia oppozitsiia v SSSR, 1923–1927: Iz archiva L'va Trotskogo v chetyrekh tomakh*, edited by Iu. Felshtinskii (Volume 2), Benson, VT.
- 1991 [1922], 'Instructions for the Representative of IKKI [ECCI] in South China', in Tony Saich, *The Origins of the First United Front in China: The Role of Sneevliet (alias Maring)*, (Volume 1), Leiden.

- 1994 [1922], 'Instruction for the Representative of ECCI in South China', *Republican China*, XIX(2): 61–63.
- 1995 [1934], 'Japanese and International Fascism', in *The Making of Modern Japan: A Reader*, edited by Tim Megarry, Dartford.
- 1996 [1926], 'Pis'mo K.B. Radeka v Politburo TsK VKP(b) ot 28 sentiabria 1926 g.', *VKP(b), Komintern i natsional'no-Revoliutsionnoe dvizhenie v Kitae*, (Volume 2), edited by M.L. Titarenko, Moscow.
- 1996 [1926], 'Pis'mo K.B. Radeka v Sekretariat TsK VKP(b) ot 31 avgusta 1926 g.', *VKP(b), Komintern i natsional'no-Revoliutsionnoe dvizhenie v Kitae*, (Volume 2), edited by M.L. Titarenko, Moscow.
- 1999 [1927], 'Perechen' vazhneishikh sobytii v Kitae i ikh otrazhenie v nashei presse, dokladakh i pr.', *Arkhiv Trotskogo*, (Volume 1), edited by Iu.G. Fel'shtinskii and G.I. Cherniavskii, Kharkov.
- 2001 [1928], 'Pis'mo [I.M.] Musinu [ot 8–12 iulia 1928]', *Archiv Trotskogo*, (Volume 2), edited by Iu.G. Fel'shtinskii and G.I. Cherniavskii, Kharkov.
- 2001 [1928], 'Pis'mo [L.D.] Trotskomu [ot 14 iuliia 1928 g.]', *Arkhiv Trotskogo*, (Volume 2), edited by Iu.G. Fel'shtinskii and G.I. Cherniavskii, Kharkov.
- 2001 [1928], 'VI kongresu Kominterna', *Archiv Trotskogo*, (Volume 2), edited by Iu.G. Fel'shtinskii and G.I. Cherniavskii, Kharkov.

Autobiography and Memoirs by K.B. Radek

- 1989, 'Avtobiografiia', in *Deiateli SSSR i revoliutsionnogo dvizheniia Rossii: Entsiklopedicheskii slovar' Granat*, Moscow.
- 1926, 'Noiabr' (Strannichka iz vospominanii)', *Krasnaia nov'*, 10: 139–75.

Literature about K.B. Radek

In Russian

Annenkov, Iu. 1926, 'Radek', in Iu. Annenkov, *Semnadtst' portretov*, Leningrad.

Artemov, V.A. 1993, 'Karl Radek: "Pust' vremia i opyt pokazhut, kto i v chem oshibalsia ..."', in *Istoricheskie portrety*, edited by G.N. Sevostianov, Moscow.

Artemov, V.A. 1999, 'Karl Radek i Germaniia (1918–1919 gg.)', in *Istoricheskie zapiski. Nauchnye trudy istoricheskogo fakul'teta VGU*, (4th edition), Voronezh.

Artemov, V.A. 2000, 'Karl Radek i voina s Pol'shei v 1920 godu', in *Rossiia v mirovoi istorii: Sbornik nauchnykh trudov prepodavatelei i aspirantov kafedry politicheskoi istorii*, Voronezh.

Artemov, V.A. 2000, *Karl Radek: Ideia i sud'ba*, Voronezh.

Bukharin, N.I. 1924, 'O tov. Radeke', *Pravda*, 30 May.
Bukharin, N.I. 1927, *Voprosy kitaiskoi revoliutsii*, Moscow-Leningrad.
Drakon 1921, 'Roman Karla Radeka s "poslednei kukharkoi"', *Sotsialisticheskii vestnik*, 8: 29.
Efimov, B. 1999, 'Kto takoi Karl Radek?', *L'Chaim*, 5(85): 25–27.
Fel'shtinskii, Iu. 1997, 'Byl li prichasten K. Radek k gibeli K. Libknekhta i R. Liuksemburg?', *Voprosy istorii*, 9: 3–35; 10: 3–33; 11: 3–24.
Fel'shtinskii, Iu. 1998, 'Byl li prichasten K. Radek k gibeli K. Libknekhta i R. Liuksemburg?', *Voprosy istorii*, 2: 3–29.
Fel'shtinskii, Iu. and G.I. Cherniavskii, 2019, *Karl Radek. Povest' o beschislennykh oblich'iakh revoliutsionera, diplomata i politika, tsinika i ostroslova, oppozitsionera i kholopa*, Moscow.
Gorelov, I.E. 1995, '"V Anglii ... Teper' Reshaiushchii Boi": Pis'mo V.I. Lenina K.B. Radeku', 1922 g.', *Istoricheskii Arkhiv*, 1: 4–5.
Grigor'ev, A.M. 1993, 'Bor'ba v VKP(b) i Kominterne po voprosam politiki v Kitae (1926–1927)', *Problemy Dal'nego Vostoka*, 2: 123–34; 3: 112–28.
Guseinov, E. and V. Sirotkin 1989, 'Litso i maski Karla Radeka', *Moskovskaia pravda*, 14 May.
Khazanov, B.Ia. 1993, 'Radek, Karl Berngardovich', in *Politicheskie deiateli Rossii. 1917: Biograficheskii slovar'*, Moscow.
1988, *Kommunisticheskaia oppozitsiia v SSSR. 1923–1927. Iz archiva L'va Trotskogo v chetyrekh tomakh*, (4 volumes), edited by Yu. Fel'shtinskii, Benson, VT.
Medvedev, F.N. 1990, 'Sof'ia Radek o svoem ottse i o sebe', in *Tsena prozreniia: spetsial'ny korrespondent Ogon'ka beret interv'iu. 1986–1988*, Moscow.
1995, 'Naznachit' revoliutsiiu v Germanii na 9 noiabria', *Istochnik*, 6: 142–53.
2001, 'Ne publikovavshaiasia rech' I.V. Stalin o Kitae', *Problemy Dal'nego Vostoka*, 1: 149–59.
Nikiforov, V.N. 1970, *Sovetskie istoriki o problemakh Kitaia*, Moscow.
1927, 'O "puteshestvii" tov. Radeka po Kitaiu, ili "ser'eznoe revoliutsionnoe otnoshenie" k problemam kitaiskoi revoliutsii', *Pravda*, 29 April.
Pantsov, A.V. 2001, *Tainaia istoriia sovetsko-kitaiskikh otnoshenii. Bol'sheviki i kitaiskaia revoliutsiia (1919–1927)*, Moscow.
1991, 'Parallel'ny antisovietskii trotskistskii tsentr', in *Reabilitatsiia. Politicheskie protsessy 30–50-kh godov*, edited by A.N. Yakovlev, Moscow.
Pechenkin, S.V. 1999, 'Karl Radek i "rozlamovskaia oppozitsiia" v SDKPiL', in *Rossiia i Germaniia v XX veke: Mezhvuzovsky sbornik nauchnykh trudov*, Voronezh.
Pechenkin, S.V. 2001, 'K. Radek: Partiino-gosudarstvennaia deiatel'nost', 1904–1936 gg.', Ph.D. Thesis, Voronezh.
1995, *Pis'ma I.V. Stalina V.M. Molotovu 1925–1936 gg. Sbornik dokumentov*, compiled by L. Kosheleva et al., Moscow.

1927, 'Politicheskaia fizionomiia russkoi oppozitsii', *Kommunisticheskii Internatsional*, 41(115): 10–24.

Sokolov, M.V. 1988, 'Voina i mir Karla Radeka', *Sobesednik*, 48: 50.

Stalin, I.V. 1953, 'Beseda so studentami Universiteta Sun Yat-sena', *Sochineniia*, (Volume 9), Moscow.

Stalin, I.V. 1953, 'Voprosy kitaiskoi revoliutsii. Tezisy dlia propagandistov, odobrennye TsK VKP(b)', *Sochineniia*, (Volume 9), Moscow.

Stalin, I.V. 1953, 'K voprosam kitaiskoi revoliutsii. Otvet t. Marchulinu', *Sochineniia*, (Volume 9), Moscow.

1937, *Sudebnyi otchet po delu antisovietskogo trotskistskogo tsentra, rassmotrennogo Voennoi Kollegiei Verkhovnogo suda Soiuza SSR 23–30 ianvaria 1937 g. Po obvineniiu Piatakova, Iu.L., Radeka, K.B., Sokol'nikova, G.Ia. i dr.*, Moscow.

Torchinov, V.A. and A.M. Leontiuk 2000, 'Radek (Sobel'son) Karl Berngardovich', in *Vokrug Stalina. Istoriko-biograficheskii spravochnik*, St. Petersburg.

Trotskii, L. 1929, 'Po povodu tezisov t.[ov]. Radeka', *Biulleten' oppozitsii*, 1/2: 11–14; Ditto 1995, *Pis'ma iz ssylki. 1928*, edited by Yu. Fel'shtinskii, Moscow.

Trotskii, L. 1929, 'Radek i oppozitsiia', *Biulleten' oppozitsii*, 1/2: 10–11.

1994, *VKP(b), Komintern i natsional'no-revoliutsionnoe dvizhenie v Kitae. Dokumenty*, edited by M.L. Titarenko, (Volume 1), Moscow.

1996, *VKP(b), Komintern i natsional'no-revoliutsionnoe dvizhenie v Kitae. Dokumenty*, edited by M.L. Titarenko, (Volume 2), Moscow.

1927, *XV konferentsiia Vsesoiuznoi Kommunisticheskoi partii (b). 26 oktiabria–3 noiabria 1926 g. Stenograficheskii otchet*, Moscow-Leningrad.

1927, *XV s"ezd Vsesoiuznoi Kommunisticheskoi partii (b)*, Moscow-Leningrad.

In Western European Languages

Arenstam, A. 1937, 'Karl Radek', *Living Age*, April.

Artemov, V.A. 1991, 'Im Banne von Dogmen oder auf der Suche nach einer neuen Taktik (1918/1919)?', in *Beiträge zur Geschichte der deutschen Arbeiterbewegung*, (Volume 2).

Balabanoff, A. 1938, *My Life as a Rebel*, New York.

Becker, B.K. 1956, *Karl Radek in Germany 1918–1923*, PhD Thesis, Urbana-Champagne, IL.

Becker, J., T. Bergmann and A. Watlin 1993, *Das erste Tribunal. Das Moskauer Parteiverfahren gegen Brandler, Thalheimer und Radek*, Mainz.

Borkenau, F. 1962, *World Communism: A History of the Communist International*, Ann Arbor, MI.

Brandt, C. 1958, *Stalin's Failure in China*, Cambridge, MA.

Broué, P. 1966, 'Note sur l'action de Karl Radek jusqu'en 1923', *Les Annales ESC*, XXI, 681–90.

Broué, P. 1976, *La Question Chinoise dans l'Internationale Communiste*, Paris.

Broué, P. 1977, 'Karl Radek ou la Confusion des Genres?', in *Révolution en Allemagne (1917–1923)*, Paris.
Broué, P. 1997, *Histoire de l'Internationale Communiste, 1919–1943*, Paris.
Carr, E.H. 1971, *A History of Soviet Russia: Foundations of a Planned Economy, 1926–1929*, (Volume 1, in 2 parts), London.
Carr, E.H. 1951/52, 'Radek's "Political Saloon" in Berlin 1919', *Soviet Studies*, III(4): 411–30.
1956–1965, *The Communist International: 1919–1943: Documents*, edited by Jane Degras (3 volumes), London.
Collard, D. 1937, *Soviet Justice and the Trial of Radek and Others*, London.
Cummings, A.J. 1935, 'Karl Radek', in *Portraits and Pamphlets*, by K. Radek, New York.
Daniels, R. 1960, *The Conscience of the Revolution: Communist Opposition in Soviet Russia*, Cambridge, MA.
Deutscher, I. 1989, *The Prophet Unarmed. Trotsky. 1921–1929*, New York.
Deutscher Oktober 1923: Ein Revolutionsplan und sein Scheitern 2003, edited by Bernhard H. Bayerlein, Berlin.
Eudin, X.J. and R.C. North 1957, *Soviet Russia and the East, 1920–1927. A Documentary Survey*, Stanford, CA.
Fanger, D.M. 1953, *Radek's Role in the Soviet Opposition*, Master's Thesis, Department of History, University of California, Berkeley, CA.
Fayet, J.-F. 2004, *Karl Radek (1885–1939): Biographie politique*, Bern.
Foster, W.Z. 1937, *Questions and Answers on the Piatakov-Radek Trial*, New York.
Frank, P. 1979, *Histoire de l'Internationale Communiste, 1919–1943*, (2 volumes), Paris.
Franz, R. 1919–20, 'Der Fall Radek in 1913', *Das Forum*, 4(1): 389–93.
Getty, A.J. and O.V. Naumov 1999, *The Road to Terror: Stalin and the Self-Destruction of the Bolsheviks, 1932–1939*, New Haven, CT.
Goldbach, M.-L. 1973, *Karl Radek und die deutsch-sowjetischen Beziehungen 1918–1923*, Bonn-Bad Godesberg.
Gruber, H. 1969, *International Communism in the Era of Lenin*, New York.
Gruber, H. 1974, *Soviet Russia Masters the Comintern*, Garden City, NY.
Heisler, F. 1937, *The First Two Moscow Trials: Why?* Chicago, IL.
Heym, S. 1995, *Radek*, Munich.
Kahan, V. 1976, 'The Communist International, 1919–1943. The Personnel of Its Highest Bodies', *International Review of Social History*, 21: 152–6.
Kochanski, A. 1986, 'Radek', *Polski Słownik Biograficzny*, XXIX: 680–8, Kraków.
Lazitch, B. with M.M. Drachkovich 1986, 'Karl Radek', in *Biographical Dictionary of the Comintern*, by B. Lazitch and M.M. Drachkovich, Stanford, CA.
Legters, L.H. von 1959, *Karl Radek als Sprachrohr des Bolschewismus*, Berlin.
1937, *Letter of an Old Bolshevik: A Key to the Moscow Trials*, New York.
1938, *Letter of an Old Bolshevik: A Key to the Moscow Trials*, London.
Lerner, W. 1963, 'Karl Radek and the Chinese Revolution, 1925–1927', in *Essays in Russian*

and Soviet History in Honor of G. Tanquary Robinson, edited by John Shelton Curtiss, New York.

Lerner, W. 1970, *Karl Radek: The Last Internationalist*, Stanford, CA.

Leviné-Meyer, Rosa 1977, 'Radek', in *Inside German Communism: memoirs of Party life in the Weimar Republic*, by Rosa Leviné-Meyer, London.

Luban, O. 2000, 'Karl Radek im Januaraufstand 1919 in Berlin. Drei Dokumente', *Internationale Wissenschaftliche Korrespondenz zur Geschichte der deutschen Arbeiterbewegung*, 3: 388–97.

Micalef, C. 2004, 'Le KPD et le Comintern (1919–1933)', *Le Bulletin de l'Institut Pierre Renouvin*, 20: 73–92.

Möller, D. 1976, *Karl Radek in Deutschland: Revolutionär, Intrigant, Diplomat*, Köln.

North, R.C. 1953, *Moscow and the Chinese Communists*, Stanford, CA.

Pantsov, A. and G. Benton 1994, 'Did Trotsky Oppose Entering the Guomindang "From the First"?', *Republican China*, XIX(2): 52–66.

Pawel, E. 1964–65, 'Karl Radek and the German Revolution' I–II, *Survey*, 53: 59–69; 55: 126–40.

Saich, T. 1991, *The Origins of the First United Front in China. The Role of Sneevliet (alias Maring)*, (Volume 1), Leiden.

Schüddekopf, O.-E. 1962, 'Karl Radek in Berlin: Ein Kapital deutsch-russischer Beziehungen im Jahre 1919', *Archiv für Sozialgeschichte*, 2: 87–166.

Schurer, H. 1964–65, 'Radek and the German Revolution', *Survey*, 53: 59–69; 55: 126–40.

Shaynfeld, S. 1954, 'Der yunger Karol Radek', *Torne: Kiyum un Khrbun fun a yidischer shtot*, Tel Aviv.

Sheng Yueh 1971, *Sun Yat-sen University in Moscow and the Chinese Revolution: A Personal Account*, Lawrence, KS.

Steffen, J. 1977, *Auf zum Letzten Verhör: Erkenntnisse des verantwortlichen Hofnarren der Revolution Karl Radek*, Munich.

Stratz, H. 1920, *Drei Monate als Geisel für Radek. Persönliche Erlebnisse in der Ukraine und Sowjetrussland*, Berlin.

1937, *Traitors Accused: Indictment of the Piatakov-Radek Trotskyite Group*, New York.

Trotsky, L. 1962, *Problems of the Chinese Revolution*, (2nd edition), Ann Arbor, MI.

Trotsky, L. 1976, *Leon Trotsky on China*, New York.

Trotsky, L. 1980, *The Challenge of the Left Opposition. 1926–1927*, New York.

Trotsky, L. 1990, 'Schriften', (Volume 2), *Über China*, Hamburg.

Tuck, J. 1988, *Engine of Mischief: An Analytical Biography of Karl Radek*, Westport, CT.

Vatlin, A. 'Die Krise unserer Partei bedroht die Weltrevolution: Karl Radek zwischen sowjetischem Politbüro und deutscher Revolution', https://www.degruyter.com/view/journals/frm/1/2/article-p135.xml.

Wehner, Markus 1992, 'Karl Radek (1885–1939): biographische Notizen', *Internationale Wissenschaftliche Korrespondenz zur Geschichte der deutschen Arbeiterbewegung*, 28(3): 395–406.

Wehrlin Th. 1923, 'Brief an Radek,' *Das Tage-Buch*, 29 September.
Werner, A. 1973, *Stillborn Revolution: The Communist Bid for Power in Germany 1919–1923*, (2 volumes), Princeton, NJ.
1937, *Why Did They Confess? A Study of the Piatakov-Radek Trial*, New York.
1980, 'The 14 November 1918 Teleprinter Conversation of Hugo Haase with Georgii Chicherin and Karl Radek: Document and Commentary', *Canadian-American Slavic Studies*, 14(4): 513–34.

Index

absolutism   16, 58, 61, 64, 66, 152, 322
agrarian question   72, 142, 192, 198–99, 201, 206, 209, 216, 253, 259, 269, 281, 284, 351, 354–55, 358, 361, 378, 380, 401–3
agrarian revolution   355, 358, 379, 388, 390–91, 393–95, 398–99, 402–4, 414, 422
alienation   31
anarchism   447, 456
Andreev, Mikhail Georgievich   258, 264, 434
anti-imperialism   8, 237, 277, 320, 336
Anti-Imperialist League   461
ARCEC (All-Russian Central Executive Committee)   1, 4, 438, 445, 455, 460–61, 463
aristocracy   30, 51, 56, 58, 60, 61, 93, 105–6, 254
armed forces   31, 79, 118, 125, 151, 185, 391, 414
artisans   16–17, 20–21, 218, 220, 223, 228, 231, 237–38, 244, 250, 257, 307, 322, 350, 352, 355, 357, 365, 367, 372, 402
AUCP(b) (All-Union Communist Party [Bolsheviks])   1–2, 5, 7, 11, 13, 15, 287, 307, 342, 344, 349, 368, 423–32, 437, 439, 443, 450, 455, 459
Austria-Hungary   3, 97, 99, 106, 117–18, 123, 146, 164, 360, 451

Baku   393, 408
Bakunin, Michael Aleksandrovich   107, 435
Baldwin, Stanley   87, 435
banditism   219, 268, 304, 313
bankers   35, 87, 124, 127, 175, 204, 271, 322, 398
banks   38, 42–43, 49, 75, 88, 127–28, 132, 134, 136, 167, 169, 170, 174–75, 178, 180, 181, 192–94, 203, 229, 260, 269, 286, 316, 320, 362, 376, 401, 420, 457, 461
Belgium   176, 266, 322
Bismarck, Otto von,   435
Bolshevism   1, 277, 336, 349, 363, 399, 407, 447
Borodin, Mikhail Markovich,   236, 373, 392, 414, 436
bourgeois revolution   9–10, 17, 226–27, 238, 242–43, 248, 252, 279, 281, 293, 309, 321, 323, 350–51, 371, 399, 400, 416

bourgeoisie   7, 9, 10, 16–19, 22, 41–42, 46, 64, 66–68, 75, 77–79, 82, 88, 104, 117–18, 120–21, 123–26, 142, 152, 158, 167, 169, 170, 172, 181, 185, 188–91, 194, 204, 206, 210, 220, 222–24, 227–32, 234–35, 240, 241–42, 244, 248–250, 253–54, 256–57, 261, 266–67, 274–78, 280–1, 285, 287–90, 292–98, 302–4, 306–7, 309, 311–12, 315–16, 318–24, 329, 331, 333, 335–36, 338, 340–42, 345–48, 350–59, 361–66, 368, 370–76, 378, 381–84, 388, 391, 394, 396–97, 399, 400, 402–6, 408–10, 416–17, 421, 425
Boxer Rebellion   100, 114, 138–39, 154–60, 162–68, 176–77, 183, 193–94, 206, 209, 228–29, 250–51, 254–55, 260, 272, 466, 468
Brandler, Heinrich   276, 436
Brandt, Max August Scipio von   100, 177, 437, 471, 487
Brest-Litovsk   4, 18
British imperialism   226, 229, 245, 304–5, 411, 430
Bücher, Karl Wilhelm   68–69, 437
Bukharin, Nikolai Ivanovich   4, 11, 242, 247, 278, 295, 298, 302, 310, 342, 345, 348–60, 365, 372, 375, 383, 385–94, 397, 399–401, 402–6, 407–9, 411–17, 421, 422, 424, 426–28, 430, 437
bureaucracy   36, 44, 46, 48, 53–54, 56–58, 60, 64–66, 70–71, 74–75, 77, 87, 93–94, 96, 97, 103, 131, 140–41, 150–53, 163, 169, 185, 195, 216, 218, 251, 256, 258, 271

Canton (Guangzhou)   6, 19, 22, 38–39, 42–43, 79–80, 98, 120, 166–67, 176, 180, 199, 205, 236–41, 244, 248, 259, 261–71, 273–74, 284–87, 290, 296–97, 300, 302–3, 306–18, 327–29, 334, 338–40, 350, 351–53, 363–64, 373, 375–77, 379, 382, 400, 404, 424, 437, 439, 444, 448–49, 461–63, 467–69
capital   8, 9, 16, 35, 40, 41–44, 50, 53–55, 57, 59, 61–68, 75–76, 78, 81–82, 85–89, 93–94, 96, 105–6, 111, 113, 120, 126–27, 137–38, 158, 165, 167–69, 171, 174, 176–77,

179–81, 183–85, 187–92, 194–95, 197–98, 201–4, 215–23, 228–30, 232, 234–35, 249–51, 253, 255–57, 259–60, 264, 269, 272, 275, 295, 350, 352, 355, 357–58, 362, 366, 372, 376, 401
accumulation 35, 44, 74, 189, 204, 221, 355, 401
capitalist development 17, 64, 77, 96, 119, 123, 165, 171, 182, 184, 187, 192, 204–5, 208, 223, 229, 242, 248–49, 251–52, 257, 260, 267, 278, 320, 322, 359, 400, 402, 409
CC (Central Committee) 1, 4, 7, 13, 15, 241, 278, 296, 307, 344, 368, 385, 389, 391, 395–96, 406, 412, 423–31, 434, 436–38, 440–41, 443, 445–47, 449–51, 453–55, 457–66, 468–69, 470
CCP (Chinese Communist Party) 5–13, 18, 20, 208, 224, 237, 241, 244, 265, 273, 276–77, 285, 311, 303, 311, 313, 317, 325–27, 329, 332–34, 336, 338, 352–53, 363, 371, 373, 377, 381–83, 391, 394, 396–97, 405, 411, 414–16, 421, 426, 430, 437–38, 448–49, 458, 461–63, 468–69
Chen Duxiu 309–10, 319, 336–38, 343, 371–75, 377, 379, 381, 390, 392–93, 395, 396, 394, 395, 400–1, 408, 414, 437, 435, 438, 439
Chiang Ching-kuo 289, 438
Chiang Kai-shek 6, 10–12, 239, 265, 270, 271, 277, 286–90, 293, 296, 298–99, 303, 306–11, 313–23, 316, 329–38, 340, 342–47, 364, 367–71, 373–82, 385–91, 398–99, 403–4, 406–7, 413–15, 424–26
Chirol, Valentin 98–99, 101, 103, 140, 192, 258, 439
civil wars 19, 25, 46, 119–20, 255, 276, 280, 290, 371, 401, 443, 449, 454–55, 460, 462, 467
Cixi, Empress Dowager 100, 151, 154, 155, 163, 251, 439, 442, 468
class interests 45, 66, 315, 323, 325, 352
class struggle 1, 16, 46, 48, 49, 51, 71, 227, 231, 277, 280, 284, 293, 331, 336, 353, 358, 369, 400, 425
Collins, William Frederick 39, 185, 251, 439
Comintern 1, 2, 4–7, 11–12, 15, 199, 236, 265, 267, 274, 277–78, 280–81, 288–93, 295, 298–302, 307–8, 311, 319, 324–29, 331–

35, 340–44, 346–51, 354–56, 359–60, 362–64, 366, 371–72, 376, 385–86, 393, 396, 401, 405–6, 408–9, 410–11, 414, 417, 421, 423–24, 426–27, 429–32, 434, 436, 440, 443, 451, 454, 457, 461, 470
commune 36, 48, 51–53, 59–60, 71–72, 216
Communism 32, 52, 75, 245, 264, 276–77, 328, 329, 335–37, 360, 368, 432
competition 16, 40, 89, 170, 175, 180, 189, 190, 192, 197, 203, 229, 232, 256–57
compradors 16, 82, 85–88, 194, 228, 250, 255, 296, 316, 334–35, 352, 355, 362, 365, 372, 375
Confucianism 45–46, 142–43, 209
Confucius 45–46, 56, 58, 77, 142–43, 148, 150, 210–11, 215, 439, 452
Conrady, Auguste 209, 213, 215, 439
Constantinople 98, 105–7, 109, 115–16
coolies 196, 233, 245, 258, 314, 373, 380
Cordier, Henry 152, 213, 439
cotton 33–34, 38, 39, 41, 81, 88, 89, 90, 95–96, 183–84, 187, 197, 232, 234, 249, 257, 317
counter-revolution 118, 120, 273, 301, 308, 310, 323, 360–61, 363, 368, 382, 389, 391, 410, 414
countryside 9, 16–17, 20, 35–37, 41, 60, 74–75, 77, 85–86, 90, 188, 192, 198, 200, 204–6, 232–34, 238, 240, 244, 247, 250, 252, 256–57, 259–60, 268, 284, 308–9, 312, 338, 352, 356–58, 361, 362, 390, 397, 402, 403
Crimean War 106
crisis 198, 248, 267, 287–89, 299, 345, 358, 361, 370, 380, 382, 432
Cromwell, Oliver 321–22

Dalin, Sergei Alekseevich 11, 263, 298, 301, 440
Denmark 117, 288, 457
Dewey, John 149, 440
dictatorship 6, 9, 10, 17, 238, 243, 244, 252–53, 264, 267, 275–76, 278–80, 287, 290, 293–96, 300, 312, 320, 321, 326, 332, 341–43, 346–48, 363, 365, 367, 370, 377, 379, 390, 410, 416
diplomacy 110–11, 124, 125–26, 128, 163, 170, 174–75, 299
Duan 156–57, 164, 440

ECCI (Executive Committee of the Communist International) 1, 4–7, 11, 15, 20, 242, 278, 280, 286, 294, 307–8, 311–12, 319, 325, 340, 344–46, 349, 353, 364–65, 372, 393, 423–27, 429, 432, 434, 436–37, 443, 446, 448, 450–54, 456–58, 460–62, 465, 469
economic development 5, 31, 44, 61, 95, 111, 114, 119, 189, 221, 361
Engels, Friedrich 9, 104, 292, 360, 371, 384, 441
Evdokimov, Grigorii Eremeevich 368, 385, 412, 417, 441
exploitation 5, 19, 51, 53, 57, 60, 159, 165, 170, 173–75, 180, 191–92, 196, 204, 221, 234, 248, 268, 284, 311, 320, 335, 363
exports 80, 89–92, 95–96, 102, 104–5, 114, 142, 165, 171–72, 189, 191, 229, 249, 251, 387

factories 38, 40, 41, 120, 183–84, 186, 189, 197, 228, 231–32, 234, 239, 242–43, 247, 250, 256–57, 261, 270, 279, 286, 287, 295, 317, 339, 356, 357, 380, 393
Feng Yuxiang 239, 385–87, 390, 391, 407, 413, 441, 468
feudalism 9, 26, 32–33, 40, 51–60, 64, 149, 210, 215–20, 253, 320, 350–51, 354–56, 357–60, 362, 366, 375, 378, 381, 401–2, 421–22
feudal lords 32, 46, 51–52, 54–56, 58–60, 68
First World War 3, 230, 250, 401, 434, 446, 460
foreign capital 9, 16, 78, 81–82, 87–89, 94, 126, 165, 168–69, 174, 185, 187–91, 194–95, 197, 228–30, 232, 234–35, 249–51, 255–57, 275, 350, 352, 355, 372, 401
foreign trade 35, 39, 41, 43, 83, 85, 89–90, 92, 95–96, 105–6, 190, 403, 445
France 17, 42, 51, 56, 60–61, 79, 81, 84, 87, 94, 98, 101–2, 104, 106, 109, 117–20, 123–27, 131, 137–38, 141, 145–46, 159, 164, 167, 170, 176, 178, 180, 184, 228–29, 238, 256, 266, 322, 436, 443, 446, 451, 454, 461, 463, 465, 469
Franke, Otto 24, 26–27, 97–99, 127, 139, 148, 149, 213, 441
Frederick II, the Great 42, 66, 441

Geller, Lev Naumovich 12, 15, 345, 370, 373, 381–82, 384, 442
German imperialism 101, 129, 130, 159
Germany 4, 17, 18, 26, 42, 56, 87, 94, 97, 101–2, 104, 106, 114–25, 127–31, 137, 146–47, 159–60, 163–64, 167–68, 170, 172, 177–78, 180, 184, 226, 228–30, 242, 256, 276, 421, 435–36, 443, 446, 449, 451, 460, 469
Girondins 322–23, 343, 371
Girs, Mikhail Nikolaevich 160, 442
Great Britain 79, 81, 98, 102, 106, 179, 184, 230, 266, 443, 560
Gosplan 454, 460
Gorev, Boris Isaakovich 10, 442
Guangdong 25, 34, 137, 178, 236, 237, 262–64, 267–68, 308, 310–11, 313–14, 317, 318, 327–28, 334–35, 351–52, 361, 438, 444, 448, 453, 461, 463
Guangxu, Emperor 100, 139, 150, 251, 442, 466
Guomindang (GMD) 2, 5–8, 10–13, 18–22, 120, 153, 206, 236–41, 260–65, 268, 271–74, 277–78, 285, 286–91, 296–97, 299, 302–4, 307, 308–9, 311, 313–14, 317–21, 325, 327–39, 341–45, 347, 352–54, 356–58, 362–364, 366–68, 373–77, 381, 383, 386–87, 390–93, 395–96, 400, 401, 403, 405–11, 413–16, 419, 424, 434–39, 441, 444, 448, 450–58, 461, 463–64, 466–69
  left Guomindang 6–7, 12, 19, 262, 265, 291, 299, 301, 304, 307, 314, 319, 310, 329, 364–65, 367–68, 375, 377, 378, 382–83, 385–86, 388–94, 396–97, 403–8, 410, 416, 424, 426, 466

Han dynasty 52, 54, 55, 58, 61, 62, 66–74, 76, 149, 218, 220, 223, 351, 450, 459
hegemony 7, 9–10, 208, 232, 245, 293, 333, 345, 347–48, 350, 357, 364, 401
Hindenburg, Paul von 416, 443
Hohenzollerns 117, 466
Holland 4, 39, 40, 99, 115–16, 221, 266, 451
Hong Kong 80, 98, 102, 108, 137, 166–67, 177–78, 237, 261, 264, 270, 284, 303, 306, 337, 438, 448, 462, 467, 468
Hubei province 29, 30, 34, 231, 285, 317–18, 361, 364, 365, 375, 387, 389, 448, 453, 467, 469

INDEX   493

Hunan province   83, 285, 339, 364–65, 386, 389, 392, 396, 448, 463–64, 467, 469

ideology   2, 18, 143, 150, 235, 237, 252, 335, 371
imperialism   5, 16, 17, 79, 91–92, 101, 123, 124, 129, 130, 136–37, 158–60, 164, 183, 187–92, 197, 206, 226–31, 234–35, 237, 241, 245, 248, 250, 255, 257, 261, 264–65, 268, 274–76, 279, 281, 283, 285–88, 290, 292, 294–96, 301, 304, 305–6, 308, 320–21, 323–24, 326–28, 331, 340–42, 346, 350, 353–55, 357, 361–62, 366, 368, 370, 372, 381–82, 398–99, 401–3, 409, 411, 419–20, 424, 420, 430
imports   63, 88–92, 95–96, 102, 121, 140, 181, 187, 190–91, 249
industrial revolution   37, 117, 175, 220
Italy   17, 32, 37, 39, 69, 84, 106, 115–16, 123, 141, 220–21, 226, 266, 444–45

Jacobins   247, 279, 322–23, 457
Jamieson, George   24–31, 33, 213, 445
Japan   89, 92–102, 104, 112, 118, 124–27, 130–31, 136, 138–41, 145–46, 155, 170–71, 177, 187, 189, 191–93, 229–30, 250, 266, 272, 304, 319, 331, 338, 376, 408

Kadets   248, 297, 347, 355, 357, 380, 395, 435, 452, 459, 462
Kamenev, Lev Borisovich   14, 368, 431, 445
Kamkov, Boris Davidovich   18, 445
Kantorovich, Anatolii Iakovlevich   168, 211, 217, 223, 284, 446
Kautsky, Karl   31–32, 37, 412, 446
Kerensky, Alexander Federovich   242, 332, 346–47, 377, 380, 392, 395, 397, 403, 404, 424, 434, 446
Kolchak, Alexander V.   412, 413, 434, 438
Korea   97, 98, 100–1, 110, 112, 138, 408, 452
Kornilov, Lavr Georgievich   377, 392, 395, 397, 404, 434, 446, 458
KPD (Communist Party of Germany)   1, 4, 436, 443, 446–47, 449, 451
kulaks   200, 240, 264, 275, 318, 352
KUTK (Communist University of the Toilers of China)   434, 439, 452, 459, 466
KUTV (Communist University of the Toilers of the East)   5–6, 273, 283, 303, 345, 349, 436, 449, 452, 459

landed property   24, 27–28, 53, 70, 73
landholding   23, 27–28, 30–31, 33, 36, 57, 59, 60, 71, 199, 216–17, 222
landlords   28–33, 43, 45, 53, 55–58, 60–62, 64–69, 72–74, 76–77, 93–95, 105–6, 112–14, 149, 165, 201–4
Lenin, Vladimir Ilyich   75, 199, 235, 238, 243–44, 246, 248, 252–53, 259, 262–63, 277, 279, 292, 294, 296–99, 301–2, 304, 324, 337, 341–42, 347, 366–67, 371, 380, 403, 412, 425, 429–32, 447, 465
Leninism   209, 275–76, 327, 358, 379, 408, 409
Li Dazhao   328, 448
Li Hongzhang   94–95, 97, 103, 114, 127, 132–34, 142, 151, 161, 163, 166, 177, 251, 448, 469
Li Jishen   285, 315, 317, 448
Liaodong peninsula   100–101, 104, 110, 125, 127–28, 130, 138
Liebknecht, Karl   3, 162, 449
Liebknecht, Wilhelm   162, 449
Liu Renjing   327, 449
loans   43, 70, 79, 92, 124, 126–27, 131–33, 136–38, 144, 167–71, 174–76, 179–80, 193, 202–3, 250, 255, 260, 268, 271, 272, 285–86, 294, 318, 320, 382, 390, 401
Lü Buwei   59, 218, 450
Luxemburg, Rosa   3, 296, 450

machine guns   342, 371, 382, 386
Manchu Qing dynasty   24, 40, 45, 48, 61, 64–65, 153–54, 156–57, 164–65, 185, 192, 194–96, 201, 222, 254, 439, 441–42, 448, 467
Manchuria   25, 28, 97–98, 109, 114, 118, 127–28, 131, 137, 142, 159, 170–71, 175–78, 180, 191, 203, 205, 258, 263, 449, 457
Martynov, Alexander Samoilovich   11, 274–76, 283, 295–96, 305, 342, 345–49, 356–57, 364, 373, 387, 396, 397–402, 414, 425–26, 428–30, 432–33, 452
Marx, Karl   9, 78–79, 238, 243, 292, 302, 323–24, 337, 358, 360, 371, 383, 384, 425, 452
Marxism   1, 3, 23, 154, 208, 209, 215–16, 224, 252, 283, 304, 323, 360, 405, 414, 441, 452
Meiji capitalist reforms   93, 94, 96, 141

Mensheviks 248, 283, 288, 291, 294, 297, 341, 344, 347–49, 355–56, 359, 364, 369, 379, 397, 399, 403, 405, 407–8, 416, 422, 425, 438, 440, 444, 449, 460, 462–63, 465
militarism 197, 203, 309, 331, 341, 355, 357
Miliukov, Pavel Nikolaevich 211, 404, 452
Ming dynasty 24, 31, 51, 54–55, 61, 64, 66, 69, 72, 76, 83, 218, 222–23, 467, 470
money 32–34, 44, 62–63, 65, 87, 124, 168–69, 194–95, 203, 224, 240, 253–54, 260, 269, 271–72
Mongolia 109, 142, 176, 408, 442, 444, 459–60
monopoly 35, 43, 170, 189, 190, 193–94, 255, 289, 403, 430

Nanjing 39, 79, 81, 169, 173, 178, 194, 289, 294, 321, 357, 376–77, 385–86, 389–90, 393, 412, 463, 466
national-liberation movement 5, 226, 252, 288, 306, 369
national revolution 226–27, 267, 269, 279–80, 286, 293, 306–7, 329–31, 333–34, 351–53, 371–72, 374, 380–81, 400–401, 403
Nicholas II 127, 129, 133, 158, 232, 252, 453
NRA (National Revolutionary Army) 6, 120, 237, 315, 376, 435, 438–39, 448, 463–64, 467–69

OGPU 345, 458
opium 33, 81, 88–89, 95, 140, 144, 183, 222, 249
Opium Wars 43, 79, 89, 100, 104, 115–16, 249
Ottoman Empire 97, 106, 444

peasant economy 30–31, 33, 79, 89, 197, 203, 357
peasant government 61, 69, 72, 74–76
peasant uprisings 8, 41, 54, 61, 72–73, 76, 216, 218, 219, 223, 238, 389–90, 395, 467
Pepper, John 360, 375, 454
petty bourgeoisie 9, 17–18, 20, 64, 77, 78, 117, 159, 204, 224, 227–28, 230, 232, 235, 237, 240, 243–44, 252, 256–57, 266–67, 276–78, 291, 299, 303–5, 312, 316, 323, 326, 328–29, 333, 335, 337, 341, 350, 356, 362, 365, 367, 374–75, 383–84, 393–94, 397, 403–4

Piatakov, Iuri (Georgii) Leonidovich 13, 368, 454
Piatakov-Radek Trial 13–14
Pokotilov, Dmitrii Dmitrievich 131–35, 161, 455
Pokrovskii, Mikhail Nikolaevich 10, 105, 110, 112, 149, 393, 455
Politburo 7–8, 11–12, 20, 265, 307, 344, 411, 423, 425–26, 428–31, 433, 436–37, 445–47, 449, 457, 460–64, 466, 469–70
Polo, Marco 32, 37, 61–63, 82, 213, 217, 220, 455
Port Arthur 101, 104, 110–11, 125, 128, 131–35, 137, 175, 469
ports 41, 79–81, 83–84, 89, 92, 102, 110–12, 116, 130–31, 163, 178, 183, 193, 249, 251
Portugal 266
Pravda 5, 11, 13, 262, 311–12, 345–47, 356, 359–60, 371, 378, 380, 385–87, 389, 392–94, 396, 412, 425, 427–28, 433, 437, 445
Prigozhin, Abram Grigorievich 11, 456
private property 23–27, 32, 52, 59–60, 70–72, 203, 206, 223, 324, 359
proletarian revolution 17, 242–43, 247, 275, 325, 351, 356
Prussia 67, 117, 202, 301, 435, 441

Qin dynasty 59, 61, 438, 456
Qin Shi Huangdi 54, 57–61, 67–68, 71, 77, 218, 253, 450, 456

Radek, Karl Bernhardovich 1–17, 19, 21, 32, 37, 38, 49, 54–55, 58, 59, 61, 62, 68–69, 75, 78–81, 85–86, 88, 93, 101, 105, 108, 114, 116–19, 123, 129, 134–35, 139–40, 144, 156, 163, 167, 173–74, 177–78, 186, 191, 200, 208–10, 212, 217, 221, 235–36, 242, 251, 253, 262–64, 287–88, 290–94, 298–99, 305, 310, 313, 316, 324, 325–33, 336–39, 341–42, 345, 347, 350–51, 353–60, 367, 371–72, 374, 378–79, 383, 385, 412, 417, 419–20, 423–25
railroad construction 69, 79, 86, 126, 138, 166, 169–74, 179, 183, 187–188, 205
Raskol'nikov, Fedor Fedorovich 7, 11, 252, 255, 263, 273, 277, 345, 456
Reclus, Élisée 54, 82–83, 140
Red Army 4, 120, 288, 290, 412–13, 460

INDEX 495

rent   25–26, 28, 31, 52, 201–5, 240, 253, 284, 421
Riazanov, David Borisovich   105, 457
Rafes Moisei Grigorievich   11, 280, 283, 287–89, 291–93, 300–2, 344–45, 364, 356
Richthofen, Ferdinand von   33, 35, 37, 82, 116, 182, 184, 457
Roy, Manabendra Nath   396, 457
RSDLP (Russian Social Democratic Labour Party)   3, 341, 379, 434–38, 440–45, 447, 449–66, 470
Rubach, Mikhail Abramovich   10, 457
Russia   3, 4, 6, 17–18, 36, 51, 53, 56–57, 61, 68–69, 74, 97–98, 101–102, 104–110, 112–16, 118–120, 123–29, 131, 136–38, 141, 146–47, 152, 158–60, 163–65, 170, 175–78, 180, 206, 208, 212, 216, 222, 224, 226, 228, 229, 232, 237, 242, 252, 260, 265–66, 279, 287–88, 301, 304, 307, 377, 387, 399, 444, 447, 451, 467, 469
Russian revolution   17, 24, 136, 164, 209, 235, 238, 242, 244, 246, 263–64, 301, 304, 332, 380
Russo–Chinese Bank   127, 178, 180, 457

Safarov, Georgii Ivanovich   385, 412, 417, 458
Schüler, Wilhelm   205, 268, 458
SDKPiL (Social Democracy of the Kingdom of Poland and Lithuania)   3, 485
Shang/Yin Dynasty   144, 438, 464, 469
Shao Lizi   308, 458
Shumiatskii Boris Zakharovich   11, 283, 303, 345, 459
Sermuks, Nikolai Martynovich   420, 459
silk   34, 37–39, 53, 62–63, 88–90, 95–96, 162, 171, 197, 222, 249, 258
socialism   5, 19, 22, 75, 242–43, 252, 279–80, 301–2, 320, 358, 420, 431
Sokol'nikov, Grigorii Iakovlevich   13, 368, 460
Song dynasty   147, 466, 467
Song Ziwen   261, 271, 294, 365, 376, 391, 394, 461
soviets   4, 10, 290, 297, 342–43, 346, 363, 365–67, 383, 386, 390, 393, 399, 403–5, 407, 410, 413–16, 421, 428, 434–36, 438–41, 444–45, 449, 455, 459, 461–62, 463, 465–66, 470
Spain   322, 451, 469

SRs (Socialist-Revolutionaries)   17–18, 235, 273, 296–97, 412, 445, 453, 461
Stalin, Joseph Vissarionovich   7–8, 10–11, 13, 14, 263, 266, 278, 286–87, 292, 308, 342, 343, 345–46, 365–68, 383, 385–89, 390, 393–94, 397, 399–409, 411, 414–15, 424–27, 430–31, 433, 436, 439–31, 443, 445, 448, 450, 453–54, 456, 458–59, 461, 464, 470
Suez canal   111
Sukhanov, Nikolai Nikolaevich   291, 463
Sun Chuanfang   118, 339, 350, 373, 463
Sun Fo   241, 261, 294, 307, 330, 365, 375–76, 386–87, 391, 394, 463
Sun Yat-sen   10, 18–19, 22–23, 153, 194, 228, 234–37, 241, 246, 248, 252–56, 262–65, 267, 301–3, 307, 314, 319, 329–30, 336–37, 345, 374–76, 392, 438–39, 444, 448, 458, 461–63, 466, 468

Taiping Rebellion   28–29, 81, 116, 155, 193, 249, 252, 258, 263
Tang dynasty   73
Tang Shengzhi   285–86, 290, 309, 339, 364, 386–95, 398–99, 407, 415, 464
taxes   25, 29–30, 33–34, 36, 43–44, 46, 52, 56, 60, 65–66, 70, 74, 84, 94, 144, 172, 181, 192–98, 202, 216, 219, 232, 233, 238, 254, 258, 260, 264, 268, 313, 356, 357, 372
trade unions   20, 164, 245, 270, 273, 277, 290, 315–17, 319, 329, 343–44, 361, 365, 373, 376–78, 380, 397, 407, 419, 441, 449, 451, 455–56, 462, 464
Trotsky, Lev Davidovich   4, 6, 10–14, 16, 279, 368, 385, 412, 417, 419–20, 423, 428, 430–33, 447, 459–60, 464
Trotskyism   278–79, 344, 373, 469
Tsarism   105–8, 110–11, 113–14, 124–25, 129, 136, 141, 152, 159, 163–65, 178, 227, 248, 252, 419, 421
Turkestan   98, 107–9, 142, 171, 176, 182, 183, 220, 234, 441, 460

USA (United States of America)   11, 112, 128, 149, 170, 186, 191, 241, 254, 257, 263, 266, 376, 447, 453, 459, 461
UTK (University of the Toilers of China)   2, 6, 8, 10, 11, 13, 345, 434, 440, 442, 452, 456, 459, 469

Varga, Evgenii Samuilovich   40, 45–46, 48, 51, 210–11, 465
Vasiliev, Vasilii Pavlovich   172, 182–83, 247, 465
Voitinskii, Grigorii Naumovich   20, 308, 465
Volin Mikhail   198–200, 205, 259, 264

Wang Anshi   66, 72–73, 76, 212, 218–19, 466
Wang Jingwei   6, 12, 241, 262, 265, 302, 307, 314, 320, 368, 376–78, 385, 389–91, 393–94, 399, 403–7, 413, 415–16, 466
warlords   117–18, 195, 231–33, 236, 254–55, 258, 266, 277, 463
Weber, Max   40, 45, 53–54, 64, 211, 223, 466
well-field system   52–53, 57, 59, 70, 72, 216–18, 223
Whampoa Military Academy   237, 314, 329, 331, 334, 338, 439, 449, 458
Wilhelm II   128, 129, 159, 466
Wilson, Woodrow   170, 467
Witte Sergei Iulievich   111–13, 127, 129–130, 132, 134, 177, 467
worker–peasant government   262–64, 276, 295, 300, 312, 338, 404, 413, 454
world capitalism   92, 228, 249, 252, 256–57, 402
Wuhan   241, 270, 296, 299, 365, 366–69, 380, 375–76, 382, 385–93, 398, 404, 405, 407–16, 438, 461–64, 466–69

Wu Peifu   22, 117–18, 136, 195, 231, 239–40, 248, 263, 266, 271, 285–86, 309–10, 331, 338–39, 350, 379, 467

Xinhai Revolution   45, 262, 462, 467

Yangzi River   29, 72, 83, 120, 130–31, 137–38, 159–60, 163, 168, 173, 178–79, 180, 185, 205, 239, 274, 276, 316, 381, 384, 398
Yuan dynasty   32, 40, 61–62, 82, 222
Yuan Shikai   151, 155, 163, 193–96, 251–52, 255–56, 272–73, 468

Zakharov, Ivan Ilyich   24–27, 31, 52–53, 70–71, 73, 213, 216, 468
Zhakov, Mikhail Petrovich   8, 10–11, 51, 56, 215, 469
Zhang Zuolin   22, 117, 136, 195–96, 233, 248, 258, 263, 266, 285, 287, 289, 304, 319, 331, 338, 350, 388–98, 413, 448, 469
Zhili province   151, 154–55, 185, 195, 255, 457
Zhou Dawen   11, 88, 469
Zhou dynasty   51, 56, 68, 71, 467
Zimmerwald   3
Zinoviev, Grigorii Evseevich   6, 10–14, 20, 308, 368, 385, 393, 406, 412, 417, 423, 425, 427–31, 433, 470
Zinovievist opposition   441, 443, 445, 458, 470
Zubatov, Sergei Vasilievich   164–65, 470